The End
of
European
Primacy

1871–1945

1871 – 1945

The End
of
European
Primacy

J. R. WESTERN
Lecturer in History
at Manchester University

HUMANITIES PRESS
New York

First published
in the United States 1966
by Humanities Press Inc.
303 Park Avenue South
New York, N.Y. 10010

Library of Congress Catalog Card No. 66-23177

Printed in Great Britain by
Richard Clay (The Chaucer Press), Ltd
Bungay, Suffolk

Contents

LIST OF MAPS

Drawn by A. Spark

List of Illustrations

(*between pages* 150 *and* 151)

ACKNOWLEDGEMENTS

Radio Times. Illustrations No. 1, 2, 4, 7, 13, 14, 17, 18, 19, 20, 21, 25, 26, 27, 28, 29.

Imperial War Museum. Illustrations No. 8, 15, 16, 24, 30, 31, 32.

Paul Popper. Illustrations No. 9, 10, 11, 12.

Documentation Français. Illustrations No. 3, 22.

Presse und Informationsamt der Bundesregierung. Illustration No. 23.

Introduction: The Problems of Progress

The late nineteenth century in Europe was a period unprecedented in its prosperity, tranquillity and grandeur. The pinch of poverty and the dangers of war and revolution appeared to be steadily receding. European countries completely dominated the old world and year by year they tightened their hold, steadily extinguishing the independence of non-European peoples. The new world could not be deprived of its political freedom, but economically it was very much under European influence. At the turn of the century a change began. Japan successfully defied a European power, thereby helping to save from extinction the disintegrating Chinese state. Two world wars followed in which the European countries were devastated or bled white. Already at the end of the first, the strongest power in Europe was the United States of America. At the end of the second, half the continent was at her disposal, the broken states of the west depending on her charity. Eastern Europe meanwhile passed mostly under the sway of Russia, which for most of the period since the Crimean War had figured as the victim of defeats, snubs and humiliations by her western neighbours.

The ruin of Europe in 1945 must not be taken too tragically. It did not last long. What did endure was a purely relative decline of the western European states. But this did not reflect any absolute decline in their strength, but rather the timely and energetic adoption of their methods by countries that had not fallen under their control. Even in 1871 the foundations of greatness were being laid in the United States, Russia and Japan.[1] It remains true that Europe experienced a ruinous crisis in the first half of the twentieth century and that she did so largely through internal failures. Ever since the French Revolution, the European states had been grappling with the continuous expansion of human knowledge and the accompanying changes in men's way of thinking, which brought not only economic transformation

[1] See R. F. Leslie, *The Age of Transformation*, pp. 310–14, 329–33, 382–8.

but new passions, loyalties and ambitions. In the mid nineteenth century the established governments had developed considerable skill in using the new forces constructively. Europe experienced a thorough reorganization in the thirty years beginning about 1848, not without violence but with very little violence in proportion to the changes accomplished. For a time all the believers in progress and optimism seemed justified. But gradually the secret was lost. There was a hardening of Europe's political arteries. In the twentieth century it became impossible to adjust either the frontiers or the constitutions of the greater states in a way that would satisfy both fermenting public opinion and embattled vested interests. There resulted both great wars and great revolutions. These remade Europe indeed, but they were so destructive that much of the potential benefit to humanity in the new forces which thus gained expression was lost. In particular, each upheaval tended, even if it cleared the way for constructive work, to create conditions leading to new and greater disturbances.

This book is an attempt to investigate the process described above as 'hardening of the arteries'. It is especially concerned with one theme which must here be stated. Politicians have always to work in an environment made up of several conflicting forces, be they states, classes, parties, churches or individuals. They can achieve nothing except by combining several such forces into a coalition. This is obvious enough in diplomacy, or in a country with many small parties like France. But beneath the surface it is equally the case within the apparently simpler Anglo-American tradition of two big parties or in the careers of revolutionaries and dictators like Lenin or Hitler. Sometimes—and often through no fault of his own—a politician can only build up a coalition strong enough to carry the day by adopting a policy of compromise and inactivity, keeping all his partners in a state of 'balanced dissatisfaction'. Sometimes, however, a policy is discovered which is likewise acceptable to very different sorts of people and yet is boldly enterprising, exploiting the possibilities of change instead of passing them by to the nation's eventual cost. Hitting on such policies—often more or less by accident—seeing their worth and carrying them through is the essential mark of the statesman under modern conditions. This book is very largely about the varying success of different political leaders in coalition-building and in striking a balance between dynamism and width of support.

History is a subject embracing everything that men do, and the historian must aim to study every human activity if he is to understand any one of them properly. But the study of history is too important to be left entirely to historians. Broadly speaking it is only political and to some extent economic history which are left mainly to them when the other disciplines have taken their pick. It therefore becomes the duty of general histories such as this to treat very largely of politics. The sections of this book which deal with entirely non-political subjects are meant to do no more than set the scene and to link what is said here with what may be more conveniently studied elsewhere. But politics expresses all the time the material and moral condition of the people concerned and can never be studied in isolation. Even the political chapters which follow try, therefore, to say something about European civilization in general, through the study of one particular European activity.

Part I
BISMARCK'S EUROPE—
THE END OF THE
LIBERAL ERA

1: Limits of Liberalism

Europe in the middle of the nineteenth century was being increasingly influenced by ideas that can loosely be called liberal. They may be reduced to two. First, the common good would best be served if the individual was allowed the greatest possible freedom in all activities of life. The most important practical applications of this were intellectual and religious liberty, the inviolability of private property and the removal of legal restraints on private business enterprise. Second, the government should be restrained from interfering with individual liberty by subjecting it to the control of the people's elected representatives. (Who should be allowed to join in the elections and how much power the representatives should have were matters of dispute.) A third idea, historically related to the other two but really distinct and sometimes opposed to them, was that of nationality. The truly liberal version of this is 'self-determination': people should be allowed to decide for themselves how they should be grouped together in order to form states.

Those who held liberal beliefs with real fervour in the last century commonly did so because they adhered in the main to the optimistic view of human nature which had gained ground in the century before. Men were supposed to be rational, able to discover through enquiry and argument what their interests were. And all men's interests were held to be identical. Conflict between classes, between nations, even perhaps between rulers and ruled, were due to nothing more substantial than ignorance and misunderstanding. Education and publicity would remove them, and all would link hands and move forward into a glorious future.

All this now seems so naïve that it is easy to forget how politically effective it was. Liberal ideas flourished most among the urban middle classes, always a minority and a smaller one then than now. But by what Marx rather unkindly called the 'universal brotherhood swindle'[1] they could enlist allies from other classes in their quest for

[1] In *The Eighteenth Brumaire of Louis Bonaparte*, respecting the 1848 revolution.

political power. After 1848 they were winning support both upwards and downwards in the social scale. In many places they were joined by the conservative peasantry without thereby losing touch with the radical urban workers. They penetrated the nobility and at every court there were adventurous ministers who urged their sovereigns to harness and exploit the liberals rather than suppress them. Liberal ideas were adopted with many gradations and shades of meaning. Thoroughgoing liberals achieved influence rather than power and the conservatives were far from vanquished. But the liberal tide crept steadily forward, even though largely by conservative thefts from the liberal programme. The liberals seemed bound to triumph in the end.

But in the decade after 1870 the tide turned. The liberals began to lose their power to appeal to all classes and to be the instrument of progressive adaptation to new circumstances. Where they kept their hold it was by abandoning some part of their beliefs. To some extent this merely reflected the human limitations of men who had achieved a great deal and felt themselves entitled to complacent satisfaction with their handiwork. But to some extent it was because the liberal formula could achieve no more. It had encountered conditions in which it could not operate effectively.

Geographical Limitations: the Fundamental Divisions of Europe

Throughout the period covered by this book Europe can be divided into an 'advanced' and what we nowadays call an 'underdeveloped' sector. Two things especially mark out the 'advanced' areas from the rest: a greater development of industry and commerce and a wider diffusion of property in land. An exact boundary, of course, is impossible to draw. France, the Low Countries and Germany— including the German and Czech territories of the Habsburgs— possessed by 1870 important modern industries and a numerous class of peasant proprietors. They also possessed landowning aristocracies and these became increasingly dominant on the eastern side of the region, so that the Austrian and Prussian lands had some resemblance to backward Poland and Hungary. Switzerland and Scandinavia were rather backward in 1870, but they were essentially communities of peasant proprietors and they rapidly acquired a very modern economic organization. Catalonia and the Po valley by now

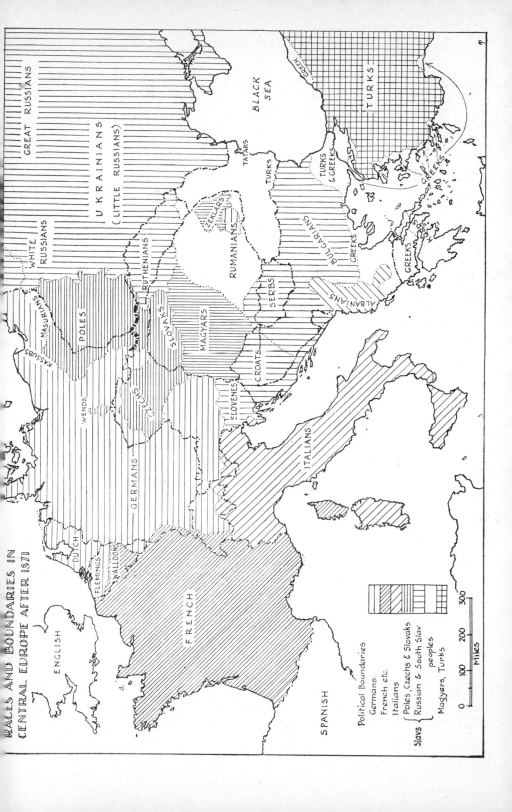

RACES AND BOUNDARIES IN
CENTRAL EUROPE AFTER 1871

GREAT RUSSIANS

U K R A I N I A N S
(LITTLE RUSSIANS)

WHITE RUSSIANS

MASURIANS

KASSUBS

POLES

WENDS

CZECHS

RUTHENIANS

SLOVAKS

MAGYARS

SZEKLERS

RUMANIANS

TATARS

BLACK SEA

TURKS

GREEK

TURKS

TURKS & GREEKS

GREEKS

BULGARIANS

SERBS

CROATS

SLOVENES

TYROL

ALBANIANS

GREEKS

GREEKS

ITALIANS

GERMANS

DUTCH

FLEMINGS

WALLOONS

FRENCH

ENGLISH

SPANISH

Political Boundaries
Germans.
French etc.
Italians
Slavs { Poles, Czechs & Slovaks
       Russian & South Slav
              peoples
Magyars, Turks

0   100   200   300
Miles

had some modern industry and they also had a body of peasant proprietors, and in the latter case an old established system of capitalist farming based on irrigation.

To the south and east of the advanced areas stretched an arc of countries where industry was only beginning and the dominant feature of society was the large landed estate: Portugal, Spain, Italy, Hungary, Poland, Russia. There were naturally regions on the borders of the area where the peasants were relatively well off and resembled those of the advanced countries: parts of Spain and Italy, the Baltic provinces of Russia. The Balkans, too, were largely a region of peasant proprietors; larger estates were found only in certain parts, notably Rumania and Bosnia. But the exploitation of this area by the Turkish administration, which still controlled most of it, was an evil comparable to landlordism. Most typical of the backward countries were the latifundia of southern Spain and southern Italy, the great estates of central Hungary and the Ukraine. These resembled the plantations of the tropics and the American south, geared to slave labour or something like it: a large area farmed as a single unit, the work done by big gangs recruited from a desperately poor rural proletariat. This was the way, too, in which the Prussian Junkers ran their estates. But it was not the only pattern. In central and northern Russia the peasants were smallholders, weighed down by heavy payments to the lords of their land, but able if they were lucky and enterprising to increase their holdings and buy the lords out. In parts of Italy and Spain particularly, large estates were cultivated by sharecropping: peasant farmers provided the labour, the landlord most of the capital, and the produce was shared between them.

It was the advanced countries of Europe that were the heartland of liberalism. Most of them had a powerful aristocracy and a large working class without property. But between the two stretched the middle classes (the plural is used advisedly), a numerous body comprising peasant farmers, shopkeepers, business and professional men. They formed a hierarchy of wealth, the poorest only just above the wage earner, the richest aspiring to enter high society. They were all conservative in that they had property and intended to keep it. But they were all progressive in that they were eager to get on in the world, and could only do so through the building up of new wealth and new institutions in society. In politics therefore it was natural for them to stand for moderate and continuous reform, and they were near enough to the classes above and below them to mediate between them, drawing all towards progressive policies which all classes could support.

The middle classes throve on industrial growth and the diffusion of landed property. Where conditions did not favour these developments the middle classes were small and society was sharply polarized into rich and very poor. The liberal formula of progress by co-operation between classes could not, therefore, work for long. Power remained in the hands of a wealthy oligarchy and little was done to benefit the poor. Sometimes a section of the middle class displaced the nobility within the oligarchy, but this did not help much. Being small, the middle classes could hope to make their fortune through control of the state and its patronage. It was only in the advanced countries that the middle classes were too numerous to rely entirely on this and had some permanent incentive to stand for progress in the general interest.

The oligarchies who ruled the backward countries of Europe long encountered little resistance from the impoverished mass of the people. But fundamentally their position was far weaker than that of the rulers of the advanced countries. In these the widespread diffusion of property made for conservatism, and by the end of the nineteenth century even the propertyless working class were in a sense conservative. The workers' wages and level of education had become high enough for them to be able to organize and seek redress by legal means for their grievances and generally inferior position. In the backward countries the masses were too destitute and ignorant to be able to organize much, and they might even have a certain superstitious reverence for constituted authority. But they entirely lacked any solid loyalty towards the established order in state and society. A small but resolute band of revolutionaries could therefore attack the ruling group with some hope of success. Henceforward, it was the backward east and south that were the main centres of revolutionary activity in Europe.

Geographically, therefore, liberal ascendancy was confined largely to the north and west. The east and south of Europe could get no farther than a sham, diluted liberalism. The real choice in those countries was between the existing order and a violent radicalism. It should be noted that certain countries were bisected by the crucial division between the two European sectors: Spain, Italy and, above all, the Habsburg monarchy, which suffered as much from this division as from the more familiar one between the nationalities. In religion and culture these divided countries belong, however, to the west—to Latin rather than Greek Christendom. In much of what follows, therefore, it is natural to treat them together with their 'advanced' neighbours.

Economic Limitations: the End of the Boom Years

There were further powerful factors which limited liberal influence not just in part of the continent but in the whole of it. The middle years of the nineteenth century had witnessed something of an 'economic miracle'. Business activity had expanded very fast and with relative ease. This represented the initial diffusion throughout Europe of the new industrial techniques developed mainly in Britain—above all the building of railways. Liberalism thrived in the atmosphere of boom. It really did seem that widening the bounds of freedom would quickly bring prosperity for all. A change set in with the economic crisis of 1873. The next quarter of a century was a period of economic difficulty everywhere. This must not be exaggerated. Trade, production and technical innovation all went forward in a massive and significant way. There was still plenty of scope for railway building, especially in eastern Europe. Mileage nearly doubled in Germany during the seventies, and more than doubled in France in the years 1871–91. The line across the Balkans to Constantinople was completed in 1888. Russia tripled her mileage in the twenty years after 1870, but it was in the nineties that railway building reached its peak there.

This great constructive effort stimulated economic activity generally. It was paralleled at sea by the building of a great new fleet of cargo steamers. Hitherto, steamships had been small and costly to run, suitable mainly for carrying passengers and mail. But from the sixties fuel consumption was steadily reduced by developing engines which used their steam two, three and even four times over in different cylinders. At the same time, steel construction enabled ships to be built much bigger. The amount of goods that could be carried by sea increased and the cost fell. World steamship tonnage rose from two million in 1870 to nearly seventeen million in 1895. Sail meanwhile fell from thirteen to nine million, though it kept first place till 1893. The cost of sending grain across the Atlantic fell from 20 cents a bushel in 1874 to 2 cents in 1904. The development of refrigeration during the same period added to the cargoes to be carried. New commodities like the banana reached Europe. Fresh meat and dairy products became important in international trade. Total world exports and imports were rising in value by over a tenth each decade, even though prices fell heavily in the last quarter of the century.

Behind the railway and the steamship stood a great new steel industry. The production of steel cheaply and in bulk was perfected (1866) in the open-hearth process of William Siemens and the Martins (two Frenchmen and an Anglo-German).[1] World output increased more than sixteenfold between 1870 and 1895. Germany advanced especially fast. The war of 1870 gave her a large share of the ores of Lorraine, and in 1878 the Gilchrist–Thomas process was developed which enabled these ores to be used for steelmaking, even though they contained phosphorus. German steel production was only 169,000 metric tons in 1870, but it was over a million by 1885 and nearly four million by 1895. Cheap steel revolutionized the construction of everything from bridges to bicycles and was the basis of a general new industrial expansion. The Eiffel Tower built for the Paris exhibition of 1889 was a fitting monument to its importance.

Meanwhile, there were important advances in electricity and chemistry. At the Vienna exhibition of 1873 occurred the famous demonstration that a dynamo could be linked to an electric motor, thus eliminating the need for a battery. In 1879 Werner Siemens built for the Berlin exhibition a little electric railway that could carry passengers. The telephone and the electric light bulb with a filament also date from this time; Marconi developed wireless telegraphy in the nineties. In Norway and the Alpine countries the turbines required for using waterfalls to make electricity were devised. Electricity was increasingly used for industrial processes like welding (1886) and the refining of metals. Aluminium, produced by electrolysis and only

---

[1] On the principle explained in R. F. Leslie, *The Age of Transformation*, p. 401.

discovered in 1828, now came into use: world production was 283 lb. in 1883 and 8,000 tons in 1902.

Chemical developments were most varied. The making of dyes from coal tar was gradually perfected. Wood pulp became the source of paper and artificial silk. The first plastic was invented, celluloid. So in 1868 was margarine. Improvements were made in the refining of mineral oil, a substance which had only just begun to displace whale oil for lamps. Chemistry and physics were allied in the refrigerator and the internal combustion engine, two rather similar machines making use of expanding gases. In the eighties Daimler developed an engine that could run on petrol instead of coal gas, and so made possible the motor car and the aeroplane; the Diesel engine followed in 1892. A more immediate impact was made by the bicycle, which took its modern shape with the invention of the 'safety' (chain-driven) type in 1876 and the pneumatic tyre in 1889. The latter helped in the rise to importance at this time of rubber. A host of other new inventions were establishing themselves in daily use, from the tin can to the typewriter.

The period therefore was not one of stagnation, but it was widely felt to be so. The most obvious reason for this was the depressed state of agriculture. The 'avalanche' of American wheat had been delayed by the Civil War, but in the seventies it was brought to Europe by train and steamer. Imports of fresh meat soon followed; the Argentine and Australasia joined in. Competition within Europe was no less important. Russia especially could now reach the western market with greater ease. There was a single world market henceforth for primary products and farmers, whether high-cost or low-cost, suffered as never before from unexpected gluts and unexpected competition from remote parts of the world. Falling prices—an average decline for all products of 40 per cent between 1873 and 1896—hit all alike, though some could survive more easily. They were especially damaging to those who borrowed heavily when prices were favourable. To make things worse, there were epidemics among sheep, cattle, vines and even silkworms—the last to the benefit of China and Japan.

Agriculture gradually recovered by adaptation. Following Anglo-American example, continental farmers steadily went over to the rotation of crops and, where they could afford it, to the use of machines. The use of artificial fertilizers greatly increased—another side to the expansion of the chemical industry. Farmers concentrated on what they could produce competitively. Sheep declined and pigs multiplied. Vegetable growing increased and so did dairy farming, helped by refrigeration and new ways of making butter: the great new export trades of Denmark and Holland were only the most notable examples. A factor, too, which helped to keep up both agricultural and industrial production was the steady growth of population—slow in France, fairly fast in most countries.

But although the farmers recovered it took time, and meanwhile they were hard pressed. This was important because almost everywhere on the continent they were the most numerous element. Even in France and Germany almost half the working population was engaged in agriculture in 1871, and more than a third still were so in 1914. To the east and south the proportion was of course much higher. The agricultural depression weighed on business and industry in all sorts of ways, restricting markets and keeping down the rate of industrial growth in backward countries that could only finance it by agricultural exports. The industries based on the new inventions did not grow quickly enough to make up for this. They needed time to establish themselves, and it was only in the nineties that the new electrical and chemical industries really started to grow rapidly.

There was thus a relative lack of investment opportunities and an industrial as well as an agricultural glut. Profits and rates of interest tended to be low, and factory prices fell just as did farm prices. They fell more than they might otherwise have done because of a limitation in the supply of money. In the seventies all continental countries that were financially sound adopted the gold standard or its equivalent, but until the nineties the supply of gold did not keep pace with the supply of goods. Not only the farmers therefore but the business community were dissatisfied. So, too, were the working class, perhaps with less reason. It has always been relatively hard to cut money wages, and though they fell in this period they did so less than prices, so that real wages rose. But periods of depression are periods of unemployment and of the destruction of inefficient firms and of the livelihood of whole bodies of workers undersold by the products of new machines. In many ways continental conditions at this time, combining the strains both of depression and of industrial expansion, recall more than they do at other times the England of the days of the Chartists.

None of this encouraged the spread of liberal optimism. There was a loss of faith both in the unaided efforts of the individual and in the working together of classes and nations in the interests of Progress. Socialist beliefs spread among the workers. Among all classes there was a growing demand for protection against foreign and sometimes against domestic competition. The state, too, was expected to aid economic development by spending public money. Socialists and protectionists commonly believed, as liberals did, in the possibility of continuous progress to the general benefit of mankind. Continental liberals for their part had never tried to limit governmental activity as strictly as had their British brethren. But what in practice underlay both socialism and protectionism was a belief hearkening back to mercantilism that classes and nations have to fight one another for their fair share of the world's wealth. This was alien to the liberal spirit, and hard to combine with forward looking policies of any kind. It pointed rather to immobility, maintained by the conflict of opposing forces. For good or ill, something like this was to come about both within the European states and in international relations.

International Limitations: the Growth of Militarism

The possibilities of international co-operation, which were to be reduced by the protectionist revival, had already been reduced by the mid-century wars which had contributed so much to the re-organization of Europe. The natural liberal preference was for peace, and until 1848 this had been shared by the conservatives, who feared that war might lead to revolution. It was the radicals who were the warmongers then. The success of the armies in putting down the revolutions of 1848 had led many conservatives, of whom Bismarck was only the most distinguished, to look to violence as a way out of tight spots. The wars that had united Italy and Germany had encouraged liberals in those countries to view fighting with more favour, and had disillusioned liberal opinion in defeated countries, especially France. Napoleon III had toyed with ideas of disarmament, and the French left in his time were ultra-pacific. After 1870 the greatest liberal nation on the continent with one accord put national defence first and was highly sceptical of the prospects of universal peace.

A misunderstanding of Bismarck's wars appears to have been the basis of most subsequent thought about the utility of war and the preparations necessary for it. These wars were short, partly because Prussia was better prepared than her opponents, but partly also because of their internal political feebleness. The cost was moderate and the disruption of society limited, especially on the winning side. The profit from Prussia's overwhelming victories was correspondingly great. Huge territories were won, and financially the war of 1870 was perhaps the most profitable ever. France had to pay an indemnity of five milliard francs and quickly did so. It was mainly used to reduce the national debts of the German states, thus releasing capital for industrial development and contributing to the feverish boom of the early seventies.

There was never any reason why the opposing sides in future wars should not be more evenly matched and the operations correspondingly longer and more costly. Since railways and modern industry had greatly increased the quantity of men and weapons that could be sent into battle, a very heavy drain of blood and treasure was indeed likely. In the American Civil War, Europe had just had before its eyes a long and sanguinary struggle foreshadowing the world wars. But that lesson was not learned. Many expected war to show easy profits, and those who disliked it readily believed that the alternatives might be worse. The Russians in 1904, the Austrians in 1914, were to hurry into war to solve their domestic difficulties. In 1914 Sir Edward Grey and Bethmann Hollweg, both in their different ways, resigned themselves to war because they thought their countries would suffer more by standing aloof. The fall of the Russian and Austrian monarchies and the devastation of Europe were due not least to the idea that the horrors of war had abated.

The expectation that war would be short and sharp led to the belief that the side best prepared beforehand would win. There was therefore a continuous 'arms race' from this time on—an attempt, that is, always to be one jump ahead of your neighbour in weapon design. The advances in chemistry meant new explosives—smokeless and stronger than gunpowder. Breechloading rifles and artillery were becoming general even in 1870, but their firepower was steadily increased. Rifles were equipped with magazines and so could be loaded with several cartridges at a time. Field guns were given a recoil mechanism, which meant that they did not have to be re-aimed after every shot. Military training of the nation's manhood in peacetime had enabled Prussia to put a surprisingly large army promptly into the field, and the Prussian system was copied by the Austrians as early as 1868 and by the other great continental powers in the seventies.

Victory was expected to go to the side which could deploy its great new forces most rapidly in the theatre of war. This was the task of the general staff, which had to make detailed plans in advance for the assembly of reservists and the movement of every unit in the army by rail to its battle station. There had to be a plan for every war the country might have to fight, and when an emergency came the plan had to be put into effect as soon as possible. A few hours gained or lost, it was held, might make the difference between victory and defeat. Hostilities must begin as soon as the plan called for the crossing of the frontier: it was commonly expected that there might be no declaration of war. If only for technical reasons, therefore, the general staff was likely to clamour for warlike measures in periods of tension. There also tended to be talk of 'preventive war' whenever a country was temporarily better prepared than its neighbours. As early as 1875 there was a 'war scare'—Germany was supposed to be going to attack France before her recovery was complete. The cult of 'preparedness' poisoned the international atmosphere.

'Preparedness' cannot be dismissed as military nonsense, but again there was a failure to realize that the experience of Bismarck's wars might not be repeated. The strength which the increasing firepower of modern weapons gave to the defence was not appreciated. This underlay the belief that an instant offensive at the outbreak of war would succeed, and it was the basis of the strong continuing element of conservatism in European military organization. The infantry were expected to fight in gaudy uniforms and dense formation, a thunderous charge of cavalry finishing off their work. There was little interest in the most deadly new weapon under development, the machine gun, and little realization that the mounting hail of bullets would have to be countered by entrenchment, concealment and dispersal. Moral fervour and cold steel were expected to carry the day. The teachings of Clausewitz were unfortunately reinforced by the experiences of 1870, when the French had not known what to do with their machine guns, and Prussia's massed ranks were preserved and carried to victory by her overwhelming superiority in artillery.

The doctrine of a swift, victorious offensive led to an undue discounting of the importance of reserves. The largest number possible of seasoned young soldiers with the colours had to be the aim. The greater the dependence on calling out reservists, the slower would be mobilization. Reservists, anyway, would be older men comfortably settled and lacking the naïve thirst for attack from which so much was expected. They would be useful in defence and for replacing casualties, but neither would be much needed in a short victorious war. Conscripts were valued less as potential reservists than because they increased the size of the regular army while undergoing training. Their period of service with the colours was made as long as possible in order to make them as like regular soldiers as possible. Both in France and in Germany the soldiers insisted on three years, which the civilians were always trying to cut down to two.

Military conservatives were strongly interested in thus keeping the army as like as possible to what it had been in pre-conscription days. They were not eager to train the whole manhood of the nation because that would mean such an increase in the number of officers that they could not all come from the nobility or even the upper class generally. They did not want short-service recruits in peacetime or reservists under their command in war because these would bring with them too much of the democratic spirit that was spreading among civilians and could only be curbed in the soldier by long training. The country which applied conscription most rigorously was France. Not only did the republicans cherish the ideal of the nation in arms but her low birthrate meant that she could only hold her own by utilizing every man. Germany, with a much larger population, contented herself with training only a large proportion of those fit and liable. This was of great importance in helping France to hold her own against Germany both in peacetime rivalry and in 1914.

Military factors thus weakened the appeal of the liberal idea of universal peace, not only or even mainly by encouraging resort to war but rather by encouraging a universal suspicion that war was being planned. They also encouraged the formation of alliances giving automatic protection in the event of sudden attack; these commitments embarrassed the powers when they had to mediate in disputes between any two of their number. But military factors were also important in arresting the disintegration of the old monarchical state machine under slow but relentless liberal attrition. The regular army, stronghold of conservatism and often of sheer reactionary folly, had everywhere to be preserved and strengthened. It inevitably wielded political and economic influence. The growing vested interests in the arms race—in the massive provision of new weapons that had to be replaced by another type before they wore out—is only the most obvious example. It and the kind of state it stood for were a possible focus of loyalty in the malaise that came with economic depression. Liberal they were not; how constructive they could be remained to be seen.

2: The Loss of Impetus in the West, 1871–9

The period of liberal and national ferment which opened in 1848 continued into the seventies. It was really closed by the Congress of Berlin (1878) which began a period of greater stability, comparable to that after the Congress of Vienna. Both before and after the dividing point, power in most countries was shared between moderate conservatives and moderate liberals. But till the end of the decade, this combination seemed to make for a fairly substantial element of change on liberal lines. Afterwards it did not, or not to the same extent. How is this change to be accounted for?

Germany: the Kulturkampf and its Abandonment

The German Empire which came into being in January 1871 was the fruit of an alliance between the old Prussian monarchy and the new German liberal nationalism. The former might seem to have contributed most: not only the best army on the continent but, in Bismarck, a diplomatic genius able to put it to the best use. But the liberal parliamentarians must not be underestimated. Without parliamentary sanction the Prussian government could raise no new taxes and, more important, could not resort to any large-scale borrowing. Till 1866 Bismarck was able to defy parliament because the existing taxes provided money enough for the government's needs. The wars against Austria and France were costly, and the Prussian king ceased to be able to 'live of his own'. Her victories, moreover, left Prussia with the task of winning the loyalty both of the territories directly annexed and of the lesser German states henceforth federated with her. The former partisans of Austria in these lands were by no means cowed by Prussia's military success and struggled hard to limit Prussian predominance in the new Germany as far as they could. Both for financial and for general political reasons, therefore, the

rulers of the new empire needed the aid of a popular political movement friendly to themselves.

The building up of the new state in its early years therefore took
the form of a triangular struggle between the Prussian emperor-
king and his servants (usually supported by the other princely
governments), the nationalists and the opponents of the new system.
The first two needed each other's help against the third, but were
themselves at odds as to the shares of power to be accorded to prince
and parliament respectively, both in the Empire and in its constituent
states.

On the governmental side a special predominance was held by
Otto von Bismarck, who was both Chancellor of the Empire and
Prime Minister of Prussia. Bismarck was fifty-five when the Empire
was founded. His services had been rewarded not only with the title of
Prince but with the rank of General in the Prussian army, and his
tall, imposing figure was henceforth commonly clad in a military
uniform. This grim giant had, however, a thin, high voice. Nor was
this the only respect in which he failed to live up to the image which
he tried to create of himself as a stern, unbending Junker. The lesser
nobility of Prussia from which he sprang were frugal, taciturn, un-
imaginative; obedient and painstaking servants of the state, both in
the army and the administration. Bismarck was loquacious, extrava-
gant and untidy. He was bad at office work and obeyed orders when
it suited him. His good qualities were those that Junkers commonly
lacked: imagination, intuition, the capacity to understand events and
movements with which he had little sympathy, and to alter his views
on any question when they did not seem to lead him to practical successes. It is hard to say whether he had any fixed principles beyond
a desire for the aggrandisement of his own country, Prussia, and
subsequently the maintenance of the Prussian character of his new
Empire. His aversion to parliamentary institutions appears to have
vanished early on and he became a skilful manipulator of public
opinion. He defended the royal prerogative against parliamentary
encroachment mainly to secure himself a free hand in diplomacy. He
had no hesitation in bringing parliamentary pressure to bear against
his sovereign and his governmental colleagues when they were unwilling to do what he wanted.

Bismarck's most reliable parliamentary supporters were the Free

Conservatives, a body of forward-looking Junkers who had come together specifically to back his plans for linking Prussia with nationalist and liberal trends. Much more numerous and influential were the National Liberals. This party, too, had been formed (1866) in response to Bismarck's espousal of nationalism and his overthrow of Austria. The more moderate liberals decided that there was more to be gained from co-operation with him than from opposition, and broke with the intransigent minority who would not compromise with a minister who had defied parliament. But it would be wrong to regard the National Liberals as mere tools of Bismarck. Their left wing in particular, led by Eduard Lasker (whom Bismarck particularly detested), meant to extract constitutional concessions in return for support of the government and gradually advance to a position of dominance within the partnership. The National Liberals were not at this time the big businessmen's party that they were to become. They were rather the party of the middle class as a whole and enjoyed wide support among the peasantry and even among the urban workers. County-court judges and other lawyers formed the backbone of the parliamentary party, and this was reflected in their strong emphasis on the need to subordinate the government to the law and render it unable to do anything not sanctioned by the laws and the constitution. This preoccupation with legality rather than with who actually held power was a weakness in practical politics; otherwise the party was well qualified to take over in due course the political direction of the nation.

German constitutional development had meanwhile reached a point midway between the desires of Bismarck and those of the National Liberals.[1] Both in the Empire and in its constituent states the monarch had abandoned legislative power to parliament, though often retaining large emergency powers: the German Emperor, for example, might proclaim a state of siege throughout the Empire, and if the Reichstag failed to vote the budget he might continue the previous year's budget in force. The representatives of the people were far, however, from having won control of affairs. In the individual states the executive remained under royal control, save in the three city republics and to some extent in south Germany. The upper chambers of the state parliaments were hereditary and conservative

[1] On what follows cf. *The Age of Transformation*, pp. 352–5.

on the English model. In the imperial constitution, likewise, the elective Reichstag was balanced by the Bundesrat (Federal Council), consisting of ambassadors of the conservative state governments.

The various elective assemblies might, nevertheless, hope to prevail because of the government's need for their support. Thus, the Reichstag took the first tentative steps towards establishing control over the imperial executive. Bismarck had at first intended this to be managed by the Bundesrat. But on the establishment of the North German Confederation in 1867, the Reichstag of the Confederation had insisted on giving the Chancellor the status of a responsible minister. The constitution of the Empire was almost identical with that of the Confederation of 1867, and the Chancellor was in theory the sole minister, though later he was given a number of Secretaries of State to be his deputies in the different departments. The Emperor might appoint whom he pleased as Chancellor and the Reichstag could not legally require his dismissal. But the establishment of a responsible minister, whose countersignature was necessary for official acts, was an essential first step towards a ministry responsible to the Reichstag.

One vital part of the executive remained, however, outside the Chancellor's control. The Emperor commanded the armed forces and their chiefs were answerable directly to him. Bismarck had hoped to make them completely independent of the Reichstag by having the necessary financial provision for them incorporated into the constitution itself. This neither the Confederal nor the later Imperial Reichstag would accept, and eventually in 1874 Bismarck negotiated a compromise between parliament and the army by which the military establishment was voted for seven years at a time. Although the soldiers won some independence by this arrangement, the Reichstag was sure of the last word, especially as extra money was often required before the seven years were up. The National Liberals had won an important victory, partly because Bismarck was growing jealous of the power of his military colleagues and was not sorry to see it curbed.

Bismarck and the National Liberals were alike in being Prussian-centred and desiring a Germany under Prussian leadership, with a strong central authority and Austria excluded. They were opposed by those who regretted the exclusion of Austria and wished to preserve as much independence as possible for the individual German states. The most important body to take this view were the Roman Catholics, from whom in 1870 the Centre Party was formed. The exclusion of Austria had hit them hardest, for it meant that they were a minority in united Germany instead of the majority. But the introduction of universal suffrage for Reichstag elections allowed them, thanks especially to the great influence of the lower clergy, to develop rapidly into a great mass party with roots in all classes. Because they were widely based, they had a special capacity for working with many other diverse groups. Their left wing included both partisans of social reform for the benefit of the working class and liberal-minded haters of Prussian absolutism. These had much in common with the nascent socialist movement and the Simon-Pure liberals unreconciled to Bismarck. The aristocratic right wing of the Catholics had, on the other hand, a close affinity with the mass of the Junkers, who mainly supported the Conservative Party. Though Protestant and Prussian, they bitterly resented Bismarck's concessions to liberalism and his breaking up of the old order. Windthorst, the first leader of the Centre Party, was personally linked with this northern conservatism, for he had been chief minister in the kingdom of Hanover, annexed by Prussia in 1866. The last of the Centre's important affinities was with the national minorities: the Poles were Catholic, and so were many in Alsace-Lorraine.

The constitution of the Empire gave on paper some encouragement to those who hoped for a fairly loose federation. It took the form of a treaty between the governments of the German states. There was a conscious rejection of the idea that sovereignty in the new nation belonged either to the German people or the German monarch. The head of state was styled German Emperor, not Emperor of Germany, for the other princes were not his subjects but his allies. But in practice it was the centralizing tendency that was uppermost. The Emperor, as King of Prussia, was sovereign over more than half the imperial territory. The competence of the imperial authorities was wide, and during the seventies many functions were taken from the state governments and vested in the Empire.

Bismarck and the National Liberals did not wait passively for a conservative onslaught on the new institutions but themselves attacked their opponents' main stronghold—the churches, and especially the Catholic Church. The National Liberals were eager for this, for they were essentially a Protestant and anticlerical party. Bismarck was reluctant to quarrel with the Catholic Church, but was impelled to do so by the difficulties made for him by the Catholics in South Germany and above all in Prussia's Polish territories. The Jesuits and other religious orders were expelled from the Empire (1872-3). Anticlerical measures were passed in the different states, notably in Prussia where the 'May laws' (1873) placed the training and appointment of clergy under state control. Bishops and clergy resisting the new laws were imprisoned. The authority of the churches was curtailed by the introduction of civil marriage. Such in outline was the Kulturkampf.

Thus, till about 1875, there was steady progress towards the National Liberals' ideal of a unified, secular and parliamentary state. After this, the economic difficulties which had begun in 1873 began to affect politics. The National Liberals were the party of free trade, and the new Empire had no protective tariff. Now there arose a general demand for Protection and liberal economics were discredited. The peasantry deserted liberalism and the economic issue placed them in the same camp as the Junkers, for whom they had no great love. A Federation of German Industry was formed in 1876 to campaign for higher tariffs. Farther left, the socialists united in a single party in 1875, and at the Reichstag elections of 1877 won nearly half a million votes. The Centre Party was sympathetic to protectionism and social reform, and it benefited greatly from the indignation which many people (some liberals included) felt at the persecution of the churches. It, too, gained ground at the 1877 elections, and the National Liberals dropped back.

Bismarck had an open mind on economic as on most other issues. By 1877 he had been converted from free trade to protectionism. His reasons were partly fiscal. Economic depression had reduced imperial revenues and new taxes were needed. Bismarck wished them to be indirect taxes. He did not wish the Reichstag, elected by manhood suffrage, to impose direct taxes because he was afraid that they would place the main burden on the wealthy. The existing direct taxes were levied by the state parliaments, elected on a limited franchise. The Reichstag could tap this source by requiring the states to pay over a 'matricular contribution'. But Bismarck was eager to give the imperial government a source of revenue entirely under its own control. Imperial indirect taxes voted by the Reichstag were therefore his solution.

The National Liberals were opposed not only to tariffs but to indirect taxes in general. In 1877 Bismarck tried to strike a bargain with them. In return for the voting of the taxes he offered the National Liberal leader, Rudolf von Bennigsen, a place in the Prussian ministry. At last the way was clearing for the invasion of the executive by parliamentary leaders. But the National Liberals stuck to their principles and refused the deal.

Bismarck decided to teach the National Liberals a lesson. In 1878 he picked a quarrel with them by proposing the legal proscription of the growing socialist movement, for which they refused to vote. His fear of socialism was sincere: he had made such proposals before. But his purpose was now tactical. He was helped by two attempts on the Emperor's life. 'Now I've got the scoundrels!' he exclaimed after the second of them. 'The Social Democrats?' he was asked. 'No!' he replied. 'The National Liberals!' The Reichstag was dissolved, and in the ensuing elections government officials throughout the country were told to use their influence against the National Liberals instead of supporting them, as they had done on previous occasions. Bismarck also took advantage of the advent of the new conciliatory Pope, Leo XIII. He met the Papal Nuncio and promised a friendlier policy towards the church.

At the elections the National Liberals lost heavily and the conservative parties gained. It was now—and not in 1866, as is often said—that there occurred a moral collapse in German liberalism and the degradation of many of its adherents into mere tools of Bismarck. The discomfited National Liberals now voted for the anti-socialist laws and (1879) for protective duties. The party was later abandoned by many of its more upright members, and it gradually declined into a small big-business pressure group. With the Conservatives—the main body of the Junkers—Bismarck was henceforth reconciled. With the Centre Party his relations remained rather distant, but the anticlerical laws gave him a hold over them. To secure their gradual repeal the Catholics needed to avoid another breach with the government. To this extent the Kulturkampf had not been in vain.

The National Liberals had failed to make the Empire a

parliamentary monarchy, and nobody was to have as good a chance for a very long time. There was no longer one party much larger than the rest and whose support was indispensable to the government. Instead, there were several parties of roughly equal size and the government held the balance between them. Though none of them really liked the government, each had experienced loss through defying it in isolation and it was almost impossible for them to combine and oppose it collectively. The Centre Party, with its unique links with other parties of all colours, was the best placed to form such a combination. But it had the fatal disadvantage of being the party of a minority. Only after 1945 could its Christian Democrat successors become the governing party in a German parliamentary republic and that only because of a further mutilation of Germany: the sundering from the rest of the Protestant territory now under Soviet control balanced the loss of Catholic Austria in 1866.

But the National Liberals' loss was not necessarily Bismarck's gain. Their fervent loyalty to the new state and their ability to appeal to all classes had fitted them perfectly to be the government's parliamentary mainstay. It was much harder to govern when majorities had to be laboriously assembled from smaller parties representing conflicting classes and interests. Moreover, it now became embarrassing, as it had not been when the liberals could appeal to all sections of the nation, that the representative system was weighted against the growing towns and the poorer classes. In both the Reichstag and the state parliaments the rural districts were over-represented and there was never any attempt to correct this disproportion. The Reichstag, elected by manhood suffrage, was increasingly out of harmony with the state parliaments, which represented mainly the propertied classes. Bismarck's successors were to find it increasingly hard to work both with the Reichstag and with the Prussian Landtag, and to maintain national and progressive policies against the attacks of the over-represented agrarian minority. Bismarck's harnessing of the German liberals to Prussian ends was a triumph of adaptation. His quarrel with them reflects a decline in his powers. The German Empire was never to be governed so vigorously again.

France: the Conservative Republic

The Third French Republic was created by the same war as was the

German Empire. But one owed its origin to victory, the other to defeat in the war of 1870. From this time until 1940 there is a special fascination in comparing the political histories of France and Germany, for they are mirror images of each other. The war of 1870 consolidated monarchy in Germany and destroyed it in France. After 1870 monarchical German governments had to work with liberal parliamentarians and were under some pressure from them; but by 1879 the liberals were in retreat. In France, meanwhile, a republican administration was matched, and for a time dominated by a parliament of monarchists; but by 1879 the monarchists had been routed. In both cases the upshot was a mildly progressive yet essentially conservative system—the emphasis in Germany more on the second, in France more on the first.

The French republicans had seized power by force in September 1870, and established a dictatorship in the hope of saving the country from the consequences of military disaster. The hero of the resistance, and the leader of the republican movement thereafter was Léon Gambetta.[1] Before the war a young lawyer on the make, he was passionate, eloquent and Bohemian. But it was his Gascon and Italian blood rather than his principles that made him thus appear the embodiment of revolutionary extremism. Although an intransigent republican, his instinctive preference was for strong government and reform, not the overthrow of the existing social order. This made him both able and eager to appeal for support among conservatives, just as personal ambition attracted him to the world of fashion. He ended his life in ostentatious luxury and the main aim of his later political career was to make republicanism respectable.

At first the republic seemed destined, like Napoleon III, to be destroyed by military defeat. The National Assembly, at length convened in 1871 to ratify the peace treaty, had an overwhelming royalist majority. The revolt of republican Paris against it was crushed. The events of 1848 seemed to be repeating themselves. But the royalists were much weaker than they had been then. During Napoleon's reign they had been steadily losing conservative votes to the followers of the Emperor, and they only recovered them in 1871 because after Sedan no Bonapartist candidate dared show his face. They were victorious, moreover, not so much because they were royalists as

For the events of 1870–1 in France see *The Age of Transformation*, pp. 418–20.

because they favoured ending the war. Their fundamental weakness was reflected in the large number of politically illiterate backwoods peers among the royalist deputies in the Assembly. Another feature of it was the division between Legitimists and Orleanists, dating from the revolution of 1830 when Charles X had been replaced by Louis Philippe. It proved possible to unite the royalists in theory because the Orleanist claimant, the Comte de Paris, was also the next in succession to the Legitimist claimant, the childless Comte de Chambord. Both groups could therefore agree to support the latter. But at heart they remained divided: the Orleanists approved of most of the changes made in France since 1789, the Legitimists mostly accepted but resented them. Chambord accentuated this division: though willing to accept a democratic constitution, he demanded the replacement of the *tricolore* by the old royal flag, white with golden lilies. An exile almost all his life, he does not seem to have been eager to claim his dangerous inheritance. At any rate, his curious request showed him to be completely out of touch with national feeling and made his restoration impossible.

Because of royalist weakness, the republicans at first retained control of the executive. The National Assembly elected Adolphe Thiers 'chief of the executive power', with authority to appoint ministers. This small, alert, pugnacious man had been a leading political figure since 1830, and was now France's most eminent elder statesman. No other member of the Assembly had anything like his moral authority, and in particular nobody else seemed likely to be able to command the respect of the European powers. Thiers was a conservative and his preference was for constitutional monarchy. But for reasons obvious enough he had come to think that 'the republic is the form of government which divides Frenchmen least'. Though he long professed himself neutral, he governed mainly with the help of moderate republicans, and at the time of the Commune made sure of their loyalty by promising not to connive at the abolition of the republic. His administration was successful. France made a rapid economic recovery, and by 1873 had paid off the large indemnity imposed on her by the Germans. The German army of occupation retained in France till payment had been made was now withdrawn. The royalists lost heavily in the many by-elections of this period, partly because there was no longer an administration which automatically helped candidates of the right against the left.

The situation of the country had so much improved by 1873 that the Assembly thought that it could safely get rid of Thiers. Marshal MacMahon was elected head of state for seven years, the intention being that he should serve until a king could be established in his place. He governed through a royalist ministry presided over by the Duc de Broglie. But the royalists were again discomfited, this time by the revival of the Bonapartists. Napoleon III died in 1873, thus allowing the revival of his party in support of the claims of the attractive young Prince Imperial, who was in no way tainted with responsibility for his father's mistakes. The peasantry remained Bonapartist at heart: they associated the royalists with the oppression they had suffered before 1789 and the republicans with social revolution and irreligion. Bonapartist candidates began to do well at by-elections. This development was profoundly disturbing to royalists and republicans alike. They had made common cause against Napoleon III, and were at one in deploring his disastrous foreign policy and the sweeping powers conferred by his political system upon the head of state. The establishment of a new permanent constitution could no longer be delayed: unless this vacuum was quickly filled, the Empire might be restored.[1]

The royalists still could not propose the restoration of the monarchy because they still could not agree on its terms with the Comte de Chambord. Many royalists were therefore willing to join the republicans in establishing republican institutions, and in 1875 this was done. Instead of the single, comprehensive written constitution customary in France, several separate acts were passed dealing with different institutions and the amendment of them was made fairly easy. This reflected the hopes of the royalists that it might later prove possible to turn this republic into a monarchy. In fact, the temporary constitution of 1875 lasted longer than any other that France has had —for sixty-five years, until 1940. In the elections of 1876 for the chamber of deputies which it established, the republicans won a large majority. President MacMahon tried to reverse this result in 1877 by holding new elections. Broglie, again premier, used all the influence of the administration against the republicans and relied heavily on the Bonapartists to organize his campaign. But this coalition against

[1] On this paragraph see especially J. Goualt, *Comment la France est devenue républicaine* (1954).

the republicans was too late and they were again victorious. In 1879 MacMahon resigned the presidency and the Prince Imperial, last presentable Bonapartist pretender, was killed fighting for the British against the Zulus. The republicans were henceforth in secure control of the republic.

The Third Republic was a liberal triumph, but still more was it the triumph of all who wished the government to be timid and inactive and who wanted to prevent any repetition of the bold reforming activity and aggressive foreign policy of Napoleon III. The republicans managed to seize for themselves the leadership of this conservative movement because of the incapacity of the royalists, revealed in their acceptance of a republican constitution, and because the mass of the middle class had got tired of being ruled by the nobility and a few rich commoners. In two respects the republicans were more fortunate than the German National Liberals. The defeat of the Commune meant that for the moment there was no 'social peril'. The leaders of the extreme left were imprisoned or driven underground until amnestied by the republicans in 1881. Therefore MacMahon could not appeal to the electorate, as Bismarck could, to vote against the liberals because of the need to combat the reds. Secondly, the republicans were not damaged by their attachment to free trade. The depression of the seventies was less severe in France than in Germany. The war and the indemnity had prevented an excessive French boom while superheating the German one. French tariffs had been lowered by Napoleon III and many, including Thiers, wanted them raised again. But they had never gone low enough for this to be a primary issue. The main economic question was the restoration of public credit, necessary for state aid to railway building and other utilities. Here success was achieved first by Thiers, with his loans to pay off the Germans, and then by the republicans, who were able to begin a big programme of public works in 1879. A brief general recovery began about then which might seem to justify both the republicans in France and anti-liberal trends elsewhere.

To win over conservative opinion the republicans had to abandon their preference for strong government with power concentrated in a single-chamber legislature. They were obliged to accept a constitutional monarchy in disguise, in which divisions of authority made vigorous initiatives in any direction difficult. The president was titular head of state, ruling through ministers responsible to parliament. The chamber of deputies, elected by manhood suffrage, was balanced by a senate, elected by the members of municipal and other local councils, in which the conservative rural areas were over-represented. The republicans managed at once to win a strong position in the senate by playing on the divisions among the royalists, and when they came to power they abolished the life members which it had at first contained and gave more seats to the urban areas, thus ensuring their own control. On the other hand, the power which the president had (with the consent of the senate) of dissolving the chamber of deputies was discredited by the use MacMahon made of it, and was never used again. The president himself was elected by the two chambers sitting together, and under the republicans a nonentity was usually chosen. All this gave the régime the character of a parliamentary oligarchy. A new chamber was elected every four years: between elections the deputies could arrange things much as they pleased, without fear of being suddenly called to account before the electors. It should be added that local administration remained fundamentally authoritarian. *Maires* became elective under the Third Republic, but otherwise no more was heard of the demands for local autonomy so much voiced by all the opponents of the Empire.

Parliamentary oligarchy might have served well enough under effective party discipline. Gambetta's intention was that there should be a single great republican party sustaining a strong ministry on the English model. The republicans deliberately rejected this arrangement in favour of having several parties in loose alliance. The consequence was the long series of short-lived coalition governments that characterised the Third Republic. As in Germany, the multiplicity of parties diminished the chances of vigorous governmental activity. Again it was largely to reassure conservative opinion that the republicans adopted this system. On the death of Thiers (1877), Jules Grévy was agreed on as prospective candidate for the presidency and titular leader of the whole movement. This was, in effect, a promise that the government of France would not be handed over to the forceful Gambetta, whom Grévy hated. As president, Grévy entrusted the formation of ministries mainly to timid mediocrities: when Gambetta was at length allowed to form one, it did not last three months. In 1882 Gambetta died at the early age of 42, and with him perished the prospect of a strong government on liberal lines. Weak governments were to rule France, with occasional draconian interludes, until the advent of De Gaulle's republic in 1958.

Bogus Liberalism in Southern Europe

In Spain, Portugal and Italy power was in the hands of an oligarchy of soldiers, officials and professional men. They were mildly liberal in outlook, but this reflected their connection with interests profiting from agrarian and political change and did not betoken any capacity to alleviate the misery of the people. There was, accordingly, a stronger challenge to the moderates in power from radical extremists than was the case farther north. But this radicalism was limited both in strength and aims. The masses were too wretched and ignorant to act effectively in politics. The radicals who counted came from the small middle class. However useful the measures they favoured might be in Britain or France, they had no answer to the problem of southern poverty. In the seventies the radicals at last won power for long enough for this to become clear. Discouraged, they joined the oligarchy, rendering it monolithic, and ending for a long time all possibility of significant political or social change.

Ever since the Peninsular War Spain had been troubled by the political activities of the church and the army. The church was profoundly conservative and the soldiers mainly liberal, but the important thing was that both were prepared to undermine the authority of the crown, and this led to political instability. The main result of the disturbances so far had been the emergence of a powerful new body of large landowners. But it was clear that if instability continued, there might be a general social revolution.

In 1868 a military coup overthrew Isabel II, unpopular through having fallen under the influence of the church. Power passed to the radicals, who retained the monarchy but brought in a more democratic constitution, with manhood suffrage. But they could not win support. Hardly anyone would vote in the elections they held, and they could not find a prince to fill the vacant throne. Their search, having helped to cause the war of 1870,[1] at last ended with the accession of Amadeo of Savoy, whose cousin was king of the new

[1] See *The Age of Transformation*, pp. 409-11.

Italy. But in 1873 he abdicated in despair, leaving no alternative, but to proclaim a republic.

A bid for power was now made by the federalists, whose programme resembled that of the Paris Commune. They wanted extreme decentralization of government, and coupled this with social demands: the restoration of the former common lands and woods to municipal ownership and popular use. Federalism was at first a middle-class movement, led by the Rousseau-inspired Pi y Margall. But its relevance to their needs was seen by some of the proletariat, and in 1873 there were risings in the south and east intended to establish an extreme form of federalism by direct action. In the north, meanwhile, there was a revolt of the Carlists—fanatical partisans of the church who had taken up the claims to the throne of a junior branch of the old royal house. Against these movements the army had to be used, and the republic degenerated into a military dictatorship. In 1875 the soldiers brought back Alfonso XII, son of the deposed Isabel.

The restoration brought back into power the oligarchy of new large landowners, the most powerful class in Spain, who had stood aloof from the radical régimes. Their chief political spokesman was Antonio Canovas del Castillo, a distinguished historian who had made a special study of his country's decline and whose view of the situation can be gathered from his famous remark that 'they are Spaniards who cannot be anything else'. His goal was political stability, without which the existing social system could not be preserved. His initial aim was to remove from politics the army and the church, the two great disturbers of the peace. His method was to establish a system of government at once authoritarian and broadly based. The constitution of 1876 restored parliamentary monarchy; in 1885 manhood suffrage was reintroduced. But in every constituency the *cacique*, the local boss acting for the government, exercised absolute control over the voters (mostly very poor) by bribery and police terror. The government could determine exactly the result of every election, national or local. However, Canovas did not use his power solely for the benefit of his own Conservative Party. He gave a share of office and representation to anyone who would be loyal to the régime, notably to the Liberal Party which included most of the disillusioned radicals. Sometimes Canovas would ordain the electoral defeat of his own party and hand over power to the Liberal leader, Sagasta, who in due course would return the compliment. The accord of the affable and hospitable Sagasta with the shy and haughty Canovas meant the junction of the middle class with the landed oligarchy. Thus were the army and church to be kept submissive. To make doubly sure, the army officers were well provided for and the church was allowed to keep and extend its wealth, on which the oligarchy had hitherto cast covetous eyes.

This fraudulent system must not be condemned out of hand. It is a gross error to judge the poor and backward countries of southern and eastern Europe by the standards rightly applied to Britain, France and Germany. Under the constitution of 1876 Spain enjoyed, as had been intended, many years free of coups and civil war. But insufficient use was made of this tranquillity in pressing forward the modernization of the country. In many ways the government was more of a hindrance to the work than a help. The personal liberty and rights of the individual were not secure. Even law and order were not efficiently maintained. Taxation was heavy and inequitable, ruinous to the poor and to commerce. State revenues were squandered on the inflated and inefficient army, and on the hordes of officials whose jobs existed mainly to reward political services. The traditional ills of Spain lived on under a liberal veneer, and for this reason the attempt to achieve political stability was in the long run a failure. In the twentieth century the army and the church resumed their wrecking activities and Spain was plunged into a new time of troubles.

Portugal's political development followed a course parallel to Spain's. The alternation in office of two parties with little to distinguish them but their past had the merit, as in Spain, of keeping the army out of politics. But the 'rotativist' system failed to cure the grave financial weakness of the state, and in the nineties a new period of crisis began.

Italian unification was completed in 1870, when the withdrawal of French troops made possible the annexation of Rome. Like the new Germany, the new Italy had been formed by an alliance between an old princely state—that of the house of Savoy—and the new nationalism. In appearance, Italy had the more liberal régime of the two—a parliamentary monarchy with parliamentary ministers. In practice King Victor Emmanuel was no less powerful than the German sovereigns. The constitution did not prescribe any degree of control by the legislature over the ministry, and the politicians were agreed in allowing the king a pretty free hand in the choice of ministers. The crown retained extensive powers to legislate by decree and these were often extended by parliament, which thus avoided the odium of unpopular legislation. The senate consisted of royal nominees. The chamber of deputies was elected at first on a narrow franchise. This was extended in 1882 to all literate males, and in 1913 to all men over 30, but until the introduction of proportional representation in 1919 the local agents of the government could 'make' the elections by bribing and bullying the electors. Whoever was in office during a general election could count on winning it. In Italy, as in Spain, the system of government was described by the coining of the phrase 'parliamentary dictatorship'.

However, the opposition to the new order in Italy was far stronger than that to the Prussian remaking of Germany. In both countries it was the Catholic Church that had suffered most from unification. The Pope had been deprived of his temporal principality by the new Italian state. The Italian government tried to make amends by granting the Pope a large income and the personal status of an independent sovereign. But successive Popes regarded themselves as being held prisoner by the new rulers of Rome, and in token of this they insisted on passing their entire lives after their accession within the precincts of the Vatican. More important, they forbade the faithful to take any part in the political life of the new Italy, either by holding office or by voting in elections. Although Italy remained an overwhelmingly catholic country, this prohibition was not as fatal to the new régime as might have been expected. The easy-going Italians did not take the Pope's quarrel with their government very seriously and, in particular, church schools were not as formidable rivals to those controlled by the state as was the case in France. But convinced catholics did abstain from politics, and this intensified the oligarchic nature of the new political system.

Unlike Prussia, the Kingdom of Sardinia, over which Victor Emmanuel had ruled before unification, had been neither a great power nor in possession of a large proportion of Italian territory. It was therefore a less suitable foundation for the new national state. Nor could the house of Savoy make use, as Prussia did, of the other princely states that had hitherto ruled the national territory. The Italian princes were too weak and too pro-Austrian. So while the new Germany was a federation, the new Italy had to be a unitary state. It was, however, unfortunate, and not an inevitable corollary of the unitary solution, that Sardinian institutions were imposed en bloc throughout the new kingdom. This did not work too badly in the northern half of the country, for there the social and economic system was much as it was in the mainland territories of Sardinia, and there was a good deal of nationalist feeling in the upper and middle classes. But the south was much more backward than the north, and more or less devoid of nationalist feeling. Unification had been accepted as the only alternative to political and social collapse. It brought heavy burdens. The new Italy inherited from Sardinia a large national debt and heavy military expenditure, both of which increased as the new state tried to win a place among the great powers. Heavy taxes resulted, which were more easily borne in the north than in the poorer south. At the same time, the establishment of internal free trade meant the ruin of southern industry by the competition of the more efficient northerners. The imposition of northern institutions and the fact that most important posts in the administration went to northerners were the last straw. In the sixties there had been massive resistance to the authority of the new government. This was eventually crushed; from the seventies, the misery of the south found expression mainly in massive emigration.

Till the mid-seventies, the new Kingdom was governed by the heirs of Cavour, known (not very meaningfully) as the Right—as conservatives. They were a loosely connected body of northern noblemen and businessmen, mildly liberal in outlook. Their main aim now was to balance the budget, which was achieved in 1876. Against them were the radicals, representing the tradition of Mazzini and Garibaldi. Their two ablest leaders, Agostino Depretis and Francesco Crispi, had been used by Garibaldi to administer the southern territories which he conquered in 1860. A party of the professional and lower middle class, they had started as republicans but had ceased to be so. They dominated the parliamentary representation of the south, mainly because the conservatives there were catholic and anti-nationalist and abstained from politics. They therefore campaigned for the redress of southern grievances and especially for the abolition of the hated grist tax. In 1875 quarrels among the conservatives led to the appointment of Depretis as prime minister and he 'made' the elections of 1876 and gave his friends a parliamentary majority.

Depretis thus became the leading figure in Italian politics, and remained so until his death (1887), when his position passed to Crispi. He was a modest man, living in a small top-floor flat even when prime minister. Conciliatory, a good administrator, he seemed to have no very definite principles. His ministries were radical neither in measures nor in personnel. They were coalitions of radicals and conservatives, and their policy was little more than routine administration. Italian parties had never been much more than loose associations of important personalities, each with his own following. Now significant party divisions disappeared and politics were entirely dominated by personal rivalries within the oligarchy. This decline of party, scornfully labelled 'transformism', reflected the fact that the radicals had no effective remedy to put forward for the country's ills. Only the ministries of Cairoli (1878–9) seriously attempted a fresh start. Their idealism shamed their successors into repealing the grist tax, but their unaggressive foreign policy was so unpopular that their attempt to allow more political freedom to the masses ended in disastrous rioting, and the new king, Humbert, was nearly assassinated. The only radical reform of real importance was compulsory education (1877), and that applied only in communes that could afford a school. A few posts in the state tobacco monopoly had, it was said, reconciled the radicals of the south to the established order.

Once again, the intractability of southern Europe's problems makes it wrong to condemn the politicians too severely. The transformist era has been defended by no less an authority than the great historian and philosopher Benedetto Croce. He saw it as bringing to an end the political divisions related to the problems of achieving unification, and clearing the way for new thinking about the entirely different problems that arose when the country was united. New thinking there was indeed (and in Spain as well as in Italy), as we shall see. But the fact remains that the Italian political system, as it developed from now on, contributed only modestly to the wellbeing of the country. Unification brought some prosperity to the north but very little to the south, which after a century of national unity was still an open sore.

Sham Constitutionalism in Austria-Hungary

Unlike the countries so far discussed, Austria-Hungary was not a nation state. The two most important national groups, the Germans and the Magyars (Hungarians) each amounted to a quarter or less of the total population. The peoples of the Monarchy were held together by their allegiance to a common sovereign. Emperor Francis Joseph had been raised to the throne in 1848, at the age of eighteen, because it was thought that only a young and vigorous prince could weather the revolutions. Weather them he did, and ruled for almost seventy years, not dying till 1916. Pious, austere and fanatically industrious, he had the highest sense of public duty and continued to the last to serve the state unwearyingly, undismayed by public calamity and hideous private misfortunes—the suicide of his only son, the assassination of his wife and later of his nephew, Francis Ferdinand. But he was the most rigid of conservatives, even to the extent of conserving oil lamps and old-fashioned plumbing in his palaces. He was also quite unusually devoid of human warmth, having no intimates, and dismissing faithful advisers without a shadow of regret if the political situation seemed to require it. As a result he could not see beyond *raison d'état*, and though ready to sanction the most sweeping changes in order to preserve the Monarchy, he was unable to sympathize with any constructive plan for its regeneration. Asking no more about his subjects than 'is he a patriot for me?' he was more concerned to maintain his own power by exploiting their divisions than to foster a common loyalty to the Monarchy that might have brought the danger of a common front against the monarch. It was this rather than some inevitable force that doomed the Monarchy: its inhabitants, long and closely associated, did not readily think in terms of breaking it up.

The earlier events of his reign had convinced the Emperor that he could only survive if he came to terms with the national movement of the Magyars. Taken in 1865, this decision was reinforced by defeat in the ensuing war against Prussia and was never thereafter departed from. It resulted in the Compromise (*Ausgleich*) of 1867,[1] which brought into being, as in Germany and Italy, a partnership between

---

[1] For a fuller account of this see *The Age of Transformation*, pp. 355-9.

an old dynasty and the nationalists. Constitutional government was restored in Hungary, and she achieved virtual independence. A separate constitutional régime was set up for the other half of the Monarchy, and certain joint institutions were set up for the common affairs of the two halves. But although in appearance there was equality between Hungary and the rest, in practice there was Magyar supremacy, tempered only by the powerful position retained by the Emperor. In demonstrating this and showing its consequences, it will be best to begin with Hungary.

The Magyars comprised only half the population of the old Kingdom of Hungary, the rest consisting of Rumanians and various Slav peoples. But most of the land was in the hands of the Magyar nobility, and they alone possessed a continuous political tradition. Since medieval times they had administered the country through elective local magistrates, and possessed in the two-chambered diet a means of restraining the sovereign. The revolution of 1848 had been for them only a continuation of the long struggle to limit the power of the crown. Its failure had led to the ascendancy of the moderates in Magyar counsels, and it was they who had made the *Ausgleich*. Francis Deak was their greatest leader, but in 1867 he retired in favour of Count Julius Andrassy, prime minister of Hungary till 1873 and then foreign minister of the whole Monarchy. Andrassy had once been a radical, and though a great nobleman he retained to the end a wild and gipsy-like appearance and an excitable demeanour. But he and Deak were probably the sanest statesmen in Central Europe. They fought for two things essential for the well-being of the Monarchy: amicable co-operation between Hungary and the other Habsburg lands, and better relations between the Magyars and the other nationalities within the Hungarian realm itself.

Under the *Ausgleich*, the Emperor was crowned as King of Hungary and the laws of 1848 reforming the old constitution were put in force. A ministry responsible to parliament took charge of the affairs of the kingdom. The Magyars thus won power: but they proceeded to compromise with the other nationalities in Hungary. The Croats received provincial autonomy. Other laws provided that non-Magyar languages might be used in local government and education.

The concessions which the moderates made both to the Emperor and to the non-Magyar nationalities were odious to the radicals in

Hungary, disciples of Kossuth. They wanted a more intransigently nationalist attitude towards both. They were mainly a party of the lesser nobility and their most important leader was Count Koloman Tisza. Like Kossuth and many earlier anti-Habsburg extremists, he was a Calvinist. Small and unkempt, he had both the debating skills of the parliamentarian and the iron will that makes a dictator. His chance came with the economic crisis of 1873, which embarrassed the Hungarian ministry and made a broader coalition necessary to pull the country through. In 1875 the bulk of the radicals and of the moderates merged in a new Liberal Party, and with its support Tisza formed a government.

As in Spain and Italy, the main parties had merged into a single oligarchy. The franchise was narrow, and so here, too, the elections were 'made' and the rulers perpetuated their own power. Another resemblance was that the radicals accepted the existing system once they were in power. But in Hungary there were important exceptions to this rule. The rise of the radicals did mean a turn for the worse for the non-Magyars. The concessions made to them were either withdrawn or ignored. The Magyar language gained almost a monopoly in the administration and the schools. There was also a turn for the worse in the administration of the common affairs of the whole Monarchy, as will be shown in due course. The Hungarian version of 'parliamentary dictatorship' was not a do-nothing affair, incapable of important reforms; it was a strong and actively hostile opponent of measures of conciliation, essential to draw the peoples of the Monarchy together and promote stability and contentment.

The main Hungarian concessions under the Compromise of 1867 were that defence and foreign policy should be managed as the common concern of the whole Monarchy. There continued, therefore, to be a single army and navy, and there were joint ministers of war and foreign affairs, as well as one for the joint finances. The main Hungarian concern had been to ensure that the joint institutions should never become powerful enough to threaten Hungarian independence. The two halves of the Monarchy, therefore, conserved separate militias in addition to the joint army. There was no joint parliament: instead, two small delegations met occasionally to oversee the joint ministers and vote a budget. The delegations sat separately and communicated with each other in writing: joint sessions were held only to resolve differences of opinion by a silent vote. The Hungarian delegation was elected by the parliament of that country; the other delegation consisted of delegates separately elected for each province, and so in any joint vote the monolithic Hungarians were likely to prevail. This curious institution never had much vitality, and so the Emperor and the joint ministers whom he appointed gained a fairly free hand. The main check upon them was that in practice they had to consult and carry with them the prime ministers of the two halves of the Monarchy. A final limitation upon the joint organs of government was that common economic concerns were dealt with not by them but by direct negotiations between Budapest and Vienna. Every ten years an agreement was required to prolong the customs union between the two halves of the Monarchy and settle the share of the joint expenses to be borne by each. On these occasions the Hungarian radicals always demanded better terms, showing little concern for anyone's interest but their own. It was especially in this way that they made the government of the Monarchy as a whole more difficult.

At first sight, the provinces which continued to be ruled from Vienna after 1867 had a constitution very like that of Hungary. There was a two-chamber parliament and, for some years at least, a parliamentary ministry. But the Hungarian constitution was as old and revered as the British, protected by the loyalty of the whole Magyar nation irrespective of party divisions. The constitution in force at Vienna was merely the latest of several arrangements promulgated in the space of a few years by imperial decree. The Germans divided for and against these successive arrangements according to their party affiliations. Their only common loyalty was to the dynasty, to Austria as a great power; they were agreed only in deploring Hungarian independence. All this is reflected in the fact that the area under Viennese rule was never even given a proper name: 'Austria' continued to refer to the Monarchy as a whole, even when hyphenated with 'Hungary'. The divisions among the Germans were highly beneficial to the Slav peoples who made up half the population of the nameless area. They never fell into the same subjection as their opposite numbers in Hungary. The Emperor, too, could exploit German divisions for his own benefit, and he retained much more power at Vienna than he did at Budapest.

From the *Ausgleich* until 1879, the German liberals were predominant at Vienna. They were a nationalist and anticlerical party like the Hungarian radicals and drew their strength mainly from the urban middle class. They favoured the centralization of authority in Vienna and, like their opposite numbers in Germany, were opposed by a catholic and largely aristocratic party who wanted a looser federal structure. Like the German Centre, the Austrian clericals had democratic as well as conservative affinities. In particular, they were able to make common cause with the Slav nationalists. Both expected to gain by the granting of more power to the provincial assemblies, at the expense of the government in Vienna.

The liberals owed their power to the decision of the Emperor. In 1867 he gave the constitution a centralizing tendency and the electoral system, both national and provincial, heavily favoured the towns (mainly German and liberal) at the expense of the country districts (mainly clerical or Slav). A special feature of the system was the separate representation of the large, landed proprietors: these were mostly noblemen and many of them voted as the Emperor wished, thus giving him a sort of casting vote in the chamber and the provincial assemblies. The successive ministries of liberal parliamentarians betokened a constitutionalism that was more apparent than real, and their triumph was as insubstantial as it was fraudulent.

The Emperor had favoured them chiefly to please the Hungarian moderates, who wished to see like-minded people in charge at Vienna. He had also intended to make a good impression on the liberals in Germany, preparatory to a revival of Austrian influence there. The war of 1870 ended all hope of such a thing and it was accordingly followed by the dismissal of the Austrian liberal ministers and preparations to remake the constitution on federal lines. It was largely the intervention of the Hungarian premier, Andrassy, that led to the abandonment of this experiment and the recall of the liberals. Its only permanent result was the granting of very full autonomy to the Poles of Galicia. The Polish nation was unique among the western Slavs in possessing a numerous body of nobles, who provided its political leaders. Haters of Russia above all, themselves the oppressors of another Slav people, the Ruthenes, the Polish nobles had strong affinities with the Magyars and even the Germans: they were henceforth a loyal element in the Monarchy.

The German liberals were finished by the economic crisis of the seventies. The general crash of 1873 actually began at Vienna, and not only upset Austrian finances but was accompanied by various commercial scandals involving liberal ministers. It also led to radical ascendancy in Hungary, and the radicals, unlike Andrassy, did not care how or by whom the other half of the Monarchy was governed: this was part of their general egoistic concentration on the immediate interests of their own land. The Emperor had not found the liberals intrinsically useful—they were mostly tiresome, doctrinaire, academic pedants. He delayed their dismissal only until a really workable alternative could be produced. This was done by the formation of Count Taaffe's ministry in 1879, with Slav and clerical support. The difficulties in the way of this solution and how they were overcome are better described in the next chapter.

The events of 1879 ended even the pretence of parliamentary control over the government at Vienna, and there now began a period of weak government based on multi-party wrangling, as in France and Germany. The Magyars were more than ever the strongest element in the Monarchy and the only ones at all satisfied. The Germans remained powerful in the army and administration, and above all in economic life. In 1907 the Germans comprised 35·8 per cent of the population of their half of the monarchy but paid 63·4 per cent of the direct taxes. But the liberal middle class was henceforth excluded from political power and became increasingly discontented. The view that Austro-Hungarian Dualism was a partnership between Germans and Magyars is really true only for the years down to 1879. The Slavs gained what the Germans lost, but in wealth and political influence they remained well behind the ruling races; in Hungary their position was getting worse. Dominated by its backward Hungarian half, the Monarchy was at the mercy of a self-centred and shortsighted oligarchy such as ruled in all the backward countries. It is clear in retrospect that the Magyars needed the Monarchy if they were not to sink into insignificance between Slav and German. But they blocked all reforms that might have maintained its vitality. The resulting mass of dissatisfaction in central Europe endangered the equilibrium of the whole continent.

3: The Slavonic Ferment and the Eastern Question

The unification of Germany and Italy led to an eastward movement of the main European storm centre to the Russian and Ottoman Empires and the shaky realm of the Habsburgs. From 1875 events there developed in a way that seemed to threaten both a gigantic revolutionary upheaval and a general European war. The trends that led to the conflict of 1914 and the Russian revolutions of 1917 were already visible, or at least curiously prefigured. But the forces pressing that way were as yet impressive because of their novelty rather than because of their strength. By the early eighties order had been restored. The revolutionaries were suppressed and the more moderate advocates of change obtained only modest satisfaction in the new system. The threat of war had passed and peace and stability in the area were assured by something very like a revival of the Holy Alliance.

The Dawn of Revolution in Russia

Defeat in the Crimean War had shown the tsarist government that it was essential to modernize Russia and an attempt was made to do so on lines which recall Prussia's 'revolution from above' after Napoleon's victory at Jena.[1] Serfdom was abolished. Local administration was entrusted to elective bodies: the town councils, and the provincial and district *zemstva*, in which representatives of the towns and peasants sat with those of the still dominant nobility. The judicial system was westernized: judges were irremovable, trials were public and there was a jury in criminal cases. The censorship became less severe and newspapers were allowed to discuss political questions.

There thus came into being the possibility of collaboration, as in the west, between enlightened conservative administrators and the liberal middle class. This was the method accepted by most of those, nobles

[1] See further, *The Age of Transformation*, pp. 310–14.

or bourgeois, who wished to reform Russia. The *zemstva* were their most fruitful field of activity. By the end of the century they were beginning to make notable progress in the creation of a national education system and a public health service. They also did something for the education of the peasants in new agricultural methods. The new judicial system brought into being a well-trained body of professional lawyers, upholder of the rights of the citizen against the state. An active and relatively free intellectual life was reflected in the growth of newspapers, now seeking to influence the government in the name of public opinion.

But there was no true partnership between government and liberals. Parliamentary institutions had not been introduced, though the government had several times considered doing so. Arrest and detention without trial remained legal, and government officials could not be prosecuted at law without the consent of their superiors. The middle class had been given a chance to show its dissatisfaction, but very little had been done to satisfy it. Consequently, despite its weakness and moderation, it did not rally to the government and abandon its hostility to authority, as did its opposite numbers in the comparable conditions of Italy and Spain. Instead, it remained politically neutral: not daring to rebel against the government itself, but rather inclining to sympathize with those who did become revolutionaries.

The peasants, too, were not fundamentally loyal to the government. Serfdom had been abolished on terms onerous to them and favourable to the nobility. Where land was valuable, they had been given little of it. Where it was not, they had been given more, but the compensation paid to the lord for it, everywhere high, was here excessively so. This compensation was paid to the lord by the state and gradually recovered from the peasants in annual instalments. This was a heavy burden: in 1880 the peasants were already in arrears to the extent of 27 per cent of the annual payment. Moreover, each village was collectively responsible for the compensation payable on its lands. A peasant was commonly not allowed to dispose of his holding unless he could pay to the village a large lump sum towards the discharge of the debt outstanding on it. Thus, the peasants remained in practice tied to the soil, and it was difficult for the more enterprising of them to add to their holdings by buying from the rest. Poor, anyway, because of technical backwardness and, in some places, over-population, the peasants were thus doubly wretched, and it was especially important that there was little incentive for the better-off among them to make common cause with the authorities: they had their grievances no less than the poorest. The depression of the seventies hurt Russian agriculture, competitive though it was, and the war with Turkey in 1877 undid much of the good work of the reform period in restoring Russian finances.

Such were the conditions which made Russia, alone among the great powers after 1870, a country where a violent and radical revolution might succeed. Russia had a revolutionary tradition of sorts going back to the Decembrists of 1825, and in the sixties and seventies agitation became more or less continuous. Drawn at first from the nobility, the revolutionaries were now largely middle-class and were beginning to include workers and peasants. But almost all were young students and they had no solid support in any class. They had to struggle both against popular apathy and ignorance, and against the huge police apparatus of the autocracy. To overcome the former, they needed time, but after a year or two the police always caught up with them. The barbarous inefficiency of the government delayed their capture but increased their subsequent sufferings. Many died in prison (mostly of consumption); not a few went mad; the strongest returned to normal life many years later, in old age. Several generations of revolutionary leaders were thus removed from the scene in a few years. Each time their successors had to start from scratch: there was little chance of learning what mistakes to avoid.

Till 1870 the main emphasis had been on plans to seize power by a conspiracy. The last representatives of this tradition were Tkachev, who did much to make Marx's ideas known in Russia, and Nechaev. The latter's personal magnetism was so intense that when at length imprisoned, he converted his guards to the revolutionary cause. But he was devious and untruthful, with a positive relish for winning supporters by blackmail and intimidation. When he and his followers murdered one of their number suspected of betraying them, it was supposed (though no proof exists) that he knew the victim to be innocent but wished to cement his band together by common complicity in a crime. The doctrine of a ruthless minority as the chosen instrument of revolution was the enduring legacy of his generation.

But the main trend of the seventies was away from Nechaev, partly in conscious revulsion against his unsavoury methods but still more because it was clear that no revolution could succeed until it could count on mass support. Efforts therefore began to educate both peasants and factory workers, and from 1873 these took the form particularly of what was called 'going to the people'. Students abandoned the university and went to live in villages or industrial slums. They earned their living either by learning and practising a trade, or by using their existing skills when these could benefit the people, as for instance with medical students. They tried to win the confidence of their new neighbours and then to instruct them politically. The pioneers tended to rely on inflammatory speeches delivered over a wide area. But the peasants were either shocked or bewildered, and the authorities soon stepped in. It proved more rewarding to settle in one place and to try at first to teach rather than convert.

Behind this activity lay certain beliefs about Russian rural society. The Russian village was governed by a peasant council (*obshchina*) which controlled the common land, managed the system of cultivation, and in many cases reallocated the cultivable land among the families from time to time, to take account of the formation of new ones and the fluctuations of the rest in size. This system was retained and remodelled after the emancipation of the serfs, being required among other things for ensuring the compensation payments to the government. The importance of such a communal organization in the system of land tenure led to the quite erroneous belief that the peasants, when left to themselves, favoured the common ownership of land. Among the urban artisans there was an equivalent to the *obshchina* in the *artel*, or co-operative workshop. These institutions had at first been celebrated mainly by conservative writers, who argued from their existence that Russian society was totally different from that of the west and could never be reorganized on liberal lines. Increasingly it was the revolutionaries who used this argument. They said that their traditional beliefs made the Russian masses ripe for conversion to the most advanced doctrines of socialism. Once they could be rid of their superstitious respect for authority, they would rise and destroy not only the government but the whole system of private property. Russia would pass directly to socialism without the need for a lengthy period of development on western capitalist lines.

The revolutionaries therefore had no interest in supporting the middle class against the autocracy or taking up the traditional middle-class demands for a parliamentary constitution. They rightly thought that any successes along these lines would benefit mainly the middle classes and turn them into defenders of the status quo, to the disadvantage of the masses. They believed in liberty and democracy, but only as part of a social revolution. In the earlier seventies, they tended to think that preaching to the people was enough: once they were converted, they would be invincible. But they were driven to more violent measures by the severity of police persecution, which almost brought their propaganda to a halt. They began to try to resist arrest, to organize escapes from prison, finally to assassinate officials in reprisal for the maltreatment of those under arrest. These measures were not directed to the seizure of power but rather to holding the ring, containing the government forces while propaganda went forward. They called for more organization than there had been hitherto, and in 1877 a disciplined secret society, Land and Liberty, was set up.

Such was the party known as the Populists (*Narodniki*). Among their leaders may be mentioned Alexander Mikhailov, if only for the contrast he presents to Nechaev. His childhood was happy. He loved nature and said that he had become a socialist in part because he wished to see 'humanity as harmonious, as beautiful as nature'. Even in prison, awaiting sentence of death, he declared his life to have been 'quite exceptional for active happiness'. Some of his missionary work was among the *raskolniki* (dissenting sects), who seemed promising material to the revolutionaries because they suffered legal disabilities and had some of the stern independence of the western Protestants. He made himself amazingly expert in their doctrines, and clearly felt a deep affinity with their religious views. This man excelled both as a political strategist and an organizer of assassination.

Such success as the Populists had was in directions at variance with their hopes. They made little headway with the peasants—their biggest success, the organizing of a guerilla band in the Ukraine, was only achieved by pretending to be agents of the Tsar. Among the workers in the new factories they did better: there were strikes in St Petersburg, and workers began to form independent organizations of their own. But their real achievement, the only thing which really frightened the government, was their impact on the middle classes. The authorities were alarmed at the sympathy shown by local notables to students 'going to the people'. The government tried in 1877 to discredit the revolutionaries by the two mass trials of 'the 50' and 'the 193'. They hoped to show that their opponents intended to deluge the country in blood. But the accused had the best of it: their speeches showed them averse to violence, driven to it by the intensity of repression, anxious to rescue the nation from an intolerable impasse. The trials enabled their views, normally little heard because of the censorship, to be widely publicized. In 1878 there followed the trial of Vera Zasulich for the attempted murder of the governor of St Petersburg. The mass trials had been conducted by special courts and only partly in public. But the government mistakenly thought that Vera Zasulich's crime was non-political—that she had been the mistress of a student who had been flogged until he went mad. Her case was therefore tried by an ordinary criminal court, with a jury. The result was a triumphant acquittal in the teeth of the evidence. The *zemstva* began to ask for reforms, and some of their leaders even negotiated with some of the revolutionaries. The middle classes were standing aside and letting the government and the revolutionaries fight it out.

The government gradually made the machinery of repression more efficient, by such measures as the appointment of military governors-general and the entrusting of all political trials to military tribunals. At the same time it tried desperately to think of ways of making itself popular. Both trends were a grave threat to the revolutionaries. Their ranks thinned rapidly under intensified repression. The prospect of reform—or even the survival of tsardom without reform—they identified with the strengthening of the middle classes in town and country, the growth of the 'capitalist sector' in industry and agriculture, and the decay of the traditional peasant and artisan communities out of which they had hoped to build a socialist society. The main body of the revolutionaries therefore concluded that the autocracy must be destroyed quickly at all costs. For this the only weapon at their disposal was assassination, and they now proposed to turn it against the Tsar. Some, however, of whom Plekhanov was the most important, rejected this return to the old tradition of a conspiracy to seize power. They rightly argued that even if the autocracy was thus broken, only the middle classes were strong enough to assume power. They saw no alternative to the gradual proselytizing of the masses, whatever its disadvantages, and they began to have more hope of the urban workers than of the inert peasants. In 1879 the movement split into two new bodies: the ultra-terrorist 'People's Will' and the gradualist 'Black Partition'.[1] The latter, by natural development of their ideas, reached the orthodox Marxist position: that a capitalist phase must precede the development of socialism and that the main revolutionary force must come from the urban workers rather than the peasants. They were the ancestors of the later Social Democrats and Bolsheviks.

Even before the split an attempt had been made on the Tsar's life, and in February 1880 the revolutionaries almost succeeded in blowing him up at dinner. A 'dictatorship of heart and mind' was now established under an Armenian general, Loris Melikov, who created for the first time a unified command over all the security forces. He showed equal determination in seeking to isolate the revolutionaries from the middle class. Several measures were taken to conciliate the latter, and at length he proposed that legislation should in future be discussed by a Council of State and preparatory commissions in which elected popular representatives were to sit with the nominees of the Tsar. The vigour of the new measures enabled the government at last to win its duel with the revolutionaries and crush them completely. But with their dying blow they destroyed the constructive side of Loris Melikov's work. In March 1881 Alexander II was at length assassinated. Alexander III was a more unbending conservative than his father. After two months' hesitation he pronounced against the proposed reforms and declared his resolve to maintain the autocracy. This he and his son succeeded in doing for more than twenty years. But government and middle classes had not come together, and so the revolutionaries were to have another chance.

Russia in the seventies reached an impasse closely resembling that in the other underdeveloped parts of Europe, notably Italy and Spain. Small though it was, the middle class alone was strong enough to promote reforms effectively, and the schemes in which it was interested were unlikely to do much to relieve the misery of the people. Unlike the Italian and Spanish oligarchies, the Russian government

---

[1] I.e. for partitioning the rich black earth among the peasants.

had not felt it necessary to conciliate middle-class radicals and so they remained in opposition. But they could not join with the revolutionaries to put pressure on the government: the two were kept apart by misguided efforts to learn from the past. The middle classes everywhere now inclined towards moderation because they had seen that revolutions commonly brought a threat to private property. Similarly, the Russian revolutionaries, having seen that the middle classes of the west were turning against revolution, shrank from doing anything that might help their own middle class for fear of tipping the political balance against themselves. Until this impasse could be overcome and an alliance of masses and middle class brought into being, the Russian autocracy was safe, little though it might deserve it.

Slav Nationalism

Nationalism and Marxism, which have proved the two most potent political ideas among the underdeveloped peoples, are both in effect of German origin. Already in the seventies the Russian revolutionaries were attracted by Marx, and the debt of the Slav nationalists to their German counterparts was very much greater. It was principally from the German writers of the period of national intellectual revival in the late eighteenth century that there came the idea that the different Slav peoples, and the Slavs collectively, had a distinctive and important culture of their own. It was largely German and German-trained scholars whose researches into Slav languages and antiquities provided a solid basis for this new idea. Lastly, it was the progress of the German national cause which led the Slav equivalents to acquire a political character and importance. The German revolutions of 1848, including that at Vienna, were rather ineffectively answered by the convening of a Slav congress in Prague.[1] There was a similar response to the events of 1866, which brought a German empire within sight and led to the supremacy within the Habsburg territories of the German nationalists and their Magyar friends. The Slav subjects of the Habsburgs had hitherto hoped to gain power by a partnership with their ruler. On several occasions (the last in 1871) Francis Joseph made them an offer, only to disappoint them by withdrawing it. They now began, therefore, to think of seeking help from Russia,

---

[1] *The Age of Transformation*, p. 257.

although most of them were Catholic and essentially western peoples and looked on the tsarist state as both barbarous and heretical. The Czechs in particular, whose growing industrial and professional middle class made them the strongest among the Slavs of the Monarchy, now went into irreconcilable opposition. In protest against the unjust electoral system, their deputies refused to sit in the Vienna parliament or the provincial assemblies. The Emperor's broken promise to have himself crowned in Prague was reprinted on specially thin paper, for use in Czech lavatories.

In Russia there was a parallel increase of interest in the other Slav peoples. There had long been a 'slavophile' school of thought in that country, mainly but not entirely conservative, which had believed in the uniqueness of Russian civilization and the undesirability of introducing western institutions, liberal or otherwise. There were also 'panslavs', who applied these ideas to the Slavs as a whole and sometimes drew the conclusion that Russia should establish political control over the other Slav peoples. But not even all the 'slavophiles' were 'panslavs', and the Russian government, which to some extent found 'slavophile' ideas useful as conservative propaganda, fought shy of 'panslavism' as disruptive of conservative solidarity with the neighbouring monarchies. But from 1866 there was a growing feeling that Russia needed to take strong measures against the establishment of German supremacy throughout central Europe and panslav ideas became increasingly popular among the Russian middle class. In 1871 was published the most important panslav work *Russia and Europe* by the biologist Nicholas Danilevsky. He saw human history as dominated by a succession of 'civilizations', of which the 'Teutono-Romance' was the latest. But he thought it was now in decline and destined to be replaced by that of the Slavs. Though Constantinople was to be the capital of his projected Slav federation, there was to be a westward advance as well: the Slavs under Habsburg rule, even the Magyars, were to be included. Panslav ideas, emphasizing racial more than religious differences, tended to make Austria-Hungary rather than the Turks the main enemies of Russia.

The new Slav trends were given expression by the Ethnographic Exhibition in Moscow in 1867—in fact, a Slav cultural congress under the patronage of the Russian government and attended by representatives of most of the Slav peoples, from the Austrian and

Ottoman as well as the Russian realms. But for the time being there was no prospect of the clash between Slav and Teuton and the Slav offensive against Austria which this portended. The Russian administration now contained some panslav sympathizers, and it was not averse to private Russian activity in aid of the Slavs abroad, if only because this distracted the Russian middle classes from their domestic grievances. But both government and opinion in Russia were highly suspicious of the Catholic, western Slavs and doubted if they would prove loyal friends. The Poles had lately been crushed anew after an unusually sustained attempt to throw off Russian rule. They were not represented at the 1867 conference and the Czechs annoyed the Russians by reproaching them for the way in which the Poles had been treated. For their part, the Czechs and other Slav peoples under Habsburg rule made common cause, as already noted, with the aristocratic, conservative opposition in the Dual Monarchy. As the German liberal ministry at Vienna got weaker, their influence increased and the need to turn to Russia lessened.

It was therefore the Ottoman Empire which bore the brunt of the Slav revival. The Crimean War had been fought by the western powers to win for the Turks a breathing space, in which to regenerate their empire before the Russian advance was resumed. The Turks had indeed grown stronger since 1856. Western capital had developed the resources of the empire, built railways and increased the revenue. The armed forces had been made stronger and more efficient. But not much had been done, except on paper, to make Moslem rule less oppressive to the christians, and the growth of prosperity in the area strengthened the christian peoples no less than it did the Turks. By 1870 Rumania and Serbia had achieved independence in all but name. Each was ruled by a Prince, whose power was only mildly restrained by constitutions in appearance rather democratic. Charles of Rumania was a Hohenzollern, whose ties were with the great European dynasties. He resented the suzerainty of the Sultan and kept Rumania hostile to the Turks to a degree not warranted by the small number of Rumanians still under direct Turkish rule. Milan of Serbia, still a minor in 1870, was of a native family, but he was a pleasure-loving cosmopolitan and turned out a puppet of the Austrians.

The christians remaining under Ottoman control received help in their struggle for emancipation not only from the Russians but from

3—E.E.P.

the Slavs and conservatives associated within the Dual Monarchy. At Constantinople the Russian ambassador was Count Paul Ignatiev, one of the few high officials who had embraced panslavism. Numerous Russian consuls were spread through Turkey in Europe, though Russian trade with the area was small: their main activity was to encourage local national feeling. Ignatiev was particularly interested in the Bulgars, the only numerous Balkan nationality still without an autonomous principality of their own. Because of their backwardness, the Russians hoped to maintain an ascendancy over them and benefit from their advance: the other Balkan nationalities showed an ungrateful tendency to turn from Russia to the west once started on the road to independence. So backward were the Bulgars that their first demands were cultural rather than political, and were directed against the Greeks, not the Turks. The Orthodox Church in the Balkans, under the Patriarch of Constantinople, was controlled by the Greeks. They used their resulting control of the christian educational system to propagate their own culture, to the detriment of Slav languages and literatures. In 1870, with Ignatiev's help, the Bulgars won from the Sultan an independent church organization under their own Exarch. Some of this church's affairs were managed by elected bodies of laymen, and this gave the Bulgars the ghost of a political existence. The Exarchate affair showed that quarrels between the christian peoples were destined to overlay their common struggle with the Turk. The Greeks were pressing their own claims against the Turks vigorously, especially in Crete. But they stood aside from the conflicts between Slav and Turk, and some even took the Turkish side. Foolishly, the Kingdom of the Hellenes did not enter the Russo-Turkish war till it was almost too late to share in the spoils. The Ottoman Empire showed its Byzantine origin in the privileged position of the Greeks compared to the other christians. They would lose something by its complete disruption.

It was the Serbs and not the Greeks or the Bulgars who began the direct challenge to Turkish authority in the seventies, and although the Russians were interested in them, the help which they received from Habsburg territory is more striking. The westernmost Turkish provinces, Bosnia and the Herzegovina, were surrounded by Habsburg lands on two sides and by autonomous Serbia on a third. The christian peasants, Serb and Croat, had to support Moslem landlords as well as Turkish governors and they lived on some of the most barren land in Europe. The tiny independent principality of Montenegro was next to them, and every few years a miniature war took place between its troops and the Turks, accompanied by risings on Turkish territory. The national movement had other focal points on Habsburg soil. The Serbs of south Hungary, who included a prosperous mercantile element, had started a society, the *omladina*, for propaganda on both sides of the border. Croatia enjoyed some autonomy within Hungary, as already noted, and from 1873 had a moderate nationalist, Mazuranic, as its Ban (governor). In Bishop Strossmeyer the Croats possessed the leading Slav statesman of the Dual Monarchy and the only one of European importance. He dreamed of a union of the south Slavs round Croatia and the South Slav Academy, which he had founded in 1867, gave cultural expression to this idea. Of greater political importance was the traditional loyalty of the Croats to the dynasty. They had fought for it against the Hungarian revolutionaries of 1848, and among the Croat nationalists were noblemen and army officers close to the court. The army command, in general, had some sympathy for the Croat desire for expansion into Bosnia-Herzegovina. These provinces were the hinterland of Austrian Dalmatia and would be important for its defence in the event of a war of revenge against Italy—always the dream of Austrian soldiers and conservatives. In 1875 Francis Joseph was induced to make an important demonstration helpful to the conservative and Croat expansionists. He visited Dalmatia and representative Bosnians came and appealed to him for help.

Thus encouraged, the people of Bosnia-Herzegovina rebelled against the Turks in 1875. Simultaneously, the Turks began to feel the effects of the great economic depression. Their finances had become increasingly dependent on loans from the west, easily raised in the boom years of the mid-century. The crash of 1873 made investors more wary, and the Turks, with their unbalanced budget, could borrow no more. In 1875 they suspended payment of interest on their debts—the unwisdom of which they might have divined from the fact that no less a person than Ignatiev advised it. Financial prostration was to be fatal to the Ottoman Empire's chances of survival as a respectable second-class power. She could not properly pay for her own defence, and the great powers constantly interfered in her financial arrangements, to the detriment of her independence.

For the moment, however, it was the toughness and not the weakness of the Turks that was in evidence. The revolt in the west was followed in the spring of 1876 by a Bulgar rising, organized by refugees in Rumania. In July, Montenegro and Serbia declared war on the Turks, the latter because Prince Milan feared the wrath of his people if he did not. The famous Bulgarian atrocities, in which the then impressive total of 12,000 people were slaughtered, were the Turks' first response to the spread of rebellion. But it was not only the Christians who suffered. There were student riots at Constantinople. Two sultans were deposed in quick succession. By the autumn of 1876 power was in the hands of the wily Sultan Abdul-Hamid and Midhat Pasha, an able administrator who was the leader of the small band of Turkish liberals. The latter only lasted a few months, but in that time he proved a serviceable barrier against intervention by the great powers. These had several times tried to restore quiet by proposing reforms, but the Turks had evaded foreign interference. Midhat explicitly refused to allow it, but also gave this a plausible justification. In December 1876 the Sultan granted his subjects a constitution: there was to be a two-chamber parliament and equal rights for Christians and Moslems. This was window-dressing, but it is interesting that in the new assembly Greeks and Armenians joined the Turks in rejecting the plans of the powers for the benefit of the Slavs. Meanwhile, Prince Milan's forces had been defeated and Serbia was obliged to make peace. The Turks had proved a match for their Balkan opponents. The question now was whether the great powers, for humanitarian or political reasons, would intervene to redress the balance. The further development of the 'eastern question' depended on the state of relations between the powers.

The Diplomatic Consequences of German Unification

(i) To 1875

From 1866 the progress of German unification had something of the same effect on Austrian and Russian policy that it had on Slav nationalism. Both Austria and Russia were losers by German unification, for the influence which both had had among the smaller German states was now supplanted by the control of Prussia, and the Hohen-zollern realm became the strongest instead of the weakest of the three. Russia had all along hoped to gain compensating advantages for this in the Balkans. The rise of Prussia weakened both France and Austria, who had acted against Russia in the days of the Crimean War. Russia therefore looked forward to recovering what she had lost after that war: southern Bessarabia (which had given her access to the Danube) and the right to have a fleet on the Black Sea. The Austrians, too, now hoped to make up for their German losses by ex-panding their Balkan influence and the prospect therefore opened up of intensified great power rivalry in the area, with the possibility of Slav gains at Turkish expense.

France, too, was driven towards the Balkans by the Prussian vic-tory in 1866. Napoleon III tried to retrieve his diplomatic fortunes by exploiting Austro-Russian rivalry. If France acquired an ally by this means there was a chance, though rather a remote one, that she might try to reopen the German question. Bismarck therefore tried to keep the Austrians and Russians from quarrelling, and to this end offered to join them in a sort of revived Holy Alliance. He proposed this as early as 1867, and it was first achieved in the Three Emperors' League of 1873. To facilitate it was one of the objects of war in 1870: by crushing France while she was still isolated, Bismarck made her unavailable for an anti-Russian alliance in the Balkans.[1] The war at once enabled Russia to get rid of the prohibition of naval construction in the Black Sea,[2] and France was left too weak to send an army to the east, as she had in the Crimean War. Austria-Hungary had to aban-don the hope of challenging Russia along with that of challenging Germany, and to make friends with both her neighbours.

It is wrong, however, to think that Austro-Russian conflict was prevented only by the activity of Bismarck or that it constituted the sole danger for Germany. The Emperors' League followed spon-taneous Austria and Russian efforts ever since 1866 to keep together in order to watch Bismarck. It was primarily an accord between Austria-Hungary and Russia, Germany only joining later.[3] The

---

[1] See C. W. Clark, "Bismarck, Russia and the Origins of the War of 1870": *Journal of Modern History*, Vol. XIV (1942), pp. 195–208.
[2] *The Age of Transformation*, p. 421.
[3] There was also a Russo-German military convention which Bismarck never ratified.

Austrians and Russians agreed to seek a peaceful solution to their differences in the interests of conservative solidarity: it was hard to believe assertions that the enemy in view was Marx's moribund Worker's International. Bismarck was still the really important revolutionary. His conservative and clerical opponents in the new Germany were the friends of Austria, and they received encouragement from the Russian ambassador, Oubril. The conservative partnership of Russia and Austria-Hungary even had its application in Balkan affairs. The Austrian conservatives who favoured it were also the friends of the Slavs and the partisans of Austrian territorial expansion in the Balkans. The even balance between the two powers there might end in amicable co-operation. The revival of France gave added point to the conservative trend. Contrary to expectation, she freed herself of the German occupation and indemnity as early as 1873. She also acquired a royalist government, another would-be protector of clerical opponents of nationalism, whether in Italy or Germany. It is arguable that Bismarck needlessly made the peaceable French into implacable enemies by depriving them of Alsace-Lorraine. Perhaps he was right in thinking that the French would never cheerfully accept second place on the continent, and the only safe thing to do was to strengthen the German frontier. But it does seem that the complete abasement of France to some extent worked against his desire to keep her isolated. Russia and Britain, in particular, showed themselves unwilling to see her sink any lower.

This became clear in the 'war-scare' of 1875. It seems impossible to discover if there really was a Bismarckian plan to crush France anew by preventive war or only loud-mouthed talk by German officials in response to French pinpricks. What was important was the European response. The French royalist cabinet and its ambassadors were an aristocratic body, and they were able to appeal not only to the governments but directly to the sovereigns of the great powers for protection. Bismarck received warning from all sides to be moderate. He hastened to close the crisis by peaceful assurances, but the episode rankled. It showed that there was a tacit sympathy between the conservative opponents of the new Germany, which any false move by Germany might suddenly bring to life. Bismarck had his answer to this in the sympathy of the liberal beneficiaries of his victorious wars: the Italian nationalists, the Magyars whose leader

Andrassy was now foreign minister of the Dual Monarchy, and not least, the French republicans. Their triumphs after 1875 were of great benefit to him, for they had no wish to patronize clericalism in central Europe and could not, like their noble predecessors, hobnob with royalty to his disadvantage. But most liberals were fiercely anti-Russian and could endanger the status quo another way, by re-opening the Austro-Russian quarrel. In diplomacy, as at home, Bismarck had to maintain an uneasy balance between liberal and conservative forces.

(ii) 1875–8

In the eastern crisis which opened in 1875, immediately after the war scare, it was for long conservative forces of various kinds that were in the ascendent, and this made for peace between the powers and the advancement of the slav cause. Andrassy hoped that European Turkey could be pacified by the intervention of the Three Emperors' League. Russia insisted that France be brought in as well. Partly this was for fear lest France join Britain against the Emperors, but Russia also attempted to win French support when she differed from Austria-Hungary or Britain. France did not respond, however, and calling her in made it impossible to exclude Italy and Britain from the joint representations to the Turks. Britain used her influence to reduce the pressure on them. Russia found herself still mainly dependent on the support of the other Emperors for effective action in the Balkans.

Local mediation by the consuls of the powers and the Andrassy Note recommending reforms to the Porte in December 1875 came to nothing. In May 1876 Bismarck, Andrassy and the Russian foreign minister Gorchakov met in Berlin and adopted a further memorandum on reforms to be asked for by the powers. Gorchakov induced the others to accept a vague addition threatening the Turks with European intervention if they did not implement the reforms proposed. Britain rejected the Berlin memorandum and sent a fleet to encourage Turkish resistance by its presence. Gorchakov met Andrassy again at Reichstadt in July, after Serbia and Montenegro had attacked the Turks. They made a very vague agreement about the territories which their respective empires were to seize in the event of

THE BALKANS
1912 ~ 1913

RUMANIA

BOSNIA

Belgrade

Bucharest

Silistria
(From Bulgaria)

DOBRUJA

Sarajevo

R. Danube

Plevna

Varna

BLACK
SEA

Novibazar

(Acq. From Turkey)

Nish

BULGARIA

MONTENEGRO

Sofia

SERBIA

Scutari

Kumanovo
(Acquired From
Turkey)

(Acquired from Turkey)

Adrianople

Constantinople

THRACE

Dedeagach

MACEDONIA

Monastir

ALBANIA

Florina
(Acquired From
Turkey)

Salonica

Enos

TURKEY

Janina

G
R
E
E
C
E

Athens

DODECANESE
(Ital. Occup.)

CRETE
(Gr. Acq. From Turkey)

0   100
Miles

Turkish defeat. The Turkish revival, which in fact took place, brought Russia a much solider agreement with Austria-Hungary and better relations with Britain. The defeat of Serbia intensified the Russian tendency to concern themselves mainly with the eastern Balkans— with the Bulgars. They became more ready to give the Austrians a free hand in the west, while the Serbs had shown themselves not strong enough to thwart Austrian wishes in the event of a clash. Gladstone's denunciation of the 'Bulgarian atrocities' made the further defence of Ottoman intransigence too embarrassing for the British government. In November 1876 they proposed themselves that a conference of the powers at Constantinople should advise the Turks on reform.

When therefore the Tsar decided in the autumn of 1876 that his honour required him to go to the help of his Slav brethren, the way was beginning to clear. The British representative at the Constantinople conference in December was Lord Salisbury. He was no partisan of the Turks like his chief, Beaconsfield. The erstwhile Disraeli was essentially a rabble-rouser and his policy was really inherited from Palmerston—oppose the Holy Alliance and therefore protect Turkey. Salisbury was a real conservative. He despaired of Turkey and, like Aberdeen earlier, he wanted an amicable settlement with Russia concerning her future. His attitude was not so very different from that of Gladstone, who had been a follower of Aberdeen. He was therefore able to agree with Ignatiev on a reform programme, the central feature of which was the creation of two large Bulgar principalities. The British government endorsed this programme, though they continued to reject the idea of imposing it on the Turks by force.

Meanwhile Bismarck had warned both Austria-Hungary and Russia that he could not allow either to inflict a decisive military defeat on the other. Germany thus forced the two powers to continue along the path of compromise agreements, and early in 1877 the Budapest agreements were signed between them, Austria-Hungary agreed to remain neutral in a Russo-Turkish war and Russia promised that in the event of victory the Dual Monarchy should receive Bosnia-Herzegovina and 'no great compact state Slav or other' would be established in Turkey's place. Russia had isolated the Ottoman Empire and could now declare war (April 1877).

Now at last the toughness of the Turks, which had hitherto served them so ill, had its reward. It was not in vain that the western powers had fought the Crimean War and tried to build up Ottoman power. Though Russia had recovered the right to have ships on the Black Sea, she had built none and so the readiest way of attacking Constantinople was closed to her. The Turkish army in 1853 had been almost useless; in 1877 it met the Russians on something like equal terms. The fortress of Plevna held out against them for four months and it was only in January 1878 that the Russians at last reached Constantinople by the land route. Had the Turks received any help from the west, they could not have been beaten: it was the war of 1870 that caused their downfall, not their own shortcomings, grave though these were. Even though they were defeated, their valiant resistance helped them in two ways. British public opinion rallied in their favour, and the fact that they had not simply collapsed made it possible for their friends to attempt their restoration by means of pressure on Russia.

The Russians might still have triumphed had they played their cards correctly. The British navy was sent to Constantinople, but could do nothing beyond preventing a Russian occupation of the city. The Austrians dared not give the British military help, and there was in any case no reason why they should. The Russians had promised to respect their interests in the western Balkans, and they were little concerned with what mattered most to both the British and the Russians—Bulgaria, Constantinople and the control of the Straits. Russia now made the mistake of gratuitously quarrelling with Austria-Hungary. The reason perhaps is to be found in the great age of Gorchakov, now at the end of a brilliant career and seemingly exercising inadequate control over his subordinates. He entrusted the making of peace with the Turks to Ignatiev, who dictated to them at San Stefano, in March 1878, a treaty which took no account of Russia's delicate European position. Bulgarian autonomy was established within the frontiers agreed by the Constantinople conference of 1876. But there was to be a single large Bulgarian principality, instead of the two (eastern and western) envisaged by the powers. Nothing was said of Austrian claims to Bosnia, and the territories given to the two Serb principalities made them almost contiguous and pointed to eventual Serb unity. All this damaged Austria-Hungary's position in the western Balkans.

Ignatiev was sent on to Vienna late in March to win Austrian acceptance of the peace. He brought home a statement of Andrassy's terms, and eventually agreed to undo the unification of Bulgaria and create a western principality under Austrian influence.[1] But he would not reduce the territories to be given to the Serbs, and this for Austria-Hungary was the most important question, and so remained until 1914: any Serb advance threatened the very existence of the Dual Monarchy. Andrassy was probably glad of an excuse to resume an anti-Russian policy. He had already appealed to a congress of the powers. Russia did not feel strong enough to defy Europe, and had to content herself with what the other powers would accept.

Conservative alignments now began to favour the Turks, as might have been expected, instead of the Slavs. Having failed with the Austrians, Russia tried to appease the British. Salisbury was now foreign minister and his liking for conservative concord was shared by Shuvalov, the Russian ambassador, who disliked the Panslav disruptionists and had already tried for a compromise in 1877. This plan was now revised and adopted by the two powers in a secret treaty. Its main feature was a new partition of Bulgaria, this time into a northern and southern principality. The latter (Eastern Rumelia) was to continue to have a Turkish garrison, and the point of the arrangement was that the Turks would thereby be enabled to hold the line of Balkan mountains, the natural defence of Constantinople, which formed the boundary between the two Bulgar states.

Austria-Hungary was also now eager for the support of Britain, and a second secret treaty promised British support for her claims in Bosnia-Herzegovina and for the handing back of Macedonia from the Bulgars to Turkey. The British were not eager for this treaty and concluded it to please Bismarck: this again shows how the Russians had foolishly let slip a chance to keep their Balkan opponents apart. Instead of making concessions to one only, they had to give ground to both. The Congress of Berlin in the summer of 1878 settled the Balkans much on the lines of the secret treaties. Russia attempted to get round them and again divide her opponents. But Andrassy stuck to Britain because he wanted her help in securing a European mandate for the occupation of Bosnia-Herzegovina: public opinion in

---

[1] Nobody complained at the inclusion of many non-Bulgars within the new Bulgarian frontiers because nobody realized that this had been done.

the Dual Monarchy was more likely to accept it if it seemed to be generally desired by the powers. Russia gained a slice of Turkish territory in Asia. To balance this, Britain had concluded a further secret treaty with the Turks, allowing her to occupy Cyprus as a base and to maintain 'military consuls' in Turkish Asia, who were supposed to reinvigorate the local administration. Russia also regained southern Bessarabia and Rumania was given part of the Dobrudja, on the opposite bank of the Danube, in compensation for it. Serbia and Montenegro also received some territory, and all three were formally recognized as independent. But the Serbs lost in a way more than they gained by the Austro-Hungarian occupation of Bosnia-Herzegovina, which was carried through against bitter Serb resistance. The Austrians also henceforth kept garrisons in the Sanjak of Novibazar, the corridor of land dividing the two Serb states, to ensure that divided they should remain. Austrian doubts about the wisdom of helping to break up the Ottoman Empire were reflected in the fact that these territories were occupied but not formally annexed. In the Sanjak, Turkish administration persisted.

(iii) 1879–81

After the congress Bismarck began to play an increasingly active diplomatic role. Hitherto, he had effaced himself whenever possible and let others make the running. Now he increasingly tried to direct European affairs in the fashion of Metternich. The reason was that the eastern crisis had made his neighbours dangerously restless. The Russians were very angry because they thought that Germany had not repaid, as she should have done, the help which Russia had given in her unification. There was a bitter panslav press campaign on the theme that Germans were the natural hereditary foes of the Slavs. The Tsar was personally hurt, and there were even unaccountable concentrations of troops in Russian Poland. All this was unfair, for it is quite wrong to suppose that at this time Bismarck suddenly and firmly decided to support Austria-Hungary against Russia. Indifferent in Balkan questions, he sought to keep the peace between them, and avoid the disruption that must come if either was worsted in a great war. At the Congress and in the lengthy work of the frontier commissions which worked out its decisions in detail, German influence was commonly on the side of the Russians. Germany's refusal to allow either power to defeat the other decisively was, it is true, anti-Russian in effect, because it was supposed, rightly or wrongly, that Russia would be victorious in a conflict between the two. But it was not meant to frustrate Russia in the Balkans, and it was in fact Russia's mistakes, not anything Germany did, which had that effect. The fact remained that the Russians had expected something more than benevolent neutrality and Germany was in danger of losing her warmest friend.

Austria-Hungary meanwhile was suffering a political convulsion as a result of the Congress. The occupation of Bosnia-Herzegovina was resented by both the German and the Magyar nationalists because it meant more Slavs under Habsburg rule. The German liberals at Vienna protested loudly, and at length refused to vote money for the occupation. The Emperor was bitterly offended: the new territory pleased him because it was the first time in his reign that land had been gained instead of lost. (The Magyars sensed this and prudently kept quiet.) Meanwhile the Slavs of the Monarchy had been greatly encouraged by the success of their Russian brethren, and concluded that their hour might be at hand. For this reason the Czechs now returned to parliamentary life. They calculated that they would soon have a chance to defeat the German liberals and they were right. Francis Joseph now had a strong enough motive and a good enough opportunity to dismiss the liberals. In May 1879 Taaffe's ministry was formed with Slav and clerical German backing. In the autumn Andrassy left the foreign office. Germany's friends in the Dual Monarchy were losing ground. There was an obvious likelihood that this might revive attempts at an Austro-Russian entente hostile to the new Germany, perhaps with France making a third. There were, indeed, some moves towards a rapprochement between the two eastern empires. But the new Austro-Hungarian foreign minister, Haymerle, was hostile to Russia—his point in common with the conservatives was his wish for expansion in the Balkans. What Austria-Hungary mainly did, therefore, was to draw closer to the western powers.

Bismarck responded to the situation by the building up of a system of alliances under his own control which lasted the rest of his life. His first move was to offer an alliance to Austria-Hungary, eventually concluded in October 1879. His motives for concluding this remain something of a mystery. He claimed that its purpose was to separate Austria-Hungary from the western powers, and this probably was its main purpose. Its terms were very favourable to the weaker party: Austria-Hungary was promised help if Russia attacked her, but had herself only to promise neutrality if Germany was at war with any other power (i.e. France). For this reason there was no difficulty in getting the Austrians to accept. But having constituted herself the protector of the Dual Monarchy, Germany could demand that the Austrians should not involve her in needless danger by provoking Russia. Bismarck, in fact, established a hold over them which enabled him to force them into an accord with Russia in the following years. At the same time, Bismarck was impressed by the fact that all the other powers were backing Austria-Hungary against Russia, and seems to have wished to avoid isolation at her side; he considered getting on closer terms with Britain as well. He also voiced considerable alarm at the way things were going inside Russia, notably in a memorandum (1880) to Radowitz, his ambassador in Athens, in which he prophetically said 'revolutionized slavdom . . . will ever be the ally of revolutionary elements not only in France but also in Italy, in Spain, even perhaps in England.' But this was mainly to impress his own Emperor, who objected strongly to an alliance with his old enemy, Austria, against his old friend, Russia, and only consented to it when his Prussian ministers threatened resignation. A final factor which may well have influenced Bismarck was that he was now carrying through a reconciliation with the German clericals who were, as noted already, pro-Austrian. Windthorst their leader had in fact objected to Bismarck's neutrality between Austrians and Russians.

Bismarck next proceeded to resurrect the Three Emperors' League. He was helped and given an extra incentive in this by Gladstone's return to power in Britain (1880). Gladstone continued the reconciliation with Russia really begun by Salisbury. With no faith in bankrupt Turkey, he abandoned the attempt to reform and dominate the Turkish administration in Asia. Having no money, the Turks made no attempt to occupy the defensive position which the British had won for them in Rumelia. Gladstone also abandoned the forward policy in Afghanistan—another of Disraeli's anti-Russian moves. The positive side of his policy was a rather tepid belief in a 'concert of Europe' to solve problems by great-power co-operation. The application of this brought Britain more into touch than before both with Russia and with France. They were especially active in forcing the Turks to give Dulcigno to Montenegro and Thessaly to Greece. The powers had decided in 1878 that these states should be enlarged, but the Turks were understandably reluctant to give up land they had not lost in battle, and it took three years' pressure to make them comply. Bismarck was absurdly angry at the new combination. No large diplomatic designs lay behind it and German suspicions had no larger foundation than Bismarck's personal dislike of Gorchakov and Gladstone. But it remains true that it was a combination with revolutionary potential: these were the powers whose accord had made possible the liberation of Greece and Italy, and was later to destroy Germany's ascendancy in Europe.

Despite panslav frothings, official Russia's main desire was to win back the friendship of Germany, whose military might she could not hope to equal. Saburov, the new ambassador in Berlin, was, like Shuvalov in London, an opponent of the panslavs and a believer in conservative solidarity. He courted Bismarck assiduously. Bismarck was therefore able to work out with him a moderate policy on future Balkan problems, which he then proceeded to force on Austria-Hungary. Since he could hope for no support from Gladstone, Haymerle had no real alternative but to accept it. Just as he did so, Alexander II was assassinated. The new Tsar hesitated a few months and then joined in. He was a panslav of sorts himself, and not pro-German like his father. But he was an even stiffer conservative and was well suited by a conservative alliance.

The Three Emperors' League of 1881 was primarily a Balkan agreement. Russia was not to be opposed if she sought to join the two Bulgar states, nor Austria-Hungary if she formally annexed Bosnia-Herzegovina. The three powers promised each other benevolent neutrality in the event of war with a fourth power (in the case of Turkey, only by prior agreement). It was a war between Russia and Britain that was envisaged here, as also in the agreement to make Turkey enforce the closure of the Straits to foreign warships in time of war. The British in 1878 had said that they would recognize only an 'unfettered decision' of the Sultan to close the Straits, and this had been taken to mean that if they wished to sail through and attack Russia, they would do so. As Austria-Hungary did not wish to annexe Bosnia, the agreement benefited Russia mainly, but it helped her mainly against Britain. It was balanced by the Austro-German alliance, but since that alliance was defensive there was no contradiction between them. Its real intent was to partition the Balkans down the middle, into Austrian and Russian spheres. The Austrians set to work to accomplish this by concluding a treaty of commerce with Serbia, which almost reduced her to a colony. This was forced on his ministers by the servile Prince Milan, soon to take the style of king.

Bismarck became a builder of alliance systems in order to prevent a Balkan explosion which might cause central Europe also to erupt. His new policy now seems of questionable value and based on outdated fears. In the last resort the powers were not prepared to fight each other about the Balkans, and resentment against German unification was dying down. Bismarck was probably still trying to guarantee his German settlement, but this was no longer called for, and the part of central Europe which he did effectively guarantee was Austria-Hungary. The two things were linked, however, owing to the limitations inherent in Bismarck's attempt to domesticate German nationalism. Prussia needed the Habsburg monarchy: if it collapsed, the Austrians would return to Germany and so would Catholic preponderance. At home and abroad, therefore, Bismarck had to bind himself more closely to intractable conservative elements. The fluidity of mid-century diplomacy gave way to a stalemate between balancing groups, just as in the politics of several countries there was appearing a deadlock between an opposing multiplicity of roughly equal parties. Fruitful change was becoming more difficult.

Part II
BISMARCK'S EUROPE— IMPERIALISM AND CONSERVATIVE EXPERIMENT

1: The New Remedies

Behind the slackening appeal of classical liberal ideas there lay inertia and disillusionment, but also new thinking about how to control and make fruitful the continuing ferment in society. The new ideas were of all kinds, revolutionary, reformist and reactionary. But until the end of the century the important ones were those that could sway the liberal and conservative groups that possessed political influence, and suggest new ways in which they might co-operate. That is what the developments discussed below have in common.

The Emergence of Christian Democracy; Leo XIII

One of the most important features of recent European history has been the mass movement in politics based on religious allegiance. Religion, of course, has always had great political importance, but this particular form of it only began to gain ground around 1870, the German Centre Party already described being the most potent example. Confessional parties owed much at the start to aristocratic patronage, but what made them powerful was the conjunction of clerical influence with the widening of the suffrage. The parish clergy were a ready-made electoral machine and, where the people would listen to them, the party they supported had a head start in organizing the new mass electorate. At first the main object of confessional politicians was simply to defend the churches against secularizing legislation by the liberals—especially in the fields of education and the marriage laws. But gradually they built up positive views in opposition to the liberal notion of how the world should be organized. Their supporters came mainly from the peasantry, small businessmen and skilled workmen—classes at first drawn strongly to liberalism but tending to lose their enthusiasm for it in the harsher economic climate of the later nineteenth century.

Church-based parties seem to flourish best in an area stretching from the Low Countries to the Po valley, and also comprising the

German Rhinelands, Bavaria, much Austrian territory, Switzerland and parts of north-eastern France.[1] Perhaps this reflects the strength and militancy of Calvinism and the Counter-Reformation in these areas in the sixteenth century. Belgium was long the country most strongly influenced by the movement. The catholics were politically organized and important from the foundation of the kingdom, even though the franchise was narrow. They had a majority in the chamber in 1870–8, and continuously from 1884 to 1914. The introduction in 1893 of manhood suffrage with extra votes for the wealthier and better educated made it overwhelming. After the abolition of plural voting in 1919 they lost it, but have almost always been the largest party. In Holland and Switzerland there have been Protestant as well as Catholic parties, and the German Centre Party was in theory undenominational and had some Protestant members. There was also a separate Lutheran movement, in which the most important figure was Adolf Stöcker, once an army chaplain and later (1874–90) one at court, where he was able to interest high political and military personages in his conservative version of social reform. In the Orthodox Church the work of such men as Father Gapon (below, pp. 197–8) echoed the Christian Democracy of the west.

But it was especially with the Catholic church that the movement was connected, and the promulgation of the dogma of Papal infallibility in 1870 gave it a decisive impetus. Bitterly disliked by liberals both inside and outside the church, the new dogma was nevertheless not really conservative. Ultramontanism had always been associated with resistance to the overweening claims of the great European monarchs. Among Catholic politicians, the ultramontanes were often radicals, eager for the church to abandon its subservience to kings and nobles, and strike out on its own in alliance with the new democratic forces.

In 1878 there came to the Papal throne a great man who, within limits, was to encourage them to do this. Gioacchino Pecci, who took the title of Leo XIII, was born in 1810, the son of an officer who had served Napoleon. For thirty years he had been an enlightened but little noticed Archbishop of Perugia and he was elected as a stopgap, not being expected to live long. He survived, however, until 1903.

---

[1] M. P. Fogarty, *Christian Democracy in Europe, 1820–1953*, pp. 6–11.

An accomplished latinist, both in prose and verse, he was also interested in the natural sciences, and was a munificent patron of research in both the sciences and the humanities. His famous encyclicals reaffirmed uncompromisingly the traditional teaching of the church, but showed how it could be applied in a modern and progressive spirit. *Aeterni Patris* (1879) argued that the claims of faith and reason were not opposed, pointing especially in this connection to the work of St Thomas Aquinas. By encouraging Thomist studies, the Pope tried to undermine the liberal belief that the church was the enemy of scientific progress. *Immortale Dei* (1885) and *Libertas* (1888) asserted that the authority of the state derives from God and not from the people, and that there should be no freedom to propagate 'lying opinions'. But they also affirmed that liberty within permissible limits was of the highest value, that democratic forms of government were as lawful as any other, and that catholics ought to participate in public affairs unless there were special reasons to the contrary. Except in Italy, Leo XIII expected catholics to accept the new liberal political institutions and work within them.

In social questions similarly, *Rerum Novarum* (1891) began on a highly conservative note. Not only were private property and the family inviolable but class divisions were part of the natural order, inequality inevitable and 'to suffer and to endure is the lot of humanity'. But in medieval style the covetousness of the rich was condemned, and mutual aid for the protection of the poor, in the manner of the old guilds, commended. The poor were entitled to a living wage, to hours and conditions of work that would not injure their health, and to enough leisure for their spiritual needs to be satisfied. Catholic trade unions, insurance and welfare associations were needed. The poor must be helped to acquire property. It was the duty of the rich to join in the fight against poverty and the state too must intervene, though private initiative was preferable. *Graves de Communi* (1901) commended the name of Christian Democracy for this sort of endeavour, stressing, however, that it in no way presupposed a democratic political order.

The Leonine vision of society had the same naïvety but also the same constructive potential as the liberals' 'universal brotherhood'. Recognizing the gulf between the classes, it tried to make a shared Christian belief the basis of co-operation between them in social reform. It combined collective action with respect for the property and initiative of the individual, which met exactly the desires of middle-class people not satisfied with liberalism. Its concern for the industrial workers derived from an already long tradition of catholic philanthropy, represented by such men as Bishop Ketteler in Germany and Count Albert de Mun in France. These were the continental equivalents of Lord Shaftesbury and the factory acts on the English model which spread over the continent after 1870 owed much to clerical initiative. The important French acts were passed in 1874 when they were in power, and in 1892 when they were recovering influence. Hours of work for children were limited to ten hours, for women to eleven, for men to twelve a day. The German and Austrian cases are noted in the next chapter. A more specifically conservative reform in the German lands was the attempt to reinvigorate the craft guilds by legislation.

Christian Democracy was well fitted to forward certain initiatives owing more at first to liberals or socialists. Christian trade unions remained a minority movement, but this was very much the case with unions in general before 1900. It was the liberals who pushed forward compulsory elementary education, achieved at this time in the advanced western countries and also in theory in Italy and Austria-Hungary. But the clericals remained strongly entrenched in the schools and it should be noted that the multiplying tribe of schoolmasters provided in many countries the backbone of the new democratic parties whether nationalist, clerical or anticlerical. In the co-operative movement, the clericals were very strong: catholic Belgium underwent perhaps the intensest development of co-operatives of all kinds. Co-operation appealed very strongly to farmers as a remedy for their increasing difficulties after 1870. Their most remarkable growth was in Denmark, where co-operatives for the processing and export of dairy and pig products began to spread in the eighties. By 1900 every second parish had a co-operative dairy, and co-operatives handled 60 per cent of the pigs killed for export. Credit co-operatives had been pioneered in Germany by Raiffeisen from 1862. These organizations to lend money to peasants who otherwise could borrow not at all or only on ruinous terms were probably the most popular type of co-operative. There were 3,000 of them in the whole of Europe by 1900, and many governments set up special banks to support them or provide credit to farmers in other ways. Another very widespread type of co-operative was that for purchasing fertilizers, machinery and other supplies at a discount, cutting out the middleman. Co-operatives were relatively weak in the Latin countries but caught on well in Russia, where they harmonized with the tradition of communal organization mentioned earlier.

Strong in votes and fertile in social initiatives, the clerical parties yet failed to make a political impact commensurate with their size. The conservative backers of the movement provided it with a large body of support ready made, but as leaders they were an incubus. Mostly they were aristocrats who disliked the new industrial world and lacked the political skill, born of long experience, of their British equivalent. Only slowly did democratic and forward-looking leaders, like Lueger in Austria or Erzberger in Germany, rise from the humbler ranks of the movement to positions of influence. In the Low Countries and Switzerland the leaders were more capable, but also more like the liberal bourgeoisie and less receptive to new social ideas.

A parallel problem was the relations of catholic politicians with the church. The politicians insisted that they could not work effectively if they were under ecclesiastical control, especially as they hoped to win the votes of many not committed to the church. The Centre Party leaders were very angry when Leo XIII negotiated with Bismarck behind their backs, and in 1887 declared that they would follow the hierarchy only on purely ecclesiastical issues. The French leaders were equally though less reasonably recalcitrant when Leo tried to force a reconciliation with the republic on them. For its part the church was justifiably afraid that the politicians, constantly dealing with and trying to influence non-catholics, might become tainted with heresy. This happened in Italy to Romulo Murri, a priest in the style of Lamennais who began working in the nineties for a christian party of the far left. In France Marc Sagnier's movement, the *sillon*, which to some extent combined educational and political work, was condemned by the church in 1910 because of the dangers this involved. Only slowly was this curious conflict of spiritual and lay authority within the christian movement appeased as each came to see what functions were best left to the other.

The leadership of the Christian parties therefore tended to be indecisive when only extreme skill could have made their position an advantage rather than a drawback. Drawn from all classes, they had the option of being a party either of the left or of the right. Their initial impetus was anti-liberal and they won much of their support because of growing fears of socialism, to which they seemed to offer a constructive alternative. But opposition to the free working of the market economy, which had started off as a conservative position, became a radical one once liberalism had become the ruling orthodoxy. The more it was stressed and the more the christian social movement grew, the more likelihood there was of socialists and christians working together for specific social reforms. The christians were, indeed, a Centre Party, and by throwing their weight either way they could hope to make society adaptable while avoiding disorder. But it was a long time before they acquired the skill and maturity to do this with full effect. Only since 1945 has Christian Democracy really come into its own.

Protectionism

Social reformers whether clerical or liberal did not aspire to direct the economy. They took its workings for granted and tried to protect the weak against them. It was in the same spirit that governments under clerical and other protectionist influences formulated their economic policies. The lack of any determined will to interfere is well exemplified in the bimetallist agitation. It will be remembered that the adoption of the gold standard had contributed to the worldwide decline in prices and so to the atmosphere, at least, of depression. Many people thought that this was the major cause of trouble. But there was little interest in the idea of a 'managed' currency, the volume of which would be varied by the government in accordance with changing economic needs. Countries such as Spain, Austria-Hungary and Russia long had an inconvertible paper currency, but this was because the government could find no other means to pay its way. The most that opponents of the gold standard ventured to urge was that silver should be made the basis of the currency as well as gold, instead of being used in limited amounts for small change. A bimetallic standard would have increased the supply of money, especially as silver production had risen sharply in the seventies. It became the nostrum of impoverished agrarian groups everywhere, quaintly bringing a similarity of view between American farmers and Prussian Junkers. But even this was too daring for any state to adopt. There was a revival of legislation against usury, and the violence of economic fluctuations lessened a little as the volume of credit came to be more controlled by the central banks. But the problem of the money supply was left to solve itself, which it eventually did through the discovery of new goldfields.

Protective tariffs on the other hand spread everywhere. The 'national historical' school of economists, which arose in Germany and acquired disciples everywhere, provided them with a theoretical justification. In 1872 the German leaders had published the 'Eisenach manifesto', in which they demanded a comprehensive regulation of economic life to promote the greatness of the new Empire. Russia, Italy and Spain raised their tariffs in 1876–8, Germany adopted protection as we have seen in 1879, France raised her duties mildly in 1881 and Austria-Hungary increased hers in 1878 and 1882. There were increases all round in 1885–7, and a steep increase in France and Russia from 1892. Holland, Denmark, Finland and Turkey were the only free-trade countries left on the continent, though Germany led a short-lived movement in the liberal direction with her commercial treaties of the nineties. Tariffs, however, were low by later standards. Particular commodities were greatly affected, but in 1910 the average rate on all imports (including those untaxed) was 8 per cent in France, 8·4 per cent in Germany and 9·6 per cent in Italy. Russia's average, 38·9 per cent, was unique. There were, of course, high tariffs outside Europe, notably those of the United States and the British self-governing colonies.

Tariffs were increasingly supplemented by subsidies, most notably and generally in the encouragement of beet sugar production and exports. This resulted in so much 'dumping' that it was limited by international agreement in 1903. There was also a notable increase in publicly owned industrial enterprises, mainly in the sector of transport and public utilities. Continental countries commonly had some state railways from the start, and except in southern Europe there was a massive increase in state ownership in the later nineteenth century. Italy followed suit after 1900, and France had some state lines, though the republicans largely succeeded in leasing the lines they had built to private firms. Railway building on the continent had normally to be subsidized in any case, and by taking over the railways the government benefited itself financially and put itself in a position to stimulate economic growth, as will be more particularly shown in the case of Russia. The manipulation of railway rates could also be used to encourage exports and discourage imports. But even in Russia the government did not really take command of the economy. The attempt was still rather to alter its working in detail.

The alterations brought limited gains to the mass of the people. They had to pay higher prices and heavier taxes, but employment was safeguarded a little by the preservation of decaying branches of production and the stimulus to infant industries. The safeguard was insecure: 'tariff wars' resulted from the attempt to export misfortune, and while some industries conquered the home market, others lost their customers abroad. Protection helped the cause of social reform to some extent. The poor had a moral claim to benefit from the extra taxes they had to pay, and protection lessened the force of the argument that concessions to the workers could not be afforded because of foreign competition. It will be shown below how Bismarck's national insurance proposals were connected with unpopular tax plans, and how in 1902 German tariff increases were palliated by appropriating the extra revenue to insurance funds. State insurance schemes for the workers were among the most important inventions of their time, and before 1900 Bismarck's initiative had been copied in Austria, Belgium, Switzerland and Italy. It was destined to spread everywhere, and gradually the benefits were increased and the application of the schemes was extended from the factory workers to the population at large. But it is notable that for a long time there was no protection against strictly economic misfortune. Sickness, accident and old age came to be covered (some states obliged employers to compensate injured workmen without specifically adopting the insurance principle). But until the British act of 1911 there was no national scheme of insurance against unemployment. Governments here again were afraid to grasp the economic nettle firmly.

The big gains from state interference were made by certain classes and sections of the economy at the expense of the rest. It was, in any case, the fostering of military greatness rather than simple economic prosperity which was for many the main justification of protectionism. This meant the disproportionate fostering of heavy industry, in which Germany led the way. Her steelmakers, charging high prices at home and underselling competitors abroad, exposed other German industries to competition from imports made with cheap German steel. French steel production trebled after the 1892 tariff, increasing now as fast as Germany's instead of much slower. The sensational case of Russia is discussed in more detail below. The nationalization of railways was partly due to their strategic importance, and many uneconomic lines were built for strategic reasons (many were also built to win votes). It was big business that benefited from the encouragement given to heavy industry, and similarly it was the large landowners who did best out of agricultural protection: the Junkers, the Hungarian nobles, the great landlords of Spain. Their staple products, like grain, were the best looked after. The peasant farmer might suffer from the tariff if he did not grow enough to feed himself and his animals. The Russian government, which kept grain prices down to stimulate exports, could claim that this benefited the majority of the rural population. It was a further grievance that agriculture as a whole was less well protected than industry. The whole system was developed and perpetuated by the building up of powerful lobbies, financed by the wealthy producers, whose propaganda and secret influence played on state officials, parliaments and public alike. Cartels likewise flourished: having excluded the foreigner, the native producers could more easily agree among themselves to limit competition. The different pressure groups often had strongly diverging interests, but in that case, too, it was often easiest to strike a bargain at the expense of the consumer. Whatever the merits therefore of protectionism as an economic system, its political effects in the later nineteenth century were bad. It intensified whatever trend there might be towards oligarchy in the state, encouraged the belief that it existed to benefit the rich and created organizations well fitted to oppose reform should that not be in the protectionists' interests.

Imperialism and Navalism

Imperial expansion had been a feature of European history since later medieval times, but it was only at the end of the nineteenth century that it was turned to as a general solution of Europe's problems. In diplomacy it was Bismarck in particular who began this. He hoped to appease the resentments created by German unification by interesting his neighbours in compensating expansion in remoter regions. He encouraged Austrian penetration in the Balkans, Russian expansion in the east generally and the colonial ventures of France. Within the different states it was the liberals, often those of advanced views, who were the champions of imperialism. Chamberlain in Britain was matched by Crispi in Italy and republicans such as Ferry in France. In the older monarchies it was naturally conservative ministers who took the lead. But the National Liberals were the great supporters of colonialism in Germany, and the imperialism of Witte in Russia was linked with his patronage of liberal elements in economic matters. In Austria-Hungary it is true, conservatives were the partisans of territorial expansion and the liberals wanted to prop up Turkey against Russia. But their reasons were in part imperialist—they wanted to turn Turkey into an economic dependency, developed by Austrian capital.

The liberals were naturally interested in colonial expansion because they were the party of business. The conservatives viewed it with suspicion because they were still the party of agriculture, and did not want the nation's capital invested in the planter abroad rather than the farmer at home. They only slowly changed their views as they came to see the value of imperialism as a vote-getter. There were obvious economic reasons why the business community should turn its attention more to distant regions at this time: the need for more remunerative outlets for capital in a period of depression, the new possibilities of long-distance trade opened up by the steamship in conjunction with the railway, the new importance of tropical products like bananas, rubber and vegetable oils. There were three reasons why this economic interest in distant territories should be increasingly associated with demands for political penetration. First, territories were increasingly being opened up in Africa and the Pacific whose political system was too rudimentary to ensure the free passage of trade. Second, the more economic development there was, the higher the standard of government required. The building of railways, harbours and telegraph lines was impossible without a government able and willing to grant a firm concession to the builders and uphold the concessionaires against attempts by rivals to dislodge them. In practice, too, European capitalists would not embark on great public works in distant countries without a subsidy or a guarantee of a specified minimum income from their investment. Governments had therefore to be efficient enough to raise taxes and loans for these purposes.

The third reason, closely connected with the last, was once more the depression of the seventies. In the palmy days of the mid-century boom, shaky enterprises of all kinds had been supported by gullible investors and ramshackle governments had not found it hard to borrow. In the seventies there was no more easy money and enterprises that could only keep afloat by perpetual borrowing to pay their old debts collapsed. The Ottoman bankruptcy has already been noticed, and it was followed by that of Egypt and similar happenings elsewhere. The European creditors asked their own governments to oblige the defaulters to put their finances in order. The result was that many states were forced to allow the establishment of international commissions to control the levying of all or part of their revenues and the raising of loans. Most of the remaining independent Afro-Asian states suffered this tutelage, and so did the Balkan states and Portugal. (The Monroe doctrine made it rather harder to coerce debtors in the New World.) Where a state's finances could be reformed in this way, it retained the shadow of independence; the more incorrigible or easily dominated ones became colonies or protectorates.

But there was now much more to imperialism than simple capitalist self-interest. It was a natural extension of nationalism. Publicists everywhere appealed to the belief in a distinctive and superior national culture, and drew the conclusion—not entirely new—that inferior races would benefit from the diffusion of this among them and the exclusion of rival brands of superior culture. More generally, imperialism could be presented as the wider diffusion of all the benefits which the liberal era had bestowed on Europe, the latest chapter in the progress of mankind. The active role of the missionaries of all countries in Europe's outward penetration helped to endow it with a spiritual character, and for many of the clericals it was a kind of crusade. This was what made French missionary leaders like Lavigerie eager for reconciliation between the republic and the church, and it helped to interest the Centre Party in the German colonies and navy. It was also an extension of nationalism on the material side, for the people were taught that a nation could only grow in wealth and numbers if it had markets, sources of extra food and raw materials, and places where part of the growing population could settle. Instead of fighting each other at home, the different classes should collaborate in promoting national expansion, which would make room for all. Imperialism was to make up for the shortcomings of simple protectionism as an economic nostrum, and it was also yet another alternative to 'universal brotherhood' notions as a means of uniting all classes in the pursuit of progress. It was a means of promoting harmony within states just as Bismarck hoped to make it promote harmony between them.

There has been much argument[1] about the character and relative importance of the political and economic components of imperialism. Its foes, radical and otherwise, have seen capitalist enterprise and greed as its mainspring, and inveighed against the waste of national resources and the enslavement of subject peoples undertaken to promote the interest of a single class or even of a few influential intriguers in that class. Against this it can be said that imperial expansion was often promoted not primarily by businessmen but by enthusiasts whose motives were patriotic or ideological: explorers, soldiers, missionaries, consular officials. These people sometimes promoted economic enterprises, but only as a convenient vehicle and pretext for economic penetration. A good example of this was Bezobrazov's timber concession in Korea, which had much to do with the outbreak of war between Russia and Japan in 1904. With similar intent, governments sometimes induced reluctant capitalists to invest their money in places where they did not much want it to go—the Italians, for instance, in Tripoli.[2]

But the economic side of imperialism has sometimes been rather too much written down. It is true that imperial ventures often began as political stunts and that political factors largely determined the direction in which capital moved. French capitalists, for instance, were forbidden to invest in Germany and later encouraged to invest in Russia and discouraged from investing in Italy. It is also true that the native capitalists of backward countries like these last two were permanently dependent on government patronage and protection, and imperial ventures were just one aspect of this. But the desire of

---

[1] See the bibliography.   [2] Now Libya.

the business world in general to trade and invest in underdeveloped countries was genuine, and so was its need of political protection. This need sometimes made it rather dependent on the whim of governments, and so at first the politicians tended to set the pace in imperial expansion. But once it was under way, great economic interests were created which the politicians had to defend whether they wanted to or not. The eighties and nineties were a great period of preparation and the marking out of claims. In the late nineties there began a great new boom in overseas investment, and economically imperialism was becoming increasingly important just as the political quarrels to which it had given rise were being resolved.

For imperialism proved a source of discord as well as of harmony among nations and there has been much debate over its role as a cause of war. (This debate cut across the one about whether imperialism was primarily economic or political: among the Marxists, Kautsky thought that imperialism would promote peace and Lenin argued the opposite.) On the whole the businessmen and politicians who were seriously engaged in colonial development wanted peace among the great powers and were prepared to be conciliatory within large limits in order to get it. (They did not necessarily have the same objection to wars against minor powers.) The reason was that a big war would mean that there would not be money and soldiers enough for imperial tasks. Also, it might mean competition among the imperial powers for the loyalty of the colonial peoples, and this would lead to unrest and the making of economic bargains unfavourable to the imperialists.

Imperialism, therefore, did not produce war in Europe except in subordination to other factors. But like militarism it did produce tension and instability in international relations. Its great value to diplomats lay in its capacity for producing reversals of alliances. Sworn foes could be turned into allies by the emergence of some new imperial issue on which it was in their interests to co-operate against a third power. This was what Bismarck counted on, and it enabled him in the eighties to promote reconciliation between France and Germany and between the Italians and Austrians. But what had happened once could happen again as the focus of imperial interests changed. Especially was this so because imperial projects were of the nature of the South Sea Bubble, arousing absurd hopes of quick profits which proved quite illusory. The resulting revulsion might extend to the allies acquired to help the project forward. Add to this the imperial quarrels that sundered old friends like Britain and France or later Germany and Russia, and it will be seen that imperialism promoted international anarchy, the incessant intriguing of all against all. It did do something to promote cohesion within the imperial states by building up national enterprises in which all could share. But it did this at the cost of increasing international ill-feeling and making it harder for the great powers to co-operate.

Imperialism also intensified the bad effects of the arms race by its fomenting of naval rivalry. Navies were relatively neglected in the seventies, but Russia and France began to spend more on their fleets in the mid eighties as their imperial conflicts with Britain sharpened. Britain followed suit, and the process was intensified in the early nineties by the conclusion of the Franco-Russian alliance. German naval expansion began in 1898, and from this time also the European powers had to take account of the growing navies of the United States and Japan. The writings of the American Captain A. T. Mahan helped to establish the idea that at sea as on land the fortunes of war would be decided by a great battle, fought early on after a quick jockey for advantage. Every country therefore tried to have as many battleships as possible, and there was a rapid increase in size, speed and armament which rendered these great vessels quickly obsolete. The *Dreadnought* (1906), with ten big guns instead of four, could virtually have taken on all the other battleships then in existence. Heavier guns were countered by thicker armour plate. The torpedo was perfected, and by 1900 the submarine was in being. Naval building gave far more work to industry and the technologist than did making weapons for the army, and it seemed to protect not merely the nation's territory but also its possibilities of expansion. The business community favoured it both because of the gains to industry in naval construction and because trade would be protected. At the same time, fears of sudden attack were even more powerfully stimulated by the steamship than by the use of the railway to move armies. By the end of the century the long continuance of peace seems to have made land armaments less alarming. But even the most landlocked states went in terror of a 'bolt from the blue' by fast steamers assembled secretly in some unfrequented quarter of the ocean.

Navalism completed what militarism had begun in unstringing Europe's nerves.

The Beginnings of Racialism and the Superman

The inspiration behind the new departures described above was mainly liberal or christian or both. On the whole, the men who moulded opinion continued to hope that humanity could learn to live in freedom and peace. But mingled with this, ideas began to gain ground which would turn the retreat from classical liberalism into a retreat from humane views in general, making the jungle rather than the ordered city the model for men to copy.

It was rather unfortunate that Charles Darwin's works on *The Origin of Species* (1859) and *The Descent of Man* (1874) coincided with Bismarck's wars and were followed by an economic depression. His picture of the conflict between living species for a limited food supply was inspired by the theories of Malthus on human population and had an obvious resemblance to human affairs. He believed (erroneously in most cases) that the individuals whose special fitness enabled them to survive in the struggle could transmit their virtues to their descendants. From this it was an easy step to regard the struggle as the instrument of progress and struggles between humans as the way to produce better sorts of man. English Darwinians like Herbert Spencer might emphasize peaceful competition, but the obvious application was to war. Nations would struggle for the limited resources of the globe, the fittest would win and increase in numbers, the others would eventually die out. War was no longer a survival of a crueller past, but a permanent and beneficial part of the human condition.

Such ideas became very widely fashionable at the end of the century, and some went farther and tried to make politics a strictly biological affair—a conflict of races. It was traditional in France to regard the old nobility as descended from the Frankish invaders, and as early as 1854 Count de Gobineau had produced an *Essay on the Inequality of the Human Races*, in which the nobility figured as pure Aryans and the French masses as degenerate mongrels. The defeat of 1870 allowed Taine to argue in the many volumes of the *Origines de la France Contemporaine* that France had been ruined since 1789 by the revolt of the mongrels against the thoroughbreds, and could only be saved by restoring control to the latter. Vacher de Lapouge was one of many who tried to strengthen the scientific foundations of such ideas by comparative studies of human anatomy. He distinguished three physical types among the Europeans—European proper (i.e. Teutonic), Alpine and Mediterranean. The first were the best and the last were the worst. France had all three, but the better stock was unfortunately getting rarer.

Gobineau's ideas were welcome in Germany, for they seemed to prove the superiority of that Aryan nation to France. Here racialism was radical and even democratic rather than conservative and aristocratic. The whole people could claim to belong to the master race, they had newly proved their virility in war and confidently awaited fresh opportunities to expand. But the aristocratic element, the search for an élite, was present in German racialism too. H. S. Chamberlain, its most famous prophet, was an Englishman by birth, and he almost turned the idea on its head by claiming Aryan descent for a variety of great men from many nations. It was in Habsburg territories that German racialism was most obviously relevant, for there Germans were in retreat before the other nationalities after 1879. A radical nationalist movement appeared among them whose most important leader was George von Schönerer. Despising their Slav neighbours as cattle, they reserved their greatest hatred for those forces that tended to give the monarchy a non-national character and so destroy their German consciousness. The dynasty and the Catholic church were chief among these. Many therefore urged the Germans to cut loose from the Habsburgs and put themselves under the Hohenzollerns. Some became Protestants, in order to belong to a 'national' church; others abjured christianity and adopted old pagan German names like Siegfried and Baldur. The party had little success among the Austrian Germans, who, whatever their grievances, were not eager to be ruled from Berlin. But it achieved importance in the person of its greatest disciple—Adolf Hitler.

Antisemitism was an important feature of racialist thinking, but not of it alone. Suffering severe disabilities everywhere on the continent under the old order and feeling no necessary loyalty to laws and customs deriving from christian tradition, the Jews were natural supporters of liberalism. It was equally natural that the rising clerical parties should be hostile to them, as an element that could not be reabsorbed in a rebuilt, modernized christian community. In France the Jews and the Protestants (many of whom were of foreign origin) were classed together as a cosmopolitan and unpatriotic element bent on the exploitation of the people and using the republican government as their tool. Edouard Drumont's books, beginning with *La France Juive* (1886), and his newspaper *La Libre Parole* (1892), made antisemitism an important feature of right-wing propaganda. In the nineties the Panama scandal and the Dreyfus affair provided sitting targets. Stöcker founded an antisemitic party in Germany in 1887 which won a number of seats and became the ginger group of the extreme right. For them, too, the Jews were a cosmopolitan force destroying the nation in pursuit of gain. It is noteworthy that at first even the socialists paid some heed to such arguments.

It was, however, in eastern Europe that antisemitism was really strong, for here it had some relevance to actual conditions. The Jews of western Europe were almost all fully assimilated into the nations in which they lived. It was sheer calumny to accuse them of lack of patriotism, and there is no reason to suppose that they were harsher as employers and creditors than the christians. In much of eastern Europe the Jews were in effect a national minority, living apart with their own language (Yiddish) and customs. A mainly urban element in overwhelmingly agricultural communities, they encountered not only simple national antipathy but also the customary animosity of the farmer towards middlemen and moneylenders. Conditions in Germany were really intermediate, for there the Jews had been emancipated and the ghettos abolished much later than in France. Things were worst in Rumania and Russia, where the Jews were still denied full rights of citizenship. The Congress of Berlin required the Balkan governments to give equal rights to all their subjects. But such was the Rumanian peasants' hatred of the Jews that the government dared not make more than limited concessions to them. In Russia the reforms of Alexander II had included measures in favour of the Jews. The educated and the artisans among them were no longer confined to their original home, the 'pale of settlement' (broadly speaking, the territories acquired in the partition of Poland). Jews became eligible for public service and it became easier for them to own land. Under Alexander III, however, all these changes were partly undone and a limit was placed on the number of Jews to be admitted to secondary and higher education. Anti-Jewish riots (pogroms) took place, notably in 1891 and 1903, and the authorities failed to suppress and even connived at them. It was the official view that the Jews were unpatriotic and it was a Russian who invented the notorious 'protocols of Zion', supposed evidence of a Jewish conspiracy to master the world.

Austria-Hungary presented another transitional picture. The Jews there were in process of losing their painfully separate identity under the pressure of industrialization. But the migration of very large numbers of them—including many from Russia—to the growing industrial towns was not very welcome to the Christians. The Jews who accepted assimilation were unique in being the only subject people of the Monarchy willing to give up their identity and throw in their lot with the ruling Germans and Magyars. This did not save them from the hostility of Schönerer and his like, for whom these valuable supporters of the Monarchy were yet another cosmopolitan, international force. Both in Russia and Austria-Hungary, some Jews came to think that in an increasingly nationalist world the Jews had no option but to become a true nation. A few went to live in Palestine. In 1896 Theodore Herzl, a Hungarian Jew, who had formerly believed in assimilation, published *der Judenstaat*, advocating a return to the promised land. The first Zionist congress met in 1897.

Ideas of race were strong among the Teutonic peoples and had some effect on the Slav nationalists, whose intellectual formation was essentially German, but relatively little on the Latins. But racialism was not the only source of the cruel philosophy which condemned men to eternal strife against their fellows. It is rather unfair that Friedrich Nietzsche has to be mentioned in this connection. Though he served in the Franco-Prussian war (as a medical orderly), he was essentially unpolitical and loathed the philistinism of the new German Empire. 'The German spirit,' he wrote in 1888, 'for eighteen years a contradiction in terms.' He broke with the super-patriotic Wagner partly because he disliked the appeal to mass hysteria which he detected in his operas. The many references to fighting in his works are metaphorical. Born in 1844, he had a distinguished academic career which he gave up (1879) to devote himself to prophetic writing. He lived henceforth mainly in seclusion, his health was bad and his career ended (1889) in incurable insanity. His writings of the eighties were at first completely neglected and have mostly been misunderstood. Proclaiming that 'God is dead', he sought to put human vitality in His place as the source of meaning in life. Men were to dedicate themselves to high adventure and find fulfilment in the excitement of the struggle: seeking to turn themselves into 'supermen', they were not to waste pity on those who had not strength for the attempt.

The hermit's quest for individual perfection was what underlay the teachings of this academic recluse, but they helped to breed enthusiasm for other prophets who put forward similar ideas in a way applicable to national as well as personal life. Thus, for the Italian poet Gabriele d'Annunzio, the poet was the superman and the obvious field for heroic action was the struggle for national glory. War could give meaning to life and d'Annunzio was to fight with enthusiasm in the First World War, besides acting as a harbinger of Facism afterwards. In France Maurice Barrès mixed the racialism of Taine with a similar call to the individual to identify himself with the struggles of the nation as a means of personal fulfilment. For both, this meant abnegation and unqualified submission to a leader. This was a sort of spiritualized Darwinism, based on personal choice and organized warfare instead of biological necessity and individual competition.

Conclusion

The last quarter of the nineteenth century was a period of great constructive importance, for the foundations were then laid of the all-embracing modern state, dedicated to 'welfare' and 'planning'. The Europeanizing of a large part of the globe hitherto free from Europeans was part of the same process. In continental Europe what essentially happened was that new thinking preserved and reanimated the paternalistic traditions of the old monarchies, not least the Papacy. But the new ideas, like the liberal ones which they replaced, were based on rather simple-minded and often backward-looking views of man and society. The new state machine would stand little chance of working well until it had passed into the hands of leaders with deeper understanding. Unfortunately there were signs that the heirs of the existing rulers would rather be men who had pushed their baser thoughts to their logical conclusion.

2: Experiments in Reform and Adaptation

New thinking gave the great European states a chance to keep up the dynamic pace of change characteristic of the liberal era, attention being now directed to questions which the liberals had overlooked or could not solve. Italy and Spain had already reached an impasse, and nothing much was done there which made any difference, except for the imperial enterprises recorded in the next chapter. The other great states all made interesting experiments with important consequences for their future. But by the beginning of the twentieth century they, too, had reached an impasse, and in two cases were under the threat of revolution.

Germany: from Social Reform to the Big Navy

Bismarck's last decade in office was taken up with trying to escape from the difficulties he had created for himself by his breach with the National Liberals. He could hope for little support on the left, where the socialists were proscribed and intransigent and the liberals weakened and increasingly divided, the attitudes of the different sections ranging from hostility to grudging support on questions of national importance. In theory he could achieve a majority in the Reichstag by combining the conservatives and the Centre. But as already explained, the clerical politicians were by no means as willing to be reconciled with him as the Pope was. Their behaviour on financial questions was highly unsatisfactory. In calling for substantial customs duties in 1879, Bismark had hoped to secure an independent revenue for the Empire, collected by its own officers and not requiring an annual parliamentary vote. The Centre voted for the tariff because they believed in protection. But they were also responsible for the 'Franckenstein clause', by which the extra revenue from the new duties went to the states and not the Empire. If the money was needed for imperial purposes, it had to be reclaimed by a matricular contribution levied by the Reichstag on the states. Bismarck had also hoped to increase the imperial revenue by instituting monopolies and excise duties, but he had no more success with these projects after his breach with the liberals than before. The vital vote of the army establishment for a further seven years in 1881 was carried by National Liberal, not clerical, votes.

Bismarck and his successor both tried to rebuild a government majority round policies of social reform which might wean the masses from the extreme left and incidentally constitute a point of agreement with the Centre. This was the genesis of Bismarck's famous plans of social insurance. His first project (1881) was for the compensation of workers in certain industries injured at work. The Reichstag had passed an act as early as 1871 placing the liability to do this upon employers. This had proved hard to enforce, and almost everyone accepted Bismarck's view that the solution lay in compulsory insurance. The simplest arrangement, supported by the National Liberals, would have been to retain the liability of the employers and oblige them to insure themselves privately. Bismarck proposed instead a state insurance organization, controlled by representatives of the employers. This appealed to the Centre, who believed that industries ought to have governing bodies capable of regulating them as the guilds once had. He also proposed that a third of the premiums should be paid by the workers and that supplementary benefits should be paid by the state. With these bribes to both employers and workers, the scheme was put forward in an election year; later Bismarck tried to link the state contribution with his unpopular plan to raise a revenue through a state tobacco monopoly. For the present this political finesse was of no avail. In the accident insurance scheme finally enacted in 1884, the whole cost was to be borne by the employers, as the National Liberals proposed. But Bismarck's plan for an employers' insurance organization was carried in deference to the Centre.

Meanwhile, a sickness insurance scheme had been enacted after lengthy discussions in 1883, providing benefits for workers unable to earn and in need of medical care through illness. Two-thirds of the cost was met by the workers and one-third by the employers. Once again the National Liberals proposed compulsory membership of private insurance organizations, and Bismarck stood out for a single state scheme. In 1889, again after lengthy preparatory discussions, a bill was introduced establishing pensions for the aged and infirm. The bulk of the cost was equally divided between employers and workers, but this time the state also contributed. Bismarck's parliamentary position was now stronger, and he carried the scheme against the opposition of both left and Centre.

Bismarck's insurance schemes are among his greatest achievements. Though no more a christian socialist than he had been a liberal, he again showed a masterly perception and skill in recognizing and harnessing to his own rather devious purposes the most important constructive thinking of the time. The insurance laws bound the working class to the state, undemocratic though it was. The radicals and socialists were their bitterest opponents because they realized this ulterior political purpose, but they were powerless against the tide. But the laws did not stop the workers voting for the Social Democrats. On the contrary, the socialist vote rose steadily at each Reichstag election, although socialist propaganda and organization was now illegal and they could do no more than put forward parliamentary candidates. Already, in 1890, the socialists were the largest party in terms of votes, though they only had thirty-five seats. This was because Bismarck's conversion to social reform was half-hearted and barely atoned for his measures against the working class, like the food taxes and the anti-socialist laws. He failed to support the proposals of Hertling of the Centre Party for more extensive factory legislation. He was strongly opposed to the statutory limitation of hours of work in factories, and he restricted as far as he could the supervision of working conditions by government inspectors which had been introduced in the seventies. The rights even of non-socialist working men to assemble and organize were severely restricted by the law. The working class therefore grew increasingly resentful, withdrawing support steadily from the more compliant bourgeois parties. The more they did this, the more Bismarck and his successors were forced to look to the right for their parliamentary backing and truckle to the increasingly impossible conservatives.

Bismarck was able for a time to escape from these perplexities because of a drift of the middle class towards the right. 1884 was a parting of the ways for the liberals. In March, those who had left the

National Liberals on the issue of protection joined the radicals in a new *Freisinnige* (freethinking) party, while the main body of the National Liberals reorganized themselves on a frankly protectionist basis. At the ensuing elections the radicals did badly, but the National Liberals had government help and gained a few seats. For the 1887 elections Bismarck formed a 'cartel' between the National Liberals and the conservatives, and by the use of his personal prestige and the cry of 'the fatherland in danger', they won a majority. The immediate purpose of this combination was to vote the army establishment for a further seven years, and on a bigger scale. But Bismarck had a more personal reason—the approaching demise of the nonagenarian Emperor, which took place in fact in 1888. The new Emperor Frederick was mildly liberal and had welcomed the formation of the new radical party. Bismarck, who had begun his career as a chief minister by defying a parliamentary majority on his sovereign's behalf, now wanted a reliable parliamentary majority to keep his sovereign dependent on himself. As it happened, the new Emperor was mortally ill on his accession and died within a few months. But Bismarck was well served by the 'cartel' all the same, for it rid him of dependence on the Centre and enabled him at last to carry an adequate number of new taxes. In 1889, however, he overplayed his hand by trying to get the anti-socialist law, soon to expire, made permanent. The National Liberals refused to perpetuate the clause allowing socialists to be deported from their homes. The conservatives refused to vote for the bill unless it contained this clause, and so it was defeated. The truth was that the cartel partners had by no means forgotten that they had lately been on opposite sides. In the elections of February 1890 they lost their majority.

Bismarck was now replaced by someone willing to revive the impetus of reform. He could have survived electoral defeat, but the ruling class of the Empire had also come to see the need for change and were extremely tired of him personally. His growing parliamentary difficulties in the eighties had made him increasingly despotic and arbitrary: he had purged the administration of all who showed independence, demanded that all public servants should unreservedly support the government at elections, repeatedly used the sovereign's name to overawe opponents and tried to brand all who opposed him as traitors. The young Emperor William II was influenced by Protestant representatives of Christian democracy like Stöcker. He also heeded military men like Count Waldersee, Chief of Staff from 1888, who saw himself as a possible successor to Bismarck and wanted a policy more actively anti-Russian. Early in 1890 the Emperor demanded certain measures of social reform. Bismarck eventually agreed to sponsor them, but not without many attempts at sabotage and obstruction, in the course of which the Emperor found that his ministers were more afraid of Bismarck than of himself. Outraged, he harried the great man into resignation: the main pretext for this was his demand that the other Prussian ministers be allowed to discuss policy with him without Bismarck's participation or prior approval.

In March 1890, therefore, William II found himself, at the age of thirty, master in his own house. Talented but lazy and without firmness of purpose, the Emperor never really grew up. He had an exaggerated, indeed a fairy-tale idea of the greatness of his dynasty, his office and himself. His parents were liberals (Frederick had married the eldest daughter of Queen Victoria). Reacting against them—and also perhaps against his physical infirmity, a disabled left arm—he was a professed worshipper of force. His troops were to enforce his will at home and abroad. They were to shoot their fathers and brothers if he commanded it and equal the Huns in ferocity.[1] His little fleet he was determined from the first to build up, extending his power over another element. But this worship of war was insincere. When real trouble was brewing, he was always for peace and compromise. It was appropriate that he had demanded factory legislation when Bismarck offered him class war. For many in his own day he passed as a villain. But later generations have seen real villainy and can pronounce him only a nuisance.

William's new Chancellor and Minister President of Prussia was General Leo von Caprivi. His family originated in Austria but had become Prussian with the conquest of Silesia in the 1740s, and since then had provided Prussia with many soldiers and officials. Now nearing sixty, the General had parliamentary experience as head of the admiralty, from which post he had lately resigned on a point of principle. His integrity made him an outstanding figure among the spineless Bismarckian bureaucrats and was his chief merit. He was as conservative as his predecessor, and no less afraid of socialism.

[1] Speeches to recruits in 1891 and to the troops sent to China in 1900.

But he believed much more strongly than Bismarck did that the really conservative policy was to co-operate with and satisfy all classes in the nation. Unlike Bismarck, a substantial industrial and agricultural proprietor, Caprivi had only his pay, and once remarked that he owned 'not an acre, not a blade of straw'. He accordingly found it easier to transcend class prejudices.

Caprivi proposed to govern with the aid of all parties and the trend of his measures was to the left. But to some extent he tried to have two separate majorities available, one left and one right-inclined, to carry different measures—just as Bismarck in the early eighties had relied now on the Centre and now on the National Liberals. Responding to the Emperor's wish, he organized an international conference on labour questions and subsequently brought in legislation. Sunday work was prohibited, the hours which women and children might work were limited and arbitration courts set up. The factory inspectorate was greatly strengthened. From 1891 a series of commercial treaties had the effect of lowering Germany's tariff. Reflecting Caprivi's belief that 'Germany must export goods or men', they were made essential by the bad harvest of 1891 and the expiry in 1892 of many commercial treaties concluded earlier by France, which had kept down European tariffs to Germany's benefit. The school bill introduced in the Prussian parliament in 1892 represented the right wing of the new administration's policies. In effect, it placed elementary education under the control of the clergy, catholic and protestant. This pleased both the conservatives and the Centre, and its great political point was to induce the Centre to vote for the increase in the army which was judged necessary in view of the growing intimacy of Russia and France.

This policy of working with everyone became increasingly difficult to carry on. The school bill aroused the fury of the liberals, whether of the radical or the National Liberal stripe. The Emperor panicked and ordered it to be dropped. The Centre therefore remained unwilling to vote for a larger army. Caprivi tried to produce a plan palatable to Centre and left: military service was reduced from three to two years, and the army establishment was to be voted for five years instead of seven.[1] But his bill was defeated in the Reichstag in 1893

---

[1] The life of the Reichstag had recently been extended from three years to five, so each Reichstag would normally have a chance to vote on the army.

and only carried after a general election in which the parties of the right gained ground.

This development in the long run was to Caprivi's disadvantage. The radicals had split over the army bill: those who had come to the party from the National Liberals in the eighties wished to support it. Divided, they lost half their seats. The gains of the right were due to a furious agitation against Caprivi's commercial treaties, conducted by a formidable organization which they had called into being, the Agrarian League (*Bund der Landwirte*). The Agrarians were especially associated with the conservatives and the new antisemitic party, but they penetrated other parties as well. At the end of 1893 they nearly defeated Caprivi in the Reichstag over the last and most radical of his treaties—those with Rumania and Russia, producers of cheap grain. On the Rumanian treaty, Caprivi was saved by the votes of the socialists. He was in danger of having either to work with them or become a prisoner of the right.

Developments in Prussia, however, enabled the right actually to overthrow him. After the withdrawal of the school bill, he had resigned the Minister-Presidency there to Count Eulenburg. This made manifest a growing divergency between the old Prussia and the new Reich. After 1890 the conservatives and National Liberals never controlled the Reichstag, but they continued to dominate the Prussian landtag. Ironically, it was now that the National Liberals won a dominant place in Prussian ministry in the person of Miquel, minister of finance from 1890. Miquel reformed the finances on liberal lines, introducing a progressive income tax. But he believed in co-operation with the conservatives and had largely inspired his party's rightward move in the eighties. Everything was now done to please the Junkers. A democratic reform of local government was not applied to their estates: the land-tax revenues now handed over for local purposes were thus in part a free gift to them. A good deal of money was voted for agricultural improvements in the nineties, and legislation regulated the market in the interest of producers. Important national projects were held up because they were supposed to be against agricultural interests, notably the building of the Mittelland Canal across the North German plain. It is not surprising that there was growing friction between Caprivi and the Prussian government. In 1894 anarchist outrages led to a general demand for a new law against revolutionaries. Caprivi and Eulenburg found it almost impossible to agree on the terms of such a measure, and in the end both resigned and were replaced by Prince Hohenlohe, elderly, self-effacing and conciliatory.

Both at this time and during the crisis of 1890 there was talk of establishing right-wing supremacy in the Reich by a coup d'état. The Reichstag was to be asked to abolish universal suffrage and in effect bring itself into line with the Prussian landtag. If it refused, the princely governments, by whose authority the Reich constitution had been established, would annul and revise it in the desired sense. In the event, this was never tried. There are signs that Bismarck was working towards it in his last months of office, but no evidence that he was ever committed to it. William II uttered fierce words at times but had not the courage for it, even when the Reichstag in 1895 refused to pass the new measure against revolutionaries. Conservatives and democrats went on trying to live together.

This was made possible for the time being by the emergence of the naval question. Tirpitz was placed at the head of the admiralty in 1897, and bills providing for the creation of a large fleet over a term of twenty years were passed in 1898 and 1900. A Navy League founded in 1898 was as effective as the agrarians in building up a body of support within the several parties. It was the business community and hence the National Liberals who most desired a big navy, both for economic reasons and because many sons of the middle class would find a career as naval officers and thereby achieve something of the same prestige as the mainly aristocratic officers of the army. The Centre contained enough people of this way of thinking to be brought to favour the fleet. The conservatives on the other hand, an agrarian and aristocratic body, had no natural sympathy for it; they were inclined to fear that it would detract from the building up of the army. But they were themselves opposed to increasing the land forces too much: Caprivi had failed to do so to the maximum extent possible in 1892, for fear of democratizing the army by the inevitable influx of plebeian officers. This meant that there were financial resources to spare which could be devoted to the navy.[1] The conservatives were prepared to vote the funds for a price: the revision in a

[1] See G. Howe, 'Gedanken zur deutschen Wehrpolitik zwischen 1871 und 1914' in W. Schüssler (ed.), *Weltmachtstreben und Flottenbau* (1954).

protectionist sense of Caprivi's commercial treaties, which expired in 1902. Accordingly, in 1901 a new high tariff was voted by a Reichstag majority of conservatives, National Liberals and Centre. The Centre stipulated that the extra revenue expected under it should go to the national insurance funds.

Bismarck and Caprivi had both, in their different ways, tried to promote the development of German society in a way satisfying to the mass of the people. They had succeeded well enough to make any attempt at revolution extremely unlikely. They had failed, however, to create a tradition of effective, forward-looking government. There was a total lack of good political leaders and strong political groupings, able to sustain a constructive but controversial policy. The failure to find a way to co-operate with organized labour meant that power had to go to some combination of conservatives and moderates and left the field free to those like Miquel, whose political thinking was limited to the alliance of big business and big agriculture. This oligarchy was strong enough to keep control of the apparatus of government but too weak to govern the Empire without help. Agrarian and naval agitation could win them this, but the result was policies damaging to Germany's international position. Germany quarrelled with Britain over her new navy and with Russia over the tariff of 1902, while military conservatism kept her army too weak to win in 1914. Naïve and disastrous patriotic commonplaces dominated policy-making because nobody had the political skill to make Germans agree on anything else.

France: Anticlericalism and the Failure of the Ralliement

France, like Germany, fell increasingly under the control of an oligarchy whose elements could not work together easily and which found it hard to offer bold constructive leadership. In both countries there was an attempt to escape from the impasse by broadening the support available to the government—in Germany to the left, in France to the right. In each case the clericals played an important role in the experiment, and in each case it failed.

French politics, in danger of torpor once the republicans had won power by wooing the conservatives, were kept lively by the issues connected with education. Like liberals everywhere, the republicans regarded the diffusion of knowledge as the secret of progress and the strongest weapon against both reaction and social revolution. Free and compulsory primary schooling was therefore instituted in 1881–2. But the republicans were unwilling to leave the expanding educational system under the control of the clergy. The catholic church had been fairly consistently hostile to them and the parish priest was a ready-made electoral agent for the royalists in every village. Secular education would be a counterweight to church influence, both by propagating different ideas and by establishing a lay schoolmaster in each village as a counterweight to the priest. Qualified laymen were too few for the last to be possible. For many years the bulk of the teaching was done by clergy and nuns. But religious instruction was banned from state schools in 1882, and in 1879–80 the establishment of state secondary schools and teachers' training colleges for girls broke the complete monopoly which the church had had of female education. The state also reserved to itself the power of granting degrees, the pupils of private colleges having to take a state examination.

The main executant of this programme was Jules Ferry, successively minister of education and twice prime minister in 1879–85. A dour Lorrainer, he had married into a protestant family and drew some of his advisers from this venerable anticlerical body. Besides his work for education, he gave France firm government and notably expanded her colonial empire. The more cautious republicans had in him a leader worthy to stand beside his rival, Gambetta. But his austere personality did not endear him to the public and made him a ready target for radical charges that he was a reactionary at heart and was diverting the national energies from necessary reforms to useless imperial adventures.

The most contentious question raised by the educational reform was that of the religious orders in France. Since 1804 a distinction had been made between orders merely tolerated and those authorized by the government, which alone were allowed to own property. Broadly speaking, nuns and missionaries had received official encouragement, the former being valuable in education, the latter in imperial expansion. But most of the male orders had been merely tolerated. Essentially international in their loyalties and organization, they were at variance with the whole French tradition of centralization, adhered to by royalists and imperialists (when in power) no less than by republicans. In 1880 the Chamber tried to forbid by law the holding of teaching posts by members of unauthorized religious orders. The more conservative Senate would not accept this, and so the government took advantage of the questionable legal status of the orders concerned to decree their dissolution, refusing to allow the legality of this to be tested in the courts. This dissolution was half-hearted, however. The Jesuits were completely banned and 261 religious houses were closed. But the property of the orders was not sold and the regular clergy were gradually allowed to repossess it. The government had really only asserted its power to persecute or tolerate the orders as it chose, and which was to be done remained a vital political issue for twenty years. The opening of this question aroused the demoralized conservatives to do battle again with the republicans.

They were helped by a worsening of the economic situation. France encountered the worst effects of the 'great depression' in the eighties. The conservatives were especially enraged by the collapse (1882) of the Union Générale, a large new bank which had been founded with the avowed intention of reducing the influence of Jewish and protestant bankers: the promoters had thus secured the help of the catholic clergy in selling their shares and the support of rich conservatives. The collapse of the enterprise was put down to the hostility of non-catholic financiers in league with the republicans and soon antisemitism became an important feature of conservative propaganda, as noted earlier. Economic difficulties beset the republicans directly. They had tried to win popularity by a large programme of public works and they had tried to relieve the poorer taxpayers not by heavier taxes on the rich (which then seemed dangerously radical) but by slackness in the assessing and collecting of taxes. The result was a deficit (1882) as soon as recession set in and the conservatives accused the republicans of extravagance.

In the crucial elections of 1885 the republicans were hindered by two further factors. One was a military defeat in Indo-China which brought down Ferry's second government. The other was their own changing of the electoral law. Single-member constituencies (*scrutin d'arrondissement*) were replaced by large constituencies returning many members (*scrutin de liste*). Like proportional representation, this system gave more scope to the minority parties and it seems to have encouraged monarchist voters of all shades to come to the polls in greater force. There were nearly as many conservative votes as republican. Fortunately for themselves, the republicans had retained the system of a second ballot where no party had won an absolute majority. At the second ballot, rival republican candidates stood down in each other's favour and the republicans presented a single list in each constituency. Their opponents did the same, but the republicans commonly had a slight majority in votes and so ended with a comfortable majority in parliament. But this had only been made possible by an alliance between the moderate republicans and the growing number of radicals, who objected to the sacrifices of principle that had been made in the seventies in order to secure the establishment of the republic and demanded a more democratic constitution, the separation of church and state, and social reform. The moderates no longer had a parliamentary majority on their own and most of the ministries from 1886 to 1893 were coalitions of moderates and radicals, embarrassing for both since the radicals were not strong enough to carry their programme, but never gave up trying to force the moderates to vote for it.

On many questions there was now more in common between the moderates and conservatives than between the moderates and radicals. Accordingly, 1887 saw the experiment of a moderate ministry, under Rouvier, with conservative support. Its policy was budgetary economy and 'appeasement': the church was not to be worried, in particular unauthorized religious orders were not to be harassed. Rouvier promised to resign if he did not have the support not only of a majority in the Chamber but of the majority of republicans in it. No conservative entered the ministry, but conservative leaders had negotiated with the President. The prospect opened of the final closing of the constitutional question by the rallying of the conservatives to the republic. In the long run this would benefit the radicals no less than the moderates. Freed from the incubus of having to help the moderates defend the régime, they could devote all their energies to agitation for their own programme.

For the remainder of the nineteenth century, the great question in French politics was whether the conservatives would rally to the democratic republic. The answer was to be negative. The rising generation on the right did not share the feeling of the older men that parliamentary government was the best, or at any rate the only practicable, system. In 1887 the Comte de Paris, the only pretender left who counted, adopted what was really the Bonapartist programme: a strong royal executive independent of parliament and able to appeal to the people by plebiscite. His action was given point by the career of General Boulanger. This led the conservatives to look to the army for salvation and to seek popularity by demanding an aggressive foreign policy and denouncing the peace-loving republicans as betrayers of the national honour. This attitude was doubtless encouraged by the fact that the officers of the army were becoming an increasingly conservative body. Military service had not been popular as a career for the sons of the upper classes before 1848, but it had become so under Napoleon III and still more so under the republicans, who reserved jobs in the civil administration for their own supporters. The army became a royalist refuge, and the conservatives began to dream of a military dictatorship.

Boulanger himself represented the older type of rather plebeian officer and he seems to have had no firm political convictions and to have been interested only in his own advancement. At first he toadied to royalists in high command. Then he professed himself a radical, and it was the radicals who insisted on his being made minister of war in 1886. He rapidly made himself extremely popular by measures both to democratize the army and to make it ready for combat with Germany. Turned out of office and the army by the alarmed republicans, he emerged in 1888 at the head of a new movement for a revision of the constitution which would have given very large powers to the president. Ironically, Boulanger was helped by the disgrace and resignation of the existing President, Grévy, whose son-in-law Wilson was found to have been selling decorations; Rouvier's ministry disappeared in the uproar and there was a return to 'republican concentration'—the partnership of radicals and moderates. Boulanger stood in a number of by-elections and was repeatedly elected. Mostly they were conservative constituencies and his large funds came from rich royalists. But his organization was largely run by a body of radicals who had remained loyal to him and his greatest victory was in radical Paris (January 1889). Enormous demonstrations followed the announcement of the result and his friends urged him to seize power by force. His refusal probably saved the régime. Soon afterwards he foolishly fled abroad, fearing a prosecution, and his movement collapsed. The terrified republicans restored the *scrutin d'arrondissement* for the elections of 1889 and retained their majority.

An effort was now made to undo the harm that Boulanger had done and bring the conservatives back to moderation. The *ralliement* was the work of the church: it represented Leo XIII's general policy of trying to come to terms with the new political system in Europe, and also his desire to exploit the growing enmity between France and his greatest foe, the kingdom of Italy. In 1890 a speech by Cardinal Lavigerie, Archbishop of Algiers and the leading figure in French missionary activity, told catholics that it was their duty to adhere to a form of government clearly desired by the people and in no way contrary to christian principles. In 1892 a papal encyclical again urged the faithful to rally to the republic. Leo XIII later said that they should 'accept the constitution in order to change the legislation', i.e. against the church.

The moment was well chosen to exploit the shock which Boulanger had given the republicans. Lavigerie, indeed, had spoken only after negotiating with the ministers and in the belief that they desired better relations with the church. The voting of a high tariff in 1892 was a republican attempt at conciliation. The conservative rural areas had long felt that they received less protection than the left-inclined industrial towns. Jules Méline, now minister of agriculture, had encouraged farmers and industrialists to forget their quarrels and combine to demand high protection for both. The new tariff was the result, calculated to forge a bond between moderates and conservatives. It was followed in 1893 by the Panama scandal. The company (since bankrupted) for building a Panama Canal had promoted the sale of its shares by means of a lottery. Legislation had been required to allow this, and it was found that various politicians had been improperly rewarded for promoting the bill. Clemenceau and Floquet, the radical leaders, were the worst hit, but all the older generation of politicians suffered: new men came forward, more ready to consider new ideas like working with the conservatives.

The republicans were ready for the experiment but the conservatives were not. Like the German Centre, they refused to be told by the Pope what their political line should be. A catholic republican movement was set going, but was never anything but weak. However, all went well for a time. The elections of 1893 weakened the right and strengthened the moderates: catholic republicans helped them in the vote against the radicals. At the same time, the socialists and 'socialist radicals' became for the first time, with about fifty seats, strong enough to count. All the parties began to promise social reform, but there was growing hostility between radicals desirous of alliance with the working-class movement and moderates afraid of the red peril. The picture was confused by the unwillingness of many moderates to break with the radicals, but there was a clear move towards a two-party system with both parties loyal to the republic: in 1893–5 moderate ministries and anti-revolutionary legislation; in 1895–6 a short-lived ministry composed entirely of radicals (because nobody else would join) and proposing what in France was a revolutionary measure—an income tax. Finally, from 1896 till 1898 there was Méline's moderate ministry tolerant towards the church and maintaining itself for an unprecedented twenty-six months, mainly by inaction.

A death blow to the *ralliement* and all that went with it was given by the Dreyfus case. There is not space enough here for a proper telling of this fascinating detective story. Let it suffice that Captain Dreyfus, an officer of the general staff, was unjustly condemned to life imprisonment in 1894 for betraying information to a foreign power. The only evidence against him was a letter to the German military attaché (recovered from his waste-paper basket) which had really been written by another officer, Esterhazy. To ensure his conviction by a court-martial, further evidence was fabricated. When his friends set going a campaign for his retrial, still more evidence was forged to frustrate them. In January 1898 Emile Zola managed to arouse public concern over the case by his sensational open letter to the President, *j'accuse*. Zola was successfully prosecuted, and Colonel Picquart, who had more or less unravelled the mystery, was placed under arrest. But the evidence inevitably came under closer scrutiny and its falsity was soon discovered: the forger, Major Henry, was arrested and committed suicide.

The political effect of the Dreyfus case was to swing a section of the moderates from a rightward to a leftward inclination. Dreyfus came from a wealthy Jewish family. He was automatically anathema to the conservatives, who continued to believe in his guilt. Henry's 'patriotic forgeries' were said to have been necessary because the real evidence could not be revealed without endangering the state. The revision of the sentence and punishment of those responsible for it were opposed as damaging to the prestige and morale of the army and so to national security. The radicals, likewise, disliked the rich, suspected their patriotism and were more than a little antisemitic. In 1898 they were further compromised by a junction with some of the nationalists, by which they succeeded in overthrowing Méline. It was among the moderates that the strongest champions of the rights of the individual were to be found: this made them hostile to socialism and an income tax, but neither would they sacrifice an individual in the supposed interests of the army. From this quarter came most of the parliamentary pressure for a reopening of the case. After the death of Henry this could no longer be withstood and the matter was referred to the Court of Cassation, which ordered a retrial; Dreyfus was pardoned in 1899, although he was not fully rehabilitated until 1906.[1] The progress of the revisonist cause in the year following Henry's death was accompanied by furious demonstrations against Dreyfus by right-wing nationalists, especially in Paris where they seem now to have been in a majority. It was clear that the threat to public order now came from the right and a fatal breach opened between moderates and conservatives. In October 1898 the republicans in the Senate—always a moderate stronghold—demanded a government based on the union of all republicans and resolute in repressing unconstitutional agitation and upholding the supremacy of the civil power and the independence of the judiciary. In June 1899 (after a demonstrator had knocked the President's hat off) a strong government of 'republican defence' was formed under Waldeck-Rousseau, a stern unbending minister in the mould of Ferry and Gambetta. Himself taking the ministry of the interior, he put an end to disorder.

Waldeck and most of his ministers were moderates, but their parliamentary majority consisted largely of radicals and socialists, and for the first time a socialist (Millerand) entered the government.

[1] He was retried in 1899 by a military court at Rennes, which absurdly found him guilty of treason with extenuating circumstances.

It was clear that the new situation was favourable to the left and in the elections of 1902 radicals and socialists made large gains. Not wishing to continue at the head of the radicalized majority, Waldeck gave place to Emile Combes, a rather obscure radical in whose ministry radicals predominated. On the purely political plane the triumph of the left was pretty complete. Combes had started life as a theologian, had entered politics rather late, and was reproached with governing more like a Bonapartist than a republican. He was highly authoritarian, and his almost sole interest was in breaking the political power of the church. He was unprecedentedly ruthless in enforcing the reservation of all the patronage and favours of the government in every part of the country to loyal republicans. To republicanize the army, patronage there was taken out of the soldiers' hands and vested in the minister of war. From 1900 this was André, a general but remarkable in being a republican. Under his authority, the political sympathies of officers were systematically investigated and promotions went accordingly. Civilian supporters of the government provided most of the information, and it was assembled and passed on by the freemasons, closely associated in France with radical anticlericalism. The public discovery of this system at the end of 1904 so discredited the Combes ministry that it fell soon afterwards. It did more to demoralize the army than to republicanize it, and all that can be said in its favour is that the clerical generals previously in control had done much the same thing.

The religious orders had become more unpopular than ever on the left. A small, new one, the Assumptionists, had been actively engaged in right-wing political agitation and was dissolved by administrative decree. The rest were suspected not only of political subversion but of having amassed ill-gotten fortunes: this was because some of them engaged in trade, notably the Carthusian makers of the famous *chartreuse*. Waldeck promoted a measure of conciliation—a law on associations which provided that those which were international or wished to be able to hold property had to be sanctioned by the government. His intention was to sanction orders that were inoffensive. But his radical allies insisted on making the sanction of religious orders dependent on a parliamentary vote, and when Combes and his friends came to power they refused to sanction any. The unauthorized orders were dissolved, their schools closed. In 1904 a further law required the dissolution even of the teaching orders that had been authorized and forbade any member of any religious order to teach. Since this would then have meant the breakdown of the educational system, ten years' grace was given. These measures of religious intolerance pointed directly to the separation of church and state which came in 1905, though not even Combes seems to have desired this.

But despite these affronts to conservative men and institutions, the fact remained that it was the moderates who had put the left in power. The final effect of the Dreyfus case was therefore to reaffirm the conservative character of the republic. A few social reforms were carried by Millerand, but not many: model conditions of work in factories supplying the government and a ten-hour day in plants employing women and children were the most important. A certain amount was done to strengthen the government by reforms in parliamentary procedure and by closer co-operation (for the moment) between the parties supporting the ministry. The governments of Waldeck–Rousseau, Combes and one or two more lasted quite a long time. But governments had to be middle-of-the road coalitions incapable as a rule of pursuing any decided policy because of the need for all republicans to hold together against the disloyal right. The socialists were increasingly regarded as part of the republican majority, but they were its prisoners: they had no more real power than the defeated conservatives. The radicals gradually forgot that they had begun as the ardent critics of the conservatism of the constitution they now defended. The 1890s in France had held some promise of a new political system at once stable and dynamic. It looked as if there would be two parties, of the left and of the right, both loyal to the régime and advancing the reordering of society by peaceful conflict. The growth of extremism on the right had made this impossible. But since extremism breeds extremism, the republicans themselves, with their anticlerical fanaticism, must share some of the blame.

Austria-Hungary: Taaffe's Iron Ring and its Breaking

The Austrian lands were another fruitful source of clerical experiment, but the attempt at political regeneration was even less successful here than in the west. By 1900 the Monarchy had reached the point at which its dissolution began to be spoken of not as a distant possibility but as an imminent probability.

Count Edward Taaffe, who took over from the German liberals at Vienna in May 1879, came of a family of Irish catholic origin long in the imperial service. His manner was that of a jovial, frivolous worldling, but his exterior was belied by a long and distinguished career as an administrator. He had the administrator's indifference to party politics: earlier he had served in liberal ministries and even presided over one. His first act now was to secure a parliamentary majority by means of a general election. But he declared himself to be a 'Kaiserminister', standing above the parties on whose support he relied and not dependent on them for office. The coalition of German clericals, Czechs, Poles and southern Slavs, which he had formed would indeed have been a weak support for a truly parliamentary minister. United only in hating the German liberals and centralization, they scarcely merited their title of 'iron ring'. Taaffe did not really try to give them a common constructive purpose: his avowed aim was to keep all the nationalities in a balanced state of dissatisfaction. What he in fact did was moderately to favour the Slavs. An extension of the franchise (1882) gave them more parliamentary seats. Two Poles and a Czech became ministers. In Bohemia and Moravia, trials were to be conducted in the language of the accused and government officials were to communicate with citizens in their own language. This meant that government servants in the Czech provinces had henceforth to know both German and Czech. As educated Czechs knew German but few Germans knew Czech, the result was that Germans lost ground to Czechs in the civil service. Similar gains were made by the Slovenes in the southern province of Carniola.

This policy satisfied extremists on neither side. The Germans were naturally the most annoyed and a radical nationalist movement appeared among them as already explained. Far more effective, however, were the Young Czechs, the extremists on the other side. Industrial expansion in the Czech lands meant that the Czechs were growing in wealth and numbers, and they consequently looked on the concessions made to them only as a first instalment. They never gave up their main aim of reconstituting the ancient kingdom of Bohemia as an independent unit within the Monarchy. In 1890 Taaffe tried to satisfy both nationalities by a measure of partition, which would have meant Czech administration in Czech-speaking areas and a corresponding arrangement for the Germans. The moderates in both national groups agreed to this. But to the Young Czechs it was intolerable, for it meant a partition of the ancient Bohemian territories and so compromised the aim of restoring the ancient kingdom. In the general election of 1891, the Czech voters showed their agreement with this view by deserting the moderates and voting for the Young Czechs. This was the beginning of the end of Taaffe's parliamentary majority.

There was a social as well as a national protest against Taaffe's policies of compromise: more boldness was demanded in redressing the wrongs of the unprivileged classes. The Taaffe ministry imitated Bismarck by introducing schemes of insurance against sickness, and factory acts of 1884–5 established a maximum of eleven hours for the working day and regulated closely the amount of work to be done by women and children. But neither this nor periodic bouts of severe repression prevented the eventual formation of a Social Democratic party in 1888. Of more immediate importance were the Christian Socialists, who were now going beyond the old conservative clericals in opposing liberalism strongly on the economic side and calling for social reforms. Their most significant leader was Karl Lueger, a lawyer of humble origin who became the 'uncrowned king of Vienna'. He came to the fore through attacks on municipal corruption. Eloquent and handsome, he was also supremely good at mixing with the ordinary voters and making himself liked. In 1895 his party won the Viennese municipal elections, amid such furious propaganda against the business community that the grain market was actually moved to Budapest. The government was afraid to confirm Lueger's election as mayor, but when he had been re-elected four times it gave way (1897). He remained in office until his death in 1910 and made his city a showpiece of municipal socialism: gas, electricity and water supplies came into public ownership, many welfare services were started, parks were developed, schools and hospitals built.

The only point on which the newer political groupings were agreed was that there should be a further extension of the franchise. In

1893 Taaffe tried to satisfy them, only to arouse the hostility of his more conservative supporters. He therefore retired, and power passed to a combination of those who disliked universal suffrage and would only make limited concessions to the demand for it: the German liberals and conservatives and the Poles. In 1895 the premiership passed to a Pole, Count Casimir Badeni, who had been governor of Galicia. (The smallest of the Monarchy's master-races also provided the minister of finance, Bilinski, and the joint minister of foreign affairs, Goluchowski.) Badeni managed to carry through a reform of the suffrage in 1897, by which seventy-two members elected by the male population at large were added to those elected on a narrower franchise. He now needed to broaden his parliamentary support and tried to win over the Young Czechs. Language ordinances extended the concession made earlier in the Bohemian lands by positively requiring that from 1901 all state servants must know both German and Czech and by extending the number of instances in which the use of the Czech language was required.

The tumult resulting from the Badeni ordinances was so violent that parliamentary government became impossible at Vienna. Save for brief intervals, it remained so until the Monarchy collapsed. The Germans demonstrated violently against Badeni both in the streets of Vienna and in parliament, bringing business to a standstill. When Badeni retired in consequence, it was the turn of the Czechs to make violent counter-demonstrations. Ordinary legislation became impossible—the ministers had to govern by decree. Koeber's ministry (1900–4) restored harmony in parliament for a time by concentrating on popular measures of economic development. But it fell in the end after yet another national question had boiled over—the quarrel of Germans and Italians in the Tyrol. It was clear that only drastic measures could make the Austrian provinces governable again.

The troubles of the ministry at Vienna were due not a little to its difficulties in dealing with its opposite number at Budapest. Every ten years the economic and financial agreements between the two halves of the Monarchy had to be renewed. The Hungarians always demanded better terms, and almost always got their way: this reflected the Emperor's determination never, in the last resort, to quarrel with them. In 1878 the Austrian state bank was turned into an Austro-Hungarian institution. Hungary contributed less than a third to the cost of the jointly provided services like defence and foreign relations, though she had an equal if not decisive voice in their control; after much complaint, a nominal increase in her contribution was made in 1898. In the period 1878–87 the Monarchy gradually adopted a strongly protective tariff. This accorded with the desires of both halves and of all the major economic interests. But whereas Hungary gained by it a privileged position for her agriculture in the supplying of the great Austrian industrial areas, Austrian manufactures did not gain an equivalent advantage in Hungary. The Magyars were determined to develop their own industries, and did so by means of subsidies, discrimination in government purchasing and the manipulation of freight rates on the railways, which during this period were purchased by the state. The Hungarians even developed the port of Fiume, virtually from scratch, so as to have their own outlet to the sea, independent of the Austrian Trieste. There was mounting resentment in the Austrian provinces at the way in which they were being treated, and the Vienna parliament could only be induced to ratify the successive accords by the judicious bestowing of favours on the different national groups within it. Badeni's concessions to the Czechs in 1897 were made to secure their votes for this purpose: in vain, since the ensuing parliamentary breakdown made it necessary to ratify the new Hungarian agreement by decree. The Hungarian factor made it impossible for the ministers at Vienna to adopt a really strong policy of reconciliation between the nationalities under their rule: if they ever had been really reconciled, they would have joined in demanding a fairer deal from Hungary and so made relations with Budapest even worse.

For the Hungarians were not content with their privileges. The renewal of the accords in 1897 met with noisy obstruction in the Budapest parliament, no less than at Vienna. The tariff negotiations were only completed several years after the expiry of the old agreement and amid loud demands for the ending of the customs union and the erecting of a protective tariff between Hungary and the Austrian lands. This agitation reflected the survival of an intransigent Magyar nationalist movement, hostile to the Austrian partnership. Kossuth, the hero of 1848 who lived on in exile till 1894, was its patron saint, and his son was its nominal leader. The expansion of the army, which was going forward in the Monarchy as elsewhere, gave the nationalists a convenient issue. They demanded that Magyar replace German as the language of command for troops raised in Hungary. Behind this were other demands, such as that Hungarian troops should always be commanded by Magyar officers. The clear intention was to create a truly Hungarian army, which could be added to the means available for Magyarizing the subject peoples of the Hungarian kingdom.

Already, in 1890, a rumpus over an army bill had led the redoubtable Tisza to retire from the premiership, after fifteen years of office. In 1902 a bill for the further expansion of the army was brought to a halt in the Hungarian chamber by violent obstruction. Determined to preserve the unity of this army, Francis Joseph appointed as Hungarian prime minister Stephen Tisza, the son of the great longlasting premier. Tisza managed to get the rules of procedure in the chamber altered so as to curb obstruction. But in doing so, he alienated a section of the ruling oligarchy, the Liberal party which the elder Tisza had established in seemingly unending power. The government appealed to the country and in the elections of 1905 it was defeated. The Independence party led by the younger Kossuth was the strongest in the new chamber.

Other things besides Liberal divisions and nationalist frenzy had led to this unprecedented failure of the Hungarian government to manage the elections to its own advantage. The Liberals were an anticlerical and partly protestant party, and they had instituted compulsory civil marriage and legalized divorce in 1894. A catholic party had grown up to oppose them on this issue. The Liberals had also attacked the influence of the higher nobility. A good many of them had been excluded from the hereditary upper chamber, which was limited to the wealthiest section. The electoral system worked against them. A great many deputies came from constituencies in the non-Magyar areas, where few were entitled to vote and most of those were government officials. It was this that enabled the Liberal ministers to manage the elections so effectively, and the Liberals increasingly became a party of bureaucrats, recruited from the lesser nobility. In the Magyar-speaking areas, where most of the electorate lived, it was the territorial influence of the great landed magnates that predominated. A fairer electoral system would have given them more power.

By 1905 constitutional government had broken down in both halves of the monarchy (Tisza was succeeded by a non-parliamentary ministry). The conflicts between the two halves and between Czechs and Germans seemed an impassable barrier to fruitful reorganization. Francis Joseph was back very much with the situation with which he started in 1848. On that occasion the Habsburg monarchy had escaped what looked like the certainty of dissolution, and it could not be said for certain that the trick was unrepeatable. The very quarrels of the nationalities always ensured that the initiative lay with the Emperor, as long as there was one. But only a bold and radical, even reckless, new policy was likely to end the impasse.

The Beginning of Russia's Industrial Greatness

Alexander III (1881–94) was the last Tsar who was at all equal to his terrible responsibilities. Tall and powerfully built, he was rather unintelligent but had a strength of character fully answering to his appearance. His son Nicholas II, the last of his line, was less stupid and his personal charm seems to have enchanted those who served him, even when he treated them badly. But he entirely lacked his father's fixity of purpose and was constantly falling under the influence of personalities stronger than his own. His views tended to be those of the person to whom he had last spoken, and in a pure autocracy this was fatal to the stability of government. Even his simplicity and his devotion to his family, his most appealing characteristics, were a political handicap. Hating court life, he withdrew increasingly into his family circle and farther from contact with the nation. Both monarchs were extreme conservatives, disliking even the modest reforms already introduced under Alexander II. Typical of their reigns was the ascendancy of Pobedonostsev, for many years Procurator of the Holy Synod (in effect, minister for church affairs), who declared in a famous phrase that parliamentary institutions were 'the great lie of our time'. Even the few liberties allowed to Russia's peoples were curtailed. In 1889–90 the elective local justices of the peace were replaced by nominated 'land captains' and the proportion of peasants' representatives in the zemstva (local councils) was reduced. The independence of the judiciary was limited by a system of instructions to judges. The press and the universities lost some of the freedom that they had gained under Alexander II. The non-Russian peoples were worse treated, especially the Jews. Finland, which remarkably enjoyed home rule under a parliamentary constitution, was subjected to the Russian system of conscription in 1901, and in 1903 its constitution was suspended.

Economic advancement was another matter. The government had to promote this if Russia was to retain her position among the great powers. The lesson of the Crimean War in this respect had been powerfully reinforced by the war of 1877. Defeat in the former had forced Russia off the gold standard. The latter ruined her reviving credit; a large issue of paper money was required to finance it and the rouble depreciated sharply in relation to the other main currencies. The able finance minister, Reutern, resigned in despair. His eventual successor, Bunge, likewise resigned in 1886 after another catastrophic run on the rouble caused by the crisis over Bulgaria described in the next chapter. Russian public finance had to be put on a sounder footing; if her military power was not to suffer, this could only be done by some remarkable increase in her productive power and hence her revenue.

Remarkable efforts were made in these directions by the two next finance ministers, both of whom were personally closer to the world of commerce than their predecessors: though in no sense liberals, they represented an important challenge to aristocratic and agrarian dominance in the Russian state. The first, Vyshnegradsky, was an engineer and company director. His philosophy was really the classic liberal one of economy and a balanced budget. He aimed at putting Russia back on the gold standard, thereby benefiting both the state and private enterprise by making it easier for them to borrow abroad. To this end he cut expenditure, even of productive kinds like railway development. But the steps he took to increase revenue and improve credit were to be more important for the future. It was he who built up the links with the French money market henceforth vital to Russian finances. Another measure was the tariff of 1891, which made Russia the most strongly protectionist country in Europe. Although Vyshnegradsky defended it as encouraging native industry, its real purposes were to increase the revenue and improve Russia's balance of payments by limiting imports. Bunge and Reutern had already introduced less drastic measures of the same kind for these purposes. Both of them were further served by the screwing up of taxes on the peasants. Not only did these bring in more money but they forced the peasants to sell more of their crops in order to pay them and thereby increased the amount available for export. A notable refinement was that the payment of taxes was demanded at harvest time. This obliged the peasants to sell when prices were low and so improved Russia's competitive position in world markets.

Vyshnegradsky's policy worked only in the short run. It squeezed the taxpayer dry and left him without sufficient resources to withstand normal economic hazards. In 1891 there were widespread crop failures. The peasants were without adequate reserves of grain and money, and the result was a severe famine, followed by outbreaks of cholera. The government had to disgorge some of its increased revenue to relieve the sufferers. The moral effect of the famine was profound. The minister of finance had to retire and there now began to develop the first stirrings of new opposition movements that were to culminate in the revolution of 1905.

But Vyshnegradsky's methods were capable of yielding better results if they were applied not merely to increasing the revenue but to developing production as well. This was the policy of the next finance minister, Sergei Julevich Witte. Born in 1849 he was the son of a Lutheran German from the Baltic provinces of the empire who had married into the Russian noble family of Fadeev. Compelled by poverty to work hard for his living, he received a technical education and entered the state railway administration. Later he became manager of the large privately owned South Western Railway and made it highly profitable by a skilfully designed freight tariff. Entering the ministry of finance under Vyshnegradsky, he was the man mainly responsible for planning the Trans-Siberian railway, the building of which was to be the great monument of his later career as minister. Though he was a Russian nobleman, his outlook was western and his personality was that of a self-made business tycoon— pugnacious, uncultured but full of ideas. His clumsy appearance— a massive head and body on short legs—fitted his character.

It seems to have been only in 1889 that Witte adopted the economic philosophy that he was to follow as minister. In that year he published a pamphlet summarizing and commenting on Friedrich List's *National System of Political Economy*. Writing before German unification, List had argued that agricultural states were doomed to ever-increasing inferiority and subordination to the great industrial powers. They must build up industry at all costs, the government helping in every way. Even agriculture would benefit from this, by an increase in its domestic market and by the growth of national efficiency. In commenting on these views, Witte argued that they were reflected in the protectionist policies of Bismarck: German industrial greatness was being fostered in the interests of her military power.

The distinctive feature of Witte's policy was that he spent money rather than saving it. The government undertook a huge programme of public works, in particular a massive extension of the railway system. The supplying of materials for this, coupled with the new high tariff, was a powerful stimulus to Russian industrial development. Of course, the improvement of transportation worked directly in the same way, improving the access to markets not only inside the country but in China and Central Asia, where Witte dreamed of establishing a huge empire by economic penetration. Witte borrowed heavily abroad, especially from France. He also took steps to make more capital available to private industry. In 1894 the State Bank was empowered to make industrial loans, and a large amount of the state debt in Russian hands was paid off by means of money borrowed abroad, thus freeing Russian funds for industrial investment. The nationalization (at fancy prices) of many privately owned railways also served this purpose, besides increasing the revenue. To pay interest on the new loans, taxes had also be to increased and in 1894 a state monopoly in the sale of spirits was set up to bring in more money. Besides spending lavishly, Witte built up a large gold reserve, and in 1897 this enabled him to achieve the long-cherished aim of his predecessors and put Russia back on the gold standard.

The achievements of the Witte era were impressive. Railway mileage increased by 46 per cent between 1892 and 1902, and industrial output more or less doubled. Although we shall see that progress was checked by a depression at the turn of the century, there was further rapid expansion after Witte's fall, from 1908 onwards. Though small by western standards, Russian industry was expanding in the two decades before 1914 faster even than in Germany. The impetus given by Witte was particularly seen in the basic industries. Coal production more than doubled between 1892 and 1902, the output of pig iron trebled, oil production quadrupled. The chemical and metal-working industries (including machine-making) increased by over 170 per cent. Two great new industrial areas sprang up in the south from quite small beginnings: the coal and steel centres of the Ukraine and the oilfields of the Caucasus. Though Russian industry as a whole remained rather backward, many of the new plants were as modern as any in the world and many were very large. There was a notable investment of foreign capital in private industrial enterprises. In 1900 there were said to be 269 foreign-owned companies in Russia, of which all but sixteen had been founded since 1888. Foreign capital, on its own or in partnership with Russians, was especially important in the fastest-growing areas and industries. Foreigners owned 67 per cent of the shares in all metallurgical companies in 1900 and no less than 85 per cent in those making iron and steel in the Ukraine. But it is wrong to suppose that expansion was confined to basic industries, large enterprises and foreign-owned concerns. The consumption of raw cotton by Russian mills doubled between 1892 and 1902. Nine-tenths of the industrial enterprises founded in the nineties employed less than a hundred workers in 1900. Two-thirds of the money for the great railway building projects came from native sources.

The progress of Russian education at this time may fairly be linked to Witte's achievements, since he realized its importance for economic advance and himself promoted the foundation of over a hundred technical schools and three advanced institutions of technology. The financial resources of the *zemstva* were considerably increased and expenditure on both primary and secondary education increased rapidly after 1890. In 1903 it was estimated that a doubling of the existing provision would make universal primary education possible. From the turn of the century there was also a notable improvement in the public medical services.

But all Witte's plans were decisively limited by the backward state of Russian agriculture. It was impossible to relieve the peasantry of the taxes which ultimately paid for both the heavy public spending and the strengthening of the currency: the industrial sector was not big enough to finance its own expansion. The agricultural position was not completely impossible: production of cereals and potatoes seems to have been increasing about twice as fast as the population.

Attempts were made to relieve the peasants by abolishing the direct taxes which they paid (notably the poll tax in 1886) and substituting indirect taxes. But these, too, were largely paid by the peasants, especially as they began to use more manufactured products like matches and oil lamps, and they continued liable to local land taxes and the redemption payments for their former landlords. They suffered from the fall of world agricultural prices in the earlier nineties, and no sooner had prices recovered than there were a series of bad harvests, notably in 1897 and 1901. Many signs appeared that the peasants were being pressed too hard. In 1900 arrears of redemption payments exceeded the total theoretically payable each year. The number of horses and other farm animals was declining. Rural wages fell after 1900. In the spring of 1902 there were peasant risings against the landlords in several southern areas.

The bad harvests unfortunately coincided with a tightening of the world money market. Witte could neither borrow nor spend on the scale he would have wished. From 1899 till 1903 there was an industrial recession in Russia: the new heavy industry and the new industrial areas were the worst hit, and many firms concerned in these went bankrupt. Witte had reached the same impasse as his predecessors.

His remedy was to try to modernize agriculture and bring it into line with industry. Industrial development itself did something to relieve rural overpopulation by providing alternative employment in the towns and facilitating emigration to less-congested areas, such as Siberia. But for further improvement the government was undecided whether to rely on the more enterprising peasants or on the nobility. In 1883 a Peasants' Land Bank had been set up to finance peasant purchases of land still belonging to the nobles, but in 1885 a Nobles' Land Bank was established which helped impoverished nobles to avoid the need to sell. Nobles were allowed to borrow more cheaply than peasants and were favoured in many other ways too. This was justified on political grounds: the nobility were the mainstay of the monarchy. Economically it made little sense. Some nobles had large farms run on the most modern lines, but noble estates as a whole were not very efficient. Witte strongly resisted subsidies to the nobles, and the whole idea of 'a throne not based on the entire nation but on separate classes'. In 1896 he said that 'capitalist development' was the way forward for Russian agriculture.

What this implied was encouragement for the more enterprising peasants to acquire more land, either from nobles or other peasants: on these enlarged farms it would be profitable to use more efficient methods and invest more capital. This process had been going forward steadily since emancipation: by 1905 the nobles had lost a third of the land left to them in 1861, though not all of it went to peasants. Peasant holdings were also increased by the extensive renting of land. Within the peasantry, the larger farmers were gaining ground at the expense of the rest, though to what extent is in dispute.[1] What is certain is that the communal element widely prevalent, as noted earlier, in Russian land tenure impeded the process. There were restrictions both on the free sale of land and on innovations in the way that it was managed. Witte came out increasingly strongly in favour of the abolition of the communal system (though he never dared to avow this openly) and the establishment of true private property in land. Many official enquiries took place, and in 1902 Witte himself was placed at the head of a 'special conference on the needs of agriculture'. But he only achieved one reform: the abolition (1903) of the collective responsibility of the villages for the redemption debt. In the same year he was dismissed from the ministry of finance and 'kicked upstairs' to a higher but largely honorific office.

Witte failed to overcome his difficulties because his political position was not strong enough. This partly resulted from confusion in his own ideas. He was passionately conservative in his devotion to the monarchy and the orthodox faith, and he distrusted representative institutions even at local level. But he could not hope to reconstruct Russian society unless he could arouse public enthusiasm. This he realized. A famous memorandum prepared at his order in 1899 argued that centralized autocratic rule was more efficient than the *zemstva*. But it also called for greater personal freedom and said that the ministry of finance 'always listened to public opinion and let the public take an interest in its activities'. Witte, in fact, supported his plans by massive propaganda both at home and abroad. The annual reports of his ministries were comprehensive economic surveys, addressed to the nation no less than to the Tsar. He encouraged the free discussion of economic issues. The business community was

---

[1] The Marxists emphasize it because it exemplifies their belief that under capitalism the rich get richer and the poor poorer.

allowed to organize and express its views: besides private associations there were official local committees of trade and industry, national business conferences and various consultative bodies attached to the finance ministry. When Witte was allowed to take up the peasant problem in 1902, he at once established local committees to advise him in every province and district. But he remained committed to the old political framework and all the limitations that implied.

However, Witte's aversion to liberal political institutions is hardly surprising in view of the fact that his policies were bitterly and almost universally unpopular. His whole system was opposed by the agricultural interest, to whom it meant both high taxes and high prices for manufactures. This hostility came not only from the peasants but also from the nobility, for whom Witte had little use, but who were the dominant element in court and administration. The supposedly liberal forces in the country did not favour the sort of changes that Witte wanted. The *zemstva*, representing mainly nobility and peasants, spoke for agriculture. Liberal intellectuals still believed in free trade. The business community was divided: some industries, such as textiles, did not especially benefit from the new policy, and new factories put many technically backward producers out of business. Economic advance took place mainly in the peripheral areas. The central provinces of European Russia, where both industry and agriculture tended to be comparatively old-fashioned, were a depressed region and generally discontented. There was universal resentment at the way in which foreigners were gaining control of Russian economic life. Jews, too, were prominent in the more prosperous enterprises and this also was disliked. There was much antipathy to Witte personally. He steadily extended the range of his activities until they embraced virtually the whole economic and social life of the country. His financial management involved a great deal of shady manoeuvring and manipulation of figures, to bolster the shaky credit of the state.

The strength of the opposition appears clearly in the history of Witte's greatest measure, the introduction of the gold standard in 1897. After lengthy deliberations within the bureaucracy, it was rejected by the State Council (a sort of officials' parliament) and introduced over their heads by imperial ukase. The servants of the autocracy protested at the disregard of normal legislative procedure! The greatest centre of opposition was the ministry of the interior, which tended to oppose economic changes because they endangered public tranquillity. Basically this ministry stood for the conservative nobility, against the new middle class fostered by the ministry of finance. But Witte's unpopularity allowed successive ministers of the interior to pose as liberals: Goremykin championed the *zemstva* against him and Sipyagin, enlisting their aid, set going a rival project of peasant emancipation in 1902.

Witte's downfall finally resulted from the growing tension at home and abroad. He resisted the drift towards war with Japan, described in the next chapter. Although he believed in imperial expansion, he also believed in the need for peace—for the world in general, and especially for rickety Russia. The powerful military party did not understand the economics of power and regarded him as an obstacle to national advance. The crisis in the government and the economy encouraged the revival of opposition to the autocracy. From the mid nineties unofficial national congresses began to be held both of *zemstva* representatives and of professional men in the service of *zemstva*—doctors, teachers and so forth. These were the nucleus of a liberal political movement. Peasant rioting has already been noticed, and now the industrial workers began to stir. Towards them the government's attitude had been undecided. Bunge had introduced a factory inspectorate and regulated child labour. A law of 1897 established a universal maximum of $11\frac{1}{2}$ hours' work a day. But after Bunge's fall there was a tendency for the ministry of finance to take the employers' part against the workers in the interests of efficiency. As in other matters, the ministry of the interior took the opposite line. The police authorities were coming to believe that unless the condition of the working class improved it would be impossible to keep order in the towns. From 1901, the police began to encourage the formation of working-class societies. In 1902 the appointment of Plehve as minister of the interior brought Witte a formidable new adversary and in 1903 he promoted a law obliging employers to care for their workers in sickness. Proper trade unions were illegal, but in the boom years of the nineties they appeared nevertheless: the workers were well placed to demand higher wages. With the onset of the slump, this ceased to be the case. The workers came increasingly to believe, therefore, that only political changes could help them. The officially tolerated societies became disloyal. Strikes became political and violent. In 1902–3 there were a series of local general strikes in the new industrial centres of the south. Not only did these help in the final ruin of Witte but the growing disorder in town and country encouraged as we shall see the growth of organized revolutionary activity. From 1901 there was a series of remarkable political assassinations, carrying off three ministers and a Grand Duke. The troubles of the seventies had returned.

The Witte régime had effectively started the growth of Russia as an industrial great power, and had demonstrated the formula by which it could be done: the screw must be put on the peasants to pay for the creation of basic industries whose products brought them little immediate benefit. The Soviet régime has simply carried on where Witte left off: being unable to borrow abroad, it has had to bear even harder on the peasants. What has not endured has been Witte's reliance on private capitalist enterprise. This reflects the fact that the development of capitalism did not, as had been both hoped and feared, strengthen the Tsars against revolution. Economic growth was proving painful as well as profitable. The peasantry and middle class were still estranged from the government by the absence of political and social reform. Worse, the signs were that in order to industrialize, the government would need to become more rather than less authoritarian and unpopular. Industrial growth, on the other hand, was increasing the numbers of the most revolutionary class—the urban proletariat. It can even be argued that since much of the capital behind the new industries was foreign, the Russian proletariat was growing relatively faster than the Russian bourgeoisie. The revolutionaries were to have another chance. The idiocy of the government in launching a country in crisis on an unnecessary war with Japan ensured that the chance was to come soon.

3: The Diplomacy of Imperialism

Already in the seventies Bismarck had been trying to reduce the diplomatic pressure in Europe by encouraging the powers to devote themselves to colonial expansion, and to avoid conflicts in the process by agreeing beforehand as to their respective shares. With the Congress of Berlin he began to succeed. In 1881, as a result of informal understandings reached there, France added Tunisia to her north African empire. In the same year, as we have seen, the Balkans were secretly partitioned into Russian and Austrian spheres. For the next two decades the powers competed for colonies and Germany's European position was strengthened thereby. But then a change came. The resistance of Balkan and Afro-Asian peoples to colonial penetration had already disrupted some of Bismarck's plans by destroying the advantages proposed under them for particular European powers. Now this resistance intensified, and for this and other reasons the powers tired of colonial rivalries. They were increasingly eager to end them amicably, even if it meant limiting their territorial gains. But at the same time Germany had become tired of taking less than her fair share of colonies in order to safeguard her European position, and so it was hard to fit her in. A network of colonial agreements emerged from which Germany was largely excluded, and this altered the situation in Europe no less than in the colonial world. In the late nineteenth century colonial rivalries had helped to secure European peace. At the beginning of the twentieth colonial rivalries were ended only at the cost of making war in Europe more likely.

Towards a Continental League, 1881–5

Bismarck's plans tended for a time to assume the very simple form of encouraging the continental powers to co-operate against Britain on colonial questions—a sort of peacetime version of Napoleon's continental system, appealing to continental jealousy of British maritime and colonial supremacy. Bismarck seems to have turned against Britain because Gladstone was in power there. Bismarck

THE BALKANS
1878

RUSSIA

HELD BY RUMANIA
1856-1878,
THEN RUSSIA

AUSTRIA - HUNGARY

Belgrade

RUMANIA
INDEPT. 1878

•Bucharest

BOSNIA
AUSTRIAN OCCUPATION
1878
ANNEXATION, 1908.
Sarajevo
HERZEGOVINIA

SERBIA

1878

Novibazar   Nish

•Plevna

Varna 1913

MONTENEGRO

BULGARIA

IND.
1878

Kumanovo

•Sofia   E. RUMELIA

Dulcigno

Adrianople

Midia

Durazzo

Monastir

Kavalla

Enos

Constantinople

Salonica

Janina

GREECE

Smyrna

Athens

Bulgarian frontier by
treaty of SAN STEPHANO   ············
Boundaries 1871   —·—·—·—
    "   1878   —··—··—

0   100
Miles

detested Gladstone and a quarrel with liberal England might help him to retain power on the accession of the liberal and anglophile Prince Frederick: as we have seen, he was trying during the eighties to build up a strong body of conservative and nationalist opinion behind himself for this purpose. But there were also good diplomatic reasons for turning against Gladstone. He desired to keep down Britain's foreign commitments, and unlike the conservatives he was unwilling to help Austria-Hungary to hold back Russia. Bismarck was to prove not unwilling to see Russia restrained when he did not have to do it himself. But when Britain could not be used against Russia, it became much more important for the Germans to prevent the reopening of the Russo-Austrian quarrel in the Balkans. The revived Three Emperors' League had been designed to encourage the Russians to turn their attention to central Asia or the Far East, where they could be helped to overcome the resistance of Britain.

That Bismarck was at first none too firmly committed to this policy is suggested by the conclusion of the Triple Alliance. This arose from Italian resentment at the French occupation of Tunis. Italy had many colonists there and coveted the area for herself. There were furious jingoistic outbursts, and the Italian government sought an alliance with the Austrians—not so much in the hope of action against France but rather to bolster its prestige at home. The essential weakness of the Italian political system had been revealed by the nationalist uproar and the King felt the need of a protector. The Austrians snubbed the Italians, but in 1882 Bismarck induced them to change their mind. The Triple Alliance bound Austria-Hungary and Germany to come to Italy's help if she was attacked by France. If one of the partners was at war with some other fourth power, the other two were to remain neutral. This was the most important provision, for it meant that if Austria-Hungary was at war with Russia, Italy was pledged not to attack her in the rear. The anti-Russian character of the alliance was sharpened by a provision, insisted on by the Italians, that it was not to be operative against Britain. Still more anti-Russian was the defensive alliance concluded by Germany and Austria-Hungary with Rumania in 1883. Thus Bismarck, while seeking a good understanding with each of his neighbours, was also seeking to play them off against each other. This was to prove a useful precaution when the policy of general good understanding broke down.

What made a league against Britain more desirable was the development of the Egyptian question. Egypt, in theory, was part of the Ottoman Empire, but enjoyed virtual independence under a hereditary Khedive. The enterprising Khedive Ismail had encouraged foreign investment in the boom years of the mid-century, but, like the Sultan himself, he had been forced into bankruptcy by the depression of the seventies. The British and French governments, whose nationals held most of the Egyptian foreign debt, established a joint control over the finances of the country to ensure that the bondholders were paid. Imposed not by armed force but by diplomatic pressure, this control was bitterly unpopular, and in 1881 it was threatened by an army coup which brought the embryonic nationalist movement to power. The French and British had now to use force or back down. Only the British were prepared to use force, and in September 1882 their army destroyed the nationalists at Tel-el-Kebir, and thereafter remained in control of the country until after the Second World War.

The failure of the Anglo-French financial control is a notable instance of the way in which the collapse of an imperial experiment produced a diplomatic revolution. Britain and France had been friends for most of the nineteenth century. Their failure to agree on a new Egyptian policy estranged them for twenty years. The French resented British occupation of a country where their own economic interests had predominated. They had not felt strong enough to occupy it themselves; still less did they feel strong enough to fight the British over it. Short of that, they tried as hard as they could to get the British out. The British professed themselves ready to withdraw as soon as internal order could be maintained without them, which came in the end to mean never. The truth was that control of Egypt was now the best way to safeguard the short route to India and the British position in the eastern Mediterranean. Britain had originally gone there to deny control to others. But as it became clearer that the Ottoman Empire could no longer resist Russia and was likely to be dominated by some other power than Britain, the control of Egypt became positively desirable to the British as a substitute.

Bismarck's attitude to the Egyptian question is mysterious. He had long encouraged the British to take Egypt for themselves. He had, however, expressed approval of good Anglo-French relations: Britain would restrain France from action against Germany and

France would restrain Britain from action against Russia. In 1879 he had intervened to uphold the financial condominium when Khedive Ismail had tried to get rid of it (Ismail was deposed by the Sultan). But in 1882 he discouraged the French from joining in military intervention in Egypt (they could only safely do this if they could be certain that there would be no quarrel with Germany during the expedition). Thereafter he encouraged the British when they acted alone, thereby helping to create the Anglo-French rift.

It seems possible that Gambetta's brief ministry (November 1881–January 1882) may have been responsible for Bismarck's inconsistencies, both over Egypt and over the Triple Alliance. Bismarck feared Gambetta, linking him oddly with his other pet aversions, Gladstone and Gorchakov, in a 'revolutionary quarter in G' (the fourth was Garibaldi). Gambetta in power was certainly likely to mean a more ambitious French policy in some direction and it inspired the visit to France of a Panslav enthusiast, General Skobelev, who enjoyed some official favour. Bismarck's moves to separate Britain from France and ally with Italy against her were a natural response, though Gambetta removed this particular need for them by dying at the end of the year.

At odds with Great Britain, France was free to turn to Russia. This could best be discouraged if Bismarck supported not only Russia but France as well against the British. In March 1884 the Three Emperors' League was renewed, and for the next year Bismarck tried to induce the French to enter a sort of continental naval alliance to put pressure on Britain, which he compared to the League of Armed Neutrality which Catherine the Great had formed for this purpose during the American War of Independence. It was at this time that he acquired, almost by a stroke of the pen, a huge colonial empire for Germany in west, east and south Africa and in the Pacific. Exactly why he did so is not clear, but it seems likely that he wanted to turn to account the dependence of the British on him for support in Egypt, and thereby achieve something that would help the government's supporters in the Reichstag election of 1884. In the event, he had trouble with the British, especially over Angra Pequena in south-west Africa. He started to work with the French against them. Germany helped French plans for the establishment of a central African empire on the north bank of the

Congo. The British tried to block this in February 1884 by recognizing a dormant Portuguese claim to the mouth of the river. In June they were forced to retract, and at the end of the year an international conference settled the status of the Congo Basin. Most of it was recognized as belonging to the International Association dominated in his private capacity by the villainous King Leopold II of the Belgians and the trade of the area was opened to all nations on equal terms. This really suited the free-trade British better than the protectionist French. Of more value perhaps to France was Bismarck's support of their other great colonial venture in Indo-China. Germany did her best to dissuade the Chinese government from interfering against the French.

But the most important manifestation of the continental league benefited Russia, not France. Russian expansion in central Asia had at last reached Afghanistan, whose forces they defeated at Pendjeh in March 1885. Only this buffer state lay between them and India. Gladstone had given up Disraeli's attempt to conquer it, but he was determined to defend it—colonial reverses, such as the recent failure to relieve Gordon at Khartoum, were making him unpopular. Parliament voted funds for military action. The easiest place for the British to attack Russia was still the Black Sea, and in 1878 they had virtually reserved the right to send their fleet into it through the Straits whenever it suited them. Bismarck always professed himself ready to protect Russia from attack in this quarter and now he was as good as his word. Under his leadership, the continental powers warned the Sultan not to let the British through. The Sultan was glad of an excuse not to and the British did not venture to defy the rest of Europe.

No sooner had the continental league won this famous victory than it fell to pieces. Neither France nor Russia had ever wished to commit themselves too closely to Bismarck. France had not accepted his plans for an alliance, and Russia used her Straits success to come to a compromise settlement with Britain. Now each of them suffered colonial reverses which disenchanted them with Germany, just as difficulties in Egypt had taken the shine off Anglo-French co-operation. In March 1885 the French forces in Indo-China were beaten by the Chinese at Lang-son. The defeat at first seemed more serious than it really was and it led to the triumph of those for whom colonial ventures were a waste of national resources. Ferry, the main promoter of colonial expansion since 1881, fell: the autumn elections strengthened the nationalists and radicals, and there followed the rise of General Boulanger.

That same autumn the Russians began to lose control of Bulgaria. Austrian and German recognition of their predominance there had been one of their main gains from the Three Emperors' League. The like recognition was not forthcoming from the Bulgars. They had no wish to fall under Russian domination, having only just escaped from that of Turkey. They were also affected by Austrian economic penetration, notably the building of the great railway across the Balkans to Constantinople. Backward Russia could not contribute nearly so much to the economic development of the area. In 1879 Prince Alexander of Battenburg was established on the Bulgar throne with a democratic constitution. In 1881, following the reaction in Russia, the Prince amended the constitution in a conservative direction. But in 1883 he cancelled these amendments and came to terms with the liberals. From that time onward the Russians were his enemies. In September 1885 there was a revolution in Eastern Rumelia and its union with Bulgaria (prevented by the powers in 1878) was proclaimed. This was supposed to be what the Russians wanted, but they were so angry with the Bulgars that they proposed that the powers should intervene to restore the status quo. The Germans and Austrians were willing, but Salisbury, who had now taken over from Gladstone in Britain, demurred.

This was Britain's revenge for the closing of the Straits in the spring. The Three Emperors did not dare to act on their own. They were further embarrassed when the Austrian puppet, Serbia, attacked Bulgaria in order to win compensation for Bulgarian enlargement. The Serbs were defeated and then protected from Bulgar rage by the Austrians. In the spring of 1886 the powers accepted Salisbury's plan for Bulgaria: the Prince became Governor of Eastern Rumelia as well and the division between the two was quietly forgotten. But the Russians were still sore. In August Prince Alexander was kidnapped by Russian officers and later bullied into abdication. The Austrians would not stand for this and pledged themselves to protect Bulgarian independence. The Bulgarian liberals, however, managed to stand up to Russian threats unaided and retained control: in November 1886 the Russians broke off relations with the principality. The Three Emperors' League had died a second time, for there had ceased to be even a pretence of a common Austro-Russian policy for the Balkans. With this there evaporated the last vestiges of the continental alliance.

Germany Between Britain and Russia

In appearance Bismarck's position was now a very dangerous one, with Russia likely to fight his ally Austria-Hungary over Bulgaria and a more nationalist France likely to come to Russia's help. In fact, the danger was not too acute and was important to Bismarck mainly in helping to win the Reichstag elections of January 1887 and so bring about the voting of a larger military budget. After the money was voted, Bismarck rapidly reduced the tension which had been building up with France by his correct attitude in the Schnaebele incident, when a French frontier official was improperly arrested by the Germans. The French moderates never lost control and French policy was not hostile to Germany but extremely reserved.

As for Russia, Bismarck's life was made much easier by the displacement of Gladstone by Salisbury, definitive in 1886. Salisbury was ready, as Gladstone was not, to resist Russia. Bismarck could therefore shed the main burden of keeping her quiet, which he had hitherto done by helping, and might otherwise have had to do by fighting her. Salisbury and Bismarck both wished to avoid appearing as Russia's main enemy, and each urged the other to step forward in support of Austria-Hungary. Bismarck used the ferment in France as his excuse for not being able to do so and it was Salisbury who gave way, probably because he also needed help against France over Egypt. In February 1887 he came to an informal understanding with Italy for diplomatic co-operation to preserve the status quo in the Mediterranean. Austria-Hungary was brought in immediately afterwards and the agreement extended to cover the Aegean and Black Seas. Simultaneously, the Triple Alliance, due for renewal, was revamped at Bismarck's instigation. Till the breach between Russia and the Austrians it had remained very much a dead letter and the Italians were tired of it. Bismarck wished now to make something of it, as an underpinning for the new combination emerging round

Britain. Additional agreements bound Germany to help Italy if she clashed with France in North Africa and pledged Italy and Austria-Hungary to back each other's claims to compensation if there were territorial changes in the Balkans.

These arrangements were directed almost wholly against France, and for that reason were accepted with great reluctance by Austria-Hungary. They protected Britain in Egypt. They gave Italy some hope of eventually gaining Tripoli, now her main North African objective, and the courage rapidly to lay hands on Eritrea and Somaliland in the African 'horn'. But meanwhile, in July 1887, the Bulgars elected a new Prince, Ferdinand of Coburg, and violent Russian action against him was expected. At the end of the year, therefore, a so-called 'second Mediterranean agreement' was concluded between Britain, Italy and Austria-Hungary. They agreed to work together to protect the status quo in the Near East—notably in Asia Minor and Bulgaria—and the free passage of the Straits.

The natural result of these developments was that France and Russia began to edge closer together.[1] Russia had still not quarrelled directly with Germany, and in January 1887 Peter Shuvalov brought to Berlin a plan in which Russia offered neutrality in a German war with France. But this was soon withdrawn and Bismarck was later told that Russia needed France in order to maintain the naval balance against Britain. In May, Drummond Wolff for Britain signed an agreement with the Sultan regularizing the British position in Egypt and providing for their eventual withdrawal. The French and Russians jointly used influence at Constantinople to prevent the ratification of this agreement. In 1888 the first of the great Russian loans was floated in France: Bismarck had driven the Russians to this by impeding the sale of their securities in Germany. In 1889 the Russians ordered a large quantity of French rifles, promising that they would never be used against France.

A new diplomatic system was appearing, based on the rivalry of two roughly balanced groups. Bismarck had alliances with the powers associated with Britain. He balanced these by the new Reinsurance Treaty with Russia, concluded in June 1887. The two powers promised each other neutrality except in two cases: a Russian attack on Austria-Hungary and a German attack on France. The Germans further

[1] But note that the Mediterranean Agreements themselves remained a close secret.

promised to support Russia in Bulgaria and at the Straits. This they successfully, though uselessly, did early in 1888. The Russians asked the Sultan to declare Prince Ferdinand's election illegal. They were supported by both Germany and France and they succeeded against the opposition of the 'Mediterranean' powers. But this remained a paper victory.

Germany was now emerging as the arbiter between two groups of powers, rivals on imperial questions and both fairly friendly to the great central European power and hoping for her support. This basic situation endured until the early twentieth century and gave the German Empire as much security in Europe as it ever had. The basis of the system were laid in Bismarck's time, in part by Bismarck himself, and the system long survived his dismissal. All this has commonly been denied. On the one hand, it has been said, ever since Bismarck's fall in 1890, that the Reinsurance Treaty was dishonest and that only his remarkable cunning could keep the system to which it belonged from collapsing. But the Reinsurance Treaty was not in conflict with the purely defensive Austro-German alliance[1] (which Bismarck actually published in 1888, to undeceive Russophobes as to its terms). It was in conflict with the Mediterranean Agreements, but though Bismarck had encouraged these he had not joined them, and he refused Salisbury's request to abandon the support of Russia on the Straits question. Of course the fact remains that by protecting Austria-Hungary Germany was denying Russia a triumph in the Balkans. But this was no secret and it did not prevent Germany and Russia from seeking each other's friendship and with some success. In this respect Bismarck's successors soon returned to the central Bismarckian policy.

On the other hand, Bismarck accused his successors—and others have done so since—of driving Russia into the arms of France by not renewing the Reinsurance Treaty. But it can be seen that Russia and France were already drawing together in 1887 and that the terms of the Reinsurance Treaty themselves reflect this. The truth is that Russia had never been prepared to see Germany crush France again except perhaps in return for a free hand against the Austrians. At the same time, Franco-Russian intimacy was not really the threat to

[1] The Austro-German defensive alliances with Rumania were against the terms of the Three Emperors' League, which placed that country in Russia's sphere.

Germany that it is usually made out to have been. It developed mainly against Britain, and over Mediterranean questions. The Russians were ready to protect France against Germany in order to be able to use her against Britain, but by the same token they had no wish to see her fight Germany or to do so themselves. It may be added that for similar reasons the French had no wish to see the Russians fight the British: for them the enemy was Germany, though they dared do nothing against her. Britain and France were likewise careful to keep their own antagonism from going as far as war: even in 1887 they were able to join in an international agreement neutralizing the Suez Canal and making it permanently open to the ships of all nations. The Franco-Russian alliance, when it came, did not therefore make for war or the upsetting of Germany's position in Europe.

Within the new diplomatic system, Germany threw her weight now to one side, now to the other. At first she drew closer to the 'Mediterranean' group. This tendency was accentuated by the fall of Bismarck, but it began with his own proposal in 1889 for a defensive alliance with Britain against France. Abruptly made for no very obvious reason, this plan got nowhere and may have been intended only as a sop to Bismarck's Russophobe critics. But it showed ingenuity in neutralizing the growing Russo-French combination without involving a direct clash between Germany and Russia. Within Germany, Bismarck was faced with a demand for a preventive war against Russia: the General Staff under Waldersee's leadership did not think it possible to conquer France again and so responded in this way to the supposed threat of Boulanger and of a Franco-Russian alliance. This was not the issue on which Bismarck fell, though for propagandist reasons he liked to pretend that it was. But the soldiers sided with his opponents, and they influenced Holstein, the foreign office official who did so much to guide German policy for the next fifteen years. An eccentric one-eyed recluse, Holstein had been used by Bismarck for various unsavoury tasks, with the result that he had been almost hounded from society. He nevertheless wielded great influence because of his capacity for intrigue, his possession of many compromising secrets and the inexperience of his new chiefs, Capivi and Foreign Secretary Marschall.

Holstein thought that he could finally nail down Russia by bringing Britain into the Triple Alliance, a plan that accorded well with

Capivi's attempt to follow a more liberal policy generally. The Reinsurance Treaty was allowed to expire and Russian requests for its renewal were refused. In July 1890 a treaty was signed by which Britain ceded the North Sea island of Heligoland to Germany and received in return the surrender of Germany's claims in Zanzibar and Uganda. This represented German help to Britain in the Egyptian question. The French were beginning to think of counterbalancing British power in Egypt by establishing themselves on the Upper Nile. There were even wild rumours that they planned to dam the river and gain control of Egypt's water supply. The British went to East Africa largely to forestall the French, and the agreement with Germany enabled them to take control of sources of the White Nile. In 1891 the Italians took the initiative in trying to move on to a full alliance between Britain and the Triplice. But the British refused to commit themselves, although the Italian premier, Rudini, led his parliament to believe that he had succeeded.

The main effect of these moves was to bring into being a formal alliance between France and Russia. It was the French who took the initiative, sending their Chief of Staff, Boisdeffre, to Russia each year in 1890–2. Russia was displeased by Germany's inclination to support Britain, but it was really her desperate need for a French loan in the famine year 1891 that led to a first agreement by exchange of notes at the end of August. They provided for diplomatic co-operation only, and were therefore directed mainly against Britain: diplomatic incidents were frequent between that country and the two allies, but neither dared argue much with Germany. In 1892 the French managed to impose something far more valuable to them on the Russians: a military convention by which the two powers agreed to mobilize if Germany or Austria-Hungary did so, and Russia promised to take the offensive against Germany if she attacked France. But Alexander III refused to ratify this convention till 1894, and the first real manifestation of the alliance was again anti-British: the visit of a Russian squadron to Toulon in October 1893, which was intended to lead to the establishment of a Russian Mediterranean fleet working from French bases. Behind the alliance lay the growing moderation of the French republicans, which made them more respectable in the eyes of the Tsar. It was even connected with the *ralliement*: Leo XIII tried to induce the Russians to be more helpful to the French, both to make himself more popular in France and in the hope that the new alliance might be a means of protecting him against the Italian government.

Germany's plan to draw closer to Britain had not produced the desired results, and it was really killed when Gladstone again became British prime minister in 1892. Gladstone could not escape, as he would have wished, from Britain's colonial quarrels and Rosebery, his foreign secretary and eventual successor, was strongly anti-French. But the Mediterranean Agreements (which had never been formal treaties) lapsed and there was no further question of Britain joining any alliance. The Franco-Russian rapprochement caused great alarm, but it was met by a massive naval building programme: Britain trusted to her own strength to see her through. When Lord Salisbury returned to power in 1895 he proved in effect to have become a Gladstonian. He had never believed that the Ottoman Empire could survive for long, and it had further discredited itself in the eyes of the British public by the massacres of the Armenians. From 1894 Britain co-operated rather ineffectively with her colonial rivals, Russia and France, in yet another attempt to reform Turkish administration. Salisbury made it known that he favoured a partition of the Turkish dominions in which Russia would take Constantinople. He also hoped for better relations with France. This plan came to nothing, but Salisbury remained pacific: his naval advisers warned him that the British fleet could no longer count on getting through the Straits to Constantinople should the Russians attack it.

The Germans therefore turned away from Britain and towards the Franco-Russian alliance: the continental league began to revive. Since the new alliance was only marginally anti-German, there was nothing incongruous in this. The new policy was first seen in Africa in 1893–4. The Germans declined to claim the territory east of their colony in the Cameroons, leaving the French free to advance towards the Nile from Equatorial Africa. The British tried to block this route by a treaty with the Congo Free State: King Leopold recognized their title to the Upper Nile and leased from them most of what is now the south Sudan. This transaction was absurd because the British were not in possession of the land they leased, and they 'granted' it to Leopold because he had a better chance than they of getting there before the French. The Germans joined the French in protesting, although the British were so angry that they soon withdrew; it was because of the French protests that Leopold finally abandoned his lease.

Germany's new attitude was dictated, like Bismarck's pro-Russian policy a decade before, by Britain's unavailability as an ally, and it owed much to a feeling that Britain was now on the weaker side in the colonial struggle. This was partly caused by a misunderstanding in 1893. The British and French were in process of making an agreement over Siam, the buffer between their respective Asian possessions. At the last moment, a false alarm of a military clash in the area led the British to ask for German support. The alarm came to nothing and the agreement was made, but it left the Germans with the totally false impression that the British had capitulated to the French. To some extent this made them think it safer to help the French and Russians, but it also gave them the idea that by so doing they could make Britain so afraid that she would join the Triple Alliance as originally intended. In 1894 the fall of Caprivi, under conservative pressure, strengthened the new line, and so did the death of Alexander III. It was his strength of character that had really created the Russo-French alliance because he was enraged by Russia's weakness in the face of Germany. The weak Nicholas II did not mind, any more than Alexander II had done. He was to fall very much under the influence of the lively young German Emperor.[1]

The Emergence of Japan and the *Entente Cordiale*

Russian involvement in the Far East was to dominate international relations for the next decade. It was not new, but it was given new point by Witte's ambitious policy of economic penetration and by the financial side of the Russo-French alliance, which made possible such great projects as the Trans-Siberian railway. The decaying empires of China and Persia were coming within Russia's reach, the more so as their capitals, Pekin and Teheran, were fairly near her territory. She could not well expand much farther in Central Asia without an undesired war with Britain,[2] but the Far East seemed open. It was

[1] Their famous correspondence was conducted in English, and they signed themselves 'Willy' and 'Nicky' respectively.

[2] From 1895 Indian and Russian territory met on the inaccessible Pamirs.

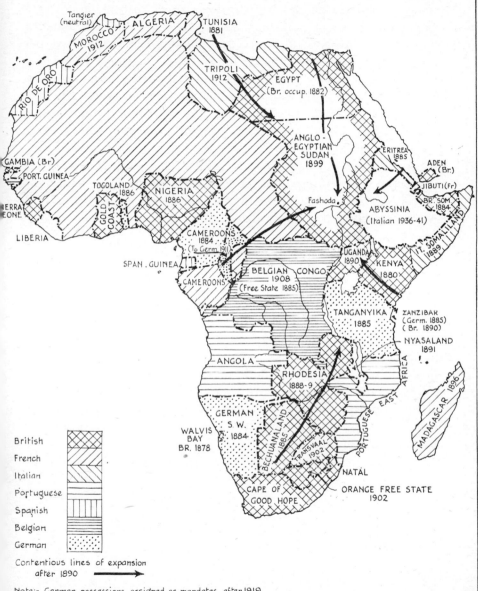

THE SCRAMBLE FOR AFRICA

Tangier (neutral)
ALGERIA
TUNISIA 1881
MOROCCO 1912
TRIPOLI 1912
EGYPT (Br. occup. 1882)
RIO DE ORO
ERITREA 1885
ADEN (Br.)
ANGLO-EGYPTIAN SUDAN 1899
JIBUTI (Fr)
GAMBIA (Br)
PORT. GUINEA
BR. SOM. 1884
TOGOLAND 1886
NIGERIA 1886
Fashoda
ABYSSINIA (Italian 1936-41)
ERRA EONE
GOLD COAST
CAMEROONS 1884 (To Germ. 1911)
UGANDA 1890
KENYA 1880
LIBERIA
SPAN. GUINEA
BR. SOMALILAND 1889
CAMEROONS
BELGIAN CONGO 1908 (Free State 1885)
TANGANYIKA 1885
ZANZIBAR (Germ. 1885) (Br. 1890)
NYASALAND 1891
ANGOLA
PORTUGUESE EAST AFRICA
RHODESIA 1888-9
MADAGASCAR 1896
WALVIS BAY BR. 1878
GERMAN S.W. 1884
BECHUANALAND 1885
TRANSVAAL 1902
NATAL
CAPE OF GOOD HOPE
ORANGE FREE STATE 1902

British
French
Italian
Portuguese
Spanish
Belgian
German

Contentious lines of expansion after 1890 →

Note:- German possessions assigned as mandates after 1919
Togoland (Fr & Br) Cameroons (Fr & Br) S.W Africa. (Union of S.A.) East Africa (Br & Bel)

0   200 400 600
Miles

now, however, that Japan became a significant factor in diplomacy. The modernization of the country begun in 1868[1] had now gone far enough to enable her to practise imperialism, instead of falling a victim to it as had once seemed likely. In 1894–5 she fought China for the control of Korea and the lands adjoining. Her victory gave her Port Arthur, the sea gateway to Manchuria. Russia found her expansion blocked by a new power on her doorstep. The new situation accorded perfectly with the increasing German need to distract Russia from the Balkans. While she was expanding in the Caspian region, Russia could not entirely neglect Constantinople, for the great trade routes to central Asia ran through or near Asiatic Turkey. It was different when China was the goal, and so the Germans set themselves to encourage Russia in the Far East. They joined the French in backing Russia's demand that Japan should leave Port Arthur, largely so that the Franco-Russian alliance should not receive a baptism of fire. Japan gave way and was compensated with Formosa, well out of Russia's way. It was to be of some importance later that Britain had not joined in coercing Japan, but the only reason was the liberal ministry's dislike of foreign entanglements.

The Russians did not at once forget the Near East. In 1895–6 the disturbed state of Turkey due to the Armenian crisis tempted them to seize Constantinople by a naval coup. This would have protected them from British attack in a war over some Asian question, and would have given them the beginning of a sea route to the Far East, for use until the railways were ready. The British dared attempt no stroke of their own without an absolute promise that the French navy would not intervene. The Austrians were displeased at British inaction and the Germans tried to frighten them out of it. At the end of 1895 Jameson's attempt to overthrow the South African Republic by force was defeated. The German Emperor sent a famous telegram of congratulation to President Kruger, and his government tried to induce the other continental powers to help defend Boer independence against the British. But though nothing came of this except British anger, their inactivity was balanced by the unwillingness of the French to see the Balkan situation disturbed. In April 1897, therefore, Russia and Austria-Hungary made an agreement to co-operate in maintaining the status quo in the Balkans.

[1] *The Age of Transformation*, pp. 387–8.

This was a return to the original basis of the Three Emperors' League and it probably saved Austria-Hungary from collapse during the grave internal convulsion now beginning there. It freed Germany from the perils involved in defending the Dual Monarchy, yet it was spontaneous and no embarrassing diplomatic manoeuvres by Germany had been needed to bring it about. This was the diplomatic apogee of the Second Reich.

Germany, however, soon began the undermining of her own position by her own increasing colonial appetite. Bismarck had acquired colonies chiefly as a political gesture and seems at the end to have seriously thought of giving them up. His successors on the contrary wanted more. In 1897 Bülow became Foreign Secretary and made colonial expansion (*Weltpolitik*) the order of the day. Germany's arbitral position in Europe was to be used not to maintain the balance of power but to extract colonial concessions. This was the justification for expanding the fleet. Tirpitz intended it to be, not the biggest, but so big that the biggest could not destroy it without suffering crippling loss. Therefore it would hold the balance between the British navy and those of France and Russia, and enable Germany to intervene more effectively in colonial disputes. This did not mean that Germany became permanently aggressive and without friends. It did mean that Germany made unwise changes of friends, fitting the colonial but not the European situation, and that her friendships were more ephemeral and a higher price was charged for them. Coupled with the mounting difficulties of the other colonial powers, this eventually produced a diplomatic revolution.

What Germany did in the main was to draw a little away from the continental powers without really making friends with Britain. Bülow's first move (1897) was to secure the port of Kiao-Chou in the northern Chinese province of Shantung and when, in 1898, the United States went to war with Spain over Cuba he hastened to lay hands on the lesser Spanish islands in the Pacific. German action in China annoyed both Britain and Russia. Both had wished to keep China intact, the British because they had hitherto dominated its trade, the Russians because they hoped to dominate its government. Witte had established a defensive alliance and (with French money) a Russo-Chinese Bank. The Chinese followed the view of Li Hung-Chang that Russian protection would preserve the failing empire.

But now the military party in Russia insisted that Germany's advance must be countered by the seizure of Port Arthur. Britain and France also demanded bits of Chinese territory, and there was a general hunt for railway concessions. This made nonsense of Witte's previous policy and it also threatened to break up Britain's market in China into a number of sectors reserved each to a different power.

The British mostly expected Russia to be the chief gainer by this, and Joseph Chamberlain in particular pressed Salisbury to seek a German alliance against them. The Germans, for reasons to be explained, were not very interested in this plan, but they were willing to give the British some negative help in the decisive conflicts now pending in Africa. In the south the British had prevented the Portuguese (1891) from linking Angola and Mozambique and were now moving towards a collision with the Boer republics. In 1898 Portuguese finances were collapsing and the British were anxious to ensure that their territory, which gave the Boers their only outlet to the sea not in British possession, should not fall into unfriendly hands. Portugal's other creditors, notably France, were correspondingly suspicious of Britain. The Germans tried to work with France against Britain, but changed sides when they found the British willing to sign a treaty partitioning Portuguese Africa with them in the event of Portugal raising a fresh loan from Britain and Germany and then defaulting on it. This absurdly hypothetical agreement (August 1898) was rendered nugatory by the Portuguese raising money in Paris instead. But it kept Germany quiet during the Fashoda crisis.

This decisive event in the north was due ultimately to the successful defence of their independence by the Abyssinians. In 1896 they defeated an Italian invasion at Adowa. This was a blow in the battle for the Nile. Abyssinia was friendly with France and it was the British who had encouraged the Italians to establish themselves in the territories round her. In 1895, with Russian encouragement, the French had sent out an expedition under Captain Marchand to try and reach the Nile from the west. Now there was a chance that the disencumbered Abyssinians might advance down the Blue Nile to meet them. This led the British to reconquer the Sudan. They had allowed it to establish its independence of Egypt in 1884 because the cost of reconquest would have made it impossible to restore Egypt's finances. By 1896 this had been done, but the other powers would not allow Britain to use Egypt's money to attack the Sudanese. The British decided that they must foot the bill themselves. In 1898 the Sudanese forces were overthrown at Omdurman, and it was Kitchener's army which Marchand encountered on the Nile at Fashoda and not the Abyssinians (who had never moved). The British demanded the withdrawal of Marchand, and the French had to decide whether to abandon the chance of annoying the British from the Upper Nile or defend their right to be there by force. But they received encouragement neither from Germany nor from their ally Russia. They gave in and thus lost all hope of ever getting anywhere in the Egyptian question.

It was the same story when at length the British went to war with the Boers in 1899. European opinion was unfavourable to them, and there was loose talk, mainly Russian, of a new continental league. The Germans were now quarrelling with Britain and the United States over the share each was to get in the partitioning of Samoa. Later the British annoyed them by searching German ships for arms consigned to the Boers. On each occasion Germany began to encourage continental solidarity, but the first time she turned round on getting her way in Samoa, and the second time (March 1900) she made a mutual guarantee of territory a condition of action against Britain—i.e. France would have to renounce Alsace-Lorraine for good and all.

Colonial developments had led Germany into a half-friendship with Britain, but Far Eastern developments were to make the British feel that this was almost worse than enmity. In 1900 took place the Boxer rebellion, an ill-organized nationalist protest against the recent European moves to break up China. The rebels seized Pekin and besieged the foreign legations. The powers had to organize an international force to rescue them, and the whole episode brought China one step nearer collapse and partition. Russian troops occupied Manchuria and there were signs that Britain was preparing to take over the Yang-tze valley. From this arose the so-called Yang-tze agreement between Britain and Germany in October 1900. The two powers promised to maintain the 'open door' in China 'as far as they can exercise influence'. For Britain, this was a measure to push back the Russians. It represented the defeat of the cautious Salisbury by the younger men in the government who looked to Chamberlain and believed (as Salisbury had once believed) that Britain could not defend her interests without allies. Salisbury now gave the younger men their head by handing over the foreign office to Lansdowne, though he remained prime minister till 1902. But it was only on the British side that the way was open for a German alliance. The Germans had signed the agreement of 1900 to restrain, not the Russians, but the British in the Yang-tze. In March 1901 Bülow (now Chancellor) made it clear that they did not think that they could exercise any influence in Manchuria. Though the British continued to seek a German alliance, the shock to them was great: henceforth Lansdowne and his colleagues gradually interested themselves in other ways of escaping from isolation.

Germany has often been criticized by observers and later historians for failing to make anything of the various chances of an alliance with Britain which arose in the years 1898–1902. But Bülow and his advisers saw that it would have been too dangerous to do so. Germany would have been required to defend British interests in China—where her own interests were secondary—at the risk of a major war on her eastern frontier. Germany could equally not offer her alliance to Russia: her colonies and infant navy would then be in danger of destruction by the British. Britain and Russia virtually could not get at each other. Germany would be the worst sufferer if she joined in a war between them on either side, and it could never be worth her while to incur this risk while the bone of contention between them was something so remote from her vital interests as the Far East. In 1901 the Germans tried to exploit Britain's needs by raising their traditional demand that she should join the Triple Alliance. But such a commitment to oppose Russia in the Balkans was more remote from British interests than ever, as was shown at the end of 1902. The Russians then got Turkish permission to send some ships through the Straits, on the way to the Far East. The British tried in vain to get the Austrians to join them in pressing the Turks to keep the Straits closed. Then they decided that now that they controlled Egypt the question was no longer important.

The abstention of Germany left Britain in an increasingly exposed and uncomfortable position in the Far East. It was the Japanese who were angriest at Russia's presence in Manchuria, and in spite of the absence of effective European support they demanded in the strongest terms the withdrawal of an agreement on the subject which Russia was trying to impose on China. Russia was torn between the pacific policy of Witte and the bellicose attitude of the military party. Eventually she dropped the agreement, though she remained in Manchuria. In the autumn of 1901 Ito, a senior Japanese statesman, visited Europe, and with French backing tried to make a deal with the Russians. He would concede them Manchuria in return for a free hand in Korea. The military party were strong enough to prevent such a concession, and so the Russians turned down a plan which would have left no real obstacle to their mastery of northern China. The British meanwhile had also been negotiating with the Russians (as they did intermittently all through these years) over both China and Persia, but got nowhere. Increasingly they feared a Russo-Japanese rapprochement which would leave them alone in the Far East except for the platonic support of the United States. They therefore offered Japan an alliance, concluded in January 1902. It was a very bad bargain—virtually a unilateral pledge to come to the aid of Japan if she was at war with two powers. The British cabinet probably only accepted it because it gave naval superiority over France and Russia in Far Eastern waters. The Japanese were now spoiling for a fight, but nobody yet expected them to win. Britain had escaped from isolation in the east, but she had made war more likely by her pledge to Japan and the war would most probably bring her trouble.

There was still a last chance that Germany might be brought into some sort of alignment against Russia. She was officially told of the Anglo-Japanese alliance and welcomed it. A new issue arose which for the first time brought a direct clash of interest between Russia and herself—the Baghdad railway. A German enterprise had built some lines in western Asia Minor in the early nineties, and in 1899 the Sultan gave them permission to plan a railway right across his Asian territories to the Persian Gulf. This project was part of much more general growth of German trade with Turkey, fostered politically by such things as the Kaiser's visits to the Sultan and the distinguished work of Marschall, who had passed from the German foreign office to the embassy at Constantinople. Germany's interest in the Ottoman Empire seems to have been economic, not political. But either way it inevitably aroused the hostility of Russia, whose interest was that Turkey should remain weak and so easily bullied by herself. The building of railways would strengthen the authority of the Sultan and make it easier in every way to turn Turkey into a base for anti-Russian action. The Russians opposed the new railway plans all they could, and in 1900 secured an agreement giving themselves a monopoly of railway construction in the part of Asiatic Turkey adjacent to Russia: their intention was that none should be built.

The Germans could not finance the building of their railway from their own capital resources alone and so tried to interest investors in other nations. French financiers were interested, but were held back by their government in deference to Russia. The British attitude was more complicated. They did not wish to see any power established on the Persian Gulf, at India's back door. But they did not believe that they could oppose all the powers at once there, and it was Russia of whom they were most afraid. A railway (completed 1904) was being built from Orenburg to Tashkent which would link Moscow to the Afghan border and bring nearer the day when Russia could mount a serious attack on India. Meanwhile, the Russian position was being strengthened by the disintegration of Persia. A German railway to the Persian Gulf might counterbalance this, especially if Britain was Germany's partner. But there was a growing feeling that Germany would not really help the British against Russia, and when Lansdowne took up the plan in 1902–3 it was with the idea of bringing in the Russians as well. They were to be connected to the international railway by a line through Persia and so given a neutralized outlet on the Gulf. But the scheme was killed by a popular uproar, encouraged by business interests hostile to its promoters and backed in the cabinet by Chamberlain. Always for bold policies, he had reacted to the failure of German alliance plans by demanding something diametrically opposite.[1]

This was nothing less than an energetic attempt to liquidate all big disputes between the major colonial rivals—Britain and Italy, France and Russia. Such an attempt had already been begun by Theophile Delcassé who became French Foreign Minister in 1898. He managed to remain so in successive ministries till 1905, and in a lesser and less sinister way he paralleled the influence of Holstein

---

[1] In 1902 Britain and Germany co-operated in forcing Venezuela to pay some debts. The United States objected, and there was bad feeling all round.

on German policy. He, too, was of a studious, retiring disposition and worked as privately as he could. He referred as little as possible to his cabinet colleagues and they gave him a free hand: the left-inclined cabinets of the Dreyfus era were indifferent to foreign affairs. Once a young protégé of Gambetta, he was on record in support of his master's plans for a French revival in alliance with Britain and Russia. But as colonial minister he had energetically struggled against the British. If there had been a chance of continuing the struggle, he might have taken it.

As it was, his tenure of the foreign ministry began with the Fashoda crisis, which showed that France could not hope to fight Britain and could not entirely rely on her Russian ally. He therefore tried to strengthen the bond with Russia, but also to forward colonial expansion by agreement rather than conflict with rivals. In 1899 he visited Russia and carried through an important modification of the alliance: it was declared to be for the maintenance of the balance of power in Europe and it was not to end automatically with the dissolution of the Triple Alliance. These changes reflected the belief that the Habsburg monarchy might soon collapse and that the allies should work together in the consequent reordering of Europe. Already in March 1899 an Anglo-French agreement had drawn a boundary west of the Nile between the spheres of influence of the two countries. Delcassé's next objective was to round out France's North African possessions by gaining control of Morocco. Britain had protected the independence of this territory because of its strategic importance: it stood at the gateway both of the Mediterranean and the South Atlantic. But the native government was now collapsing, and from 1900 the French were pressing forward on the landward side. Paul Cambon, their ambassador in London, tried to interest the British in some plan that would give France Morocco but neutralize the seaward side of the country. But he was met with polite inattention.

It was otherwise with Italy. Adowa naturally had directer and profounder consequences there than anywhere else. The imperialist Crispi fell from power, there was a period of severe internal crisis and also second thoughts about the policy of siding with Germany against France. This had meant in particular that Italy could no longer borrow from the French, and had led to a tariff war between the two countries in which Italy was almost ruined. In 1898 a commercial treaty between them showed the Italian wish for better relations. The Anglo-French agreement of 1899 made Italians fear that the British would cease to support their claim to Tripoli. They were therefore willing to sign an agreement with France (December 1900) acknowledging her right eventually to take Morocco, in which event France was to let them take Tripoli. In 1902 the French tried to induce them to take the logical final step of reconciliation by withdrawing from the Triple Alliance, but they dared do no more than declare that it did not bind them to go to war with France.[1] This was the first time that a colonial entente damaged Germany's position in Europe, though the semi-desertion of a half-great power did not damage her much.

Events in both Africa and China now forced Britain also to listen to Delcassé. At the end of 1902 the government of Morocco irretrievably collapsed, and the British could no longer hope to keep the French out by giving it a little cheap encouragement. Then the Russians failed to keep the promise made in 1902 to leave Manchuria. Witte fell from power, the soldiers triumphed, and in August 1903 Admiral Alexeiev was made Viceroy in the Far East with powers to defend Russian interests without reference to the foreign office. The Japanese accordingly made ready to fight: if France entered the war on the side of Russia, Britain would have to fight too. British efforts to conciliate France included an exchange of State Visits, of which King Edward's to Paris is the more famous, but President Loubet's to London (with Delcassé) was the more important. Bad news from the Far East prompted Lansdowne to propose a general settlement of issues to Delcassé. They agreed on the outlines of a Moroccan settlement, and Delcassé held out the hope that this might lead on to something which the British had only just thought of making their equivalent—the liquidation of the Egyptian question. But it was the settling of quarrels with Russia, not those with France, that was the prime British concern. They were trying hard to do it by direct negotiation, and their great hope was that France could now be brought to use her influence with Russia to make such negotiations succeed.

Delcassé's interests were the same as Lansdowne's. He had failed

[1] Italy was pledged to help Germany if France attacked her, but the reverse was of course much more likely.

to make a separate accord with Spain, the other Moroccan power, in 1902, and so he could not safely act there without Britain. He had been obliged by the Russians to join in a public declaration of a common line of action in face of the Anglo-Japanese alliance, but the last thing he wanted was to be drawn into a war over the Far East, where French interests, though greater than Germany's, were nevertheless secondary. After some five months of detailed negotiations, therefore, an Anglo-French agreement was signed in April 1904. The *entente cordiale* ended a considerable number of colonial disputes, but its centrepiece was that France and Britain were to help each other to predominance in Egypt and Morocco respectively. British troops were to stay in Egypt and the international debt commission, through which France had been able to impede the British administration, was to lose its powers over the Egyptian government. Britain was not to hinder the establishment of French control in Morocco, but it was agreed that Spain should be given a share and that the 'open door' should be preserved for thirty years.

The entente failed to achieve what was perhaps its most important immediate object. In February 1904 there began the war between Russia and Japan—the biggest since 1870. But the war was to complete what the entente had begun. The military party in Russia were given their chance and failed miserably. Japan annihilated most of the Russian navy, captured Port Arthur and drove the Russians half out of Manchuria. Russia was shaken to the core, the cautious counsels of Witte were justified, and a defensive policy was adopted. It was for this reason that the system of ententes which by 1904 already joined Britain, France, Italy and Spain,[1] eventually grew to include Russia and Japan. Germany continued to play no real part in Far Eastern events (except for some platonic encouragement to Russia during the war) and so the ententes continued to be made without her.

It is quite wrong to suppose that the ententes were directed against Germany or grew mainly out of hostility to her. Their main cause was an intensification of that disillusionment with colonial adventure that had already brought so many diplomatic revolutions. This was largely due in turn to stronger resistance by Afro-Asian peoples—the Japanese and the Abyssinians especially, to whom

[1] France and Spain agreed on spheres of influence in Morocco by a treaty of November 1904.

incongruously must be added the Boers. Though they admitted defeat in 1902, they tied up so much of the British army for three years that they made isolation seem doubly alarming. At the same time, the blank spaces on the map were disappearing and the powers could no longer hope to increase their shares without serious fighting. They gradually decided to content themselves with what they had. Germany caused some annoyance with her own colonial demands, but her main contribution to the ententes was refusing to take sides firmly between the colonial rivals. Either side would have accepted her alliance had it been available, and might then have been tempted into a colonial fight to the finish. Not only were the ententes not directed against her, they were at first not even alliances at all. Rather were they non-aggression pacts that simply brought peace in the colonial world. But when that had been done the colonies could no longer be Europe's safety valve, and Russia in particular was no longer distracted by China from the Balkans. The territorial settlement in the centre of the continent was no longer quite safe. Bismarck's Europe was no more.

1 The Congress of Berlin, 1878. Standing at rear table, l. to r. Beaconsfield, Andrassy, Bismarck. Salisbury sits on Beaconsfield's right.

2 Constantinople Conference, 1876. Salisbury standing 2nd from left. Ignatiev sitting 3rd from left.

3 Thiers is acclaimed in the Chamber of Deputies under the Third Republic.

4 ADOLPHE THIERS, 1787–1877.

5 Bismarck and the parties (the Liberal spoke says he will soon be on top again.
Cartoon from *Kladderadatsch*).

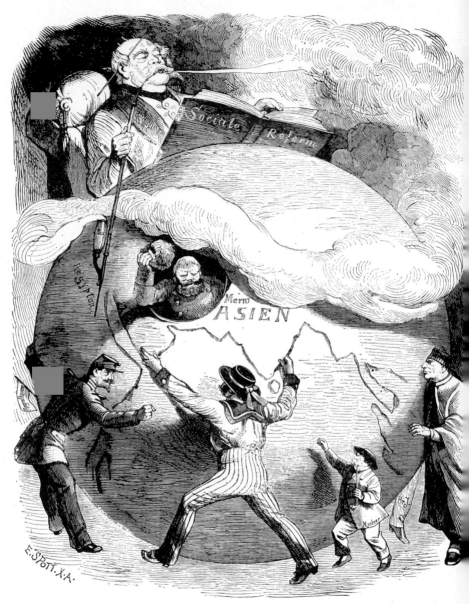

6 Bismarck's Europe: peace and reform at home while the other powers fight for colonies. (Cartoon from *Kladderadatsch.*)

7 The Russian railway from the Caspian to Samarkand, 1888.

8 The *Dreadnought* (1906).

9 Pope Leo XIII in 1878.

10 Kaiser Wilhelm II (with raised fist) entertains guests at prewar manoeuvres.

11 First transatlantic wireless message, 1901. The transmitter in Cornwall.

12 Marconi with the receiver in Newfoundland.

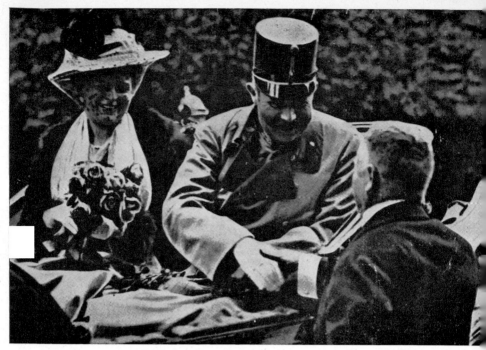

13 Francis Ferdinand and his wife just before their murder, 28 June 1914.

14 Hunting their assassins.

15 Trench warfare 1914–1918.

16 Inside a U-boat.

17 American troops in France, 1918.

18 American engineers in a ruined French village, 1918.

19 A. F. KERENSKY.

20 V. I. LENIN.

21 The Bolsheviks woo the all-important peasants: Kalinin in 1921.

22 Peacemaking, 1919: Wilson (handkerchief showing) has on his left
Clemenceau, Balfour, Orlando.

23 Reconciliation, 1926: Stresemann addresses the League of Nations.

24 ADOLF HITLER.

25 Hitler acclaimed by his people, 1938.

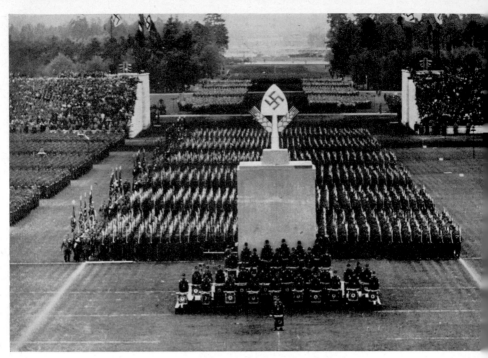

26 Totalitarian theatricalism: the Nuremberg Rally, 1938.

27 Appeasement in action: Halifax and Chamberlain in Rome, January 1939.

28 Nazi persecution: the Jews starved in Ghettoes.

29 Nazi persecution: the Jews humiliated.

30 Nazi persecution: the burning of the books.

31 Hitler watches the invasion of Poland, 1 September, 1939.

32 Germans taken prisoner at Stalingrad.

Part III

REVOLUTION WITHOUT BETTERMENT— GIOLITTI AND STOLYPIN

1: The Beginning of the Twentieth Century

At first sight it seems naïve to think of the opening of a new century in 1901 as the start of a new epoch. Obviously, it was the war of 1914 that made the real break in European life. But the post-war world was shaped not just by the war but by other revolutionary factors which, as it happens, were coming into action around 1900. This part of the book tries to determine what effects they could produce unaided; the next part considers the effects which they had in conjunction with the war. By comparing the two, some idea can be formed of the effect of the war itself. The present chapter describes the new forces, and the following two describe the attempts of the governments down to 1914 to turn them to good account. Failures in this respect led on, as will then be shown, to the war.

The Economic Revival, 1896–1914

Europe's economic growth had by no means ceased after 1870, but most people found the difficulties more apparent than the progress. From the mid nineties, however, expansion greatly speeded up and there was a return to the economic atmosphere of the revolutionary generation after 1848. This owed something to the increasing economic activity of governments, both in fostering particular industries and in stimulating demand by their growing expenditure on armaments and public works. But it must be remembered that government interference often burdened one side of the economy while helping others. This can be seen in the economic development of Russia already studied. Similarly, the building of the German fleet stimulated heavy industry, but the state loans by which it was mainly financed intensified the shortage of capital that was a hindrance to German industrial growth. It was probably the colonial activities of governments that did most to benefit the economy, by opening up new territories to capitalist enterprise. The increase in overseas investment and the stimulus it gave to trade and exports was one of the foundations of the boom. From 1904 new British investment abroad was averaging over £100 million a year, having previously seldom reached half that. French foreign investments have been estimated at 20 milliard Francs in 1900 and 45 milliards in 1914. The Germans were short of capital to invest, but their total also increased. World trade doubled between 1900 and 1913, and in 1895–1915 the world tonnage of steamships almost trebled. A notable instance of overseas development was the growth of rubber plantations, which only began in this period but by 1914 had displaced the collection of wild rubber as the main source of supply. But it should be emphasized that much of the economic expansion outside Europe was in independent or at least autonomous countries. It is to their governments that credit must go in those cases for making the conditions ripe for the building of railways, the first factories and so forth.

For the rest, the boom was due to the simultaneous overcoming of various obstacles in the economy. Monetary stringency was removed by a great increase in gold production. New deposits were discovered in South Africa, the Klondike and elsewhere, and the cyanide process of refining increased the proportion that could be recovered from the ores. Prices consequently recovered much of the ground lost since 1870. The efforts to make agriculture more efficient were now bearing fruit, and new industries that had previously been in the experimental stage were now beginning to produce on a large scale. In 1914 the motor industry was important only in the United States, and the aeroplane, an invention of the new century,[1] had yet to give rise to an industry. But electric trams spread everywhere from the nineties, and the agricultural revival meant more fertilizers. Electricity and chemicals boomed, and Germany was the most important European centre in each case. World electric generating capacity rose from $2\frac{1}{2}$ million kW. in 1900 to over 10 million in 1910. The German occupational census of 1895 was the first to note the electrical industry, which then employed 26,000 men. In 1907 this had risen to 107,000. German potash production trebled in the nineties and again in the following decade. Exports of dyestuffs made from

---

[1] The Wright brothers' machine of 1903 was by no means the first to fly under power, but it was the first that could be properly steered.

coal tar were some 35,000 tons in 1897 and nearly 100,000 in 1912. In 1900–13 both France and Germany nearly doubled their output of sulphuric acid, again important for fertilizers, Italy trebled hers and Russia became a producer for the first time.

New investment abroad (and in the more backward parts of Europe) and new industries at home led to expansion all round. Coal production in Germany and Russia more than doubled between the late nineties and 1914. Russian steel production was 2·2 million metric tons in 1900 and 4·8 million in 1913. The German advance was from 6·6 million to 18·9 million, and the French from 1·6 million to 4·7 million. The Russian cotton industry (excluding Poland) had 6 million spindles in 1900 and 9·6 million by 1917. The story seems to have been much the same in all countries and fields of activity. But how stable the new prosperity was, it is hard to say. There were brief recessions around 1902 and 1908, and another had begun in 1914. The war ended it, and there is no means of telling if recovery would have come anyway.

Politically, the effect of economic expansion was to raise the temperature all round. Well-fed optimism characterized the upper classes and made them more pugnacious. This may have encouraged liberal movements in the backward parts of Europe, but what it mostly encouraged was militant nationalism and conservatism, movements nurtured in depression but firmly rooted enough to survive it. The industrial workers gained a new political importance. They were increasing rapidly in numbers, labour was in demand, and so they were well placed to fight for better conditions. They also had a greater need to fight: the recovery of prices diminished the value of their pay. There was thus both the need and the opportunity for militant trade unionism and the period saw a notable growth of organized labour. The German trade unions (christian, liberal and socialist) multiplied tenfold between 1891 and 1913, ending with three million members. The French confederation of labour founded in 1895 was a much smaller affair, but its constituent unions nearly trebled their membership in the years 1904–12, reaching 400,000. Of course, there was organization on the other side as well, and as the class war intensified it was natural that political movements among the workers should grow stronger. For the first time socialism became a force really to be reckoned with.

Socialism

Socialist ideas have a pedigree stretching back to antiquity, and a continuous tradition of socialist thought began at the end of the eighteenth century. As a movement, though much divided and persecuted, continental socialism was in existence from 1840 at least, and participated in the revolutions of 1848 and subsequent upheavals. But until the twentieth century its main importance was as a bogey. It was too weak in numbers and strategy to accomplish much, but the propertied classes were afraid of it, and more than one government owed its power to the protection it was supposed to give against the red peril. The foundation of the Second (socialist) International in 1889 conveniently marks the point at which socialism began to be something more. Many of the parties represented at its conferences were tiny. But in the nineties every continental parliament that was at all democratic in character came to have a significant body of socialists in it, and elsewhere revolutionary movements began to emerge, fired by the progress of their parliamentary brethren in happier lands.

By this time Marxism was the mainstream of socialism and 'social democrat', the title favoured by Marxists, had much the same emotional connotations as 'communist' today. Marx[1] had believed that the exploitation of the worker was not merely a feature but the essential feature of the capitalist system. This meant that there could be no compromise with the capitalists: their overthrow and expropriation by revolution was essential. Not only could the worker never hope for justice from them but society could not survive unless they were got rid of. Because employers necessarily paid the workers less than the value of their labour, the economic system was bound eventually to collapse for lack of purchasing power to buy the increasing volume of goods produced. But though revolution was essential to prevent this, it might not be too difficult to achieve. Marx expected the capitalists to dwindle in number as the small business went to the wall and property fell increasingly into the hands of a few monopolists. The proletariat would eventually comprise the overwhelming bulk of the population and become irresistible. Marxists tended to stop thinking of revolution in terms of violence and expect rather an

---

[1] Karl Marx died in 1883, and his associate Friedrich Engels in 1895.

economic collapse leading to a general recognition that certain changes were historically inevitable. There was much in this of the liberal belief in human progress through the spreading recognition of what was in mankind's real interests. Marxists hated liberals bitterly, but they inherited their optimism and it could often turn in both cases into a credulous and rather enervating belief in the inevitability of progress.

Capitalism has so far not collapsed in the manner foretold by Marx. This in itself is not so important, for capitalist development has been near enough to his picture to encourage a great development of socialism. Great concentrations of economic power have come into being and the concentration of workers in factories has, as Marx expected, enabled and encouraged them to band together in self-defence. What has been far more damaging to Marxist prospects has been the failure of society to polarize into monopolists and pro-letarians. Though many small farms and businesses have disappeared, continental Europe has continued to have a massive population of peasant farmers whose outlook has differed from that of the industrial workers. The urban middle class, too, has survived and increased, the growth of salaried employment more than compensating for any diminution of small entrepreneurs. To gain power the socialists, like any other party, have needed to find a strategy capable of creating alliances between divergent social groups. Nor have they ever succeeded when they have left historical inevitability to do their work for them: somebody else has always seized the initiative. Socialists have needed to be more accommodating but also more forceful, even violent, than classic Marxist doctrine would allow.

Most socialists in the early twentieth century had failed to see this, and so their influence in the greater part of Europe was by no means in proportion to their growing strength. The movement lacked constructive policies of its own. Believing that human action is necessarily governed by historical development rather than abstract thinking, Marx had rejected as 'utopian' any attempt to decide in advance how society should be organized after the overthrow of capitalism. Socialist parties therefore adjourned the real planning for a better society until after the revolution. For electoral purposes they had a so-called 'minimum' programme, comprising the practical demands of the workers for shorter hours, better conditions and so forth, plus those political objectives of the middle-class radicals that were unachieved in the country concerned. These included such things as the abolition of monarchies and standing armies and fairer electoral laws. Individual socialists might think beyond this, but the party leaders had a fine excuse for not committing themselves on the tricky subject of how to run society when power was achieved. This hindered the acceptance of the socialists as a national party rather than a working-class pressure group. A special case of it was the socialists' belief that it was their mission to deal with one particular problem—the breakdown of capitalism through underconsumption. They thought that this problem mattered more than all the rest, but others just as severe turned up—notably that of physical devastation and impoverishment after the First World War. The socialists had really no remedy to offer for this (even in the Soviet Union) except the revival of capitalism. It was the capitalists' historical role to expand production, and the socialists expected to step in only when this had been achieved.

This rather negative attitude intensified the natural tendency of all the socialist parties to be profoundly affected by the character of the régime they were opposing. How fruitful their development was therefore depended on their environment. Three patterns can be seen. Wherever they could make gains by doing so, socialists made common cause with the 'bourgeois' parties even if it meant postponing indefinitely their revolutionary objectives. This was only natural since there was a middle-class element in every socialist party, and especially in the leadership. In Britain, the Low Countries and Scandinavia this was always the rule, and it enabled the socialists to play an important constructive role, though their successes did not lead to socialism and have benefited others besides themselves. Belgium affords an interesting example. The socialists there have been almost the only ones to make successful use of the general strike as a political weapon—the dream of almost all labour movements. In the pre-1914 period it was used in the struggle for manhood suffrage, and it succeeded because the socialists had middle-class allies. In 1893 the chamber of deputies was fairly evenly divided on the merits of suffrage reform and a general strike tipped the balance. In 1902 the socialists struck again, to get rid of the system of plural voting with which manhood suffrage had been tempered. But they had no allies and were beaten. In 1912, however, they fought the general election in alliance with the liberals. The allies failed to win a majority for reform, and so in 1913 there was a third strike. This led the government to promise the measure desired, though the war delayed its introduction till 1919. The socialists did not destroy the power of the dominant clericals by these efforts, but they gained increased representation for the forces making for social reform, notably the left wing of the clericals themselves.

In most of Europe, however, experiments of this kind were impossible because of the tendency towards oligarchy, with the older parties linked together against outsiders, which has been studied in the earlier part of this book. Socialism here was a protest against this very system, but this second pattern, like the thing it opposed, was essentially sterile—a sullen and intransigent opposition. That socialist behaviour varied according to the scope allowed to them for constructive action within the existing system is well shown by the cases of Germany and France. In the south German states (and the Austrian half of the Dual Monarchy) the franchise was fairly wide and parliament exercised some control over the ministry. The socialists there co-operated with 'bourgeois' parties and entered the government if they could. In Prussia and the other north German states the franchise was narrow and parliament did not control the executive. The socialists there were an intransigent opposition and it was their attitude which prevailed at the national German level, because both the party and the imperial constitution were predominantly 'northern' in character. By 1900 there was a strong 'revisionist' movement, headed by Eduard Bernstein, that wanted the whole party to follow the line of the south, but it did not prevail. In France there was a fully parliamentary régime and the socialists were always split into two or more parties on the issue of how much to work with the 'bourgeois' politicians. In the nineties, when there was a likelihood of a radical–socialist alliance against the moderates, even the intransigent group of Guesde interested itself in policies appealing to the peasantry and other radical elements. But when radicals and moderates came together over the Dreyfus case, significant gains by the socialists became less likely. Guesde bitterly attacked the participation of the independent socialist Millerand in the government and the strong support which Jaurès and his friends gave to the Dreyfusard ministries. The International intervened in these French disputes and its congress of 1900 (in Paris) condemned the joining of bourgeois ministries. International mediation succeeded in uniting all but a few independent French socialists into one large intransigent party (1905). But though intransigence was henceforth an international orthodoxy, the issue was not closed in practice as we shall see.

Intransigence did not commonly imply any recrudescence of belief in violence. The militant socialists, both personally and collectively, had far more to lose than their chains. Those of them who were not 'bourgeois' themselves came mostly from the better-paid section of the working class. The bourgeois virtues of thrift and self-help were strong among them: without these qualities they could never have built up their organizations. The trade unions, co-operatives, newspapers and educational services that they created gave them not only a weapon against the bosses but a stake in the established order. They benefited from protectionism—its fostering of heavy industry meant more large factories and so a faster growth of their own movements. Those in charge of these prosperous and growing concerns (and increasingly they became paid officials) had little desire as a rule to risk them in any perilous bid for power.

The second pattern of socialism then combined intransigence and non-violence. It was a gamble on history doing the socialists' work for them, and it did not come off. The pattern of gradualist reform was an improvement on this, but there were few countries where it could work. It was a third pattern that was to give the most striking results. At the opposite pole to gradualism, it resembled it in preferring action to expectant waiting and stressing co-operation with elements outside the industrial proletariat. This was a pattern belonging especially to Russia and southern Europe, where the peasantry was a potential revolutionary force and the oppressiveness of governments drove radicals to violence even against their better judgment. Anarchism was its most natural expression. Living simply and too backward to be able to organize, the peasants regarded the whole structure of government with hostility and could think of no better remedy than a huge primitive uprising that would sweep away the officials and landlords and leave them on their own. In the seventies Russian Populism and Spanish Federalism had both tried to mobilize this crude peasant hatred of the social superstructure. In southern Europe a tradition had grown up of itinerant anarchist agitators, organizing strikes and riots on the big estates and begging their bread like the early friars. Populists began to organize again in the nineties, and in 1902 a conference in Switzerland formed the Socialist Revolutionary party. This carried on the tradition of the seventies by forming a terrorist section which had remarkable success in assassinating leading figures in the Russian administration. Though a member of the International, its claims to be a socialist party were dubious. It desired in practice to divide up the land among the peasants, who would have become indistinguishable from small proprietors. Its leaders were mainly middle class and readily became respectable parliamentarians when they had the chance. But for the time being it was revolutionary, whatever else it was.

Anarchism was not absent from western Europe (there had been an epidemic of bomb-throwing in the nineties) and for a time it was extensively taken up by the extreme left there in the form of syndicalism. As its name implies,[1] this was the belief that the trade unions rather than a political party should be the main political instrument of the workers and that their aim should be not to capture the state but to destroy it, thereafter organizing social life by a development of the trade-union principle. Syndicalism centred in France. The most famous writer about it was Georges Sorel, an engineer who believed in violence as a sort of social tonic and thought that the 'myth' of a great general strike to seize power would regenerate the working class by encouraging disciplined preparedness. But Sorel really belonged with the wild men of the right, lovers of combat for its own sake, and his main importance is as an antecedent of fascism. Syndicalism itself arose in the trade unions as a spontaneous protest against the dominance of the socialist movement by bourgeois intellectuals and timid parliamentarians. It was the last kick of the old Parisian tradition of insurrection which had produced the Commune. It never got anywhere in Germany, where the trade unions were much richer and more respectable than the French, and it eventually retreated to the old anarchist homeland, southern Europe.

Anarchists had a commendably greater appetite for action than socialists, but their ideas of how to prepare for revolution and what to do afterwards were even hazier. What was required was a synthesis

[1] *syndicat* is French for 'trade union'.

of anarchist verve and socialist discipline, a movement able to appeal both to organized labour and the crushed peasantry of the poorer countries. This eventually came into being within the Russian Social Democratic party, founded in 1898. This was at first a movement of expectant waiting in the German tradition. Plekhanov and his friends, whose activity led to its foundation, had concluded (above, p. 52) that terrorism was futile. Russian Marxists in the nineties were mainly anxious that capitalism should grow and so give them a chance afterwards. A section of them, the 'economists', wanted to confine themselves to organizing trade unions for peaceful bargaining with the capitalists. But as the original party manifesto said, 'the farther to the east one goes in Europe, the weaker in politics, the more cowardly and the meaner becomes the bourgeoisie, the greater are the cultural and political tasks that fall to the lot of the proletariat'. The Russian bourgeoisie was shirking its historic task (according to the Marxists) of leading the fight for freedom and democracy. Increasingly, socialists began to think that they would have to do the job instead.

Vladimir Ilyich Ulyanov, better known by his pen name of Lenin, was increasingly of this opinion. Born at Simbirsk on the Volga in 1870, he had a mother apparently of German extraction and a father who had risen from humble origins to be a provincial inspector of schools—a post which carried with it a patent of nobility. In 1887 his elder brother Alexander, whom he worshipped, was executed for attempting to revive Populism by an attempt on the Tsar's life. This event, and the prudent shunning of the stricken family by their liberal middle-class neighbours, appears to have marked the young man permanently. Although he became an orthodox Marxist, he revered the old Populists, believed in heroic action in their style and despised the lukewarm body of ordinary beings who were incapable of it. After a perfunctory attempt at a legal career he devoted himself to agitation and politically useful research work. Sent to Siberia in the nineties, he and his devoted wife thereafter spent a wandering and penurious life abroad save when recalled to Russia by revolution in 1905 and 1917. Short and slightly mongoloid in feature, his body and mind alike were powerful though without refinement. His vitality was enormous, he was a boisterous and jolly companion, enjoyed playing with children and was completely unpretentious. But he always insisted on the entire acceptance of his own ideas by those with whom he worked, and he applied those ideas without flinching at their terrible cost in human suffering.

In 1902 Lenin set forth the principles behind his early revolutionary activity in *What is to be Done?*, a pamphlet calling for a highly disciplined party of professional revolutionaries, an educated élite able 'to divert the labour movement from the unconscious tendency of trade unionism to march under the protective wings of the bourgeoisie'. He argued that socialism was not native to the working class but derived from 'philosophical, historical and economic theories which had been developed by the representatives of the well to do, the intellectuals'. At the second congress of the Social Democratic party, held in Brussels and London in 1903, Lenin's demand for a tightly organized party was on the whole endorsed, and from that time onward his supporters were known as the Bolsheviks (members of the majority), and those who wanted a looser organization as the Mensheviks (the minority). These names conceal the fact that Lenin failed to dominate the organization of the united party and therefore established a private organization of his own on strongly authoritarian lines. The Bolsheviks and Mensheviks were really distinct parties, although until 1912 there was a pretence of unity and occasional joint congresses.

Having quarrelled about party organization, the Russian socialists came also to differ about how they should advance towards power. All accepted the orthodox Marxist view that a bourgeois revolution was needed in Russia before there could be a socialist revolution, since socialism only developed in response to the transformation of society by capitalism. Only the countries of the west were already ripe for socialism. The only hopeful feature of the Russian situation was that there might soon be a socialist revolution in the west and the Russians would receive western socialist help. In 1905 a revolution began in Russia which the Marxists took to be the start of the long-awaited bourgeois bid for power. The Mensheviks were encouraged to hope that the Russian bourgeoisie was equal to its historic task after all and they were for concentrating on pushing the liberals forward against the Tsar. Lenin had no faith in the liberals and he bitterly resisted the 'liquidators' who wished the party to cease its conspiratorial work and concentrate on the parliamentary activity that became possible after the revolution. But he was interested in the rising peasant discontent after 1900, and increasingly abandoned the orthodox view of Russian Marxists (and indeed of Russian conservatives and liberals) that the peasants were a conservative force. He thought that common ground could be found with them in the slogan 'nationalization of the land', which to the peasants would mean dispossession of the landlords but to the socialists public ownership. At first the land would simply be divided among the peasants, but the ensuing 'capitalist' phase in agriculture would lead to a new concentration in the ownership of land and the poorer peasants could then be got to demand real nationalization. It was the beginnings of these ideas that lay behind Lenin's plan for a revolutionary alliance of workers and peasants set forth in *Two Tactics of Social Democracy* (1905). The insurgent masses would extirpate the old ruling class and establish a democratic republic. It would be 'bourgeois', not socialist, but its atmosphere would be revolutionary and the masses would be encouraged to take up arms to achieve their liberation and later to defend their gains. Their formidable uprising would encourage the outbreak of revolution in the west and so win them aid. In Lenin's alliance of workers and peasants the workers would be the senior partners because they would be the better educated and organized. In the Menshevik alliance with the urban middle class they would be the junior partners and in a less dynamic partnership.

Lenin and the Mensheviks were both in the awkward position of arguing that the socialists, having to ally with bourgeois groups, could at first make no demands of their own. This was largely denied by a few daring spirits of whom the most notable was Trotsky. This was the alias of Lev Davidovich Bronstein,[1] born in 1879 the son of a Jewish farmer—in Russia almost a contradiction in terms. His father was almost illiterate but he was prosperous and enterprising, and Trotsky had a good education and became a brilliant and wide-ranging thinker—much more so than the roughly practical Lenin. Their careers followed the same pattern—revolutionary activity, a spell in Siberia, flight abroad. He played a big part in the St Petersburg revolutionary movement at the end of 1905, and this experience encouraged the idea he had been forming of 'permanent

[1] He had a wife under each name.

revolution'. The proletariat was to seize political power (as it nearly had in the Russian capital in 1905) and press on with social transformation. The distinction between capitalist and socialist phases of development was largely though not entirely suppressed. As Trotsky disliked Lenin's authoritarianism and did not share his confidence in the peasantry, he stressed all the more the need for the revolution to spread if it was to succeed: only help from the west could make up for the numerical weakness of the Russian workers. The Bolshevik revolution when it came was to synthesize Lenin's and Trotsky's views. There was to be 'permanent revolution' in the sense of rapid progress in a socialist direction. But help from the west played a smaller part than any Russian socialist had expected and it was the behaviour of the peasantry that was decisive. Lenin's authoritarian views were to prevail moreover in the organizing of revolution. The disciplined élite which he had first conceived of mainly as a weapon of agitation became the basis of the new state.

The Marxists, despite their own expectations, were to triumph in eastern Europe and not (so far) in the advanced capitalist west. It was the World Wars that made their success possible; before 1914 the Russian Marxist factions were all very small beer. Under the impact of war, Lenin and those who followed him came increasingly to see themselves as a movement against imperialism, which was not only the 'highest stage' but also the international aspect of capitalism, and so as the spearhead of the colonial revolt against Europe. Leaving aside for the moment the possibility of explaining their success in those terms, it is possible to point to features of pre-war Russia which were calculated to give the nascent party there a better grounding in tactics than the more formidable movements of the west. The political situation was so grim that they were bound to prefer action to expectancy and the working class was so small that they were bound to seek allies. These were in themselves first steps towards success.

The Peace Movement

In August 1898 the Tsar annoyed the other powers by proposing an international conference for 'ensuring to all peoples the benefit of a real and durable peace and, above all, of putting an end to the progressive development of the present armaments'. The First Hague Conference (1899) managed to produce a convention for the peaceful settlement of disputes. The signatories declared that 'so far as circumstances allow', mediation should be attempted before a resort to war. A Permanent Court of Arbitration was established, consisting, however, only of a list of persons available for this work if called upon. Germany prevented an agreement to make arbitration compulsory in cases of minor importance, but the new machinery was used to good effect on a number of occasions before 1914. In 1907 there was a Second Hague Conference which made an entirely platonic declaration against the arms race and was followed in 1909 by a conference in London on safeguarding neutral commerce in time of war. The 1907 conference agreed to reconvene in eight years' time and to set up a preparatory committee two years ahead to study the proposals to be brought before it. Owing to the war, this conference never met.

Some degree of tepid internationalism was almost bound to arise in view of the increasing unity of the world in every respect but the political. By 1914 there were over thirty international authorities looking after various matters of mundane interest. The oldest was the Danube commission (1856) and the most important the International Postal (1874) and Telegraph (1865) Unions, the International Institute of Agriculture (1905) and the International Health Office (1907). Improving communications had made possible an increasing number of private international associations and conferences. Arbitration had been used quite frequently to settle international disputes in the nineteenth century, and the Geneva Conventions had sought to make war more humane, the object also of various regulations established by the Hague Conferences.

Politically much more important was the growing belief, apparent even in much orthodox diplomacy after 1900, that international rivalry was becoming increasingly unprofitable. There had been no large war in Europe since 1877. The profits to the victor in Bismarck's wars looked less striking when the inescapable burden of the resulting arms race was set against them. As for the losers, even the French were ceasing to repine. In 1897 a Russian Jewish railway magnate, I. S. Bloch, published a massive treatise on *The War of the Future* in which he accurately predicted that war under modern conditions would not be rapid and cheap but long and unbelievably costly. 'Everybody will be entrenched in the next war . . . all wars will of necessity partake of the character of siege operations . . . the ultimate decision is in the hands of famine.' Norman Angell's *The Great Illusion* (1910) argued that war could no longer pay. The international system of trade, finance and capitalist enterprise could not be disrupted without general impoverishment. It was therefore no longer possible for the victor to plunder the vanquished. This was to be the argument of J. M. Keynes in 1919 when he tried to show that massive reparations could not be expected from Germany.

Conservatives were not usually responsive to these arguments. The Tsar was interested in disarmament and peacekeeping partly from personal conviction and partly because the general development of his backward country was hindered (and has been ever since) by the need to compete with the armaments of the more advanced powers. But such ideas attracted support mainly from the left, both socialists and bourgeois. The latter propagated the old liberal belief that the interests of all nations were identical. The socialists believed similarly that the interests of all workers were identical and that national quarrels were a means of distracting them from the common struggle against the capitalists.

The left failed to avert war in 1914 and most of the radicals and socialists proved as willing to fight as the rest when the call to arms came. The pre-war peace movement has accordingly been dismissed as ineffective and remote from the real sentiments of the people. This is not entirely true. There was a very real sentiment against wars fought for the advantage of the governing class rather than the nation. In purely imperial conflicts the left was capable of united international protest. Statesmen respected and even over-valued the strength of radical pacific sentiment and this helped to prevent colonial wars. In 1906 the Kaiser told the Americans that Germany had never contemplated war over Morocco because 'the German people would not understand it', and in the second Moroccan crisis (1911) the socialists everywhere took a resolute line against war. But the fact was that colonial wars were usually not desired, even by the politicians and businessmen directly involved in colonial ventures. It was different when national security seemed threatened and statesmen and the ruling class believed war to be necessary. The left could not then sway government and opinion and the socialists always rejected plans to stop war by strikes or revolt. This was partly because they stood no chance against the powerful military states of the continent, whose generals and administrators would often have been glad of an excuse to crush them. But there was also the danger that the movement of protest would be successful only in the more advanced countries and so would promote the military success of the more backward and oppressive states. Even in the nineties Engels had said that German socialists must defend their country against backward Russia, and the French similarly felt that their republic was worth defending against Prussian Germany. In 1914 the European socialist leaders consulted together during the crisis and tried to halt it, but in the end the national parties supported the war because in every country except perhaps Austria-Hungary it could plausibly be made out to be a fight for democracy and the preservation of independence—things dear, of course, to the whole left.

The peace movement was not so much a hopeless venture as one that had not developed fast enough to be ready when it was really needed. In the nineteenth century even the parties of the left tended to regard perpetual peace as a pious aspiration unconnected with practical politics. In any case, the wars of the period were palatable to the left, being mostly for national liberation or unification, and imperialism similarly appeared to many simply as a progressive force, spreading civilization among savages. It was in the new century that the left began to see war as an urgent and terrible danger, and to realize, indeed to exaggerate, the threat of colonial rivalries to peace. In the Second International, for instance, it was only in 1907, at the Stuttgart conference, that the subject began seriously to be tackled. Constructive thinking had not gone far enough to present a serious obstacle to war in 1914, and the first really formidable effort of the peace movement was concerned with the subsequent picking up of the pieces.

Modern Art and Science

The beginning of the twentieth century was an important point of new departure in the intellectual and cultural life of Europe, and about this something must briefly be said. The new trends were too much at variance with customary ways to be readily absorbed into the thinking and feeling of ordinary people; indeed, it might be argued that the intellectual history of one era really belongs with the political and social history of the next generation, the first able to understand what has been going on. But there is no such delay in the application of scientific discoveries, and by the time of the explosion of the first atomic bomb in 1945 the pioneering stage was past, even on the aesthetic and purely intellectual side. This must be taken into account in any attempt to chart the course that Europe was taking.

It is commonly said that the idea of progress has no application to the arts, and in the sense that the best artists of one age cannot be supposed to have greater natural talent than the best in previous ages this would seem to be true. But what 'progress' has meant first and foremost to educated believers in it over the last two centuries has been the increase of knowledge and understanding. In this sense the arts have progressed just as much as the sciences and as part of the same process. Historical and archaeological research and geographic discovery have greatly increased European knowledge of the arts of other continents and of the European past. From the end of the eighteenth century there has been a steady abandonment (save where the state has interfered) of the cramping ideas that men and art should conform to one particular pattern regarded as good or normal. There has been a growing wish and ability to understand people remote from us in time and place and to enjoy their works of art. This has meant, in turn, that European artists and their public, exposed to new and ever more diverse influences, became capable of creating and enjoying artistic works beyond the scope of earlier ages.

This is not to say that the art produced was intrinsically better than that of earlier ages. The growing weight of knowledge could have a stifling as well as an inspiring effect, to say nothing of the growth of a new, wealthy but undereducated middle class. Nineteenth-century architecture was largely antiquarian: architects had found out how to work accurately in the idiom of any period specified and their clients were too excited by this to demand a new style for their own time. Literature was the art with which the middle class was most at home (in those days even poetry was popular) and painting and even music in the last century were tending to fall under literary domination. Pictures were rather expected to tell a story, like a book illustration. There was a tendency to write music that described a scene and, with the Wagnerians, to give a new importance to the words in opera and songs.

At the end of the nineteenth century the visual arts began to revolt against the domination of antiquarians and writers. In architecture the change began in Britain: disciples of William Morris stressing plain and workmanlike design aiming at usefulness rather than just showing off. *Art nouveau*, also of British derivation and more a style of decoration than of architecture, asserted the designer's right to use his imagination freely in the devising of fantastic lines and shapes. Both these developments were given point by the development of new methods of construction, using steel beams, reinforced concrete and large areas of glass. This encouraged a plain, functional style of building, but it also made easier the realization of unorthodox and fanciful designs. In the nineties Frank Lloyd Wright in America was beginning the development of the open-plan house with extensive windows and communicating as freely as possible with the garden. Before 1914 the Germans Behrens and Gropius were designing factories and offices of the characteristic modern type, with clean square lines and glass making up most of the walls and enclosing the staircases. In France Perret pioneered the use of reinforced concrete and Garnier planned in 1904 a concrete-built 'industrial city'. The new architects were eager to plan for the machine age and current attempts to improve the urban environment mainly stem from the great pre-1914 innovations.

In painting France was the great centre of innovation. From the sixties there developed impressionism, in which the aim was the rapid portrayal of a scene as it was at a particular moment. The interest centred on the momentary quality of the light and atmosphere rather than the colour and shape of the objects portrayed. The painter in all this was really trying to compete with the photographer. Further developments were in a quite different direction, away from the realism and fidelity to the seeing eye striven for by the impressionists. From the eighties such painters as Seurat, Cézanne and Gauguin were more interested in the effects that could be produced by studied composition: by particular juxtaposing of colours, balancing of masses, emphasis of lines. The conscious departure from real-life appearances began, and after 1900 there was a growing willingness to abandon the accurate representation of things seen in order to concentrate on conveying interesting visual effects suggested by them. The *fauves* painted objects the 'wrong' colour. Matisse, a master of the line, sought in his pictures to create designs that grow as a plant grows, with a natural unity. Picasso and Braque by 1914 were painting entirely abstract 'cubist' pictures, in which the interest lies in the deployment on the canvas of a number of variously shaped plane surfaces. After the war Ozenfant was to argue that the shapes to be used should not be chosen at the whim of the artist but should be 'universal'. Shapes which natural objects and machines had because of their function had this character. The architect Le Corbusier was a collaborator of Ozenfant and applied the same ideas in his own field. Much of the best modern architecture and painting have shared the same spirit of functionalism and classicism, the search for harmony and proportion.

On the other hand, there has been a parallel romantic stream in modern art, abandoning realism and convention not in order to become more abstract or formal but in order to express personal feeling with less inhibition. The writings of Freud encouraged this, but there seems to have been a general heightening of interest in the unconscious and instinctive side of human nature of which his ideas were a symptom rather than a cause. The surrealists portrayed the world of dreams, the futurists in Italy wanted an art of excitement and brutality that could accompany the new extreme nationalism, the dadaists arose during the war (1916) to cap the general insanity by abandoning sense and reason in art in order to produce something that would be the work of instinct alone. All this reflected a belief that the unconscious contained great hidden powers which could produce extraordinary results if only they could be tapped. In the resulting search a great deal of rubbish was turned up, but it had a fructifying effect, for instance in the later work of Picasso.

It is this heightened romanticism which has been the strongest force for innovation in literature. The movements just mentioned were as much literary as concerned with the visual arts. Since the French symbolists of the later nineteenth century, poets have tended to evoke rather than to describe, relying more on the subconscious effect and associations of their words on themselves and their readers than on direct statement. Novels, as with Kafka, have taken the world of dreams and subconscious tensions as their subject. But there has been far less of a break with the past in literature than in the visual arts. It had already asserted its right to be fantastic in the romantic period and attempts like Joyce's to go farther and produce something directly akin to the outpourings of the subconscious do not seem to have led anywhere. Innovation has been more important in the theatre. The drama is among other things one of the visual arts, and like the others it had been expected to copy nature accurately and had been rather in subordination to literature. Now photography (the cinema) competed with the theatre no less than with painting in the realistic portrayal of nature and this made it natural for the drama to be deliberately unrealistic. Plays thereby became less literary, less an account of something that could be read like a book and more of an occasion at which feelings could be aroused, like a public meeting or a punch and judy show. Of course the cinema, developing in the nineties, itself became a new dramatic art, and very soon had a poetry and fantasy of its own.

Music again, though many novel sounds were produced which infuriated the older listener, was not really revolutionized. There was a reaction against romantic lushness in the delicacy of Debussy or the stridency and resurgent classicism of Stravinsky. But music, like literature, had really already asserted, in the romantic period, its right to go whatever way it pleased, and the really radical experiments, like the work of Schönberg, were not of much account in the period down to 1945. In one respect, however, music led the way— in the popular acceptance of a non-European idiom. Afro-Asian influences are apparent in a host of modern artistic experiments: Gauguin's visits to the Pacific, the African masks which for a time helped Picasso, the influence of the Japanese Noh Plays on writers and dramatists, to name only a few. But the jazz of the American Negro not only interested 'highbrow' composers but appealed to the masses everywhere. It, too, reached Europe early in the twentieth century.

The work of Sigmund Freud has already been mentioned, and it forms, indeed, a bridge between the sciences and the arts. Freud was probably the last important scientific figure whose major works can be understood—as those of Darwin and even Galileo could be—by the educated layman. Consequently he had a direct influence not only on the specialists in his own field but on the whole 'climate of opinion'.[1] Born in 1856 Freud came of a struggling Moravian Jewish family which migrated, like so many others, to Vienna. He had an orthodox medical training and specialized in neurology. In the nineties he developed the technique of 'free association' in the treatment of hysteria. Patients were asked to repeat everything that came into their minds, however trivial or embarrassing, in connection with their symptoms. The interpretation of the material so collected produced a theory that proved applicable to the sane as well as to the deranged. Sexual desires were present in infancy and were repressed by education. They sought vicarious outlets in, for instance, dreams, jokes and artistic creation. Shameful feelings about them led to the wilful forgetting of what was best not remembered, and the cloaking of real resentments and desires by the display of others analogous to them but more innocent. *The Interpretation of Dreams*, Freud's most important work, appeared in 1899. By 1910 there were disciples enough to justify the foundation of an International Psychoanalytical Association. Freud's work was still a step away from a true science of the mind. He analysed mental behaviour, but could only sketchily relate this to the physical structure and workings of the organ itself. But he set going the scientific investigation of those deeper levels of the human personality of which modern man has become increasingly conscious as his liberation from external and customary restraint, which kept them in their place, has progressed. He also made it impossible, henceforth, to take human action and belief at its face value.

The beginning of the twentieth century saw the overthrow of the traditional view of the physical world as well as the fading away of the commonsense picture of human nature. The discovery of the electrically produced X-rays was followed by the discovery of natural radiation from uranium (1895–6). It was found that some of these rays consisted of helium atoms and that they could pass through thin metal foil and were sometimes, but not always, deflected by it. This suggested that the atoms in the foil were not solid all through but only in part. Already by 1899 J. J. Thompson had suggested that atoms consisted partly of electrons and in 1911–13 Rutherford and

---

[1] As W. H. Auden wrote in a poem about him.

Bohr reached the modern view of the atom as a central mass with electrons in orbit round it. It was soon found that the weight of an atom varied according to the number of electrons it contained and that this was what differentiated the atoms of different substances. In 1919 Rutherford achieved the goal of the alchemists of old—he transmuted one substance into another by knocking electrons off its atoms. In the thirties ways were discovered of splitting the nucleus of the atom and the possibility emerged of using the energy which held it together for practical purposes, good or ill. It was also discovered that fusion as well as fission was possible and that the atom contained a variety of different particles besides electrons. Every branch of science was deeply affected by these discoveries; in principle the boundary between physics and chemistry disappeared.

Behind these discoveries lay entirely new ideas about the behaviour of the physical world, of which the most important were Max Planck's quantum theory (1900) and Albert Einstein's special (1905) and general (1916) theory of relativity. The former destroyed the view that the physical forces in the universe are essentially uniform and constant. Instead, they consist of a series of discrete units. The old problem of whether to regard light as consisting of continuous waves or separate particles now applied to movement of all kinds, including that of the particles within the atom. Heisenberg in 1927 argued that the momentum and position of a particular particle cannot both be exactly specified. In place of the exactness and regularity of physical happenings on which the old science had been based, reliance had now to be on statistical probability. Einstein showed that the size and weight of objects altered according to the speed at which they moved, relative to one another, in space, that time itself was affected in the same way by velocity and gravitational attraction, that an object represented a quantity of locked-up energy, the amount of which was proportionate to its mass. In his universe the speed of light was the only constant. The new theories commonly made a practical difference only when it came to dealing with very small objects and very high speeds—hence their importance in the study of the atom and of all kinds of radiation. But the plain man's ideas of time and matter were now seen to correspond with appearance rather than reality. Behind them was a universe devoid of substance in the usual sense and consisting rather of emptiness and energy.

There has always been a tendency to link the new art and science of the twentieth century with the more mundane movements of society. The artists and the Freudians have been reviled by conservatives as precursors of Bolshevism and by Bolsheviks as bourgeois decadents. Some scientists have likewise incurred Bolshevik censure, though it has been less the physicists than the disciples of Mendel in biology who have angered them. The study of heredity, like the study of physics, has led to the idea that nature moves in jerks rather than with smooth and constant regularity, and this has upset the stricter determinists and comforted many who believe the universe to be under the direction of a personal God. But the refutation of one idea seldom proves its opposite and the new discoveries can be variously interpreted. In fact, neither the artists nor the scientists of the present century can be associated with any particular view in politics or philosophy, or even narrowly with any particular class. Their social origins and personal views of the world have been diverse. Their work would seem to be the natural flowering of an increasingly rich and free society, with rising standards of education. It points collectively in no single direction. It does, however, point away from one. Until the present century, certain comfortable certainties about the nature of man and the universe were shared by conservatives and innovators alike. Rebels against one certainty could rest on another. Those who rejected religion could look on science as a new revelation; those who rejected authority, in religion, politics or even in art, could rest on the strength of their inner convictions. But henceforth science was to be the study of probabilities rather than the discovery of certainties, inner conviction might turn out to derive from infantile sexuality, and so many old certainties about what was true or beautiful had been destroyed that not much faith could be placed in the rest. Human life in all departments was going to depend more on conscious choice and calculation and less on custom and instinct. This would make it more exciting but also more of a burden.

2: Crisis Averted in the West

At the beginning of the twentieth century all the states of Europe faced mounting discontent, and new political strategies had to be found to promote necessary change and harness or contain new movements of protest such as socialism. In the western countries there were some hopeful experiments that were cut short by the war of 1914. In France and Germany splits in the ruling circle gave a chance of penetration to those less fortunately placed. In Italy the important experiments of Giolitti had a similar effect. But especially from 1911 the deepening international crisis poisoned the political atmosphere. It did not halt but encouraged domestic political change, but this very fact casts doubt on the worth and vitality of the new trends.

France: Briand and his Consequences

The fall of the Combes ministry at the start of 1905 was the signal for a fresh departure. Moderate men were tired of the intolerance that had been shown towards real or imagined enemies of the republic in the army and the church. Paradoxically the way back to conciliation was opened by the most extreme of the anticlerical measures, the separation of church and state which took place in 1905. It was so extreme that not even Combes wanted it. But the system established by concordat between Napoleon and the Vatican had become unworkable. Combes interpreted it more rigidly than his predecessors and refused to continue the practice instituted in 1871 by which the state consulted the church before exercising its right to nominate bishops. The new Pope Pius X meanwhile reversed the liberal policies of Leo XIII and foolishly protested to the powers against a visit of the French President to the King of Italy. He further challenged the French government's control over the episcopate by forcing two bishops to resign. Diplomatic relations were broken off and church and state could no longer co-operate in ecclesiastical administration.

Since no one dared to propose a schismatic national church, the extreme left's remedy of separation had to be accepted as the only way to prevent a breakdown. The reluctant republicans were mainly intent on avoiding trouble, and abandoned the spirit of persecution which they had shown against the religious orders. Church property was mostly nationalized, but churches were to remain in perpetual and free possession of all places of worship and were allowed to retain certain endowments. The existing clergy received pensions. These arrangements were accepted by the Jews and Protestants (whom Napoleon had subjected to state control no less than the Catholics), but the Pope rejected them, chiefly because the management of church property was to be entrusted to associations of laymen. Despite a safeguard in the law against heretical takeovers, the Catholics maintained that this was a threat to the authority of the hierarchy. As a result of this, they lost their endowments in 1908, but every effort was made to find a compromise and avoid disturbing them in other ways. The clergy were left in peaceful but technically illegal possession of their churches. The law relating to public meetings was made more liberal so as to avoid the danger that services might be illegal. The lay authorities had been required by the separation law to make an inventory of church property, and when they entered churches for this purpose they met forcible resistance. At first the government met force with force and some demonstrators were killed. But at length the making of inventories was given up: Clemenceau declared that he would not kill men in order to count candlesticks.

Few would now deny that separation has been beneficial to church and state alike. The church was left to shift for itself, but it was freed from the deadening effects of state interference and faced with the challenge of maintaining its authority by its own unaided efforts. Its vitality and spiritual influence have greatly increased as a result. On the other hand, the state has accepted religious freedom as the solution to the religious problem, and this has made for a growth of tolerance in national life. Religion remains a political issue, mainly in its educational aspect, but in this respect at least France has made political progress.

The main architect of the separation was Aristide Briand. The law of 1905 was a hot potato which the ministers would hardly touch.

It was Briand, a private member, who piloted it through the chamber, and this established his political reputation. As minister of education (1906–9) he was the person mainly responsible for the conciliatory application of the law. As prime minister from 1909 to 1911 he tried to apply the same spirit of conciliation to the affairs of the nation at large, healing the wounds which the Dreyfus affair had opened and winning for the republican régime the loyalty of the nation as a whole. Born in 1862, a lawyer by profession, he entered politics as a socialist of the 'independent' stripe that refused to accept the unified party and the ban on entry into 'bourgeois' ministries. The English observer is tempted to see in him a great conservative of the stamp of Baldwin. He had the same desire to preserve the nation from the threat of disruption by class antagonisms. He had appeared for the defence in some sensational trials arising out of violent labour disputes; he had tried in these to defend the working class as a whole and win sympathy in the middle-class public for its sufferings and ways of thought. He approached sectarian quarrels in the same spirit. Like Baldwin, he was also an 'appeaser' abroad, but not when this seemed to endanger national security.

Briand did not abandon his sympathy for the left, and as prime minister came out in favour of a share for the workers in the profits and management of industry. But it was on the right rather than the left that an irreconcilable opposition to the republic existed and it was to that quarter that his 'appeasement' was chiefly directed. He therefore reinforced the trend already noticed as beginning with the Dreyfus explosion: moderate and radical republicans drew together in an all-powerful block which could prevent reform but had not itself enough common purpose to initiate it. The conservative groups in opposition shrank in the elections of 1906 and 1910, but conservatives increasingly infiltrated the parties to their left, many even becoming nominal radicals. With the ministry headed (1906–9) by Clemenceau, the fiercest of the radicals and never in office till these years, the left really seemed to have arrived. Each ministry between 1906 and 1911 was pledged to extensive social reforms and to the introduction of a progressive income tax, providing in a fair way for the constantly increasing military expenditure. But almost nothing was done except the introduction of old-age pensions and the buying-up of a notably inefficient railway at an excessive price.

There was rising anger on the left. The syndicalists were behind the wave of strikes that began in 1906, in which the strikers resorted to violence and troops were used against them. The syndicalists retaliated by spreading seditious propaganda among the troops. In 1907 the farmers of the Midi staged an unusual demonstration against the low price of wine. The municipal authorities resigned en bloc and refused to execute the laws. There was a mutiny in one of the local regiments. The employees of the state complained of victimization and political interference in appointments, dismissals and promotions. In 1909, parliament responded to a strike of postal workers by refusing to recognize the right of state employees to strike. Finally, in 1910, came the threat of a general strike on the railways. The Briand ministry prevented this by calling up all the railway workers for military service. This authoritarian measure displeased many besides the socialist and brought an open breach between the far left and the main body of the radicals. Briand, increasingly dependent on the votes of conservative republicans, resigned; Monis, who succeeded him, declared that he would 'govern with the republican majority, which ends where violence begins'. The socialists could do little but seek an alliance with the equally discontented parties of the right. Had Christian Democracy been stronger among the clericals this might have had interesting results. But this trend has almost always been weak in France and there was really only one issue on which socialists and conservatives could join—proportional representation. The existing system of single-member constituencies over-represented the radical majority at the expense of the two extremes. The radicals themselves were rather ashamed of it and had been champions of electoral reform when in opposition. A majority therefore existed in the chamber for some sort of change, but the defenders of the existing law were strong enough down to 1914, especially in the senate, to wreck every plan that was proposed.

The extreme left began to recover ground, however, as their moderate–radical opponents moved farther to the right in their policies. This would perhaps have happened anyway after the events of 1910, but the immediate cause was the worsening international situation, which caused politics, as in the Dreyfus era, to centre round the army. The Agadir crisis of 1911 brought an abrupt reaction against the policy of conciliating Germany. Joseph Caillaux, prime minister for most of the crisis, had really adopted much the same mixture of firmness and conciliation as his predecessors for several years past. But he was rightly suspected of underhand and unofficial negotiations with the Germans, and it was this that led to his fall in 1912. Raymond Poincaré, his successor, was, like Caillaux himself, a moderate who had come over to the left in the Dreyfus period, though not to the extent of supporting Combes. A Lorrainer, able, dour and arid, he was to be bitterly accused of having helped to start the First World War. That charge will be examined in due course: what is undoubtedly true is that his ministry promised to put down disorder and give the country a feeling of security against foreign attack. This was right-wing talk, and it encouraged the parties of the right and the more moderate of the radicals to work together. Candidates from the moderate right were raised to high office in spite of the radical majority: Deschanel to the presidency of the chamber, Poincaré himself to the presidency of the republic in 1913, Barthou soon afterwards to the premiership. The new president pointedly told the two chambers that the weakening of the executive was not the desire of the country. He seemed anxious to rescue his office from its inanity.

An important measure was now brought forward and carried by the resurgent moderates—the lengthening of the term of military service from two to three years. This was something genuinely desired by the military authorities in response to the plans known to be coming forward to strengthen the German army. It was the only way to counterbalance the increasing German population. But it had vital political overtones. In 1905 the length of service had been reduced from three to two years essentially as a consequence of the Dreyfus affair. The intention had been to make the army more democratic by lessening the time during which the conscripts could be isolated from the community and indoctrinated by the suspect professional soldiers. Other measures were taken for the same purpose: educated men were no longer able to serve for a shorter term than the rest, and prospective officers who had passed through St Cyr were to serve a year in the ranks. The law of 1913 was a deliberate reaction against this previous measure and reflected the usual desire of the regular soldiers to make the army as professional as possible. The socialists, on the other hand, wanted more reliance on the reservists and a larger and less professionalized army. This was partly because they rejected the generals' preference for the offensive. More in accord with the republican traditions of 1793 and 1870, their approach was also less likely to encourage warlike thinking and talking in peacetime, such as might poison the diplomatic atmosphere.

The return of three-year service was a warning to the entire left that their victories of ten years earlier were in danger of being overthrown. Caillaux took the lead in rallying the party organizations of the radicals and radical-socialists against the measure. At the end of 1913 the Barthou cabinet was replaced by another farther to the left. In the elections of 1914 the socialists and the radicals fought together against the moderates on the three-year service issue and narrowly defeated them. The 'independent' socialist Viviani became premier with the intention of trying to save the new military law but introducing an income tax by way of compensation. It was at that point that political life was transformed by the outbreak of war.

By 1914 France was returning to the hopeful political situation that had existed in the nineties. The republicans were split into a moderate left working with the socialists and a moderate right working with the conservatives. The loyalty of the two bodies of moderates was a guarantee that the republic would be safe whichever group was in office. The division of the moderates gave both the extremes a chance of gaining power and so tended to reconcile both to the existing form of government. But it was, above all, the military service law of 1913 which had brought about the new situation, and this was due not to the natural development of home politics but to the tense international atmosphere. It cannot be confidently said that the Third Republic was on the way to discovering the secret of peaceful adaptation.

Germany: the 'Bülow Bloc' and its Aftermath

Count Bernhard von Bülow succeeded the aged Hohenlohe as German Chancellor in 1900, after three years in charge of German foreign policy. Born in 1849 of a Prussian noble and bureaucratic family, he had married an Italian wife and was a polished and cultured cosmopolitan, closer in spirit to Metternich or Talleyrand than to the rough Bismarck or the austere Caprivi. His insinuating charm made him a natural courtier, but he was also an eloquent parliamentarian.

He thus had the gifts required to keep harmony between his royal master and the Reichstag and Prussian landtag. In calmer times, no one would have suited his job better. But he lacked the imaginative range and firmness of character needed to carry through the great political reconstruction that Germany was increasingly coming to need. At first he aimed at holding together the conservatives, clericals and National Liberals, whose collaboration produced the high tariff of 1902. A Prussian schools law, like that promoted by Caprivi a decade earlier, assured a strong measure of confessional control over public education. The imperial law against the Jesuits and kindred organizations, left over from the Kulturkampf, was amended. Individual members of these orders were no longer restricted in the performance of their work, although the orders themselves remained excluded from the country. These concessions did not arouse the strong united resistance among the liberals that there had been ten years before, and they meant that a majority of the same colour controlled and assured harmony between the Prussian and the imperial parliaments.

The socialists gained nearly a million votes in the Reichstag elections of 1903 but, like their French equivalent, they were helpless because they were isolated. Their gains had mainly been at the expense of their likeliest allies, the middle-class radicals, with whom they shared a belief in low tariffs and democracy. But there was a chance that they might find new friends on the left wing of the Centre. A valuable young recruit reinforced this element in the Reichstag in 1903 in the person of Matthias Erzberger. The son of a village tailor, he had made his career in journalism and the organizing of education and trade unions among catholic workers. In this work his main enemies were the socialists. But his outlook and background were very much like those of the socialist leaders and he, like them, was out of place in the patrician atmosphere of a Reichstag dominated by the older parties. He sought to make his way by hard work, and in particular concerned himself with scandals in the colonies. Misgovernment there had led to a series of revolts, and the Centre had become increasingly concerned because of its connection with Catholic missionary activities. Erzberger's campaign led to the appointment of an energetic and enlightened director of colonies, Bernhard Dernburg. In spite of this, the Centre voted against an estimate for the force destined to suppress the rising in South West Africa at the end of 1906: joining the socialists, they put the government in a minority.

Bülow's response was to hold a general election. The clericals and socialists were accused of lack of patriotism in voting against an army estimate. Bülow spoke a good deal of the menace of socialism, but it is generally supposed that his main intention was to free himself from dependence on the Centre. They always exacted a high price for their support, and now a new alliance was available. The radicals were sore at the successes of both socialists and clericals. They had been pleased by the appointment of Dernburg, a banker of mildly liberal outlook. Bülow seems to have wanted to bring them back into the governmental fold, having alienated them by adopting a higher tariff. In this way his policy remained ultimately conservative, aimed at keeping the socialists in isolation.

The socialist vote rose again in 1907 but they lost almost half their seats, partly because the radicals worked against them with the parties to their right. Though the Centre won a few seats the government now had a Reichstag majority without them, the so-called 'Bülow bloc' of conservatives, National Liberals and radicals. The implication of this was that the government would promote liberal reforms. An important one was carried in 1908: a law protecting the rights of the citizen to form associations and hold public meetings. This made the work of trade unions, political parties and the like much more secure from police interference. More important, though unproductive, was a vague remark in the royal speech at the opening of the Prussian landtag in the same year which showed that the government was considering electoral reform. This was the first official admission that the oligarchic nature of the Prussian state was incompatible with the further political development of the nation.

In basing his policy on his 'bloc', Bülow had left two things out of account: the incurable selfishness of the Junkers and the protean character of the Centre, which enabled it to form an alliance with any other party. Both groups were sore at the ascendancy of the radicals, and in 1909 an issue arose on which the aristocrats and agrarians of both parties thought alike. German finances, like those of France and indeed of most countries, were being upset by increasing expenditure, especially on armaments. In consequence, Bülow decided to make a concession to his radical friends which Bismarck had always refused to the Liberals—direct taxes levied by the Reichstag. The budget of 1909 (the year that Lloyd-George introduced surtax) proposed 500 million marks of new taxation, four-fifths of it indirect but including a plan for death duties. To protect the family estates of the landed class, conservatives and clericals joined together to defeat the government. They were helped by the Poles, whom Bülow had treated badly. Taxes on sales of land and securities were imposed instead. The socialists had voted for the government, but their losses in 1907 made them unable to save the author thereof from defeat. The new majority, the 'blue-black bloc' as it was called, was master of the field. In 1910 the clericals in the Prussian landtag voted with the conservatives to kill the government's timid plan of electoral reform for Prussia.

Meanwhile, Bülow's personal position had been ruined by a crisis in the relations of the egregious Kaiser with his subjects. In October 1908 the *Daily Telegraph* published an 'interview' with him—actually put together from several conversations. Wilhelm pictured himself as a lover of England ruling a nation which hated her. Everyone in Germany was offended: the extreme right because they were anti-British, everyone else because the Kaiser had spoken as if he was an absolute monarch who could rule as he pleased. Bülow was also blamed: the text of the interview had been sent to him and he had passed it for publication. Highly sinister motives were suggested for this, but it was discreditable enough even if it was only negligence as he claimed. The national fury was only appeased by a curious act of public penance. Bülow told the Reichstag that he was convinced that in future the Emperor would show more restraint in private utterances and that neither he nor anyone else would otherwise be willing to assume responsibility as minister. The Kaiser issued a statement afterwards, associating himself with what his Chancellor had said. On these terms he was forgiven; Bülow on the other hand resigned on the defeat of his financial plans in 1909.

Did these events mean increased parliamentary control over the executive? Bülow had resigned after a parliamentary defeat, but the real reason was that he had lost the Emperor's favour because of the *Daily Telegraph* crisis (indeed, this was what gave many conservatives the courage to vote against him.) In the crisis the Emperor had appeared to submit to the nation, but his spirits soon recovered and his remarks were soon as outrageous as ever. Bülow's successor was certainly not the man to stop him. Theobald von Bethmann-Hollweg came from a patrician family of bankers in the ancient city of Frankfort-on-Main. He had had a distinguished career in the internal administration of Prussia and the Reich and was mildly progressive, with an interest in social reform. Unlike Bülow, he was generally respected for his complete honesty. But like Bülow, he was a fair-weather minister, able to work the system but not to master or transform it. One big domestic reform stands to his credit: the voting in 1911 of a constitution for Alsace-Lorraine. Hitherto the *Reichsland* had been governed as a sort of colony, the governor being assisted by a consultative assembly and council. Henceforth, it was to be nowise inferior to any of the states in the Reich and to have a constitution more democratic than Prussia's. The imperial governor retained the executive power but shared the legislative power with a two-chamber parliament, of which the lower chamber was elected by manhood suffrage The *Reichsland* was to have representatives in the *Bundesrat*, equal in status to those of the other states. The relatively uncontentious passage of this measure boded well for Germany's future at home and abroad. It suggested a real wish to make friends with France and, far more than the events of 1908–9, it is evidence that both government and parties wished for political changes in a democratic direction.

In 1912 a way forward appeared to open by the defeat of the 'blue-black' bloc in the Reichstag elections. The radicals, split in two since 1893, had at last been reunited. For the first time they co-operated officially with the socialists, candidates of both parties standing down in certain cases to produce a united vote against clericals and conservatives. Behind this was the anger of business interests at the favour constantly shown to the agrarians, reflected in the formation of the 'Hanse league' to act as a counter pressure group. Even the National Liberals moved a little to the left. The conservatives lost seats heavily and the socialists, taking some seats from the Centre, replaced them as the largest party. One hundred and ten seats in the house of 397 and one voter in every three were now Social Democrat, yet this perhaps was less important than the signs that this great party was coming out of isolation. A new anti-clerical majority 'from Basserman to Bebel' (i.e. from National Liberal, through radical, to Social Democrat) seemed to have been formed when representatives of these parties were elected to the presidency of the new Reichstag, to the exclusion of conservatives and clericals. The effect was rather spoiled by the refusal of the socialist vice-president (Scheidemann, the future chancellor) to join in the customary visit to the Kaiser. His colleagues resigned in protest and a new presidium was elected without him.

More significant was the affair of the defence tax (*wehrbeitrag*) in 1913. This was the German counterpart to the great French agitation over three-year service. A massive increase in the German, as in the French forces was voted in the wake of the Agadir crisis. There was no shortage of men, but money was as tight as ever and it was no longer possible to avoid a massive direct imperial tax. The heavy initial expense of expansion was met by the tax already mentioned, a capital levy. Other taxes were instituted to help to meet the smaller recurring expenses. As in 1909, the conservatives voted against them. No other party dared to do so. This was, of course, a change for the Centre, but it was a bigger one for the socialists. As a protest against the whole existing political order, they always refused to vote the budget and especially did they dissociate themselves from the voting of military expenditure. Their vote for the capital levy was a decisive step away from intransigent opposition. Their justification was that the other parties would provide a majority for the voting of the increased expenditure and it was therefore their duty to see that the cost was not placed on the shoulders of the working man, in the form of extra indirect taxation. In fact, there was a majority for the direct taxes without the socialists, who voted for them because they were no longer willing to seem unpatriotic. But whatever their reasons, their intransigence was on the wane.

At the point when war broke out, the government had accepted the need for reform in Prussia, for liberal measures in the Reich and for more responsible behaviour by the Emperor. All the parties except the conservatives accepted the need for changes. But the conservatives were full of confidence and determination, as the sinister affair of Zabern showed.[1] The reformers were timid, hesitant and above all disunited. The left was more united than at any time since

---

[1] The garrison of this Alsatian town (French, Saverne) perpetrated certain acts of violence against the population, which went unpunished despite the protests of the Reichstag.

the seventies, but the two really big parties, the Centre and the Social Democrats, had not pulled together except accidentally in 1906. This was especially important because only with the help of the Centre was there a chance (though a poor one) of a reforming majority against the conservatives in the Prussian landtag. The most important gulf in the reforming ranks, however, was between the government and the socialists. Both Bülow and Bethmann-Hollweg treated these, if not altogether seriously, as enemies of the state, and wasted their energies in laborious attempts to keep the other parties united against them by yoking together conservatives and radicals. It is not surprising that they did so, for the socialists still purported to be a revolutionary party. But a man of vision would have taken their measure, as Bismarck did that of the liberals, and made use of them for reforming work as he had done with the left of his day.

The most depressing feature of the German scene was the continuing political exploitation of patriotic enthusiasm. The government had made great use of this in the elections of 1907, and both the socialists and the Centre were chary, after their defeat, of continuing the attempts which both had hitherto made to moderate the extravagance of the arms race. Too much can easily be made of this. The Pan-German League, champions of an aggressive foreign policy, were never a large organization. Bethmann-Hollweg virtuously and explicitly refused to exploit the international tension to escape from internal difficulties. But the behaviour of the socialists in 1913 made it clear that this was the easiest way to unite the parties. Foreign Secretary Kiderlen's aggressive line in the Agadir crisis (1911) was adopted in part because he hoped that it would help the government in the ensuing Reichstag elections: as we shall see, this was one of the most important mistakes in foreign policy that Germany made before 1914. Even less than in the case of France, therefore, can there be any confidence that German politics were set on a fruitful and constructive course when the First World War began.

Southern Europe: the Era of Giolitti

Within the narrow confines of Italian parliamentary politics one issue survived from which important experiments were to grow. This was the question of whether the country was to be governed in a liberal or an authoritarian spirit. The constitution, conservative but vague, could be interpreted in either way, and the issue tended to cut across what remained of the division between left and right. Francesco Crispi, born in 1818 and the dominant figure from 1887 till 1896, was at heart a man of the left, very anticlerical and still a bit inclined to be republican. His first years in power were marked by liberal measures. Mayors became elective as in France; so, too, did the chairmen of provincial (i.e. country) councils. A code of laws was adopted for the whole country, superseding the codes of the former separate states which had remained in force after unification. There were also an important public health act and, a little later, measures to protect the citizen against administrative abuse. But there were also many signs that Crispi wished to strengthen the executive. He commonly held the ministries of the interior and foreign affairs as well as the premiership, he secured for the crown the power to reorganize the ministry by decree, he carried a law restricting rights of public meeting. More important was the bizarre and volcanic personality of this Sicilian of supposed Albanian extraction. He goaded parliament and nation into feverish activity, and in his bombastic and egocentric speeches often urged the need for a strong man.

In the absence of a stable parliamentary majority based on party discipline, it was not unreasonable for Crispi to try to provide a focus of authority in his own person. What marred his rule was his inadequate idea of what his authority should be used for. Indifferent to Italy's economic weakness, he launched her on the creation of an East African empire which she could not really afford, and energetically upheld the Triple Alliance, which could be afforded even less. A tariff war with France resulted, which crippled Italy's export trade and added to her economic hardships. This encouraged the rise of the growing socialist movements, and by 1893 there was serious unrest in Sicily. Crispi responded with a turn towards authoritarian methods more decisive than any before. In 1894 martial law was proclaimed on the island and socialist organizations throughout the country were dissolved.

Crispi's career was ended by the defeat of Adowa in 1896, but his successors were more conservative than he and in face of continued unrest on the far left went farther, perhaps, than he would have done. By 1898 there were disorders in the north as well as in the south; in May there were pitched battles between workers and troops. Soon afterwards, the conservative but peaceable Rudini was succeeded as premier by a soldier, General Pelloux. In 1899 he proposed a series of exceptional laws, drastically curtailing the freedom of the press and of assembly. His chief parliamentary lieutenant was Sidney Sonnino, a man of unusual enlightenment and breadth of mind and one of the first to realize that under the existing system the south represented a permanent incubus.[1] It was the more notable that he had adopted strongly conservative views, and published a pamphlet in 1898 advocating exclusively royal control of the executive, parliament confining itself to legislative activity.

Such was the authoritarian trend in Italian politics. Though interesting in view of later developments (and Mussolini's admiration for Crispi) it never came to much. There was always a strong body of liberal opinion in the Italian parliament which deprecated harsh measures against the extreme left and saw the unwisdom of an overactive policy abroad. Crispi and his successors were always blocked before they went too far. When the far-left parties (radicals, republicans, socialists) opposed Pelloux's programme by prolonged and violent parliamentary obstruction they were successful and did not forfeit sympathy. When Pelloux appealed to the country in 1900 he failed to strengthen his parliamentary position despite the most arbitrary use of ministerial influence to 'make' the elections. His resignation was soon followed by the assassination of King Humbert, which not only removed a sovereign of a rather conservative bent but also led to a general wish for reconciliation, to protect the dynasty. An appeasing liberalism was the dominant note in Italian politics from now until the World War—which for Italy began only in 1915. Even those like Sonnino who had toyed with authoritarian ideas mostly abandoned them.

The new king, Victor Emmanuel III, soon identified himself with the new political trend by entrusting the premiership to Zanardelli. This passionate idealist had won both respect and unpopularity by the strength of his liberal beliefs. His great achievement was the code of laws enacted in the eighties. As minister of the interior under Cairoli in 1878–9, he had shown the tolerance towards the extreme

[1] He was part author of a famous work on *Sicily in 1876*.

left which had resulted in disorder. He now adopted the same policy with the same result, and in both cases his parliamentary position suffered. His ministry did not manage, however, to win the firm allegiance of the extreme left. It was to some extent a prisoner of the King, who had made Zanardelli promise to maintain continuity in foreign policy and not to cut the armed forces. He was therefore unable to appeal to radical sentiment by a really substantial cut in the more oppressive taxes. His ministry was responsible for certain popular measures: the creation of a Labour Office, the repeal of the flour tax, the building of an aqueduct in Apulia and a measure for developing the especially desolate province of Basilicata. But the premier was in declining health and had no real hold on parliament. He resigned in 1903, and it was his successor, weaker in constructive zeal but stronger in political guile, who turned the liberal trend into an entrenched system of government.

Giovanni Giolitti was born in 1842, of a professional middle-class family in the Piedmontese Alps. After a legal education, he entered the civil service of the new Italy soon after unification and for twenty years worked in various departments concerned with finance. Entering parliament for a constituency near his birthplace, thanks to the influence of his family, he was associated for a time with Crispi. But it was during an interregnum between two Crispi ministries that he first became prime minister (1893), and he distinguished himself from his former leader by trying to conciliate the Sicilian extremists that Crispi was afterwards to suppress. Falling from power mainly because of his supposed complicity in a bank scandal, he was Zanardelli's minister of the interior and the real power in the ministry; his resignation helped to seal its fate. His personality was the antithesis of what Italians and foreigners alike thought proper for an Italian. Totally averse to the theatrical either in word or deed, he was sober to the point of drabness in his parliamentary speeches and eschewed as far as he could all policies of adventure. Hard and unremitting work at everyday tasks was for him the way out of Italian backwardness. This epitome of the northerner and the bureaucrat had the large frame and robustness proper to his native mountains and lived to be nearly ninety.

His main task during and after Zanardelli's ministry was to show that the rising agitation of the socialists could be dealt with in a liberal spirit. There was a huge wave of strikes, involving both industry and agriculture. Zanardelli and Giolitti annoyed all the conservative-minded by observing strict neutrality between employers and employed. They would intervene only to preserve order and to prevent the intimidation of those who did not wish to strike. This was a statesmanlike policy, designed as Giolitti said 'to demonstrate to the people, not with words but with facts, that within our institutions all progress and all liberty is possible'. But it brought a growing risk of national disorganization. In 1903 there was a general railway strike, resulting from the repeated failure of the companies to implement promises that had been made to their employees. The government felt obliged to prevent the strike by calling up the men for military service and then to atone for this by remedying their grievance out of public funds, because of the difficulty of holding the companies to their word. In September 1904 there was a general strike, in protest against the deaths of some strikers in affrays with the police. This dangerous moment proved a turning point. The government prepared for widespread military action but held its hand; the strike collapsed in a few days.

The general election which followed was of crucial importance. Giolitti, like Zanardelli, had tried to bring the far left into his ministry, even consulting the socialists, but he, too, had failed. The socialists, discomfited by the failure of the strike, planned to join with his more conservative opponents to bring him down. Giolitti prevented this by dissolving parliament, hoping that the socialists would lose ground because of their recent extremism. In this he seems to have fallen into the same error as Pelloux, for the first results showed the socialists to have held their ground. But, as in France and Germany, there were second ballots in constituencies where no one had achieved an absolute majority, and here a revolutionary departure secured some socialist defeats. The catholic church was beginning to abandon its intransigent attitude to the new Italy. As late as the disturbances of 1898, catholic political leaders were imprisoned along with socialists. But a change came, to some degree associated with the accession of Pius X in 1903. Though more conservative than Leo XIII, he was much better versed in Italian politics. He also had neither the inclination nor the opportunity to continue his predecessor's attempts to use France against Italy. The French republicans were both attacking the church and trying to woo Italy from Germany. The visit of President Loubet to the King of Italy in Rome in 1904 was part of the latter policy, but the Vatican not unreasonably saw it as damaging to the church, and it contributed to the final rupture of 1905 already described. There were therefore practical reasons for the Pope to turn towards the Italian king, besides the general one present in everybody's mind—the emergence of the red peril, dangerous to throne and altar, liberal and conservative alike. So when (appropriately) the Italian foreign minister consulted leading catholics before the final ballot in 1904, the result was favourable. The Pope was asked by certain important laymen if they might participate in the elections in order to keep out the socialists. He replied 'do as your conscience dictates'. In the event, the socialists lost six seats, and for the first time there were two avowedly clerical members in the Italian chamber.

Henceforth, Giolitti was the master in Italian politics until the outbreak of war in 1915. Although he was not continuously in office, he was so during the general elections of the period—1904, 1909 and 1913—and his influence upon them was such that there was a 'Giolittian' majority upon which all ministries depended. As in the days of Depretis, the majority was 'transformist'—it was not a party but a collection of groups drawn from both left and right. Much of it was drawn from the south, where the poverty-stricken electors were bribed and intimidated, the prefect 'making' the election and the police condoning violence. But these methods, which earned for Giolitti the name of 'minister of the underworld' (*ministro della mala vita*), were ceasing to be applicable in the richer and more sophisticated north. Here there was transformism on an epic scale—an attempt to reconcile the ruling oligarchy with its bitterest enemies. Giolitti regarded himself as of the left and he never ceased to try and include the socialists within his majority. By protectionist measures he created a degree of prosperity in northern industry that employers and workers could share. Accordingly, the moderates had the upper hand in the socialist party for a number of years. But though his relations with some of them were good, he could never induce them to join the government and had always to be ready to treat them as enemies. Against them, he could increasingly use the catholics. They were not fully reconciled to the Italian state, and they included a left wing whose sympathies inclined somewhat towards the socialists. But the Pope would not allow a proper party of Christian Democrats for fear of its falling under heretical control. The church, on the other hand, was very tactfully treated by the government—which opposed, for instance, the spread of freemasonry—and so continued to give the ministers some support. In 1905 bishops were allowed officially to sanction participation in elections when it seemed locally desirable. In 1909 there were thirty-eight clerical deputies elected. By 1913 there was a catholic electoral union under papal control, which secretly agreed with the ministry to support liberal deputies who undertook not to patronize anticlerical measures. The Giolittian majority thus included both clericals and anticlericals and the secret character of the pact with the catholics[1] made it uncertain which were which. The heterogeneous character of the majority made it difficult for the ministry to have anything but a vague policy, and in 1905, 1909 and 1914 Giolitti had to retire from office when his position became too contradictory. To maintain his reputation as a liberal, he always tried to be succeeded by someone more conservative than himself. In each case save the last he soon returned to power.

Giolitti's experiments are of the highest interest for any student of democratic institutions. They were an attempt to govern on liberal lines a country which poverty and deep internal cleavages both social and ideological seemed to have marked out for dictatorship. Liberals in Mediterranean lands who have shown tolerance to the poor and to the church have commonly found themselves swamped by anarchy or by reaction as the case may be. Giolitti set himself to win the loyalty of both and thereby to turn a political system that was essentially an oligarchy into one that was truly national. He brought the extremes into politics, and by carefully balancing them he avoided a breakdown. He did not domesticate all the extremists, but he taught a great many to look for the satisfaction of their wants within the existing system and thereby strengthened the state.

His weakness lay in the absence of great constructive schemes which could underpin the reconciliation of old enemies by creating new common interests. Italy became more prosperous under his rule.

---

[1] It is usually called the Gentiloni Pact, after the leader of the electoral union. But it was really negotiated over his head.

The virtual absence of coal was beginning to be made good by the building of hydro-electric power stations, which by 1911 had a capacity of 500,000 kW. The total horsepower of the machines used in Italian industry rose from 430,000 in 1899 to 1,620,000 in 1915, of which nearly a million represented hydraulic power. Industrial production almost doubled in the years 1901–15; even the output of the small steel industry rose from 300,000 tons in 1900 to over a million in 1910. Giolitti was associated with two major projects which helped to make the country less dependent on foreign capital: the reduction of interest on the national debt and the establishment of a state insurance monopoly. But apart from the building up of industry in Naples he did nothing for the south—less than Zanardelli. In politics his extension of the suffrage in 1913 to illiterate men who were over thirty or had done military service seems to have made little difference to anything. As for the catholics, the secrecy of his dealings with them bespeaks the absence of constructive policy. Disillusion with his system gradually set in. Socialist disturbances never ceased. After 1910 the extremists gradually gained control of the party. In 1914 there was another general strike and in the Romagna something approaching an attempted revolution. Earlier that year, the extremist editor of *Avanti!*, the chief socialist newspaper, had told the party congress that his policy was 'intransigence on all lines, fight against kindred parties, especially the democratic. Italian democracy can never be fought sufficiently'. Thus spoke Benito Mussolini.

It was the outbreak of war in 1915 which destroyed the system of Giolitti and pointed to the overthrow of parliamentary government altogether. It showed conclusively that the existing régime rested on acquiescence only, that few believed or would devote themselves actively to it, and that it was ripe for overthrow by men of more determination, even if they were only a minority. It was the nationalists who thus humbled the parliamentary dictatorship. They had what Giolitti lacked: a plan to unite the different sections of the nation in a common cause. This was the more significant in that, like the Giolittians, they were not a party but a loose alliance of men of left, right and centre. Their oldest constituent was the irredentism associated since the eighties with the radical Imbriani. Ruthlessly kept down by Crispi in the interests of his alliance with the Austrians and Germans, it flourished in the twentieth century as Italy moved back towards

France. By that time also a body of intellectuals, of whom the most famous was the poet d'Annunzio, were denouncing the lack of purpose and virility in the parliamentary régime and trying to give the nation a sense of identity and common aims by means of an active foreign policy. The fact that Italy was a poor country from which many people had to emigrate made the demand for colonies of settlement a natural nationalist programme, but this was not really the ultimate purpose of the movement.

Opportunely the situation in the Ottoman Empire gave the nationalists a chance to show their paces. The Young Turks, who seized power in 1908, tried to resist the colonial penetration of the powers in the different provinces of their decaying realm. Italian trading interests had long predominated at Tripoli and Italy was slowly winning the assent of the other powers to her annexing it. The Turks now tried to pare down Italian influence, encouraging the enterprises of other powers such as the Germans. The government dared not abandon the little imperial influence Italy already had, and so Giolitti reluctantly undertook the conquest of Libya as soon as the diplomatic situation was favourable (1911–12). The idiotic enthusiasm aroused in almost all quarters, right and left, by this futile struggle for an almost uninhabitable tract of desert[1] showed the extent of national demoralization and the thirst among all the politically minded for a satisfying national philosophy.

With the war of 1914 the irredentist theme returned to the fore. The Salandra government, having concluded that the Central Powers were the attackers in the war, did not feel bound by the Triple Alliance to go to their aid. They decided to use the opportunity to obtain as much as they could of the Austrian lands inhabited by Italians—either by peaceful negotiation or by war. By the spring of 1915 the former policy had failed and they had concluded a treaty with Britain and France and were ready to fight. But the negotiations had been secret: the declaration of war was preceded by a struggle to make the nation accept the government's decision. Giolitti was for peace: he knew that Italy was not strong enough for a great conflict. He came out of retirement to oppose the government, and at once received promises of support from 300 deputies. If things had gone according to precedent, he would have returned to power. But the

[1] Its oil resources were unknown.

nationalists opposed him with furious demonstrations and rioting. If the clericals were unwilling to fight the catholic Austrians, many on the left now rallied to nationalism, for their sympathies were with France; not the least of these recruits was Mussolini. Encouraged with French gold, most of the press was for intervention. The ministry was sustained against parliament by the uproar out of doors: defying the Giolittian majority, it went to war. Parliament was shown not to be the real source of power, for what was expressed in parliament was less real opinion than managed elections. The importance of Giolitti the manager waned with that of parliament.

In trying to govern Italy on liberal lines, the parliamentary politicians of the pre-war era had set themselves an almost impossible task. Giolitti was not perhaps the noblest or the ablest of them, but he was the one with the greatest practical capacity. His sober character, however, was not what the situation demanded. He would have made an ideal German chancellor; for his own country someone rougher, a Witte or a Stolypin, was perhaps essential. But Giolitti must not be dismissed as a fair weather statesman. He upheld parliamentary institutions through years of daunting turbulence and only succumbed to the gravest shock of all. His achievement is perhaps best measured by comparison with the essentially similar conditions of Spain and Portugal. There, too, politics had been disrupted in the nineties by colonial reverses: Portugal's exclusion from Rhodesia in 1891, and Spain's defeat by the United States in 1898. Bankruptcy and discredit had steadily overcome the Portuguese monarchy. In 1908 the king and crown prince were assassinated, and in 1910 the monarchy was replaced by an extremely unstable republic. In Spain the young Alfonso XIII came of age in 1902, and undermined the shaky constitution by frequently changing his ministers in order to display and increase his own power. His sympathies were with the army, which thus began to creep back into politics from which Canovas, for all his faults, had been able to exclude it. The church, too, was growing in power and not diminishing in intolerance, and in Catalonia there was an unsavoury repression of national aspirations. Italy appears a paradise beside her southern neighbours: it was only the war that was to reduce her to the same level; only after the war that all three countries were to renounce the liberal path as hopeless, as will be told in its place.

3: Unavoidable Crisis in the East

The countries of western Europe faced serious problems after 1900, but except for Spain and Portugal[1] they cannot be said to have been in danger of breaking down. The war of 1914 brought calamity to them from without. The countries of eastern Europe, on the other hand, were in a state of revolutionary disintegration. The old governments hung on, like their predecessors in 1848, mainly because their enemies were divided. But their efforts to avert revolution only landed them in a major war. The catastrophe of 1914 arose naturally from the east European malaise and spilled over into the west. Europe paid the penalty for the failure of the eastern revolutions.

The Russian Revolution of 1905; Stolypin

Plehve had told Witte and Kuropatkin in 1903 that Russia needed 'a little victorious war to stop the revolutionary tide'. In July 1904 the war was already going badly, and Plehve was assassinated. Svyato-polk-Mirsky, the new minister of the interior, promised to show 'confidence in the public'. A private meeting of *zemstva* representatives was allowed at St Petersburg in November, and this formulated the orthodox liberal demands for a constitution in 'eleven theses' which became the basis of resolutions passed by *zemstva* all over the country. From the end of the year strikes began to multiply in the towns. Particularly notable was the general strike in St Petersburg in January 1905. The union which organized it had originally been encouraged by the police, but had fallen under left-wing control. Its leader was a young priest, Father Gapon, who seems to have been a sincere, naïve exponent of Christian Socialism. He thought that he could help his cause by leading a huge procession to the Tsar's palace with a petition. But the Tsar fled from his palace and his troops fired on the crowd: hundreds died on this 'Bloody Sunday'. Gapon fled abroad and for a while joined the revolutionaries. In

[1] And Britain, because of Ireland.

March 1905 peasant disturbances began and grew steadily, reaching a peak in the autumn. There was arson and the stealing of timber, and in some cases landlords were chased from their villages. Alike among peasants, workers and the middle classes, these events led to the formation of 'professional unions'. The setting up of a 'union of unions' in May 1905 symbolized the union of the different classes against the government.

The authorities were under mounting physical pressure. In February 1905 the Grand Duke Sergei, uncle to the Tsar and an unpopular governor of Moscow, was murdered. It was after this that the Tsar promised to call an elected consultative assembly. Meanwhile the Japanese defeated the Russians at Mukden and drove them out of southern Manchuria. In May the Russian Baltic fleet, having sailed to the Far East, was almost annihilated at Tsushima. Mutinies began to occur in the armed forces: that on the battleship *Potemkin* in the Black Sea is only the most famous. In August the plan for a consultative assembly was embodied in an imperial decree, but already in July a congress of *zemstva* and city representatives had met in defiance of the police and adopted a draft liberal constitution. In October there was a national railway strike—especially paralysing in a huge country like Russia—and a general strike in St Petersburg. There and in Moscow there were formed soviets (councils) representative of the workers of the city which henceforth undertook the protection of the workers' interests both political and economic; their activity and their situation in the capitals made it seem likely that they might make a bid for power.

Witte was called in to save the state. He only remained in office till the spring of 1906, but in a few months he transformed the situation. He had already performed an essential service by making the peace of Portsmouth with Japan in September, and in the course of the winter he carried through demobilization and restored order in the forces. But his first triumph was to induce the Tsar to issue the Manifesto of 30 October which gave Russia the beginnings of a parliamentary constitution and also created the office of Prime Minister, which he was given. The lower chamber, the State Duma, was to be elected by all householders. For this purpose they were divided into classes according to wealth, and each class chose its representatives, in most cases indirectly. The peasants, indeed, only joined in the election at two removes: they chose electors, who then chose further electors, who chose the representatives. The upper chamber, the State Council, consisted half of the Tsar's nominees—removable at any time—and half of the representatives of important bodies in the state, like the *zemstva*, the clergy and the universities. The two chambers shared legislative power with the Tsar, but he retained control of the executive and could legislate by decree when they were not sitting. Their financial powers were rather limited and they had no control over the budgets of the armed forces and the court.

The granting of the constitution began the splitting up of the opposition. The *zemstva* men were already divided: some insisted on a proper constitution and others would have been content with a consultative assembly. The former now formed the Constitutional Democratic party (known as the KDs—in Russian the Cadets), behind which rallied most of the professional middle class. The latter became the Octobrists, so called because the October constitution satisfied them: this party attracted big business and the more liberal bureaucrats. A much more important split took place between these parties and the working-class section of the opposition. For them, political concessions were important above all as the prelude to social change. In November 1905 the St Petersburg soviet ordered a strike for the eight-hour day. This was, of course, resisted by the employers, whereas previous strikes had had a good deal of sympathy from them. Both for this reason and because the hardships of strike action cannot be supported indefinitely, the strike failed and the strikers' movement ran down. In December the government arrested the leaders of the St Petersburg soviet and then dissolved it. The Moscow soviet rose in arms, but was eventually suppressed. It was noteworthy that the railway strike was not repeated and so troops could be sent from St Petersburg to Moscow.

The work set going by Witte had so far benefited the Tsar and the liberals fairly indifferently. His last achievement was particularly his own, and it benefited the Tsar exclusively and damaged the liberals more than anything else. In April 1906 a Russian loan of 2,250 million francs was floated in Paris—the largest ever made to a government. Imperial rivalries, in the shape of the Japanese war, had hitherto helped the revolution, but now they helped to halt it. This loan was Russia's reward for supporting France in the first Moroccan crisis. It saved the Tsar from financial collapse, and so from dependence on his people for keeping the government going. There had been a radical change since the sixties, when investors in western Europe had refused to lend to despotic Austria. Both economically and diplomatically, it now suited the ruling class in the liberal democracies that there should be a strong monarchy in the east. In fairness it should be added that the British and French governments, who both favoured the loan, favoured also the constitutional experiment in Russia, and hoped by this means to get it off to a good start. The fact remains that there is an ineluctable connection between this 'imperialism'—if that be the right word—and the failure of liberalism and ultimate triumph of totalitarian radicalism in Russia. Foreign capital tipped the balance against the native middle class and in favour both of the Tsar and the workers—by giving the former money and by causing the latter to expand faster than the middle class expanded. The foreign capitalists suffered in the end, of course: already in 1905 the Petersburg soviet warned foreign investors that a revolutionary government would not recognize debts contracted by the Tsar without the people's consent.

But for the financial factor, the first Duma which now met would have been well placed to seize the political initiative. The revolutionary parties—Socialist Revolutionaries and the two wings of the Social Democrats—had decided to boycott the elections, but they could not induce the mass of the electorate to do so. The conservatives were likewise disappointed in their hope that the mass of the peasantry would vote for them. About half the seats were won by the Cadets, and the greater part of the rest went to left-inclined independents and to socialists of various kinds who had ignored the party orders for a boycott. The Cadets and those to the left of them were agreed not only in desiring a democratic constitution but also in wanting land reform. The Duma presented an address to the throne on these lines, and when the government rejected it they passed a vote of censure and went on to consider plans for breaking up the great estates. The ministers hesitated and there were negotiations for a compromise, in which some of the parliamentary leaders would have been given office. But eventually the government decided to fight, and it had some success in putting the Duma in the wrong. An official statement warned the peasants that the break-up of large estates was a menace to private property both great and small and said that the government could do more for them than the Duma could. The Duma naturally replied with a manifesto of its own, but this was illegal and gave the government an excuse to dissolve the Duma (22 July 1906). The members of the left-wing majority fled to Viborg in Finland and published a manifesto calling on the people to refuse taxes and military service until the Duma was restored. This allowed the government to condemn them as grossly irresponsible, and those who had signed the manifesto were declared ineligible for election to future Dumas.

The second Duma, elected in February 1907, continued the discomfiture of the Cadets by the frightening of moderate opinion, thus making impossible the collaboration of the masses and the influential classes on which liberal success is commonly built. The socialist parties now saw that their boycott had been a mistake and they entered the elections in full force. The Cadets lost half their seats, and the independent socialists who had sat in the first Duma[1] were so reinforced by the socialist parties as to produce a socialist majority. The parties of the right were also strengthened. The government could safely let this assembly discredit itself in the eyes of the upper classes and thereby cure them of leanings to constitutional democracy. By June 1907 they judged the Duma sufficiently discredited to be disposed of. An alleged plot against the life of the Tsar was made the pretext for asking it to lift the immunity of the Social Democrat deputies so that they could be arrested. This request was not refused, but the Duma insisted on examining the evidence against its members itself. Before the commission of enquiry had finished its work, the Duma was dissolved.

The government now had the initiative and proceeded to reconstruction. Witte no longer headed it. His liberal measures were detested at court, and since violent repression continued to be necessary they were held to have failed. As soon as he had netted the French loan he was replaced by his old enemy Goremykin, but this elderly and spineless bureaucrat was not equal to fighting the first Duma. When the decision was taken to dissolve it, the premiership passed to the minister of the interior, Stolypin.

Peter Arkadievich Stolypin was born in 1862 and his career had been in local government: first as a marshal of the nobility, elected

[1] Known as *trudoviki* (labourites).

by the nobles and presiding over their own assembly and over the *zemstvo*, and then as a provincial governor. His rise to the ministry was due to the courage he had shown as governor of Saratov, an especially disturbed province, in 1905. Personally visiting the trouble spots, he strode into the midst of mobs and simply awed them into submission. His physical and moral stature were alike heroic, and though he had the force of character to govern as a dictator, he also had less need to do so than weaker men. When the Goremykin ministry slunk from the first Duma after suffering a vote of censure, Stolypin alone remained in his seat, for he was ready to face and fight parliamentary criticism. Opposed alike to reaction and revolution, he made the last attempt to save the throne by building up a strong body of conservative loyalists and adopting a progressive policy.

He first completed the restoration of order. With the crushing of the soviets and of the military mutinies, the government could turn to reducing the peasants to submission, and this was done with great brutality all through 1906. Then he set about remoulding the Duma, so that it could be a means of promoting co-operation between the government and the propertied classes. A high-handed decree revised the electoral law. Hitherto, although the different social classes had elected their representatives separately, the poorer voters had been represented more or less in proportion to their numbers. Now, although no one was disfranchised, the wealthier classes were given very much more than their fair share of seats. The third Duma, elected in the autumn of 1907, was totally unlike its predecessors. Cadets and socialists combined were well under a third of the house. The Octobrists were the largest party, and the extreme right were almost as numerous. Stolypin would have liked to take some of the moderate parliamentary leaders into the ministry, but this he had not influence enough to carry through. Good relations were, however, established between the more enlightened ministers and the Octobrist leaders, such as Alexander Guchkov. This made possible both some co-operation between government and Duma, and also some restraint on the reactionary side of the administration, whose policies could be shown to damage that co-operation and make the work of government needlessly hard.

But Stolypin had far bolder plans than the mere creation of a parliamentary oligarchy like those of southern Europe. He wanted to give his political experiment a mass basis by means of a great social reform. He took up and began to carry through Witte's design for the 'capitalist development' of Russian agriculture. It will be recalled that this involved the suppression of the old communal system of land tenure, so as to help the more enterprising peasants to acquire more land and manage it more efficiently. Many peasants would be driven off the land, but the prosperous farmers that remained would be more ready and able to feed the new industrial towns. What was now more important, they would become a conservative social force, like their equivalent in western Europe. Russian conservatives had hitherto resisted such reforms on the grounds that the peasants were conservative already, but the events of 1905–7 proved that this was not so, and the need for reform was therefore more generally accepted.

Stolypin's reforms were once more begun by emergency decree, in November 1906; other laws developed them in 1910–12. His main adviser was Andrew Kofoed, long in the Russian service, but born and trained in an agriculturally more advanced nation—Denmark. Several distinct processes were involved. Peasant holders were allowed to claim absolute property in the land they held, instead of being liable to have their holdings periodically increased or diminished according to the size of their families. If the system of redistribution was still in operation, they might in some cases have to pay compensation to the commune. But in 1910 it was laid down that the system should be totally abolished in any village where there had, in fact, been no redistribution since the emancipation. These measures were of little economic benefit while the holdings remained in the form of scattered strips in open fields, with the work of cultivation still largely in common. Proprietors were therefore empowered to demand the consolidation of their holdings. If two-thirds of the holders demanded it, all the land in a village was to be rearranged in this way. Before the War and further revolution put an end to the scheme, about a tenth of the 11·2 million holdings in European Russia had been consolidated, and upwards of two million had been removed from communal control. It is probable that the law of 1910 had ended redistribution in the case of as many more, while in some three million cases it had never existed. The payment of compensation for the abolition of serfdom was ended in 1906, and improving farmers received government loans and technical assistance. It must also be remembered that the rural community continued to benefit from the increasing migration to Siberia and the industrial towns and the considerable sale of nobles' and state lands to peasants, which the Peasants' Bank helped to finance.

A final feature of Stolypin's policy was his nationalism. The subject peoples of the empire had joined fully in the disturbances of 1905, had made various more or less ambitious claims to autonomy, and had been strongly actively represented in the first two Dumas. Stolypin severely restricted their representation in the third Duma and kept them in even stricter subordination than had many of his predecessors in the days of outright autocracy. He struck especially at the Finns and Poles. The attempt, already begun, to limit the very considerable antonomy and liberty enjoyed by the Finns was resumed, largely because of the needs of defence. In 1910 the Duma reserved to itself the power to legislate for Finland on a wide range of subjects, and reduced the Finnish diet to the status of a provincial assembly. The Finns resisted, and constitutional government there broke down. In 1911, *zemstvo* institutions were introduced into the western provinces of Russia which the Poles thought of as belonging to them, but where in fact only the nobility was Polish. The nobility were given less representation in the new *zemstva* than they enjoyed in those elsewhere. In 1912 a new province of Cholm, with a Ukrainian majority, was carved out of two of the Polish provinces, and in 1913 Polish towns were given councils which contained a large Russian element. Stolypin was here appealing to the strong Russian nationalist feeling among the Octobrists and conservatives in the Duma. This feeling was also apparent, as we shall see, in the more Slav-conscious foreign policy of his government.

The Stolypin experiment perished in the disasters of the First World War. What were its chances of success given the preservation of peace? Russia made notable industrial and social progress in the years before 1914. The censorship was greatly relaxed. From 1906 a law allowed the formation of trade unions, though as strikes were forbidden they were little more than friendly societies. In 1912 insurance against sickness and accident was established for industrial workers. The progress of public education among the younger people is shown by the fact that in 1914 as many as 73 per cent of army recruits were literate. The intellectuals were becoming less obsessed by politics: aesthetics and philosophy were ceasing to be treated in political or utilitarian terms, if only because political discussion was no longer completely prohibited and did not therefore have to be disguised as literary criticism and the like. But against all this remains the fact that Russia was still frantically building up her military and industrial greatness on the flimsy basis of a backward agriculture: more than half the peasant holdings were without an iron plough. A bad harvest in Russia, bringing famine; a good harvest elsewhere, bringing lower prices for Russian exports; a temporary tightness on the world's money markets—any of these commonplace happenings could produce the severest difficulties, as they had before.

What is certain, moreover, is that by 1914 the political situation was getting worse. The revolution of 1905 had helped the more progressive conservatives in some ways, but it had also stimulated the utter reactionaries. They had many sympathizers in the police and the administration, and might even reach the ear of the ruler. There was a growth of violent counter-revolutionary organizations such as 'black hundreds', who beat up intellectuals, supposed friends of the revolution and, above all, Jews. Pogroms increased during the revolutionary years, and the civil disabilities of the Jews remained though they were given the vote. It likewise remained a crime to convert anybody from the orthodox faith, though to be converted was now legal. Court reactionaries, like Trepov and Durnovo, plagued Stolypin in the Council of State, the new upper chamber. In 1911 they scored a notable success. The bill establishing *zemstva* in the western provinces already described was thrown out, because although anti-Polish it was also anti-noble. The bill had passed the Duma, and Stolypin once more resorted to the government's emergency powers to enact it. But in so doing he angered his friends in the Duma, who favoured the measure but were more interested in winning respect for the new constitutional laws. Soon afterwards (September 1911) Stolypin was assassinated at a theatre in Kiev, in the presence of the Tsar. The murderer belonged to a terrorist organization, but he was also a police spy and had got into the theatre with a police pass. There has always been a suspicion that an enemy of Stolypin's in the government was behind the deed.

Stolypin's successor was Kokovtsov, who had served as finance minister under both him and Witte. He was an enlightened but not a strong man, and he was quite unable to cope with a new disruptive influence: Rasputin. In 1904, after ten years of marriage and four daughters, the Tsarina had presented her husband with a male heir. The boy proved to be sickly and to suffer from haemophilia; it seemed unlikely that he would live. But the year after his birth, his parents found for him what they understandably came to regard as a miraculous preserver. The monk Gregory was only one of several charlatans who battened on this credulous pair, but behind his highly dubious piety there was a real power of some kind: by hypnotism or some other means he could stop the Tsarevitch bleeding, and is supposed on two occasions to have saved his life. The private character of this holy man is indicated by his nickname, for Rasputin means 'dissolute'. Not all were prepared to accept his own belief that his great sins had made for great repentance and from 1910, when his behaviour became worse, both the parliamentary leaders and the more liberal ministers strove for his removal. This aroused, in particular, the implacable fury of the Tsarina. Moderate conservatives like Guchkov, who wished to preserve the good repute of the dynasty, appeared to her to threaten her son's life; their interference in affairs of state she also resented as a threat to his right to rule autocratically, as his father had done. The Tsar tried, in defiance of the laws, to prevent the newspapers from mentioning Rasputin. In 1912 he dismissed the minister of the interior for having failed to prevent the agitation against him, and installed a hopeless reactionary. Kokovtsov's turn came early in 1914—like Witte, he was kept until he had succeeded in negotiating a huge French loan. He, too, was succeeded by the spineless Goremykin. The government was both falling to pieces and alienating the moderate conservatives who were its best hope for survival. By 1914 the Octobrists were tending to move towards the Cadets: the Duma was soon to have once more a left-centre majority in opposition.

Revolutionary activity was also beginning to revive. After 1905 there was a widespread feeling on the far left that peaceful agitation, directed against the régime but taking advantage of the new-won liberties, offered better prospects than conspiracy and violence. Lenin and his counterparts among the Socialist Revolutionaries disgusted their party comrades by the continuance of terrorism, even when the government was clearly strong enough to withstand it.

Lenin, in particular, aroused the somewhat naïve horror of socialists throughout Europe by making use of bank robberies and similar seriatim dispossessions of capitalists to swell the party funds. He was forced in 1910 to disgorge some of his ill-gotten gains, while within Russia the terrorists were increasingly worn down by the unremitting offensives of the secret police. Numerous police agents penetrated both Lenin's and the Socialist Revolutionary organizations and occupied key positions—though as we have seen, it was not always easy to tell for which side they were really working. By 1912 even the Bolsheviks seemed a little domesticated: they had a legal newspaper, *Pravda*, and their Duma deputies worked harmoniously with those of the Mensheviks. But Lenin, though increasingly desperate, never gave up. He now decided to end the pretence of unity with the Mensheviks in a single party and summoned a congress of his own supporters only at Prague, who claimed to speak for the whole Social Democratic movement but were, of course, disowned by the other factions. In 1912 there was a revival of violence which might seem to justify him. During a strike in the Lena goldfields troops fired on the workers. A series of political strikes in 1912–14 pointed to a renewal of revolutionary tension like that of ten years before.

Even had there been no war, there would almost certainly have been a great new political convulsion in Russia—which is not to say, of course, that it would have ended in a Bolshevik dictatorship. The immediate reason for this was that Stolypin had been able too readily to brush aside the oppositional Dumas. He and his more enlightened colleagues could therefore be brushed aside themselves, because they had no weapon to use against the reactionaries at court. Stolypin's experiment could only have worked if the Duma had been too strong to be set aside by the Tsar, but not strong enough, or extreme enough in its views, to seek to overwhelm him. This was the formula that lay behind Bismarck's successes in the sixties and seventies. Only the Duma of 1906 came near to fulfilling these requirements, and that is why its failure has such a significant place in the eventual and general failure of moderation in Russia.

Austria-Hungary and the South Slav Revival

Soon after the Tsar's October manifesto had initiated the Russian experiment in parliamentary government, the aged Francis Joseph made a still more daring appeal to democratic forces in the hope of saving his disintegrating realm. The campaign for a broader suffrage had always been for some a way to lessen the national antagonism within the Monarchy. The Austrian socialist Karl Renner applied to his country's affairs the classic Marxist view that workers everywhere had the same interests and should unite, and that national conflicts reflected only the interests of the bourgeoisie or else were used by them to sow discord among the workers. He called for a democratic Austria in which each national group would have autonomy in purely cultural matters. This international outlook was shared to some extent by the clerical parties: the Roman Catholic Church was not a national institution. Clericals and socialists might thus be expected to support a reforming imperial government against nationalist fanatics, and both could expect to gain seats if universal suffrage was introduced. The Russian revolution gave a certain urgency to these speculations. In November 1905 Francis Joseph declared himself converted. A manhood suffrage measure for the Vienna parliament eventually became law in 1907.

The ensuing elections produced a great weakening of the nationalist parties, as had been intended. Especially was this so because each nationality was allotted so many seats on the basis of its numbers and wealth, and they could no longer directly compete in elections. But it proved impossible to go on to satisfy the competing national claims in the government of the provinces. In 1905 Moravia had achieved such a settlement by amicable agreement between Czechs and Germans. Both seats in the provincial diet and jobs in the civil service were shared out in agreed proportions and, among other things, a two-thirds majority was required for certain kinds of legislation. Similar arrangements were eventually made in the province of Bukovina, but these remained exceptions. The rift between Czechs and Germans in Bohemia and between Ruthenians and the dominant Poles in Galicia remained particularly intractable. In the general election of 1911 nationalism recovered lost ground, the socialists in particular virtually splitting into separate national parties. Parliamentary government proved only intermittently possible, and in 1914 both Reichsrat and provincial diets were in abeyance.

But the democratic experiment in Austria was not foredoomed to failure. The nationalities continued for the most part to accept their association as inescapable. 'People have often spoken of the dissolution of Austria. I do not believe in it.' Thus in 1908 wrote Eduard Beneš who was to be one of the founders of the Czechoslovak Republic. While this was so, it remained possible to reinvigorate the state by restoring a sense of common purpose and efforts to this end continued. There was, for instance, Neoslavism, an attempt to end the religious and national quarrels among the Slavs so that they could unite against their common enemies. The reconciliation of Serbs and Croats described below was a striking instance of this, but especially important were the ramifications of the idea outside Austrian borders. After the revolution of 1905 the Poles were marginally better treated in Russia than in Germany, and a party led by Dmowski, for some time a Polish deputy in the Duma, was therefore willing to work for Russo-Polish reconciliation and Slav unity in general. As already mentioned, Russian foreign policy under Stolypin became more Slav-conscious and both Cadets and Octobrists included Slav enthusiasts. In 1908 the new idea was launched at a Slav conference at Prague, promoted by the Czech Kramar and the Slovene Hribar. Almost all the Slav peoples were represented, including the Russians and the Poles. Kramar visited Russia just before the conference to confer with his Russian sympathizers and was received by Stolypin.

Neoslavism was not an anti-Austrian movement. It envisaged a Slav predominance in a democratic Austria, which would then become the ally of Russia instead of Germany. This was by no means an impossibility. Austro-Russian relations had, in any case, been good since 1897, and the heir to the throne not only supported this policy but also had some sympathy with the Slavs at home. Francis Ferdinand was a curious paradox. Born in 1863, he was a grandson of the penultimate King of Naples and was an extreme conservative, with a distrust of humanity in general and a hatred of the Kingdom of Italy in particular. But he had contracted a morganatic marriage with a mere countess, which meant that his children were barred from the succession and that he was almost an outcast at court. He detested liberal Hungary even more than liberal Italy, and stood for the old Austrian conservative link with the Slavs. He interested himself in various plans to improve the position of the subject peoples of the Monarchy and, in particular, to raise the Rumanians and the south Slavs to equality with the Magyars. His death by violence in 1914 was not only the beginning of Europe's desolation but the end of Austria's possible regenerator.

What really brought to nought the campaign of adventurous reconstruction was Francis Joseph's continued refusal to quarrel with the obstructive Magyars. He was sorely tempted at the outset in 1905 when the refusal of the nationalist majority in the Hungarian parliament to govern in a way acceptable to him had led to the installation of a non-parliamentary ministry under General Fejervary. As in the struggle before the Ausgleich, the Magyars refused extensively to pay taxes and levy recruits. But if universal suffrage were introduced, parliament could be given a non-Magyar majority: Emperor and oppressed peoples might work together against a common enemy. Eventually the Emperor threatened to do this, if necessary by decree, and as an earnest of his intentions dissolved parliament in February 1906. The Magyar opposition at this gave in: it had, in any case, the weakness of being a coalition, some parties in which were hostile to democracy even among Magyars. It was agreed that the parliamentarians should take office, themselves reform the suffrage, and only then bring up again the army question on which they had quarrelled with the Emperor. A minor concession was made to them in the ensuing negotiations for a new economic agreement between the two halves of the Monarchy. In 1910 the nationalists split over whether to insist on a completely separate Bank of Hungary, and this enabled Stephen Tisza's reconstructed party to win a majority in the ensuing elections. Tisza became prime minister in 1913, having established a parliamentary dictatorship stronger than his father's and carried some unpopular military laws in the teeth of nationalist obstruction. In 1913 also, manhood suffrage was introduced, but so qualified as to ensure that most of the people would never vote. Dualism and Magyar supremacy had been assured.

It was essentially from the Hungarian crisis of 1905 that there arose at last a new wave of nationalism that in the last resort was against rather than within the Monarchy. This was among the southern Slavs. Since their great upheaval in the seventies (which was partly with Austrian encouragement) they had given relatively little trouble. The tendency of certain far-sighted intellectual leaders among them, like Bishop Strossmeyer, to consider them a single people had not won popularity. It was too contrary to their past history. Although closely akin in language, the Serbs belonged to the Greek and the Croats to the Roman church. This produced not only animosity but cultural estrangement: the two peoples used different alphabets. The Slovenes, who had done quite well under the Taaffe régime and increased their prosperity by a remarkable system of peasant co-operatives, concerned themselves little with the rest and tended to regard them as beyond the pale of civilization.

While they were divided, the southern Slavs were too weak to resist the Habsburgs. Croatia was supposed to be an autonomous kingdom federated with Hungary. The Austrian occupation of Bosnia in 1878 made the Croats restive: they saw a chance of expanding into a great Slav state. The Hungarian government accordingly determined to lessen Croat autonomy, and this was successfully done during the twenty-year rule of Count Charles Khuen-Hedervary, whom they appointed Ban (governor) in 1883. He managed to reduce the diet to subservience, relying on electoral corruption and the fact that some of the members were nominated and not elected. His most notable stratagem was to favour the Serb minority in Croatia against the Croat majority. A good many of them supported him against their fellow Slavs and as late as 1902 there were serious riots in which Serbs and Croats clashed. Meanwhile, the independent kingdom of Serbia remained closely dependent on the Austrians. This was the policy of the dynasty and it was supported on the whole by the urban clement in the country which was associated with the Austrian commercial enterprises engaged in its economic development. The peasant masses, represented by the Radical party, were kept in submission.

A great change began on both sides of the frontier in 1903. Khuen-Hedervary then moved to Budapest to become Hungarian prime minister, and his departure was followed by joint Serbo–Croat riots against the Hungarians. The ensuing breach between Hungary and the Emperor encouraged the Slavs to co-operate in order to take full advantage of such a golden opportunity. In 1905 Francis Supilo, a Croat leader in Fiume,[1] summoned a meeting of Croat leaders from both Austrian and Hungarian territories who called for the restoration of full Croat autonomy and the unification of Croatia and Dalmatia.

[1] The Hungarians had displeased the Croats by giving Fiume, which was dominated by Italians, virtual independence of Croatia.

They offered their support to the Magyar nationalists against
the Emperor if they would accept this programme. Even more significant, a meeting of Croatian Serbs at Zara subsequently endorsed
it, and representatives of both races finally petitioned the Emperor
to execute it. The southern Slavs had thus appealed to both sides in
the constitutional conflict, and while it continued they got fair
words from both. But when a compromise was reached, both combatants abandoned them: their reward was a new Hungarian law
making the use of Magyar obligatory in the administration of the
Croat railways. The Croats had similarly been betrayed after 1848,
and when the Emperor and Magyars had come to terms in 1867. At
last they were fully disillusioned. Henceforth, the Croatian diet was
dominated by a coalition of Serbs and Croats, and constitutional
government became impossible.

In 1903 there occurred another event which gave much more point
to these developments—the emancipation of Serbia from Austrian
tutelage. King Alexander had made himself unpopular in the ruling
clique by marrying (1900) an ambitious widow who gave him no
children and was suspected of desiring the succession for her brother.
He also exasperated the Radicals in 1903 by an illegal purge of parliament and the judiciary. Shortly afterwards he and his wife were
brutally murdered by a band of army officers. With him ended the
Obrenovich dynasty, and the throne was given to Peter Karageorgevich, whose family had a standing rival claim to it. The new king was
a picturesque old gentleman who had lived mainly abroad and
fought in two wars. With him there came to power the Radicals, and
a democratic constitution was established. But it was the officers of
the army who had carried through the revolution, and their political
power remained considerable. The regicides remained unpunished,
and in consequence several of the powers long considered the new
régime too disreputable for recognition.

The new Serbia was willing and able, as the old had not been, to
act as a rallying point for south Slav sentiment within the Dual
Monarchy. Francis Joseph hastened to recognize the new king because he was not personally hostile to the Austrians, whereas the
murdered Queen Draga had been pro-Russian. But the new government soon showed its colours by ending the old quarrel with Bulgaria
and concluding a treaty of commerce that was intended to lead to a

full customs union. The single large Slav state that the Austrians had always feared in the Balkans seemed to be coming into being at last, and the Serbs underlined the change by switching from the Austrian firm of Skoda to the French firm of Schneider for the supply of arms. In 1906, therefore, the Austrians refused to renew their treaty of commerce with the Serbs and closed their frontier to Serb products. The 'pig war', as it was called from the chief Serb export, lasted until 1908; the Serbs found other outlets for their products and eventually won a new, though less favourable, commercial treaty from the Austrians.

Even now, few aimed at complete union of the south Slavs. The Radicals of Serbia thought mainly of their fellow Serbs still under Habsburg and Turkish rule. The united Serbs and Croats of the Dual Monarchy thought less of dismembering the state in which they lived than of the achievement of autonomy, coupled with a close alliance with independent Serbia. But there was a steady trend towards closer links, especially among the younger people. In 1908 the president of the Croatian diet praised Garibaldi and the Italian *risorgimento*. Across the border the militant young nationalists of the Serb army supported a newspaper named *Piemont*, which revealed their ambition that Serbia should become the liberator of the neighbouring provinces from the Austrians, as the Cavourian kingdom had been of Lombardy-Venetia. Later, Croat students were to visit Serbia for demonstrations and hail Peter Karageorgevich as 'our king'; in 1912 many of them fought as volunteers for Serbia against the Turks. A national movement was in being which had a base on foreign soil and could seriously think of seceding from the Monarchy. Austrian fears of Serbia mounted, and increasingly perilous moves were made to put her in her place. In consequence, the Monarchy quarrelled fatally with Russia and completed the disillusionment of its own subjects. Neoslav dreams of an amicable reconstruction of eastern Europe perished. Instead, the deepening Austro-Hungarian crisis plunged Europe into the First World War.

4: The Coming of the First World War

The war of 1914 was due to the unbearable national tensions within Austria-Hungary and the attempts of that power to escape from them by action dangerous to peace. The continued existence of the Habsburg monarchy as a great power was the thing at stake in the war, at least to start with. To this extent the war was a European rather than a world conflict, and it was 'imperialist' only in the sense that Austria-Hungary had always been a multiracial state and the subject races were now rebelling against it. But the Austrian crisis could not have grown into a general war among the powers had there not been tensions among them which prevented effective co-operation in the preservation of peace. These tensions were the result of imperial rivalries, and often concerned regions far beyond Europe and hardly touched by the ensuing war.

The Background: the Completion of the Ententes

In 1904–7 Germany's diplomatic position worsened as the other powers drew closer together. But thanks to the collapse of Russia her military position had never been better. No power desired to quarrel with her, and she did not seriously try to use her military advantage to redress the diplomatic balance. Peace was not endangered.

The Anglo-French agreement of 1904 was mainly a simple settlement of differences, but contained one pointer to closer intimacy: a pledge of diplomatic co-operation to further British interests in Egypt and French in Morocco. Contrary to the common belief, it was the British who insisted on this,[1] and it first came into operation in Egypt in 1904. The other powers followed France in consenting to the abrogation of the international control over the country's finances. Germany lost her long-established power of pressure on the British by threats to vote against them in the international debt commission,

[1] G. Monger, *The End of Isolation* (1963), pp. 158–9.

and it was only rather grudgingly that the British undertook to respect German economic interests in Egypt. The Germans increasingly
feared that there might be worse to come. Russia's disasters in the Far
East might enable Delcassé to bring off a further great reconciliation
between her and Japan. The entente might become a quadruple
alignment centred on France. Another source of alarm to Germany
in 1904–5 was naval. The British public were at last fully aware of
the new German fleet, and bellicose remarks in British newspapers
and even by high personages in the Admiralty led the Germans to
fear that the British planned a surprise attack, such as the Japanese
had lately made on Port Arthur. Some Englishmen certainly would
have liked to sink the German fleet before it became strong enough
to be dangerous, but this never had a chance of becoming official
policy. The possibility of it, however, made the Germans very edgy.

A balancing policy having brought them increasing isolation, they
became anxious for a new, firm alliance. The obvious ally was Russia,
already on cordial terms both with themselves and the Austrians. The
first opportunity came with the Dogger Bank incident in October
1904. The Russian Baltic fleet, on its way to the Far East, fired on
some English fishing-boats in the North Sea on the supposition that
they were Japanese. The British demanded reparation and prepared
to intercept the Russian ships. The Kaiser suggested to the Tsar that
they joined to remind France of her obligations to her ally Russia,
thus creating a continental league against Britain. As the concrete
provisions of the Franco-Russian alliance were directed against
Germany, this was an odd suggestion and it came to nothing. The
dispute was referred to the Permanent International Court—a compliment to the Tsar who was in effect its creator. The Tsar declined
to enter an alliance with Germany without consulting France first,
which the Germans would not allow. The possibility recurred in the
summer of 1905, when the two Emperors, on their yachts, met at
Björkö, on the coast of Finland. The Kaiser's personal magnetism
drew the feebler Nicholas into the conclusion of a treaty, no minister
being present on either side. But in the autumn the Tsar once more
said that it should not apply until France had been consulted, and
later laid down that it was not to operate against France. This reflected the advent of revolution and the end of the Japanese war.
France had to be cultivated, for a French loan was essential to save

the state. Russia benefited from German friendship only when she was trying to expand in Asia. This for the time being she could not do, and anyway the Kaiser—against the wishes of Bülow and Holstein—had made his treaty inapplicable to Asia and so almost useless.

After the first failure with Russia, Germany tried to block France in Morocco. The Treaty of Madrid in 1880 had assured to all the powers most-favoured nation treatment there. In January 1905 the French sent a mission to Fez to make the Sultan reform his administration. In March the Germans replied with the Kaiser's visit to Tangier, where he declared his resolve to protect German trading interests and to treat the Sultan as an independent power. Soon afterwards an international conference was proposed, to save the country from French penetration. In appearance, the Germans were defending their treaty rights—indeed, those of all the powers. In fact, their purpose was to disenchant France with the entente by showing her that she could not win Morocco without German approval. Germany's own trade with Morocco was too small to lead her to do what she did. There was a good chance that Germany would succeed. The French radicals, now in the ascendant, were men of peace and so were those interested in French colonial expansion or—like Rouvier the prime minister—in overseas investment. They had backed the entente because it seemed a policy of peace but ceased to do so when it seemed to involve tension with Germany. In April Delcassé was so strongly attacked on both the right and the left of the chamber that he offered his resignation. He was induced to withdraw it, but the Germans encouraged the belief that his policy was making for war by refusing to negotiate with him. Behind his back, Rouvier let the Germans know his own desire for conciliation. Germany eventually announced that she would invade France if Morocco was attacked. At a Cabinet meeting on 6 June, Delcassé declared that this was bluff and France should stick to her guns. Rouvier and the other ministers disagreed with him and he resigned, the premier himself succeeding him. His departure, though rightly seen as a triumph for Germany, did not at once mean a change of policy. Rouvier had thought, with some reason, that it was the man and not the policy which had aroused hostility, and he had no wish to abandon Morocco. But when he found that the German line did not change, he gave way to their demand for a conference.

The Germans might have succeeded completely had not the second chance of a Russian alliance obliged them to reverse their policy. They had to conciliate the French in order not to antagonize the Russians, and therefore gave up the idea of forcing on them an agreed programme to be submitted to the conference. This therefore met, at Algesiras in January 1906, with the Moroccan question still wide open. The Germans hoped that most of the powers would concur with them in wishing to maintain the 'open door'. But in fact Britain, Spain and Italy were already pledged to France, Russia had decided to remain her ally, the United States was determined to keep out of European quarrels and even the Austrians gave only half-hearted support. The conference imposed a plan of reforms on the Sultan and on the question of greatest political significance followed French views and rejected those of Germany. The organization of the police in the eight chief ports was entrusted to France and Spain instead of being shared with officers from less interested powers. Germany meekly accepted the decisions of the conference, and Holstein, the main advocate of a tough policy, was dismissed. The attempt to show France that she could do nothing against German wishes had failed.

But Germany did not come empty-handed from the conference. The international regulation of Moroccan affairs meant that France could not now absorb it without concluding an agreement with Germany similiar to those with Britain, Italy and Spain. The Algesiras Act contained many concessions to German views, notably in the details of the organization of the international bank to be set up in Morocco, and in the establishment of international control over the Franco-Spanish police. France remained unwilling to quarrel with Germany, and the other powers, though they almost all refused to help Germany, were loath to help France either. This appears most interestingly in the course of Franco-British relations in 1905–6. In April 1905 Lansdowne told the French that he would be ready to join in 'strong opposition' to a rumoured plan of the Germans to press for a Moorish port. Ambassador Cambon led Delcassé to think that the British were working up to the offer of an alliance, and it was this that was Delcassé's main argument for stiffness at the fatal cabinet meeting on 6 June. But Lansdowne told Cambon explicitly that his aim was 'absolute confidence' between their governments, to prevent French concessions to Germany at Britain's expense. Both Lansdowne and his successor Grey warned the Germans that if they attacked France, public opinion would probably force the British government to come to her defence. Grey even sanctioned (without telling the cabinet) military staff talks to prepare for help to France in such an event. But Grey pressed the French as hard as he dared to make concessions to Germany and he stood by her for fear that Britain would otherwise lose her friendship and once more be isolated. The staff talks (which came to little at this time) were essentially a substitute for the pledge of armed support which the French now wanted and Grey neither would nor could give.

The ending of the Moroccan crisis left the way open for the un-rolling of the consequences of Russia's Far Eastern defeat and internal collapse, which Germany's feverish activity had been largely designed to prevent. The peace treaty of September 1905 was moderate, giving Japan Port Arthur and supremacy in Korea, but leaving Russia in control of most of Manchuria. It was preceded in August by a renewal and extension of the Anglo-Japanese alliance: Japan agreed that the alliance should cover India as well as the Far East, and Britain agreed that it should operate if either power was attacked by another power—not as before, by two powers. Russia was henceforth firmly contained, both in eastern and central Asia, and her internal situation made it essential anyway for her to keep quiet. Unfortunately, the revolution brought a new foreign minister (April 1906) only imperfectly attuned to the situation. Alexander Isvolsky was an able diplomat long marked out for promotion. He was also a liberal and nearly resigned when the first Duma was disposed of. Vain and ambitious, he thirsted for diplomatic glory at a time when his country's only need was repose and recuperation. His policy was an unhappy attempt to combine the two. He wished to put the disputes with Britain and Japan on ice in order to undertake a more ambitious policy in Russia's traditional stamping ground in the Near East. He was opposed in this particularly by the army. Partly this was because they did not wish to retire ignominiously from the existing battlefields, but even more it was because they feared a quarrel with Germany in their weakened state after the Japanese war. Isvolsky met this second objection: he had no wish to be another Delcassé.

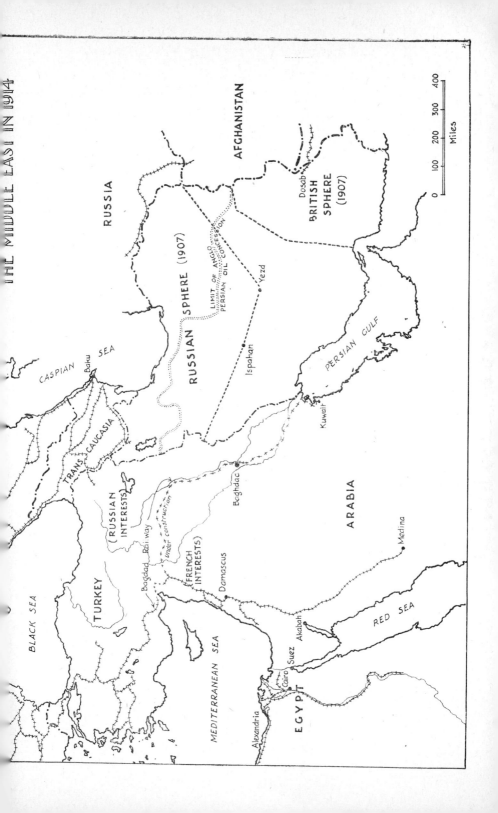

THE MIDDLE EAST IN 1914

In October 1906 he visited Germany and ascertained that there would be no objection to an agreement with Britain. In 1907 he was able to make treaties with both Britain and Japan. Manchuria was divided into Russian and Japanese spheres of influence. In Persia the British agreed not to challenge Russian ascendancy in the north, and the Russians promised not to disturb the British in Seistan, the province adjacent to India. Afghanistan and Tibet were to remain buffer states. The two treaties were essentially parts of a single operation: Isvolsky held up negotiations with the British while he was uncertain of the attitude of the Japanese and both Britain and France used their influence to make them come to terms with the Russians.

What was the forward aspect of Isvolsky's policy, to which this settling of old scores was the preliminary? In part, he wished to put himself in a good position to deal with Germany over the Baghdad railway. The Russians and British each feared that the other might do a deal with the Germans that would weaken their own position on the Persian Gulf. Isvolsky now induced the British to promise not to negotiate separately about the Baghdad railway. But he gave no undertaking to take their side against the Germans and would not include the Gulf area in Persia in the arrangement of spheres of influence, as the British wished. More important was Isvolsky's desire to see the Straits open to Russian warships. The British soon realized that they stood a much better chance of reaching an agreement if they made an offer on this question, and they unofficially declared their wish to see Russian desires fulfilled, though they thought the time not yet ripe. The opening of the Straits would have strengthened Russia's general Balkan position and probably annoyed the Central Powers. But it was really a question which interested Britain and not Austria-Hungary; there is no real evidence that Isvolsky intended with it to depart from the policy of co-operation with the Austrians followed since 1897. Russia's turn towards the west was not, therefore, a turning against either of her western neighbours. Moreover, the treaty of 1907 did not commit Britain and Russia to future diplomatic co-operation, and relations between them never became nearly as close as those between Britain and France. The growth of the ententes had unfortunate repercussions for Germany, but she was in no way 'encircled' by enemies.

The Crucial Crises: Bosnia and Agadir

It was in 1908 that the international situation began to deteriorate because of plans to use diplomacy and even war as a way out of the impasse in Austria-Hungary. There, as in Russia, a new foreign minister took office in 1906. Baron Alois Aehrenthal, the grandson of a Jewish merchant who had worked his way up to a title, was, like Isvolsky, a clever man eager to strike a great stroke. His main aim was to transform the occupation of the Turkish provinces of Bosnia and Herzegovina into an outright annexation. Once the Austrian occupation had lost the appearance of being temporary, he hoped that it would be possible to build up an autonomous south Slav unit within the Monarchy, thereby ending the agitation for union with Serbia. More generally, he wished to show by a dramatic gesture that the Dual Monarchy had not lost its vitality and was still a great power. This was also the aim of Conrad von Hötzendorf, who became chief of the Austrian general staff at this time. He called repeatedly for preventive wars against both Serbia and Italy. Aehrenthal toyed with the idea of crushing Serbia, and certainly hoped eventually to dominate it. But he did not want the embarrassment of more Slav territory for the Monarchy, and he did not want to quarrel with Russia. He had himself been ambassador at St Petersburg and one of the architects of the prevailing Austro-Russian entente. True, his first move, early in 1908, was the aggressive project of a railway through the Sanjak of Novibazar, the Austrian-occupied strip of territory between Serbia and Montenegro. This seemed to portend an Austrian offensive in the Balkans and angered the Russians, who replied with a plan for a railway from Belgrade to the Adriatic. But these railway projects soon disappeared. Aehrenthal intended from the first to evacuate the Sanjak when he annexed the other provinces, to reassure the powers and show that his aims were defensive.

Isvolsky for his part was not against the project of annexation, and hoped by agreeing to it to gain Austrian support for his plan of opening the Straits to Russian warships. After preliminary soundings in the autumn of 1907, he made a formal offer to this effect in July 1908, and in September the two ministers met and discussed it at Buchlau in Bohemia. Here a momentous misunderstanding took place. Isvolsky thought that it had been agreed to carry through the proposed programme by means of a general revision of the Berlin settlement of 1878. He accordingly went on a tour of the European capitals to win support for his Straits project. But Aehrenthal really intended to carry through the annexation by unilateral action, and this was done at the beginning of October, Isvolsky and the other powers receiving only a few days' notice. At the same time, Bulgaria threw off the suzerainty of Turkey and declared herself independent. This was with Austrian encouragement and inaugurated the Austrian policy of using Bulgaria against the Serbs.

Aehrenthal had a genuine reason for hasty action in the Young Turk revolution which had broken out in July. A military revolt forced the Sultan to restore the constitution which had been proclaimed in 1876 and almost immediately abrogated. An elected parliament met in September. The Young Turks were essentially nationalists, but at first they were strongly liberal and tried hard to befriend their Christian fellow citizens, who were given parliamentary representation. It became urgent for the Austrians to end Turkish sovereignty in the occupied provinces, lest the new government supported anti-Austrian demands for autonomy by the Slav population. But though he denied it, there is little doubt that Aehrenthal deliberately stole a march on his Russian colleague, deceiving him as to his plans if not by lying then at least by evasions. Isvolsky had so compromised himself that he could not effectively object to the annexation, but it became increasingly doubtful if he could collect the promised reward. His supposed friends the British refused to implement their half-promise to agree to the opening of the Straits. They wished to avoid a further shock to Turkey, now really bent on liberal reform (and incidentally showing signs of turning from Germany to Britain). Isvolsky was furious, and the entente with Russia which had protected the Dual Monarchy against nationalism was at an end.

But though Aehrenthal's foolish cunning had precipitated this disaster, his policy was such an affront to Slav sentiment that a serious crisis was probably inevitable. Russian opinion in and outside the government was totally averse to Isvolsky's plan (till then secret) of opening the Straits by making concessions to the Austrians at the expense of the Serbs. Stolypin threatened to resign. Isvolsky had to defend himself in the Duma against the charge of being a traitor to Slavdom. The fact was that his plan for the Straits was of small value to Russia,[1] while the concessions he had offered were totally at variance with the Slav enthusiasm strong in the government and parliament of post-revolution Russia. Aehrenthal, indeed, was able to blackmail him by threatening to reveal exactly what his offers had been.[2] Serbia meanwhile demanded the ending of annexation or something in exchange, mobilized, and established a national society (*narodna obrana*) to organize propaganda and military training among all south Slavs that could be reached. No other country was prepared to do more than protest against the annexation. But to Serbia it meant the formal ending of a possibility of territorial expansion that had at least seemed to remain open. Aehrenthal, rather reluctantly, began to prepare for war against Serbia in the spring.

Angry though the two Slav states were, there was never any real likelihood of their accepting battle. Russia had not yet recovered sufficiently to be able to come to Serbia's aid. But Germany chose to intervene and accelerate their surrender in a humiliating way. Bülow encouraged Aehrenthal to act against Serbia as strongly as he thought fit, promising German protection in all circumstances. In January 1909 Moltke, the German chief of staff (nephew of the victor of 1870), officially promised Conrad that if Austria-Hungary attacked Serbia and was herself attacked by Russia, Germany would mobilize in her defence. In February Grey tried to induce the powers to mediate between the Austrians and Serbs, but Germany insisted that the proper step was collective pressure on Serbia to submit. Isvolsky warned the Serbs that resistance was useless, and Aehrenthal let it be known that they would receive economic concessions if they gave in. Eventually Serbia renounced all claims to compensation, and promised to do whatever the powers directed. Germany now undertook to get a formal recognition of annexation from all the powers, as a preliminary to forcing the same on Serbia. Russia was asked first, and gave a reply that was conciliatory but not unequivocal. She was then told (21 March) that if she did not reply with a simple 'yes' Germany would 'withdraw and let things take their course'. She thereupon capitulated, and eventually Serbia, too, surrendered.

---

[1] The Straits were to be closed to warships not from Black Sea countries, but only one Russian ship at a time might pass through.
[2] They had included the Sanjak.

German action went beyond the letter of the Austro-German alliance, which was purely defensive, and which Bismarck had refused to interpret as obliging Germany to cover Austrian adventures in the Balkans. This change in the German interpretation of the alliance was to be of crucial importance in 1914, but was probably not what governed German policy in 1909. The Germans realized that Russia could not fight, and their March 'ultimatum' went out at a time when both Isvolsky and Aehrenthal were being conciliatory and English and Italian efforts at mediation were going well. Their concern was not so much to help Austria-Hungary as to prove to Russia that the friendship of the western powers was useless and that German friendship was essential to them. Even the Austro-German staff consultations seem to have been connected with this, for they sprang from a German fear that the Austrians were coming to see Italy as the main enemy, and that in the event of war they would take the offensive there and stand on the defensive against Russia. The Germans were trying once more to escape from isolation. By itself, Germany's action against Russia seems foolish. The disastrous Austro-Russian breach was aggravated by Russian resentment against Germany. But German policy towards Russia was given great effectiveness by simultaneous developments in German relations with Britain and France. At the very time that Bosnia was annexed, the Moroccan animosity between France and Germany broke out afresh. The German consul at Casablanca was frustrated by the French in an attempt to organize the escape of some German deserters from the foreign legion. Tempers ran high, and the dangers of this when war threatened in the Balkans was obvious. The Germans took advantage of the fact that France was still governed by the peace-loving radicals who had repudiated Delcassé. In February 1909 an agreement was signed in which Germany recognized France's claim to political predominance in Morocco, and in return France agreed that the economic development of the country—the building of railways and so forth—should be undertaken by the nationals of both countries in co-operation. Soon after this the French followed the German lead in calling for pressure on Serbia as the way to end the Bosnian crisis, and they felt safe enough to tell the Russians in no uncertain terms that they would not come to their rescue if they went to war in defence of Serbia. In other words, their attitude was the exact reverse of

Germany's towards the Austrians. The Russians were probably as angry with them as with the Austrians and Germans.

It was at this same time that British fears of the German navy reached their height. The ultimate origin of the scare was the building of the *Dreadnought* in 1905–6. She rendered all other battleships obsolete. This was as damaging to Britain as to her rivals, for she had a large superiority in old ships and a lead of only one in the new. Many English experts therefore thought it a mistake to build the *Dreadnought*, but it was probably safest to anticipate the other powers with similar plans. The fact remained that the Germans had, for the first time, a real chance to catch up. Several years of anxiety followed until it became clear that they had not the will or resources to do so. The worst scare began at the end of 1908, when the story got about that the Germans were secretly preparing to build faster. The opposition in Britain campaigned for eight new battleships instead of four, and the government eventually gave way. This led on to Lloyd George's revolutionary budget to pay for the ships, and the struggle with the house of lords. The Germans were alarmed by the coincidence of all this with the Bosnian business and by fears that they might soon face a hostile British conservative government. They began to take seriously the frequent British requests for an agreement to limit armaments. This was something quite against their principles and offended the Kaiser especially. But from 1909 they tried to interest the British in schemes by which they would promise to build neither more nor faster. The British, in return, were to promise to limit their construction and—more important—to stay neutral if Germany became involved in a European war. What they hoped to gain by this may best be considered later on. It was clearly a bad bargain for the British: they would not save money and they would anger their entente friends and risk isolation. They did not therefore accept it.

Nevertheless, relations between Russia and Britain deteriorated, though not as badly as those between Russia and France. British radical opinion was disgusted by the way in which the Russians used the free hand that the British had given them in north Persia. The nascent Persian constitutional movement, which the British would have supported but for the entente, was crushed. The Russians, for their part, were suspicious because the Anglo-German talks that had now started included negotiations about the Baghdad railway. They were, in any case, alarmed because the extension of the railway could not be delayed much longer. Britain and Russia had used the system of international controls over Turkish finance to delay the giving of the necessary financial guarantees to the German company, but this could work only for a time. The result was that the Russians made an entente with Germany parallel to that with Britain over Persia.

In September 1910 the discredited Isvolsky retired to the lucrative and influential embassy in Paris. His successor, Stolypin's brother-in-law Sergei Sazonov, was a man who gave most people the impression of not knowing his own mind. But his more cautious and colourless policy was much more appropriate to Russian weakness than Isvolsky's. He began with a visit to Germany and there concluded the 'Potsdam agreement', by which Germany recognized Russia's position in north Persia, and Russia promised not to block the ingress of German trade there and to tolerate the Baghdad railway and its linking by a branch with their own Persian railways. This agreement was similar to the one which the Germans had made with France over Morocco, but the Germans insisted on adding a Russian pledge of neutrality similar to the one they proposed to the British. Their object, indeed, was to get something which would induce the British to sign. The Russians refused this extra condition, and the agreement remained unratified. It nevertheless achieved the loosening of the bonds of the entente to the benefit of Germany. The British ministry got wind of it, and the anti-Russian radical element forced Grey to offer the Germans a 'political formula' and a colonial understanding. A little later, in 1911, the second Moroccan crisis broke out and Germany thereupon waived her demand for the promise of neutrality which had delayed ratification. In the very words which the French had used about Bosnia in 1909, the Russians now said that they could not support France in a quarrel that was no concern of theirs.

This crisis, however, was to reverse the new trend in Germany's favour. It was caused by the progressive disintegration of the Moorish government, which by 1911 had gone so far that the French felt it necessary to occupy Fez. Though this was supposed to be temporary, it was clear that the moment for the establishment of a French protectorate had come. But this meant a breach of the Algesiras Act, for which the consent of the powers was necessary. France had secured the consent of almost all the powers likely to care, but the Germans proceeded to claim compensation for the projected expansion of French power. By the standards of the day this was perfectly legitimate, but the Germans made a foolish use of their strong position. The responsibility for this lies with Kiderlen-Wächter, who had become foreign secretary in 1909. An able but brutal diplomat, relegated for many years to the Bucharest embassy because he had displeased the Kaiser, he perpetuated the bullying tradition of Holstein, supposedly derived from Bismarck. According to himself, he was the man responsible for the 'ultimatum' to Russia in 1909. He now induced the reluctant Kaiser and Chancellor to let him try and score a really big victory by a show of force. On 1 July the German gunboat *Panther* appeared off the south Moroccan port of Agadir. On 15 July Kiderlen asked for the whole of the French Congo as compensation for Morocco and threatened 'to proceed very forcibly'. Caillaux, just become French premier, was embarrassed, for his aim was friendship with Germany. He tried to put things right by private negotiations behind the back of his own foreign minister. The French foreign office, however, told the British of the German demand and asked for help in resisting it. Grey and his critics were temporarily able to work together. Grey thought that if the French gave way it would amount to putting themselves under German protection and was ready to help them in order to stiffen them. The radicals feared that the Germans would end by keeping Agadir and a slice of Morcoco and would gain a valuable naval base, for which Britain would get no equivalent. This was what Lloyd George meant in his famous speech at the Mansion House on 21 July by saying that Britain could not bear to be 'treated where her interests were vitally affected as if she were of no account in the Cabinet of nations'. France and Germany were not to do a deal at her expense.

It was as much the behaviour of Caillaux as that of Kiderlen that had made this likely, but the British do not appear to have realized till later how eager he was to settle with Germany. It was the Germans whom Grey officially warned, and they took Lloyd George's words as meant for them and were bitterly angry: Britain seemed to them to be selfishly hindering reconciliation with France. Anti-German elements in France were correspondingly encouraged.

Serious preparations began for war with Germany, and it was at this time that the commitment represented by the Anglo-French staff talks became a serious one. Hitherto, the navy had always opposed the sending of British troops to France in the event of a German war because they wanted them for amphibious operations. Even the War Office had not been keen on the idea. Now the Committee of Imperial Defence overruled the navy, and the British and French staffs were allowed to plan on the basis that British troops would be available to hold a sector of the French front in the event of war. This would make it morally much harder for the British not to come to France's help if she was at war with Germany.

War, however, was not to come this time. Even before the Mansion House speech, Kiderlen had only just managed to keep his superiors in line. After it, it was obvious that he had miscalculated badly. On 2 August he had to offer to accept part of the Congo only as compensation for a French protectorate over Morocco, and it was on this basis that an agreement between France and Germany was signed on 4 November. It was followed by an outburst of patriotic rage in both countries, and in January 1912 Caillaux was overthrown. With him there ended the policy of appeasing Germany which had ruled in France since the fall of Delcassé.

In 1909–10 Germany had almost repeated the success of Britain in escaping from 'splendid isolation' by making friends with France and thereby making it easier to drive a bargain with France's ally Russia. In view of the continuing tension resulting, as will be shown, from the south Slav problem, this combination was an important safeguard of European peace. Formerly Germany had used good relations with Russia to restrain France. Now she needed good relations with France, so that when trouble recurred in the Balkans France would, as in 1909, restrain Russia. But in the Agadir crisis the Germans put colonial ambitions above their European needs. They both offended and frightened France, and they drove Britain closer to her. Pacific sentiment in France would not henceforth counteract those many influential Russians who smarted under their worsting by Germans and Austrians. Peace had become decisively less secure.

Austrian Misfortunes in the Balkans

Meanwhile, Aehrenthal's great Bosnian stroke had produced such a building up of animosity among his neighbours that the Monarchy's Balkan position grew worse instead of better. Among those offended were the Italians, who repudiated the complacency of Tittoni, the foreign minister, in face of Austrian aggrandisement. Isvolsky's last important move as foreign minister was the making of a secret understanding with Tittoni at Racconigi in October 1909. Italy's claims in Tripoli and Russia's in the Straits question were endorsed by it, and the two powers agreed to co-operate in maintaining the *status quo* in the Balkans and the application there of the principle of nationality. Isvolsky told the Russian ministers to the three Slav states in the Balkans of this agreement, and encouraged them to promote the solidarity of those countries.

The purpose of these arrangements was defensive—against supposed Austrian ambitions for more Balkan territory. Russia hoped at first to include Turkey in the anti-Austrian front, and the purpose of the Potsdam agreement was, in part, to induce Germany to restrain Austria-Hungary. But in Italy and the Balkans interest soon shifted to Turkey. After thirty years of torpor, the old empire seemed on the point of regeneration by the Young Turks, and her neighbours were eager to take the slices of her that they had long coveted, before the opportunity vanished. As already noticed, this helps to explain the suddenness of the annexation of Bosnia and also the Italian attack on Tripoli in the autumn of 1911. All the powers had by now acknowledged her claims there, and the confusion of the second Moroccan crisis was an ideal occasion to assert them. Hostilities spread to the Aegean and aroused Balkan hopes. In September 1911 Hartwig, a rabid panslav whom Isvolsky had made Russian minister in Belgrade, induced the government there to negotiate with Bulgaria, and in March 1912 an alliance between the two countries was signed. Ostensibly it was a defensive alliance, including provision for resistance if a great power invaded Turkey. These anti-Austrian provisions were of great value to Serbia. But Bulgaria had no quarrel with the Austrians, and aimed at winning Turkish territory. Her interest was rather in the secret annexe which provided for military action against the Turks. Russia was given a say in deciding when this was appropriate, and in dividing up the conquests. Greece and Montenegro were drawn into the alliance in the summer: Greece, too, had no quarrel with Austria-Hungary, and her immediate object was to acquire Crete.[1] That same summer conservative revolts broke out against Young Turk rule, and the moment for attack had clearly come. In October the allies attacked Turkey, and in less than two months they had, to the general surprise, virtually ended Turkish rule in Europe. Only Constantinople and three fortified towns held out. The Turks had declined very far since 1877, when they had nearly beaten the Russians.

Anti-Austrian resentments had thus backfired against Turkey, and for this reason there was at this stage no real danger of European war. The Russians were not well suited by the way things turned out. Their first reaction to the Libyan war had been to offer a guarantee to Turkey in return for the opening of the Straits. When Sazonov found that his policy was leading to a Balkan war he almost panicked, and pushed forward Poincaré to propose an intervention of the powers both to reform Turkey and to protect her. Austria-Hungary had earlier made a similar proposal, and had the strongest reasons to intervene. Serbia and Montenegro, occupying the Turkish territory that lay between them, were bringing into being the solid Serb bloc, which the Austrians had always feared and which they had formerly tried to prevent by occupying the Sanjak of Novibazar themselves. This was the moment at which they could have attacked Serb nationalism with much appearance of right on their side, since the Serbs were the aggressors. But Aehrenthal had died in February and been replaced by Count Berchtold, a pleasure-loving aristocrat with little mind of his own, heavily dependent on his subordinates for knowledge and ideas. Like Aehrenthal he had been ambassador in St Petersburg, and began with a strong wish for good relations with Russia. He did not wish to fight the Serbs, and nor did anyone else except Conrad, temporarily out of office. Ultimately this was because it was realized that strong measures against them could only succeed if the Monarchy was prepared to treat its own south Slavs justly and to annexe or federate with a defeated Serbia. The dominant Magyars were not prepared to do either. Since neither Austria-Hungary nor Russia wished to follow a forward policy—though both took military measures—the other powers, too, could stay at peace: in December 1912 an international conference met in London to tidy up after the war.

[1] Crete had been autonomous under an international commissioner since 1897, when Greece had unsuccessfully attacked Turkey.

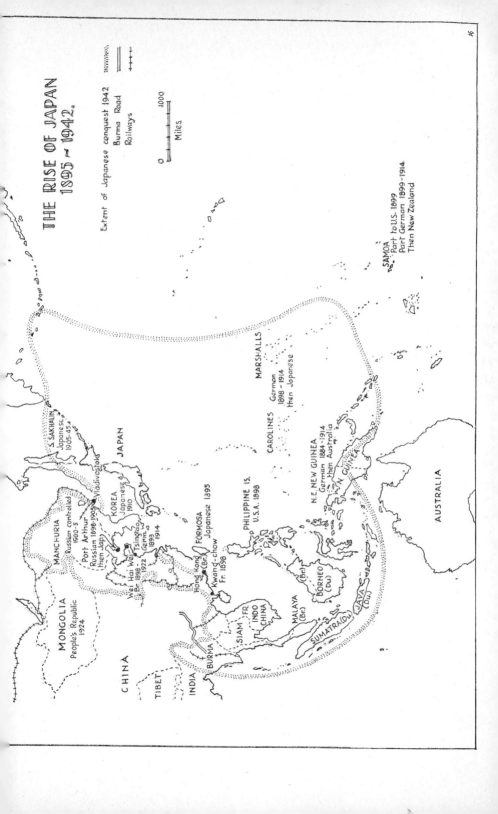

THE RISE OF JAPAN 1895 ~ 1942.

Extent of Japanese conquest 1942

Burma Road

Railways

0 — 1000
Miles

MONGOLIA
People's Republic 1924

CHINA

TIBET

INDIA

BURMA

SIAM

FR. INDO CHINA

MANCHURIA
Russian controlled 1900-5

Port Arthur
Russian 1898-1905
then Jap.

Vladivostok

S. SAKHALIN
Japanese 1905-45.

JAPAN

KOREA
Japanese 1910

Wei Hai Wei Br. 1898-1922

Tsingtao, Germ. 1899 1914

FORMOSA
Japanese 1895

Hong Kong (Br.)

Kwang-chow Fr. 1898

PHILIPPINE IS.
U.S.A. 1898

MALAYA (Br.)

SUMATRA (Du.)

BORNEO (Du.)

JAVA (Du.)

N. NEW GUINEA

N.E. NEW GUINEA
German 1884-1914 then Australia

CAROLINES
German 1898-1914 then Japanese

MARSHALLS
German 1898-1914 then Japanese

SAMOA
Part to U.S. 1899
Part German 1899-1914
Then New Zealand

AUSTRALIA

The Monarchy here made an ingenious attempt to limit the damage to her Balkan position resulting from the eclipse of Turkey in Europe, but though she received some help from the powers she ended up worse off than ever. She called for the establishment of Albania as an independent state, mainly with the object of denying to the Serbs an outlet to the Adriatic through Scutari and its port of San Giovanni di Medua. Since the Albanians were not Slavs and mainly Moslem, this was a 'nationalist' solution which Slav Russia and liberal Britain could honourably support. In the spring of 1913 Montenegro had to be bribed to leave Scutari, and in the autumn the Serbs were only got off Albanian territory by an Austrian ultimatum. But an independent Albania was brought into being, though only on paper. The disappointed Serbs sought compensation in Macedonia at the expense of Bulgaria. The peace with Turkey in May 1913 was followed by a deepening rift between the former allies over the division of this province, and at the end of June, Tsar Ferdinand of Bulgaria attacked the others without even telling his own government—a wicked and foolish move which, however, only anticipated similar plans by the Serbs. It was part of Austrian policy to use Bulgaria against the Serbs, and so Bulgaria received Austrian encouragement.

But Bulgaria was easily beaten by Serbia and Greece. Turkey joined them and recovered Adrianople. So did Rumania, which had resented the expansion of Bulgaria from the first, and had been demanding territorial compensation from her. Austrian policy was not this time supported by Germany, for three of Bulgaria's enemies were protégés of Wilhelm II: Rumania, where a Hohenzollern ruled; Greece, where his brother-in-law was king; and Turkey. After the despoiling of Bulgaria, the Balkans were dominated by Rumania, Serbia and Greece, who kept together to maintain their gains. Austro-Bulgarian friendship made this grouping anti-Austrian, quite apart from the fact that both Serbia and Rumania had large *irredenta* under Austro-Hungarian rule. The change in the attitude of Rumania, the strongest Balkan state, was especially notable. She was technically a member of the Triple Alliance, but this had never been popular and the Bulgarian war was the last straw. Her relations with Russia were notably cordial in 1914. Austria-Hungary's immediate enemy, Serbia, therefore emerged from the Balkan wars much strengthened in territory and allies.

This was the situation at the moment of the Sarajevo murders on 28 June 1914. It is customary to say that the killing of the Archduke Francis Ferdinand and his wife was only the pretext for a war for which much grander causes were really responsible. Of course, the Archduke's death was not itself sufficient to start a war, but its importance must not be underestimated. Austrian—still more Hungarian—statesmen shrank from a conclusive battle with Serbia. They were making ready at that very moment to swallow a fresh unwelcome strengthening of Serbdom—a projected union of Serbia and Montenegro—provided that they could secure the Montenegrin coast for Albania. But the Archduke's murder was both a challenge and an opportunity which could not be evaded. It was the culmination of the whole south Slav agitation, and there was little doubt from the first that Serbs were implicated. It is clear now that the assassins were supplied with weapons and smuggled into Bosnia by conspirators in the Serb army and administration, chief among whom was the head of Military Intelligence, Colonel Dragutin Dimitrievich, one of the assassins of King Alexander. There is even reason to think that the Serb premier, Pashich, got wind of the plot from a police spy and that an ineffectual attempt was made to warn the Austrians. Against the conspirators and their melodramatic secret society the Black Hand, the Serbian government was almost helpless. It had only just got through a violent quarrel with the army about the administration of the newly won Macedonian territory, which had nearly ended in a military coup. It dared not offend nationalist sentiment in the army. Although the facts of the situation could only be divined in July 1914, the Austrians were conscious that only by strong pressure on Serbia could the real instigators of the murder be reached, and that in exerting such pressure they were entitled to much sympathy from all law-abiding governments, including the hostile but monarchical government of Russia. On the other hand, if they did nothing in face of such an affront, nobody would ever take them seriously as a great power again.

The Outbreak of War

The Austrians dared not go to extremes against Serbia without German backing, which the terms of their alliance did not guarantee.

But the Germans had backed them in the previous crisis with Serbia in 1909, and were now asked to do so again. Berchtold had been compiling a memorandum for them designed to prove that the Bulgarian alliance, which they disliked, was essential to Austrian security. On the news of the assassination, he revamped it and sent it with a covering letter from his Emperor to William II. Both papers hinted at violent action against the Serbs and Count Hoyos, who took them to Berlin, explained verbally that war was contemplated. The Kaiser and Bethmann-Hollweg received the Austrian communication on 5 July and pledged their support. It was to be claimed by the Germans later that they had done this without knowing what the Austrians intended, and that they did not learn until too late the impossible severity of Austrian demands on Serbia. But there is plenty of evidence that they knew and approved of what was planned.[1] Had they wished to exercise restraint they could easily have done so, for Tisza, the Hungarian premier, held out almost to the last for making only such demands on Serbia as she could honourably accept. The Austrians were, on the contrary, spurred on by the fear that if they did not act strongly this time, Germany would never think them worth supporting again. The Germans did, indeed, think that inaction now would irretrievably undermine morale within the Monarchy, and it would become useless as an ally. Though often critical of Austrian policy, they had always been ready to back them in any action which they themselves deemed necessary for their own survival. Both at the end of 1912, when it seemed likely that Austria-Hungary might come to the aid of Turkey, and in 1913 when first Montenegro and then Serbia threatened the frontiers of Albania, the Germans were ready to stand by the Monarchy even if it meant a general war. 'If Austria must fight,' Kiderlen told the Bundesrat, 'we must go to her side lest we have later to fight alone beside a weakened Austria.' Germany could not afford to lose her only real ally, at least till she had escaped from isolation, and she still could not face having to absorb the Austrian Germans if Austria-Hungary collapsed.[2]

[1] See especially the refutation of Jagow in Albertini, *Origins of the War of 1914*, vol. ii, pp. 265–8, and Schoen's report, pp. 268–70. Cf. pp. 145, 453.

[2] Jagow, German foreign secretary from 1912, wrote on 18 July 1914 (Albertini, vol. ii, pp. 157–8) that the preservation of Austria was necessary on 'domestic and foreign' grounds and that the alliance was a poor bargain, but relations with Britain were not yet good enough to be a substitute.

The Germans did not rule out the possibility of a European war, but thought there was a good chance of avoiding it. The Agadir crisis had been by no means wholly bad for Germany's international position, since it encouraged more serious attempts to bring her into the system of colonial ententes. The British radicals in particular had come to believe that Germany had a grievance. The mission of Haldane to Berlin (1912) failed yet again to trade a naval agreement against a British pledge of neutrality. But colonial co-operation proved more feasible. There were new talks on the eventual partition of Portuguese Africa, not to speak of Grey's friendly attitude to the Austrians in the affair of Albania. In 1914 Britain, in return for certain safeguards, withdrew her opposition to Germany's extending the Baghdad railway to the Persian Gulf. This agreement was awaiting ratification when war broke out. Other understandings of the same year amicably allotted spheres of influence in Asiatic Turkey to the interested powers. In France the radical campaign against Poincaré and his friends presaged a new attempt at reconciliation with Germany. British fears of the German navy were dying down. They had shown themselves able to keep ahead, while the Germans had to restrict their own expansive plans, embodied in the law of 1912, so as to be able to spend more on the army. Anglo-Russian relations in Persia, meanwhile, were going from bad to worse and Grey in May 1914 thought it unlikely that Britain would go to Russian aid if Germany attacked her.

The Russians, however, were in no mood to listen to the call of monarchical solidarity against the anarchical Serbs. They had been thrown into a panic at the end of 1913 by the establishment of a German military mission in Turkey under General Liman von Sanders. Not only did the General have extensive powers to interfere in Turkish army organization but he was actually placed in command of the army corps at Constantinople. The Russians feared that he might one day use his position to close the Straits to their trade, while Sukhomlinov, the war minister, thought the strengthening of the Turkish army a threat to the Caucasus and wanted the mission sent away. The Germans seem, in fact, to have had no such grand designs in view, and found a way to have Liman removed from the actual command of a corps. But the Russians considered once more the forcible seizure of Constantinople, and Sazonov became so eager for a British alliance that he was ready to offer them the whole of the neutral zone in Persia in return for a naval agreement.

The French, too, thanks to Agadir, were in no position to mollify the Russians. In the crises of 1912–13 they had shown a willingness to help Russia in the Balkans quite absent in 1909. The Balkan league of 1912 annoyed the French, and they pointedly reminded the Russians that one of the obligations of their alliance was consultation before adopting an important new policy. In August Poincaré visited Russia to find out what his ally was up to. But then and subsequently, he found it advisable to assure the Russians that France would come to their aid if Germany intervened in their quarrels with the Austrians —even if Russia attacked the Austrians and Germany came to their support. Poincaré stretched the Franco-Russian alliance in just the same way that Bülow in 1909 had extended the Austro-German alliance beyond its strictly defensive terms. There has been much argument over whether Poincaré was a warmonger, dreaming of the recovery of his native Lorraine from Germany. There is no need to suppose this. Russia had shown in 1911 that she would not help her ally against Germany without an adequate return and while Franco-German relations remained distant the French were obliged to con-sider Russian susceptibilities.

The Central Powers no longer counted on the restraining influence of France. On the contrary, the ultimatum finally sent to the Serbs was timed to arrive just after the end of a state visit to St Petersburg by Poincaré and Viviani, the new premier. Their presence in Russia was expected to be inflammatory, and it was thought best that the crisis should take place while they were returning home by sea. It was Britain that was relied on to restrain her entente partners, but for this purpose she was too remote from Russia and too close to France. Anglo-French military links now had a naval counterpart. In 1912 the British responded to the new German navy law by moving many of their ships from the Mediterranean to the North Sea. The French moved many of theirs in the opposite direction, to safeguard the passage of reinforcements to France from North Africa in the event of war. The radicals in the British cabinet tried to belittle the signi-ficance of military developments. In November 1912 they forced an exchange of letters declaring that the staff talks did not represent a British commitment to come to the aid of France. But the British could not now refrain from doing so without incurring bitter French resentment.

If the Germans were prepared to accept a European war, supposing that the powers would not tolerate the chastisement of Serbia, the reason is to be found in the intensification of the arms race, which was another bad consequence of Agadir and the ensuing nationalist uproar and itself the cause of some of Germany's difficulties. The armies of Russia, France and Germany were now being increased to their maximum possible size. This meant that every little counted and so helps to explain the accent on Anglo-French co-operation and the sudden Russian concern over the Turkish army. It was also the case that Germany would reach her maximum strength before France did, and before the fruition of the Russian plans for military revival. This gave Germany an entirely new incentive to go to war rather than wait and hope that her position would improve. 'Any delay means a lessening of our chances,' Moltke told Conrad in May 1914.

Austro-German plans for localizing the conflict with Serbia were muddled from the start. The Germans seem to have expected the Austrians to invade Serbia almost at once, presenting Russia with a *fait accompli* while indignation against the Sarajevo murder was still intense. But they also urged the Austrians to have a convincing dossier of evidence against the Serbs ready for circulation to the powers before an ultimatum went out. This was not possible if action was to be prompt. The dossier that was hastily compiled was probably not convincing enough; in any case, it only reached the powers when the crisis was in full swing and nobody paid any attention to it. As for military action, the lumbering Austrian forces could not be ready without several weeks' preparation. The campaign against Serbia did not, in fact, get going till battle was furiously raging between the major powers. All that happened at first was the threat of Austrian action, against which indignation steadily grew.

The Austrians decided to begin with an ultimatum so severe that Serbia was almost bound to reject it. The Serbian government was asked to disown and suppress nationalist agitation and punish conspirators, some of whom were named. Austrian agents were to be allowed to participate in the police work. The ultimatum was delivered on Thursday, 23 July, and caused intense excitement in Russia as soon as it was known there. Mobilization against Austria-Hungary was quickly decided on in principle, and military measures preparatory to this begun. Russian general mobilization was finally ordered on the following Thursday, 30 July, and this as we shall see made war inescapable. It was in the intervening week that the diplomats had a chance to stop it.

Serbia, after appealing to the great powers, decided to accept the demands in the ultimatum except for the participation of Austrians in their execution. The wording of the reply makes it evident, however, that the Serbs intended subsequently to evade their undertakings as far as they could. Russian concern, and perhaps direct Russian advice, encouraged them: without it they would probably have accepted the whole document and trusted entirely to their skill in evading its execution. As it was, they gave the Austrians an excuse to break off diplomatic relations at the end of the forty-eight hours allowed for an answer. Berchtold was uncertain what to do next: he even sent word to Sir Edward Grey that his ultimatum was really not one but only a '*démarche* with a time limit'. But Germany pressed him to declare war on Serbia before anyone could intervene, and this he did on 28 July.

With Poincaré and Viviani at sea and only imperfectly in touch (by wireless) with events during the fatal week, France played only a limited part in the crisis. Military preparations soon began there. Britain, echoed by Italy, looked for ways in which the powers might mediate. This was the last thing the Germans wanted, for it might protect Serbia. In London and St Petersburg they encouraged instead the idea of direct friendly conversations between Russia and Austria-Hungary, but they did not press Vienna to get these going. They wanted the Austrians to act first, and meanwhile try to win Italian support. Russia was to be kept quiet by a promise to take no Serb territory. But on the 27th the Kaiser, rather to his ministers' annoyance, came home from a yachting holiday. He was very impressed by the Serb reply to the ultimatum, and considered that war would now be absurd. He hit on an ingenious way of stopping it, usually called the 'Halt in Belgrad'. The Austrians were to occupy that city and hold it as a pledge for the satisfaction of their demands, but not do more. A settlement could then be negotiated at leisure. Something like this solution also occurred to Grey and to statesmen in other countries; it was the likeliest way out of the crisis.

Unfortunately, Bethmann-Hollweg was half-hearted about it at first, and when he became really interested it was too late.

The Austrian declaration of war on Serbia on the 28th made things much worse. In Germany it roused the military authorities, who now began to doubt if war could be avoided. Moltke pointed out that Austria-Hungary would have to mobilize all her forces in order to deal with the Serbs on one side and Russian preparations on the other. War between Austria-Hungary and Russia would almost certainly follow, and Germany would be drawn in. This was something that the diplomats simply had not realized: foreign secretary Jagow had even told the Russians that it would not matter if they mobilized against the Austrians. Bethmann more or less collapsed on the 29th: he now urged Vienna to accept the 'Halt in Belgrad', warned Russia not to mobilize, and sent to London a fantastic proposal that Britain should remain neutral in a continental war in return for a promise that no territory should be taken from France and Belgium if Germany won. He had hardly done this when he received word that Grey had warned ambassador Lichnowsky that if war came, Britain would probably not remain neutral. This warning led Bethmann to redouble his efforts to hold back Vienna. It, too, resulted from the Austrian declaration of war on Serbia: Grey was disabused by it of his belief that Germany was trying to hold back the Austrians. Of course, Bethmann's neutrality plan completed his disillusionment.

Sazonov was affected by the Austrian action in the same way as Grey, the more strongly so as till then he had been rather pleased by German efforts to build a bridge between himself and Berchtold. The German warning not to mobilize was another severe shock. Meanwhile the Russian chief of staff, Janushkevich, had been convinced by his subordinates that it was impossible to carry out the decision that had been taken to mobilize only part of the army—that intended for operations against Austria-Hungary. Only one plan existed—for general mobilization against both Austria-Hungary and Germany. To attempt to improvise another would mean chaos. The upshot was that both the diplomatic and military chiefs came out in favour of general mobilization. They had a long struggle to get the Tsar to agree, especially as the Kaiser was bombarding him with telegrams urging restraint. But on the afternoon of the 30th he gave way.

The effect of Russian mobilization on the German military authorities made war unavoidable. Germany could mobilize quicker than Russia and would lose a valuable military advantage if she allowed Russia to mobilize before war began. Germany, too, had only one plan for mobilization, which was also a war plan. It was assumed that war with Russia would automatically mean war with France, and so the bulk of the forces were to be sent west through Belgium and Luxemburg in order first to crush the French—the stronger and also the more accessible opponent. So when the news of Russian mobilization came, Moltke demanded not only mobilization but war: war, moreover, against France and Belgium, with whom Germany at that moment was not even quarrelling. He sent word to Conrad, his Austrian opposite number, to mobilize at once. Coming at the same time as Bethmann's pleas for restraint, this advice led Berchtold to ask in amusement who ruled in Berlin.[1] The answer—now—was Moltke. Meekly, the German government asked the French for a pledge of neutrality; if it was given, they were to be asked to surrender Toul and Verdun for the duration of a Russo-German war. The object was to goad them into fighting, and they spared the Germans some embarrassment by saying simply that they would act in accordance with their interests. Germany and France both ordered mobilization on 1 August. Having failed to get the Russian mobilization order withdrawn, Germany declared war on Russia on 1 August, and on France on 3 August. On this day also the Belgians rejected a request for the passage of German troops and so found themselves at war. This, in turn, led to a British ultimatum to Germany next day. Britain entered the war because she was a guarantor of Belgian neutrality under the treaty of 1839.[2] Whether she would have done so otherwise can never be known. Grey considered her morally obliged to come to the aid of France, and would have resigned had this not been done. The conservative opposition felt the same, but the cabinet and its parliamentary supporters were divided. Only the invasion of Belgium made the decision certain and almost unanimous.

It will be seen that the crisis was begun by the Germans and Austrians, and most of the steps which successively intensified it were

---

[1] German mobilization was briefly halted on 2 August, when the British seemed to be offering a worthwhile mediation plan.

[2] *Age of Transformation*, p. 196.

theirs. On the other hand it was the French and Russians[1] who first took active military measures and it was the Russian mobilization that ended the chances of peaceful settlement. Russian mobilization, unlike German, did not automatically mean war and—more important—neither the Germans nor the British nor anyone else showed any anxiety at Russian military activity until it was too late. But in Russia, as in other countries, the generals assumed that mobilization and war went together, and it is likely that everyone—save perhaps the unstable Sazonov—realized that what was being done was very dangerous. Neither Britain nor France nor Italy spoke as strongly as they should have done in favour of restraint. The dismay which Grey's hint of intervention on 29 July caused among the Germans makes it evident that it might have made a great difference had it come earlier. Grey's defence was that he dared not get ahead of public opinion or arouse hopes on the other side; it can now be seen that the risk would have been worth taking.

Military men increasingly took over from the diplomats in the last stages of the crisis, and it is probably fair to say that everywhere they thought that the moment for war had come. But the soldiers did not force war on the diplomats: even Conrad, who had often tried to do so earlier, was not this time more bellicose than his foreign office. The soldiers entered the fray only when the situation seemed to them to make military action necessary in the interests of national security. It was the diplomats who allowed this situation to arise, and it was their ignorance of military matters which caused them to let things get to the point when the soldiers felt it their duty to say a word. The word, once spoken, was everywhere obeyed. We shall see in due course that the plans of the soldiers were everywhere militarily foolish. Unfortunately, in Germany they were politically foolish too. The indignation aroused by the German attack on Belgium has tended to hinder the doing of justice to the German attack on France: no less wicked and many times as absurd. Germany had no quarrel with France in 1914, and the bad feeling between them was subsiding as French radicalism revived. Russia's premature mobilization gave Germany a chance to exploit this situation: she threw it away because she had only one plan of campaign and no statesman to assert the primacy of political considerations.

[1] And the British, who kept their fleet together.

The outbreak of war in 1914 does not seem to have been inevitable. The view often expressed that the powers were dragged remorselessly into war by 'entangling alliances' is quite wrong. None went to war because of an alliance treaty, and it is clear that the closeness of alliance bonds varied greatly according to circumstances. There were certainly strong factors making for war, but the general international situation had been improving, not worsening, before the final crisis. Repeatedly, a difference for the worse was made by avoidable mistakes on the part of individuals. But it may perhaps be conceded that these individuals were bound to make mistakes. The stunted growth of Europe's constitutional systems (especially east of the Rhine) had made for clumsy remedies and incompetents in high places. This certainly did make war increasingly hard to avoid.

Part IV
REVOLUTION WITHOUT BETTERMENT— WILSON AND LENIN

1: Europe at War

Contrary to their expectations, the military commanders on both sides failed to win a decisive victory in 1914. The war became a costly stalemate and the contending states were ground to pieces. This made for a twofold revolution. Disruptive forces within Europe gained a chance to master it, and the extra-European countries could begin their escape from European tutelage. Lenin eventually took power in Russia, and eagerly awaited revolution in the west. But, instead, the United States, the greatest of the extra-European powers, entered European affairs in order to check the ever-widening spread of war and devastation. President Wilson reinforced the decaying liberalism of the old world and tried to build a new liberal order that would contain militarism and Bolshevism alike. For a time Wilson and Lenin divided Europe between them, but neither could rebuild the continent as he would have wished, and power eventually passed to more backward-looking forces, inimical to the ideals of both.

The First Three Years of Fighting

The French, Germans, Russians and Austrians all took the offensive almost as soon as the war started. The German plan was based on the work of Count Schlieffen, chief of staff 1891–1906. Almost all the available force was concentrated in the west. The actual frontier between France and Germany, in the Vosges mountains, had been well fortified, and Schlieffen had intended it to be very lightly and defensively held. The great bulk of the German forces were to move in parallel arcs through Holland, Belgium and Luxemburg, engulfing the whole of northern France, deeply outflanking the French army deployed against Germany and eventually taking it in the rear. The plan was always regarded by its author as something of a gamble and it required overwhelming numerical superiority and a commander with iron nerves. Neither was present to a sufficient degree in 1914. Large though it was, the German army had been habitually kept below the

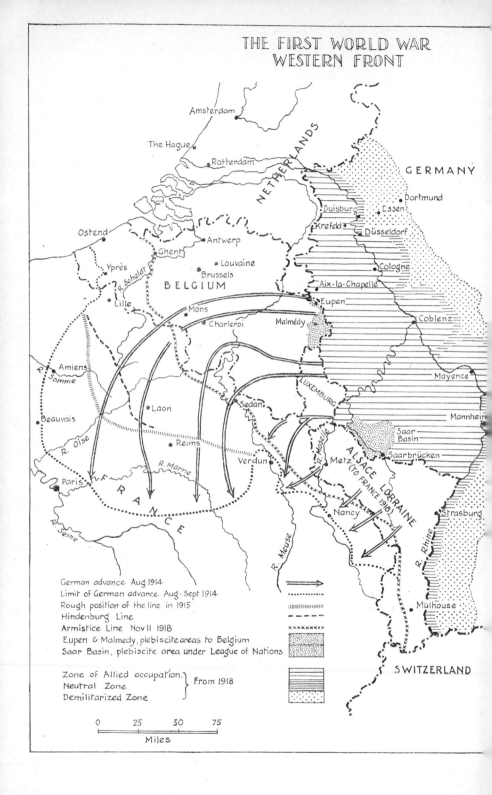

THE FIRST WORLD WAR
WESTERN FRONT

Amsterdam

The Hague

Rotterdam

NETHERLANDS

GERMANY

Dortmund

Duisburg   Essen

Krefeld   Düsseldorf

Ostend

Ghent

Antwerp

Cologne

Ypres   R. Scheldt

Louvaine

BELGIUM   Brussels

Aix-la-Chapelle

Lille   Mons

Eupen

Coblenz

Charleroi

Malmédy

Amiens   R. Somme

LUXEMBURG

Mayence

Beauvais

Laon

Sedan

Mannheim

R. Oise

Reims

Verdun

Saar Basin

Saarbrücken

R. Marne

Paris

FRANCE

Metz (to France 1918)

ALSACE LORRAINE (to France 1918)

R. Moselle

R. Seine

Nancy

Strasburg

R. Meuse

R. Rhine

German advance Aug 1914
Limit of German advance Aug-Sept 1914
Rough position of the line in 1915
Hindenburg Line
Armistice Line Nov 11 1918
Eupen & Malmedy, plebiscite areas to Belgium
Saar Basin, plebiscite area under League of Nations

Zone of Allied occupation. ⎫
Neutral Zone   ⎬ From 1918
Demilitarized Zone   ⎭

Mülhouse

SWITZERLAND

0   25   50   75
Miles

maximum strength possible, and the expansion immediately before the war had not made this good. An especially obvious deficiency was in lines-of-communication troops of all kinds. There were not enough to guard the army's rear as it advanced across Belgium, and this made commanders nervous and was a cause of the atrocities which did so much damage to Germany's reputation, especially in America. There were not enough for the installation of signalling systems, and the high command increasingly lost touch with its far-flung armies.

Schlieffen's successor was the younger Moltke, an intelligent man who had more inkling than most of what a modern war would be like, and deplored the conservative, parade-ground notions of fighting so strong in his army. But his will was not strong and it had been weakened by the political argument in the last days of peace as to whether to mobilize. He had amended his predecessor's plan by giving up the idea of invading Holland and by strengthening his left, hoping eventually to envelop the French from both flanks. The first obstacle in his path was Liége, surrounded by a ring of forts. A *coup de main* by the then obscure Ludendorff carried the town by 7 August, but the forts held out until the 16th, being destroyed by German siege guns of unprecedented size. By the 18th the German advance was gathering momentum, and by 1 September they had wheeled through ninety degrees and were facing south on a line from Amiens to Thionville. Kluck's army on the far right had covered 180 miles in fifteen days (by horse and foot).

The French had known roughly what the Germans would do and planned to reply in kind with a counterattack on the German frontier, aimed at cutting the German main body off from home. But they had expected only a fairly small German wheel through the south-east corner of Belgium, and they grossly overestimated the power of their offensive against the German frontier defences. They attacked on 14 August—having briefly captured Mulhouse on the 8th—but got nowhere and suffered 300,000 casualties in ten days—a quarter of their force. The German advance, meanwhile, was opposed by the small British force that had come over and one French army out of five. Joffre, the French commander, was a man whose phlegm was, if not greater, then at any rate more apparent than his intelligence. His extremely regular habits in eating and sleeping were undisturbed by the German avalanche; he seems to have thought he was luring them into a trap. But the Germans now began to make mistakes. A mis-directed attack failed to penetrate the French position in the Vosges and left them safe on that side. Kluck's army, instead of marching west of Paris, went to the east of it in pursuit of the troops facing him. The French government had left Paris, but a powerful garrison remained there on Kluck's flank and a new (sixth) army was being scraped together. Late on 5 September Joffre rather reluctantly sanctioned the counterattack for which Gallieni, the governor of Paris, was pressing. Kluck had to turn away from the German second army on his left to meet it, and the British opened another attack along the Marne between the two armies. The Germans reformed their line by retreating a little and then both sides tried to outflank each other, thus progressively extending the front until it reached the North Sea just east of the Franco-Belgian frontier. The Belgian forces, which had been harassing the German forces from the Ant-werp area, abandoned most of their country and took their place in the line. The Western Front was to remain in very much the same place for almost four years.

The battle of the Marne is always closely linked with the opening engagements on the Eastern Front. The Germans had placed only nine of their eighty-seven divisions there, to hold off the Russians while they beat the French. The Russians, for their part, were pledged to an immediate offensive, to relieve the pressure on their allies. Their forces were humanly splendid, but poorly equipped by western standards and often poorly commanded. Even so, they were more than a match for the Austrians, whose morale was terrible, the troops levied from the subject peoples eventually deserting en masse. The Russians ought probably to have tried to knock out Austria-Hun-gary while Germany was occupied in the west; the Germans would eventually have had to come to the rescue on a massive scale. Instead, the Russians took the offensive against both their enemies, and suc-ceeded in alarming the Germans considerably by invading East Prussia at both ends. Prittwitz, the local German commander, wanted to retire to the Vistula. But even before he was superseded by the illustrious team of Hindenburg and Ludendorff, his principal staff officer, the brilliant Colonel Hoffman, had worked out a plan which ended the danger. The Russian armies moved slowly and were not in contact. The German forces had been facing the one that was threatening Konigsberg. Almost the whole of them were quickly moved southward, where they surrounded and destroyed the other Russian army, Samsonov's, at Tannenberg (25–30 August). Ninety thousand prisoners were taken; the Russian invasion ended.

It is customary to say that this Russian sacrifice enabled the French to win at the Marne. This is true only in a recondite sense. The Germans sent two army corps to reinforce the threatened east which might have turned the scale if they had stayed in the west. But the Russians were beaten before these army corps arrived, and the German offensive against France would not have got so far anyway if the French armies had not been mainly locked up in the futile Vosges offensive. France was endangered by the stupidity of her own generals, and saved by the stupidity of the generals on the other side. She received very little help from either of her allies, and this makes the battle of the Marne all the more significant. Germany could not knock France out in single combat as she had in 1870, even though she was now much the stronger country of the two. The advantage of the defensive in war was now too great. Germany's only hope of a total victory would now be from a war of attrition, in which she would suffer almost as much as the foe.

There were other more attainable objectives than total victory, however, and in 1915 Germany concentrated on saving Austria-Hungary, the purpose for which she had really gone to war. Austrian attempts to conquer Serbia petered out in disgrace in 1914. The main Austrian forces had invaded Poland and at first been rather successful, but they had to retire when the Russian left attacked in Galicia and drove them out of the eastern half of the province. This meant that the Russians could still threaten Germany. East Prussia was invaded a second time, and Hindenburg's main force had to undertake an abortive offensive in Poland to cover Silesia. Hungary, too, was in danger. Falkenhayn, who had replaced Moltke after the Marne, remained eager to attack in the west. But as hopes of a quick victory there faded, he came to think that it would be necessary to make Russia helpless first. German troops were brought east until there were four preponderantly German armies there. After an attack by Hindenburg from East Prussia had failed to rout the Russians, Conrad's plan was adopted of breaking through on the Southern Front. On 2 May 1915 the Germans and Austrians together attacked the Russians between Gorlice and Tarnow, east of Cracow. After their line was broken, the Russians totally collapsed. Their scanty supplies of equipment had been almost used up in the earlier fighting and many of their better officers and men had been lost. What was left was a half-armed rabble. The offensive of the Central Powers lasted till September and took them right through Russian Poland. By the end of the year the front ran due north, from the eastern end of Galicia to Riga on the Baltic.

The western powers, like Falkenhayn, thought that the Western Front was the more important. But they had to do what they could to help Russia. Italy was coaxed into the war, but she only entered it on 23 May, when the Austro-German offensive was well under way, and her attacks on the Austrians in no way lessened the pressure on Russia. The Austrians were protected against Italian attack by the south-eastern extremities of the Alps, and morally they benefited from the fact that hatred of the Italians was almost the only sentiment that Germans and Slavs had in common. Germany had had a much greater success in bringing Turkey into the war. The long fostering of German influence there bore fruit in a treaty of alliance on 2 August 1914. This was strengthened when two German warships took refuge in Constantinople from the British and were then sold (with crews) to the Turkish navy. The *Goeben* and *Breslau* gave the Turks command of the Black Sea and strengthened the war party. On 28 October they bombarded Odessa and Turkey was at war. A Turkish offensive in the Caucasus came to nothing, but merely by existing, Turkey cut Russia's main supply line. But the Turkish forces were of doubtful efficiency and very dispersed. It might be possible to seize Constantinople and the Straits. The French would spare no forces for this. The Greeks were willing to undertake it, but the Russians could not bear the thought of Constantinople becoming Greek rather than Russian. Allied naval forces therefore made the first attempt (February–March), but after some progress against the forts of the Dardanelles they gave up when several ships were sunk by mines. Had they persisted, they might perhaps have got through. By this time, thanks mainly to the British navy, Germany had almost no trade or territory left outside Europe. But the allied navies proved powerless to tip the strategic balance in Europe by relieving Russia. The German fleet held the Baltic, and the British could not get into the Black Sea. The

Dardanelles were to the British navy what the Marne was to the German army.

The British army next tried to open the Straits by seizing the Gallipoli peninsula and marching from there to Constantinople. The attempt began at the end of April and only ended in January 1916. The first landings might have succeeded if the advance had begun at once, but as it was the defending forces concentrated in time and the attackers never gained more than a toehold. The forces on each side steadily increased and conditions in the tiny battle areas, mountainous and without cover, became increasingly infernal. To clear the way for reinforcements and supplies to Turkey, Falkenhayn determined to dispose of Serbia. Bulgaria was induced to join the struggle against her in September. German troops were sent to stiffen the Austrians, and in January 1916 Montenegro surrendered, while the Serb army had sought refuge in Albania. The allies tried to restrain the Bulgarians by landing a force at Salonika, but this was wasted effort.

In 1916 emphasis returned to the Western Front. Since 1914 both sides had been digging in there and their firepower had been increasing. The cavalry charges and the dense masses of infantry in gay uniforms which had still figured in 1914 gave way steadily to a war of attack and defence under cover, of heavier bombardments against steadily deepening fortified lines. Numerically, the sides became more evenly matched, with the creation of a large, though still raw, British army. Both sides attempted offensives in 1915, but they completely failed, even when the Germans enlivened them with poison gas. Both sides prepared to resume the offensive, but Falkenhayn, who had the initiative, seems to have realized that only limited gains were possible. Abler and stronger-willed than his predecessor, he was also more conservative. In thought as in appearance, he embodied the stiff and stern tradition of the old Prussia. It was natural to him to think of the object of the war as 'a good peace'—limited gains rather than total victory—for this had always been the purpose of the old dynastic struggles. His great stroke in the west was the attack on Verdun, designed not to overthrow the French army, but to bleed it until France grew weary of the struggle. This strategy arose from Falkenhayn's belief that the French will to war was weaker than that of Britain.

Verdun had long been an important frontier post, but its suitability for this had declined with the improvement of artillery and its fortifications had been neglected. It represented an awkward salient in the line, bothersome to the Germans without being very helpful to the French, but it was morally impossible to give it up without a terrible struggle. The German attack began in February 1916. Only a very limited front was assaulted, later extended but not greatly. The main feature of the attack was the very intense artillery barrage, closely and accurately synchronized with the movements of the infantry so as to clear the path before them steadily as they advanced. The French were traditionally better in attack than in defence, and for supply they were heavily dependent on one secondary road. But they stood their ground magnificently, and their guns gave as good as they got. The attacks went on until June, and the French lost heavily as planned—315,000. But German losses were 281,000, and they did not take the town.

The British, on the left of the French, were asked to take the offensive as soon as possible to relieve the pressure on Verdun, and there resulted the series of attacks known as the battle of the Somme. They took place in July, September and November, gained little ground and cost the allies 600,000 casualties, though the Germans may well have suffered more. The British had not enough artillery, and lacked the tactical skill of their foes and allies. The Russians, too, were asked for help. They had done something to restore their strength, as will be told later, and they had received some supplies over the long routes still available. Yudenich brilliantly took the offensive against the Turks in the Caucasus, but he had not the resources to contemplate knocking them out of the war. In March and in June–July there were unsuccessful attacks against the German-held part of the front. But the most striking development was Brusilov's offensive against the Austrians, which went on intermittently from June to October. The Russians again reached the confines of Hungary, and it was clear that the Austrian army was now in a very bad way: 400,000 prisoners were taken. But the offensive petered out through bad communications and lack of reinforcement, and Russian losses were also very heavy and demoralizing. The biggest gain was that Rumania, which had been waiting to see which side was going to win, decided to join the allies (August 1916). But their army was not good, and the Germans hastily improvised forces which invaded the country from Bulgaria and western Transylvania. Bucharest fell on 5 December, and the Rumanians were left with only a small tract of country adjacent to Russia. The record of stalemate in 1916 was completed by the accidental and indecisive naval battle of Jutland in May.

Then and since the cry has been raised[1] that both sides were wrong to concentrate on the Western Front; they should have sought success in some other theatre where there was more room to manoeuvre. But even if Germany had knocked Russia out of the war, she would only have been back to the situation of 1914, when she had almost all her forces in the west and had not won. The same applied to the knocking out of Italy, for which Conrad pressed. These operations would release the Austrian army, but it was not good enough to fight the French and British. As for the western allies, the events of 1915 had shown that it would be a very long job to break through Turkey and build up Russia. Anyway, as German-controlled railways were faster than British steamers, any stroke not entirely peripheral was likely to be met by a swift and superior counterstroke. The forces which really counted in the war were those of the Germans and of the British and French. They roughly balanced and so there was a stalemate. The only means immediately available for undermining this was the painful and perilous one of attrition. The only other really sound solution to the strategic problem would have been to end the war.

The attempts to do this will be discussed farther on. Their failure left the field free for attrition to do its worst, and in 1917 it began to produce the gravest effects. The weakening of the combatants was not reflected, however, in any public abandonment of faith in victorious offensives. New and more fiery commanders were, on the contrary, appointed to revive it. The cautious Falkenhayn was dismissed in August 1916; he subsequently commanded with distinction in the campaign against Rumania. He was succeeded by the partnership of Hindenburg and Ludendorff, whose protests had brought about his fall. The success of these generals on the Eastern Front (though others, in fact, had done as well) had brought to Hindenburg, in particular, a remarkable degree of trust and reverence among the German people that was to make him a national figure for the rest of his long life. Born in 1847 and in retirement when war

[1] Notably by Sir Winston Churchill.

broke out, he was a massive, paternal and by no means brilliant figure. The brains were provided by his deputy, the brilliant and unstable Erich von Ludendorff. Eighteen years the junior of his chief and born only on the fringe of the Junker class to which the old Marshal so indubitably belonged, he was a fanatical professional who thought only of war. This ultimately was his downfall. It led him to strive for total victory, achieved by the complete mobilization of the nation's resources. Before the war the champion of really universal training against the conservatives, he was now the force behind the systematic harnessing of industry to the war effort. But the supreme direction of a modern war is a political as much as a technical task, and in politics Ludendorff was a complete innocent. He was to bring his country outlawry, revolution and ruin.

His arrangements did, however, make military sense. Recognizing that the great battles of 1916 had left the troops exhausted, he prepared a new and shorter line for them to hold, heavily fortified and cutting off a corner of the old front. To this 'Hindenburg' or 'Siegfried' Line, the Germans retired in February 1917, devastating the country they abandoned. On the defensive in the west, Ludendorff did something towards knocking Russia and Italy out of the war. But though he had made most of his reputation in the east, he did not concentrate his attention on these theatres. His chosen means of beating Germany's major enemies in the west was the submarine, which was now let loose to do its worst. The plans of the other side were far less cautious. A new young general, Nivelle, had come to prominence in the defence of Verdun and now replaced Joffre. He appealed to the allied politicians because he was articulate (and could speak English). He believed that he could puncture the enemy line in a single day by a surprise attack with unprecedented concentrations both of troops and guns. Such was the impression he made (reinforced by Lloyd George's suspicions of his own commander, Haig) that he was almost given command over the British forces, till then co-operating with the French but entirely independent. His offensive took place north-west of Rheims in the latter half of April and was supported by another series of slogging British attacks, in the region of Arras. It was a total fiasco, partly because surprise was not achieved, and its moral effects were terrible. There was a series of mutinies in the French army, though mostly in the form of refusal to return to duty; there was no attempt at revolution. Pétain, who had commanded at Verdun, was made commander-in-chief and slowly nursed the army back to fighting trim. But in the meantime France was on the verge of collapse.

The British had again to take the weight off them by an offensive. Haig had long been planning an advance along the North Sea coast, turning the German flank and capturing their submarine bases in Belgium. As the submarine attacks mounted, this objective became increasingly important. The battle began with the capture of the Messines ridge in June and the British crept forward in successive attacks a little to the north of this, gaining about six miles before the offensive stopped on Passchendaele ridge in November. Lengthy preparations and rainy spells interrupted the attacks. There was little surprise, the Germans had an unusually deep system of defences, including many concrete forts, and the ground was mostly reclaimed marsh likely to flood. At the end the battlefield had virtually ceased to be land at all and men were being suffocated in liquid mud. But the British now had a skill in the attack they that had lacked in the previous year. They steadily bored their way through the fortifications, and the German troops faced them with increasing reluctance. This third battle of Yprès, with some 240,000 casualties on either side, was as near to a triumph as attrition could get.

The allies (as the entente powers were now called)[1] were hard pressed in the autumn of 1917. Russia was in revolution, with the Germans helping to speed Lenin on his homeward journey. The final Russian offensive in July was a fiasco, and in September the Germans tried to help forward the demand for peace by taking Riga. At the same time they at last listened to Austrian pleas for help against Italy.[2] German troops played the major role in the Italian defeat at Caporetto in October. The Italians had hitherto fought well, but now they collapsed and fled fifty miles to the line of the Piave, near Venice. The Central Powers did not, however, devote enough resources to the venture to knock Italy out of the war, while, thanks to the unfortunate Nivelle, the allies had plans to reinforce Italy. In the end the Italians stabilized their front on their own. There were other hopeful signs. The British had devised a new weapon to challenge

[1] They concluded an alliance in September 1914.
[2] They were not even at war with her till 1916.

the ascendancy of the defensive—the tank. Used experimentally in 1916, it made its first big appearance at Cambrai in November 1917. Its main function was to take over part of the artillery's role in clearing a path for the infantry through the barbed wire and machine guns. In that way it facilitated surprise, and at Cambrai at long last the enemy's line was punctured. But the first tanks were mechanically unreliable: 179 out of the 324 available were out of action after one day. The troops available were insufficient to exploit the success, while the Germans were quick to bring in fresh forces. Cambrai was abortive, but its importance for the future was clear. Still more so was the fate of the technological offensive on the other side. The submarine had come near to winning the war for Germany, but it had not done so, and it had brought the United States in. The European situation was about to be transformed.

The Home Fronts

Attrition had a strong direct effect on the political stability of the continental states. Those east of the Rhine, in particular, were still essentially military monarchies, their stability assured by the loyalty of strong regular armies in which conservative elements preponderated. These were the troops that bore the brunt of the earlier campaigns, and by the end of 1916 they had been substantially destroyed everywhere. The losses of seasoned NCOs and of officers of middle and junior rank were especially severe. The discipline and loyalty of the regular troops was their creation, they showed the greatest courage everywhere in leading the attack and soon few were left. All the armies became increasingly like militias, with officers and men alike newly drawn from civil life and not steeped in the old traditions. The body of the officers in particular was no longer aristocratic or necessarily conservative. The new troops fought well, but they were by no means automatically loyal to their governments when things went seriously wrong. This was awkward even for Britain and France, and it was fatal in the eastern monarchies.

The states were weakening in this way just when opposition to them was growing. The war had begun with outbursts of patriotic enthusiasm everywhere. But this waned as casualties mounted and economic conditions deteriorated. None of the continental states was at all good at the effective taxation of the rich, there were limits to what the poor could be made to pay towards the war, and anyway it was supposed to be soon over. War finance therefore tended to be improvident, and increasingly based on hopes that the enemy would pay in the end. Meanwhile, there was heavy borrowing and an increasing amount of inconvertible paper money. Inflation set in, wages rose but lagged behind prices, huge profits were made while many starved. The food supply in towns became bad almost everywhere. In the case of the Central Powers this was partly due to the blockade but it was equally apparent in Russia, where the blockade had the contrary effect of keeping the agricultural surplus at home. More important were first the effect on production of taking men for the army from the mainly unmechanized farms; second, the reluctance of the peasants to sell to the towns when all they got in return was depreciating paper money, for which few goods could be bought. Industry, of course, was increasingly diverted to war production and away from making consumer goods. Here, too, there was at first a tendency for total production to fall as men were taken away to fight. Hunger and shortages and the mounting toll of death at the front steadily bred revolutionary feeling in the towns.

At the same time, the war was creating new political and economic forces. Government control of the economy was seriously undertaken for the first time. The governments stepped in with reluctance— in 1914 there was prolonged economic confusion and much unemployment. The Central Powers led the way to some extent, because they had to counteract the dislocation of their economies by the allied blockade. Walther Rathenau, a brilliant leader in the new electrical industry, warned the German government of the danger as soon as war broke out, and he was put in charge of a 'raw materials division' in the war ministry which organized the purchase of supplies abroad where possible, the requisitioning of stock at home and in the occupied territories, and the development of home-made substitutes and home production of goods formerly imported. The distribution of scarce supplies was later undertaken by 'war companies', largely based on the existing cartels, which planned production in the different industries and obliged factories to keep to the plan by the threat of withholding supplies. Something like this institution was the basis of industrial planning in all countries. Gradually price control crept in, to counter inflation and the shortage of food. Simple price control tends merely to cut off supplies and increasingly complicated systems were needed, designed, for instance, to provide cheap food for the workers and yet give incentives to the farmers. Food shortages led to requisitioning of supplies and eventually rationing, to attempts at extending the area cultivated and the introduction of machinery to replace the departed men. Military conscription broadened into a general control of labour and the increasing employment of women was notable everywhere and, of course, a challenge to accepted notions of their place in society. Controls of shipping and of the overseas purchases which formed the cargoes became increasingly important on the allied side as the counter-blockade by submarine tightened. Eventually, inter-allied control authorities were set up. Allied governments, like their opponents, had to foster new industries to replace imported supplies and also the products of the French industrial areas under enemy occupation. While the Germans made rubber and petrol from coal, the allies were building chemical industries on the German model. Entirely new industries resulted from the war, like aircraft building. There was also a stimulus to large plants and mass production methods, especially because greater use had suddenly to be made of new, unskilled workers.

After the war, the governments were as eager to retire from economic activity as they had been reluctant to undertake it. But the belief, so very general before 1914, that they could accomplish little by interfering could hardly now be sustained. It was from the wartime experiments that the Bolsheviks first learned how to plan. The first chapter of their career in power was a civil war for which the resources of the country had to be mobilized, and it was to the work of Rathenau that they turned for guidance. Even the Bolsheviks were sceptical of planning in the twenties, but the economic crisis of the thirties brought mounting government interference in all countries, whatever their ideology.

Politically, the war unleashed the aggressive nationalism which had hitherto been kept reasonably in check. It was not the pressure of the chauvinists that brought war in 1914, but the war itself made moderation seem increasingly impossible and absurd and the chauvinists gained ground accordingly. The circumstances of Italy's entry into the war, already discussed, show this very clearly. The original belligerents did not enter the war with the object of making conquests, but once in they determined to make the most of their opportunity. Germany wanted a slice of Belgium, the rest of the Lorraine iron-field,[1] Poland and the Baltic states. Russia wanted Constantinople and territory in Turkey and Poland. France, of course, wanted Alsace-Lorraine. Behind the generals, capitalists and politicians who particularly interested themselves in these projects there was a new political force. Many of those who had entered the armed forces for the first time to fight in the war had found excitement, comradeship and a sense of purpose there which the orderly and increasingly atomized society of pre-war capitalist Europe had not offered them. Many had risen from the ranks to be officers and were better placed materially or socially than they could hope to be in civil life. These people more than anyone else had a vested interest in war, wanted it to go on and were sorry when it ended. They were to perpetuate after it the wartime annexationist programmes, and were to be the backbone of the Nazi and Fascist movements and their like everywhere.

But those who enjoyed the war were a minority, and its most important political effect was to give form and substance to the peace movement. A 'League of Nations Society' was formed in Britain in May 1915, and a 'League to Enforce Peace' appeared in America at the same time. Before the war only one statesman of note was committed to the idea of a peacekeeping organization—Léon Bourgeois. Now, besides several leading Americans, Sir Edward Grey came out in favour of the idea. His career was almost over, but the cause was taken up by a rising conservative, Lord Robert Cecil, who made it his life work. Continental conservatives continued to have less sense, but as the war neared its end even the statesmen of the Central Powers began to speak with favour of projects for a League. But the statesmen of the European belligerents thought of these as a feature of post-war reconstruction. Outside America, it was for long only uninfluential people, mainly socialists, who tried to stop the war there and then. The socialist parties of neutral Holland, Switzerland and Scandinavia were, of course, free to attempt this and they were supported by the Italians, who opposed their country's entry into the war and did not afterwards recant. In France the labour movement contained an anti-war minority, centred on the syndicalists; in

[1] Not annexed in 1871 because not discovered.

Germany, the socialist party split in 1916, and a minority voted against the war credits and in 1917 formed the Independent Social Democratic Party. The socialists of eastern Europe had not the same reasons for loyalty to their governments as those of the west and most, though not all, were anti-war.

In 1915 the Swiss and Italians convened a conference at Zimmerwald in the former country, which was attended by delegates from several nations, including exiles in Switzerland such as Lenin. It launched what was henceforth to be the main anti-war slogan: a negotiated 'peace without annexations and indemnities'. But Lenin was by no means content with this. It is noteworthy that the peace movement was at first recruited from the right rather than the left wing of the socialists. Men such as Ramsay Macdonald in Britain or Bernstein in Germany were its characteristic figures. They were against war because they had not abandoned the old idealistic liberal belief in the brotherhood of man, and their methods for seeking peace were limited to sweet reasonableness and constitutional agitation. To Lenin, this seemed useless. In 1916 he wrote *Imperialism, the highest stage of capitalism*, in which he sought to show that the growing crisis within the capitalist system leads inevitably to imperial rivalries, and thence to war. It followed that to try and make peace between capitalist states was a sheer waste of time. The only way to end the war was for the masses in all countries to turn their arms against their masters and inaugurate a general socialist revolution. In 1916 there was another socialist conference in Switzerland, at Kienthal, and it went some way towards meeting Lenin's views. 'Bourgeois pacifists' were condemned as well as the 'warmongers' within the socialist movement, and the delegates declared that 'the real durable peace will be the fruit of socialism triumphant'. There could be no end to war without 'the conquest of political power and the ownership of capital by the peoples themselves'. It was the fight for peace in this sense that Lenin thought he was starting when he led the Bolshevik revolution.

The Wider World

The war was a calamity for Europe, but it is far from clear that it was so for other continents. It increased the European demand for their products. By reducing the export of manufactures from Europe, it also stimulated their industries. Empires were overthrown, and the winning side emerged weakened and had to make concessions. Arab nationalism received some British encouragement, and there were important political concessions in India after the war. The Russo-Japanese conflict had already shaken European prestige, and by the twenties Asians in particular had a new determination to be masters in their own house. It is often said that the First World War is wrongly so called because its causes and most of the fighting lay in Europe. That is substantially true, but the war deserves its title because of its world-wide effects. The greatest of these was that the Europeans had henceforth to reckon, even in European affairs, with two non-European great powers.

(i) Japan

Japan benefited both economically and politically from the war to a notable degree. Before it she had a menacing trade deficit, owing to industrial expansion and rising population which swelled the imports of food and raw materials. Now the products of her factories and shipyards were eagerly in demand both in Europe and in the Asian countries which Europe had formerly supplied. She ended the war with a large gold reserve and, for instance, her cotton industry had 3·8 million spindles in 1920 against 2·1 million in 1910. Japan had already annexed Korea in 1910, and in 1914 she took the prudent and obvious course of declaring war on Germany in order to lay hands on her colonial possessions in the Pacific and China. Adding German-controlled Shantung to her existing possession of Port Arthur, she was well placed to attempt the subjugation of northern China as a whole. The Chinese Empire had collapsed in 1912, and been replaced by a highly unstable republic. The European powers had no wish to see Japan expand farther, but while they were at war at home they could do nothing about it. In 1915 Japan presented to China the Twenty-One Demands, which asked for the transfer to her of German rights in Shantung and for new privileges in Manchuria and Mongolia. They also called for considerable Japanese participation in the general government of China, both central and local. When the Chinese proved recalcitrant, these more radical demands were given up and the rest were then agreed to. From 1916 the Japanese built up their influence in China indirectly, by means of loans to the central and local rulers. In 1917 the allies desperately needed Japanese naval help to fight the German submarines, and in return for this they agreed to recognize Japanese claims to Shantung and to Germany's Pacific possessions north of the equator. Japan, in turn, recognized British claims to the more southerly German possessions, like Samoa and New Guinea.

Japan had the Europeans where she wanted them, but in these years she won two implacable new enemies, the Chinese and the United States. The latter had viewed her rise with sympathy, and the Chinese had, at any rate, hated her no more than their other tormentors. But the sudden revelation of huge Japanese ambitions in 1915 made the Chinese consider Japan henceforth their most dangerous enemy and aroused strong feelings in America. There were considerable American interests in China, not least the religious and educational kind typified by missionaries, and the establishment of a republic there had aroused American enthusiasm. Americans began mentally to extend the Monroe doctrine to the orient, and to think of the Japanese as the Asian equivalent of the wicked European colonialists. Racial prejudice in California did not help. The antagonism leading to the eastern half of the Second World War was beginning to appear.

(ii) The United States of America

The economic gains of the United States from the war were even more spectacular than those of Japan. A recession had begun there when war broke out and the flood of European orders for both industrial and agricultural products put an end to it. Again increasing trade with Europe was reinforced by increasing trade with markets which Europe could no longer serve. American trade and investments in Latin America made particularly important advances. Exports totalled 2·3 milliard dollars in 1914, and almost 4·3 milliard in 1917; the surplus of exports over imports rose from 435 million to nearly 2·7 milliard dollars. Steel production almost doubled in three years, and farmers had the unusual experience of selling more at a higher price. The national income had increased by 5 milliard dollars in 1910–14, but rose by 12 milliard in 1914–16.

What of the country's international position? The United States had been the world's greatest industrial power since the nineties, and a school of imperialists had arisen there which wished her to abandon isolation for power politics on a global scale. The imperialists were influential in the then dominant Republican Party, in the persons notably of Theodore Roosevelt, President from 1901 to 1909, and Senator Henry Cabot Lodge. Although expansionists, they were not eager to despoil the British like American expansionists of the past and they became increasingly anti-German. Germany was a rival in the snapping up of unappropriated colonial morsels like Samoa, and she might become one in the Americas. The American imperialists therefore favoured American participation in the war of 1914 on the allied side. But they were a minority, even among the Republicans. Having completed the settlement of their own interior, the Americans expanded sufficiently to secure their own sea frontiers. In the nineties they secured Hawaii and drove the Spaniards out of the Caribbean. They then acquired a strip of territory across the Panama Isthmus and built a canal between their two oceans, opened in 1914. Along with this went the foundation of a powerful navy. But the American public was little interested in anything farther afield. It was with reluctance that it acquiesced in the taking over of the Philippines from Spain. In 1899 the British tried to push the Americans forward as defenders of the 'open door' in China, but this came to nothing beyond a platonic exchange of notes. In 1912 the Republican Party split because the bulk of it refused to accept the novel ideas of Roosevelt—an innovator in home as much as in foreign affairs. This led to the then quite exceptional election of a Democrat as President—a near amateur in politics and with very different ideas about international relations.

Thomas Woodrow Wilson was born in 1856 in Virginia, the son of a Presbyterian minister. After trying the law, he settled for an academic career, specializing in history and politics. President of Princeton from 1902 till 1910, he made it a trail-blazer in American higher education, introducing among other things what in Britain would be called a tutorial system. But he had always yearned for a political career and had tried to make himself 'an outside force in politics', as he put it, by speaking and writing. He was now a sufficiently notable public figure to be useful to Democratic politicians, who lacked sufficiently attractive and eminent candidates for the highest offices. In that way he became Governor of New Jersey (1910–12) and then President of the United States. Of him, as of Lenin, it could be said that he lived for nothing but politics. But he had a very different conception of political activity. For him it meant primarily the rousing of moral fervour in the service of great causes, a means for giving expression to his deep religious convictions. Tall and nobly featured, he had made himself a master of the grand style of prophetic oratory associated with his great hero, Gladstone. He resembled his hero also in his mingling of conservative and radical beliefs. He was nurtured in the agricultural South's dislike of the democratic and industrial north, disliked extending the power of the state, and wanted to keep government in the hands of a morally awakened ruling class. But rural America had retained the liberal belief in free trade which rural Europe had lost, and it also had a strong distrust of big business. Wilson did not find it difficult to come out in favour of policies of social and economic reform when he found that only left-wing support was likely to carry him to office. His presidency was marked not only by a lowering of the tariff but by a renewal of legislation against monopolies (trusts) and the establishment of controls over the banks —the Federal Reserve system. In foreign affairs it was natural for him, as for the American rural voter, to reject the imperialism that went along with high tariffs and big business, and to stand in practice for isolation but in principle also for the old liberal creed of peace and universal brotherhood.

Though a latecomer to political life, Wilson was not without the skill of balancing between and combining diverse bodies of opinion, on which indeed his elevation depended. Mobilizing enlightened opinion by his own eloquence, he kept in touch through intermediaries with the disreputable political machines in the big cities on the one hand and the world of business on the other. Among the men who attended to the mundane side of politics for him, one was to be especially important in his dealings with Europe. Edward House was a Texan gentleman who bore the purely honorific title of Colonel. Small and rather feminine, he never held elective office, but had great skill as a diplomat as well as a strong taste for intrigue. Wilson was not always as well served as he was by him, however, and there was a side to his character that made it impossible sometimes for him to be served at all. Shy and aloof, he could be a patient listener, but in the last resort was dictatorial. This had eventually made Princeton too hot to hold him, and it was finally to ruin his presidency and the peace of the world. Admiring British parliamentary government, with leadership and responsibility concentrated in the Prime Minister, he chafed under the American division of authority between President and Congress. From the time that America entered the war, their relations steadily worsened to the point where the country's whole foreign policy was destroyed.

Wilson declared for neutrality in 1914, and in 1916 he was re-elected quite largely on the strength of it. His Republican opponent, Hughes, was for being tougher with the Germans and suffered for it. Nevertheless, the United States went to war in 1917 and, what was far more surprising, did not confine herself to a naval and backseat role like the Japanese but intervened with ever greater effect in European fighting and diplomacy. The simple decision to declare war was a natural and indeed almost inevitable consequence of the opening of the unrestricted German submarine campaign of 1917. Submarines, at first, had been usable only for coastal defence, but improvements in the diesel engine from 1911 made possible a long-range type able to take the offensive. Worsted on the surface of the sea, the German navy was eager to use the submarine to starve Britain into submission. German suffering from the blockade led to strong support for the navy in the Reichstag.

It was largely American influence which kept the use of the submarine within bounds until 1917, and Wilson has been accused of (or praised for) an un-neutral policy of treating the British blockade more leniently than German counter-measures. It is, in fact, entirely wrong to think of him as spiritually on the allied side. The trouble was simply that the British blockade was easier to square with international law and civilized practice than the use of the submarine. It was generally accepted as lawful to sink or capture enemy merchant vessels, but there was a corresponding obligation to ensure the safety of those on board. The Americans had always contested the right claimed especially by the British, to search neutral ships for enemy goods, but there were sound legal arguments for it, as also for the prohibiting all trade with the enemy coast. In the latter case, however, the blockader could only claim to be within the law if he was strong enough to enforce his prohibition systematically. Submarines could not, however, police the seas in the way these rules implied—they were essentially a weapon of terror, and only by giving up the advantage of submerged surprise attack could they safeguard enemy crews or search neutral cargoes. The British blockade did not involve loss of life or even destruction of property. The British could keep the Americans happy with legal argument, and when that failed they let through commodities in which the Americans were specially interested or even kept them out of German hands by buying the entire ouput themselves—as for a time with cotton.

All the same, Wilson tried desperately to be fair to both sides and by 1916 he was indeed becoming more hostile to the British, if anything, than to the Germans. Bethmann-Hollweg was anxious not to bring the Americans into the war, and he convinced the army leaders that he was right. Germany for long had too few submarines anyway to attempt to starve Britain out, so there was nothing to be gained by pushing the United States too hard. A first prohibition of trade with the British Isles in 1915 was called off. The Germans promised to spare neutral ships. After the sinking of the *Lusitania* with heavy loss of American life, Wilson rather reluctantly pressed them to sink no passenger ships at all. Eventually, after the sinking of the *Sussex* in 1916, he forced them by threat of war to give up submerged attacks and abide by the traditional rules of cruiser warfare. The allies by that time were the less compliant side. They were no longer willing to let through the modicum of German–American trade which had hitherto continued, and they used increasingly odious means to strangle it, such as a boycott of American firms trading with their enemies. They had made it harder to civilize submarine warfare by arming their merchantmen and letting them fly neutral colours— points on which Wilson tried to mediate between the belligerents. The repression of the Irish rebellion of Easter 1916 added to a growing popular feeling in America against the allies. Wilson had always been eager to preserve trade between his country and the Central Powers: he had championed, for instance, an abortive scheme for his government to take over the German merchant ships blockaded in American ports. He was now more determined than ever to insist on the rights of neutrals.

But although Wilson was not led to take sides in the war, he certainly was led by it to contemplate greater American involvement in world affairs, just as his imperialist opponents did but in a different spirit. 'The position of neutral nations,' he wrote in November 1916, 'has been rendered all but intolerable.' To check the universal repercussions which a modern total war was proving to have, he soon became convinced that all nations now needed to associate themselves in peacekeeping. His deep christian and liberal convictions made this idea come easily to him. His administration had already set to work on a Pan American Pact, joining the American republics in mutual guarantees of independence and territorial integrity. As the danger increased that America would have to take sides in the European war in order to protect her trade, Wilson became increasingly anxious to end it by mediation. The inducement that he could offer the belligerents was that the United States would join in a peacekeeping organization to protect the settlement then made. Colonel House visited Europe in 1915 and in 1916 to sound out the belligerent powers. Grey's response (September 1915) was to ask 'would the President propose that there should be a League of Nations binding themselves to side against any power which broke a treaty?' Wilson replied that he would, and in May 1916 he addressed a meeting of the League to Enforce Peace in this sense, remarking that 'we are participants, whether we would or not, in the life of the world. The interests of all nations are our own also.'

But, as Wilson later said, the United States could only underwrite a peace based on 'American principles, American policies'. This meant, in effect, a peace without annexations and indemnities, and after it 'not a balance of power, but a community of power; not organized rivalries, but an organized common peace'. Neither side in the war was yet ready even to take the first step of renouncing the hope of victory. There was more sympathy with Wilson's ideas on the allied side, and in 1916 Wilson first tried to elicit a request for mediation from them. But they had so far lost the most European territory and seemed likely to be at a disadvantage in negotiations. House would probably have liked to offer the bait of American intervention if Germany refused mediation. But Wilson would not and could not make this offer, and the most that was said was that in such a case the United States would 'probably' enter the war. The allies refused Wilson's offer, and this, too, was behind his deteriorating relations with them in 1916. He turned to the Germans.

By the end of 1916 German submarine building had gone far enough to make a complete blockade of Britain worth attempting, and Hindenburg and Ludendorff could see no other way of winning and became increasingly eager to try it. Bethmann's moderate policy was bereft of support: the Reichstag even called on him in October 1916 to follow the views of the high command in this question. He therefore became, like Wilson, eager for a negotiated peace to forestall American entry into the war. He was allowed to try for one, and the temporary ascendancy of the extreme right in Russia described below gave him a good chance to split the allies. But he was expected to hold on to as much as he could of the conquests of the Central Powers, and in November their proclamation of a puppet Polish kingdom had made a settlement with Russia impossible. Nor could Wilson be allowed to mediate, since he would never approve terms acceptable to the Central Powers. In December, therefore, Bethmann offered to negotiate, but he did not respond when Wilson asked the two sides for their terms with a view to bringing them together. The allies did reply, coming out for the first time with demands for the dismemberment of the Habsburg and Ottoman Empires. Negotiations never even got started, and on 9 January 1917 the Germans decided to begin unrestricted submarine attacks on all shipping round the British Isles and in the eastern Mediterranean at the end of the month. On 2 April the United States entered the war.

American isolationists and left-wingers long contended that the country was dragged into war by big business interests which had grown fat on supplying the allies. They had made it impossible for the United States to dispense with this trade, while giving Germany the strongest reasons for attacking it. By lending the allies money they had acquired an un-neutral vested interest in their victory. These views resulted in the attempt to keep America out of the Second World War by the Neutrality Act, which restricted belligerent trade with the United States to 'cash and carry': neither American ships nor American credit were to be involved. Wilson's government itself had similar thoughts. For almost a year after the outbreak of war they refused to allow Americans to give credit to their allied customers, and gave in only when the embargo threatened to bring trade to a stop. We shall, indeed, see in due course that European indebtedness to America kept the United States deep in European affairs in the twenties when she was eager to withdraw from them. Likewise, it is hard to see how the Americans could have remained inactive when their exports to Europe totally stopped, the goods piling up on the quaysides: this happened as soon as the submarine campaign began. Yet it is too simple to say that economic interests led the United States directly to the side of the allies, or even into war at all. The main economic aim of the Americans in 1916 was to trade with both sides, and the best way of achieving that was to restore peace. What the economic factor really determined was that the Americans could no longer hold aloof from Europe. Trade with the old world was so important—not least to the isolationist farmers—that they could not tolerate its interruption. They could not even interrupt it themselves as a reprisal against belligerents, as had been done in the Napoleonic wars. They had instead to intervene in European affairs and help to put things to rights.

The form and extent of the intervention was determined by the behaviour of the European belligerents. The Germans were in the end the more unreasonable, so intervention had to be against them. Their unreasonableness increased (or became more apparent) with time and so the American commitment to the allied cause steadily strengthened. At first Wilson had envisaged simply an armed neutrality, and war was declared partly just to regularize the position of Americans firing on submarines in self-defence. But Wilson and his people were already moving farther. The German submarine campaign was not directed primarily against American trade. Ironically, the American harvest of 1916 was bad, and what had particularly encouraged the Germans to launch their submarine attack was the strain on allied shipping resulting from reliance on more distant sources of supply, like Australia. But the Germans expected war with the United States to ensue and made plans accordingly. An absurd plot of theirs was discovered for an attack on the western states by Japan and Mexico—a great shock to that isolationist (and race-conscious) area.[1] Wilson was very shocked when he was told at last, and in confidence, what peace terms the Germans had just been contemplating. Popular anger was aroused when the submarines began in

[1] This was the affair of the Zimmermann telegram.

earnest to take a toll of American lives. The first Russian revolution (March 1917) also affected American sentiment: once the Tsar was gone, they were willing to believe that the allied cause was the cause of democracy. The declaration of war when it came was therefore not a mere token, and as early as June 1917 a few American troops reached France; as yet there were only a few available.

But Wilson was careful to style his country an 'associated', not an 'allied', power, careful even in December 1917 to say that 'we intend no wrong against the German Empire'. His allies found his attitude still that of an arbitrator rather than a belligerent. American entry into the war did not really come suddenly, with the formal declaration. It built up slowly before that event and continued to build up after it. It became complete only with the events next to be described.

2: The Russian Revolutions of 1917

In 1917 the war began to take its toll among the weaker states. Austria-Hungary (and to some extent Italy also) was preserved only by the proximity of a stronger ally. Isolated Russia succumbed. But from both conservative Austrians and revolutionary Russians came desperate initiatives to save their states by restoring peace. These aroused some revolutionary feeling in the rest of Europe and completed the process of American involvement in European affairs.

The February Revolution[1]: the Fall of the Russian Monarchy

Russia was the first great power to suffer real military disaster, and the misfortunes of war already described were intensified in her case by the primitiveness of her government and society. The slaughter and capture of the old army was especially serious in a country so short of educated men who might become officers. Aristocratic incompetence in the rear hindered the growth of the munitions industry. Large areas behind the lines were put under martial law and their administration was badly disorganized by military interference. Sukhomlinov, the war minister, was so incapable that he even told the French that he did not need their help in the supply of munitions. One of his principal associates, Colonel Myasoyedov, was hanged as a spy in April 1915, and was supposed to have said that only a German victory could save the Russian autocracy. It was common knowledge that this treasonable attitude was widespread among the extreme reactionaries.

The liberals and moderate conservatives, on the other hand, were passionately committed to the war, as they had been to the policy of Slav defence which led up to it. The Tsar, for his part, cared for nothing so much as his army and was heartbroken at its misfortunes,

---

[1] Till the Bolsheviks took power, Russia continued to use the Julian calendar, by now thirteen days behind that used elsewhere (and in this book): the February revolution really happened in March and the October revolution in November.

which, in any case, damaged the autocracy as nothing else could have done. The first effect of disaster was therefore a coming together of Tsar and reformers, and a reversal of the reactionary trend which had set in with the death of Stolypin. At the start of the war the *zemstva* and town councils had got together and set up a national Red Cross organization (*Zemgor*). This had already been done during the Japanese war, and on both occasions prominent liberals were active in the work. The reactionaries accordingly regarded *Zemgor* with great suspicion, which from their own point of view was entirely justified. The *Zemgor* officials discovered at first hand the gross mismanagement behind the front line. They found that they could not confine themselves to the medical care of the men, but had increasingly to concern themselves with their general welfare; for instance by trying to improve the food supply. The demand arose in the political circles from which they came for a new and similar organization to take over the supply of munitions. Rodzyanko the Octobrist president of the Duma—already in charge of the army's boot supply—urged the Tsar to set up a Defence Council for this purpose, on which the business community and the two houses of the legislature would be represented. In June 1915 Prince George Lvov, the liberal head of *Zemgor*, convened a conference on munitions in Moscow at which Guchkov, the ablest Octobrist leader, described in detail the want of arms and ammunition and denounced Sukhomlinov by name.

The Tsar yielded to these remonstrances. The Defence Council was established,[1] and the reactionary ministers who disliked it removed. Sukhomlinov was replaced by the able and enlightened Polivanov. The useless premier Goremykin remained, but he was subservient rather than reactionary. Guchkov was allowed to set up a network of war industry committees to organize production of the army's needs in the different industries and localities. They included representatives of both management and labour, and were thus an attempt to draw the classes together in the interest of national defence. The same impulse was seen in the Duma, which the Tsar allowed to meet after a year's virtual abeyance in August 1915. All the parties save the extreme reactionaries joined in a 'Progressive Bloc'. While pledging their support in the prosecution of the war, they came out in favour of a huge programme of reform: no more

[1] Eventually there were five councils, for different departments of national life.

punishment of political activity, the liberalizing of local government, concessions to the Poles, Finns, Ukrainians and Jews, labour legislation and the curtailment of military authority in civil affairs. A ministry of 'national confidence' was also an aim of the Bloc, though to spare the feelings of the conservatives there was no demand that it should be dependent on the Duma. What is notable about this programme is that even the conservatives and the ministers regarded it as reasonable, despite the fact that the middle of an unsuccessful war was hardly a convenient moment for the reconstruction of the state. The ministers chafed at the insubordination of the army, and Polivanov had long been on close terms with Guchkov. They would have liked to strike a bargain with the Bloc and carry on the war on that basis.

The lost opportunities of 1905–6 for a turn towards parliamentary government by a common accord of government and educated classes, conservative and progressive, had almost been re-won. But the Tsar was not prepared to respond to disaster by confessing himself unfit to wield supreme power: quite the contrary. At the end of August he personally took over the post of commander-in-chief of the forces from the Grand Duke Nicholas. This was the work of the Tsarina and Rasputin. The Tsarina had been nobly devoting herself to the care of the wounded, oblivious of politics. But she was alarmed at the triumph of the 'horrid Rodzyanko' and her pet aversion, Guchkov, and began to bombard her husband with political advice, never to stop until the throne fell. 'Be more autocratic my very own Sweetheart,' she wrote (they corresponded in rather odd colloquial English). Nicholas tried, but it was not for nothing that late in 1916 he signed a letter to her 'your poor little weak-willed hubby'. An entirely ordinary man had taken on a hero's task, and he seems to have been crushed beneath the weight of it. In the last year of his reign, he is described as exhausted and apathetic. Such capacity to rule as he had was destroyed by his attempts to do better.

His assumption of military command was especially unfortunate. Wisely he left the business of his new post to his generals, but he did insist on residing almost permanently at army headquarters at Mogilev. He was henceforth even more isolated than an autocrat usually is from popular feeling and responsible opinion. Though he did not accept the advice of his wife and Rasputin without criticism, he became far more liable to succumb to it. His ministers realized at once what a blunder he was making. With the exception of Goremykin, they besought him to change his mind, and even hinted at resigning in a body. Nicholas plucked up courage to defy them, and Goremykin now urged the prorogation of the Duma, which was done on 16 September 1915. A two-day general strike and the protests of the *Zemgor* leaders (to say nothing of many municipal resolutions in favour of the Bloc programme) were ignored. At the end of the month the Tsar met his ministers and reproved them for trying to force his hand, ordering them to confine themselves to their departmental duties.

The abortive liberal revolt of 1915 was not without result. The administrative changes remained, and the progressives were able to do much in the organizing of the war effort. Munitions production increased and the Russian army was far better equipped when the monarchy fell than when the war started. If this was partly due to allied help, the same cannot be said of Polivanov's work in improving the training of recruits. A new army, in effect, was created in place of the regular force that had been destroyed. Of course, all this work was suspect to the Tsarina, for it was in the hands of her political enemies. Polivanov was dismissed in March 1916, avowedly because he had been 'insufficiently authoritative' with the war industries committees—in other words, too friendly towards liberal elements. But the Tsar never again left the armed forces under the control of anyone as bad as Sukhomlinov.

None of this could atone, however, for the renewed ascendancy of reaction. It was not that the government became strikingly more oppressive: it did not, and had it shown the vigour necessary to do so, the day might yet have been saved. What the reactionaries did was to disorganize the administration: they could not have served the cause of revolution better had they been its paid agents. The Tsarina tried as far as she could to turn out the honest ministers who had dared to have a mind of their own in the crisis of 1915. In proposing replacements she was governed by Rasputin, and he was bound to suggest bad men because all the honest ones detested him and were bent on his destruction. Even the ministers whose careers he promoted pretended to have nothing to do with him. Such was the incapacity of the men brought forward, and so incessant were the quarrels among the adventurers who crowded in to seek their fortune, that the new ministers seldom lasted long. A ministerial instability far worse than that of republican France intensified the effects of ministerial incompetence. Rasputin particularly needed a docile minister of the interior, so that the police would not interfere with his own debaucheries and the misdeeds of his hangers-on. Hvostov, his first choice, was at least an energetic administrator, but he did not outlast the winter of 1915–16; tiring of Rasputin's patronage, he tried to have him murdered, and was dismissed soon after the story came out. Stürmer and Protopopov, who held the office for most of the monarchy's last year, were quite incapable of discharging their duties and did not seriously attempt to do so. The ministry primarily responsible for keeping order and suppressing sedition—latterly also for the food supply—was headless. Not all departments were as badly off as this: there were always some respectable ministers in the government. On the other hand, numerous lesser posts everywhere went to the creatures of Rasputin, some of whom were simply criminals.

It was not hard to build up opposition to this rotten system. Most of the adventurers fighting for power were not reactionaries for any reason but self-interest. Hvostov and Protopopov were members of the Duma, and hoped to govern in concert with it. Goremykin was pushed out in 1916 because he was unwilling to try this, and replaced by Stürmer, a court official and complete nonentity, intent only on feathering his nest. The Duma, accordingly, met briefly in February 1916, and continuously from the autumn, by which time Stürmer had taken over the foreign office and was suspected of wanting a separate peace. This, however sensible, was anathema to all the progressives. Milyukov, the leader of the Cadets, denounced the shortcomings of the government and asked concerning each one 'is this folly or treason?' As the disintegration of the state proceeded, more and more respectable conservatives went in to opposition. Purishkevich, the ablest reactionary parliamentarian, attacked Rasputin in the Duma on 2 December 1916. With him Prince Yusupov and the Grand Duke Dimitri (both related to the Tsar) formed a plot to murder the monk, and this they accomplished on 29 December. Stürmer had already been dismissed, and now the infatuated Tsar was urged not merely by Rodzyanko but by the Grand Dukes his cousins, by the heads of the General Staff, even by the British and French ambassadors, to create a ministry acceptable to public opinion. But on 7 March 1917 he left his capital for army headquarters without having done it. Duma leaders began to make plans with leading generals for a *coup d'état*. On 27 February Kerensky, leader of the *trudovik* group, openly told the Duma that the Tsar must go.

But the generals and politicians were forestalled by the workers and soldiers. Defeatism spread among them after the crisis of 1915. The increasing disorganization of government was reflected in rocketing prices and scarcity of food. As already noted, this was not due to a dearth in the country. The immediate causes were the demands of the army and the consequent strain on the railway system: there were not trains enough to move supplies to the towns. Strikes, which had almost ceased in late 1914, again became common. From October 1916 the situation in Petrograd[1] was recognized on all hands as serious. On 8 March 1917 widespread food riots began in the capital, where many strikes were already in progress. The city was full of troops as always, but now they were mostly recruits. Arms were still so scarce that their training had not got far and their morale was low. On the 12th the troops mutinied, and next day the capital was in the hands of the insurgents. As early as the 9th the ministers turned to the Duma for help, and showed themselves willing to resign at its behest. On the 11th Rodzyanko got in touch with the generals in high command at the front and assured himself of their support. Nicholas did not realize how bad things were until the 13th. He started for the capital but could get no farther than Pskov. Consulted by the chief of staff, the generals in command of "fronts" (army groups) came out in favour of his abdication and he had already decided on it when Rodzyanko, Guchkov and another conservative, Shulgin, came to ask it on behalf of the Duma. The Tsar and his advisers hoped to save the dynasty and avert civil war. Because of his son's infirmity, Nicholas abdicated in favour of his brother Michael. But because of the state of the capital, Michael did not venture to claim the throne and abdicated in his turn.

The house of Romanov had fallen because it had shown itself unfit to rule. It is not difficult to frame a defence of Nicholas II by comparing him with his Bolshevik successors. He allowed more liberty than

[1] The German name of St Petersburg had been Russified as a patriotic gesture in August 1914.

they did and the industrial and educational advances of the country were as striking in his time as under Stalin. The peasants too, who escaped from their yoke after his fall, were forced back under a heavier one after little more than a decade. But all this is entirely beside the point. A government's first duty is to maintain its authority and Nicholas had allowed the administration to go to pieces. A government that intends to survive needs also to proportion its policies to its resources. This may well serve to excuse the government of Nicholas for not having done more for Russia's internal development. But in that case the foreign policy of the last Tsar must be all the more strongly condemned. He twice launched his country into a war which she could not win, in the first case for a totally inadequate cause. It was his failures in war and diplomacy, the traditional fields of an autocrat's activity, that led to his downfall. In the end it was desired by the ruling class no less than the oppressed. It seems positively unlikely that he would have survived as long in the eighteenth century as he did in the twentieth. The Russians form of government then was "absolutism tempered by assassination," and an impossible ruler had been murdered as recently as 1801.[1] Autocracy could not survive the increasingly challenging conditions of the modern world without some such remedy. The murderers of Rasputin struck too late and killed the wrong man.[2]

The October Revolution: the Bolsheviks Gain Control

On the fall of the monarchy, the Progressive Bloc took over, forming a ministry according to plans worked out in the last months of opposition. The prime minister of the provisional government was Prince Lvov, the Red Cross leader, whose appointment was the Tsar's last official act. Kerensky was brought in to represent labour, but the other ministers were Cadets, Octobrists and conservatives. The fall of the monarchy had taken place in such a way, however, that the new government were very imperfectly in control of the situation. Conservatives and liberals had seen the need for drastic changes and had been able to organize for action in the winter of 1916–17, but they had been too timid and slow. Forestalled by insurrection from below, they had to share power with the insurgents, in the first instance with

[1] *Age of Transformation*, p. 78.
[2] The Tsar and his family were eventually murdered by the Bolsheviks in 1918.

those of Petrograd. The unrepresentative Duma naturally did not appeal to the masses as the basis of a new government and quietly disappeared from the scene. As early as 12 March a soviet (council) was elected in Petrograd, as in 1905, and it symbolically took over most of the Duma building. The other towns, and even the villages, elected soviets in imitation, and in June a national congress was held of their representatives. In contrast to the provisional government, the soviets represented the peasants and workers to the exclusion of the higher classes, and delegates who ceased to reflect their constituents' views could be withdrawn and replaced by them. More strikingly, the Petrograd soviet included, as it had not in 1905, representatives of the soldiers, and one of its first acts was to assume authority over the garrison. The famous 'order no. 1' required the election of a committee in each military and naval unit, which was to have charge of the arms and, in effect, decide what orders were to be obeyed. This was only the most striking instance of the way in which the soviets on occasion assumed governmental powers. Lenin was rightly to speak of a 'dual power', a sharing of authority between government and soviets.

But the provisional government's position was not hopeless. The soviets were dominated at first by the Socialist Revolutionaries and Mensheviks. At the national congress in June they had, respectively, 285 and 248 deputies, against 105 Bolsheviks. The Mensheviks believed, as we have seen, that a 'bourgeois' revolution had to be carried through before the struggle for socialism could begin, and so they accepted the new government. The Socialist Revolutionaries contained a revolutionary element, but included a great many moderates—rich peasants, professional men and the like—and became a haven for conservatives seeking a new political home after the revolution. Even the Petrograd soviet was dominated at first by middle-class politicians of fundamentally moderate views, notably the Duma deputies Chkheidze and Kerensky. The latter defied an order of the soviet by joining the ministry, but his action was not objected to and reflected the degree of sympathy between the two. They had no difficulty in agreeing that the future of the country should be entrusted to a constituent assembly elected by universal suffrage, which should decide on the form of government. The ministers failed, however, to consolidate their authority while they had the chance. The convening of the constituent assembly was delayed and the government therefore remained without moral basis for its power: it could not really claim to represent the people. This might not have mattered if its policies had been popular. But the ministers failed to do what the masses wished, and as their physical resources were so weak, the masses naturally came to defy them.

The main reasons for the increasing popular discontent were the delay in agrarian reform and the continuance of the war. The chief, perhaps the sole important, political aim of the peasants who made up the bulk of the Russian people was to seize the land which remained in the landlords' hands. When the revolution came, they expected to be allowed to do this. But the provisional government simply referred the question to the constituent assembly. The need for reform was generally admitted, but the propertied classes naturally wanted an orderly transfer after proper study and with compensation. The question was not on the face of it urgent: the peasants were not especially badly off, there was more food available in the countryside than before the war, it was in the towns that shortages and mass discontent had built up. But the peasants could see that their chance had come, and in the course of the summer the villages began to take over and divide up the landlords' land, burning manor houses and killing or driving out the owners. There was no way of stopping them. The police had been abolished, and the army itself was little more than a peasant mob.

Far more fatal was Russia's continuance in the war at the side of the allies. Again, this seemed at first to be obviously right. Not only were the liberals and moderate conservatives strongly patriotic, but their natural sympathies were with the western democracies just as those of the reactionaries were with the other side. The British and French ambassadors had tried, as noted already, to induce the Tsar to make liberal concessions in 1917. In 1915, likewise, Ambassador Paléologue had contributed to the fall of Sukhomlinov, and Lloyd George, by a cryptic remark in a public speech, had encouraged the Duma opposition. The new government therefore looked naturally to the entente powers for protection. A German victory was expected to mean the restoration of autocracy and a setback also to democratic forces within Germany. These last factors weighed especially with the moderate socialist leaders in the soviets and led them also

10—E.E.P.

to support the continuance of the war on a purely defensive basis. The allied governments, their backs to the wall, naturally encouraged the Russians to stay in. The improvement in the supply of munitions which had been taking place made it seem that their military chances were improving. But all these good arguments ignored the fact that the masses were now sick of the war and any government, therefore, that went on with it was doomed.

The great crises which led to the Bolshevik assumption of power were all to do with the war or the army, and they began almost as soon as the new government was formed. Milyukov, the Cadet leader, had become foreign minister, and on 18 March he promised the allies that Russia would fight on until total victory had been won. This was too much for the Petrograd soviet, and the provisional government was forced instead to come out in favour of a negotiated peace 'without annexations or reparations'. Milyukov, however, went on championing the old aggressive aims of the autocracy—especially the demand for Constantinople and the Straits—and on 1 May he repeated his former pledge to the allies. This brought the crowds back on to the streets of Petrograd, and on 18 May an entirely new government took office. Guchkov and Milyukov went out and five socialists came in, including Tseretelli and Chernov, the leaders respectively of the Mensheviks and Socialist Revolutionaries. Premier Lvov and some other liberals remained, but in effect power now passed from the Progressive Bloc to the moderate socialists—from the leaders of the old Duma to the leaders of the soviets. Henceforth, the real power in the government was Kerensky, who now moved to the war ministry. He was the very pattern of an old-style romantic revolutionary. Handsome, eloquent, looking younger than his thirty-six years, he had first won fame as a lawyer defending political prisoners, and now rose to the top through his power over the crowd. By a curious chance, he was the son of the headmaster under whom Lenin had been at school.

The new government had some chance of making a fresh start, as the agent of the soviets, the only existing bodies with any claim to represent the nation. But there were few important policy changes beyond the abandonment of Milyukov's foreign policy. The moderate soviet leaders therefore lost credit steadily with their supporters. One popular step which Kerensky did take at once (22 May) was to issue a 'declaration of the rights of the soldier', which applied to the whole army the principles of 'order no. 1'. Military discipline was already declining at the front, and now it steadily collapsed. Soldiers deserted in droves and went home. There was a connection between this and the growing disorder in the villages. Many of the deserters left the front in order to be sure of participating in the share-out of the confiscated land. The authority of the government progressively declined.

It was in this situation that the Bolsheviks set to work. For a decade they had borne the brunt of police repression, and at the start of 1917 their organization hardly existed and most of the leaders were in Siberia or abroad. Their line at first was accordingly timid and moderate. *Pravda*, it is true, which resumed publication on the fall of the monarchy, came out against the new government. But when the leaders who had been in Siberia arrived at the end of March they reversed this policy and were ready to support a defensive war. Lenin, on the other hand, denounced the new government as the tool of western imperialism. Britain and France had furthered its formation to prevent the Tsar making a separate peace, and they wished to use Russia as a tool in the furtherance of their plans of conquest and aggression. Revolt against both the war and the provisional government was the only answer. Not surprisingly, the allies were reluctant to permit Lenin to travel home from Switzerland, and the Germans were correspondingly eager that he should do so. They permitted him to cross Germany with some other revolutionaries in a sealed coach, and he reached Petrograd, via Scandinavia, on 16 April. A huge crowd and the leaders of the soviet awaited him at the Finland Station. Replying to their welcome, he said that he was 'the vanguard of the international proletarian army', and that his German opposite number, Liebknecht, would soon summon the people to 'turn their weapons against the capitalist exploiters'. Soon afterwards, *Pravda* published a summary of his views, known as the 'April theses'. As usual, he argued that a lasting peace could not be achieved by negotiation but only by a universal proletarian revolution. To this end the soviets should seize power and not permit the establishment of a parliamentary system, which the bourgeoisie would be able to control. They should take possession of land and industry and destroy the existing state machine. Since all socialist parties but his own had sold out to the bourgeoisie, he proposed for it a new name to mark it off from the renegade social-democrats. It should be called the Communist Party.

Lenin's apocalyptic views left his own followers aghast, and almost everyone else active in politics was either angry or contemptuous. Hardly anyone believed that the ignorant Russian masses could assume control of the state and economy. German military conquest seemed a more likely outcome of the attempt than an answering German revolution. Lenin came quite near to being executed as a German agent. When he told the June congress of soviets that his party was ready to take power, he was laughed at. He went on to propose an enquiry into excess profits and the arrest of a hundred important capitalists. Kerensky poured scorn on this simple-minded approach to economic problems, and very reasonably said that 'Marxism never taught such childlike and primitive means'. He warned the congress that extremism could only lead, as in the great French revolution, to the triumph of reaction.

This sort of talk was conclusive for most of the politically educated, but it was Lenin who gave voice to the dumb resentments of the war-weary masses. He soon converted his own followers to his view of the situation, and they worked hard to convince the people. Stalin, in *Pravda*, urged the peasants to seize the land. A big agitation was set on foot among the soldiers at the front. Lenin's own oratory, his terse and repetitive style and gift for slogan, was of great importance in the capital, where the Bolsheviks had a majority among the industrial workers by June. In July he was reinforced by the small but able following of Trotsky. The allies had little less suspicion of Trotsky than of Lenin, and it was some time before he was allowed to return from America. He had agreed with Lenin in his assessment of the war, and now joined him because his new ideas appeared to mark a departure from his former narrow authoritarianism.

But the Bolsheviks were still only a small minority and in their first encounter with their opponents they were decisively worsted. This next crisis of the provisional government was again due to the war. On 1 July, after Kerensky had toured the front in an effort to arouse patriotic enthusiasm, Brusilov launched the last Russian offensive of the war. It was a complete failure and by the middle of the month the enemy was counterattacking. Already on 23 June the Bolsheviks had planned a gigantic demonstration in the capital to impress the congress of soviets. The congress prohibited it, and the Bolsheviks with some difficulty restrained their supporters from defying the prohibition. On 15 July a breach took place between the Cadets and socialists in the ministry, and a reconstruction of the government became necessary. This was the signal for the Bolsheviks' supporters in Petrograd to rise and demand the assumption of full power by the soviets. On the 16th and 17th huge crowds of soldiers, sailors and workers besieged the Tauride Palace, where the Petrograd soviet met. Although defenceless, it refused to do what the insurgents demanded. The Bolshevik leaders endorsed the demands of their followers, but they did not feel strong enough to counter the soviet's refusal by seizing power themselves. The disorders therefore went on aimlessly until loyal troops arrived and put them down. The government then took the offensive against the Bolsheviks. The arrest of their leaders was ordered and they went into hiding. The headquarters of the party and *Pravda* were seized. Lenin fled to Finland. Convincing evidence came to light that Bolshevik propaganda had been largely paid for by the Germans. Meanwhile Kerensky, on 21 July, had displaced Lvov as prime minister. He kept the war ministry, and installed there as his deputy Boris Savinkov, perhaps the ablest organizer among the Socialist Revolutionaries. The death penalty was restored for crimes by soldiers at the front, and on 31 July the command of the army was given to the Cossack general Kornilov, who began vigorously to restore discipline. An attempt was under way to rebuild the power of the state.

The events of July lessened the standing of the soviets. Lenin concluded for the moment that they could be written off as a bourgeois tool. Kerensky seems to have concluded that he needed to reinforce his position with more support from the right. The Cadet element in the government was strengthened and a State Conference was convened at the end of August, consisting of members of all four Dumas and numerous other representatives of all classes and parties. It met in Moscow—almost a snub to the Petrograd soviet. Kornilov moved troops towards the two capitals, ready to deal with soviet insubordination, Bolshevik or otherwise. This third attempt at a stable provisional government turned out, however, even worse than its predecessors, for it was based on the collaboration of elements that were drifting apart. At the State Conference the left were behind Kerensky, but the right applauded Kornilov and were clearly beginning to hope for the repression of anarchy by a strong man. Kornilov seems to have wanted the establishment of a strong government based on the power of a reconstructed army, but including Kerensky as well as himself and perhaps not authoritarian in character. He was a stupid man, however, and his entourage were more obviously reactionary than he was. In September he negotiated with Kerensky from headquarters, demanding control of the troops in the capital, while Kerensky, for his part, asked for the dissolution of reactionary organizations among the officers. On 20 September, Kornilov asked for a new government with dictatorial powers, headed by the commander-in-chief. Apparently he did so because he had been led to believe that Kerensky would agree. But on the 22nd Kerensky dismissed him, and he responded by trying to march on the capital. Kerensky perforce appealed to the left against him, and Bolsheviks and their opponents were hastily reconciled. Kornilov's rising collapsed at once. His troops would not follow him, the railwaymen would not transport them, and he was soon under arrest.

This fresh crisis left Kerensky with the task of re-securing his government with left wing support. On 27 September Russia was officially proclaimed a republic. Serious preparations for the constituent assembly at last began. Another consultative conference, the Preliminary Parliament, met on 20 October—this time in Petrograd. The Bolshevik leaders were released. Such measures might have pointed the way to stability in June, but they were now too late. The peasants were hard at work seizing land and needed a government that would endorse them without ceremony. The collapse of government meant, of course, that economic conditions in the towns got even worse, transport and industry breaking down and food being scarcer than ever. The Kornilov affair, which was followed by a massacre of officers, almost finished the army. The soldiers and industrial workers needed no more to win them for Communism, and in September the Bolsheviks won a majority in the Petrograd soviet. The left wing, both in the Menshevik and Socialist Revolutionary parties, now thought it necessary to work with the Bolsheviks to defeat the reactionaries. A new rumour of counter-revolution arose—that the government was thinking of handing over its turbulent capital to the Germans. To prevent this the Petrograd soviet, on a Menshevik motion, established a Military Revolutionary Committee on 26 October and the chairmanship of both the committee and the soviet were entrusted to Trotsky. On 3 November the regiments of the capital decided to recognize the committee as the effective commanders of the garrison.

After the fall of Kornilov, Lenin, from his Finnish hideout, began to urge his followers to seize power. He took seriously the German danger to the capital, and also the attempts being made in the west for a compromise peace, which would enable the imperialists to combine against the Russian revolution. As the Bolsheviks now had a majority not only in the Petrograd but also in the Moscow soviet, they must strike at once. The party leadership was not so sure. They doubted their capacity to govern, and wanted at least to wait till the forthcoming national congress of soviets. Lenin wrote in a pamphlet at this time that there were 240,000 Bolsheviks, while the old aristocracy had only numbered 130,000. He concluded that his party was strong enough to retain control. He threatened to resign from the central committee of the party if his view was not adopted, and at last returned to the capital and carried the committee with him, after an all-night sitting on 23 October. A subcommittee was established to organize the rising—in that way there began the Politburo, destined at length to be the real ruler of the country.

It was, however, Trotsky's committee which directed the seizure of the capital by the garrison on 7 November. There was virtually no resistance. On the 6th Kerensky had appealed to both the Provisional Parliament and the Cossack troops in the city for support. But the former called for an entirely new administration, and the latter stood aloof: they considered that their loyalty in July had been ill repaid by the subsequent turn to the left. Only the Winter Palace, where the ministers were in session, held out till late on the 7th, and had to be bombarded by a cruiser from the river. Kerensky had escaped to army headquarters, and attempted to march on the capital. He had little support, and the railwaymen refused to transport the forces of either side. On the 13th he fled abroad. In Moscow the Bolsheviks rose, but at first were beaten back by loyal troops. But on the 13th they, too, surrendered, finding themselves unsupported.

The national congress of soviets met on the 7th. The Bolsheviks had timed their rising to coincide with this, intending that the congress should legitimize it. Fortunately for them, Kerensky's activity on the 6th had forced them to change their plan and act before instead of after the meeting. For they still had no national majority, and the congress would not have endorsed anything but a *fait accompli*. As it was, the Mensheviks and most of the Socialist Revolutionaries seceded in disgust. The Bolsheviks and the left wing of the Socialist Revolutionaries were left in control, and they formally assumed power and set up a new ministry, under the title of Soviet of People's Commissars. As early as the 8th decrees were issued giving the land to those who tilled it, and calling on the nations of the world for immediate peace without annexations and indemnities. Soldiers were ordered to fraternize with the enemy, and General Dukhonin, the chief of staff, was told to seek an armistice. On his refusal to do so, he was deposed by a detachment sent from the capital and then murdered. An armistice was concluded on 15 December.

Vigour on the side of policy was matched by vigour in asserting the authority of the new government. From the first it was tolerably clear that it was to be a one-party dictatorship. Some of the Bolsheviks were still afraid that this could not work. Several of the People's Commissars resigned on 17 November because Lenin would not join in a coalition with all the socialist parties. But Lenin was bent on destroying every organized political group but his own. As early as 9 November the suppression of newspapers began, and virtually none but Bolshevik papers were allowed to continue. On 11 December the Cadet party was declared illegal. On 20 December an 'extraordinary commission for the suppression of the counter revolution' was set up under Felix Dzierzynski. This quiet, efficient, fanatical Pole proceeded to organize a terror against all, high or low, who might make things difficult for the government. Arbitrary arrests and executions came thick and fast. There was not even a pretence of justice—violence, endemic all through the revolution but hitherto casual, was now organized for the benefit of the new régime. Lenin did, it is true, broaden his government at the end of November by the inclusion of the left Socialist Revolutionaries. But this merely enabled him to split the biggest party opposed to him, the one that appealed most to the peasant masses, and falsely claim that it was on his side.

He was helped thereby to deal with the one serious political embarrassment left over from the period before his revolution. The previous government had belatedly ordered elections for a constituent assembly. The Bolsheviks had chided their predecessors for failing to do this sooner, and this issue, along with the greater ones of land and peace, had helped to win them popularity. They dared not cancel the elections or prevent the meeting of the assembly. It speaks volumes for the incompetence of the other parties that they had let the Bolsheviks get away with the claim—sincerely made at least by some—that they would win a majority in free elections. When voting at length took place on 25 November it was the Socialist Revolutionaries who secured a majority—21 million votes and 370 seats against 9 million and 175 for the Bolsheviks, to which must be added the 40 seats of the dissident Socialist Revolutionaries.[1] When the assembly met on 18 January 1918 the Bolshevik position was parlous. They had shown great political vigour, but had nothing done to arrest the collapse of the ordinary administration and the economy. The soldiers and workers in the capital did not like the dictatorial ways of their new masters, and many of them were hostile or indifferent. But the moderate parties in the assembly failed to exploit this situation, and even refused offers of help from some of the troops. Lenin strengthened his forces in the capital by bringing in reliable bodies of sailors and Latvian sharpshooters, and for the rest relied on his terrorist organisation, which packed the galleries of the assembly when it met and made such an uproar that business was almost impossible. In spite of this, the assembly transacted business for a day and a night before adjourning. The government refused to let it meet again. The Bolsheviks claimed that the soviets represented a purer form of democracy and that the dissident Socialist Revolutionaries would have received most of that party's votes if the election had taken place after the decisive split. But Lenin rejoiced at 'the complete and open repudiation of the democratic idea in favour of the dictatorship concept. That will be a valuable lesson.'

The Bolsheviks had prevailed because the victors in the February revolution had not been able to solve the problem of 'dual power' resulting from it. The leaders of the Progressive Bloc had failed to dominate the soviets, and from May onward they virtually abdicated

[1] There were only sixteen Mensheviks and seventeen Cadets.

in favour of the moderate socialists. These, however, were not prepared to dethrone the higher classes completely, and so they steadily lost the sympathy of the rebellious peasants and mutinous soldiers without compensating gains elsewhere The failure of the Cadets and Octobrists either to seize power unaided or to retain it bears out the dictum in the first pronouncement of the Russian Social Democratic party in 1898 that the farther east one went, the more cowardly and ineffectual did the bourgeoisie become. The failure of the moderate socialists was, of course, judged by the Bolsheviks in the same light, but this is not entirely fair. Kerensky and his like were often socialists more in word than deed, but they sincerely believed in liberty and democracy, and could not share Lenin's trust in violence (in the forms both of anarchy and of dictatorship) because they could not believe that it could benefit the people. However, there is much substance in the argument that the backwardness of Russia justified Lenin's rejection of democracy. It was not that the Russian people were too ignorant of democratic procedures to operate them. The fatal thing was the deep social cleavages, which make it hard to believe that any government could have been freely obeyed by the willing consensus of all classes—the real characteristic of a democratic system. The Cadets and Octobrists might conceivably have established a sham democracy like that of Italy, for they had friends among the army officers who might have created a reliable force and held down the discontented masses without attempting to overthrow the liberal institutions set up by their political associates. Kerensky could not even do this, for the regenerated army was almost bound to overthrow him.

There remained the possibility of ending 'dual power' by unequivocal reliance on the insurgent masses. Lenin was left with a monopoly of this solution because hardly anyone else believed that the socialists could run the country without the co-operation of at least the bulk of the upper classes. This, it has been seen, tended to be the view of the Bolshevik leadership itself when not under Lenin's eye. Lenin differed from the rest partly because his approach was military rather than sociological. He considered not the strength of the social forces in presence but their dispositions: good tactics might make up for weak numbers. He made the capture of the government his sole objective, not worrying about the battles that would then ensue, because he was confident that he could devise new tactics to meet emergencies as they arose. Having defined his objective simply, he subordinated everything to achieving it, regardless of consistency. He championed the soviets because they were large bodies and the members were mostly inexperienced, and he thought, therefore, that his party could easily control them; when it turned out otherwise in July he was for a time for dropping them.

But the thing above all which impelled Lenin to rush in where the moderate socialists feared to tread was his internationalism. They were internationalists, too, but in practice they thought of what could be done in Russia and for Russia. Lenin, the returned exile, continued to work for a great international proletarian insurrection against the war. The moderates wanted co-operation with the Russian upper classes and Russia's allies abroad because they feared the Germans. Lenin thought that revolution would take care of that danger. The moderates feared that if the Russian proletariat tried to seize power for itself alone it would be crushed beneath the sheer weight of opposing numbers. In the last resort Lenin did not mind if it was: its example would encourage other nations and hasten the day of a universal proletarian outbreak, from which Russia would benefit in due course.

For the Bolsheviks, therefore, the seizure of power was only the first act in the drama. The state having almost broken down, there was indeed little power to seize. What it would lead to depended much on their ingenuity in using what they had won. But still more it depended on whether the international situation developed as Lenin expected it to.

The Attempts at a Peace of Reconciliation

Conservative Austria-Hungary showed more sense than conservative Russia in seeking peace before it was too late. Francis Joseph died at last in November 1916. The new emperor, Charles, was faced with the first allied declarations presaging a break-up of his realms, and with the fact that Hindenburg and Ludendorff had virtually deprived the Austrian forces of their independence. The Monarchy seemed doomed to destruction either by friends or by foes unless peace could be made. Charles negotiated with the western allies behind the back of

Germany through his brother-in-law, Prince Sixte of Bourbon-Parma. The allied reverses of 1917 made the moment propitious. In France there was a considerable defeatist campaign, financed in part with German money. Caillaux came out in favour of a compromise peace, and so did Lansdowne in Britain. But the allies saw little point in a separate peace with Austria-Hungary, even supposing that Charles would or could escape from his ally. The secret negotiations petered out.

More important were Austrian attempts to soften Germany. Czernin, the new Austrian foreign minister, approached Bethmann-Hollweg, who gave a hopeful reply, but was unwilling to defy the military leaders. The Austrians had better luck with their friends, the German clericals. The increasingly influential Erzberger was in close touch with the new Emperor and his government. Well informed about the submarine campaign, which he had tried to prevent, he knew that its results had not come up to expectation. He was worried by the growth of the 'independent' socialists, and wished to help the 'majority' socialists against them by forming a coalition for making peace which they could join. Early in July he made two important speeches in the main committee of the Reichstag, exposing the submarine situation and calling for a repudiation of annexationist war aims. On the 19th the Centre, radicals and 'majority' socialists carried a resolution in the full Reichstag reaffirming that the object of the war, as Germany had claimed at the start, was defensive, and calling for a peace without 'forced cessions' and 'extortions'. Erzberger next tried to get rid of Bethmann, himself a moderate, but too weak to fight for the policy he believed in. Unfortunately, Erzberger rather absurdly allied himself for this purpose to the high command of the army, which had long wished to dispose of Bethmann for quite contrary reasons. The result was a new chancellor indeed, but he was a complete nonentity—Michaelis, till then undersecretary in charge of food supplies. He accepted the peace resolution 'as I understand it' and the army rightly expected no trouble from him.

The German Centre were not the only catholics to come to the aid of Austria-Hungary, the last surviving catholic great power. Erzberger had been spurred on by the papal as well as the Austrian authorities, and in August Pope Benedict XV proposed to the belligerents a peace on the basis of the restoration of Belgium and of the *status quo* of 1914. The Pope, however, was not well placed to mediate, since protestant Britain was the only allied power represented at the Vatican, and anticlerical France and Italy protested when she tried to respond. Michaelis consulted a Reichstag committee on the terms of the German reply, but he managed to cheat them by letting the Pope understand that Germany was not willing to give up Belgium entirely. What might be called the Austrian-inspired peace moves came really to an end in October, when the Germans announced that they would never give up Alsace-Lorraine, and Lloyd George responded by making the recovery of these provinces a British war aim.

Behind the conservative campaign for peace there lay the fact that anti-war propaganda was at last making headway among the socialists, and the first Russian revolution made it a force to be reckoned with and, if possible, anticipated by the governments. In the spring of 1917 the Dutch and Scandinavian socialists undertook the convening of a conference of all socialist parties at Stockholm, to discuss terms of peace. The Petrograd soviet came out in favour of a similar plan, and after some confusion the two initiatives were fused. The conference never took place, but a great many delegates from different countries and parties visited Stockholm to confer with the committee that was trying to organize it, and there were also contacts between the Russian socialists and those of the west. In Britain and France the pro-war socialists, though under pressure, were still in the ascendent, but quite a revulsion was caused by the decision of the governments there not to allow delegates to attend the proposed conference, at which, of course, they would have sat down with the enemy. Arthur Henderson retired from the Lloyd George coalition, and though he was replaced the French socialists left their government for good. Meanwhile, the Kerensky government was urging its western allies to join in a revision of war aims, but its request was refused.

The situation when Lenin came to power in Russia was therefore ripe for some kind of revolutionary offensive for peace. Feeling against the war was growing in widely different quarters, but as yet the belligerent governments were holding their own. The Bolsheviks at once tried to supply the initiative required, but they were not the only ones. Wilson also intervened with the same purpose in view, and what Lenin achieved in the end was not a proletarian revolution in the west, as he had hoped, but the furthering and moulding of Wilson's plans for peace.

On 8 November a manifesto of the new Bolshevik government reaffirmed its predecessor's policy of a peace without annexations or indemnities and called for an armistice on all fronts. It was addressed to peoples as well as governments, and specifically to the working classes of Britain, France and Germany. In December the Bolsheviks published the secret treaties which the allies had made among themselves during the war. They included the treaty of London (1915) by which Italy had been induced to come in: in it she was promised Albania, the south Tyrol, Istria and Dalmatia, all with large non-Italian populations. There were also treaties of 1915–16 partitioning the bulk of the Ottoman Empire among the allies. The Bolsheviks hoped by this to open the eyes of the masses everywhere to the selfish greed of their rulers. Their negotiations with the Central Powers for an armistice were accompanied by pleas to the allies to join in, and a separate armistice was signed only when it became clear that the allies would not do so.

The Central Powers responded to the Bolsheviks in a reasonably amicable way. The German upheaval in the summer had brought to the foreign office Kühlmann, who desired a compromise peace with moderate gains and thought that this might be the way to it. Ludendorff gave him some latitude because he was increasingly anxious to send his troops in Russia against France. The German and Austrian food shortages were bad enough to produce riots early in 1918, and the Austrians in particular were desperately anxious to get corn from the Ukraine by the spring. These considerations pointed to a quick, amicable settlement with Russia. The Bolsheviks' willingness to provide one was almost their only card in the subsequent negotiations.

An armistice having been concluded, therefore, representatives of the Central Powers met a Bolshevik delegation at Brest Litovsk, Germany's eastern military headquarters, to consider the making of peace. On Christmas Day the Central Powers accepted Bolshevik proposals for a territorial settlement on the basis of self-determination, provided that the western allied powers would accept them too. But they soon made it clear that they would not apply this to 'national groups which possess no political independence' (such as the peoples of Austria-Hungary) and also that they expected it to lead to the detaching from Russia of the areas they had conquered. On 28 December discussion was adjourned till 9 January 1918, to see if the western powers would join in. Trotsky, now People's Commissar for Foreign Affairs, once more begged these powers not to 'sabotage the course of a general peace'. He threatened them with a separate peace if they did so, and urged the workers, in that case, to deprive them of power.

Meanwhile Wilson too was eager for action towards peace. He had regretted being able to make nothing of the papal initiative, and in September he had assembled a body of academics (known as the Inquiry) to investigate in detail how Europe might be reconstructed on liberal lines by a peace settlement. House went to Europe to induce the allies to make a joint, enlightened declaration of war aims. He failed, but American efforts were now seconded by Bolshevik propaganda of which the Brest conference itself—held in public at Bolshevik insistence—was an important part. In December the British labour party came out with a peace plan reflecting the resurgent idealism of the left. On 5 January 1918 Lloyd George addressed labour leaders on the need for sterner measures of conscription, and to make these more palatable he pledged his government to a peace programme similar to Labour's, the work of Lord Robert Cecil. The British urged Wilson, too, to make a statement, and he was very willing. The Brest negotiations had revealed to the public that aggressive aims lay behind the professed moderation of the Central Powers. The German supporters of a negotiated peace could no longer be deluded by their own government and began to protest. A skilful declaration from the west could be used to encourage the desire for peace in the enemy countries, and also the desire to resist among the Russian people, who surely would not submit to the Central Powers once it was clear that only the western nations would treat them fairly.

On 8 January 1918, therefore, Wilson went before congress. He spoke of the Brest negotiations, where the Russian representatives, having 'very justly, very wisely' insisted on treating in public, had been faced with terms reflecting the views of 'the military and imperialistic minority' in power in the enemy countries. There followed his statement of war aims, the Fourteen Points. The evacuation of Russia by the enemy was one of these (evacuation of Belgium was another), and Wilson said that 'the treatment accorded to Russia by her sister nations in the months to come will be the acid test of their good will'. Territorial changes which 'should' take place included the return of Alsace-Lorraine to France and comparable gains by Italy, the creation of an independent Poland with access to the sea, and autonomy for the subject peoples in the Habsburg and Ottoman Empires. The Straits should be internationalized. More essential than these were the general points aimed against the imperialist rapacity which Wilson, like the Bolsheviks, took to be the cause of the war: freedom of the seas in peace and war, general disarmament, removal of trade barriers, impartial settlement of colonial claims and the establishment of a League of Nations. The Americans in Russia at once set to work making the terms generally known by means of posters and leaflets. The Russian troops still at the front received them, and so did the Germans facing them. The Bolsheviks had made the free exchange of propaganda one of the terms of the armistice, and of this the Americans were now able to take advantage.

The Fourteen Points were a real triumph for the Bolshevik peace initiative. The second Russian revolution had decisively strengthened Wilson's hand against the warmongers in both camps. But he could not and did not wish to force the allies to join in the dubious conference at Brest. It therefore reconvened on 9 January without the western powers. The Central Powers were ready to conclude a separate peace, but no longer considered themselves bound by the conditions which the Bolsheviks had proposed, and which they had accepted (on paper) for the case of a peace between all the belligerents. The Bolsheviks were forced back to what was really their own distinctive policy—peace at any price. Lenin was prepared to accept this. He saw that his army was so disorganized that resistance was impossible. He believed that a few months' respite was essential to enable his government to establish firm control of the country. He continued to hope for proletarian revolutions elsewhere, but meanwhile the only thing to do was to hold on and wait. But he found that, even within his own party, most favoured the resumption of war rather than the acceptance of hopelessly unjust terms. For the moment a compromise policy was adopted. Trotsky took over the negotiations in person and tried so to conduct them that opprobrium increasingly fell on the other side, and time was given for the forces of peace to strengthen themselves in the enemy countries. What this meant at first was that he made innumerable long speeches, addressed to the world rather than the conference, in which he demonstrated the wicked egoism which underlay the enemy's terms.

This strategy might have succeeded better, but for another great problem which had all the time confronted the new Russian government, and which was dealt with by the Brest conference only in part— the relations of the Russians with the non-Russian peoples within the borders of the former Empire. On this question, as on others, Lenin and his followers were more uncompromisingly internationalist than any other party. On 15 November 1917 the new government had published a declaration promising not only equal rights for all national groups within Russia but also the right of any national group that wished it to proclaim its independence. The real meaning of this was rather obscured by the Bolshevik conception of politics as an international class war. Where a national group was divided by a civil war between classes, the Russian Bolsheviks did not consider it as contrary to the principle of self-determination if they intervened on the proletarian side. The Germans, in the large non-Russian territories which they had conquered from the Tsar, had been following a similar principle. By threats and promises they had tried to win the allegiance of the upper classes (who in the Baltic area were German, anyway), and then to claim for them the right to speak for their countries, which might thus be brought under German control by 'self-determination'.

A triangular contest thus arose between the various nationalist movements, the Germans and the Bolsheviks. In the territory held by the Central Powers a kingdom of Poland existed at least on paper, and preparations were also going forward to annexe the Baltic provinces to Germany. After the October revolution, the new government's authority was rejected in most of the non-Russian lands remaining unconquered. Finland, the Ukraine and large parts of the Caucasus seceded. Central Asia relapsed into anarchy. The Don Cossacks east of the Ukraine also broke away, though this was in part an attempt by officers of the old army to start a counter-revolution. The Bolsheviks, however, had their supporters in these places, who counterattacked. A civil war raged in Finland between Whites and Reds, although the Bolsheviks had actually acknowledged Finnish independence. With German help, the Whites were victorious by May 1918. The Ukrainian Rada in control at Kiev was challenged by a soviet government set up at Kharkov, in the industrial area farther east, where the Bolsheviks had more sympathizers. Early in February the soviet forces were strong enough to drive the Rada out of its capital.

The Germans befriended the Rada as they did the Finns, and to much more purpose. Here was a way of bypassing Bolshevik obstruction and laying hands on the grain of the south. The Austrians were so desperate for this that the Bolsheviks might have gained something otherwise by delay. But the German response was to open separate negotiations with the Rada, whose delegation had been brought into the resumed conference on their demand. On 8 February a peace treaty was signed with them. The Bolsheviks, who had by now produced a Ukrainian delegation of their own, refused to recognize this. But nothing was to be gained by further speechmaking, and on the 10th Trotsky delivered what he thought would be a master stroke. Withdrawing from the conference he declared that Russia would sign no treaty, but would consider the war at an end. The protocol-ridden Germans were floored by this, as Trotsky had intended: 'unheard of', gasped Hoffmann, the military plenipotentiary, victor of Tannenberg. The civilians, afraid all along of being put in the wrong with liberal opinion at home and abroad, were for acquiescence. But on military insistence the armistice was ended and the army began a quick unopposed advance on Petrograd. Lenin now demanded capitulation. Trotsky had agreed to support him if his experiment failed, and their combined influence produced a bare majority for it in the central committee of the Communist party. The treaty of Brest-Litovsk was eventually signed on 3 March. Continuing its policy of putting the enemy in the wrong, the soviet delegation signed the treaty without discussion, making clear that it bowed to force.

The treaty deprived Russia of the Baltic states, Finland, the Ukraine and Poland. Trotsky's final experiment added Estonia and Livonia to her losses. Turkey recovered the Asian territory she lost in 1878. A supplementary agreement in August provided for the removal of German troops from what remained of Russian territory, but imposed an indemnity of six milliard marks. Russia lost a third of her population, half her industrial undertakings and nine-tenths of her coal mines. Austro-German forces occupied the Ukraine in the name of the Rada. They then quarrelled with it, and superseded it by a nominee of their own, a Tsarist officer named Skoropadsky. Under his shadowy authority, landlords and capitalists began to re-establish themselves in the area. In Russia itself, the erstwhile liberals, who looked to the erstwhile expansionist Milyukov for leadership, now planned a counter-revolution with German support. Germans and Turks overran the Caucasus. Considering also the bitter quarrels within Russia resulting from the overwhelming unpopularity of the peace, it can be said that Lenin barely achieved his objective of a breathing space.

But the Central Powers did not profit from their severity, and the Bolsheviks richly achieved their objective of discrediting them in the eyes of the world. Thanks to the passive resistance of the peasantry, they never managed to get much food from the conquered territory, nor were they able to withdraw as many troops from the area as they had hoped. The statesmen of the Central Powers, meanwhile, had spoken in respectful terms of the Fourteen Points, but their deeds belied them. What was more, anti-war sentiment in their own countries proved quite unable to restrain them. In Germany the extreme left called a general strike in protest against the Brest terms. The 'majority' socialist leaders were so alarmed that they joined in to domesticate it, and in this they succeeded. The Reichstag swallowed the treaties. It was clear that they would not insist on a just peace if they could get victory. This at last led Wilson to the conclusion that only victory could bring peace. He had no interest in the defeat of Germany as such, but henceforth it seemed the essential preliminary to the establishment of a just and therefore durable world order. He spoke in a way he had never done before of 'force, force to the utmost, force without stint or limit, the righteous and triumphant force which shall make Right the law of the world and cast every selfish dominion down in the dust'. The entry of the United States into the war was, as it were, complete at last—just as large American forces were beginning to land in Europe. Thanks to the Bolshevik stimulus, the Americans had forced a programme on their allies and now had the will to force it on their foes. They would attempt to remake Europe on liberal lines, while the Bolsheviks sought to revolutionize it. The global struggle of the two ideologies had begun.

3: The Collapse of the Central Powers

The last year of war saw a final German attempt to win a total victory in the west, followed by a steady German collapse in the face of the mounting weight of men and metal brought against them by the European allies and the Americans. It was German power that had kept Germany's feeble allies in the field, and two of them, the Habsburg and Ottoman Empires, therefore disappeared at once from history. Germany (and Bulgaria) were in no real danger of doing this. The loyalties of the peoples and the principles of the victor powers alike required a Europe organized in nation states, the vanquished among them. But the German Emperor and other sovereigns were brought down by defeat, and the country's political future became highly uncertain: liberal, Bolshevik and reactionary trends all had a chance to prevail.

The End of the War and of the Multinational Empires

Hindenburg and Ludendorff had hoped to end the war in Europe by defeating Britain through the submarine blockade. They had counted on American entry into the war, but had assumed that the Americans would never send large forces to Europe, or at least could not get them there soon enough to make a difference. These calculations proved wrong. The Germans employed 90 to 100 submarines in the seas round Britain for most of 1917, their most important operating area being between Ireland and Spain. They sank 212 ships in February, the first month of blockade, rising to 335 in April. But in May the use of convoys began. Naval opinion had hitherto regarded these as too difficult to organize, and too vulnerable to attack anyway. But Beatty, now British commander-in-chief, was in favour of them, and so was the principal American commander, Admiral Sims. By August there was a regular system of eastbound convoys across the Atlantic—three different kinds of ships of different speeds—and westbound convoys were then started as well. Ships lost fell to 148 in August and 103 in November. They remained over 90 a month for most of 1918, but sinkings in the latter year were only 879 against 2,122 in 1917, and in 1918, moreover, they began to be exceeded by new construction. In the Mediterranean, where 844 ships were sunk in 1917, the convoy system was less successful, and it put a great strain on the British fleet, which was at last in some danger of not being able to contain the German surface forces. But it received important reinforcements from the Americans in home waters and the Japanese in the Mediterranean. Spectacular attempts of doubtful value were made to blockade the submarines themselves: barrages of mines across the North Sea and of nets across the Adriatic, and raids on Zeebrugge and Ostend (April–May 1918) where the smaller submarines were based.

The Americans had only a small regular army when war broke out, and Wilson had taken only belated and modest steps to expand it (1916), while declaring that they must have a navy 'second to none'. But he wisely insisted on conscription rather than haphazard voluntary effort to expand it when war started, and though it took a year to get any substantial numbers of troops to the fighting line, they then built up very quickly. Twenty-seven divisions were in Europe by the end of July 1918, and two million men crossed the Atlantic before the Armistice.

As early as November 1917, therefore, Ludendorff concluded that a new plan was necessary: the land war in Europe must be won before the Americans arrived in force. The collapse of Russia and the subsequent making of peace gave some hope that this could be done by allowing the Western Front to be reinforced. In May 1917 Germany had had ninety-nine divisions on the Eastern Front and 141 on the Western. In 1918 she eventually had over 200 in the west. Even so, her margin of superiority over the allies was only about 10 per cent and reserves were inadequate. It was decided to strike at the British, now stronger than the French (and also, Ludendorff claimed, less skilful). Their section of the line was only a little way from the coast and it was hoped to drive them into the sea. Because of the Flanders mud, the offensive started a little to the south, east of Amiens. On 21 March 1918 when the offensive began, seventy-one German divisions faced twenty-six British in this sector. A huge hole was torn in the line, and the Germans advanced some twenty miles in five days. But the biggest gains were southwestwards, away from the Channel ports, and on the 28th an attempt to widen the gap northward failed, and ended the advance. On 9 April, however, a second offensive was opened, as planned, in Flanders. It happened that a bit of the line there was held by some Portuguese (for Britain's oldest ally had joined her in the war) and they were quickly thrust aside. The new offensive began much nearer the ports, and it led to Haig's famous order of the day, calling for a fight to the finish 'with our backs to the wall'.

The British were apprehensive at the passive attitude of the French when the attack began, and had nothing changed in France since the Nivelle fiasco they might now have been beaten to pieces. But in November 1917 Georges Clemenceau had become prime minister. Born in 1841, originally a doctor by profession, he had been for many years the custodian of Simon-Purity among the republicans and the great destroyer of compromising ministries. The 'tiger' was feared not only for his eloquence in speech and writing but also for his marksmanship—opponents who pressed him too hard were challenged to a duel. Though he had kept out of office, he was implicated in the Panama scandal and greatly damaged, but recovered and eventually came to head a ministry (1906). This had been strongly pacific in foreign affairs, in the then radical tradition. But the war revealed in Clemenceau the older belligerent and dictatorial radicalism of the Jacobins, and it was to save the republic that he was again made premier, by Poincaré. He disposed summarily of the defeatists, had Caillaux, the most eminent of them, put in prison, and rallied the nation for a fight to the finish. The French republic was to survive, perhaps by a hairsbreadth, while the German Empire, and later liberal Italy (not to speak of the states farther east), went under.

At the same time, allied co-operation improved. A supreme allied war council, consisting of heads of governments, was established in November 1917 and henceforth gave some general direction to allied planning, not only in war but afterwards, in the shaping of Europe. In response to the German offensive a conference of senior soldiers and statesmen was held at Doullens (26 March), at which Poincaré took the chair and Clemenceau was present. It was decided to give Foch, the French chief of staff, the task of 'co-ordinating' the action of the allied armies, and he gradually came to have something like the position of commander-in-chief in the west. Foch was readier to help the British than was Pétain, who remained as French commander-in-chief. By the end of April the Flanders offensive was halted, and the Germans decided that they must damage the French before trying once more against the British. The resulting attack (27 May) was more successful than expected, and brought the Germans once more to the Marne and within striking range of Paris. But attacks to the east and west in June and July failed to widen the narrow bulge which they had pushed forward, and Ludendorff had already decided to withdraw when a counterattack on 18 July pushed them back. In consequence, their plans for a further attack in Flanders were postponed, as it turned out, for good.

Ludendorff had done remarkable damage to the allied front, but he lacked the reserves and transport to widen and deepen the breaches and turn them into a general advance. His troops were left in an exposed position, holding lengthened lines that were not properly fortified. On 8 August, which Ludendorff was to call 'the black day of the German army', the British attacked them east of Amiens, and on the 20th the French joined in a little to the south. The Germans were completely unable to hold their gains of the spring, and early in September they were back more or less in their old positions, including the heavy fortifications of the Hindenburg Line. Foch now called for a general offensive which, largely under the influence of Haig, he tried to give something of the character of an enveloping movement. Besides attacks in the centre, there was to be one on the right, in the region of Verdun, intended to menace the enemy's rail communications with Germany. Another was added at the other extreme, in Flanders. In the event, the last was spoiled by the usual mud, and the Americans on the right, though they pinched out a German salient to the east of Verdun, were able to advance only slowly in the Argonne, farther west. It was the battle in the centre that was decisive. The British opened the attack on 27 September, and on 4 October they broke right through the Hindenburg Line.

This was really the end of the war: on 29 September Ludendorff, his nerve destroyed, told his government that peace must be sought. He believed that his army was in imminent danger of collapse, and though at that moment this was an exaggeration, he was fundamentally right. The British, in particular, had shown great skill in the attack, notably in developing the concerted use of infantry and tanks. But successes were achieved against strong fortifications and with little numerical superiority, which would have been unthinkable earlier in the war. The storming of the Hindenburg Line was a frontal attack, with prolonged artillery preparation and consequently no surprise. The British government expected another futile massacre, and Haig had to go to London to win their consent to it. The story was different this time, because the Germans were hungry, short of equipment and certain now that they could not win the war. The allies, thanks to the Americans, were more numerous than ever, they at last had unity of command, and their advance was accelerated by a great increase in motor transport. The final victory was one of attrition, though generalship was not lacking. A declining force on one side was overwhelmed by a growing force on the other.

The final defeat of Germany was accompanied by the overthrow of her Near Eastern allies. The western powers continued to keep forces in Salonika, and an offensive in May 1918 suggested that the Bulgars were tired of the war. On 15 September an all-out attack was launched, and on the 30th the Bulgars were granted an armistice, agreeing to evacuate their neighbours' territory and put their own at the allies' disposal. The British had had to keep forces in Egypt to protect the Suez Canal, and to invade Mesopotamia to safeguard their position in the Persian Gulf. From this they were led to recommence the conquest of Turkey, this time the hard and slow way, from the extremities. Jerusalem fell in December 1917, and on 19 September 1918 the Turks were routed north of Jaffa; the whole of Syria was quickly occupied. The defection of Bulgaria broke Turkish communications with Germany and made an armistice imperative. This was concluded on 30 October with the British naval commander in the Mediterranean, by which time the Turks had lost almost all their remaining non-Turkish territory. Meanwhile Serbia was reconstituted, and Rumania (which had made peace soon after Russia) re-entered the war, and in December took over Transylvania. Austria-Hungary was menaced on all sides.

The allies had not finally lost interest in the idea of preserving the Monarchy until the Austrian failure in the role of peacemaker in 1917. In the summer of 1918 they recognized a provisional Czechoslovak government in exile under Masaryk. South Slav claims had

no such recognition, but in 1917 Pashich and Trumbich, the main
Serb and Croat leaders in exile, had agreed that a single south Slav
state should be formed under the King of Serbia. The Emperor
Charles did his best to conciliate the Slavs, reconvening the Vienna
parliament in 1917 in order to consult with them, and issuing in
October 1918 a proclamation establishing a federal form of government in accordance with their wishes. But even in this the integrity of
the kingdom of Hungary was safeguarded, and the Slavs in the Vienna
parliament had already made it clear in 1917 that they required it to
be broken up, so allowing the union of the south Slavs and of the
Czechs and Slovaks.

Charles was under no direct military pressure till the very end, for
the Italians long refused to take the offensive. But he took the German
reverses to be decisive, and as early as 14 September launched an
appeal for peace that was generally ignored. On 4 October, simultaneously with Germany, he accepted the Fourteen Points as a basis
for peace and even left Wilson to determine their application to his
realms. Wilson, in replying to the Austrians, declared that the
Czechoslovaks and the south Slavs, not himself, should be the judges
of that. This was the cue for these peoples to establish their states.
National councils of Czechs, Slovaks and south Slavs assumed power
in their respective territories on 28–30 October. On the 23rd the
Italians had at last plucked up courage to attack, and on the 27th the
Austrians were driven from their line on the Piave. Even the ruling
races now abandoned the Habsburgs, hoping to fare better with the
allies in a democratic guise. On the 31st Michael Karolyi, a Hungarian
nobleman but a real radical, was appointed his country's prime
minister, and three days later he declared its independence of the
monarch who had appointed him. The German members of the Vienna
parliament—including, of course, those from territory claimed by the
Czechs—formed a national assembly, and on 30 October proclaimed
themselves a state. Charles and the Hungarians made separate armistices with the allies on 4 and 10 November. The other ruling race, the
Poles, were more fortunately placed since they had some claims to be
considered as belonging to the victors' camp: their national aspirations had after all been included in the Fourteen Points. They, too,
set about establishing their own state from the territories of the
empires between which they had been partitioned. By the time that

the peace conference met in 1919, a new system of states was already in being in east-central Europe. Only the exact demarcation of frontiers remained to be done.

From Empire to Republic in Germany

The sheer magnitude of events in the war had steadily reduced to insignificance the ridiculous German Emperor and the timid bureaucrats who conducted his government. From 1916 effective power passed increasingly to the two groups in the country that had some real political strength behind them—the army commanders and the party leaders. There was little sympathy between the two. The generals were authoritarian, aristocratic and conservative. The politicians who counted were mildly liberal and progressive to various degrees, and often extremely plebeian. But a curious bond of co-operation grew up all the same, and it dominated the German scene until Hitler, destroying all rival politicians and reducing the army to submission, established a one-man rule surpassing that of Bismarck.

At first it was the generals—ultimately Ludendorff—who ruled. Even the moderate and progressive politicians had become eager for conquests in the early years of war, and their greed and their confidence in the army were slow to abate. They had helped the high command first to dominate and then to get rid of Bethmann. They asserted themselves a little more in the autumn of 1917. Michaelis, the new chancellor, was so obviously unequal to his post that their criticism sufficed to remove him. His successor was Count Hertling, the Bavarian premier, who had formerly been a leader of the Centre party in the Reichstag. He adopted a programme of peace and reform in consultation with the moderate party leaders, and made two of them, Payer and Friedberg, his deputies in the governments of the Empire and Prussia respectively. But there was no more than the appearance of parliamentary government. Hertling's personal views were extremely conservative, almost those of a Junker, and he was too old to do much work. The army continued to rule the roost. High officials who believed in a negotiated peace, like Kühlmann, were removed. A new attempt to reform the Prussian electoral system had been started by Bethmann in consequence of the first Russian revolution, but it now petered out. The moderate party leaders proved themselves as incapable as their opposite numbers in Russia of acting vigorously against the obstinate folly of the ruling circle, and so of forestalling the final disasters of defeat and revolution. An important reason for this was their personal insignificance: it is noteworthy that while the monarchy lasted they never tried to claim the chancellorship for one of their own number.

Only the military collapse changed the situation. By the end of September 1918 the parties which had supported Hertling were pressing for a true parliamentary ministry. The 'majority' socialists made the removal of Hertling a condition of themselves entering the government. The Centre and radicals regarded full socialist co-operation as essential in the worsening emergency, and so supported them. Hertling was preparing to resign when the politicians suddenly found themselves again in step with the generals. Ludendorff, having decided that the fighting must be stopped at all costs, demanded that the government approach Wilson for the negotiation of an armistice and the making of peace on the basis of the Fourteen Points. In order to make the approach more convincing, Germany was to be given a liberal ministry and democratic constitutional reforms. Thus it came about that Prince Max of Baden took office at the beginning of October with a cabinet in which the parliamentary, and notably the socialist, leadership was represented, and the imperial constitution was hastily amended to allow Reichstag members to become ministers without giving up their seats.

Ludendorff's new strategy was the result of nervous collapse induced by defeat, but it had a certain mad streak of genius about it. An armistice might allow the German army to withdraw and regroup. Wilson was not supposed to desire the total victory of either side, and the appeal to him was in effect an attempt to get him to resume his role of mediation. Germany might therefore expect reasonable terms, and if they were not good enough (Ludendorff was an annexationist to the last) the fighting might be resumed with some chance of bettering them. But this sort of reasoning failed to take account of Wilson's growing hostility to Germany. On 23 October he told the German government that he was ready to discuss the question of an armistice with his allies, but could only propose such terms as would make it impossible for Germany to resume hostilities subsequently. He also said that if the United States had to deal with 'the military masters and monarchical autocrats of Germany now' they 'must demand not peace negotiations but surrender'. Not only did Wilson refuse to play Ludendorff's game but in effect he invited the German people to remove the Kaiser and his generals in order to get better terms. Ludendorff, who was no longer quite so pessimistic about the military situation, responded by calling for continued resistance. But now a further miscalculation of his revealed itself: the war-weary ministers and people would not continue to fight once there was a real chance of peace. The hold of the high command was broken. Prince Max demanded and obtained the dismissal of Ludendorff, though he felt it necessary to retain Hindenburg.

Revolution broke out because the old rulers of the country could not be got to submit fast enough to the new. The battle fleet, unlike the army, was still intact, and the naval command thought that its chance had come to improve Germany's position by seeking battle. But the sailors had no wish to go out to certain death in a battle that might at best postpone defeat. At the beginning of November the fleet mutinied, and the mutiny spread to the soldiers sent to put it down and so inland through north Germany. Bavaria, meanwhile, was faced with the hitherto undreamed-of prospect of invasion through the collapse of Germany's allies. The natural dislike of the easygoing southerners for the Prussian military monarchy was exacerbated and on 7 November Kurt Eisner, an 'independent' socialist, was able to proclaim the republic in Munich. The princely dynasties everywhere toppled—they had become little more than appendages of Prussia. All this time the new government in Berlin had been trying to get the Kaiser to abdicate in favour of his grandson, in order to save the dynasty. Nobody wished to keep him once it was clear that better terms could be got without him: as early as 24 October Noske, on the extreme right of the 'majority' socialists, called in the Reichstag for 'a unique grand gesture on the part of the crown'. The Kaiser evaded the issue (rather as the Tsar had done) by going to army headquarters in Belgium. But growing disorders in the army made it clear that even there he was not safe, and on 9 November he abdicated on the advice of his generals. But in Berlin the socialists had decided on the 7th to withdraw from the government unless the abdication took place next day. Only in this way could they prevent their followers in the capital from going over to the 'independents'.

On the 9th Berlin was full of demonstrating crowds. Even before he had heard from the Kaiser, Prince Max found it necessary to announce that the thrones had been vacated,[1] and to hand over the Chancellorship to the 'majority' socialist leader, Ebert. But Liebknecht, one of the few truly revolutionary socialists, was now preparing to proclaim the republic. To forestall him Scheidemann, Ebert's partner in the 'majority' socialist leadership, did so at once. The armistice negotiations were already well under way, conducted on the German side by Erzberger: hostilities ended on the 11th.

The revolution gave the socialists the initiative, and at first they followed the soviet model. Workers', soldiers' and peasants' councils sprang up. The new government, formed by the 'majority' and 'independent' socialists, took the title of 'council of people's representatives'. A large and disorderly congress of councils in the Berlin area on 10 November confirmed it in office, and established an executive council to watch over it. But only a few as yet really wished to imitate the Bolsheviks. The 'majority' socialists believed, in Scheidemann's words, that 'Russian–Asiatic Bolshevism' was only a 'Barbarian–Asiatic caricature of scientific socialism'. They realized that Russian social organization had as good as collapsed, and they wished above all to prevent such a catastrophe in Germany. This was what Ebert meant when he said of social revolution 'I hate it like sin.' To preserve order the 'majority' socialists wished to work with the old army and bureaucracy. The future of the country they wished to entrust to a constituent assembly elected by universal suffrage. The 'independent' socialists did at least want to see all power vested in the representatives of the councils. But they felt too weak after the revolution to claim power for themselves, and agreed instead to share it with the moderates, leaving the question of a constituent assembly open. Many of them indeed (as already explained) were themselves moderate on most questions and radical only on the issue of war. Kurt Eisner, the Bavarian revolutionary, saw little prospect of socialist measures in November 1918 because, owing to wartime destruction, 'there is hardly anything left to socialize'. Some real revolutionaries had joined the 'independents' because their own organizations were proscribed. But they were really quite distinct. Their opposition to the war had begun early and, like Lenin's, it was not 'bourgeois pacifist', but

---

[1] The Kaiser, absurdly, had not renounced the Prussian throne.

based on international proletarian solidarity, which was to end the fighting by revolution. Their most important leaders were Liebknecht and Rosa Luxemburg, both of whom spent much of the war in prison.[1] At the end of 1918 they formed the German Communist Party.

The 'majority' socialists were able without too much difficulty to rouse opinion in the nation in favour of the rapid handing over of power to a constitutent assembly. On 25 November a conference of state premiers met and debated the question, rather indecisively. In December a national congress of councils was held, and in this moderation triumphed. The 'majority' socialists resoundingly justified their name in the elections, and the congress voted for the immediate summoning of a national assembly, electing a new executive council to supervise the government meanwhile. A general election had, in fact, been ordered on 30 November, and polling took place on 19 January. This time, rather to their surprise, the 'majority' socialists did not win the day. The two socialist parties together received only 45 per cent of the vote. The makers of the November revolution were outnumbered in the new parliament.

But this would not have been decisive if insurgent workers and soldiers had retained control of the streets. Ebert and his colleagues had kept in touch with the army command, where Ludendorff's successor, Groener, was very ready to work with them. Not a Junker but a relatively liberal Swabian, he had earned much respect and confidence in the labour movement while helping to organize war production. But although the army at the front had kept its discipline while the fighting lasted, its withdrawal under the armistice terms led to a complete collapse, the troops simply leaving their units and going home. The garrisons in the rear that had joined the revolution consisted of recruits, deserters and, in general, the unfittest portion of the army (like the equivalent Russian garrisons in 1917), and obeyed the government as long as it suited them. The December congress of councils issued something very like the Petrograd 'order no. 1', requiring army officers henceforth to be elective. Attempts in December to restore order in the Berlin garrison by using troops supplied by the high command were ineffectual: the incoming troops proved no more obedient. After one such attempt at the end of Decem-

---

[1] Their group was known as the spartacists, after their periodical the *Spartacus Letters*, published 1916–18.

ber, the 'independent' socialists retired from the government. On 4 January 1919, Eichhorn the 'independent' chief of the Berlin police was dismissed, and next day there were massive demonstrations of protest in the capital. The 'independent' and Communist leaders decided to attempt the overthrow of the 'majority' socialist government by force.

That they did not succeed was due to the rapid creation of an entirely new army, consisting of volunteers hostile to Bolshevism, and commanded by professional officers from the old army now in dissolution. These 'free corps' had first emerged for the defence of the eastern territories against the new Polish national state. They now went into action in Berlin under the orders of Noske, appointed defence commissioner. After heavy street fighting, they mastered Berlin (by 11 January); soon afterwards Liebknecht and Rosa Luxemburg were captured and murdered. The opening months of 1919 witnessed a series of similar battles between the extreme left and the free corps, whom the national assembly quickly made into the basis of a 'provisional Reichswehr'. The defeat of the socialists in the general election was a great shock to the working classes, and was followed by widespread strikes and demonstrations in the northern industrial areas, which were ruthlessly suppressed. In Bavaria, where the state elections had a result similar to the national ones, the murder of Eisner led to a further rising in Munich and the formation of a soviet republic. This egregious body was not capable of anything beyond chasing out the state parliament. It was dispersed by the army in May. The partisan and part-amateur character of the governmental forces led to casualties out of all proportion to the resistance which they encountered. The Bavarian soviet republic had taken only 12 lives but its suppression cost 700, including the massacre of 21 catholic youths mistaken for Communists. In March 1919 some 1,200 people were put to death in Berlin after martial law had been proclaimed, on the unfounded pretext that 50 policemen had been murdered.

It was to escape disorder that the national assembly met not in Berlin but in the little town of Weimar, famous as the centre of Germany's literary revival in the days of Goethe. Three-quarters of the seats were held by the parties of the progressive majority in the last Reichstag—the 'majority' socialists, the Centre and the

Democrats (radicals). Ebert was elected president of the republic, and Scheidemann became chancellor in a coalition cabinet. A constitutional draft had already been prepared by Dr Hugo Preuss, a noted authority on the development of German institutions, whose Jewish blood and democratic beliefs had restricted his academic advancement to a chair in the *commercial* university at Berlin. It was referred to an all-party commission, and the result of their labours became law on 11 August. The constitution had but a few years to live and has found but few admirers. But it usefully charts the stage which German political development had reached. A democratic and parliamentary system was created, with the government responsible to the legislature and the vote extended to women and younger men. The old federal states were preserved: they were required to give themselves democratic constitutions and their governments, as before, sent representatives to form the second chamber.[1] The opportunity to create new local units less geographically absurd was lost. This reflected in part the strength of local feeling (especially in Bavaria), and partly the desire to retain a supposedly conservative force. But the second chamber was given only a suspensive veto on legislation, and the national authorities received a great increase of power at the expense of the states, which might even in certain circumstances be dissolved and reorganized by the Reich. The central government used its new powers almost at once to take over from them the railway system and the administration of almost all the taxes.

Three features of the constitution which it is customary to condemn were the direct election of the president by the people, the introduction of a strict form of proportional representation (obligatory also on the states) and the provisions for direct participation in lawmaking by the electorate. Parliament had to consider a bill if a certain number of electors requested it, and bills might also be referred to the electorate for acceptance or rejection. These last provisions reflected the traditional ultra-radicalism of the socialists and were little used. The other two also look like ultra-radical points, but they were really concessions to conservatism. Proportional representation prevented the old upper-class parties from being squeezed out by the rich mass parties—the socialists and catholics. It is reproached with encourag-

[1] Half Prussia's representatives were elected by the individual provinces of Prussia.

ing small parties, but it would be sounder to reproach the German upper classes for being afraid of big ones. The direct election of a president, who might dissolve parliament and could sometimes rule by emergency decree, reflected a traditional dislike among German liberals for the third French republic. This was seen with some reason, as a self-seeking and self-perpetuating parliamentary oligarchy. A need was felt for someone outside parliament, who could call it to order: the truth was that even the 'majority' socialists regretted the passing of the monarchy. The substitute king created at Weimar was rather uncomfortably like a dictator, but it was a mark of wisdom to create an institution that might save the country if the experiment of a parliamentary system should fail to work.

The constitution included consolations for the extreme left as well as for the conservatives. To subdue the strike movement of early 1919, the government had had to promise the strikers that the social changes which they had hoped for from the revolution would at least in part be achieved. A promise of nationalization measures came to nothing. But factory councils, at which workers and management were supposed to consult about the management of the enterprise, were provided for by a law of January 1920. The constitution provided in theory for a national council on the same lines and one for each industry. More important to the workers of the country was a private agreement come to between the trade unions and the main employers' associations in November 1918. This, too, provided for joint factory and industry-wide committees, but it also established the eight-hour day, collective bargaining and arbitration in disputes and the re-employment of returning ex-service men. Company unions and restrictions on union organization were abolished. These were the practical benefits to the working class of the revolution.

The German social system had survived the inital shock of revolution. That it did not perish like its Russian equivalent reflects, of course, the far greater strength of conservative forces in Germany. The peasants owned their farms in much of the country and were upholders of private property. The middle classes were far more numerous than in Russia, and much more spirited in defence of their interests, as the rapid forming of the free corps shows. The workers were well off by Russian standards, and they had long been allowed to organize: their leaders were too sophisticated to expect an automatic millennium through confiscation. But no less important was the simple inadequacy of the socialists, who had the initiative in 1918–19 and made little use of it to change society. Those who believed in violence had plenty of supporters in the big cities—more than Lenin had, and little less anarchy than he to exploit. But they had not trained themselves, as the Bolsheviks had, for revolutionary activity, and so were not equal to their opportunity. Those who believed in liberal democracy should not really be blamed, as they often are, for the forcible suppression of the extremists: a government must establish its authority, and if it has none to start with, the process is bound to be unpleasant. If Noske used the free corps, Trotsky used Tsarist officers. The 'majority' socialists and the Reichstag politicians may more justly be blamed for not averting the horrors of revolution by stronger and earlier resistance to Ludendorff.

Still more may the 'majority' socialists be blamed for the lack of constructive social policies calculated to endear the new republic to the masses. This has often been excused on the grounds that even the national assembly of 1919 had a non-socialist majority. But one of the socialist ministers, David, explicitly said that the non-socialists in the ruling coalition had not made difficulties for socialist plans.[1] As already explained, however, the socialists believed that the re-building of the shattered German economy was really work for capitalism and free enterprise. 'No socialist régime,' wrote Karl Kautsky, then an 'independent', in 1918, 'can lift the misery which is due to general want in society. It can only lift the misery of want amidst abundance.'[2] Erzberger of the Centre party was more interested than many socialists in plans for the corporate organization of economic life, growing out of the new system of councils in industry. Wissell, the socialist Minister of the Economy in 1919, was not followed by his party in his enthusiasm for such schemes. Thus the Weimar republic committed itself to the existing economic system, and its survival came to depend on whether that system (dominated by men who disliked the Republic) worked well.

But the political situation in Germany did not result solely from what Germans did. It depended very largely on the actions of the

[1] A. J. Berlau, *The German Social Democratic Party, 1914–21* (Columbia, 1949), p. 253.
[2] *Ibid.*, p. 266.

victorious enemy. Wilson had done more than anyone to bring down the monarchy and the wisdom of this may be doubted. Only the revolutionary left really wanted a republic; what the bulk of the left and centre wanted was simply a democracy. If the old ruling classes were not to be forcibly extirpated there was nothing for it but to win them over to this, and it was more likely to be done if the monarchy was retained and high society strongly represented in the government. A later American administration was to show more tact in dealing with the Emperor of Japan. But far more important was the character of the peace which the victors were to impose on Germany. The Germans had gone over to democracy in the hope of getting better terms. The republican régime was likely to survive if it proved internationally rewarding. If not, it was sure to find itself under pressure both from the frustrated revolutionary left and from the far from republican elements still in control of the army, business and the bureaucracy.

4: The Paris Peace Conference of 1919

When Wilson came to Europe in December 1918 to attend the peace conference he received a popular welcome in the allied countries that probably had no precedent in Europe's past. On his tours of France and Italy he was acclaimed by huge and fervent crowds as a prophet and a saviour. His welcome in England was without this excitement, but there, too, he raised great hopes. In January 1919 the adoption in outline of a plan for a League of Nations and the defeat of the extremists in the German elections seemed to herald a secure liberal peace. But the peace settlement was not a clear liberal victory. It was not as oppressive as many then claimed, but it was something worse—it was unstable. Its provisions were not loyally accepted by the defeated side, and some at least of them were unworkable. The guarantee of the United States essential for their maintenance was withdrawn. The peacemakers failed to make peace with the Bolsheviks, or to crush them either. The great new revolutionary power stood behind the dissatisfied and defeated countries that were hostile to the settlement.

The League of Nations

The peacemakers were faced with a tragically impossible task. Europe east of the Rhine was in a state of revolutionary collapse. Governments and the economy were breaking down, starvation was spreading. A peace imposed by the victors would meet little organized opposition, but might be very hard to enforce in the face of anarchy. The soldiers and peoples of the victorious alliance were tired of fighting, and it was questionable if the terms of the treaties could be carried into execution before the victorious armies had to be demobilized. All this suggested the need for a moderate peace quickly made. The carrying out of such a settlement would not depend too much on allied military superiority and might anyway be accomplished before that superiority began to decline. But, unfortunately, among the victor nations hatred of war was evenly matched with hatred of the enemy. In the United States Wilson's Republican opponents won the congressional elections of November 1918, and although they included isolationists the predominant element among them were the imperialists who had been clamouring for the 'unconditional surrender' of Germany. The British elections of 1918 were won by L oyd George and his followers to the accompaniment of such famous cries as 'hang the Kaiser!' and 'squeeze Germany till the pips squeak!' Organized opinion in Italy and France was no less belligerent. The statesmen who assembled in Paris were under pressure to enforce on the enemy a peace of impossible severity, which could only have been carried out by strong exertions of military power for many years.

The French probably had the most level-headed idea of how to deal with this situation. They wanted a carefully organized agenda for the peace conference, and they desired to impose preliminary peace terms on Germany without discussion and then proceed at leisure to the elaboration of a European settlement. This, in effect, would have put off the real work of peacemaking to a point when the war had definitely ended and tempers had begun to cool. Also valuable was the French suggestion that the embarrassing secret treaties between the allies should be suspended. The Anglo-Saxons brushed aside the French plans, largely it seems because Wilson found them redolent of the old diplomacy. The conference started slowly and without an agenda. After some weeks the plan of a preliminary peace was revived as the need for speed became increasingly obvious. But Wilson again vetoed it because he could not afford, as will be explained, to have a peace treaty that did not include the League of Nations Covenant. The preparation of the final peace terms was therefore pressed forward with breathless haste. It was this need to finish the work before there was a general revolutionary cataclysm that led to the peace being 'dictated'. The Paris conference had at first been intended only to draw up terms which would be discussed with the enemy at a subsequent conference; the terms were intentionally made stiff for bargaining purposes. But to save time the Germans were eventually only allowed to make written submissions, within a given period. The allies' terms, as amended in the light of these, were then imposed on them. Haste was achieved but vindictiveness was not avoided: much of the work had to be done again.

The shortcomings of the settlement have often been explained by saying that an idealistic Wilson was bamboozled by the worldly politicians of Europe. This is to mistake the nature of the contrast. Wilson was very much an expert both in the theory and the craft of politics. He had, it is true, been a practising politician for a relatively short time, but he was far more readily deceived by himself than by others. Nor were his principal European colleagues very distant from him in their aspirations. The Italian Orlando strongly sympathized with his liberal principles in international affairs. Clemenceau and Lloyd George were bourgeois radicals in politics as he was. The cynical old Frenchman and the self-seeking opportunist Welshman were so unlike him personally that there was little cordiality between them. But they all shared the old progressive dream of a world of free and independent states living in harmony. The great difference arose from the fact that the European statesmen all depended for their position on parliamentary support, and their parliaments were bent on a peace of revenge. Lloyd George had faced a general election before the conference, and Clemenceau faced one after it, at which the right-wing nationalists whom he had fought all his life made big gains. Wilson had exactly the same parliamentary troubles as the rest, but he was not dependent on parliament for office. He alone, therefore, could approach diplomacy with something of the detachment possible for Bismarck and the other monarchical statesmen of prewar Europe. Of course, this independence lasted only until there was a treaty to be ratified, and the action of the United States Senate after the conference was as disastrous as that of the European parliaments during it.

The detached Wilson, representing moreover a country without territorial claims, could afford to strive for a just peace. But his was not the only or always the strongest voice for moderation. Lloyd George believed that the peace would not last if it was too harsh, and he strove for moderation as hard as his parliament would let him. This often led him to support Wilson against Clemenceau, but sometimes he found himself alone against them. For Wilson believed that the Germans had grievously sinned, that they ought to be punished—in short, that the basis of world order was not mere clemency but the rule of law and the triumph of justice. It was Lloyd George who made 'appeasement' a slogan; Wilson would never have done so.

This contrast between British and American policy persists to some extent in our own day.

As between Lloyd George and Clemenceau, there was a contrast reflecting different national interests. Nothing clearly could take priority for France over security against another German attack. Nothing but strong military guarantees could satisfy her because she was the weaker power even in 1914, and had become weaker still by her great loss of life and the devastation of her chief industrial regions. Germany had suffered no such destruction and could better bear heavy casualties. British interests were rather different. The surrender of most of the German fleet at the armistice, and its scuttling at Scapa Flow in 1919 ended her immediate security problem in a decisive way that no single event could possibly do for France. It was the Bolsheviks, with their dreams of revolution not only in Europe but in Asia too, who were now the obvious threat to the British Empire. The French hated the Bolsheviks far more virulently than the Anglo-Saxons did, and were mainly responsible for sabotaging negotiations with them. But it was largely British resources that kept a civil war going in Russia against Bolshevik rule, and it was the British who most feared the consequences of Germany going Bolshevik. A Russo-German tie-up had, of course, always been dangerous to British interests, even before the revolutionary factor was introduced.

The first victories in the peacemaking went to Wilson. As already noted, he was approached by the Germans in October 1918 in the hope that he would persist in his detachment from European passions and mediate between them and his allies. This in effect he did, but he managed to retain his allies' confidence and avoid favours to the Germans. He stipulated that the Germans must not be left in a position to resume the war—in effect, for German disarmament. But he agreed to their wish that the Fourteen Points be taken as the basis of the peace, which was not entirely welcome to the allies. Only after Colonel House had had a memorandum prepared which showed how readily their demands might be squared with the Points were they satisfied. Britain reserved her position regarding the freedom of the seas, and there were also afterthoughts about reparations which will need attention later. On these bases the allied military command was authorized to conclude an armistice, which took from Germany a huge quantity of naval and military equipment and brought the allied armies to the Rhine.

The so-called 'preliminary peace conference' among the allies did not begin until January. Of the five great powers present, the Japanese were only interested in the East, the war-torn Latin states, France and Italy, were decidedly poor relations. Wilson had both moral and physical ascendancy, and the British Empire was also well placed; never before had Europe been dominated by English-speaking armies. It was a French success that Paris was the seat of the conference, but, unprecedentedly in Europe and to their chagrin, English as well as French was an official language there. The self-governing white 'Dominions' of the Empire had their own representatives for the first time, and they and still dependent India were to be separate members of the League. It was largely in deference to Anglo-Saxon ascendancy that idealistic and extra-European issues were the first considered. The assigning of the enemies' colonies and dependencies as 'mandates' to trustee powers internationally accountable for their welfare was an Anglo-American idea. The main opposition was also English-speaking: South Africa, Australia and New Zealand wanted to make certain of their security by annexing the German territories adjacent to them outright. General Smuts of South Africa had, however, devised a compromise. Mandates were divided into three classes. Some were to be given independence after a brief interval, others to be administered as colonies, others to be governed as an integral part of the mandatory power. The three southern dominions received mandates of the last kind, and so did Japan for the German Pacific islands north of the Equator. The first kind was used for the Arab territories of Turkey. The dominions had made their mark in a big way, and Smuts was to emerge as a leading figure of the conference. The system of mandates has been decried ever since as a contemptible blind for annexation. It is perhaps more realistic to regard it as a step in the growth of international concern for dependent peoples (a concern that had begun when the Congress of Vienna prohibited the slave trade). It was a useful precedent that some colonial governments could be held to account at the League of Nations.

The League was not a solely Anglo-American idea, but the form which it finally took was. The French plan, prepared under the direction of Léon Bourgeois, was for a glorified defensive alliance of the victor powers, with forces under international command and control. At the opposite extreme were the British plans, essentially an attempt to systematize the informal concert of the powers which had kept the peace as best it could until 1914. They provided for mediation in disputes, the referring of cases to the International Court and so forth. Powers involved in a dispute would have to seek some such way of settling it. If a power complying with this obligation was attacked, the members of the League were to come to its aid by imposing sanctions on the attacker. There was no attempt to guarantee existing frontiers: on the contrary, the League was to recommend frontier changes when it seemed desirable, A deliberate attempt was made to avoid having a defensive alliance, protecting some powers against others, and to concentrate on the avoidance of war by giving every state a fair chance to safeguard its interests peacefully.

With this approach Wilson agreed, and he also went with the British in thinking that sanctions could be primarily economic and moral, with only a limited, exceptional use of force. The universality of the League was expected to mean that nobody would dare to defy it. Wilson defended it at home by saying that heavier armaments would be necessary if the United States did *not* join. He did not like the French plan for an international army, anyway—it seemed to him to be only the replacement of 'national' by 'international militarism'. The French plan disappeared in face of Anglo-Saxon disapproval and the only concession to their view was that the League was given a body of military advisers. But Wilson's starting-point was totally at variance with British thinking: all the members of the League were to guarantee each other's independence and territorial integrity, and violation of these in any case was to be deemed an act of war against them all. The British had to swallow this, and it entered the League Covenant beside their own very different ideas. They consoled themselves with Article XIX, which incorporated their wish that the League might recommend territorial changes. But as League decisions had to be unanimous (save that sometimes the parties to a dispute might not vote), this did not amount to much. Wilson wanted the guarantee because as a liberal he believed that civilization depended on the sanctity of property: to secure the 'land titles of the world' was essential. But this put him fundamentally on the side of the French, who wanted an alliance to guarantee the new territorial settlement. French 'international militarism' was the natural corollary of such an idea, and the Anglo-Saxons were eventually to be won over to it. The United Nations Charter drawn up after the Second World War contained provision for international military forces. In 1919 there was only one significant practical concession to the view that the League might eventually become a sort of world government. At the suggestion of Smuts it was given a Council, consisting of representatives of the great powers and of a few smaller ones. This ancestor of the Security Council might be expected to act with more vigour than the numerous Body of Delegates of the members as a whole.

It was a further triumph for Wilson that the conference accepted his wish that the League Covenant should be an integral part of the treaties of peace. To him it was their most important feature, taking precedence of the territorial arrangements because it rather than they guaranteed the world against a return of war. Having achieved what to him was the essential item in his programme, he went home briefly in February 1919 to catch up with presidential business. From this time on, things began to go seriously wrong. Firstly, Wilson's opponents in Congress began to make it really clear that they would not accept his policy as it stood. Rather unwillingly the President met the foreign relations committees of the two houses at dinner, but it did little good. Just before he returned to Europe, a declaration known as the Round Robin was signed by thirty-nine Republican senators. It declared the League of Nations unacceptable 'in its present form', and called for the making of peace with Germany first and consideration of the League afterwards. These thirty-nine senators had votes enough to block the ratification of a treaty, which requires a two-thirds majority in the Senate. Wilson thought that he had dealt with them to some extent by incorporating the Covenant in the peace treaty: he did not think that they would dare to reject the latter. But he concluded that four amendments must be made to the Covenant to assuage American opinion: members must be able to withdraw from the League and to refuse mandates; there must be no League interference in domestic affairs or in those of the Western hemisphere, safeguarded from European meddling by the Monroe doctrine. There was as yet no reason to believe that the United States would not join the League, and Wilson got the amendments accepted without very great difficulty: he declared his confidence that no country would ever withdraw. But Wilson had to appear as a suppliant, and American willingness to assume real responsibilities under the League was now much in doubt. His own prestige and that of his creation were severely shaken.

The Treaty of Versailles with Germany

It was in this atmosphere that peacemaking with Germany seriously began. Wilson was furious on finding when he returned to Europe that House had been planning with the allies a preliminary peace without the Covenant. But haste was urgent: the military authorities were worried by German restlessness. At every renewal of the armistice further surrenders of arms were therefore insisted on and the blockade was maintained, adding to the starvation and misery in the new republic. The peace treaty was therefore drawn up in barely two months, and presented to the Germans before the allied delegations themselves had had time to study the complete text. The different sections of it were the work of different specialists working in isolation, and their cumulative harshness was to some extent simply the result of poor liaison. Wilson's health, moreover, began to give way under the strain of overwork, and he became less able to control and moderate his colleagues.

The French showed their lack of faith in the League as it was developing by demanding that the left bank of the Rhine remain in the possession of their forces. No difficulty was made, of course, in restoring Alsace-Lorraine to them, but German Rhenish territory was another matter. France wished to annexe the Saar for the sake of its coal, and toyed with the idea of an independent Rhenish republic. Anglo-American opinion was firmly against this Alsace-Lorraine in reverse. Lloyd George persuaded Wilson to offer France instead a guarantee by their two countries against German attack. The French were to receive the Saar coalmines, to atone for the German destruction of their own, but not the territory. The French refused to budge until Wilson threatened to pack up and go home. Eventually, they were conceded the perpetual demilitarization of the Rhineland up to fifty kilometres east of the river and a fifteen-year occupation of the west bank and some bridgeheads by the allies, together with League administration of the Saar pending a plebiscite. The offer of the treaty of guarantee on which all turned was a blunder: there was no real chance that the United States Senate would ratify it, and British ratification was made dependent on American. This part of the settlement therefore damaged Germany without giving France the security she craved. The only real satisfaction to France was that she was permitted to prolong the occupation if she did not consider herself secure: this was some consolation when the treaty of guarantee failed to be ratified.

There was general agreement that Germany should be disarmed, but only on the point itself. The treaty eventually said that the intention was to facilitate general disarmament, and this reflected Anglo-American views far more than French. The British and Americans were especially hostile to conscription. Foch, on the other hand, had the professional soldier's contempt for short-term conscripts and thought a small professional army more dangerous. The French plan for a small German army of one-year conscripts was finally rejected in favour of a long-service professional army. But the French insisted, in return, that it be very small indeed—only 100,000, which was barely sufficient for internal security. Tanks, military aeroplanes and submarines were forbidden to the Germans, but they were allowed a navy with six battleships. The eastern as well as the western borders were demilitarized.

On reparations it was for once the British who were most for severity. When the allies agreed to the offer of an armistice on the basis of the Fourteen Points they made it clear that they would expect compensation 'for all damage done to the civilian population of the allies and their property'. The strict application of this principle would have meant that Germany would have paid a fairly moderate amount, mainly to France and Belgium. The European allies were far from satisfied with this: their finances were in ruins, and they would have liked to recover from Germany something towards the general cost of the war. The French insisted on a clause in the armistice by which 'future demands' of the allies were to be 'unaffected' by its financial terms. At the conference the demand for the recovery of war costs was formally made, only to be sternly repulsed by Wilson. This was not too bad for the French, since they could expect a good deal anyway. But the British could not claim much, although they could and did secure a large part of the German merchant fleet to make up for their shipping losses. It was especially from the British side that the demand came that civilian damage be taken to include the cost of allowances to soldiers' families, and pensions payable on account of their death or disablement. Smuts convinced Wilson of the justice of this by asking why damage to a peasant's hut should be paid for and not damage to the peasant.

The ultimate effect of including pensions was to almost treble the bill presented to Germany. Smuts and Wilson did not expect this because they expected that the total demanded would be related to Germany's capacity to pay. But the conference would accept this only in principle. Lloyd George at least saw the need to fix a modest sum, but he was under such overwhelming parliamentary pressure that the best he could consent to was the stating of an exorbitant one which could later be abandoned. Attempts to agree on a sum, or on a term of years to which payment might be limited, failed. In the end the total was left for subsequent fixing by a Reparations Commission on the basis of certain categories of damage. To satisfy public opinion further, Germany was declared to be liable for the full cost of the war but was excused it. This was the reason for the famous war guilt clause (article 231 of the final treaty) which spoke of the war as 'imposed' on the victors by 'the aggression of Germany and her allies'. The workability of the reparations settlement will be considered later. But the treaty provisions themselves can be faulted at once. They contributed to unrest by leaving the question in partial suspense and by making the Germans avow their own guilt. This may have been deserved, but it served no useful purpose and not only infuriated the vanquished but gave them the absurd idea that they could evade the terms of the peace if they could prove that they had not started the war.

Germany's new eastern frontiers were a simple negation of the principle of self-determination which underlay the peace. The reconstitution of Poland, with access to the sea, had been promised in the Fourteen Points, and the Germans would no doubt have been sore at it even had only Polish-inhabited land been taken from them. But to give the Poles a port, the German city of Danzig was also detached, though it was made a city republic under League protection. Upper Silesia was a more contentious problem. Though it was largely

Polish in population, its great industries were a German creation. But no doubts can arise about the Czech and Austrian borders. Here, in effect, the frontier created by Bimarck when he excluded Austria from Germany by force was preserved by the anti-Bismarcks of Versailles in the teeth of protests from the Germans of the Habsburg lands. The remains of Austria reluctantly accepted independence and the separate peace treaty of St. Germain (September 1919). This, of course, pleased the French, but it is notable that at first even they seem to have expected rump-Austria to go to Germany, and it is hard to see why Wilson did not fight harder for this solution. In the case of Poland and Czechoslovakia, he was convinced by his experts that German areas had to be incorporated in the new Slav states in order to make them economically viable. This he was ready to do, for he was by no means the doctrinaire nationalist of legend.[1]

The treaty was presented to a hastily summoned German delegation on 7 May. Foreign minister Brockdorff-Rantzau, who headed it, had private knowledge of the treaty's character and delivered an angry speech against it—seated. The Germans then set furiously to work, and within the short time allowed they produced a huge memorandum exhaustively criticizing the peace terms. Though understandable, this Teutonic mixture of arrogance and pedantry in their response did them little good. Not only was Clemenceau unmoved but so too was Wilson. All that happened was that the British panicked: they were now afraid that the Germans would not sign and the cataclysm would not be avoided after all. They demanded concessions, of which one important one was adopted. A plebiscite was held in upper Silesia, and eventually most of it was given back to Germany, though Poland received the industrially richest part. The Germans were given a week to accept the revised treaty and it was signed on 28 June. Two clauses almost led to rejection: that respecting war guilt and one requiring all accused of war crimes to be handed over to the allies for punishment. Ironically, this last was never implemented. The Kaiser was safe in Holland, which would not hand him over, and Foch refused out of professional solidarity to take any measures for the arrest and trial of German generals.

The Germans claimed that the treaty of Versailles was a 'swindle'.

[1] North Slesvig was returned to Denmark after a plebiscite: a Prussian pledge of 1866, repudiated in 1878. Belgium gained the towns of Eupen and Malmedy.

They had been induced to lay down their arms by the hope of a peace based on the Fourteen Points and they had then been savagely plundered. They had lost all their colonies in spite of the promise of an 'absolutely impartial adjustment of all colonial claims'. They were being saddled with war costs in spite of all that had been said to the contrary. Disarmament and self-determination were applied only in such a way as to harm them. They were not admitted for the time being to the League of Nations. The fundamental reason for all this was that not only Clemenceau but Wilson also thought that they deserved severe punishment, and only the shifty Lloyd George stood between them and public opinion. Strictly speaking, they were not cheated because they accepted not only the Fourteen Points but Wilson's subsequent pronouncements as the basis for peace, and these included such sweeping items as that every 'arbitrary power' which might 'disturb the peace of the world' must be 'destroyed' or reduced to 'virtual impotence'. Nor can it be supposed that they would have been much less sore if the peace had been less harsh, or that they could have gone on fighting much longer if they had known how harsh the final treaty was to be. But a terrible mistake had been made. Wilson was counting on liberal opinion throughout the world to support the peace and the League. But Germany was given grievances enough to enable her to win liberal opinion over. Already in the autumn there appeared J. M. Keynes' famous tract on *the Economic Consequences of the Peace*, which helped to persuade the Americans not to join the League and made many converts in all countries to the cause of treaty revision in Germany's favour. A harsh peace required stronger military measures to support it than were acceptable to Wilson; in so far as it was to rest on the force of opinion, the moral position of the victors needed to be unassailable. These lessons were to be heeded the next time peace had to be imposed on Germany. President Roosevelt in particular was to do what Wilson's republican opponents had vainly urged in 1918 and insist on Germany's 'unconditional surrender'.

Italy and Japan; America Fails to Ratify

At the same time that they were making peace with Germany, the allied statesmen had to set the rest of the world to rights as well.

Since Keynes wrote, the gravest charge against them has commonly been that they broke up the economic units of pre-war Europe in the name of doctrinaire nationalism. This was not really so. Keynes was wrong in expecting the detachment of Silesia and Lorraine to be fatal to Germany, and to the provinces themselves. The Balkans were 'balkanized' already in 1914, Asiatic Turkey was backward even before it was carved up, and the collapse of the Habsburg monarchy was a *fait accompli* which the conference could not undo. The economic damage which certainly did result from it was minimized rather than accentuated by the drawing of the frontiers. Wilson had behind him, as already explained, the able body of advisers known as the Inquiry. They had worked hard on proposals for frontiers and commanded great respect among the European delegations, themselves well equipped with experts. As noted already, they did not confine themselves to the ethnic aspect but took economic and geographical factors fully into account in constructing boundaries for the new states. Czechoslovakia emerged in consequence as a polyglot miniature version of the Habsburg monarchy from which it had been carved. It has been computed that the number of Europeans under foreign rule fell at this time roughly from 60 millions to 30 millions. Attempts were made to protect the rest by the conclusion of minority treaties, which obliged the countries of east-central Europe to report to the League on this matter. But the truth is that there would have been less political trouble if the boundary-drawers had considered economics less and ethnic lines more. All the same, it is remarkable how many of the 1919 frontiers survive. One reason is that once national states became the norm everywhere the expulsion of minorities became the simplest method of readjustment. Ataturk was soon to discover this, as we shall see.

The main trouble in 1919 came from the conflict of self-determination, not with economics but with the secret treaties made by the allies during the war. In 1915 Italy had been promised territories inhabited by Germans, south Slavs and Albanians. They were not large but they were appreciable and there was no other tangible reward that Italy could claim for the destruction she had suffered in the war. One of Wilson's first acts was to promise the Italians the Tyrol, with its 200,000 Germans. Nothing did more to convince liberals that he was a dupe or a fraud; he seems, in fact, to have acted in simple ignorance. The Italians also had little difficulty in securing the mainly Slav peninsula of Istria, but Wilson made an inordinate fuss when they claimed Fiume. This creation of the Hungarians had an Italian population but a Slav hinterland and was the best port on the coast still left to the Slavs. It had not been promised to Italy in 1915, and so Britain and France supported Wilson in objecting to the Italian claim, which their treaty obligations debarred them from doing elsewhere. Yet on 23 April Wilson foolishly issued a public statement which appealed in effect to the Italian people over the heads of their government. It urged Italy to conform to the principles on which the peace was being constructed and assure herself thereby of south Slav friendship. The Italians left the peace conference and received a triumphant welcome at home. If Wilson had counted on his popularity with the Italian masses, he had indeed been deceived. His prestige was nevertheless enough to prevent an Adriatic settlement that he did not like. It was only after the election of his successor that the Yugoslavs were sufficiently discouraged to yield. The treaty of Rapallo in November 1920 made Fiume a free state, connected to Italy, and with Italians in control of the town. Italy failed to get more than a fragment of Dalmatia, and gave up her toehold in Albania in disgust. Wilson's appeal to her had, of course, been right in principle: her great gain from the war was the disappearance of Austria-Hungary and her best policy now was to befriend the weak Balkan states and bind them to her by peaceful penetration.

Japan raised only one demand not related to the Pacific area, and even this was judged in Pacific terms. She asked for a clause in the League Covenant requiring 'alien nationals' of member states to be given 'equal and just treatment' without 'distinction . . . on account of their race or nationality'. The Japanese seem to have been sincerely concerned over the principle of racial equality, but in Australia and California this was taken as an attempt to remove restrictions on Japanese immigration. Premier Hughes of Australia bitterly attacked it and Wilson dared not oppose him; it was France, for once, that championed liberal principles, but once more the Anglo-American view prevailed. For the rest, Japan contented herself with claiming her share of the German colonies, and here the Chinese were the obstacle. Japan intended to keep the German mines and railways in Shantung. Their port of Kiao-Chou she did not need, since she already had Port Arthur as a naval base, and she merely asked to be allowed to restore it to China herself instead of through the general settlement. These proposals aroused the ire of liberals everywhere, but Britain and France were bound by secret treaties and Wilson finally gave in for fear that the Japanese might refuse to join the League. As a result, the Chinese had the solitary honour of refusing to sign the peace treaty. It can be argued that the Japanese were only asking for modest economic concessions, plus something to save 'face'. But on the other hand, Japan was the only imperial power that made really significant gains at this time, though before rather than by the peace treaty.

The final hurdle had now to be surmounted—the ratification of the treaty by the United States Senate. To this there were enormous and growing obstacles. The simple isolationists were reinforced by Americans of German and Italian origin who resented the wrongs done to their countries. To these the Irish Americans were added by the foolish British delay in applying self-determination to Ireland. (Nothing perhaps did the cause of the League more harm in America than the fact that the British Empire was to have six votes in it, though as all decisions had to be unanimous this did not mean much.) Liberal sentiment tended to desert Wilson, suspected of abandoning his principles either because he was a knave or simply because he had been swindled. Especially, and very unfairly, he was accused of giving part of a republic, China, to the last great military empire Japan.

But still American opinion seems to have been preponderantly in favour of accepting in some form the most controversial part of the treaty—the League (the rest of it most people were prepared to swallow, despite its shortcomings). There were no public opinion polls in those days but there was a poll of newspaper editors, run by the *Literary Digest*. In April it published the results of a question about the League which showed that papers with a circulation of nearly 10 millions were in favour, others with a circulation of $6\frac{3}{4}$ millions were in favour with reservations, while the circulation of papers unreservedly opposed was only some $4\frac{1}{4}$ millions. It was conditional approval that finally won the day with the Republican majority in the Senate. They included imperialists and internationalists as well as isolationists. Henry Cabot Lodge, their leader, was in the first category and he would have welcomed a straightforward alliance with Britain and France. In the end they came out in favour of accepting the treaty and the League with reservations.

The philosophy behind these was compounded of two ideas— that the obligations of the Covenant were too diffuse and that Wilson and his successors could not be trusted. For the last Wilson had only himself to thank. He had appealed (unsuccessfully) in November 1918 for a Democratic victory in the elections to give him the moral authority to conclude peace. He had been his own chief delegate at the conference, and the American delegation had included no other important political figure and no representative of the Senate majority. Wilson consulted the parliamentarians little and reluctantly, and he made no secret of his intention to ram the treaty down their reluctant throats. He thus envenomed the suspicion between executive and legislature which, anyway, is almost written in to the American constitution. As for the treaty which he had helped to make, the territorial guarantee in Article X of the Covenant obliged the United States in effect to uphold all the frontiers in the world and to uphold them for ever. It was mistaken in thus trying to prevent change, and unreasonable in expecting the United States or any other great power to interfere in matters not threatening their vital interests or the general peace of the world. Moreover, the Covenant deprived the United States of the power to decide in a given case whether it would go to war or not.

The reservations eventually offered by the Republicans in the Senate laid down that under Article X and in other cases, too, the United States reserved for itself the right to decide what action to take in each case, irrespective of the terms of the Covenant or the wishes of the League. But what was more, they gave this right not to the President but to Congress, which was also, for instance, to control the appointment of the American delegation to the League. This was an assertion of the rights of Congress against both the League and the President and it recalls an attempt made early in 1918 to take the organizing of the war effort out of presidential hands and vest it in a three-man directory. The old bogies concerning the Monroe doctrine and interference in domestic affairs which Wilson had tried to lay reappeared in the reservations, while the Shantung clauses of the treaty were repudiated. American ratification of the treaty was only to take effect when three of the other four great powers had accepted the reservations.

Wilson's main reliance for beating down his opponents was in the nationwide tour which he undertook in the summer of 1919 to arouse popular enthusiasm in favour of the treaty. But he also negotiated with some moderate Republican senators and allowed the Democrats in the Senate to put forward some reassuring reservations of their own. His case against the Republican reservations was that by them the United States avoided assuming any binding obligations at all, and so failed to contribute to the maintenance of security and stability in the world, by which alone war could be prevented. He argued that the obligations under the Covenant as it stood were not burthensome. The United States would not be called on to interfere in every local upset: the resources of the area concerned, under League direction, would suffice to restore order. The rule of unanimity in League decisions ensured, anyway, that the United States could not be forced into action against her will. One of the Democratic reservations extended this point by remarking that the League Council was only empowered to *advise* action in support of the territorial guarantee and the member governments remained free to decide whether to take any. It will be seen that Wilson's interpretation of the Covenant is open to much the same objection as the Republican reservations: the difference between them was really mostly a matter of the degree of latitude left to the President.

The tragedy and absurdity which marked so much of the peace conference characterized also the American debate on ratification. Wilson's health was finally ruined by his nationwide tour. In September he had a stroke, from which he slowly recovered but which seems to have made his mind more inflexible than ever. In November the Republicans carried their reservations in the Senate with isolationist support. Wilson refused to accept them, and so the Democrats then voted with the isolationists to defeat ratification altogether. This result horrified all thinking men, and the winter was spent in attempts to draft reservations that all could accept. The European powers made it clear that they would prefer ratification on any terms rather than none at all. But Wilson would not compromise, and spoke apocalyptically of renewing the appeal to the people and running for president a third time. In March 1920 the treaty was again presented for ratification, with the Republican reservations amended but substantially unaltered. The bulk of the Republicans voted for ratification and

21 Democrats broke ranks and joined them. But 23 more again voted with the extreme isolationists. There were 49 votes for ratification and 35 against. But the constitution required a two-thirds majority, which the 'ayes' fell short of by 7 votes. This was all that kept the United States out of the League. The issue did not immediately die, but Warren Harding, who captured the presidency for the Republicans in the autumn of 1920, effectively buried it by avoiding commitment either way. The United States made a separate peace with Germany in 1921. Wilson was a spent force; he died in 1924.

The shortcomings of the peace settlement of 1919 are easily explained. It was too severe to be a peace of reconciliation, and not severe enough if the intention was to impose on the enemy a settlement against which he would never have the power to rebel. This would have required the dismemberment of Germany and a strong military alliance among the victors. Neither a harsh nor a soft peace had much chance of lasting without the support of the United States, for either was likely to be strongly challenged by imperialists and Bolsheviks if it seemed to be the work only of the exhausted powers of western Europe. It was the biggest shortcoming of all that a settlement so largely shaped by American ideas—especially in the paradox of punishing Germany without crushing her—was denied the American guarantee which might have upheld it. The mixture of harshness and softness was probably unavoidable: it reflected the conflicting emotions of anger and war-weariness in the belligerent peoples. Any settlement made in 1919 was almost bound to need rapid revision. The failure of American ratification must be attributed to Wilson, with his doctrinaire insistence on the party system and the supremacy of the executive in foreign affairs and his failure to accept what he could get. He misjudged nothing in Europe as badly as he misjudged his own country.

But in measuring the significance of Wilson's failure it is important not to exaggerate the extent to which American involvement in Europe was feasible. Wilson and Harding alike were opposed to the American involvement in power politics which was desired by imperialists like Lodge or Theodore Roosevelt. If Wilson was an internationalist, it was partly because he underestimated the burdens of internationalism. If the Americans had entered the League, even without the famous Reservations, it is entirely uncertain whether they would in practice have done any more to uphold the peace settlement than they did from outside. A concrete commitment like a French alliance would no doubt have been respected, but there was less chance of approval for that than for the Covenant. This to some extent justifies the line that Wilson took. The Covenant did not really commit the Americans to very much on paper, but Wilson tried to give ratification the character of a great moral commitment and so give it real meaning. For the rest, he trusted to the educative effect of belonging to the League to bring the American people to a growing acceptance of international responsibilities. In presenting the Covenant to the peace conference he had said 'a living thing is born', and he valued the document only as an instrument for spreading acceptance of the moral principles which stood behind it.

By not joining the League the Americans had lost one chance of being educated, but others remained. They could not escape the contraction of the world and the growing entanglement of European and American affairs. Like the final character of the peace settlement, the extent of American involvement in it was essentially undecided by the events of 1919. For Europe this was an evil, since it meant insecurity. But it was insecurity mixed with hope.

5: Liberal Reverses: The Threat from the East

Wilson left Europe for good before peace had been made with Germany's allies, and the Americans left Europe to its fate just as the difficulties of enforcing and administering the new settlement were beginning. The Bolsheviks beat off the rather half-hearted allied attempts to dislodge them in Russia and stood behind the challenge to Anglo-French ascendancy that came both from the peoples of Asia and the defeated side in Europe. By 1923 one of the defeated powers, Turkey, had managed to get her peace terms revised. Germany was resisting the reparations provisions of the peace settlement with increasing fervour, and as a result was relapsing into anarchy. Central Europe was threatened with the revolutionary overthrow of democracy, just at the point when liberal institutions, as the next chapter tells, were being destroyed in the south.

The Russian Civil War

The treaty of Brest Litovsk seemed at first more likely to destroy the Bolshevik régime than to win it a breathing space. The shameful terms brought a split in Lenin's party and the secession of the left Socialist Revolutionaries from his government. In March and July 1918 Lenin met furious opposition in the national congress of soviets, and after the latter meeting the new German ambassador, Mirbach, was murdered in an attempt to restart the war. Socialist Revolutionary risings followed all over the country. One took place in Moscow, but the most formidable one was in Yaroslavl, directed by Savinkov. At Samara on the Volga some of the SR deputies to the constituent assembly gathered under the lead of Victor Chernov, head of the party and president at the assembly's only session. They tried to establish a provisional government in its name. The old SR tactic of assassination was revived. Uritsky, the head of the Petrograd secret police, was killed, and Lenin was seriously wounded.

THE TERRITORIAL SETTLEMENT
IN THE EAST AFTER 1918.

NORWAY
Bergen
Oslo
Stavanger
Stockholm
SWEDEN

FINLAND
Abo — Viborg
Helsinki
Tallinn
Leningrad
Pskov

Territory from Russia
„ „ Germany
„ „ Austria & Hungary
„ „ Turkey-thus SYRIA
Spheres of influence projected
by secret treaties
1915 – 1917   ----
MANDATES
French : Syria
British: Iraq,
Transjordan
Palestine

ESTONIA
LATVIA
Dvinsk
Memel
LITHUANIA
Kaunas
E. PRUSSIA
Vilna
Warsaw
POLAND — Brest-Litovsk

• Moscow
• Smolensk
U. S. S. R.
• Minsk

Hamburg
Bremen
Stettin
Essen
GERMAN
REPUBLIC

Prague
Pilsen — CZECHOSLOVAKIA
Munich
Brno
Cracow • Lvov
Linz
Vienna
AUSTRIA
Graz
Budapest
HUNGARY
Zagreb
ISTRIA
Fiume
Venice
Zara (It.)
(It.)
YUGOSLAVIA
Florence
Rome
ITALY
Naples
Bari
ALBANIA
Monastir
Nish • Sofia
BULGARIA
GREECE
Salonika
To Greece
GREEK 1920-3
Palermo

• Kief
Kamenets Podolsk
Czernowitz
BESSARABIA
RUMANIA
Galatz
Ploesti
• Bucharest
Varna
Burgas

BLACK SEA
Projected U.S. 1918
Kars

Constantinople
(Russian)
• Ankara
T U R K E Y
To
(Italian)
To TURKEY 1939
(French)
Mosul
• Aleppo
Kirkuk
RHODES (ITALIAN)
(British)
Beirut
SYRIA
(International) Haifa
PALESTINE
IRAQ
(British)
TRANSJORDAN

MEDITERRANEAN SEA
Alexandria
Cairo
Suez
ARABIA

CAS

0   500
Miles

Equally serious, the peace failed to end foreign invasion. The Germans were only kept out by renewed concessions, and Russia's former allies had already begun to consider marching in. The Japanese had plans to occupy eastern Siberia in the event of a total German victory in Russia, in order to safeguard their Chinese position. Wilson was strongly against any occupation of Russian territory, especially one conducted by the aggressive Japanese. But the British and French, fighting with their backs to the wall in the spring of 1918, had the ridiculous idea that if the Japanese went to Siberia they could be induced to march right across Russia and attack the Germans. Defensively, they wished to deny the Germans the great natural resources of Russia and the vast dumps of munitions from the west piled in her ports. The British also feared a German–Turkish threat to India. None of this at first involved hostility to the Bolsheviks. The British, at any rate, wished to avoid interference in Russian internal affairs, and were willing to work with the new government, if only because it was not expected to survive for long. In the spring of 1918 the British established themselves at Murmansk (to protect stores) with the connivance of the local soviet, and for a time supported the Red Finns against the Whites because the latter had German backing. In the summer a British force tried to keep the Turks from Baku, and only orders from Moscow prevented their working with the local Bolsheviks. But the British wished also to work with those local rulers who did not acknowledge Bolshevik authority, such as the Cossacks in the north Caucasus, and could not quite see why the Bolsheviks minded. The soviet government, for its part, tried to keep the western powers amicable by offers of cooperation, at first fairly seriously meant because it seemed possible that the Germans would refuse to make peace. After the treaty of Brest, the Bolsheviks continued to conciliate the allies in order to prevent a Japanese invasion, of which they were mortally afraid. But they had no intention of returning to the war, and so the allies increasingly regarded them as German tools.

But intervention against them might have remained on a small scale had it not been for an accidental factor, the workings of which illustrate perfectly how much could then be accomplished in Russia— as Lenin realized and his opponents did not—by a smallish body of resolute and disciplined men. A great many of the Czechs and Slovaks drafted into the Austrian army had deserted on reaching the front and enrolled in the Russian service to fight for the liberation of their country. There were 40,000 of these Czech troops in Russia when the war in the east ended, and they wished to go to France and continue the fight. The soviet government agreed, and they set off on the Trans-Siberian railway. After clashes en route however (notably with Hungarian prisoners going home in the opposite direction), the Bolsheviks decided that the Czechs must be disarmed. The Czechs resisted, and in May seized the whole railway from the Volga to Irkutsk. The Bolsheviks had already been contending with much local resistance in Siberia and this now triumphed. At the same time, Wilson was at last brought to agree to intervention, in order to rescue the Czechs. The Japanese, accompanied by British and American troops to keep them in order, seized eastern Siberia. In the north the British advanced to Archangel, partly with the idea that the Czechs might get out that way. Mushroom Russian governments sprouted everywhere.

From this apparently hopeless position the Bolsheviks managed to fight their way out. Two important steps were taken immediately after the peace of Brest. The capital was moved to Moscow, since Petrograd had become a dangerously exposed frontier town: the undoing of Peter the Great's work, the restriction of Russian power to the ancient limits of Muscovy, was thus neatly symbolized. Trotsky meanwhile became Commissar for War, and the creation of an effective army was seriously taken in hand. A Red Guard had been founded soon after the October revolution, but it was at first no improvement on the decaying old army. Now orthodox military discipline was restored and a large number of Tsarist officers were induced to serve, partly to save their skins and partly because they were thus able to defend Russia from dissolution. Political commissars attached to each unit replaced the soldiers' soviets as the safeguard against officers' plots. The experiment was a dangerous one and not all the officers proved loyal, but it worked well enough. In September the Czechs and Whites advancing from Siberia were checked at Kazan. Meanwhile, an army organized by Stalin and Voroshilov, to some degree in rivalry with Trotsky, had been holding the Cossacks in check in the region of Tsaritsyn, better known as Stalingrad. The junction of the White forces in the east and the south was thus prevented, and

Moscow was able to go on drawing provisions from the Caucasus. The Socialist Revolutionary revolts in the heart of Russia had quickly been put down, and a merciless terror was unleashed, amounting to a massacre of those elements thought to be capable of organizing resistance. The German military collapse ended the danger from that side. On 9 November the Soviet government denounced the treaty of Brest. In the course of the winter the Ukraine was recovered.

The peacemakers were very conscious that their work would be half done if Russia was not somehow brought into it. For want of their presence, indeed, the frontiers between Russia and her western neighbours could not be defined in 1919. Lloyd George was prepared to invite the Soviet government to the conference. He believed that it was securely in power, and that foreign hostility to it would only make it more popular. Wilson similarly regarded Bolshevism as a natural though horrible response to intolerable conditions, and did not believe that foreign bayonets could thrust it aside. The French, however, were implacably hostile to the Bolsheviks, and even proposed that Russia be represented at the conference by some distinguished émigrés. British ministers and opinion for the most part followed not Lloyd George but Churchill, who believed that the Bolsheviks would be crushingly repudiated by the Russian people if a little foreign help was forthcoming. Lloyd George, with Wilson's support, managed to induce the allies to propose (January 1919) a conference between the Bolsheviks and their opponents at Prinkipo, on an island in the Sea of Marmora. The Bolsheviks accepted the invitation, and generally did all they could to appease the allies. The Whites, encouraged by the French, refused.

The collapse of the Central Powers allowed Britain and France, if they so wished, to intervene directly in western Russia. By the end of 1918 British troops had moved into the Caucasus, French troops were at Odessa trying to support a new attempt at an independent Ukrainian government under Simon Petlura, and a British fleet on the Baltic was trying ineffectually to cope with Bolshevik forces and unwithdrawn German troops. Foch produced a grandiose plan for the reconquest of Russia under a French high command. But at the end of March 1919 the allies, on American insistence, turned it down. Soon afterwards the French forces in Odessa, who had shown signs of mutinous sympathy with the enemy, were withdrawn.

Thereafter, intervention mainly took the form of supplying munitions to Russian forces thought to deserve aid. Most of this help was British.

In the autumn of 1918 a White government more imposing than the rest had emerged at Omsk by the merger of the Siberians with the Socialist Revolutionaries established at Samara. Before long a coup ousted these in favour of the dictatorship of Admiral Kolchak. This youngish and enterprising sailor had served with distinction in the Baltic, and offered his sword to the allies when Russia left the war. He was little qualified for generalship or political office. In May the allies decided that it would be right to help him if he showed himself to be a democrat. He was asked for pledges regarding land reform, personal liberty and equality, the calling of a constituent assembly and support for the League. He gave satisfactory answers, and in June was accorded a sort of semi-recognition.

By that time an offensive was under way from several directions against the Bolshevik-held area round the two capitals. Kolchak's forces had again reached the Volga, while from the Don Cossack regions powerful new formations advanced in the direction of Moscow under General Denikin. Another White army was formed in Estonia, and in the summer it advanced towards Petrograd under General Yudenich. By October Denikin had occupied the Ukraine and was threatening Tula, not far south of Moscow, while Yudenich was at the very gates of Petrograd. But the White forces never joined up. Kolchak and Denikin could almost certainly have done so, and Denikin's forces did succeed in taking Tsaritsyn, which had stood between the southern and eastern Whites in 1918. But the main weight of Kolchak's offensive was farther north, probably with the hope of linking up with the Whites in Archangel. Bolshevik forces under Frunze pushed him away from the southern Volga. Denikin's main thrust, similarly, was away from Kolchak and towards the more distant Yudenich. Late in 1919 the Red armies went over everywhere to the offensive, and not only did they win battles but the whole White movement disintegrated. By February 1920 Siberia had been occupied as far east as Irkustsk, and Kolchak was captured and shot. In March the remains of Denikin's forces were confined to the Crimea. Yudenich's army was demobilized in February. In the course of 1920 the Bolsheviks made peace with Finland and the little Baltic states— Estonia, Latvia and Lithuania—which had somehow managed to create themselves and (with allied help) to get rid of the Germans as well.

The last episode in the civil war was really a straightforward national struggle between Russia and Poland, notable indeed for a rallying of patriotic Russians to the Bolsheviks. The former commander-in-chief, Brusilov, appealed to all old officers to join them. The Poles were eager to exploit Russian weakness in order to achieve as far as they could their historic frontiers before the partitions—which had embraced much of the Ukraine, White Russia and Latvia. In December 1919 the allies designated a frontier—the Curzon Line—which roughly corresponded to the ethnic border between the Poles and their neighbours.[1] But the Poles had already pushed beyond this, taking Vilna from the Lithuanians, and in 1920 advancing to Gomel and Kiev, the Ukrainian leader Petlura putting himself under their protection. But in the summer of 1920 the Russians counterattacked and drove the Poles to the gates of Warsaw. Had their forces in Galicia obeyed orders to help those farther north, they might have taken it. As it was the Poles, helped by French supplies and officers, completely routed the attack. Peace was made in March 1921, the Russians accepting a frontier considerably east of the Curzon Line.

The Polish war gave an opening to the Whites remaining in the Crimea. They were now commanded by Baron Wrangel, more conservative and aristocratic than Denikin and Kolchak but more efficient also. He established strict old-style discipline in his forces, and tried to win over the peasants with an edict giving them a large share of land, the work of the pre-war minister of agriculture, Krivoshein. When the Poles invaded the Ukraine, he marched into it from the other side. His fate was sealed, however, when the Russians and Poles concluded an armistice in October. After little more than a month the Crimea was reconquered.

This was the end of the war, but it took some time to recover the extremities of Russia. British forces remained in the Caucasus till 1920, and the independent Georgian republic (stronghold of the Mensheviks) was only destroyed by invasion in 1921. The Japanese left Siberia fairly readily, but Eastern Siberia was an independent republic from 1920 till 1922: the Bolsheviks were content to leave it as a friendly buffer state until the neighbouring powers became less

[1] And to the post-1945 frontier.

afraid of them. Russian authority in Central Asia was shadowy for some time.

It was the civil war rather than the October revolution which resulted in Bolshevik mastery of Russia. At the end of 1917 they really only controlled the capitals. At the end of 1920 they effectively ruled almost the whole country. The basis of their success was their good strategic position, arising from their control of the central area around the two capitals. This area had voted heavily for them in the elections to the constituent assembly and was willing to some extent to fight for them too. Their opponents were strongest, both in the elections and the war, in the periphery of the country. The non-Russian nationalities tended to want independence. The farmers of Siberia were more prosperous and so more conservative than many elsewhere; so were the Cossack peasants, who had been deliberately privileged by the Tsars because of their military value. It is also worth remembering how the periphery had prospered more than the centre in the pre-war industrial revolution.

The Bolsheviks won, in the second place, because the rift between the left and the right wing among their opponents, strongly working in their favour ever since the Kornilov episode, was never healed. This was fatal to both wings, since they could not work in isolation. The peasants, the bulk of the population, had been conciliated by the Bolsheviks, who had acknowledged their right to the land. But even supposing that they were not disillusioned by the dispersal of the constituent assembly, they certainly were so by the forceful requisitioning of their crops. The ruination of economic life and the need to devote what industry there was to arms production for the civil war meant that there was no other way in which the Bolsheviks could feed their towns and their army. But the defecting peasants were unable to organize a régime of their own. The Socialist Revolutionaries, who at least purported to be their spokesmen, were pushed aside in 1918 not only in Bolshevik territory but by the other Whites with whom they tried to co-operate. Too scattered, ignorant and ill-organized to come to their rescue, the peasants were reduced to the negative role of choosing whether to give their support to the Bolsheviks or the more conservative Whites. Their only authentic and effective political expression was henceforth in the guerilla bands that sprang up everywhere to resist brutality and spoliation by the authorities. The most famous of the guerilla leaders was Nestor Makhno, who for a time dominated large areas of the Ukraine. Though he sometimes contributed decisively to the fighting against the Bolsheviks, he was really not against them alone but against government in general. A thoroughgoing anarchist, he even printed money with an inscription permitting anyone who wished to forge it.

Over the heads of the sceptical peasants, the battle was fought between two urban minorities—the Bolsheviks and their working-class followers on the one hand, the upper and middle classes on the other. Invertebrate and relatively few in numbers, the latter showed themselves unable to conquer the revolutionaries once they had lost the support of the old state machine. It was not only that they failed to exploit the disenchantment of the peasants with the Bolsheviks by offering them firm guarantees of their land and liberty. They failed more simply to maintain law and order, and keep discipline among their troops. Everywhere, peasant communities, having welcomed the Whites in revulsion against Bolshevik rapine, ended by turning against them because they behaved badly too. The Bolsheviks bore much of the responsibility for reducing the country to chaos, but they showed much more skill and vigour in restoring order again. In particular, they showed far more determination than the Whites in winning over hostile elements whose friendship was essential for survival. Against the White failure with the peasants must be set the considerable measure of Red success in using Tsarist officers in their army, and middle-class managers and technicians in the factories which, though at their last gasp, did produce the necessary weapons.

A final shortcoming of the Whites was that they tended to be Great Russian nationalists, unable to co-operate with the non-Russians, who were really the staunchest anti-Bolsheviks. The Ukrainians, Poles, Baltic peoples and even Cossacks viewed them with suspicion if not dislike. Here, too, the Bolsheviks learned their lesson quicker, and made a timely peace with western neighbours.

Allied intervention did not cause the civil war, but it grievously prolonged it without in any way benefiting Russia. It began as a muddled attempt to halt the Germans, and later policy was distorted by just the forces that warped the peace terms for Germany. The statesmanship of Lloyd George and Wilson could not work freely in face of the fury of organized opinion in the victor nations, as strong against the Bolsheviks as it was against the Germans. The result was enough intervention to keep the war going, but not enough to beat the Bolsheviks. It must be said, however, that anti-Bolshevik sentiment did not result merely from anti-capitalist measures like the expropriation of capitalist concerns without compensation and the repudiation of the Russian state debt in February 1918. It was largely due to the savagery of the Bolsheviks, and their repudiation of democracy evident in the suppression of the constituent assembly. Moreover, it was the allies' defeat of Germany, and not spontaneous revolution there as Lenin expected, that saved Russia from German rapacity.

Allied intervention of some sort was inevitable, anyway, in view of the patent determination of the Bolsheviks to export their revolution. Despite a specific undertaking in the treaty of Brest, they had done their best to undermine the governments of the Central Powers by propaganda, and Joffe, the first soviet ambassador to Germany, was expelled shortly before the fall of the monarchy there for this reason. The allied powers fared no better—indeed, it came naturally to the Bolsheviks to regard Britain, the greatest capitalist power, as their chief enemy. As early as 3 December 1917 the Soviet government had called on the peoples of the east to 'overthrow these robbers and enslavers' of their countries, 'the rapacious European plunderers'. British rule in India was particularly mentioned, and the British were sufficiently worried to try as far as possible to prevent the publication of the appeal.[1] Had the Bolsheviks not been contained at home they could have helped the proletarian forces to considerable effect throughout east-central Europe. There was a strong Red element in the Baltic and some Balkan states. The invasion of Poland in 1920 was undertaken with the object of installing a Red government there, and success would have brought the Bolsheviks into contact with the industrial west and the rising communist movements of Germany and Czechoslovakia. From February to August 1919, Hungary had actually experienced a communist régime, under Bela Kun. Born of an unholy alliance between the Bolsheviks and army officers of the opposite political extreme, who would support any government that would not surrender Hungary's non-Magyar territory, it was finally destroyed by a Rumanian invasion. The allies had some trouble in

---

[1] R. P. Ullman, *Intervention and the War* (Princeton, 1961), pp. 28–9 and n. 93.

getting the Rumanians to leave, and it was only in 1920 that they could conclude with the new Hungarian government the treaty of Trianon, reducing that once-proud kingdom to a Magyar-inhabited rump.

The mistake of the allies was in attempting the overthrow of the Bolsheviks inside Russia. Such was the internal disorganization of the country that this was not necessary to prevent aggression. What was required was the defence of self-determination among the non-Russian peoples once subject to the Tsar. This was successfully done in the west, and here the Bolsheviks' only outlets, henceforth, were ideological and diplomatic. It might well have been attempted in the Ukraine and the Caucasus. For want of persistence here, Russia's doors into Asia were soon open again.

Russia and Asia: the Problems of Turkey

The Soviet authorities undertook the penetration of Asia concurrently with the task of recovering the Asian and Caucasian conquests of the Tsars. The moving spirit in both was Joseph Stalin, who as Commissar for Nationalities had general charge of relations with the non-Russian national groups concerned. In two articles written at the end of 1918 (one challengingly called 'ex oriente lux') he had argued that the chances of Communist expansion among the down-trodden Asian victims of imperialism were unusually good. Certainly Communist expansion, halted for many years as it turned out on the European frontier of Russia, very soon began again on the Asian frontier. As early as 1921 a 'People's Republic' was founded in Outer Mongolia, and the economic penetration of Chinese Turkestan began. In China there emerged in the twenties both an effective communist party and a powerful new nationalist party, the Kuomintang. This resembled the communist and fascist movements of the west in seeing the establishment of a one-party state as a necessary condition of national progress. Gradually expanding the territory under its control, it began the long task of restoring central authority. For the time being the Soviet government remained on good terms with its leaders and gave them much help, and the Chinese communists therefore, with some reluctance, co-operated with them.

It was in western Asia that Soviet policy most obviously began to

12—E.E.P.

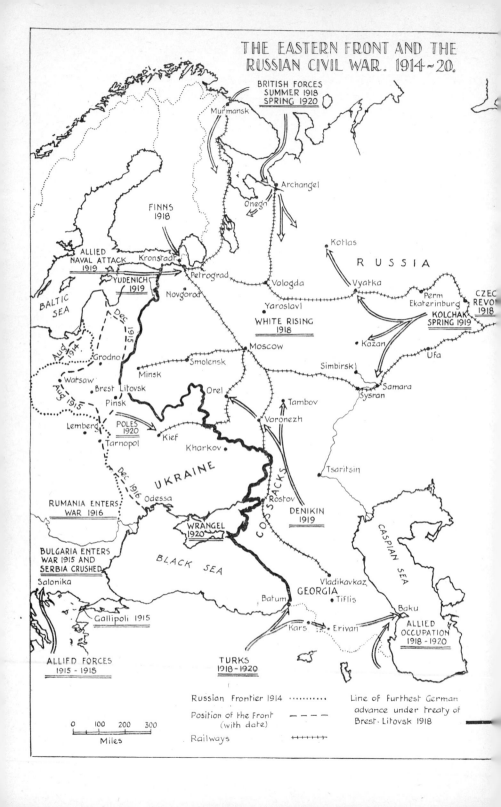

THE EASTERN FRONT AND THE RUSSIAN CIVIL WAR. 1914~20.

BRITISH FORCES
SUMMER 1918
SPRING 1920

Murmansk

Archangel

Onega

FINNS
1918

Kotlas

R U S S I A

Vologda

Vyatka

CZEC
REVO
1918

ALLIED
NAVAL ATTACK
1919

Kronstadt

YUDENICH
1919

Petrograd

Novgorod

Yaroslavl

Perm
Ekaterinburg

KOLCHAK
SPRING 1919

BALTIC
SEA

Dec 1915

Aug 1914

WHITE RISING
1918

Moscow

Kazan

Ufa

Grodno

Smolensk

Simbirsk

Samara

Minsk

Warsaw

Aug 1915

Brest Litovsk

Orel

Sysran

Pinsk

Tambov

Voronezh

Tsaritsin

Lemberg

POLES
1920

Kief

Tarnopol

Kharkov

Dec 1916

UKRAINE

Odessa

C O S S A C K S

Rostov

RUMANIA ENTERS
WAR 1916

DENIKIN
1919

WRANGEL
1920

CASPIAN
SEA

BULGARIA ENTERS
WAR 1915 AND
SERBIA CRUSHED

BLACK SEA

Salonika

Vladikavkaz

GEORGIA

Batum

Tiflis

Baku

Gallipoli 1915

Kars

Erivan

ALLIED
OCCUPATION
1918 - 1920

ALLIED FORCES
1915 - 1918

TURKS
1918 - 1920

Russian Frontier 1914 ··········

Position of the Front
(with date) — — —

Railways +++++++++

Line of furthest German
advance under treaty of
Brest·Litovsk 1918

0   100   200   300
Miles

menace the greatest of the imperial powers, Britain. A striking demonstration, though of limited practical importance, was the Congress of Peoples of the Orient at Baku in 1920. As there was only a little organized political activity in Asia at that time, this was little more than a gathering of private individuals. But early in 1921 the Soviet authorities entered into treaties with the governments of Afghanistan, Persia and Turkey. The collapse of Russian power had left Persia very much under British control, and the treaty of 1919, by which Britain sought to consolidate her position, was so much resented that it was never ratified. In 1921 power passed to the nationalists after a military coup by Riza Khan, who became Shah in 1925. The Soviet-Persian agreement ended Russia's former privileges in return for more ordinary commercial concessions and the right to march into the country if it came to be used as a base for military operations against the Soviets. This was clearly anti-British, as was the treaty with the new Amir Amanullah of Afghanistan, who had lately attacked India. With Turkey the Soviet authorities had a joint interest in the subjugation of the Caucasian peoples. They had co-operated in the suppression of the Armenians in 1920, and the ensuing treaty restored to the Turks some of the territory which the Tsars had taken from them.

The former Ottoman territories in Asia were the scene of strong nationalist upsurges among both Turks and Arabs. The allies had shared them out in advance of conquest by secret treaties, and occupied most of the area after the war. But promises had been made to the Arabs, and there had also been the Balfour Declaration (1917) in favour of a Jewish 'national home'. The system of mandates, with eventual independence in prospect, was a way out of these contradictions. Mandates for Armenia and for the eternally contentious Constantinople area were at first designed for the United States, whose rule would neutralize them in European quarrels. It was the hostility of American opinion to this that led to the American demand that League members be not obliged to accept mandates. The San Remo conference (1920), which continued the work of peacemaking, followed the secret Sykes-Picot agreement of 1916 in granting mandates to France for Syria, and to Britain for Mesopotamia and Palestine, where a Jewish national home was to be established. But the agreement had envisaged native states under European protection as covering most of the hinterland between the Mediterranean and the Persian Gulf, and the simple decision for a mandate did not settle the relations between the mandatories and the Arab nationalists. The British had, in fact, handed over the interior of Syria to their protégé Feisal in 1919. But he weakened his diplomatic position by claiming Palestine as well, and the French on the coast now picked a quarrel with him and drove him out. By way of atonement, the British established the kingdom of Iraq for him out of their own mandate of Mesopotamia, to which the French in 1919 had agreed to add Mosul from their share. The hinterland of Palestine similarly became the Emirate of Transjordan under Feisal's brother; these states became formally independent in 1930 and 1946. Feisal's father ruled farther south, in the Hejaz, until turned out by Ibn Saud in 1924. Egypt attained formal independence in 1922. Arab nationalists thus received some rewards for their help to the allied cause. But Syria and Palestine, in effect, were colonies, and elsewhere British military occupation remained. It was rather like the German settlement of eastern Europe after Brest Litovsk.

The so-called treaty of Sèvres that was drawn up in the spring of 1920 for signature by Turkey deprived her not only of her Arab territories but of Armenia; the nearby Kurds were to receive autonomy. In the west the terms were a personal triumph for the Greek premier, Eleutherios Venizelos. This distinguished Cretan had carried through the union of his native land with Greece and her enlargement by participation in the Balkan war of 1912. Espousing the cause of the allies in the World War, he became premier in 1917 on the deposition of King Constantine the Kaiser's brother-in-law, under allied pressure. His charm and skill at the peace conference won him much influence, especially with Lloyd George. This he put to especially good use when Italy quarrelled with the major allies in the spring of 1919. Italy was already establishing herself in the south of Asia Minor, awarded her by secret agreement in 1917. To contain her, a Greek force was allowed to be landed in Smyrna. The treaty of Sèvres placed this region under Greek authority for five years, after which its future was to be settled by plebiscite. The peace treaty of Neuilly with Bulgaria (November 1919) was another success for Venizelos. Not only did the Bulgars lose their wartime conquests but Greece acquired their short Aegean coastline, and added to this in 1920 all that was left of European Turkey except Constantinople itself. Only the advance of the Greek forces in Asia Minor forced the Turks to accept the peace treaty in August 1920—without thereby halting the Greek advance.

But the Greek landing in Asia was followed by a great upsurge of Turkish nationalism, which found a leader in Mustafa Kemal, the defender of Gallipoli against the British in 1915. Gaining power early in 1920, the new movement showed itself far more strictly nationalist than the Young Turks, to whom it was the successor. Renouncing the attempt to maintain the old cosmopolitan empire, it laid claim only to those territories which were inhabited by Turks. This trend was accentuated when the allies responded to the emergence of the new government by the occupation of Constantinople. The seat of government was accordingly moved from this cosmopolitan city to Ankara, in the heart of the Turkish lands of Asia Minor. The Sultan remained in Constantinople under allied protection. On Kemal's final triumph he was deposed, and in 1923 Turkey became a republic with Kemal as president. The Sultan's son was at first recognized as Caliph, but in 1924 this essentially international office of headship of Islam was abolished. The government of Kemal Ataturk, as he came to be called, was henceforth anticlerical, and it sought to abolish such distinctive Moslem customs as the seclusion of women, and to make Turkey a European rather than an Asiatic country. Constitutionally it was a one-party dictatorship, but attempts were made to move towards a true parliamentary system, and this was achieved, though rather insecurely, after the Second World War.

Kemal was quickly able to set aside the treaty of Sèvres. In October 1920 King Alexander of Greece died from the bite of a pet monkey. Elections followed, in which Venizelos was completely defeated, and in December a plebiscite recalled King Constantine. The allies now had no reason to regard the Greek government as more friendly than the Turkish. Italy and France, who had both done badly in the area compared with the British, increasingly supported the latter. In September 1921 the Greek army in Asia, having almost reached Ankara, was defeated. In October France made a new peace with Turkey, withdrawing from Asia Minor and ceding a strip of Syria which contained part of the Baghdad railway. Italy also withdrew, and made peace the following April, by which time the allies had agreed to revise the 1920 treaty. In September 1922 the Turks recovered Smyrna, and the Italians and French withdrew their forces from the region of the Straits, leaving the British to hold on if they would and could. An armistice followed, and in 1923 the treaty of Lausanne revised the Turkish settlement, confirming Kemal's gains and restoring European Turkey roughly as it had been in 1914. The Straits and the Greek–Turkish frontier were demilitarized. Turkey retained Armenia, although her efforts to recover southern Kurdistan from Iraq failed. The Greeks drew the correct moral by again chasing out King Constantine, and in 1924 established a republic. A feature of this settlement was a Greek–Turkish agreement for the exchange of minorities. Most of the Greeks in Asia Minor (where both Greeks and Turks had committed atrocities) had fled, in any case, when the Turks reconquered Smyrna. To make room for them the Greeks expelled not only their Moslem minorities but Serbs and Bulgars too. This was a new twist to the principle of self-determination: frontiers were to determine population instead of the other way round. The expulsion of the Germans from east-central Europe in 1945 was to apply this on a large scale. The establishment of the Jewish National Home similarly pointed to a new way of dividing up the earth among its inhabitants not based on existing occupation.

After the First as after the Second World War there was a general Asian revolt against European domination. It secured a modest measure of success. The Bolsheviks allied themselves with it, and already showed themselves more adept at fighting the imperialism of the capitalist powers than at opposing capitalism direct. They met more response in Asia than in Europe, and even there less in China, where there were some factories, than in Mongolia and western Asia, where there were almost none. Of course, this reflects in some measure the fact that the Bolsheviks had stepped into the shoes of the Tsars. They continued some Tsarist enterprises, like the Manchurian railways, and inherited Tsarist resources. Like the French revolutionaries after 1792, they more and more pursued old monarchical ambitions strengthened with new ideological weapons.

The Reparations Muddle: Rapallo and the Ruhr Occupation

In Europe the Bolsheviks could appeal for support, as they could not in Asia, to a labour movement already organized and in most countries devoted, if only theoretically, to the cause of proletarian revolution. Although its interests were world-wide, it is therefore in European affairs that the foundation of the Comintern (Communist or Third International) in 1919 is important. Its first meeting was not much more than a gesture, but the second, in the summer of 1920, took place when the civil war had almost been won, and adopted twenty-one resolutions composed by Lenin to which all parties wishing to belong to it were called on to adhere. These called for the establishment of an authoritarian and international movement, the member parties modelling themselves on the Russian Bolsheviks, taking their orders from the Comintern, and having nothing to do with bourgeois and reformist parties. It was these resolutions which really faced the Social Democrats of the west with the question whether they were uncompromising revolutionaries or not, and many, even on the left, refused them. In France a majority of the socialist party adhered to the Comintern, but only a minority of their followers adhered to the new communist party. In Germany, on the other hand, only a minority of the 'independent' socialists became communists, but they took most of the 'independent' voters with them. The rest of that hybrid party went back to the 'majority' Social Democrats. In Italy only a minority of the socialist movement became communists, but the majority of those that were left remained in a hybrid state, revolutionary in sentiment but not in any practical way. Gradually the labour movement polarized into rival parties supporting the Third and the revived Second International respectively, though there was much feeling against a split expressed, for instance, in the attempt to set up an all-embracing association inevitably dubbed the Two and a Half International.

There was now an organized communist movement which might attempt to win power in the west. Their chances depended on the speed of post-war recovery in the area. Economically, it had suffered no shock to compare with the consequences of territorial break-up in Austria-Hungary and the total disintegration of society in Russia. But there had been extensive devastation, especially in France and Belgium, and frontier changes had taken from Germany 36 per cent of her coal deposits and 72 per cent of her iron ore. A large proportion of the thirteen million combatants who died in the war and of the very large number disabled came from the west. Industrial plant had worn out and not been replaced, and the fertility of the land had declined for want of chemical fertilizers. In 1920 the volume of industrial production per head of the population was 61 per cent of pre-war in Germany and 66 per cent in France. For agriculture the figures were 62 per cent and 83 per cent.

There was little inclination to use the wartime machinery of economic controls for anything beyond emergency relief work in the famines and dislocation that immediately followed the war. For long-term recovery, reliance was placed on the recovery of confidence and enterprise among businessmen and the restoration of the free flow of international trade. Both were held to depend on getting rid of the depreciating wartime paper money and restoring sound currencies based on gold, and therefore stable in value in relation both to goods and to each other. The great obstacle to this was the international indebtedness resulting from the war: reparations obligations on the one hand and inter-allied debts on the other. These represented a heavy incubus on the balance of payments of almost all the European countries, and with everyone's gold reserves in danger of depletion, the return to sound money seemed a long way off.

Effective international co-operation was required to deal with the problem, and the political conditions for it were long wanting. A moratorium on inter-allied debts would have been a great help, and this was what Britain and France proposed: they were both in debt to the United States and creditors of the other allies, and so they were relatively impartial.[1] But the Americans, the chief creditors to the tune of 10 milliard dollars, insisted with one voice on the sanctity of contract. This intensified the pressure on Germany for reparations, already great because of the economic and political condition of France. This in turn intensified the political instability of Germany and her inclination to turn to Russia. Neither France nor Germany seemed to have statesmen heroic enough to chart a new course (almost bound to be unpopular) out of the impasse.

France and Belgium were bound to press hard for reparations, not only because of their debts but because the needs of reconstruction required the government to spend heavily. The French had a deficit of 29 milliard francs in 1919 and 17 milliards in 1920. This

---

[1] Britain was a net creditor to the extent of some 4·5 milliard dollars, and France a net debtor for about 3·5 milliards.

fell to 3 milliards by 1922, but the treasury was left with a floating debt of 60 milliards, which it could not cut down: this amount had in effect to be re-borrowed each year as short-term loans fell due for repayment. Heavy tax increases were voted in 1920, but by 1923 the Chamber was refusing to vote any more. So the French budget came to include a section of 'recoverable expenses', which could be met by borrowing because the Germans would eventually pay. French policy, however, became much more unreasonable than it might otherwise have been because of the success of the parties of the right in the elections of 1919. The radicals and socialists had been unable to combine against them. They themselves had presented a united front, and they had profited from the introduction at long last of a form of proportional representation. Their victory was nothing less than a revolution—elements excluded from power since the Dreyfus case, and even since the seventies were now ascendent. The republic was not endangered: the right was partly clerical and aristocratic, but it was monarchist no longer. Its most important leader, Millerand, premier and later president from 1920, had begun as a socialist, and republicans to the left joined in his and later ministries. But the right remained ultra-nationalist, it stirred up all it could the hatreds and rancours aroused by the war, and French intransigence mounted accordingly.

The treaty of Versailles was a severe blow to the Weimar republic because it had been established in the hope of winning thereby a more lenient peace. The national assembly refused to ratify the treaty, army officers threatened to revolt if it was accepted, the ministry resigned. Eventually, Groener told Ebert that there was no possibility of successful military resistance, and promised to keep the army in order. The socialists and catholics in parliament assumed the odium of voting for the treaty, and the other parties declared publicly their belief that this action had been inspired by entirely patriotic motives. This high-minded attitude did not last, partly because the practical hardships brought by the treaty soon began to be felt. In the autumn of 1919 Erzberger, now finance minister, brought in a series of heavy taxes on the wealthier classes, including a huge capital levy to be collected in thirty annual instalments. These measures were justified by the poor state of the finances, but they were nevertheless hated by the rich, and they were not popular with the nation at large, for the proceeds were expected to go largely in reparations. At the same time, the freshly recreated army had to be halved in size to reach the exiguous figure laid down at Versailles. Though already small by pre-war standards, it was twice the permitted size. Many officers were laid off: the upper class faced not only high taxes but unemployment!

It was now that army officers, nationalists and conservatives began the cry that the war had been lost because the army was 'stabbed in the back' by the politicians who passed the peace resolution of 1917, concluded the armistice and brought in the republic. The behaviour of the high command in Ludendorff's time, though pretty certainly foolish, had the merit of providing the perfect background to this strategic recovery. Ludendorff had made no concessions to moderation till defeat came, and he had then suddenly fallen, leaving the shame of capitulation to his opponents. He and all the rest could therefore say that he would have won had not the agitation against annexations damped German morale and encouraged that of the allies. Care soon came to be taken to preserve the reputation of the war leaders from any taint of association with their 'defeatist' successors. Thus it was Groener, not his chief Hindenburg, who assumed the odium of telling Ebert that the army could not fight against the peace terms. Erzberger, a key man in all the changes since 1917, was particularly aimed at, and eventually had to bring a libel action against the former vice-chancellor, Helfferich, who had constantly accused him of corruption and dishonesty. His indifferent success in the long trial early in 1920 led to his retirement from office: he was not dishonest, but had entirely failed to observe the proprieties which ensure that a man is not thought so. He was on the way to rehabilitation when he was assassinated in 1921. Thus died one of the few German politicians with vigour and imagination enough to unite a diversity of parties for a constructive purpose.

In March 1920 the right-wing revival reached a sudden climax in the Kapp putsch. Some units due for dissolution under the peace treaty marched on Berlin. They had the sympathy of General Lüttwitz the local military commander and encountered no resistance. The immediate outcome was a triumph for the republic. The conservative bureaucracy which continued to staff the ministries in Berlin would have nothing to do with so insignificant a movement. Dr Kapp, who was proclaimed chancellor, was an obscure provincial official with no political skill. The republican government retired to Stuttgart and the trade unions called a general strike. The putsch collapsed in four days. But the aftermath was less happy. The communists tried to turn the general strike in the Ruhr in a revolutionary direction and both their activities and the repression of them involved bloodshed and terror. The Berlin putsch inspired one in Munich which turned the socialists out of the government and left the new Bavaria People's Party in power, a separatist and partly royalist breakaway from the Centre. This government was popular enough to retain office, and by its protection of seditious nationalists and virtual defiance of the Berlin government it called the very existence of the state in question. There was, indeed, a general failure by those in responsible positions to protect the republic against forcible attack by its enemies. Of 354 political murders by such people in the early years of the republic, 326 remained unpunished, and in 23 cases there were acquittals though the accused pleaded guilty.[1]

To strengthen their position, the government yielded in 1920 to the growing demand from the right for a new general election. But this deprived the coalition of Centre, Democrats and 'majority' socialists that had dominated parliament since 1917 of their majority. The Democrats lost half their votes, mostly to the People's Party (formerly the National Liberals). The 'majority' socialists lost getting on for half theirs to the 'independents'. This was a protest against the 'majority' party's loss of its revolutionary character: most of these votes went to the communists after the 'independent' party disappeared in 1922. The 'majority' socialists tried to recover lost ground by leaving the ministry without going into opposition. The new ministry included the People's Party instead. There was a fresh political convulsion when the total to be paid in reparations was announced in 1921. Wirth of the Centre then formed a ministry with both socialist parties, but this collapsed after a year. The next ministry was that of Cuno, whose career had been in business and administration, not politics, and it consisted of people like himself. Parliamentary government was breaking down. The moderate parties were so intimidated by the growth of the extremes that they were increasingly afraid either to compromise with each other to make a majority or to assume responsibility in government.

[1] Berlau, *The German Social Democratic Party, 1914–21*, p. 253.

Such was the situation in France and Germany when haggling over reparations began. The treaty of Versailles left the fixing of the total bill to a Reparations Commission, which was to do it by May 1921. Meanwhile the Germans had to pay 20 milliard gold marks towards reparations and occupation costs, and make certain payments in kind, notably of coal to France, Belgium and Italy. The Germans were allowed to make an offer in respect of their total liability, and the wish of the allied governments, who realized that reparations were never likely to come up to what the public expected, was to strike a bargain. In July 1920 allied and German representatives conferred at Spa, but nothing came of it except a sensible arrangement by which coal deliveries were to be paid for in gold, to provide food for the German miners. Another agreement of August 1921 facilitated the repair of war damage in France by German deliveries in kind. Early in that year the allies made an 'offer' to fix the German obligations at the fabulous figure of 226 milliard marks plus 12 per cent of German exports for forty-two years. The Germans made a counter offer of 30 milliards all told. The allies regarded this not as bargaining but defiance. They seized the Rhenish towns of Düsseldorf, Duisburg and Ruhrort, and sequestrated part of Germany's receipts for exports and the duties levied on imports through the occupied areas. There was no more time for bargaining before May 1921, when the Reparations Commission duly fixed the total payable at 132 milliard gold marks (£6·6 milliard; far below the allies 'offer') and called on Germany to pay 2 milliards a years for thirty years plus 26 per cent of the proceeds of her exports and reparations in kind. The first milliard was paid by the end of August by means of a foreign loan. Despite new taxes the repayment of this caused the mark to slump from 60 to the dollar in July to over 200 to the dollar in November. Germany declared herself unable to make the further payments due in the new year.

The French premiership had now devolved on the conciliatory Briand, henceforth the outstanding champion of reconciliation in western Europe. He and Lloyd George produced a plan for a moratorium linked to controls over German finances. Lloyd George hoped to induce the French to adopt a conciliatory policy by offering them a defensive alliance in return. But the French nationalists overthrew Briand and replaced him by the intransigent Poincaré. All the same,

Germany's obligation for 1922 had to be reduced to 720 million gold marks and 1,450 millions in goods.

Interest was now shifting to wider plans for restoring the world economy. Success here would make the reparations problem less intractable. The British were particularly interested in this approach, for their greatest loss through the war had been in their overseas markets. British exports had fallen to half their pre-war value. World economic recovery could not really be achieved without bringing in the Americans and the Russians, and the main effect of the attempts made at it in 1922 was to strengthen the position of the Bolsheviks. The western powers' need to export to Russia made them lift their blockade on Soviet ports in 1920. In 1921 there was an Anglo-Soviet trade agreement, even though Britain did not recognize the Soviet government. Then Rathenau and Loucheur, the ministers responsible for reconstruction in Germany and France respectively, produced a grandiose plan for an international European corporation for economic development in Russia. The Bolsheviks, for their part, knew that they could not develop their country without western help, and for want of a revolution there they were eager to encourage the return of the foreign capitalist enterprises that they had driven out. In April 1922, therefore, there was a world economic conference at Genoa, of which the centrepiece was negotiation between the Russians and the west about the conditions on which the capitalists would return—in particular, about the compensation which would have to be given to the expropriated owners of Russian factories and state securities in order to reassure the business world. These talks were curiously similar to the haggle about reparations. Like the Germans, the Russians did not deny their obligation, but they protested that they could not pay unless help was given in restoring their economy. In both cases Poincaré was against concessions, while the British were for moderation. In both cases the British tried to get the Americans to help and were rebuffed. The United States was not represented at Genoa, and gave its moral support to the uncompromising line of France and Belgium. The Americans were inclined to believe that the European capitalists were making bargains with the Bolsheviks detrimental to American business interests. They also failed to respond to mounting British pressure for the cancelling of war debts, so that the French could be induced to accept less in reparations. By December the British were ready to risk paying the Americans more themselves than they could recover from their allies and Germany, if only the United States would reduce its total demand on Europe—but in vain.

No progress, therefore, was made in 1922 in settling reparations or in achieving prosperity by healing the breach with Russia. The first consequence was a spectacular though essentially limited drawing together of Russia and Germany. From 1920 at least, Germany had resumed the attempt to exploit Bolshevism for her own purposes. The Russian advance into Poland was welcome to her, and she was rather ostentatiously neutral. Maltzan, the able head of the foreign ministry's eastern division, pushed reconciliation as a means of diplomatic revival. The army became increasingly interested because it proved possible to establish on Russian soil factories for the manufacture of weapons that Germany was now forbidden to own. Already in 1921 a commercial treaty was concluded, which recognized the Soviets as the only legitimate authority in Russia. Chicherin, the Russian foreign minister, visited Berlin on his way to the Genoa conference and pressed for a further treaty. Rathenau, now foreign minister, would not agree. But at the conference Chicherin threatened to conclude a treaty with the west at Germany's expense, taking a slice of reparations. Rathenau yielded to the pressure of Maltzan and Chancellor Wirth, and the two delegations to the conference concluded the treaty of Rapallo during the adjournment for Easter Sunday. There was a mutal renunciation of claims for reparations and compensation, and a full resumption of diplomatic relations was agreed on. The Soviets enjoyed friendly political and economic relations with Germany henceforth, until the rise of Hitler.

The other consequence of the impasse was the steady worsening of the German situation. The republic was shaken by the murder of Rathenau in July, and sapped by the advent of the feeble Cuno ministry. The mark fell from 350 to the dollar to 4,500 to the dollar by the end of October. Germany could raise no more foreign loans. The moderate Lloyd George fell after the Greek fiasco, and in Italy power passed to an apostle of violence, Mussolini. Poincaré insisted on 'productive guarantees' as a condition of any further leniency to Germany. The allies were to take possession of some of her physical resources and appropriate the profit from them. The British objected, but in December 1922 the Reparations Commission declared Germany in default, even on her reduced payments under the existing moratorium: she had failed to deliver 100,000 telegraph poles. The British delegate, with a famous remark about a similar use of wood in the Trojan horse, voted against France, but she was supported by Belgium and Fascist Italy. In January 1923 French and Belgian forces occupied the Ruhr. Germany responded with passive resistance. The coal syndicate withdrew its offices to Hamburg, the managers and workers refused to collaborate with the invader. The German government endorsed this and promised to make good any loss it caused. Eventually, the French and Belgians established their own organization for working factories and mines, and managed to get production going again. But they put a customs barrier between the Ruhr and the rest of Germany, the economic life of which, deprived of its great power-house, became heavily dependent on imports. Under these pressures the currency collapsed altogether and virtually ceased to have any value. Profits and some wages and salaries could keep pace with the inflation. But pensions, small savings and any investment yielding a fixed return became worthless. The middle class suffered worst and the enduring political effects of this were very bad. Nationalism would, no doubt, have been rampant in any case. But the lesson of the inflation was that the traditional middle-class virtues of prudence and moderation did not pay. The natural supporters of order henceforth would not need much to tempt them into support of a radical adventurer, such as Hitler.

Radical adventure was under way in 1923 itself and seemed destined to tear Germany apart. Nationalists in the west tried to start a guerilla war against the occupying forces, which was met not only with severe repression but the encouragement for some time of the small Rhenish separatist movement. Armed bands in the style of the free corps multiplied elsewhere, especially in Bavaria where the counter-revolution of 1919–20 had never really stopped. The Bavarian government had long failed to dissolve the 'home guards' kept on foot in defiance of the Versailles provisions for disarmament. A state of emergency continued which allowed the arbitrary repression of liberals and socialists by 'people's courts'. On the other hand, measures taken to protect the republic after the murders of Erzberger and Rathenau were largely inoperative in Bavaria. Even Lossow, the local military commander, was demoralized, and told his superiors in May 1923 that he could not suppress the nationalists, who had more arms than he had. A march on Berlin in the style of Mussolini was being increasingly talked of, especially by the fieriest local leader, Hitler himself.

The mistakes of the western democracies had further given the Bolsheviks a new chance to extend their revolution to Germany. The communists there went to work in two ways. They sought the alliance of social democrats to resist the danger of a new military coup from the right. Defensive fronts began to be organized in Saxony and Thuringia which might form the basis of a revolution. At the same time the communists tried to woo the nationalists themselves, seeking as in Asia a common front against the arch-imperialists, Britain and France. Under Chicherin, who was Soviet foreign minister from 1918 till 1930, there was indeed a fairly constant Soviet preference for good relations with Germany, even a non-communist Germany; nor was it so very different afterwards. The communists have been much reproached for their collaboration with right-wing nationalist forces in Germany. But it should be said that they were thereby continuing traditional Russian policy, from which the only complete departure, in the era of the First World War, had been disastrous. Russia and Germany had a common interest in the suppression of Poland. Germany was the nearest great power to Russia in the west, and it was common prudence to keep her friendly, disarmed though she was. Reconciliation between Germany and the western powers threatened to isolate Russia and might well be attained by common measures against her. After, as before, 1917 it was the German socialists and liberals who hated Russia and wanted friendship with the west; Junkers and nationalists who hated the democracies never abandoned the hope of using Russia against them. It therefore had to be the policy of the Bolsheviks no less than the Tsars to ally with the German reactionaries.

Allied mistakes were an important cause of the dangerous vacuum that had emerged in central Europe. The allies had failed to make it clear that a republican constitution would not win the Germans easy peace terms. This increased the disillusionment with the republic, and made it even weaker than it would otherwise have been. The demand for massive reparations with very large payments from the start was mistaken. In 1920 German exports, the financial basis of reparations payments, were only a quarter of what they had been before the war and the attempts of the feeble republic to pay produced political and financial chaos. This is not to say, as Keynes did, that massive reparations were in principle economically impossible. Contrary to his expectations, the German economy recovered quite quickly: the depreciation of the mark produced by the threat of reparations at first helped this by stimulating exports. There was much to be said for the view prevailing in France that the Germans were being evasive and could pay much more if they tried. Petty duplicity was the keynote of German dealings with the Reparations Commission. Their payments down to 1924 were claimed by them to represent over 42 milliard gold marks, but even neutral investigators valued them at only 26 milliards, and the Commission believed them to be worth only 10 milliards. There was likewise a failure to execute loyally the Versailles provisions respecting disarmament and the punishment of war criminals: as late as 1925 the allies had to enforce the completion of disarmament by prolonging the occupation of their bridgehead opposite Cologne. The annual amount of reparations demanded has been shown to be similar to what Hitler managed to extract from France and to what the German people spent on rearmament under his rule (it must be remembered that the disarmament of Germany meant a great financial saving to her).

It was politically that French intransigence was misguided. The German delegation at Versailles had argued that the reparations demanded could not be exacted without complete allied political and economic control of Germany. The allies, in reply, had specifically disavowed any intention of interfering in German political and economic affairs. Poincaré's demand for material guarantees and his resort to military occupation proved the Germans right. The allies might have been able to collect reparations if they had been prepared to behave like Hitler and turn Germany into a colony. But this would really have meant that exhausted France would have had to defend central Europe against the Bolsheviks in perpetuity, and nobody seems to have contemplated it. Further, massive reparations payments implied huge, unrequited German exports at rock-bottom prices. This would damage other exporters, notably Britain. Justly or not,

France and Belgium would get part of their reparations from their allies rather than Germany.

The western powers, in short, had committed themselves to the rebuilding of the world on the basis of democracy, national independence and orthodox capitalist economics. Really massive reparations were in contradiction with all these. What could be extracted had to be limited to what would be paid fairly quickly and willingly, in order to ransom the defeated nation from occupation and subjection. The amount which the defeated power would offer could be stepped up a little by a display of sternness, and this in the end was what Poincaré may have achieved. But much of the financial burden of the war had to be shouldered by the victors, and shared out as fairly as it could be. On these lines a reconciling settlement had at length to be sought.

6: Liberal Reverses: Dictatorship in Southern Europe

In the early twenties Wilsonian liberalism was already in retreat in eastern Europe. It fared no better in the other great underdeveloped region of the continent, the south. Liberal institutions had hitherto held their own in Italy and Iberia, although it was the form rather than the substance of democracy that was upheld. The strains of the post-war world made it impossible to keep up the pretence any longer, and the ruling groups in each country established outright dictatorships. This boded ill for the future of free institutions in Europe, but for the time being it did not threaten the new international order. Even Mussolini's bark was worse than his bite, and the assimilation of the southern dictatorships did not seem as thorny a problem as relations with Soviet Russia.

The Rise of Mussolini

Italy had entered the war for no very good reason, and came out of it with small tangible gains and large tangible losses—over half a million dead, industrial production down by a quarter and a war debt of 48 milliard gold lire. The weakness of the Italian economy had meant that its considerable war effort had only been kept going at the end by large credits from the allies; all the same, the amount of paper money in circulation had doubled during the last year of war and there was a deficit of 8 milliards in the first financial year after the peace. Popular discontent with the sufferings of war and the prospect of stringency after it was increased by the fact that in Italy it had never been strongly supported by the mass of the people. Obviously an imperialist venture by the wealthier classes, it had been openly fought by most of the socialists. The catholics had disliked (much as in 1848) a war against Austria-Hungary, the great catholic power. Workers and peasants had thus been united in the desire for peace, and their discontent so unnerved the ruling classes that there was a widespread expectation that Italy would become a republic. In all this the Italian situation was very similar to that in Russia.

To satisfy the growing popular forces, the electoral law was changed and proportional representation introduced. The large constituencies which this required could not readily be controlled by the corrupt machinations of the old party bosses. In consequence, the socialists won 156 seats out of 508, and the People's Party, newly formed by the catholics, won 99 when elections were held in November 1919. The Socialist party was now completely dominated by the 'maximalist' wing. Their current programme, put out during the war, demanded, besides international reconciliation, such things as a republic, the election of high officials, a minimum wage and the expropriation of ill-cultivated land. But what was more important was their virtual repudiation of loyalty to the existing state. They did not rebel against it, but essentially their policy was to await its collapse and to assume that their aims would then be painlessly achieved. The formation of the People's Party resulted from the Vatican's final abandonment of restrictions on catholic political activity in Italy. To some extent this was due to the fear of socialism: much of the strength of the new party was due to the wealthy catholics who supported it for this reason. Its main parliamentary leader, Filippo Meda, was of this stamp: in the general interests of conservatism he had, indeed, supported entry into the war and served in the wartime ministries. But its secretary and founder, Don Luigi Sturzo, had quite different views. He came from Sicily, where he was mayor of his home town. Besides being an expert in municipal administration, he had been closely in touch with the catholic trade unions and youth movement. His aim was a centre party which could work with and restrain the parties of the left as well as of the right. It was a misfortune that this young nobleman with wide culture and statesmanlike views should be debarred from parliament and ministerial office because he was a priest.

But the mass parties, mainly hostile to the late war, were not the only movement of discontent. The nationalists who had been eager for war were naturally most disappointed at its meagre fruits. They were not numerous and did not do well in the 1919 elections. But their mobbing tactics had intimidated the representatives of the people into accepting war in 1915, and they had many friends in high places. Their rank and file consisted largely of soldiers who had enjoyed the war: men of the lower middle class who had served in crack regiments or become officers and did not relish a return to their humbler peacetime status. There were also, however, some old anarchists and syndicalists who were drawn to this party because they had always regarded violent destruction as the beginning of salvation. Because of its violence the movement at first attracted only some of the conservatives, but more and more sympathized with it as the heightening revolutionary tension made their tempers fray. What it could do was seen already in 1919. Fiume, claimed by Italy without success, was under international occupation. In September the poet d'Annunzio invaded and conquered it with an irregular force. What was striking was that the Italian authorities had done nothing to stop the organizing of this expedition on Italian soil, and that it included many deserters from the regular Italian forces, notably from a unit recently sent away from Fiume by the allied command because it was thought to be meditating a coup.

The old-established body of parliamentary politicians still held nearly half the seats in the chamber, but it was no longer strong enough either in parliament or the country to govern alone. In view of the irresponsible violence of the socialists and nationalists, the most sensible outcome would probably have been a coalition with the People's Party. The populists did indeed support or even join the various governments which held office till the establishment of Mussolini. But there was no love lost between these allies, for they represented in effect the two sides in the struggle for the making of the Italian kingdom. The old parliamentary liberals would rather deal with the socialists than the catholics, and in negotiating with organized labour it was their practice to ignore the catholic trade unions and allow them to be victimized by their socialist rivals. Bad blood also resulted from Giolitti's plan in 1920 to stop tax evasion by compelling disclosure of the ownership of bearer bonds. Many of these were held by ecclesiastical bodies whose legal right to own property was uncertain. It was unfortunate that Meda would never try the experiment of forming a ministry himself with liberal support. Instead, there was a succession of liberal premiers, none of whom could rely on his majority.

A renewed effort to domesticate the socialists was therefore in order. This was the policy especially associated with Giolitti, and in the summer of 1920 he returned to power. He was better placed in one respect than his predecessors to work with the new mass parties, for like them he had been against war. But it seemed unlikely that he could work with the left. 1919–20 witnessed a huge wave of strikes, accompanied by a good deal of violence, raids on food shops, sometimes the seizure of factories or uncultivated land. By 1920 the war boom in industrial activity was subsiding and the employers were resisting wage demands more strongly. The metal workers tried to conserve their resources by calling a series of partial strikes instead of a general one, and in August the employers replied to this strategy with a lockout. The union responded by ordering its members to occupy the factories, and this was done throughout the country. The revolution seemed to have begun. But the socialist leaders had no plan for exploiting the situation, and the aim of the union seems to have been the narrow one of using the factories to earn revenue and so gain resources to support their members in the dispute. Giolitti was able to play his chosen role of peacemaker, not using force and letting the storm blow itself out. The employers naturally did not press him when he ironically offered to bombard their factories, and the workers found that they could not produce much without the managers and technicians. The government finally negotiated a compromise by which workers' committees were to join the employers in the management of the factories.

In other quarters Giolitti set himself vigorously to the work of reconstruction. The previous government had already carried heavy new direct taxes, and Giolitti made an essential contribution to a balanced budget by abolishing the bread subsidy. In his year of office he reduced the deficit by half, to $4\frac{1}{2}$ milliards for the year. Abroad he ended the costly and unfruitful policy of adventure. Attempts to expand east of the Adriatic were given up. Fiume became a free city. D'Annunzio wished to continue in control of the town, making it the nucleus of a nationalist new order, but Italian troops chased him out. At the opposite political extreme, the more furious of the socialists seceded to form an Italian Communist Party early in 1921. But there seems to have been no corresponding increase in the left's understanding of revolutionary techniques.

It was at this point that the fascist movement emerged as the main focus of nationalism. Benito Mussolini, its leader, was born in 1883, the son of a blacksmith in the Romagna. His family held radical views and he quite naturally became a socialist. But his only real beliefs seem to have been in violence and in self-advancement. It was the tradition of violence on the left, exemplified in Blanqui and Sorel, that appealed to him rather than the rationalizing tradition carried on by the Marxists. He managed to qualify as an elementary school-master, but his political violence led to several years of exile and almost of destitution in Switzerland. He became a notable socialist journalist, but his taste for violence, as we have seen, led him not only to attack his party's subservience to Giolitti but also to desire Italian participation in the World War. His breach with the socialists over this issue was embittered by suspicions regarding the source of the funds behind the paper which he now founded, the *Popolo d'Italia*. Having played a notable part in the agitation for war, he enlisted himself, and was seriously wounded in 1917 and thus enabled to return to journalism. The front page of his paper carried two quotations which aptly express his beliefs at all times in his career: 'whoever has iron, has bread' (Blanqui); 'revolution is an idea that has found bayonets' (Napoleon).

The fascists were founded in 1919, and at first had a left-wing pro-gramme. Mussolini applauded the first (syndicalist) attempt to occupy a factory in 1919, and he supported the nation-wide factory seizures of 1920. But he needed money for his movement, not to speak of his own now very comfortable style of living. This could only come from wealthy conservatives, and so Mussolini changed his line and became an outspoken champion of private enterprise, opposing all state in-terference in economic life. But in this he was perhaps even less sin-cere than in his socialism and it was by no means his last word. He cleverly tried to avoid commitment to any views that would hinder his freedom of manoeuvre among the other parties. He justified this by saying that the fascists had no principles, that their only principle was to act, that they were not a party but an anti-party. The fascists were, indeed, not organized as a party but on military lines. Instead of local party branches there were the *fasci di combattimento*, from which their name came[1]—'combat groups', ready to act in the man-ner of the German free corps.

[1] The fasces were the bundles of rods carried before the Roman consuls to symbol-ize their power to punish. The reference intended here was to the binding together, symbol of discipline.

In the winter of 1920–1 the socialists had lost the initiative, and the frightened upper class was eager to teach them a lesson and to revenge themselves for the humiliation they had endured. The 'black-shirts' of the *fasci* were willing to do this for them. Their activities eventually covered the whole of the north, down to Tuscany, and also Apulia, the 'heel ' of Italy. The rest of the south and the centre was still so apathetic that there had been little danger of revolution there, and so no need for counter-revolution. Violence in these areas was still mostly on the side of the liberals against the catholics. It was especially in the rural districts that the fascists won their early suc-cesses. Here the socialists had gradually managed to organize the large landless proletariat and build up an impressive organization of co-operatives and labour exchanges. There were far too many men for the work to be done, but agreements were forced on the em-ployers which ensured that each man had work some of the time— commonly not more than 120–130 days a year—and was paid enough then to maintain him and his family while he was unemployed. This system of poor relief at the employers' expense was, of course, much resented by them, and it also tended to be disliked by the more enter-prising peasants who were or wished to become smallholders. Small farms employed no hired labour, and so could not be brought into the system. It was therefore in the socialists' interest to keep down the area they covered as much as possible.

The blackshirts broke up the socialist organization by force. A body of them would descend on a township by lorry, seize and burn down the premises of all the local socialist organizations and beat up everyone they encountered there. Organizers of the labour movement who escaped with their lives usually had to flee the area on pain of further reprisal. The agricultural labourers were thereafter at their employers' mercy. Later the fascists began to organize their own unions in the place of those they had destroyed, often using the workers they organized to break strikes called by the socialists. This technique of terrorism had originally been developed in 1920 in the area round Trieste and used largely against the Slav minority there. It took advantage of the dispersal of the rural workers. The fascists had money and so they could make up for lack of numbers by superior mobility. Squads could be brought considerable distances by lorry in order to concentrate against a single township, and as the area under fascist control increased its resources could be turned against the area still to be conquered. But the fascists did not confine themselves to rural areas or private socialist organizations. They attacked the socialists in the big towns: the offices of the great socialist newspaper *Avanti!* in Milan were burned down three times. Above all, they took action against the large and growing number of municipal councils which had come under socialist control. Town halls were occupied and socialist councillors beaten up and forced to resign. In all their undertakings the fascists received much quiet help from sympathetic officials and military commanders. They were often able to borrow weapons and lorries from government stores.

Giolitti's attitude to fascist violence was much what it had been to socialist violence. He hoped that if it was handled with tolerance it would blow itself out. His main concern was to press on with financial reconstruction, and for that purpose to create a parliamentary majority on which he could rely as surely as on that which had existed before 1914. For this purpose the fascists had their uses—if the wild socialists were intimidated, they would feel the need of his protection. He wanted to bring them both into the government, and to hold new elections in which, as before the war, government support would be given to candidates of all opinions from left to right, united only in their availability for Giolitti's purpose of the moment. The elections were duly held in May 1921. With the fascists Giolitti was able to do a deal. Their acts of violence were ratified—the municipalities which they had broken up were dissolved in the interests of public order. This condoning of violence and suspending of local elective authorities was again nothing new for Giolitti: all that was novel was its application in the progressive north instead of the backward south. The fascists fought the elections as government candidates, and aided by this and their own violence they won a modest thirty seats. But Giolitti was not able to do a deal with the still much more important mass parties. The populists would not stand on a single list with other government supporters. The socialists would not enter the government. The mass parties returned from the elections as strong and unbiddable as ever. Giolitti found increasing difficulty in putting through his programme of economies, and soon afterwards resigned in favour of Bonomi, another old parliamentarian a little to his left.

Mussolini had entered parliament at the election and he now set seriously about the winning of power. The fascists were furiously multiplying: in October 1920 there were only 190 squads, in November 1921 there were 2,300 with 320,000 members, a third of them fighters. But they were not strong enough to govern alone, and opinion was beginning to harden against them. Bonomi made some attempt to halt their atrocities, the Reds began to arm and fight back, and several incidents showed that the fascists were no use against serious resistance. At Sarzana in July a body of fascists clamouring for the release of some of their number from prison were fired on by the gendarmerie and fled in all directions. The people of the area at once rose and lynched every fascist they could find. Mussolini needed allies. He tried to get them by splitting the mass parties. In parliament he appealed to the trade union movement to work with him, and drew a sharp distinction between them and the wicked socialists. He also spoke with great respect of the church, drawing a veil over the atheistic provenance of himself and his chief associates. Here he was appealing to the hierarchy and conservative catholics over the heads of christian democrats like Don Sturzo. He called for a pact of pacification with the populists and socialists. Such a document was actually signed by fascists and socialists on 2 August.

Mussolini's plan misfired however, for it was disowned by his own movement. Atrocities did not cease, and Mussolini retired in disgust from the fascist national executive. After a decent interval he climbed down and, in the absence of rivals equally gifted, resumed the leadership. His argument had been that the fascists were not a party but a more specialized organization, and so could share power with other organizations of different kinds. Now he was forced to come out in favour of turning the fascists into a party, and this was done: his followers were not keen to share power.

Fortunately for the fascists, the other groups remained unable to co-operate effectively. Under communist pressure, the bulk of the socialists remained unwilling to work with the government in return for action against fascism. Bonomi was turned out by socialist and fascist votes in February 1922. A long ministerial crisis was followed by the purely stopgap ministry of Facta. By the summer many of the socialist deputies were ready to behave more responsibly, but Giolitti was now saying that it was impossible to govern against the fascists—it would mean civil war. This reflected especially the breach between Giolitti and Don Sturzo: neither could bear to support the other, and so an effective ministry was impossible. Rather than work with the moderate parties, the socialists tried all through to defend themselves by means of general strikes, which were carried out with heroic discipline but had no effect except to irritate. The last was in the summer of 1922, and the fascists called the socialists' bluff by saying that if the government would not suppress it they would do so themselves. The strike was called off before the fascist ultimatum expired. The fascists went on to seize control in the great socialist strongholds of Milan and Genoa. In the latter they destroyed an imposing dock labour organization, which had controlled employment much as the agricultural unions had done but made itself rather unpopular by reserving jobs for a privileged body of workers. The fascists now felt strong enough to defy and insult the prefects who dared to oppose them, calling for their dismissal and ordering shops and factories to close in protest.

Mussolini was therefore able to take the initiative in moves to restore effective government. He negotiated in turn with Giolitti, with Nitti (premier in 1919) and with Salandra, offering a coalition with himself as junior partner. They all accepted, but did not offer him good enough terms. In October 1922 the 'march on Rome' brought him the premiership. The rather disorderly and ill-provisioned fascist columns that moved on the capital through the cold, wet weather would have been no match for the available regular forces had these opened fire. But they gave Facta the excuse he needed to hand over to Mussolini, and provided a good argument that could be used to induce the king to offer him the premiership. Summoned by telegram from Milan, where he had prudently stayed, he formed a cabinet which included four liberals and two populists. He was dissuaded only at the last minute from including a socialist trade-unionist.

For the time being, indeed, it was not clear what effect his advent would have. The half-liberty remaining in Italy was not much diminished. Mussolini tried unsuccessfully to incorporate his 'blackshirts' in the regular army, and it was thought that he might part company with them now that he had found more respectable friends. His first big political change was an electoral reform which retained the forms of proportional representation but allowed a list winning a quarter of the votes to take two-thirds of the seats. But this could be

construed as a measure to restore efficiency to parliament by creating
a stable majority, and opposition to it was not wholehearted. In the
event, the government list at the elections of April 1924 was as variegated as those of the Giolitti era, even including anti-fascists. It
secured 60 per cent of the vote—4¼ millions against 3 millions—and
the opposition had only 133 seats out of 535. But the fascists were
not yet in control of parliament.

A decisive change took place immediately afterwards. On the re-
assembly of parliament Matteotti, a leader of the sensible socialists
who would have saved liberal democracy if they could, delivered a
long attack on the malpractices of the government at the elections.
Soon afterwards he was murdered. Mussolini condemned the deed
strongly and publicly, but it was clear that it had been instigated by
himself or by someone highly placed. Fascists in high office were dismissed or prosecuted. The moderate men who had been working
with Mussolini in the hope of domesticating him were disenchanted,
and began to look towards the opposition. Mussolini was faced with
the choice of retiring or setting up a pure-fascist government without
the help of the old parliamentarians. The opposition made things easy
for him by retiring from parliament, weakening the hands of any
who might wish to oppose him from the government benches; they
returned in the autumn of 1925 when it was too late. Attempts were
made to get the king to dismiss the government, but in vain. In
January 1925 Mussolini announced his intention of establishing a
dictatorship, and proclaimed his solidarity with the fascists and their
violent methods. Restrictions on political liberty came thick and
fast, and the democratic leaders were exiled, imprisoned or killed.
At the end of 1926 the remains of the opposition were expelled from
parliament *en bloc*. Nobody dared oppose the force—regular and
irregular—at the disposal of the fascists. In December 1925 the head
of the government was made, in effect, the sole minister, his colleagues becoming subordinate executants of his will. In January 1926
he was given plenary powers to legislate by decree and the rule of
Mussolini as *Duce* began.

Mussolini embodied in his earlier career two political traditions of
united Italy. He was a dictatorial hero like Garibaldi and Crispi,
sweeping aside the talkers and eager for great deeds. But he was also
a 'transformist' like Cavour, Depretis or Giolitti, avoiding commit-

ment to a party programme, and sacrificing everything to the building up of a strong body of support, gathered together from the most variegated sources. The deep religious and social divisions in the country gravely impeded the co-operation of its larger political movements, and his small, disciplined party was able to manoeuvre among them and survive and eventually triumph because of their cleavages. To this extent backward Italy was like backward Russia, the fascists were like the Bolsheviks and Mussolini was like Lenin. Both men started as social democrats, for both the quest for power was primary and this caused them to leave the party, to make several radical shifts in their views, and to try and build up a small and obedient following who would accept these shifts without question. The way in which the Italian workers were treated and the Italian parliament finally thrust aside similarly recalls the fate of the Russian constituent assembly and the sufferings of the Russian peasants in the civil war. The German free corps never had so much latitude for evil doing, for there the gulf between the classes was not so wide, and there were more moderate men on both sides to defend the cause of amity between them.

The Italian socialists made the cardinal error of failing to decide whether they were a revolutionary or a reformist movement. They did enough to enrage the upper classes, but not enough to intimidate them. Which they should have chosen to be, the historian may excuse himself from deciding, but a decision was essential. Whichever way it went, more attention should have been paid to what Lenin would have called the 'middle peasantry' and its urban equivalent—the backbone of the populists—whose help was needed in standing up to the rich. The failure of Italian socialism sprang from the incongruity of political freedom in a socially backward country. The one meant that the socialist leaders were parliamentarians; the other meant that the rank and file would not long be content with speechmaking and piecemeal reform, but would demand strong measure of which the parliamentarians were incapable. Because there had been freedom in Italy there were no real Bolsheviks there, and the socialists could be put down when they became too dangerous. Had the government of the Tsars taken a leaf or two from the Italian book, it too might have survived. But the Italian ruling class would have been well advised to think of something beyond mere survival. It failed to produce a constructive policy at home capable of broadening loyalty to the new kingdom, and instead had plunged the country into useless war to which succeeded years of demoralizing anarchy. It might have derived a new impetus from an alliance with christian democracy; but this movement came so late upon the scene that it had not the maturity and cohesion to take over from the faltering liberals.

The Fascist System in Italy

When they were first established, the institutions of the fascist state enjoyed something of a vogue, and were much studied by foreign observers in search of a cure for the world's ills. In retrospect they do not seem especially novel or fruitful, and so are only briefly discussed here.

Mussolini's main political task was to come to some settlement with the two organizations that had shown themselves capable (as the fascists had not) of moving the masses—the church and the labour movement. The fascists had acquired, almost by accident, a trade union organization of its own, and in 1923 this concluded an agreement with the Italian employers' organization providing for co-operation for the national good and explicitly repudiating the idea of the class struggle. A further agreement of 1925 gave the fascist unions the sole right to speak for the workers in collective bargaining. A law of 1926 organized unions and employers into 'corporations', empowered to levy funds from workers and employers and to settle wages and working conditions by negotiation, even for non-members. Strikes and lockouts were forbidden. Unofficial unions were allowed as well in theory, but as there was little that they were allowed to do they soon died out. The corporations were taken very seriously as the foundation of the new state. A ministry and a council of corporations were set up. The local and regional associations were grouped into thirteen national confederations—six of employers, six of workers and one for the professions—and these in turn into two general confederations. A new electoral law of 1928 gave the confederations power to select candidates for the chamber of deputies. The Fascist Grand Council had then to select 400 from the names suggested, and present them to the electorate for approval in a plebiscite. In 1938 the chamber was abolished and replaced by one in which sat the members of the national councils of the Fascist party and of the corporations. In practice, the corporations were so dominated by the Fascist party that their usefulness to the workers was dubious and their autonomous life exiguous. They were a bureaucratic incubus performing certain welfare functions and not much more.

This, perhaps, was because the Fascist party itself was not much better. Although in theory it directed the state in the way that the Communists controlled Russia, in practice it was a channel for graft and enthusiasm but not for policy making. The successive secretaries-general of the party were all stupid men, the Fascist Grand Council, created in 1928 and containing the leading men in the different sections of the movement, seldom met. Effective power lay with Mussolini and his associates personally, and with the ordinary heads of the administration and the armed forces. Of course, the fascists believed explicitly in personal leadership, and did not have a mystique of the Party to nearly the extent that the communists did.

Mussolini suppressed the christian democrats and catholic trade unions and co-operatives with the same brutality as their socialist equivalents. But he did everything he could to get on good terms with the church. A crucifix was ordered to be displayed in every school and government office, religious teaching in schools became compulsory. An examination was instituted which could be taken at the end of their career by children both in church and in state schools—thus ending discrimination against the former. There were numerous other favours and courtesies. Mussolini was fortunate in the elevation of Achille Ratti to the papal throne as Pius XI in 1922. He came of a northern landowning family and had a particular horror of communism, whose westward thrust he had just witnessed as nuncio in Warsaw. He was alarmed at the growing schism among politically active catholics between those who went with fascism and those who wanted a socialist alliance in defence of democracy. The People's Party seemed to him a dangerous experiment, and he preferred the previous system of strict ecclesiastical control over catholic politicians. This was the background to the Lateran Treaty of 1929. Italy recognized the Vatican City as a tiny sovereign state and gave extra-territorial status to various buildings elsewhere in papal possession. The church accepted an indemnity for the loss of its other possessions. Its activities were to be completely free and under state protection.

Clergy were exempt from military service, religious orders were to enjoy the fullest legal rights, there was to be a catholic university in Milan with power to confer degrees. The catholic faith was to be the religion of the state, and other religions were merely tolerated. Catholic priests (but not those of other faiths) were empowered to celebrate marriages without the need of a separate civil ceremony or registration. In return the church at last recognized the Kingdom of Italy, and agreed to consult it in the nomination of Italian bishops.

The policy of reconciliation with the church did not begin with Mussolini as we have seen, and in most of its aspects he was continuing experiments begun by his predecessors. Nevertheless, the treaty of 1929 is the one great and lasting achievement which should be remembered to his credit. It finally healed a deep cleavage which had done much to give the new Italian state the character of a conquered territory in the power of an aggressive minority. Very wisely, the settlement was confirmed when the Italian Republic was created after the Second World War, even the communists voting in favour of it.

Apart from conceding freedom of action to the church, the fascists sought to dominate the entire spiritual life of the country. Control of the press, radio and films was established in 1925. The Balilla youth movement was founded in 1926, enrolling in different sections boys and girls from eight to eighteen. Physical training and the Duce's speeches bulked large in its educational programme. A workers' leisure organization (*dopolavoro*) organized adult education and the provision of cheap holidays. The large funds at the disposal of the corporations allowed a fair provision of social services. A special organization was created to care for the health and well-being of mothers and children. For Mussolini, Italy's expanding population was not an incubus but a source of national power, and he wished to encourage its growth.

In economic matters Mussolini had the common dictator's love of grandiose public works, and under his rule there was much building of roads and embellishment of towns, not always in very good taste. His desire for military strength was reflected in a rise of iron and steel production in the twenties from about 1 million to over 2 million tons a year, and in the 'battle for wheat'. This reduced very considerably the dependence of Italy on imports for her bread supply, but at the cost of lower production of other commodities. (The results of collectivizing Russian agriculture were to be rather similar.) Italy was the largest European producer of artificial silk, and production increased tenfold in the first five years of Mussolini's rule. Production of hydro-electric power increased in the same period from 6·9 milliard to 8·4 milliard kWh; in 1937 it was 14·4 milliards. But this development was under way before Mussolini gained power. More to the credit of the régime were the laws, notably that of 1928 which established for the first time a national plan for the improvement of the land by the draining of marshes and the afforestation of mountains. The areas requiring development were defined, and the contributions to be expected from the state and from the local landowners were laid down. Mussolini's most famous exploit in this direction, the draining of the Pontine Marshes round Rome, was an addition to the plan in the thirties.

In the twenties, however, fascist economic policy, like that of the Soviet Union as we shall see, was essentially cautious and unoriginal, adhering closely to capitalist orthodoxy. As in France and Germany, a period of physical reconstruction after the war led to increased production but also to inflation. There followed (1926–7) strong measures to protect the lire, which led for a time to depression. Italy did not do significantly better or worse than her neighbours. The main fascist contribution was in balancing the budget. An authoritarian régime could cut expenditure more readily than a democratic one, and Giolitti, before his fall in 1921, had been demanding power to make economies by decree. The fascists were also able to decree reductions in wages, rents and interest as an alternative to devaluing the lire.

In foreign affairs Mussolini continued to profess himself a fervent nationalist and to decry the ideals of the League, putting his trust as always in force and violence. But it is completely wrong to regard him as having blazed the trail back to unbridled international anarchy. That he has been so regarded has been due largely to his first notable essay in foreign policy, the Corfu affair of 1923. The Italian members of a commission established by the allied powers to determine the frontiers of Albania had been murdered on Greek soil. Mussolini sent an ultimatum to Greece requiring reparation and the punishment of the guilty, which in its threat to Greek sovereignty resembled the Austrian ultimatum to Serbia in 1914. The reply being unsatisfactory, Corfu was bombarded and occupied, and Mussolini declined to allow the League to interfere. But he was prepared to accept the interposition of the conference of allied ambassadors which had set up the boundary commission. The Council of the League therefore suggested a solution which was taken up by the conference of ambassadors. By a show of intransigence, Mussolini got them to improve the terms and then accepted them. The affair rightly aroused great concern among the idealists and small powers that supported the League. But as a threat to European stability it was chicken feed beside the French occupation of the Ruhr then in progress, which the League was powerless to prevent. One of the features of the crisis was that the French government was receiving Italian support over the Ruhr, and accordingly was not inclined to thwart them in Corfu.

Ensuing events, moreover, suggested that Mussolini's violence had just been a beginner's blunder. He had at first protested at the settlements which his predecessors had made with Yugoslavia, and threatened to regard Yugoslav registration of the treaties with the League as an unfriendly act. Now the two countries joined in registering them, and early in 1924 a treaty of friendship was signed by which Fiume at last became part of Italy, but with the Slav-inhabited territories hitherto joined to it going to Yugoslavia. Good relations were re-established with Greece in 1926, and Italy cultivated the friendship of all the smaller states in and around the Balkans. Relations with Yugoslavia became distant again, however, mainly because of Albania where the rivalry of the two powers succeeded that of the Italians and Austrians. In 1925 Ahmed Zogu became Albania's president and succeeded for the first time in setting up an orderly government there; he made himself King Zog in 1928. Originally a Yugoslav protégé, he turned to the Italians because they could better undertake the economic development of his country. Defence and economic agreements in 1926–7 made him virtually an Italian puppet. The winning of a protectorate over Albania gave Italy the keys of the Adriatic, and was a solid success won at little cost. It was Mussolini's most worthwhile victory in foreign affairs, though not his biggest.

More generally, Mussolini's policy was one of rivalry in the Mediterranean with France and good relations with Britain. These two powers compensated Italy for the non-fulfilment of their promises of 1915 by the cession of some useless territory adjoining Libya and

Somaliland. Mussolini played a satisfactory part in the pacification of Europe after 1923. He was the first to follow Ramsay Macdonald in recognizing the Soviet Union—another sign that his left-wing origins were not forgotten—and he came briefly to Locarno, in which settlement Italy had an important role. As a victorious but unsatisfied power, Italy was bound to have a rather restless post-war policy even under democratic rule, but at the same time was well placed to mediate between victors and vanquished.

Mussolini's régime was the first serious attempt to set up a totalitarian state in western Europe, and though it was brutal and repressive there was always something a little half-hearted about the experiment. The settlement with the church involved a renunciation of that total control over the spiritual life of the nation which is an essential totalitarian characteristic. Of course, the relations between clergy and fascists were often excellent, but the church as in the past was a sanctuary of sorts against the lay tyrant. De Gasperi, future premier of the Italian Republic, spent the fascist era as a librarian in the Vatican. The social changes wrought by the régime were likewise limited, especially in the countryside. The reason may be sought in the paucity of Italy's resources and her exposed position. She could not hope for the industrial greatness of Germany or of Stalin's Russia, and could not therefore embark on the ruthless imperial expansion which such greatness alone could make possible. Mussolini desired imperial grandeur more than anything, but he was long sensible enough not to attempt it. He therefore had no incentive to overturn existing Italian society. The rise of Hitler tempted him to depart from wisdom, to seek imperial greatness and to attempt the transformation of Italy in order to make her strong. This belated expansion of his megalomania from words to deeds did not succeed for long and brought his career to a rapid and inglorious end.

Primo de Rivera and Salazar

Neutral in the First World War, Spain was nevertheless touched by the economic dislocations of the war years, as she had already been by the growth of new political forces before 1914. A notable result of this was that it became increasingly hard for the ruling group to give itself a title to power by means of faked elections. Deputies got into the Cortes who did not belong to any of the parties within the oligarchy, and official candidates carried the day only by increasing use of intimidation and by extensive bribery, which had hitherto been unnecessary. In 1917 a Renovation Movement appeared, the object of which was to depose the oligarchy and call a constituent assembly. It had the support of 71 members out of 760 in the two houses of the Cortes, and they tried to form themselves into a provisional assembly for the direction of the campaign.

But the opposition was too heterogeneous to hold together. Its main elements were the product of industrial growth: an expanding class of businessmen impatient with the inefficiency of the mainly agrarian oligarchy and an emerging labour movement, mainly syndicalist. The two were essentially enemies. The only possible point of union was that both were especially strong in Catalonia, which was almost a separate nation and resented being ruled from Madrid. But Catalan nationalism was left mainly to the middle class, and the ruling oligarchy showed remarkable unscrupulousness in fomenting animosity between its opponents. Barcelona endured several spells of strikes, riots and assassinations in which the authorities, instead of restoring order, encouraged violence through their own agents and by the arrest of moderate leaders. Just as Giolitti tried to domesticate the socialists by letting the fascists loose, so the Spanish rulers with more success domesticated their middle-class opponents by increasing the danger to them from the left. The Catalan element was further appeased by a minor grant of autonomy, which did not last, and heavier protective duties on their products. The reforming movement of 1917 broke up; the far left was isolated.

But the prestige of the parliamentary system was shaken beyond repair, and the way was open for military rule. The army played a major part in the increasingly violent struggles between capital and labour, and the military commanders increasingly adopted a strategy of their own in dealing with them at variance with the orders of their civil superiors. A feature of the movement of 1917 was the spread of a species of trade union among the officers, the object of which included both the improvement of pay and conditions and the checking of corruption in the state. Behind the army stood the King. Alfonso XIII, who had the unusual distinction of having reached the throne while still in the womb (1885), was a flamboyant personality, a little in the style of Emperor William II. He liked military men, disliked parliamentary politicians and was eager for opportunities to increase his personal power. In the end, it was not so much an opportunity as a necessity that arose. The partition of Morocco between France and Spain in 1911 was long and bitterly resisted by the natives, who found a notable leader in Abd-el-Krim. The Spanish army did consistently badly in Morocco, and in 1921 suffered a bad defeat at Annual. Silvestre, the defeated commander, was a protégé of the King, who had directed his operations personally, and had hoped that his victory might be the prelude to the abolition of parliamentary rule. A lengthy enquiry threatened to expose the royal responsibility; just before its report was published, power was seized by Primo de Rivera, the military commander in Catalonia (September 1923).

The new dictator was a Spanish nobleman, intelligent but ignorant, bohemian and disreputable. Like Mussolini, he began by trying to win support in almost all quarters, and for this reason his rule enjoyed very general acceptance. Identifying himself with the growing desire for Regeneration, he made energetic attempts to clean up the government and deprive the old gang of their ill-gotten gains. He promoted conciliation between workers and employers, abandoning the wicked policy of fomenting class war, and tried to encourage the respectable and moderate socialists in order to reduce the strength of the violent syndicalists. An eight-hour day had been ordained in 1918, and a ministry of labour set up in 1920. Government action for the protection of the workers really began at this time. Spain benefited from the economic revival, which allowed an ambitious programme of public works. Above all, the Moroccan war was ended. Primo at first planned to do this by retreat, but the Moroccans made the mistake of attacking the French before they had finished with Spain and they were completely defeated by 1926.

But Primo did not succeed as Mussolini did in advancing from general but transient popularity to enduring power. His reforming activity was unsystematic, his financial management bad. He failed in the attempt to build a political party to support him, and he did not really enjoy the loyalty of the king and the army. Alfonso had no more wish to be second fiddle to a dictator than he had to be a constitutional monarch; he would not efface himself as Victor Emmanuel did under Mussolini. The army had accepted Primo, but it did not identify itself with him and was quite ready to see him over-thrown if he did badly. In the late twenties he was under constant attack despite a censorship, and in 1930 he fell. The suppression of parliamentary government had not brought tranquillity to Spain.

Portugal on the other hand acquired the most enduring, because the most sensible, of all the southern dictators. Nor did he come to power by force, though that was the basis of his rule. The Portuguese republic established in 1910 was distracted by conflicts between the moderates and the middle-class radicals, whose main aim was to separate church and state, and who persecuted the hierarchy with considerable vigour. Violence played an increasing part in the alterna-tion of the parties in power, and in 1917–18 an army officer, Sidonio Pais, made an abortive attempt to establish a strong presidential government. After the war there was extreme ministerial instability and at length, in 1926, the army seized power. But as in Spain, the soldiers did no better than the politicians—above all, they were un-able to remedy the chronic insolvency of Portugal which had existed as long as anyone could remember. In 1928 they had to ask the League of Nations for a loan, only to refuse it when controls over Portuguese finances were made a condition. It was then that they turned to a man who had already been asked to be finance minister, but would only take the job if he was given plenary authority over expenditure and economic affairs. Dr Antonio Salazar, born in 1889, was a noted professional economist and belonged to the small Por-tuguese christian democrat movement. By economy and good man-agement he succeeded in putting Portuguese finances in order, restor-ing her credit and so making possible a halving of the rate of interest payable on her debt. The plenary power over expenditure that he insisted was necessary to achieve this made him the most powerful man in the state. In 1932 he became prime minister, and in 1936 minister of foreign affairs and war.

Salazar, like the fascists, was well placed to cut expenditure because he did not have to fear a consequent loss of votes in parliament. The general policies which he sponsored as his power increased recall fascism. From 1929 there was an attempt at self-sufficiency in wheat and in 1936 a modest Fifteen-Year development plan began. Cor-porative organizations of workers and employers were set up, at first among producers of important exports, like port and sardines, and then voluntarily over a wider field. In 1933 came compulsory fixing of working conditions by negotiation between these corporate bodies, and they also sent representatives to a national consultative chamber. A president and national assembly elected by popular vote were established at the same time, but the government was to decide what candidates might stand. A single political party, the National Union, was established in 1930. But it was the christian faith which was declared in the new constitution to be the basis of these arrangements, and Salazar remained a christian democrat not a fascist—it is, of course, to be remembered (see above, p. 75) that christian democracy is a social and not a political doctrine, and can exist without political democracy. The practical difference that this made was that Salazar was under no temptation to embark on imperial adventures like Mussolini. Portugal had not been deterred by her smallness from doing this in the eighties and in the First World War,[1] but now she concentrated on the retention of her considerable holdings. Prudently avoiding the second world conflict, Salazar remains at the time of writing comfortably in power.

[1] She gained a small bit of German East Africa.

7: The Return to Normalcy in East and West

The confusion in the west was not at this time so great as to force the abandonment of liberal solutions. The economic collapse which threatened to result from it brought everyone to their senses. Moderate counsels prevailed in France and Germany. America returned to the European scene, economically in the main but politically too, although she never joined the League. A workable settlement to the great problems of the area emerged. There were important consequences in this for Russia. The failure of her revolution to spread had already led to the adoption of milder courses at home. Now it was manifest that the chance of world revolution opened by the First World War had been finally lost, and the Soviet government accordingly came to behave increasingly like any other government. But this return to normalcy was not a return to stability. It was a precarious equilibrium based on the insecure foundation of an American boom. Chauvinist and revolutionary forces would soon dominate the scene again.

The Dawes Plan and the Triumph of Moderation in the West

In August 1923 the German chancellorship passed from the ineffective Cuno to a real statesman, capable, like Bismarck, of subordinating his prejudices and preferences to the necessities of finding policies that would work, and of winning support enough to carry them through. Gustav Stresemann was the leader first of the National Liberal party and then of its reconstructed Weimar version, the People's Party. Outwardly a loud-mouthed, square-headed Prussian, he has always seemed to many the perfect head and spokesman for the party of big business. During the war he had been an ardent annexationist, and his aim after it was always to obtain for Germany the German-speaking lands to the east, though he seems increasingly to have accepted the need to do this by peaceful means. But there was another side to him. Born in 1878, the year when his party's fortunes began to decline, he came from the lower middle class and never felt at home in conservative high society. Deeply read in the German classics, he represented the idealistic past of his party rather than its materialist present, and had long favoured parliamentary control of the executive. By the time he became chancellor (the first and last National Liberal to do so) he had decided that the French must be appeased and the Weimar constitution must be supported against its enemies. His party was to dislike his truckling to the allies and the German socialists as much as the Junkers had hated Bismarck's working with the liberals, but he saw that the opposite policies meant only ruin and confusion.

Stresemann formed a government of all the moderate parties, including the socialists. On 26 September it announced 'the bitter necessity of ceasing our struggle' in the Ruhr, and at once had to fight for its life against the extremists. The Bavarian government proclaimed a state of emergency, and gave plenary powers to Kahr, who had been removed from the premiership in 1921 because even the Bavarians considered his disobedience of the national authorities excessive. The national government had also to proclaim a state of emergency, and all now depended on the behaviour of the armed forces and of their commander, General Seeckt. He it was who had moulded the semi-irregular bands that had sprung up after the war into an efficient regular army, very small but therefore increasingly select. His professed aim was to keep the new Reichswehr out of politics. But while in normal times this meant loyalty to the republic, in times of trouble it might mean that with the cry of 'Reichswehr does not fire on Reichswehr' the unpolitical soldiers stood aside and let any who were so inclined fight it out with whatever weapons they chose. Further, Seeckt jealously upheld the traditional independence of the army from civil control. The republican constitution had theoretically ended this, but Gessler, a titular Democrat and minister of defence for eight years, acted as an efficient screen against parliamentary interference. Seeckt, likewise, was in touch with politicians, and occasionally dreamed of political power for himself. But though his monocle and staccato sarcasm betoken the Prussian officer, he was essentially a civilized man with a cultivated mind. He did not, therefore, become a prey to nationalist absurdity to the extent that Ludendorff, a monomaniac barbarian, did. Late in September he told President Ebert that his forces could not repress enemies both to left and to right, and a truce would have to be made with one side; Bavaria was obviously in his mind. Pressed, he declared that Stresemann was too unpopular to govern, and he repeated this to Stresemann himself, but he did no more.

On 1 October a rising of the 'black Reichswehr', a semi-official irregular force, at Kustrin near Berlin was suppressed. Then the communists induced the social democrats in Saxony and Thuringia to form coalition governments with them to ward off the danger from the right. The national government deposed the two ministries by force at the end of October. They had first tried to persuade the socialists to resign, and allowed them to resume office without their new allies. The Reichstag socialists were displeased that there was no corresponding action against Bavaria and retired from the government. But the action against the communists was mainly intended to deprive the Bavarians of a pretext for marching on Berlin, besides concentrating national forces to block their path in Thuringia. Kahr, indeed, was disconcerted. He had formed an alliance with Lossow, commanding the regular troops in Bavaria, and on 27 October demanded the resignation of the Reich government. Now he temporized, arousing the suspicion of the nationalist groups that had united behind Hitler. They resolved to force the issue by a coup. On 8 November the seizure of Munich began, and Hitler interrupted a meeting where Kahr was speaking, and forced him, Lossow and police chief Seisser at pistol point to agree to a revolution. But he stupidly allowed them to leave the meeting unguarded, and they at once began to organize resistance. On the morning of the 9th a large body of nationalists moved across the city to relieve a detachment under Röhm that was being besieged in the War Office. To their surprise they were fired on, and all fled in panic except for Ludendorff, whom Hitler was using as a figurehead. Meanwhile the national government had transferred the plenary powers under the emergency from Gessler to Sccckt, and he issued a proclamation declaring that disorder would be suppressed by the Reichswehr from whatever quarter it might come. This was really the end of the danger of revolt. A communist rising in Hamburg collapsed. In February 1924 Bavaria came to terms with Berlin, and its semi-independence ended; not, however, before one of its 'people's courts' had imposed a totally inadequate sentence on Hitler.

Meanwhile economic recovery had begun. The ending of resistance in the Ruhr was the vital step towards restoring the value of money, for the government had only been able to finance it by printing more notes. But it remained to create a new currency which people would believe in, backed by the balancing of expenditure by new taxes. The difficulty was that an inconvertible currency would not be trusted, but Germany did not have gold enough to go back to the gold standard. It was Helfferich who produced the solution of creating a mortgage on all the industrial and agricultural land in Germany and issuing interest-bearing notes (the Rentenmark) whose value was guaranteed by the revenue yielded by this mortgage. Helfferich was so hostile to the republic that he could not safely be given office under it, and it was the famous Dr Schacht who carried through his plan, first as currency commissioner and then as president of the Reichsbank. Schacht was to become memorable as Hitler's financial arm, but he had helped to found the Democratic party and was then seeking his political fortune through alliance with the left. The new currency was introduced in November, one Rentenmark being worth a billion old marks. The amount that could be issued, and the amount that could be credited to the government, were limited by law. To keep the government going, numerous new taxes were imposed. Two enabling acts gave the government plenary powers to carry through these measures. This set a dangerous precedent, of which more was to be heard; even at this time, the bureaucracy abused the powers it was given by introducing all sorts of changes not relating to the economic crisis— for instance, the radical revision of the system of trial by jury. It was also sinister that though the Social Democrats voted for the enabling measures they dodged their share of the responsibility in applying them. This was mainly because the People's Party in particular insisted on the abrogation under them of the workers' great gain of 1918—the eight-hour day. The socialists, for their part, wanted heavier taxes on the rich than the People's Party could stomach. Stresemann was unable to achieve his goal of consolidating the republic by forming a 'great coalition' stretching between the two.

Recovery might seem unlikely to get far in any case. It was based on surrender to France, from which severe economic consequences was to be expected. The end of passive resistance was followed by a private agreement between the occupying powers and the Ruhr industrialists, who escaped from the stranglehold imposed upon them by promising to hand over 30 per cent of their production and make substantial money payments. It is worth emphasizing that this agreement was observed until the adoption of the Dawes plan in the following year, and it did not ruin Germany as everyone expected it to. It did much to justify the French claim that the Germans would pay if squeezed, especially as the German currency was restored at the same time. But German currency reform struck France a shrewd blow. French finances was now tottering, and the fruits of German surrender was too meagre to save the day—in fact, they were not really an improvement on what had gone before. In 1922 the French received 11½ milliard francs from Germany; early in 1924 they were getting 350 millions a month. Bankers and investors now considered German finances in better shape than the French. Those who had been making short-term loans to the French treasury would do so no longer. A flight from the franc began, and depreciation set in. The French government had to raise a big loan in Britain and America, which meant that they could no longer afford to ignore Anglo-Saxon opinion. To uphold their credit, they had to balance the budget and demand yet more heavy taxes. The left had already been made uneasy by proposals to give financial support to catholic schools. Elections were now due, and the radicals hastened to attack the right and its new unpopular taxes. One of these was especially odious to the socialists: the match industry was to be denationalized and a match tax imposed instead. Radicals and socialists made common cause and won the elections of May 1924. Poincaré, already in search of a compromise over reparations, fell; Millerand, who had spoken out in favour of the outgoing majority, was obliged to resign the Presidency.

Fortunately Britain and the United States had gained not only the influence necessary for mediation but a new desire to use it constructively. Lord Curzon, British foreign secretary during most of the Ruhr crisis, had lacked this: he had been simply anti-French. Baldwin, who became premier in the summer of 1923, genuinely wanted pacification, and so still more did Ramsay Macdonald, who both headed and took the foreign office in the Labour government of 1924. His nine-month tenure of these offices was of great importance. Almost alone among prominent political figures in Europe, he had stood out against entry into war in 1914. He was determined to give a new impetus to international reconciliation. Among his first acts was official recognition of the Soviet government, and his example was followed by the major allied powers. His measures to revivify the League of Nations will be considered below. Naturally, he wished for reconciliation with Germany, but he also wanted better relations with France, and hastened to get on friendly terms with Poincaré.

Meanwhile, British efforts to bring the Americans back on to the scene were at last bearing fruit. In December 1922 Charles Hughes, the secretary of state—Wilson's interventionist opponent in the elections of 1916—declared that Europe's problems 'are world problems and we cannot escape the injurious consequences of a failure to settle them'. He suggested an impartial enquiry by financial experts to determine how much Germany could pay in reparations, and by what means. In October 1923 Britain asked the Americans if they would join in such an enquiry, supposing that her European allies would accept it. The United States agreed, and so eventually did Poincaré. Subcommittees of the Reparations Commission were set up to investigate the balancing of the German budget and the flight from the mark. American financiers sat on them. They first reported in April 1924, and produced a plan for the payment of reparations always known by the name of the chief American representative, Dawes. It strongly repudiated any idea that Germany's liabilities were unjust and its practical proposals combined the British desire for moderation with the French demand for guarantees. Germany's capacity to pay was assessed at $2\frac{1}{2}$ milliard marks a year, but she was not asked to pay so much for the first four years, while, on the other hand, she was to be called on for more if her general prosperity increased. The total amount of her obligations was left undetermined. Payments were to be made either in kind or in German currency to an Agent General of Reparations, who would send money abroad only to the extent that it could be done without endangering the German balance of payments. Revenue-bearing assets were handed over to the creditors. The German state railways were turned over to an international company which issued interest-bearing bonds.

A mortgage was established over part of German industry. Certain taxes were appropriated for reparations. As a final safeguard, the Reichsbank was given an international board of management. Most important of all, it was suggested that Germany receive a foreign loan of 800 million gold marks (which would have to come mainly from the United States).

The acceptance of this plan by the London conference in July 1924 was the first step towards real peace in Europe. Essential to this result was the moderation of the new French government under Herriot, which undertook to withdraw from the Ruhr in the course of the year. But the tractability of the Germans and the return of the Americans to Europe were no less essential, and to this the protests of France as well as the pleas of the British had made their contribution. Further progress on the new course depended on whether men who believed in it ruled in France and Germany. The 'cartel des Gauches', which won the French elections of 1924, ran into the same difficulties as Stresemann when it came to restoring the value of the currency. Heavy taxes and forced loans were demanded by the socialists. A balanced budget and other measures to reassure capitalists were the quite contrary remedies of the Right, with which the radicals had more sympathy. There proved to be no majority for the socialist solution, partly because the communists voted against every government and would not support the moderate left against the right. The left was now suffering, as the right had before 1914, from the existence of a body within it hostile to the whole régime. Not until the middle of 1926 was the conclusion drawn that a renewed alliance of radicals and conservatives was the only way out: Poincaré then formed a ministry on that basis which quickly ended the mounting inflation by heavy taxes and an attack on the floating debt. He remained in office until 1929 and the parties of the right regained their majority in the elections of 1928,[1] and were in power almost continuously until 1932. But past mistakes were not repeated. The conciliatory Briand remained in charge of foreign affairs, and his spirit also ruled at home: a comprehensive scheme of social insurance came into force in 1930 and family allowances were introduced in 1932.

In Germany it was touch and go if the violent protests of 1923 against Stresemann's adoption of a moderate policy would be

---

[1] Proportional representation had been abolished.

pudiated by the electorate. The elections of May 1924 were virtually a plebiscite on the Dawes plan. 7½ million voters supported the nationalists of various kinds and 3·7 million the communists. The socialists lost 71 seats. But the moderate parties were left with a working majority, if they stuck together. A further election was held at the end of the year, and in this the communists and nazis both lost a million votes, though the other nationalists gained somewhat. The socialists, however, were still too afraid of communist competition to join any ministry not uncompromisingly favourable to the working class. It seemed desirable, in any case, to have the nationalists in the government if at all possible, in order to make German acceptance of pacification more whole-hearted and convincing. Stresemann did all he could to placate them, notably by obstinacy and occasional demagogic gestures in his negotiations with the western powers. They were tempted by the fruits of office in 1925, only to return to the more congenial role of opposition and patriotic denunciation by the end of the year. They returned in 1927 because of the prospect of co-operation with the Centre in furthering the cause of confessional schools. Minority governments were the rule at other times. The elections of 1928 brought an improvement. They were largely fought on the relatively harmless issue of confessional schools, and the anticlericals won. The nationalists lost two million votes, the Centre half a million. The socialists and communists gained two millions, and the socialist Hermann Müller was induced to form a government in which representatives of the other parties sat in a private capacity.

The nationalists thus remained without much power, but in 1925 they had scored a great success—the election of Hindenburg as President on the death of Ebert. This was the first popular election to the presidency; Ebert had been installed provisionally, by parliamentary vote. No party, at first, had a really distinguished candidate, and on the first ballot the nationalist polled 10·7 million votes, three moderate candidates about 12¾ millions and the communists 1·8 millions. A second ballot was required when no candidate had an absolute majority. The moderates united behind Marx of the Centre, and the nationalists in desperation ran Hindenburg. He received 14·6 million votes and Marx 13·7 million. The communist Thälmann remained a candidate, and received about as many votes as before. An absolute majority was not required in this ballot and so, in effect, the communists let Hindenburg in, just as they helped to bring back Poincaré in France. The Field Marshal was nearly seventy-eight and knew nothing about politics. He discharged his new duties with dignity, honesty and propriety, but he was too straightforward to be able to disguise his sympathy for the nationalists. The absence of a true parliamentary majority obliged him from the start to assume important functions. He had to find chancellors and bully the moderate parties into the unwelcome task of joining in minority governments. Germany thus began to move back towards a monarchy. The only real counterpoise was that parliamentary government worked rather better at state level, notably in Prussia, where coalitions of the moderate parties provided a stable administration until 1932. This at least ensured that the main responsibility for law and order in most of the Reich was in democratic hands.

Moderation therefore prevailed in France and Germany alike. The divisions of the left made for conservative ascendancy, but events had discredited the extreme nationalists in both countries. But this was a precarious balance, based on scepticism, not faith in a new order. Its strongest element was the return of prosperity. Physical reconstruction of war damage was completed at about the same time as the restoration of French and German finances. Europe, everywhere, had got back to something like the pre-war economic position. But behind this was the biggest uncertainty of all. American capital had been needed to make the Dawes plan work, and the Americans were rewarded by the settlement of the inter-allied debt problem once reparations began to flow. The Americans, British and French all concluded agreements with their debtors. American money lent to Germany financed reparations, and these in turn allowed interallied payments, most of the money eventually going back to America. The Americans were encouraged to invest more in Europe, particularly in Germany. The municipalities were especially big borrowers there, and the houses and social amenities which they built, along with the expansion of the health service and the introduction of unemployment insurance, gave the Weimar republic a considerable reputation as a welfare state. But there was danger in the creation of burdens for the taxpayer, and especially for the balance of payments, without an offsetting increase in productive resources. Europe was again contracting with America a larger debt than she could conveniently service. It would take little to bring economic disaster, and political disaster was almost bound to follow.

Russia: the NEP and Socialism in One Country

The civil war had completely ruined the Russian economy. Industrial production was down at its end to 13 per cent of the pre-war figure, and grain production had been more than halved. Many had fled from the starving towns, so that under the 'dictatorship of the proletariat' the urban working class had actually got smaller. In 1921–2 the misfortunes of Russia revealed themselves in the classic form of a famine, in which millions died. Peasant fury at the requisitions, by which alone the towns could be fed, was now concentrated solely against the Reds, victors in the civil war, and large areas of country hardly obeyed the government. In March 1921 there was a particularly striking danger signal in the revolt of the naval base of Kronstadt, just outside Petrograd. The sailors had been the loyalest supporters of the Bolsheviks. Now they had to be crushed in a great battle with the Red Army, which managed to reach the rebel island across the ice just before the thaw, and conquered it in hard fighting.

The sailors' demands had in the first instance been political—more freedom, 'soviets without communists'. But to the tenth congress of the Party soon afterwards, Lenin proposed an economic remedy. He wished to conciliate the peasantry by replacing requisitions by a fixed levy on what they produced. This eventually settled down at 10 per cent of each farmer's output, and was paid at first in kind but later in money, as an ordinary tax. The peasant could dispose of the rest of his product as he wished. From this one change there resulted a complete economic reorganization—the New Economic Policy (NEP). The country's industries remained nationalized, but they could no longer be kept going by the requisitioning of food and raw materials, nor was the new tax on the peasants enough to subsidize their growth to the extent that the Tsars had done. They tried to make up for this by raising their prices to the peasant, at a time when his own were falling as agriculture recovered. But the resulting 'scissors crisis' (1922–3) threatened to infuriate the peasants again, and the government insisted on greater efficiency and lower prices from its factories.

Industrial enterprises had to pay their way by selling in a free market. The tendency to restore them to the control of managers trained under the capitalist system was already under way, and now ran its full course. As in former times, they sought to make a profit, kept wages down if they could, and dismissed redundant workers. Trade unions existed to protect the workers, but at all times the communist-dominated Russian trade unions have done this only so far as it has fitted state policy. Under the stimulus of peasant demand, industries making consumer goods recovered quickly. But heavy industry had relied much on state protection, and it recovered very slowly; here there was much unemployment.

In trade and finance it was natural to apply free-enterprise principles thoroughly once industry and agriculture were ruled by the profit motive. Wholesale and retail trade was handed back to private enterprise; a class of prosperous traders, the 'nepmen', emerged. The state bank, dominated by bourgeois economists, demanded a stable currency and a balanced budget. In 1924 a new gold-based currency was introduced. Not only foreign trade but foreign investment was desired, as already explained. Even before the NEP, generous concessions was being offered to exploit Russia's timber, ores and oil. Now expropriated concerns were virtually offered their own businesses back (or similar ones) on lease, and with financial help that amounted to compensation. Little came of these offers, but otherwise capitalism had returned to Russia, and liberal economic principles were better observed than they had been by the Tsars, because the Soviets had not the resources required for the artificial fostering of heavy industry. The return to a Gladstonian 'normalcy' in economic affairs was thus characteristic of the Soviet as well as the western lands in the twenties, just as the change to 'planning' in the thirties took place in the west as well as in Russia. Important though the differences are between Red and White, it must not be forgotten that they inhabit the same world and to some extent are commanded by the same circumstances.

The return to 'capitalism', however, was rightly seen by the Bolsheviks as threatening their dictatorship. They had given the peasants what they wanted, and they had partly restored the middle class. But neither element had any real affection for them, and they felt sure only of the support of the depressed class of workers. To secure themselves in power they therefore balanced the economic concessions by making their régime more dictatorial. During the civil war the Mensheviks had been allowed to continue with some political activity, and within the Communist Party there had been a good deal of free debate. An organized left wing had risen in protest against the shameful peace of Brest, and it criticized such things as the growing use of bourgeois specialists and the increasing power of the administrative machine. By 1920 there was also a 'workers' opposition' which wanted to transfer power from the party to the trade unions. But in 1921 the Menshevik leaders were driven into exile, and the same happened to the Socialist Revolutionary leaders in 1922 after a sensational trial for treason. The Communist Party congress of 1921 which took the first steps towards the NEP also prohibited factions within the party, and authorized the central committee to expel members who disregarded this. A purge of the party later that year removed a third of the members. Control of the membership passed increasingly to the secretariat of the party, in the first instance at local level but subject to control from the top. The party ceased therefore to be a free association and became a species of army, the officers recruiting and discharging the rank and file as it suited their purposes.

In 1922 Bolshevik rule took on the form familiar to us of a Union of Soviet Socialist Republics. In 1918 Russia had been constituted a socialist, federal republic, and other soviet republics had been established as the Ukraine and Caucasus were recovered, which in theory were independent. Now the republics were combined in a federal union, retaining in theory the right to secede. A congress of soviets was the formal holder of supreme power in each republic and in the Union. Delegates to congresses, and to the similar bodies responsible for local administration, were indirectly elected, and the towns were heavily over-represented—arrangements very similar to those by which Stolypin had tried to secure a tractable Duma. But the congresses were, in any case, too numerous, and met too seldom to exercise effective power. They elected large executive committees which met more regularly and did more of the work, including the appointment of ministers. The Union constitution, adopted in 1924, provided for a committee divided into two Councils, the Council of Nationalities representing the different national groups more or less equally, while the Council of the Union represented the population without national distinction. But even the executive committees were largely a façade, and it was the ministry—the people's commissars— who wielded effective power. The Communist Party was not mentioned in the constitution, but needless to say it controlled all elections and took all the political decisions; the government was only the administrative machine. The structure of the party was similar to that of the state: the party congress tended to lose power to an increasingly large central committee, and this in turn came to be overshadowed by the small Politburo, in which the leaders sat.

The Bolsheviks believed the whole new system that they had created to be essentially transitory. They thought that they could not survive unless they could resume the expansion of industry and build up the working class. But how to do this when the civil war had been won but the proletarian revolution had failed to spread? It was as they were reaching this problem that the genius of their leader was lost to them. In the spring of 1922 Lenin had a stroke, and though he recovered and returned to work, his health soon broke down again. He died in January 1924, the same year as Wilson. Of the leaders who remained, none seemed fit to rank above the rest—all, indeed, were best fitted to serve rather than to lead, which was why Lenin had chosen them as his colleagues. Zinoviev and Kamenev headed the party organizations in the two capitals, Leningrad (as it was now renamed) and Moscow; Zinoviev was also president of the Comintern. Both were talkers and writers rather than doers, and their timidity showed itself in their frequent opposition to Lenin when he demanded revolutionary action in 1917. Trotsky, on the other hand, had been the great man of action of the revolution and civil war. But until 1917 he had opposed the Bolsheviks, and this and his arrogance and intellectual brilliance made him suspect. Bukharin also had intellectual distinction, and was described by Lenin in his testament as 'the favourite of the whole party'. But he lacked real force of character.

The eventual victor in the struggle for power was already in high office, but nobody regarded him as a serious candidate for supremacy. Joseph Vissarionovich Djugashvili was a Georgian. Born in 1879, the son of a poor shoemaker, he had worked his way to the theological seminary at Tiflis, and while there became a Marxist. Expelled in

1899, he became a professional revolutionary, active in the labour movement at Batum, and later in organizing the stealing of money for Bolshevik funds. It was at this latter time that he acquired the alias of Steel Man (Stalin) by which he has since been known. His early work was by no means as important as official writers were to claim in his days of power, and he became one of Lenin's inner circle largely because, as a non-Russian, he was especially fit for propagating Lenin's very strong belief in the right of national self-determination. After visiting Lenin at Cracow, and some research at Vienna in 1912–13, he wrote his famous work on *Marxism and the National Question*. He naturally became commissar for nationalities in 1917, and played a notable part as already noticed in the recovery of the non-Russian territories formerly held by the Tsars. The constitution of 1924, mainly an attempt to solve the national question, was his work.

Stalin had had some education, but he lacked intellectual distinction. He resembled the rank and file of his party far more than did most of its leaders, who tended to be men of considerable culture from the educated classes, often widely travelled in the course of political exile. He was given the boring jobs which his colleagues did not care to do, and generally treated with the contempt of the incorrigibly intellectual for the merely practical man. In this way he acquired a most influential position, notably as general secretary to the central committee of the party and head of the 'workers' and peasants' inspectorate' (Rabkrin). The former position enabled him to pack the party with his supporters and dispose of his opponents. Rabkrin had been set up to oversee the state bureaucracy and check abuses: it served rather to let Stalin poke his nose in everywhere and build up a following in the state bureaucracy also.

At the end of his life Lenin became extremely discontented with Stalin and the bureaucracy under his control. He was particularly incensed at the oppressive way in which Stalin was imposing Bolshevik rule on Georgia, his reconquered native country. His will, in which he attempted to offer guidance to his successors, gave critical but friendly assessments of most of his colleagues, but a postscript roundly condemned Stalin. Just before his political activity finally ended in March 1923, he was planning an attack on him in alliance with Trotsky. The moment was a critical one: the 'scissors crisis' brought strong complaints against the oppression of the workers and the lack of freedom at the party congress of 1923 and, later, a manifesto—'the platform of the 46'—against bureaucracy. Without Lenin to support him, Trotsky did not venture to endorse this opposition, though he finally came out with an anti-bureaucratic manifesto of his own. Among the party leaders he was isolated. Zinoviev and Kamenev hated him, and Stalin discreetly supported them, though without quarrelling with Trotsky. This 'triumvirate' dominated the Politburo. At the end of 1923 they gave ground by encouraging a free discussion of issues that were worrying party members. But by the time of the party congress in 1924 the economic situation had improved and there was an obvious need to close ranks following the death of Lenin. Trotsky was called on to recant. He made the extraordinary reply that though to do this would be insincere, 'I know that one must not be right against the party. One can only be right with the party . . . history has created no other road for the realization of what is right.' Later in the year he made the blunder of referring at length in a pamphlet to the pusillanimity of Zinoviev and Kamenev in 1917. His own opposition to Lenin before that was at once urged against him in reply; the Politburo meanwhile had decided to suppress Lenin's testament, and Trotsky did not challenge this. In January 1925, likewise, he was removed from the Commissariat of War, and so lost the one weapon that might have defeated Stalin's bureaucratic power—the Red Army which he had created. Though he remained in the Politburo some time longer, he was now a spent force.

It was now that the debate on the country's future really got under way. It had much to do with Trotsky's ideas, but was relatively little connected with the decline in his personal fortunes. The communists set great store by the great German crisis of 1923, and hoped that their revolution would now begin to spread. The failure of the German communists and the subsequent reconciliation of the western powers were deeply disturbing to the Soviet authorities. In his attack on Zinoviev and Kamenev Trotsky pointed out that by choosing to seize power in 1917, Lenin had accepted his own view of a 'permanent revolution', destined to succeed in Russia because it would engulf the world. He blamed Zinoviev, as head of the Comintern, for the failure of the revolution to spread. Stalin drew quite different conclusions from the way things were going. When Lenin died he had still professed to believe that the revolution could only be saved by its further triumphs in advanced industrial countries. Now, in *Problems of Leninism*, he argued that it was possible to have 'socialism in one country'. If the capitalist powers could be kept at bay, the Russian working class could slowly develop the vast resources of their country until it became an industrial, and so securely socialist, community. This was essentially a practical man's view of the situation. Whatever the theoreticians might have predicted, the fact was that the Bolsheviks had managed to master Russia and had not managed to gain power elsewhere. It was common sense, therefore, to develop what they held as best they could. Stalin was, indeed, supported in the subsequent argument by two men who might be expected to be in touch with daily realities—Rykov the prime minister (chairman of the council of commissars) and Tomsky the head of the trade unions. But it is notable that he was also supported by Bukharin, the party's leading theoretician and former leader of the extreme left. 'We shall creep at a snail's pace,' he said, but 'we are building socialism and . . . we shall complete the building of it.'

In March 1925 a party congress approved the line of 'socialism in one country', and Zinoviev and Kamenev suddenly realized that it was not they who were in control of the party. To retrieve their fortunes, they began an attack on Stalin in the name of orthodoxy. Zinoviev published *Leninism*, in which he attacked the NEP as a policy of retreat from socialism and called for an attack on the richer peasants. In December 1925 an attack on Stalin at the party congress failed. Kamenev was demoted from the Politburo, and Stalin sent Kirov to destroy Zinoviev's control of the Leningrad party organization. In 1926 Trotsky and his two former enemies joined forces in what Stalin aptly called a 'mutual amnesty', but it was too late. Trotsky and Zinoviev were removed from the Politburo, and Bukharin replaced the latter at the Comintern. The party congress in December censured the opposition for 'social democratic' deviation. But in 1927 the international situation, which had provided the real argument for 'socialism in one country', began to help its opponents. The Chinese nationalists, alliance with whom had been one of Stalin's favourite policies, broke with the communists and expelled them, moving towards friendlier relations with Britain. As a result of the General Strike, the British conservative government became more hostile than ever to communism, and broke off relations with Russia. Everyone feared a new war of intervention, and Trotsky spoke of the need for a 'Clemenceau' to organize the national defence. The allusion to his own role in the civil war was plain.

Stalin replied by having Trotsky and Zinoviev expelled from the central committee, and after they had led a street demonstration on the anniversary of the October revolution they were expelled from the party. In December 1927 the party congress expelled the whole of the opposition. Zinoviev and Kamenev thereupon recanted and were allowed back. Trotsky was exiled, first to central Asia and, later, from the Soviet Union. Once more he became the leader of a political movement in exile, and Stalin pursued him with a vindictiveness that was no doubt personal as much as political. In 1940 he was assassinated in Mexico by a Soviet agent.

Stalin had won power by packing the party organs with his adherents, while the other leaders quarrelled over policy. His own views were flexible, or at least he did not allow them to obtrude till he was strong enough to impose them. By 1928 he was firmly in the saddle, and those who helped him against Zinoviev and Kamenev found themselves removed in turn when they quarrelled with him about his plans for further industrialization. Till then there was still enough personal freedom for party members to make opposition better than hopeless. But the party had made Stalin's task easy by outlawing opposition movements both inside and outside itself. The leaders showed the greatest reluctance to fight back once they found themselves in a minority, and the reorganization of the party left them with few resources. Zinoviev's and Kamenev's followings in the two capitals were simply the members of the local party machines, not different from those who followed Stalin and by no means a revolutionary force on their own. The Bolsheviks were here the prisoners of circumstances: they had no chance of retaining power unless they made themselves into a disciplined hierarchy, and anyone who controlled this had its members at their mercy. The same thing comes out another way in the form which the party debates took. There was virtually a standard opposition programme, adhered to by the protest movement in 1920-3, and then by the party leaders on going into opposition. It reflected the discontents of the working-class faithfuls who still formed the inner bastion of the movement and called for more favour to industry and greater personal freedom. But as the former was bound to annoy the peasants, the majority of the population, it could not be combined with the latter.

The evolution of Russia in the twenties has been most variously interpreted. Stalin's opponents feared, and foreign observers hoped, that his rise marked the Thermidor[1] of the Russian revolution and would confirm the trend of the NEP back towards the old order. Certainly Russian traditions could be seen reasserting themselves. Repulsed in her European enterprises, the old Russia had repeatedly turned to Asia and to internal development. These, too, were Stalin's interests, and his sturdy belief that Russia could do without the west was one that he shared with Slavophiles. It was no accident that his opponents were especially strong in westward-looking Leningrad. They belonged to the other Russian tradition, of seeking help from the more enlightened west as the means of salvation. The resemblance of Bolshevik foreign policy to that of the Tsars has already been noted.

In recent years much has been made of the contrast between Lenin and Stalin, who is supposed to have perverted his master's policies. It is certainly hard to imagine Lenin espousing Stalin's central idea, the turning away from revolutionary prospects in the west. In other ways, too, they were very different. Lenin was essentially a rationalist, with no use for mystification or personal glory. Stalin commemorated Lenin's death by an address to the congress of soviets, which would seem to reflect his theological training and sounds like part of a religious liturgy. In repetitive phrasing the 'commands' of Lenin were recited, each time followed with a 'vow' by the living to fulfil what was commanded. Reason, indeed, was to give way increasingly to incantation as Stalin's hold tightened. As for what is now called the 'cult of personality', Lenin's successors foreswore it. But in the exhibition of his embalmed remains in a sumptuous tomb, they departed at once from his example of personal modesty, and almost at once there began the naming of towns after *living* Soviet leaders: Zinoviev was the first so honoured. Here, too, may plausibly be seen a revival of the traditional Russia of saints and ikons.

But it is dangerous to argue that Stalin was turning his back on Lenin and the revolution. It is hard to see how Stalin was departing

[1] Meaning the fall of Robespierre in 1794.

from Lenin as he became more oppressive and arbitrary. Lenin, throughout his career, had insisted on the strictest maintenance of centralized control in party and state as the only road to revolutionary victory. For him all politics was war, and all opposition had to be broken or cowed by force, without regard to the suffering and injustice inflicted on individuals. He constantly insisted on this with the utmost brutality. The most that it seems possible to argue is that if he had lived longer he might have become more aware of the evils of bureaucracy. 'Socialism in one country' is a much more specifically Stalinist idea, but Lenin, too, was fundamentally opposed to the 'westerners', and eager for Russians to act instead of waiting patiently until they had in some way 'caught up'. Stalin developed Lenin's characteristic approach, though not in the only possible way.

Stalin did in a sense turn Russia back into a monarchy: at any rate, his patient work did much to ensure that it went on being ruled by a hierarchic, bureaucratic despotism. That this did not lead him to be in any very meaningful sense a conservative is perhaps because in the eastern lands of which Russia formed a part, absolute monarchy had not yet lost its progressive role, exemplified in Peter the Great. Ministers of the Tsar like Witte had taken important steps to modernize the Russian economy, by methods that were cruel but effective. By the time that Stalin had established his power, the Russian economy and the administrative machine had at last got back to roughly their pre-war state of efficiency, and it was natural therefore for Stalin to continue Witte's work and by very comparable means. Abroad, Russia had always been a patron of revolutionary movements, and it was natural for Stalin not to abandon this useful way of making up for Russian military weakness. Like the Tsars, he used it strictly as an adjunct to Russian foreign policy. But he was able to be far less inhibited in its use than the Tsars, if only because he had fewer friends.

Thus in Russia as in the west, the return to normalcy in the twenties was deceptive. Disruptive forces were barely contained, and began indeed to burst out even before the renewed western collapse. Not the least important failure of the western powers in the twenties was in not turning Soviet economic weakness to good account. Unwilling to provide economic help when the Bolsheviks ardently desired it, the capitalist countries lost a chance of strengthening the moderate element among them at a time when Stalin himself was ready to be moderate if it seemed wise. Russia was left with no path of economic advance except the horrible one soon to be associated with Stalin's name.

Locarno and After

Behind the reparations problem was the far greater one of security. Germany was at her neighbours' mercy, but she remained united and was a far stronger nation than any of them. The French had secured neither the Rhine frontier nor the Anglo-American alliance. They had concluded alliances with Belgium in 1920, Poland in 1921 and Czechoslovakia in 1924. But these by no means made up for the loss of the Russian alliance, itself an inadequate counterweight to Germany, and the truth, ill-recognized by the French, was that France would have to protect, rather than be protected by, her allies.

Would an idealistic Wilsonian approach prove better? Events on the other side of the world suggested that it might. The Americans, as already explained, were highly suspicious of the gains which Japan had made during the war. But in Japan, liberalism and caution were in the ascendant. She was therefore ready to co-operate at the international conference which met in Washington on American invitation in August 1921, and which resulted in important agreements respecting both naval armaments and security in the Pacific. The latter was the subject of a treaty between Britain, the United States, Japan and France, and also of a nine-power treaty guaranteeing China. Japan gave up her preferential position in Shantung, and limitations were placed on the building of bases in the Pacific area. In effect, Japan was conceded military and naval superiority in the western Pacific (at least till Russia revived) in return for undertakings to respect Chinese independence—a variant on the traditional imperialist theme of spheres of influence.

For the naval agreement Italy joined the four great Pacific powers. The number of battleships was restricted, and so was the total tonnage of aircraft carriers and the size and armament of battleships, aircraft carriers and cruisers. On world level, Britain and the United States were left equal, with Japan as third largest naval power. But in European waters Britain was overwhelmingly superior. In the Pacific the British abandoned their alliance with Japan, thus ensuring superiority to the Americans. As the United States could have out-built anyone had she chosen to, these were sensible arrangements creating a naval balance of power; the treaty was to run till 1936.

These arrangements really testify to the continuance of the pre-war situation, whereby imperial quarrels were more easily settled than European ones. But they encouraged the United States to resume an interest in peacekeeping on Wilsonian lines, and even in the League of Nations. The fruitfulness of the Washington conference also revived interest in disarmament. A 'temporary mixed commission' had been established by the League to study this question in 1920, and Lord Esher, one of the British delegates, now produced a plan to fix the size of armies in Europe.

The discussions which followed revealed a divergence of opinion on the related questions of armaments and security between Germany's immediate neighbours and the remoter members of the League. This had revealed itself already at the drafting of the Covenant, and it was to persist until after the rise of Hitler and to be exploited by him. Events before 1914 had convinced English-speaking countries especially that competition in armaments and the resulting mutual fears were a major cause of war. Limitation of forces sufficient to make it impossible for anyone to attack anyone else was therefore expected to make war very unlikely. Even if one broke out, there could at first be little real fighting, and so there would be a good opportunity for mediation. Many objections might be brought against this, such as that limitation of forces by treaty could easily be evaded. But the great argument of Germany's neighbours, which liberal opinion elsewhere never really appreciated, was that such an arrangement restored German military superiority. Because Germany was larger and industrially stronger than her neighbours, she was bound to beat them in a war if she had a chance to develop her resources. They could only regard themselves safe if they had military superiority enough to overrun her before this could be done. They received little encouragement to rely instead on international protection. Within the League, the 'British' thesis that its purpose was conciliation rather than collective security was in the ascendant, upheld especially by the isolationist Dominions. The British offer of a guarantee to France in 1922 was limited to a German invasion and did not cover remilitarization or eastern Europe.

But in the 'temporary mixed commission' a compromise began to emerge between the British and French representatives, associated in particular with Colonel Requin of the French general staff and Lord Robert Cecil. Nations willing to disarm were to receive international guarantees for their security. Approved in principle by the League assembly in 1922, this idea was developed in a draft Treaty of Mutual Assistance in 1923. It envisaged both regional security pacts and wider action by the Council of the League. Each member might be called on by the Council to supply forces for use against aggression within the limits of its own continent. These proposals were too ambitious for most of the members, though they were approved by France and (save for regional pacts) by Mussolini's Italy.

In 1924 Ramsay Macdonald and Herriot sponsored the drafting of a new instrument, the Geneva Protocol. The two premiers virtually set a precedent by attending the League assembly in person, and never before had so many important political figures represented their countries there. The new leading idea was to make more systematic provision for arbitration in the case of disputes. This would not only correct the vagueness of the Covenant but make it possible instantly to determine who was the aggressor—viz. the power that refused arbitration. States were to undertake to refer all suitable disputes to the International Court. Other disputes were to be decided by the Council or, if they could not agree, by arbitrators appointed by them. Signatories were to come to the help of the victim of aggression, but only to the extent that was geographically and militarily reasonable; the Council was merely given power to ask them what forces they could supply. A disarmament conference was to be held in 1925, and the Protocol was not to come into force until disarmament had been achieved.

This plan was welcomed all round, and France, Poland and Czechoslovakia ratified it on the spot. But it was killed by the subsequent refusal of the British Empire to adhere. The immediate reason for this was the replacement of Macdonald by the Conservatives. But Baldwin and his government (which included Cecil) were not hostile to the League, and rejection was probably inevitable. Besides the isolationism of the Dominions there were two important reasons. Enquiry had shown that the United States would probably insist on her rights as a neutral in a League war, and so the British navy would have to uphold a blockade of the aggressor against the Americans. Further, the British remained unhappy about what was essentially another guarantee of the territorial status quo, and particularly averse to endorsing Germany's eastern frontier. 'For the Polish corridor,' said Austen Chamberlain the new foreign secretary, 'no British government ever will or ever can risk the bones of a British grenadier.'

The rejection of the Protocol was sad rather than important. It led the powers to turn from universal and idealistic schemes to a limited one aimed at preserving security in the region where it was actually lacking, Europe. It was Stresemann, no longer chancellor but foreign minister, who took the initiative early in 1925 by confidentially offering to Britain and France a treaty guaranteeing Germany's western boundary and the demilitarized zone. He thereby forestalled an offer by Chamberlain of an alliance with France, which would have suited Germany less well. Germany's eastern frontiers were pointedly not included, but Stresemann offered to enter into treaties of arbitration concerning them, and Chamberlain took this as a promise not to make war to change them. The French were more sceptical. Briand who soon became foreign minister, insisted on a further guarantee: Germany must enter the League and accept the obligations of the Covenant. This had formed part of the great peace plan of 1924, and Stresemann had already begun to sound the League about it. Now it sensibly figured as a demand rather than a concession of the allies. At length, in October 1925, a conference met at Locarno, at which Italy, Poland, Belgium and Czechoslovakia were represented as well as the three western powers. Several treaties were concluded which amounted to a fragmentary and local application of the Geneva Protocol. By the main agreement Germany, France and Belgium bound themselves to respect their common frontiers and the demilitarized zone, and never go to war with each other. They accepted the Protocol's provisions for the settlement of disputes between them, and the Council of the League was to pronounce the guilt of any party violating the treaty. Britain and Italy bound themselves in that case to come to the aid of the party attacked. Germany signed arbitration treaties with Poland and Czechoslovakia as well as with France and Belgium, but the eastern pair renounced war only by implication, and there was no guarantee of the frontier. France tried to make up for this by new treaties of alliance with Poland and Czechoslovakia, but it was clear that the eastern settlement was in no way as definitive as that in the west. In many ways Locarno anticipated Munich.

The contingent admission of Germany to the League took place in 1926, not without difficulty. Stresemann had stipulated from the start that she be made a permanent member of the Council, and no objection was made to this acknowledgment of great power status. But Poland, Spain and Brazil demanded seats as well. Germany would not accept a permanent seat devalued by other admissions, and eventually Poland accepted a new elective seat and Spain and Brazil resigned in a huff. More lastingly important was German objection to Article XVI of the Covenant, binding them to participate in sanctions. The ostensible ground for this was that it was not safe for a disarmed state to do so. The real reason was the fear of being forced to help in measures against Russia. The Soviet government regarded the whole Locarno experiment as a British plot to create a great new alliance for their extirpation and Chicherin came to Berlin just before the conference to hold Germany to her Rapallo agreement. Stresemann did not believe in this danger, but he had no wish to take sides between his neighbours, and valued the Russian connection. At Locarno Germany was given an assurance by the other powers that they considered the obligation to impose sanctions binding only to the extent that a country's circumstances enabled it to help. But Russia, strongly seconded by German opinion, insisted on a new treaty with Germany (April 1926) in which the two powers promised not to co-operate in measures against each other.

The Dawes plan and the Locarno settlement constitute the real end of the First World War. They were accepted by Germany, however reluctantly, with the intention that they should be observed, and so paved the way for a return to normal international relations. Stresemann, Briand and Chamberlain were able to keep up the momentum in this direction. They remained in charge of their foreign offices, Briand till 1932, and the others till 1929 (when Stresemann died). They became increasingly united by friendship, and by a common devotion, if for different reasons, to the League. Following the lead of Chamberlain, they attended its meetings in person and made its Council the centre of their diplomacy. The League, which had spent its early years in useful but rather secondary relief work and conciliation, became politically important. But this was really because it had changed its nature: no longer the rather utopian instrument of the lesser powers, it now continued much more directly the tradition of co-operation of the great powers in the European concert. The Assembly, to its chagrin, found itself overshadowed by the private deliberations of the great men.

The pacification of the west encouraged the League to continue the search for a universal system of peacekeeping and disarmament, and its rising prestige brought it support from the great outsiders, the United States and Soviet Russia. In December 1925 a Preparatory Commission was set up to make ready for a general disarmament conference. The Americans were in it from the start, and the Russians came in in 1927. But the measures so far taken to achieve security were not enough to encourage disarmament. France insisted that a system of verification by inspection be part of any treaty, but Italy and the United States categorically refused to accept such a thing. France also wished a country's war potential as well as its actual forces to be taken into consideration, though inconsistently she resisted limitations on the size of reserves trained by conscription. In 1927 a naval conference broke down because the British insisted on keeping a specified number of cruisers for trade protection, whatever reductions were made by other powers. At London in 1930, the United States, Britain and Japan at length extended the agreement of 1922 by fixing the amount (by total tonnage) of their cruisers, destroyers and submarines. But France and Italy could not be got to accept anything so embracing and only joined in lesser restrictions, notably a 'holiday' in the construction of capital ships. Only in 1930 did the Preparatory Commission venture to put forward a general plan of disarmament, based on limitation partly of the size of forces and partly of what might be spent on them.

Further measures to ensure security were evidently needed as a condition of disarmament. In 1927 the League assembly passed a Polish resolution prohibiting wars of aggression, and eventually a new treaty was produced binding signatories to accept various procedures of arbitration and conciliation in settlement of disputes. A few states adhered to this, but much more important was the Kellogg Peace Pact because, though only a pious declaration, it again brought in the Americans and Russians. Like the Geneva Protocol, it was largely inspired by the researches of Americans enthusiastic for the League, notably Professor J. T. Shotwell. It began with a suggestion of Briand that France and the United States renounce war as an instrument of policy between them. This platonic gesture was intended to celebrate the tenth anniversary of America's entry into the war. But in December 1927 Kellogg, the secretary of state, proposed instead that all countries be invited to make such a renunciation. The treaty of 1928 was eventually acceded to by almost every country in the world. It contained no sanctions, did not apply to wars of self-defence and was signed with reservations: Britain, for instance, excepted certain areas whose 'welfare and integrity' were vital 'for our peace and safety'. But its potential importance could be seen in the words of the noted isolationist Senator Borah that it was 'inconceivable' that they could 'stand idly by in case of a grave breach' of it. Russian enthusiasm was even more notable. As early as the Genoa conference of 1922 they had been eager to talk about disarmament, noting that their own armaments were being used to justify the failure of the west to disarm. In December 1922 they proposed far-reaching disarmament and pacts of non-aggression to the states on their western borders. In this there was a large propagandist element, as there was in Litvinov's suggestion to the Preparatory Commission in 1927 for the total abolition of armed forces. But there was also a desire, shown in other negotiations too, for more normal relations with their neighbours. Litvinov was able to invoke the Kellogg Pact for this same purpose. In December 1928 he proposed to Poland and Lithuania that they bring it immediately into force in their area by means of a separate treaty. To this instrument Rumania, Latvia and Estonia were also parties. A Locarno-type stability was thus extended to the eastern as well as the western frontiers of central Europe; more specifically, this marks, in effect, Soviet acceptance of Rumania's seizure of Bessarabia which prevented normal relations between the two countries.

In 1929–30 the era of pacification culminated in what then seemed the final closing of the reparations question and the evacuation of German territory by the allies. The Dawes plan had left undecided the total amount payable in reparations. The Agent General appointed under the plan (an American banker, Parker Gilbert) believed that there was no chance of a final settlement unless action was taken before demands began (under the Dawes terms) for Germany to pay

14—E.E.P.

more as she got richer. The end of occupation (due to last till 1935) was claimed by Germany as required by the treaty of Versailles when she had fulfilled all her obligations. Strictly this could only mean when reparations had been paid, not when the system of payment had been settled, but at the end of 1928 the allies agreed to discuss both questions. An expert committee chaired by another American banker, Owen Young, who had been the moving spirit of the Dawes Committee, proposed that Germany should pay 34 milliard gold marks—only a quarter of what was demanded in 1921.[1] Annual payments were to rise from 1.7 milliard to 2.4 milliard marks; after 1966 lesser amounts would be payable till 1987, to cover allied war indebtedness. Germany had to pay 660 millions of each annuity on time, but could put off the rest for two years; a third was to be in kind. The international controls were abolished, and a Bank for International Settlements was established to manage the payments. The Nazis and nationalists campaigned against this plan, and invoked the machinery of initiative and referendum to put forward a law to stop it. But under six million in an electorate of forty million voted for this. The Hague conference of 1929 accepted both the Young Plan (scaling up the payments a little) and the evacuation of German territory.

In the late twenties prosperity and stability of a kind had returned to the countries of Europe. The leading statesmen had the opportunity and inclination to devote their energies to plans for maintaining universal peace, and even those suspicious outsiders the United States and the Soviet Union were joining in. But the new stability was to prove precarious and the work of the peacemakers too slow to take advantage of it. The experiment was to fail, and it was to be the last conducted on liberal lines. In 1929 military and economic power was overwhelmingly on the side of the western democracies. Japan was inclined to be liberal, and the dictators of Italy and Russia were respectful. After this, a major share of world power was to be held by totalitarian states—the Axis, the Soviets, the Chinese. The liberal order might survive in the west, but the chance of a liberal world, such as it was, had gone.

---

[1] But in both cases interest was payable while the debt remained outstanding. The total, with interest, proposed in 1929 was 121 milliards.

Part V
AN IRON AGE—
HITLER AND STALIN

1: Violent Solutions

The tentative moves towards a Pax Americana came to an end in the west with the collapse of the American economy, and they had never got far towards including Russia at all. There was a massive return to the methods and beliefs that had dominated Europe at the height of the First World War and Bolshevik Russia during the civil war. Economic life was increasingly dominated by state planning and controls. As the states proved unable to co-ordinate their plans, growing economic barriers between them were required to make these work, and there was something like a return to the blockade conditions of wartime. Gradually there grew up also a belief that war was needed to resolve the tensions of the world. The discredited annexationist ambitions of the war years came into their own again, and they were encouraged by advances in the art of war which seemed to promise that the next conflict would not be a near-stalemate like the last. There was intense psychological preparation for the Second World War as there had not been for the First. States suppressed opposition with a ruthlessness hitherto only experienced in wartime. Adventurous men found in preparedness, as they had found in war itself, a welcome outlet for energy and ambition. The rest, as in wartime, submitted out of fatalism or in a spirit of patriotic dedication to the demands of the state.

Economic Collapse and 'Planned' Economies

During the twenties the United States experienced an almost continuous boom. She had benefited from the economic stimulus of war without experiencing its ill effects. This redoubled the impetus to growth given by the rise of new industries already developing before the war—notably the manufacture of motor-cars and the various applications of electricity. The unprecedented prosperity led to such a volume of optimistic speculation in securities (and, indeed, in everything else) that the ordinary measures of restraint at the disposal of the Federal Reserve Banks[1] were powerless to check it, at least without making things worse. At length, the immediate opportunities for genuinely profitable investment in new plant and enterprises began to diminish, and in due course this had its effects on the speculators and produced a monumental crash (1929). The resulting shock to business confidence might not have been too serious had it not been for deeper economic weaknesses and, in particular, for the fact that the economies of the other countries of the world were not as strong as that of the United States and were less well able to take a strain. The prices of primary products had already been weak during the boom. European agricultural production had recovered after the war, but production in the rest of the world, stimulated in wartime, had not diminished. The onset of depression brought a catastrophic fall in prices: wheat, for instance, fell 19 per cent in 1929–30, and coffee 43 per cent. Already in these years primary producing countries like Hungary, Australia and Brazil were having to devalue their currencies.

European, and especially German, prosperity had been kept up, as we have seen, by American loans. This source began to dry up even before the crash, as American money went home to take part in the ever more feverish speculation. As most of it was lent for short terms, there was nothing to stop it quickly trickling away. By March 1930 German unemployment was so bad that the new unemployment insurance system was insolvent. The Social Democrats retired from office rather than contemplate a cut in benefits, and once again there was a minority government, under Brüning of the Centre. He followed an unpopular policy of deflation and economy, enforced by presidential decree. The remaining American money seems mostly to have stayed. But the other great financial power at this time was France, which had lately been concentrating on strengthening the franc and had built up a large reserve of gold. The French were worried by the rise of the Nazis, to which the German depression led, and began to withdraw their money from central Europe, as did lesser European countries. Worse hit than Germany was the little republic of Austria. Comprising the former imperial capital and its 'home counties', this new state was as unviable as a head severed from its body. It was given some chance of life by a League of Nations loan

---

[1] Equivalent to the Bank of England and other central banks.

in 1922. In May 1931 its principal bank, the Creditanstalt für Handel und Gewerbe, was declared insolvent. The Germans tried to help Austria by promoting a customs union between the two countries. The project naturally encountered the furious opposition of France and her eastern allies, and had to be dropped. It seems to have been put forward largely to appease nationalist sentiment in Germany and because the desperate Austrians were showing signs of prejudicing Germany's future chances by seeking closer links with their other neighbours.[1] The Germans also opened a diplomatic offensive for a partial moratorium on reparations, for which the Young Plan provided on certain conditions. In June 1931 they issued a manifesto declaring that the German people had been squeezed to the utmost to maintain payments, and no more could be expected of them.

These events in Germany and Austria finally ruined confidence. There was a flight from the mark and a run on the German banks, not only by foreign but by German investors. The Americans were afraid that this panic would spread to their own country, and in July President Hoover spontaneously proposed a year's moratorium on inter-governmental payments (reparations and inter-allied debts) to relieve the pressure on German finances. This was eventually agreed on, but the French delayed it by haggling about the terms and the German government could not wait. It closed the banks for a time and imposed controls in foreign exchange dealings: money could not leave the country. This was especially serious for the British, who had large sums invested in central Europe and could not now withdraw them to meet their own increasing difficulties. Britain therefore underwent a severe crisis, and in September came off the gold standard. In June 1932 a conference met at Lausanne to consider the perpetuation of the moratorium in order to promote recovery. By now even France was willing to cancel reparations, but as usual only if inter-allied debts were also cancelled. The Americans rejected this once more, and were not at the conference. In the end the Germans escaped from further reparations, except to some extent from part that had been 'commercialized' by the raising of ordinary long-term loans to pay it off. They seem to have paid about 37.5 milliard gold reichmarks in all

---

[1] It does not seem true, as is often said, that the French deliberately sabotaged the Creditanstalt to prevent the Customs Union. See E. W. Bennett, *Germany and the Diplomacy of the Financial Crisis, 1931* (Harvard, 1962).

including interest—under a third even of the principal fixed in 1921. Europe's war debts to the Americans were repudiated. American investment subsequent to this date was withdrawn, despite restrictions on the movement of money. By 1934 Europe was again a net investor in America, largely owing to the flight of refugees with their money from Nazi persecution. A world economic conference was held in 1933 in a last effort to lower tariffs, restore the gold standard and encourage international lending. The League had had modest success with such conferences in the late twenties, but this one was a fiasco. Thus every attempt to restore the cosmopolitan capitalist economy to working order by international economic collaboration had failed.

The first measures to stem depression on a national basis were the traditional ones of higher tariffs. These were reasonable to some extent when debtor countries tried to reduce imports in order to pay their debts without upsetting their balance of payments. But when creditor countries raised their tariffs, as the United States, in particular, did with the Smoot-Hawley tariff of 1930, they made it impossible for their debtors to pay them and therefore rendered the existing system unworkable. More revolutionary was the interference with currency and the physical movement of trade. This could go along with a clinging to orthodoxy in the shape of the gold standard. Both France and Germany were anxious, after their experiences of the twenties, to defend their currencies at all costs. But for the former in 1931 this meant restrictions on the quantity of goods to be imported, while in Germany it meant not only this but control over all movement of money out of the country, besides the cutting of wages, prices and interest by degree in December. Physical controls over the movement of goods and currency spread throughout Europe. All the same, the abandonment of the gold standard was the most radical step of all, especially when the lead in it passed from Britain to the United States. Britain had gone off gold because of the strain on her reserves. President Franklin Roosevelt had no such problem when he took office in 1933, and he went off gold in the spirit of the bimetallists, to devalue the currency and raise prices. This was a worse blow to international economic co-operation than the Smoot-Hawley tariff, and it ruined the world conference of 1933. With currencies fluctuating in value according to the domestic needs of governments, and with competitive devaluation as a weapon in the export drive, international trade was in the greatest confusion. The countries still on gold had to abandon it or see their exports dry up. France came off in 1936, and there was then an attempt by Britain, France and the United States to keep their currencies stable relative to each other and avoid competition in this particular field. But order had not really been restored when war broke out.

The attempt to find shelter from the international economic blizzard landed governments with increasing economic powers which they had to learn to use in a constructive way. Internationally, this meant the conclusion of economic alliances between governments sufficiently like-minded to be able to work together. The French colonial empire was a natural economic unit of this larger kind, and still more so was what was now called the British Commonwealth of Nations, which in 1932 adopted the system of 'imperial preference'. The more general expedient was bilateral treaties by which the contracting powers agreed to allow quantities of goods roughly equal in value pass through the barrier between them. Sometimes it was laid down that no money should pass. Either there was simple barter or payment for exports was made in the receiving country, and the money could only be spent there. Germany made up for her lack of a colonial empire by a notable system of such agreements with the east European countries and South America.

Within the insulated national economic units, governments were expected to take the lead in restoring and surpassing the former levels of production. Government interference became so multiform that it was natural to seek for continuity and co-ordination by means of a National Plan stretching over several years. Soviet Russia set the pace here. Since 1921 she had possessed a National Planning Commission (Gosplan). This was a very lowly organ at first, but in 1926 it was told to draw up a plan for the development of the whole economy. The first Five Year Plan covered 1928–33 and it was formally adopted in 1929. The Nazis had Four Year Plans, beginning in 1933. Mussolini's government was slow to discard its economic liberalism, and only from 1934 did exchange and import controls multiply. But in that year Mussolini announced 'the end of liberal capitalism' and the corporations were reorganized, twenty-two groups being established for different branches of production, and including representatives of the state as well as management and labour. Intended to regulate production and labour relations in various ways, they took over in 1937 the control of prices and the planning of industrial development so as to increase self-sufficiency. Countries which did not have plans at any rate advanced towards comprehensive government intervention in internal as well as external economic affairs. This stage was reached in France with the advent of the Popular Front government in 1936.

The Soviet and western Plans had much in common. The starting point for both was withdrawal from an international system of trade and payments, and great government boldness in giving financial help to industrial expansion. From 1926 the Russians found it impossible to keep up the value of their currency in the international market without deflation at home, and they abandoned their remarkable monetary orthodoxy, refusing any longer to exchange roubles freely for gold and foreign currencies. There was, therefore, no international discipline to inhibit them from financing their plans by inflation, and they expanded the supply of money very considerably, with the classic results of shortages and rising prices which had to be met by price controls and rationing. Eventually, the rouble was officially devalued in terms of gold (1935), and a great attempt was made to balance the heavy investment in industry by heavy taxes. Purchasing power was mopped up, and so rationing could end and price control be relaxed. In Germany, similarly, the exchange controls of 1931 paved the way for reflation without the fear of a flight of capital abroad. In 1932 Papen's government initiated a large programme of public works, and also stimulated demand by issuing certificates to taxpayers which could be used to pay taxes in future years. They could be sold for cash to others who might then use them for this purpose, and in this way were a means of raising capital at the ultimate expense of the state. The Nazis used the same methods on a bigger scale, adding new tax reliefs and the compulsory employment of young men on public works, even before military conscription was restored. The public works were financed by an expansion of credit, and as there was much slack in the economy there was little danger of inflation. But price controls had been brought in as part of the deflation of 1931, and the system was extended until in 1936 it became universal. The need to restrict imports also led to rationing.

From 1936 the economy was becoming overloaded owing to the needs of rearmament, but inflation was now checked by rising tax revenues, as in Russia.

If Russian industry was nationalized, industry to the west by now included a substantial public sector as we have seen, and its expansion was paid for by public money. Even in 1926 the German government had industrial holdings (not counting public utilities) worth 128 million marks, and it added to these steadily, notably in 1932 when Papen bought a huge steel concern, the Vereinigte Stahlwerke, which was in danger of passing under French control. Italy from 1932 was establishing cartels by compulsion to rationalize production, and several state corporations were established to invest funds in industry. Russian planning might appear to have more precision than that of the west, for the latter still had to take into account, indeed to encourage, private saving and investment, which had to be predicted rather than controlled. But Russian planners, too, had to predict important imponderables, like the state of world trade and the willingness and ability of the workers to increase productivity, and they often got them wrong.

Russian planning differed, however, from that of the west in aiming at an economic and social revolution, while the western plans rather served to revive the impetus in the existing economic machine. Russia was collectivizing agriculture in an effort to squeeze more from the peasant at less cost. Nazi Germany and the France of the Popular Front were alike in seeking to raise agricultural prices and save the present farmer from extinction. Russia was bent on having more industry and increased production. But some of the planning in the west was intended to adjust industry to economic stagnation. The Italian government took power to control factory building in order to prevent too many factories being built. One feature of the first Nazi Plan was loans to newly married couples—conditional on the wife giving up her job and so reducing the over-large labour force. There was another important difference, this time between planning in the totalitarian countries and economic policy in the remaining democracies. In the former the trade unions were, in effect, state controlled, and the government was able to keep down wages and exercise considerable control over labour. Even in 1931, under a democratic constitution, Brüning had cut wages by decree. This made planning in general and expansion without inflation in particular much easier. In France, on the other hand, there were wage increases as soon as the Popular Front came to power, and the task of restoring the economy was made much harder for it by the need to consider the desires of labour as well as the possibilities for expansion.

The economic story must be continued in the separate national chapters, but a general impression can be given here of the results of the universal change in economic system that took place in the thirties. By 1932 industrial production in Europe outside the Soviet Union was less than three-quarters of what it had been in 1929. World prices had declined by 37 per cent for manufactures, 56 per cent for raw materials and 48 per cent for foodstuffs. Germany and the United States were the countries worst hit: industrial production there had halved. There were six million unemployed in Germany and a million in Italy. French industrial production had fallen by almost 30 per cent, but unemployment there was never high: many immigrants had come in to take the place of the men killed in the war, and these were sent home. By the end of the thirties world industrial production had more than made up the lost ground, and was something like a third greater than a decade before. But world trade had barely recovered its former volume and was worth only about half what it had been. This was due to the many obstacles that had been erected in its path, and to the lack of international investment to promote it. More fundamentally, it resulted from the continuing low prices of primary products, which kept down the amount of manufactures that their producers could buy. Primary production had not fallen nearly as much as industrial output, and so prices fell farther instead. Industrial capitalists responded to falling prices by cutting production and limiting competition. The farmers of the world were too numerous, ignorant and dispersed to do this at all effectively; anyway, they commonly had to sell at any price to pay debts and taxes. Behind these was the desire of states, especially the Soviet Union, to export at any cost and so procure the means of industrialization.

For the other side to stagnation in world trade was increasing self-sufficiency as the more backward nations of the world caught up with the industrialized west. During the thirties the former were advancing while the latter stood still. Soviet Russia, of course, led the way. Her planners were striving to increase industrial production at the unheard-of rate of 27 per cent a year just when the slump was at its worst elsewhere. The increase actually achieved in the thirties amounted to the trebling of output at least,[1] and heavy industry grew even more. Pig iron production, for instance, was 3.3 million tons in 1927–8 and 15 millions in 1940. But the achievements of Japan, much more dependent on foreign trade, were equally notable. Industrial production hardly fell during the slump, and by 1937 was 70 per cent above 1929. Wage-cutting, drastic devaluation and a switch from textiles to other products maintained exports at a sufficient level to keep the economy going. Russia's neighbours to the west also made considerable though less spectacular progress. In 1937 Swedish industrial production was almost half as much again as in 1929, while Bulgaria, Rumania, Jugoslavia and Greece together had achieved an increase of 37 per cent by 1938. By contrast, industrial production in western Europe (France, Britain, Belgium, Germany) was only 1 per cent greater in 1938 than in 1929. Germany was 17 per cent up, Italy half as much and France was still nearly 20 per cent down. Britain, France and Germany had accounted for 36 per cent of world imports and exports in 1913. In 1938 this had fallen below 27 per cent. The picture was brightened by the growth of new industries. Electricity production increased fourfold in Germany in the years under consideration, and nearly doubled in France. Europe began to reduce the long lead of the United States in car production, which was only an eighth of the American figure in 1929 but a quarter in 1937. But all the same, the slump years were an important stage in the ending of the economic primacy of western Europe.

The new economics pointed pretty directly to war. It is not true that economic recovery was made possible by expenditure on armaments. German recovery was approaching completion when rearmament really got going, and it was a burden on the economy more than a help. Mussolini's Abyssinian adventure involved him in economic difficulty because of the League's attempt at sanctions against him. Fortunately for him, he had just begun the change from liberal to 'planned' economics, and by hastening the process he weathered the storm. In Japan deflation was certainly prevented by the vested interest of the military in high expenditure, but economically

---

[1] The exact amount is uncertain.

this expenditure was a problem rather than a solution. Politically, however, the Japanese situation was typical. The partisans of expansion through self-sufficiency and state planning mostly aimed thereby to increase the state's military power: this is as true of Stalin as of anyone. With international trade increasingly state-controlled, war seemed the only way to get a bigger share of raw materials and markets. The old British Empire had no tariff round it. Now the Germans, and still more the Japanese, were fenced out. The end of economic liberalism gave a new sense and importance to imperial rivalries, just as autarky transformed ideological rivalry into the competition of different national economic systems. Lastly, if recovery was not due to rearmament, it cannot be shown that it could have continued without it. Though not a brilliant year, 1937 proved the peak of a boom. Recovery had owed much to governments spending heavily and unbalancing their budgets. Nobody was happy at this departure from respectability and there was a return to orthodoxy everywhere, not least in Russia. Attempts to balance the American budget, along with a new decline in prices of primary products, led to a fresh depression there. Because the world had largely ceased to be an economic unit, the repercussions were nowhere near as serious as in 1929. But the Second, like the First, World War, broke out during a recession. It was war production that put an end to it, and since then there has been no opportunity to see if prosperity can be maintained without heavy expenditure on armaments.

The Revival in the Art of War

The First World War had destroyed for the time being the belief previously common that modern wars would be rapid and reasonably cheap, with great profit to the winning side. The character of the conflict had given moderate and reasonable men everywhere, whatever their political sympathies, a new eagerness to co-operate in the preservation of peace. But this situation, which is a recurrent one,[1] is essentially impermanent. New military thinkers arise, with a fresh formula for quick decisive victory which may indeed work until it is copied by the other side. Aggression again becomes fashionable.

The 1914 war saw the development of three really important new

[1] Cf. Europe after 1763 and Italy after 1454.

weapons—the long-range submarine, the aeroplane and the tank. Only the first of these was far enough advanced to have a full chance to prove its worth during the war.[1] Military aeroplanes were few and primitive in 1914; airships, which were rather more developed, proved only of limited value. Gradually, more powerful and faster machines were developed, capable of carrying machine-guns and an increasing weight of bombs. Invaluable for reconnaissance, they became increasingly important as a means of circumventing the impenetrable enemy line, destroying communications and supply dumps. The Germans also used them, like the submarines, to attack the otherwise inviolable British Isles. These early air raids on centres of population were physically trivial, but their moral effect was great. Factories shut down, trains stopped running and had the attacks been more continuous they might well have produced a universal panic. The British were taught the value of air power, and they led the way in establishing an independent air force. By the end of the war they had multi-engined bombers with a long enough range to cross the protective belt of German-occupied territory and attack the German cities. The armistice, however, prevented the full fruition of British revenge.

It was an Italian, General Giulio Douhet, who made the most notable attempt to develop a strategic doctrine for the new weapon. In *Command of the Air* he tried to show that it could dominate future wars and restore the primacy of the offensive. Whoever achieved air supremacy could win a quick victory. He argued that there was no effective defence against air attack—that, as Baldwin was to say later, 'the bomber will always get through'. Anti-aircraft artillery was of little use (which was true at that date). In the air, fire-power was more important than speed, and heavily armed bombers would be able to destroy the fast fighters sent after them. Douhet imagined that on land there would be the same stalemate in future wars as in the last one. But in the air, one side would rapidly establish its supremacy. It would then maintain a continuous attack on the enemy's cities. The moral and physical effects of this would be so great that society would collapse, perhaps even before the land forces were fully mobilized. The forces required for this would not be large. If 50 or 100 or even 20 aircraft of 6,000 h.p. could be kept in the air, the war would

---

[1] Flame-throwers were less important, and gas has not been much used since.

be won. A thousand tons of bombs (explosive, gas and incendiary) would suffice to destroy London or Paris.

The air forces of the world adopted Douhet's views, which were probably more representative than original. They made the prospect of war more terrible than ever, but they also made it seem that attack was the best defence. Air attack was the spearhead of aggression in the thirties, and down to 1940 it did seem to disintegrate opposition in the way that Douhet had predicted. But his views were not really sound. Given proper organization and leadership among the civil population, and a certain amount of dispersal of industry, a modern industrial society proved able to withstand a remarkable weight of air assault without collapsing. The British air offensive against Germany in the Second World War was an attempt to disrupt such a society, as Douhet had planned, with a force specially designed for that purpose. The bombardment was far intenser than Douhet had called for. Nevertheless, German morale did not crack, and war production continued to rise till 1944. Selective attacks on objectives of more immediate military relevance were to show far more important results. Fortunately for themselves, the British had already refuted another of Douhet's doctrines—that there was no defence against the bomber. The development of radar in the thirties and of faster and very heavily armed fighters had warded off the German air offensive against Britain in 1940–1. The British air force had accepted with some reluctance the effort to strengthen the defensive in the air. Its success really refuted the idea that the aeroplane had restored the primacy to the offensive in war.

Tanks had won battles in 1917–18, but they could only crawl along, and usually broke down before the day was out. As with the aeroplane, the war cut short experiments with better types and bolder plans. Like the aeroplane also, the tank was of especial interest to the British, who had invented it. It was a British officer, J. F. C. Fuller, who made the most notable attempt at that time to base a war-winning strategy on the tank. He called for a vehicle that could go at 20 m.p.h., and he wished to use it not in conjunction with ordinary infantry but independently, in order to take full advantage of its mobility. His plan was for bodies of tanks to cross the enemy line and ravage his rear; in particular, capturing the headquarters of his armies and disrupting their communications with the front. The decapitated enemy forces would then be finished off by an orthodox infantry attack. The air force was to work closely with the tanks, keeping the different bodies in touch and providing them with supplies.

The British army retained an interest in such ideas. From 1927 it experimented with the use of tanks in independent groups, and in 1934 organized a tank brigade. But it was a small army and little money was spent on it: only in 1940 did it have an armoured division. The French army was the largest after 1918, and it had adopted the tank with enthusiasm. But the terrible experience of the war had left army and nation with little offensive spirit. What there was died after the occupation of the Ruhr had been succeeded by Locarno, pacification and retrenchment. In 1930 there began the construction of the Maginot Line, covering the frontier from Switzerland to Longwy. These huge fortifications did not by themselves betoken an unenterprising defensive. They left the Belgian frontier uncovered. Their purpose was to allow the field army freedom of manoeuvre here, its flank protected, if the Germans again came that way (as they did). But at the same time (1928) the term of service for conscripts was reduced to one year. The army approached the socialist ideal of a militia capable only of defensive action. This was of the greatest significance. It would now be rather harder to intervene in Germany to prevent infractions of the peace treaty; harder still to take offensive action to help France's allies in eastern Europe. In the more narrowly military sphere, it meant little interest in the massing of tanks for a rapid, independent offensive. Tanks were confined to their original role of supporting the foot-soldier. The French tanks in 1940, dispersed among the infantry, had no chance of opposing the massed German armour. The youthful Charles de Gaulle had no success in his advocacy of fast, heavy tanks, and a small, mobile professional army.

It was left to the defeated powers in the 1914 war to develop a new offensive system. The Red Army had a natural advantage in this task. It regarded itself as the vanguard of world proletarian revolution, destined to take the offensive when the moment was ripe and sweep away the old order. Already in 1920 there had been the attack on Poland, and for the rest, Russia's wide spaces had promoted a war of movement both before 1917 and in the civil war. The Reds had owed much to their cavalry. Russia's lack of industrial resources and trained men made it hard to develop the technical arms, especially as the Bolsheviks tried to make their army as proletarian as they could and so had to tolerate a low level of education among the officers. But with the Five Year Plans, this began to change. Military expenditure greatly increased: 1·5 milliard roubles in 1933, it was 14·8 milliards in 1936. The technical proficiency of the officers also improved. The Germans, conducting on Soviet soil experiments with weapons forbidden them at Versailles, taught the Russians a good deal. Their own inventiveness is shown in the development of airborne troops. They were the first (1931) to experiment with the dropping of considerable forces by parachute. They were ahead also in the thirties in developing heavier tanks with greater firepower. The Red Army retained a good deal of weakness and crudity. It was badly disorganized by the great purge of 1937–8, which removed 90 per cent of the generals and 80 per cent of the colonels. In terms of military thinking, however, this may have been a gain. Tukhashevsky, the deposed commander-in-chief, believed that his army need have no reserves, for they would be provided by the insurgent proletariat of the countries they attacked. He deprecated too much reliance on tanks, saying with some justice that their advocates were men who wished for political reasons to avoid using the mass of the people in war. The development of more efficient and modern military principles was the work of a new generation, centred on the new chief of staff, Shaposhnikov. In 1941 the Russians relied on offensives that were impetuous rather than scientific and used their tanks, as the German General Halder said, 'a little everywhere'. They were beaten, but they were within reach of mastering the new way of fighting.

This in the end had been perfected first by the Germans. They had done almost nothing about tanks down to 1918, and they were then forbidden to have them. In 1928 they began to use imitation tanks in exercises, but even in 1933 the official doctrine was still that tanks were to be allotted in small groups among the formations of more orthodox troops. The German army of the Weimar period had by no means cast away conservatism to the extent often supposed; it seems to have been Hitler who made the cavalry get rid of their horses (1933). But there was an 'inspector of motorized troops', General

Lutz, who among other things controlled an experimental and train-ing station in Russia, where tanks acquired from several countries were tried out. It was his chief of staff, Colonel Heinz Guderian, who developed and eventually applied with success the independent offensive use of tanks. No longer confined, as in Fuller's plan, to preparatory disorganizing of the enemy force, they were to break through his front and advance boldly into his territory, spreading confusion and ignoring forces too slow to catch them. For this pur-pose independent armoured divisions were needed, combining tanks with motorized infantry and artillery in support. It was only late in 1935 that these views prevailed in the German army and the first three armoured divisions were ordered to be formed. The cavalry was abolished in 1936. Another decision vital to the success of the new system seems to have been made by Hitler: the reconstructed German air force was not allowed to make the destruction of enemy cities its first priority, in the style of Douhet. It had to concentrate on the direct support of the army. Of course, in a war of movement, aimed above all at disruption and confusion, this still meant plenty of attacks on the civilian population.

The skilful combination of tanks and air power brought the Ger-mans their brilliant *blitzkrieg* victories of 1939–41, and the Second World War in general was to be a war of movement and decisive battles, very unlike that of 1914. First the possibility and then the reality of decisive military victories electrified international relations. But this resurgence of military effectiveness was more transitory than that which had brought the triumph of Bismarck. Once again it largely depended on the enemy being unprepared and politically weak. Britain, Russia and the United States were just strong enough, aided by geographical factors, to withstand the first onslaught, and thereafter the two sides reached a rough technical equality, victory going as in the First World War to the physically stronger. Moreover, just as a strong defensive proved possible in the air, so too could the tank be stopped by the pillbox and the anti-tank gun. Tanks had to hide in trenches, like infantry. The Second World War might well have ended as a war of positions had not its emphasis been so much on the spacious eastern front, where the fighting had remained mobile even after 1914. As in the First World War, the development of new weapons seemed, when the fighting ended, to be restoring the shaken primacy of the offensive. But the combination of nuclear explosives and long-range rockets appears to have given unlimited power to the offensives of both sides, mutual annihilation replacing victory. As yet military thinking has found no clear and obvious path round this difficulty. Thus the thirties saw a great revival in the effectiveness of war as an instrument of state policy, and in the early forties this fact dominated the world. But the revival was not long-lived, and the search for universal peace was destined to be resumed.

The Totalitarian Environment

The new economic system involved increasing interference with people's daily lives and measures calculated to arouse bitter resentment in wide sections of the community: the cutting of wages by decree in Germany, the collectivization of Soviet agriculture and so on. Behind everything was the growing expectation of, and preparation for, a war. From this situation arose a desire on the part of governments for a greater degree of obedience from their subjects than had satisfied them in the past. Outward conformity was no longer enough: the citizen must obey in his heart as well, accepting and believing in the policy of the state as if it were the teaching of a church. Propaganda and terror were used in conjunction to achieve this result. In the former field the object was to make the individual uncritical and ready to believe what he was told. The great processions and mass meetings characteristic of the new Italy, Germany and Russia alike were designed for this purpose. The people were harangued by spellbinding orators, and there was no opportunity for questions, heckling and discussion to break the spell. The incantation of slogans and the skilful use of pageantry, with banners, flaming torches and military pomp, helped in the subjugation of reason to emotional enthusiasm. Huge numbers of people took part in these demonstrations: 460,000 at the Nazi rally at Nuremberg in 1934. But it was important that new means of communication came in to reinforce their effect. The use of radio for broadcasting news and entertainment began everywhere around 1920. By 1925 there were ninety broadcasting stations in Europe, and by 1938 this had become 300. The Bolsheviks tried from the outset to send propaganda by wireless—it was often their only means of reaching the outside world.

By placing loudspeakers in the streets, a totalitarian government could make its propaganda inescapable. The cinema, though dumb until the thirties, could obviously work in the same way as the great rallies: its audiences were amorphous, passive and suggestible, unable to establish the critical relationship with the performers possible in a 'live' theatre.

The content of the propaganda varied according to the country, but an invariable feature was the building up of the national leader into a figure of overwhelming importance. Owing his position to his personal merits and often of humble origin, he possessed extraordinary wisdom and energy and so should be accorded complete trust. At the same time, he was one of the people, shared their feelings and aspirations, and was completely their representative even if they had not elected him. To obey him was therefore to be one with the people. Hitler and Mussolini owed their position in the first instance to the skill with which they could play the role of leader in the propagandist drama. If they had more serious political gifts, it was really by the way. Stalin began as something quite different, a self-effacing bureaucrat. But he, too, became a showpiece leader, the ceremonious marking of his fiftieth birthday in 1929 helping to set the trend.

Behind the simple propaganda was the ever stricter and more purposeful control of education and intellectual activity. Continental states had commonly been eager to control the schools. But the growth of youth movements extended this control to children in their leisure hours and there was much more direct teaching of a political faith. The aim everywhere was to make the young feel that their primary human loyalty was to the state and what it stood for: children proved ready sometimes to denounce their parents to the secret police, and this example was held up as worthy of imitation. Censorship again was nothing new, but it had been on the decline and governments had contented themselves with suppressing views hostile to them and encouraging writers who would come to their defence. Lenin had been quite ruthless in gagging his opponents, and he had attacked what he regarded as erroneous philosophical views in his own party. But even he had assumed that art, science and literature needed to function autonomously. Now the state set itself up as arbiter of taste, philosophical soundness and even scientific

truth. There was an official style in the visual arts, adopted for ideological reasons and mostly very dreary. Writers were not just cen-
sored, they were organized, disciplined and assigned their tasks.
Scientists could not be interfered with too much because their constructive work was too important for the state. But they were put in
their place when they became awkward, and biology in particular,
with its inconvenient relevance to disputes about human nature,
suffered at both Nazi and Soviet hands. Thus the state tried to take
over the forming of moral and intellectual standards at its deepest level.

Terror was used to break any inner unwillingness to accept the
methods and purposes of the state that remained after the efforts of
the propagandists. Secret police and political prisoners were not a
new, though they had fortunately been a declining, element in the
European scene. But hitherto the main purpose behind them was the
breaking up of conspiracies against the state. Now the moral effect
on the population at large was increasingly the important thing. It
was not new for people innocent of conspiracy to be arrested because
of careless talk on ticklish subjects, or as the Japanese said, 'dangerous thoughts'. But this was now done on a much bigger scale, and
there was a new interest in repentance and the avowal of crimes by
the prisoner. The propagandist purpose of this is obvious. It was also
meant to break the wills of the prisoners, as was life in concentration
camps, with its combination of brutality and capricious favours.
Inmates developed a slave mentality and could be returned to the
outside world. It was the Soviet authorities who developed this
system most highly. The Nazis were too interested in the massacre
of entirely innocent people, whose only offence was their race, to be
really scientific. But the Nazis had their propagandist Reichstag Fire
trial, and later their 'people's court'. Violence was used by Hitler
(save at the beginning and end of his career) above all for its moral
effect, as we shall see.

The Nazi and Soviet régimes were unequalled in Europe as expon-
ents of the totalitarian principle, but paler imitations ruled in an increasing number of European states. Even the democracies were not
entirely without parallel trends. The appeal to the irrational represented by mass-circulation journalism and commercial advertising
grew first and furthest in the Anglo-Saxon world, and on the
continent in France. For this reason among others, allied propaganda

was superior to German in the First World War. Hitler in *Mein Kampf* speaks of the need to copy allied methods, and it was in 1916 that a nationalist industrialist, Alfred Hugenberg, began the building of a newspaper and film empire that under Weimar tried to do so. In the thirties it was only in a few of the smaller continental countries that democracy seemed to flourish. In the old French and new Spanish republics, notable democratic experiments were made, but they did not work well. Hence, opposition to the totalitarian trend was mostly feeble, though it was furious under the prick of poverty in Spain and Russia.

It was the churches and the armies, organized corporations commanding among their members the sort of inner loyalty that the totalitarian states were out to establish, that best resisted their claims. The dictators, as a rule, were very anxious to have the soldiers and priests on their side, and were accordingly less well placed for keeping them in order. Soviet Russia was better placed in a way by being strongly anticlerical and having an army entirely of its own creation. But Stalin found it necessary to purge his army, greatly to the detriment of his military strength, and in the Second World War he found it expedient to establish more friendly relations with the church. Hitler concluded a concordat with the catholic church when he came to power and he did not try to replace the existing army. But though both provided a certain degree of sanctuary for those out of sympathy with the régime, attempts to make them active centres of opposition had little success; generals not entirely reliable were steadily weeded out. By contrast, the Italian church enjoyed a privileged position under fascism, as has been explained, and the army had in the king a focus of loyalty other than the dictator which the German army lacked after the death of Hindenburg. Mussolini was therefore turned out in 1943 when things had gone badly wrong, whereas Hitler survived a similar plot in 1944. In Spain the church and the army were even stronger, but this meant that when a dictatorship was established it was mainly their instrument. Franco was primarily an army leader, and the Falangist movement, equivalent to the parties of Hitler and Mussolini, has always taken second place in his system of government. It has therefore been less monolithic, though not perhaps less oppressive, than the others.

When it did not result from simple physical suffering or corporate loyalties, opposition to the dictators was usually inspired by some faith which made it possible to retain a belief in the primary importance of the individual and of individual judgment. Only a very strong faith of this kind could inspire constant resistance to the pressure to conform. To some extent the idea of a ruling élite, possessed of some kind of superior wisdom, could serve as a basis of opposition to totalitarian régimes which were themselves largely based on it. Revolutionary Marxists, believing it their duty to be the conspiratorial, iron-hard vanguard of the proletariat, were psychologically prepared to fight dictators when the 'party line' required it. Claus Schenk von Stauffenberg, who tried to assassinate Hitler in 1944, was a disciple of the poet Stefan George. A spiritual élite was what George and his friends aspired to be—they would redeem the nation from corruption and philistinism by being themselves an example of purity and devotion to beauty. Christian belief gave some the strength for the fight, and among both Christians and non-Christians the philosophy of existentialism helped to inspire resistance. Rejecting complicated ideological systems and conventional beliefs, it attached importance only to the individual and his personal decisions in an environment that was beyond his control, brutal and absurd. Christians and existentialists were not inevitable opponents of the dictators. The bulk of the German protestants continued their traditional subservience to the ruler. Martin Heidegger, the leading existentialist philosopher, supported the Nazis. But Karl Barth, the noted protestant existentialist, sponsored a manifesto rejecting state ascendancy in the spiritual field as early as 1934. During the war none were braver in opposition than the protestant pastors Niemöller and Bonhöffer or the catholic bishop of Münster.

But the domestic opponents of the dictators were always weak in organization, and usually also in numbers. External force alone, it seemed, could shake their grip on the continent.

2: Stalin and his Neighbours

In the industrial and military advance of the thirties Russia and Japan were the pacemakers. Their mutual suspicions, and the fears and hopes aroused in the west by both of them, were an essential but sometimes inconspicuous undercurrent in the relations between Germany and the other western powers. Equally important in forming the background to these was the state of Russia's western neighbours. The dissolution of the multinational empires had not brought amity to that part of Europe, and it remained, as in 1914, a serious source of international instability.

The Russia of the Five Year Plans

Stalin had long been a moderate in economic matters, but three things made him increasingly a partisan of hectic industrialization, mainly at the expense of the peasants. By 1926 Russian industry had expanded as much as it could by more orthodox methods. Abroad, Russia was increasingly isolated (at least in Stalin's view) by the failure of the revolution to spread, and the growing aggressiveness and military power of Germany and Japan in the thirties made this isolation really dangerous. In 1931 Stalin said 'we are fifty to a hundred years behind the advanced countries. We must cover this distance in ten years. Either we do this or they will crush us.' Internally, too, industrial expansion was felt to be politically necessary. Stagnation there would be a great strategic victory for the anti-Bolshevik peasantry, whose continued preponderance in Russian society would thereby be assured. In 1929 Stalin spoke of the need to make the 'socialist sector' of the economy prevail over the 'capitalist sector', and said that a Five Year Plan which failed to take account of this 'central idea' would be only 'a Five Year Absurdity'.

It was in 1927 that the food supply showed itself clearly insufficient to sustain further industrial advance. The state could not buy as much grain as it wished to ensure supplies for the towns. There was some return to civil war methods of requisitioning, and the stirring up of poorer peasants to help in seizing the stocks of the richer ones. It was decided to encourage peasants to enter collectives, and to begin to create large state farms, worked by wage labour. In 1928 there was no need for extraordinary measures. But in 1929 the harvest was worse, and the government wanted to buy considerably more. Its purchases were therefore given the character of requisitions, non-compliance with which carried considerable penalties. In the autumn an all-out drive began to get the peasants to enter collectives. It was the culmination of the drive already under way against the 'kulaks' or richer peasants, who were blamed for the shortages. This made little economic sense. The 'kulaks' were little different from the other peasants (indeed, they tended to be simply anyone who made trouble for the authorities), and it was they who were able to provision the towns, because they had a surplus for sale. The real trouble was that the revolution had increased the holdings of the poorer peasants, who sold less of their crop because they needed it to feed themselves. But the campaign against the 'kulaks' made political sense because the other peasants could be given their land and stock as a reward for entering the collectives. Once the authorities really put pressure on the peasants remarkable results were achieved, and by March 1930 55 per cent of holdings had been collectivized. But so much force had been used that Stalin found it prudent to call for moderation (in an article entitled 'dizziness from success'), and by the autumn half the collectivized holdings had reverted to private possession. But the pressure was resumed, more cautiously. By 1932 over 60 per cent of holdings were collectivized, and by 1936 over 90 per cent.

The collective farms from the government's point of view were a a second best. They failed to get far in the creation of large state farms under their complete control. These were too unpopular, and there were not enough skilled managers. From 1933 state farms actually got fewer. The collectives belonged in theory to the peasants, who usually retained a little land and stock in their individual possession. They could, at least in theory, dispose freely of what they produced separately and also of some of their collective produce. In the war years, especially, some farmers did well. But the authorities put the management of the collectives in reliable hands, and were thus able to requisition a large proportion of the produce at low prices. The struggle for control was long and costly. At first 25,000 industrial workers were sent out with the idea of organizing the farms on factory lines. These men knew little as a rule about either agriculture or organization. The peasants, bitterly hostile at what amounted to dispossession and loss of income, kept production down to their essential needs. But the government took no account of declining output in its demands on them, and the result was yet another terrible famine (1932). Five million people died at least, and the decline in livestock in these years was catastrophic. There were 35.5 million horses in Russia in 1928, and only 15.7 millions in 1934. Cattle declined from 67.1 millions in 1929 to 38.4 millions in 1933. Gradually better management and the introduction of modern methods, notably a great increase in the number of tractors, restored the situation. It is only fair to say that the large farms created by collectivization were better suited than smallholdings to the use of modern implements. But their immediate value was political rather than economic. It was the government, not the collectives, that owned the tractors. The peasants could no longer work the land with their own resources, and had to pay heavily for the use of government equipment. By the outbreak of war agriculture had caught up and a little surpassed the level reached before collectivization. Cereals available for consumption totalled 614 million quintals in 1928–9, fell to 551 millions in 1933–4 and rose to 693 millions in 1939–40—just keeping level with the rise in population. But the state's ability to take a larger share made all the difference. Its collections and purchases rose from 112 million quintals in 1928 to 350 millions in 1940. Similarly, the cattle population had only recovered to 63.2 millions in 1938, but the state was collecting twice as much meat as a decade before.

The industrial advance which this policy made possible—and especially the growth in heavy industry, the last easily financed by selling its products to willing peasant buyers—has already been indicated. The social consequence of this advance was not entirely what Bolshevik theorists had originally hoped for. The industrial working class became for the first time a really large element of the population, but the middle classes also began to achieve something like the same degree of importance as in western Europe, and 'bourgeois' methods and standards were increasingly found to be a necessary condition of industrial advance. Between 1927 and 1937 the urban population increased from under 27 millions to 51 millions and the population dependent on agriculture fell by almost 40 millions, in a total population that had risen to 170 millions. In 1939 Molotov found that managers, technicians and salaried and professional people of all kinds numbered almost 10 millions. A basic feature of the Five Year Plans was a great expansion in education, especially technical education. Students in universities and higher technical schools numbered 177,000 in 1929, and 603,000 ten years later. The new middle class wanted and got better pay than had hitherto been customary. The higher ranks were very well off indeed. They were, moreover, not by any means all members of the Communist Party, and the influence in industrial management of party stalwarts with little technical knowledge was reduced. The ordinary workers, meanwhile, were subjected to the pressures both of a capitalist and of a socialist system. From 1929 they gradually received encouragement to compete against each other, in order to speed up the tempo of work. Piecework gradually spread, differentials between skilled and unskilled men increased. In 1933 the collective fixing of wages between unions and management ceased. Unemployment relief had been abolished. In 1935 propaganda took up the tale, trumpeting the achievements of a champion coalminer, Alexei Stakhanov. 'Stakhanovite' workers who set new records in production were given rewards and medals. In the light of their achievements, the amount that ordinary workers were expected to do was increased.

These expedients, and the constant exhortations of government spokesmen to produce more, were better calculated to increase the quantity than the quality of production. Bad quality was one of the worst failings of Russian industry during its breakneck expansion, and to check it the state intervened with heavy punishments for 'sabotage'. To prevent absenteeism and maintain discipline, a system of passports and detailed records of each worker's performance was introduced. From 1930 the direction of labour was developed to ensure that workers went where they were needed, and stayed there. The migration of workers from the countryside was largely achieved by contracts, in which collective farms undertook to supply industrial enterprises with men surplus to their own requirements. Besides harsher conditions at work, the industrial population had to endure bad living conditions in the very rapidly growing towns. Especially was this so because the Five Year Plans involved important changes in the geographical distribution of industry. A new industrial complex was created, based on the iron of the Urals and the coal of Kuznetsk, in central Siberia. The long haul between them made this a rather uneconomic proposition, but eventually iron mines were developed near Kuznetsk, and the Urals were similarly furnished with coal from nearer at hand. The tendency of Witte's time to develop the periphery of Russia more than the centre was made up for.

There had already been a considerable return to bourgeois ways under the NEP, but there had been some attempt to counter this by keeping society as egalitarian as possible and giving important positions to ordinary workers. Under the Five Year Plans there was a much more radical departure from equality, and the ordinary workers, unless they were enterprising and rose into the new middle class, counted for little. Most of them, anyway, were now new recruits from the peasantry, and in no way specially loyal to the Soviet state. Russian politics and society therefore took on in some respects an increasingly bourgeois character, especially in the derogatory sense of becoming more stuffy and hypocritical. In the twenties there had been some Soviet patronage of doctrines emphasizing experiment and free expression of the personality, both in the arts and in education. In the thirties not only were writers expected to be narrowly propagandist but music and the visual arts were confined to the conventional and academic. In the schools there was a return to discipline and hard work, and in 1940 secondary and university education ceased to be free. The Russian past was gradually rehabilitated. Stalin rejected the contempt which the leading Soviet historian, Pokrovsky, had shown for the Tsars and their annexations. He demanded that justice be done to Tsars who were 'progressive for their time'. When war came, a strong appeal was made to national patriotism and traditions, and Stalin began also to speak of foreign policy in terms of traditional Russian desires—for instance, for a warm-water port in the Far East. During the war, too (1943), the Orthodox Church was again accorded state recognition and support, though anticlerical propaganda was never abandoned. The church still had many followers, and had for some time been buying toleration by political complaisance. The war made a formal reconciliation expedient.

In 1936, likewise, the Soviet Union was given a new constitution. The name of soviet was retained, but the Supreme Soviet was henceforth an ordinary parliament of two chambers, directly elected by universal suffrage. The Supreme Soviet elects a Presidium, whose chairman acts as head of state, and this appoints the Council of Ministers: the title of 'people's commissar' was dropped. The new parliament had no power, and, anyway, the authorities had complete control of who was elected. But its creation was ideologically significant. It was supposed to mark the end of violent class struggle inside the Soviet Union. Hitherto the government had avowedly been a dictatorship, directed explicitly against the enemies of the working masses. Now it was supposed to be a workers' and peasants' democracy, with freedom for all except individual traitors. The dictatorship had become hypocritical: the ruling oligarchy was beginning to try to hide behind parliamentary forms, in the way so long prevalent in southern Europe.

But the Soviet government was not merely an oligarchy, it was kept going by terror. The central political fact of the thirties was not growing respectability but the great purges. The inception of the Five Year Plans led to the downgrading (1929-30) of the last important communist leaders who were not Stalin's creatures, but had hitherto taken his side. Of this so-called 'right-wing opposition', Bukharin objected especially to the oppression of the peasants. Tomsky, less well fitted by the label, disliked the downgrading of the trade unions which he led into mere welfare organizations. Rykov, their associate, was replaced as prime minister by Molotov. At about the same time (1929-31) there was a series of spectacular trials of bourgeois experts in Soviet service, such as Professors Ramzin and Groman, who were accused of disloyalty. This was fairly clearly to intimidate the rest of the tribe into obedience during the hard time ahead. Simultaneously the wholesale traders ('nepmen') who had been allowed to flourish during the NEP were liquidated, largely for the sake of the wealth they had accumulated. After this it was mainly on the poor peasants and workers that the weight of the terror fell. But in 1934 Kirov, the head of the party organization in Leningrad, was murdered. This was laid at the door of Zinoviev's followers there, and it eventually led to the liquidation of all Stalin's defeated opponents, who had hitherto been allowed to lead a fairly quiet life.

In August 1936 Zinoviev and Kamenev and fourteen others were tried and condemned. A new chief of the secret police, Yezhov, was appointed in September. It is supposed that the Central Committee of the party objected to further measures for some time. But in January 1937 came the trial of seventeen alleged followers of Trotsky, in June it was the turn of Tukhashevsky and other army chiefs and in March 1938 Bukharin and Rykov were disposed of (Tomsky committed suicide). By this time the purge was turning into a general clearance of the higher administrative ranks. Thirty-five thousand army officers are said to have been disposed of, 70 per cent of those elected to the Party Central Committee in 1934 and 90 per cent of the higher trade union leadership. But humbler people were not spared: it has been estimated that eight million people at least were arrested during the purges. All those actually brought to trial 'confessed'. The purge petered out slowly after December 1938, when Yezhov was dismissed. He was subsequently put to death himself and made the scapegoat for all injustices committed.

Nobody really knows the purpose of the purges. Indeed, all the political history of the Stalin era is still a matter on which there can only be informed guesswork. Once started, they became something of a vested interest. Personal scores were settled, and the secret police built up great industrial enterprises run by slave labour. It seems natural to look for the original impetus in the general terrorism needed to implement the Five Year Plans. But the bitterest struggles arising from the economic revolution were in the early thirties; the purges came when things were a little easier. Indeed, it is temping to regard them as the next item on Stalin's agenda. The important political and military figures who were removed were either men who did not owe their advancement to him or men who seem to have shown insufficient firmness in carrying out his wishes. They disliked certain features of his policies, and the growth of a new privileged class might give them the strength to oppose him if they were not got rid of in time. The army officers are a case in point. Like their civilian equivalents, they had been growing in technical knowledge, independence and prestige. In 1935 the old military ranks were restored, discipline and smartness were increasingly insisted on as in Tsarist times, officer candidates no longer had to be of working-class origin and the higher commanders could no longer be arrested by the civil authorities.

The political commissars had been downgraded to a merely educational role under the supervision of the military commanders. (After the purge they were restored.) Commanding mainly peasant conscripts, the officers were hostile to collectivization, and the commander-in-chief in the Far East even managed to get it slowed down there. It is supposed that the military members of the party Central Committee were among those that opposed the purge. This was the kind of independent, privileged group that went under. In their place young men on the make were promoted who owed everything to Stalin and his policies, and saw their interest in unquestioning loyalty. The solidifying of the Soviet system and consequent loss of the dictator's personal power was delayed until after Stalin's death.

In the thirties many people in the west believed that Russia was a workers' paradise. It was not. But this should not prevent (as it often has) a fair judgment of the Stalin era on its actual merits. With its growing population, primitive agriculture and limited industrial growth, the Russia of the twenties was in danger of impoverishment, starvation and foreign conquest. Industrial expansion was needed to prevent all three, and it hard to see how it could have been achieved without great hardships. That is not to say that things need have been as bad as they were: the number of obvious and self-confessed mistakes by the Soviet authorities strongly suggests the contrary. At the same time, industrial growth has been continuous through the Stalin era and since;[1] previous attempts to promote it, after as before 1917, had got some way and then lost impetus. The Soviet Union gains, too, if it is compared, not with the non-existent utopias of the left, but with its actual neighbours in eastern Europe. Industrialization there was less feverish. But all the same there was dire poverty, oppression and confusion in politics, and no escape in the end from foreign conquest, first by Germany and then by the Soviet Union itself.

East-Central Europe between the Wars

Two countries here perpetuated the old order of large landed estates with political power in the hands of their owners: Hungary and Poland. After the episode of Bela Kun, what was left of Hungary reverted more or less to the political and social condition of 1914,

---

[1] Not counting wartime devastation.

save that there was now a regent (Admiral Horthy) instead of an emperor-king. Room was made in parliament for a few socialists, representing the small urban working class, and in the thirties there was a modest growth of fascism and a good deal of fascist talk. The rural masses gained neither political power nor social concessions. The Polish republic had been established by agreement between exiles who had looked to the allies for liberation and those who had stayed at home and tried to work with the Central Powers. The most important of the latter was Pilsudski, a revolutionary who had organized a legion to fight the Russians, in the spirit of Garibaldi. The former were headed by Dmowski, former Polish leader in the Duma. Poland received a parliamentary constitution, and Dmowski's conservative, clerical National Democrats emerged as the largest party. There were also sizeable Peasant Parties and a land reform measure was passed. But parliamentary government did not work well and a deflationary policy made it unpopular. In 1926 Pilsudski, who had been living in retirement, came to power by a military coup. Although he had formerly been a socialist and was supported by the left in his revolt, once in power he turned to the right. The redistribution of land was slowed down and the landed aristocracy returned to public life. Power was henceforth shared between them and Pilsudski's friends—the military freebooters who had led his revolutionary legion. The appearance of parliamentary government was maintained, but the elections were increasingly rigged, and just before Pilsudski's death (1935) the constitution was altered in an authoritarian sense. The oligarchy was never as secure as in Hungary. In 1937 there was a massive 'strike' of peasants, who refused to bring food to the towns. In 1938 the socialists did very well in municipal elections. The Government restarted agrarian reform and liberal gestures were made. On the other hand, the Poles continued to suppress the Ruthenes in Galicia, as they had when under the Habsburgs. The German minority was not well treated, and anti-semitism was rampant. Fascist movements made headway in the ruling circles.

The other states in the area all firmly adopted the principle of distributing the land among the peasants after 1918, and most of them made a serious effort to establish political democracy.[1] Serbia,

[1] None of this applies to the primitive tribal society of Albania.

Bulgaria and Greece were already countries of peasant proprietors in 1914. Rumania was the reverse, but a radical land reform measure was passed in 1918. The proximity and danger of the Bolshevik revolution largely account for this, and it was most quickly and thoroughly applied in the province of Bessarabia which was taken from the Russians. In the former Habsburg territories the large estates had belonged to members of the ruling races, and it was natural that the German and Magyar nobles, as also the Croat nobility and the moslem landlords of Bosnia, should be dispossessed by Rumania, Czechoslovakia and Yugoslavia. This was all very well for the prosperous Czech and Slovene farmers, living in what were in effect parts of the advanced, western half of Europe. But elsewhere the peasants were poor and ignorant, the amount of good soil was limited, the rural population was growing fast and the custom of dividing each holding among the owner's children at his death tended to increase the number too small for efficient working. The governments did little to educate or financially support the peasants, and they were increasingly at the mercy of the village moneylenders. Their economic position became catastrophic in the world crisis of the thirties.

The economic life of the area had, of course, already been disrupted by the break-up of the Habsburg monarchy. But the backwardness of most of it meant that disruption was less serious than it would have been farther west. Hungary, like Austria, suffered a complete collapse, but it, too, was rescued by a League of Nations loan and thereafter was able to borrow heavily abroad. Their obvious economic difficulties made it easy for the lesser Central Powers to get relief from their undertakings to pay reparations. It was more serious that all the states of the region desired not only industrialization but self-sufficiency, and at first could barely be prevailed on to trade with each other at all. The situation improved in the twenties, but deteriorated when the depression set in, notably in the ending of the important trade between Hungary and Czechoslovakia. The raising of capital abroad likewise became impossible and, as in Russia, this meant that the burden of industrialization fell with increasing severity on the peasants. At the same time the collapse of world agricultural prices greatly reduced their already exiguous incomes. As in Witte's system, industry was both protected by very high tariffs and subsidized from the proceeds of taxation. The peasants had to contend with lower prices for what they sold, higher prices for what they needed to buy, ruinous taxes and a mounting burden of debt.

Political democracy did not flourish in these conditions and had already proved a sickly growth in the twenties. Czechoslovakia was an exception to this. With their extensive industrial development and large educated middle class, the Czech lands were well suited to the parliamentary republic that was established there, and it survived and worked well until destroyed by Hitler. But like the Habsburg monarchy, Czechoslovakia not only contained many nationalities but was divided into a prosperous western and a backward eastern half. The Slovak and Ruthene territories that were taken over from Hungary had no wish to return to Magyar rule and were too small, poor and lacking in educated men to form states on their own. But the Czechs did not keep the promises of autonomy made to them. Czech officials dominated the government, the Slovak industries fostered by the Hungarians were ruined by Czech competition, the poor Slovak peasantry received no special help: it was the story of southern Italy in a milder form. Further, the Czechs were anticlerical, revering the memory of Hus and associating the catholic church with the defunct monarchy. There were some Lutherans in Slovakia who were loyal to the republic, but most of the peasants were devout catholics. A strong Slovak People's Party emerged under clerical leadership, hostile to democracy and the republic. By contrast the large German minority at first accepted Slav supremacy fairly quietly, and from 1926 the German parties were included in the coalition ministries by which the country was governed. But the great economic crisis affected Czechoslovakia almost as badly as Germany and Austria, and the German industrial areas were as badly hit as the agrarian east. In 1934 a Sudeten German movement was founded by Konrad Henlein, a teacher of gymnastics like some of the original German nationalists of Napoleonic times. In 1935 it swept the other German parties aside in the elections and became the second largest party in the republic. Though it professed to be loyal and democratic, its sympathies in fact were with the new Nazi Reich. Another feature of the scene disquieting for liberals was that from 1920 the Communists were the largest party among the working class. They were especially strong in the backward eastern territories.

The Balkan states were too backward socially for real democracy to be possible there, and at best they followed the pattern already familiar to us of oligarchy behind a democratic and parliamentary façade. The oligarchies were not aristocratic, as in Hungary, but consisted mainly of self-made men, like the rulers of Soviet Russia. Though largely of peasant origin and sometimes even forming specifically Peasant Parties, they tended to be less connected with agriculture than with the business groups who thrived on state protection. In Bulgaria a real attempt to do something for the peasants, both economically and politically, was made by Stamboliski, who came to power as a consequence of the nation's defeat in 1918. He was also a believer in the old ideal of Slav unity, and had not only opposed war against Russia but desired reconciliation with the Serbs and the union of all the Balkan Slavs. He was therefore disliked both by the privileged groups in the country and by the extreme nationalists who wanted to reconquer Macedonia. He was removed and murdered in a sanguinary revolt in 1923, and thereafter the army and the nationalist terrorists were in the ascendant. Elections were sometimes held, but there was little political freedom for those outside the ruling circle. From 1935 King Boris governed personally, with only an intermittent pretence of parliamentary sanction. Yugoslavia was dominated by the Serbs, who provided its king, and in defiance of the wishes of the other peoples it received a centralist constitution. Croat opposition to this was led by Stephen Radich, leader of the Peasant Party, who, like Stamboliski, wanted some sort of free union of all the Balkan Slavs. In 1928 he was shot dead in parliament by another member, and parliamentary government came to an end. King Alexander, a stern military man who already controlled the army, took power. A sham parliamentary constitution was established in 1931, and it became a little more real when the king was assassinated in 1934 and his cousin Prince Paul became regent. Cosmopolitan and little interested in politics, Paul had no special liking for the Serbs. He governed in concert with the Slovene and Moslem political leaders, and in 1939 Croatia was given extensive autonomy. As in Slovakia, however, there was a growing catholic and ultra-nationalist movement that wanted something more. In this case it was the adherence of the dominant Serbs to the Greek church that gave religious offence. Both Bulgaria and Yugoslavia had sizeable suppressed communist movements.

The new Rumania, like Yugoslavia, was divided to some extent by differences between the regions on the opposite sides of the pre-war frontier. Those who had been under Habsburg rule—the Transylvanians, the Croats and Slovenes—regarded themselves as more civilized and expected higher standards in government than those who had not. The Transylvanian leader Maniu succeeded in allying himself with the peasants in opposition to the Liberals of the old kingdom. It was they who at first dominated post-war Rumania, and they had favoured industry at the expense of agriculture and denied autonomy to Transylvania. But in 1927 Maniu's new National Peasant Party won the elections and made a serious effort to help the farmers, notably by trying to finance industrial expansion by foreign borrowing instead of by directly squeezing them. At the same time, however, a strong though rather amorphous fascist terrorist movement was growing up. This was nourished by the national hatred of the Jews, and by the fear arising from the nearness of the Soviet Union: left-wing movements were ruthlessly suppressed, and in this the terrorists helped the police. In 1930 the throne was successfully claimed by Prince Carol, who had been barred from the succession in favour of his infant son because of a morganatic marriage. Carol was a flamboyant character in the tradition of his relation, the last Kaiser. He set about the acquisition of personal power, sowing discord within the big parties, flirting with the terrorists, and relying on the administration's power to 'make' the elections in favour of whatever ministers were appointed. In 1937, however, the terrorists and the Peasant Party banded together in opposition, and the ministry lost the elections: intimidation from the other side neutralized pressure by the government. Carol shortly afterwards abrogated the constitution. His personal assumption of power was legitimized by a new one, approved by plebiscite, and he tried to strengthen it by establishing a single political party in the fascist style. The history of the Greek republic was no happier than that of the Balkan kingdoms. Military coups punctuated its history. In 1935, a plebiscite restored the monarchy, but behind this was the military dictatorship of General Metaxas.

The political as well as the economic situation of east-central Europe was made very much worse by the inability of its constituent states to unite. Hungary, and as a rule Bulgaria also, remained implacably opposed to the new territorial settlement and dreamed of revenge. Attempts at a Habsburg restoration in Hungary led (1920–1) to the establishment of the 'little entente', a system of defensive alliances linking Czechoslovakia, Rumania and Yugoslavia. In 1934 a Balkan entente linked the latter powers with Greece and Turkey. This owed much to Turkish initiative. She had become reconciled with Greece, and wished to forget old scores and promote a general Balkan union for defence against outside aggression. But her one-time ally Bulgaria would not show the same wisdom, and so the entente came to be directed against the Bulgars. This meant that the Balkan states made a sort of chessboard pattern, each tending to be on good terms with the next but one. The pattern was completed by the disastrous failure of Poland and Czechoslovakia to be friends. Though Poland was not one of the defeated powers in the First World War, the affinities of the Polish ruling class had always been with the Germans and Magyars rather than the democratic and pro-Russian Czechs. In addition, the two countries both claimed the industrial district of Teschen, awarded to the Czechs by the allied powers in 1920. Both states had an alliance with France, and Poland also had an alliance (1921) with Rumania against Russia. But their relations remained distant, and this estrangement was fatal to the future independence of east-central Europe. They were the only countries in the area which had advanced at all far in industrial development. Poland made a notable further advance in the thirties by developing new industries in her interior, less vulnerable to attack than the Silesian region which she had acquired from Germany. Combined, they would have had the weight of a great power. Isolated, they easily fell to Hitler, and he acquired in his first blows the industrial areas which were vital to any defence of east-central Europe by its own independent strength.

In 1939, therefore, the area was as ramshackle as the realms of the Habsburgs had ever been, and it was ripe for conquest by any powers with the opportunity and inclination to undertake it.

The Japanese Advance

Japan had participated in the liberal revival of the twenties and followed a policy of peace and retrenchment. Universal suffrage was introduced, and the parliamentary politicians were steadily gaining control of the government. But from 1930 a strong counter-movement built up, stemming from several causes. The gradual establishment of an effective nationalist government in China threatened to arrest the growth of Japanese influence in Manchuria and Shantung. Japanese troops landed in the latter province in 1927–8 without much avail, and relations between the two countries deteriorated. Manchuria remained virtually independent under the control of a local war-lord, but in 1928 this potentate was murdered by the Japanese, and his son and successor made a show of joining the nationalists. The Japanese army increasingly desired a strong forward policy. But the politicians increasingly committed themselves to disarmament, which took a step forward with the naval agreement of 1930. This was bitterly opposed in Japan, and the army feared that its turn would come next. In the same year the economic crisis reached the country, the farmers especially being hit by the collapse of the market for raw silk. As in Russia, the army officers sympathized with the sufferings of the peasantry from whom so many of their men came. They were rather hostile to big business, with which the main political parties were closely linked, and wanted an end to deflation and retrenchment, and the restoration of prosperity by means of vigorous national aggrandizement. Naturally these views were widely popular. Even a section of the socialists supported the army.

The Japanese had been in occupation of the southern tip of Manchuria ever since 1905. In September 1931, just as the European financial system was collapsing, they began to expand northwards, and gradually occupied the whole territory. At first the army acted without consulting the government, which told the world that it would retire when order had been established. But in 1932 the state of Manchukuo was created, theoretically independent under the sovereignty of the last Chinese Emperor, but in fact governed by Japanese 'advisers'. In Japan the prime minister was assassinated— the culmination of several attempts at a coup. Henceforward the party politicians no longer held office, and ministries consisted of officials and dignitaries acceptable to the army. The Chinese had, of course, appealed to the Council of the League of Nations, which accomplished little beyond sending out a commission of enquiry, whose report (September 1932) completely upheld the Chinese complaint. In the spring of 1932 China took the matter to the Assembly of the League. An extension of Japanese aggression to Shanghai was checked, partly through League intervention. The Japanese forces could make little headway there against strong Chinese resistance, which had been lacking in Manchuria. They horrified world opinion by bombing civilians, and their new invasion was in an area where other imperial powers had large interests. They therefore retired, but in Manchuria they stood firm. In February 1933 the League Assembly, after long and judicious consideration, endorsed the report of the commission of enquiry. It called on China and Japan to negotiate a settlement restoring Chinese sovereignty in Manchuria. Japan's response was to leave the League, in March. Their military expansion began to threaten Peking, and so in May the Chinese accepted an armistice—the Tangku Truce—which for the moment safeguarded their remaining territory. In 1934 Japan denounced the treaty limitations on her naval armaments.

These events were a serious blow to the system of peacekeeping represented by the League and the Kellogg Pact. (As Japan claimed to be acting in self-defence, there was no overt breach of the latter.) The poor showing of the League was due to the apathy of the European powers, who had more pressing economic and political problems at home and were not without sympathy with Japan. Britain and France, too, were imperial powers; their influence, too, was diminished by the rise of the Chinese nationalists and Japan had been their ally in the war. The smaller powers were eager for action and this explains the unprecedented transfer of the affair from the Council to the Assembly, which began to recover its importance as the great powers lost interest. But there was little prospect of forcible measures if the great powers would not join in. A more constructive feature of the affair was that the great outsiders, Russia and the United States, continued to draw closer to the League. The United States was asked to associate itself with the League's action at every stage and did show consistent sympathy, an American representative actually joining the meetings of the Council for a time. The Americans were, of course, more concerned at Japanese expansion than Britain and France, and in January 1932 Stimson, the secretary of state, declared that he would not recognize any Sino-Japanese agreements that infringed American treaty rights or was obtained by means contrary to the Kellogg Pact. He tried in vain to get Britain and France to follow his lead. Russia was very directly threatened by the Japanese advance, and she was invited, like the United States, to join the committee set up to try and enforce the League resolution of 1933. She did not venture thus to offend her close and powerful neighbour, which in view of the remote prospects of help against her is hardly surprising. But she made a polite reply, and soon began to consider joining the League. The benefit to China of League action remained meagre. Shanghai was left alone for the moment, League members would not recognize Manchukuo, and China had made a dignified protest, saving her honour without having to go to war. But for the League machinery there would have been no other way to save 'face'. A war however would have destroyed the new state.

The Manchurian affair was not perhaps in itself a serious threat to peace. It was only the latest of a series of imperialist escapades since 1918, all of which, however unsavoury, proved digestible by the international system. But the League's moral authority had been committed in the affair and successfully defied—a fatal precedent. Also, a good chance had been missed of encouraging positive action by the United States.

The further action of Japan was largely governed by the conflict of two factions within the army, one of which saw Russia as the main enemy, while the other wanted good relations with her, as the basis for further penetration in China. The Russians still ran the railways of northern Manchuria jointly with the Chinese, but in 1935 this possible bone of contention was removed by their selling out to the Japanese. In 1936 there was a revolt of young Japanese officers of the party hostile to Russia. They murdered some leading men opposed to them, but eventually they were suppressed. In 1937 a full-scale Japanese invasion of China began. This seems once more to have been a reaction to the growing strength of the Chinese government, which had continued all the time to increase its authority within the country and was now able to offer much tougher opposition to Japanese penetration than in 1931. But they were not able to withstand a full-scale invasion. In 1937 the Japanese took Shanghai and Nanking. In 1938 they landed in the south and took Canton. The cities and railways in the eastern half of China gradually fell into their hands, and Chiang Kai-shek, the nationalist leader, had to set up his capital at Chungking, deep in the interior. The Japanese maintained throughout that the war was a mere measure of police, and they eventually tried to set up a new Chinese government dependent on themselves.

Although the main Japanese effort was turned against China, relations with Russia remained delicate. In the summer of 1938 there was a pitched battle for possession of a hill where Siberia and Korea join. From May until September 1939 there was more extensive fighting between Russians and Japanese on the border between Manchuria and Outer Mongolia. The Japanese got the worst of it. In 1941 a non-aggression pact was concluded between the two countries. But when Hitler attacked Russia soon afterwards, Matsuoka, the very man who had signed the pact, was in favour of joining in.

Japanese aggression did something to inspire the rampaging of dictators in Europe. This in turn made it seem safe for the Japanese to embark on the long task of subduing China: by 1937 the European powers were more than ever taken up with affairs in their own continent. The further Japanese advance once more smoothed the path for European aggressors. Russia could not afford to be indifferent to it, and it had now gone so far that Britain also had to regard it as a possible danger to her Asian possessions, and even to Australia and New Zealand. Hitler was to find them both more pliable than they might otherwise have been.

3: The Rise of Hitler and the Decline of France

The moderate politicians in France and Germany had failed after 1918, as they had before 1914, to rediscover the secret of orderly progress which they seem to have possessed in the middle of the nineteenth century. They could not find policies that were positive and dynamic, and yet at the same time capable of winning support among very diverse groups in society. There was enough grudging co-operation between different classes and parties in the twenties to preserve the existing political and social system. But the thirties demanded something much more dynamic, and there was not enough unity of thought and purpose in the two nations to provide it by democratic means. German democracy collapsed in 1930–2. France's situation worsened more slowly, and there was time for one more important democratic experiment, the Popular Front. But this quickly lost its impetus, and the Third Republic was in a hopelessly enfeebled state when it succumbed to military defeat in 1940. Dictatorships in each case seemed the only way out.

The Rise of the Nazis

Adolf Hitler was born in 1889, the son of a minor Austrian customs official. His father, though not unduly strict, was a heavy parent of the old school; his mother was more indulgent. Adolf wanted to be an artist and resisted his father's wish that he, too, should enter the government service. Perhaps because of these tensions, he did badly at school. When his father died, his mother paid for him to go to Vienna and study art. But he did badly at this too, and when his mother died and her money was used up, he sank into destitution. He eventually moved to Munich—apparently to evade military service. But when war came he volunteered for the German army and served bravely, rising to the rank of corporal. He ended the war in hospital, nearly blinded by gas.

Curiously, this biographical notice is also an index of his political beliefs and talents. Because of his father's job, he was born near the frontier: at Braunau on the Inn, where Germany and Austria adjoin. This artificial boundary between people of the same nationality he became eager to sweep away. Vienna fascinated and appalled him. A glittering, cosmopolitan city full of Jews and Slavs, it brought home to him the non-national character of the Habsburg monarchy. He adopted the views of Schönerer's radicals, that the Germans must secede from it in order to preserve their national character. He developed an intense hatred of the Jews, representative of the denationalizing principle. He saw the socialists as their tools. But living among the poorest people, he saw also that both the socialists and the clericals had a far better grasp of the needs of the masses and of how to move them than had the socialists. He particularly admired the work of Lueger, the great mayor of Vienna. He wanted a nationalist movement based on the masses instead of on the educated classes. He had himself the talents needed in such a movement. His artistic gifts were real, but they were practical. Advertising, not creative art, was his vocation. It was he who designed the excellent Nazi flag, with its swastika emblem, and the effective stage-management which was so important in Nazi demonstrations was in the first instance his work. He also proved to be a demagogic orator of the highest power. As is often the case in men with such talents, his private personality was rather rudimentary. He had few friends and only one serious love-affair (with his niece), though he enjoyed the society of women. He was a vegetarian and lived very simply, though in his days of power he liked cream cakes, fast cars and luxurious houses. Monumental rages, tears and pathos, and displays of great personal charm alternated in his behaviour. But all seem to have been largely artificial. Behind them was a passionate temperament controlled by a powerful will and increasingly centred on the sole object of gaining power. This intense devotion to his destiny gave him a profound and almost uncanny ascendancy over those who worked with him.

Hitler was one of those to whom the war had brought steady employment and who had no job to return to in 1918. He was kept on for a time in the army for propaganda work, and it was then that he discovered in Munich an insignificant nationalist group called the National Socialist German Workers' Party. He took this over and built it up, with the aid of sympathizers in the army and elsewhere. It included a body of 'storm-troopers', organized on military lines ostensibly for the protection of its meetings against left-wing violence. In 1923 it took part, with kindred organizations, in the unsuccessful coup already described. Hitler was imprisoned for his part of this— briefly and comfortably. He spent much of the time dictating *Mein Kampf*,[1] a pretentious and repetitive collection of ideas and reminiscences. Written to prove that he was no mere rabble-rouser but a serious political figure, it provides a history, not always reliable, of his political development and an account of his aims for Germany. He believed that the day of the nation state was over and the future belonged to states on a continental scale, like Russia, the United States and the British Empire. Germany must become such a state if she was to survive. The Kaiser's government had attempted to expand peacefully, by acquiring tropical colonies. Hitler believed that German expansion to the extent necessary would never be accepted by the other nations without a war. He did not much want overseas colonies. They implied a mainly industrial Germany, and he knew at first hand the evils of slum life and thought that the nation could only be healthy if it was mainly agricultural. To gain new land on which Germans could settle as farmers, he wanted the conquest of eastern Europe. The Soviet state he regarded as too weak to offer much opposition, and France is portrayed as the main obstacle to expansion. By contrast, Britain is referred to with considerable respect in *Mein Kampf*, and a quarrel with her in the foreseeable future is not envisaged. Hitler's Austrian origins are no doubt reflected in his preference of eastward to seaward expansion, and France very obviously was the chief enemy at the moment when he was writing. An entirely personal belief which he championed consistently for the rest of his life was that Italy was Germany's natural ally. How far he applied the rest of the strategy contained in *Mein Kampf* when he came to power is a mystery about which more must be said in its place.

Hitler spent the rest of the twenties restoring his party and extending its activities to north Germany. The failure of his revolt in 1923 had convinced him that he could only reach power by legal means—with the army, not against it. He rebuilt and expanded his army of stormtroopers, but their constant violence was intended by

[1] 'My Struggle.'

him to have a moral rather than a direct political effect. There was to be no direct seizure of power, but opponents were to be demoralized and silenced by being beaten up, until it appeared that almost everyone agreed with the Nazis. Hitler claimed to have learned this technique of intimidation from the socialists. Many of his followers did not appreciate its subtlety, and wanted something more forceful. Hitler had an embarrassing time before and even after he took office, trying to appear respectable enough to be taken into partnership by the army and bureaucracy without losing the revolutionary fervour which made him popular. This difficulty was especially apparent in the economic policy of the party. As its name implied, it had originally been anti-capitalist as well as nationalist, and many of its members regarded it as mainly intended to defend the small man against big business. The brothers Otto and Gregor Strasser were the most important representatives of this view, and for a time they were supported by Joseph Goebbels, a brilliant young propagandist whose intellectual and academic distinction was well above the party's average. Hitler was concerned, if only for tactical reasons, at the economic plight of the people. But his remedy for it was expansion abroad, and he had no wish to be committed to measures of socialization because he wanted to use big business as a source of party funds. By 1933 he was finding it hard to do this while vying with the Communists as an opponent of the mounting economic misery.

The unsuccessful campaign against the Young Plan in 1929 enabled the Nazis to publicize themselves on a big scale. Party membership rose dramatically, and from October they began to gain ground in state elections. Businessmen became interested, and the funds available to the party steadily increased. This enabled it to spend heavily on publicity and electoral campaigning. In the presidential election of 1932 the Führer took the then unusual and dramatic step of going on an election tour by air, on one occasion arousing admiration by flying when all other aircraft were grounded. But mounting funds also allowed the multiplication of the brown-shirted stormtroopers (the SA) who in 1932 numbered 400,000—four times as many as the regular soldiers. It was unemployment that allowed the recruitment of this huge force. The men were subsisted by the party (partly at their own expense, for they turned their unemployment pay over to it), and having no work to do they occupied their time in rioting and lynching. The strength of the Communists increased at the same time and in the same way. Pitched battles between the rival armies of totalitarians were common. It was his appeal to the generation just reaching manhood that gave Hitler much of his strength, both in elections and on the streets. A sensational trial in 1930 showed that young officers in the army were also being affected. The aloofness of the army from politicians, even those with whom it sympathized or co-operated, was no longer complete.

The economic crisis meanwhile, destroying both the popularity of the moderate parties and their ability to work together, transferred effective power to the President and the generals. Hindenburg was now too old as well as too simple to control events himself, and his power was largely exercised by his personal entourage. The most important figures in this were his son Oskar, the head of his chancellery[1] Otto Meisner and, above all, General Kurt von Schleicher. This lively, intelligent, wily but fundamentally unstable and even naïve man had become the army's chief expert on relations with the politicians. He was a follower of the wise Groener, who had been minister of defence since 1928 and had appointed him head of the ministerial office— virtually his second-in-command. He was also a crony of Oskar von Hindenburg, and this gave him access to the President.

The influence of these men became important in March 1930, when the breach between the socialists and the other parties made a return to minority governments necessary. Heinrich Brüning the new chancellor was their choice. Austere and strong of will, he had served at the front in the war, and had considerable sympathy with the conservatives and a sentimental, soldierly loyalty to the old President. It was clear from the outset that he owed his office to the President rather than the party politicians, and could count on strong presidential backing. But the ministry was essentially parliamentary. Brüning was a leader of the Centre, and his colleagues were the non-socialists of the outgoing ministry. The first plan was simply a parliamentary move to the right, the Nationalists replacing the Socialists in the governmental majority. For this reason the sternly deflationary policy of the ministry was coupled with generous concessions to agriculture. But the Nationalists were afraid of voting for deflation because they might lose votes to the Nazis—just as the Socialists similarly feared

[1] Equivalent to a principal private secretary.

losing ground to the Communists. Both these fears were justified, and the Nationalists were so divided on whether to help or hinder the government of the republic that the party steadily dwindled. In the summer of 1930, therefore, Brüning found himself without a majority for his deflationary budget, and enacted it by invoking the president's power to issue emergency decrees. But there proved to be a small majority in the Reichstag for annulling the presidential order, and so Brüning went to the country in September. This allowed the Nazis to emerge as a great parliamentary power. They won over six million votes and instead of 12 seats had 107. They were now the second strongest party, after the Socialists. The Communists with 77 seats came third.

Brüning's immediate position was strengthened by the elections because the socialists saw that the republic was now in danger and were no longer prepared to vote against his use of emergency powers. To avoid losing votes to the Communists they did not positively endorse the government's policy, but they gave it in effect the benefit of a parliamentary majority. But the respite was temporary, for the economic crisis was deepening. The President's advisers, moreover, were not pleased to see the government depend on socialist rather than Nationalist votes. Not only did they dislike the socialists but there had developed an important difference with them on a question of policy. Groener and Schleicher were eager to take advantage of Germany's improving political position to begin serious preparations for rearmament. The Socialists were inclined to oppose this: in particular, they delayed plans for building 'pocket battleships' for the navy. Schleicher, in particular, therefore began to turn wistful glances towards the Nazis. The conservative generals and bureaucrats had no more love for Hitler than for the Socialists and Communists—all to them were parties of the gutter, and it was obvious that the Nazis were capable of dangerous violence. But Hitler incessantly proclaimed his determination to seek power by legal means alone, and occasionally reprimanded or disavowed his subordinates when it became too obvious that they were preparing to go farther. It was tempting to regard the Nazis as misguided patriots who might be induced to lend their many votes to the support of a sound conservative government.

Brüning might perhaps have survived on his precarious perch until the economic tide had turned but for the unfortunate accident that the term of office of the President, on which his power depended, ran out in 1932. His first idea was to ask the Reichstag to prolong it. But this would be a constitutional amendment, requiring a two-thirds majority. From the autumn of 1931, therefore, there were negotiations with the Nazis and Nationalists with the object of securing their votes. Hitler was interested, but he eventually insisted on new Reichstag elections in return, which he expected to win. The negotiations broke down, but the idea of striking a bargain with him did not die. Meanwhile the ancient Field Marshal was induced to stand again for popular election, and the Centre and Socialists against whom he had stood in 1925 supported his candidature. As in 1925, two ballots proved necessary, and these were the first of no less than five national votes in 1932–3 which raised the country to a revolutionary pitch of excitement. Hitler and the Communist Thälmann were the other main candidates for the presidency, and on the second ballot (April 1932) Hitler won over thirteen million votes, double as many as the already hugely swollen Nazi total of 1930. Thälmann had four million supporters, but Hindenburg topped them both with nineteen million. His victory, however, did not settle but made more acute the question whether the government should lean to the right or to the left. The activities of the SA had naturally intensified during the elections, and it was clear that they were preparing for a coup in the event of Hitler's victory. The state governments bore the chief responsibility for law and order, and they were still controlled by the parliamentary politicians. They demanded that the Reich government suppress the SA. Groener, who in 1931 had added the Reich ministry of the interior to his defence portfolio, agreed. The ban was ordered on 13 April, and it was completely effective. But neither Schleicher nor Hindenburg liked the breach with the right which this implied. The old President was also upset by some rather odd schemes being mooted by the government for breaking up the great estates of the Junkers and settling some of the unemployed on the land. Hindenburg was of Junker stock, and in 1927 had been presented by national subscription with the estate of Neudeck, which his family had had to sell. His Junker neighbours easily persuaded him that a more conservative government was imperative.

In May, therefore, first Groener and then Brüning were driven to resign, Schleicher telling the former that he had lost the confidence of the army. Schleicher himself became minister of defence, and the new chancellor, Franz von Papen, was his nominee. Events soon showed just how much political understanding was possessed by the army's chief political expert. The new chancellor was a wealthy political amateur, nominally a member of the Centre, which he had been striving to give a strongly conservative orientation. His cabinet, like himself, were distinguished figures in high society, and not taken seriously as politicians. The moderate parties in the Reichstag would have nothing to do with them. Schleicher had hoped that Papen's own party, the Centre, would support him, but it was particularly incensed against the supplanter of the real party leader, Brüning. Schleicher had also been trying to bring the Nazis to the support of Papen. He offered the end of the ban on the SA and new elections. He received only the vaguest promise of support in return. The result of the elections might have been foreseen, not only from the presidential contests but from the important vote in Prussia in April, where the Centre and Socialists had lost their parliamentary majority and the extremists (Nazi and Communist) outnumbered them. The Reichstag elections in July followed the same pattern. The Nazis won 230 seats out of 608; the Communists 89. The parties loyal to the republic had lost control of the legislature as well as the executive. Papen added to their discomfiture by deposing the republican coalition ministry in Prussia, which had stayed in office because the Nazis and Communists could not combine against it. The pretext for this was the growing violence of the Nazis, but the consequence was that the maintenance of law and order in the greater part of Germany was no longer in democratic hands. Neither socialist party nor trade unions dared attempt any resistance to this latest extension of presidential dictatorship. But if Papen could stamp on the left, he was at the mercy of the right. Hitler was too near an absolute majority to be willing to accept the second place designed for him by the presidential advisers. He demanded the chancellorship and plenary powers. The Reichstag met in September, only to be dissolved at once. Papen's parliamentary strength had proved to be thirty-two. He had nobody behind him except the President and the army.

But Papen's position was stronger than it might seem. For one thing, the ministers were personally congenial to the old President in a way that the previous cabinets of politicians had never been, and

Papen himself was a far better courtier than he was a politician and soon held first place in the old man's favour. Hindenburg would not part with him unless he was forced to, and Hitler's ability to use force was beginning to decline. He had spent a great deal of money in the many elections, and he was finding it increasingly hard to hold together his revolutionary followers and financial backers. In 1930 Hitler had severely restrained the left wing of his followers. He had driven Otto Strasser out of the party because he had supported the trade unions in a strike in Saxony, and he had restrained his Reichstag followers from introducing a measure to nationalize the banks. Even then he was troubled by mutinies in the SA, and in 1932 he was obliged to be more radical in order to keep up with what were increasingly his most serious competitors—the Communists. In November there was a transport strike in Berlin, in protest against the reactionary ministry and its cutting of wages. The Communists started it, but the Nazis had to join in. Such moves alienated financial backers and respectable conservatives were increasingly disgusted by the frequent murders now committed by stormtroopers, and by Hitler's outspoken contempt for Papen. In the November elections the Nazis lost thirty-four seats and two million votes; the Communists and the Nationalists gained, and the former now had one hundred seats. The Nazis had failed in 1931 to make an alliance with the Nationalists, and they now failed in attempts to come to terms with the Centre. They were so short of money that the stormtroopers took to begging their bread in the streets. It seemed that they might have shot their bolt.

The fact remained that the existing ministry was without parliamentary supporters, and if it wished to stay in office it would have to abrogate the constitution. This was what Papen now prepared to do. On his ministers' insistence, he offered his resignation to allow it to be discovered if there was any possibility of a combination of parties with a majority in the new Reichstag. When it proved that there was not, he proposed to Hindenburg that if the Reichstag would not support his government it should be dispensed with for the time being, and a way should be found of altering the constitution. This was too much for Schleicher, though exactly why is something of a mystery. His ostensible reason was that it would cause Nazis and Communists to rise together against the government, as in the Berlin transport strike, and the army would not then be able to maintain order. But he had become personally jealous of Papen's growing influence, and he probably realized that he had mistaken his man. Papen wanted a pure conservative régime ruling in the teeth of the entire population, and Schleicher saw that this was absurd. He believed that a more popular and conciliatory approach would win at least the toleration of the new Reichstag. Early in December, therefore, he declared that the army could not undertake the execution of Papen's policy, and he was himself appointed chancellor to carry through his proposed alternative.

Schleicher tried to retrace his steps and move back to the left— farther to the left than Brüning. He pledged himself to reduce unemployment, and appealed to the moderate left and also to the left wing of the Nazis. He had long considered circumventing the intractability of Hitler by trying to detach some of his followers from him, and he had similar plans to appeal to the trade unions over the heads of the socialist politicians. But his plans did not work. The left, in view of his past record, stayed aloof. Gregor Strasser tried hard to bring the Nazis behind Schleicher. He was the principal party organizer, and was acutely conscious of their loss of votes and need to capitalize their success before it was too late. But he failed to convince the more important leaders and went off to Italy in a huff; while he was away, Hitler destroyed his influence in the party. Schleicher eventually had to confess that he could not govern with the existing Reichstag—in other words, that he had been wrong and had failed. Meanwhile, the conservative old guard, brought by Papen within sight of the promised land, were furious and afraid at the change of course. Papen reconciled himself with Hitler, and on the revival of plans for the breaking up of the Junker estates so, too, did the Nationalists. The influences playing on Hindenburg were at last favourable to a Hitler government as the least of evils, and so at the end of January 1933 a coalition came into office with Hitler as chancellor, Papen as vice-chancellor and Hugenberg the Nationalist leader as minister of the economy, food and agriculture. The president allowed them to hold new elections, and Nazi violence now had full freedom in the intimidation of voters. Even so, the voting in March gave the Nazis and Nationalists together only a bare majority: 288 and 52 seats out of 647. The Nazis won 17 million votes, 43.9 per cent of the total. For the grant of the plenary powers which they desired from the Reichstag they needed something more—the two-thirds majority required for a constitutional amendment. But the supporters of the republic were tired of the fight: the Centre voted for the government and carried the day.

The rise of Hitler was due to the progressive failure of the democratic system to work. This was above all a failure of leadership. Hitler had his own distinctive policies, but they were to be applied much later. When he first took office his policies in economic matters and other things besides were those that his predecessors had evolved in the previous year or two. But he applied them with much greater vigour, and he took responsibility for them. The parliamentary politicians had fumbled their way very slowly towards the way out of the economic collapse, and they had shunned responsibility, sheltering behind the president's emergency powers. This reflected their inability to produce constructive policies and 'sell' them dynamically to the nation as Hitler sold his. The old conservative ruling class, who had lost power for the same reason, attempted a come-back when the politicians proved no better than they had been. But they had learned little. They were no better than the politicians at making an appeal to the nation, their ablest leader was yet another wire-puller, Schleicher, and they could provide no effective presidential candidate under the age of eighty. At the end they were reduced to governing by force alone. Hitler owed a great deal of his power to the skilful use of violence, but he owed much more to his mastery of the art of appealing to the people that is part of the equipment of every democratic statesman worthy of the name. He could lead the people; the democratic politicians and the old guard could not. So the old guard, having taken power from the politicians, handed it to him.

Did Hitler come to power by the choice of the German people? In the literal sense, no. The Nazis never won a majority in a free election, and the Socialists and Centre retained most of their votes to the end. But negatively, the Germans certainly did reject democracy. The Nazis and the Communists had a majority between them at the end, which becomes substantial if there be added the scarcely more democratic Nationalists. The democrats became increasingly demoralized and unwilling to fight for their rights—witness the socialist apathy at the suppression of democratic Prussia and the Centrist vote for the Nazi enabling act. A dictatorial method had been adopted already for the solution of the economic problem—not only was the economy regulated by decree but this was already being done in a notably arbitrary spirit, especially by the cutting of wages. The establishment of the Weimar republic had been by a similar negative process: labour had declined to set up a dictatorship, the army and bureaucracy had not supported the Kapp putsch or Hitler's in 1923, and so democracy came into being, though it aroused little enthusiasm. Now that there was a clear retreat from democracy, the passing of power to the strongest non-democratic movement was the obvious next step. Hitler, in conclusion, owed his political importance to his popularity—to the fact that a great many people voted for him, even though not a majority. In this respect he was very unlike Mussolini, for whom few people ever voted from choice, or Lenin, who won power rather because he had a majority of votes in certain key places. Germany is perhaps the only country where the ballot box has played so large a part in bringing a dictator to power.

The Moulding of the Third Reich

Hitler had taken office with respectable conservatives whose intention was to keep him under control and use him for their own purposes. He was allowed to bring only two colleagues with him into the new Reich cabinet. Frick, the humdrum parliamentary leader of the party, had the then not very important ministry of the interior. Göring, the deputy leader of the Nazis, was minister without portfolio. In the great state of Prussia, still under Reich control, Papen was minister-president, though Göring was minister of the interior. When the 'law for removing the distress of the people of the Reich' invested the government with dictatorial powers, the Nationalists and the Centre considered that the personal ascendancy of Hitler had been guarded against by the clause which preserved intact the prerogatives of the president.

But Hitler had no intention of playing Ramsay Macdonald to Papen's Baldwin. The conservatives by whom he was surrounded were second-rate men without popular support, all parties except his own and perhaps the Communists were thoroughly demoralized, and now that a parade of respectability had won him office he had no scruples about the unbridled use of revolutionary violence to demolish what opposition remained. Göring's Prussian ministry controlled the police in the greater part of Germany, and he at once saw that it was put into safe hands and enrolled a large section of the Nazi private army as auxiliary police. There was now no protection for anyone whom the Nazis wished to terrorize. On 27 February 1933 the Reichstag building in Berlin burned down. This was so convenient for the Nazis that they were long suspected—it seems unjustly—of having started the fire themselves. Next day a presidential decree suspended the guarantees of personal liberty under the constitution and empowered the national government to take over the administration in any of the states. The latter provision at once gave enormous potential power to Frick's ministry of the interior, hitherto confined to overseeing its state equivalents. On 9 March the Nazis in Munich seized control of the Bavarian government by a revolutionary coup, and a month later Hitler appointed Reich governors in all the states, with powers to remove the existing authorities, dissolve the parliaments and promulgate state laws. He assumed this office himself in Prussia, and at once appointed Göring in Papen's place at the head of the government. In January 1934 the state parliaments and legislative powers were formally abolished, and Germany lost her federal character and became, as she had never been before, a fully centralized autocracy.

The Reichstag fire was claimed by the Nazis to be the first incident in a bloody Communist insurrection, and the systematic proscription of that party began at once, although it was not officially abolished till May. By that time the Nazis felt strong enough to strike at the moderate left also, and the trade unions and the socialist party were also abolished. The assets of the former were given to a new organization, the Labour Front, set up under the Nazi Dr Ley. Collective bargaining was abolished and the state undertook the fixing of wages and conditions of work. In the course of the summer the remaining political parties, even Hitler's supposed allies in the Reichstag, the Centre and the Nationalists, went into voluntary liquidation. A law declared the Nazis to be the only legal party. Hugenberg resigned from the government. The old conservatives had their own body of stormtroopers, the Stahlhelm, who had hitherto been on very bad terms with the SA. They were now induced to merge with it. The catholic church was compensated for the loss of its political arm by the conclusion of the concordat with the Reich government. Among the protestants there was a considerable body sympathetic to Nazism. The state churches were now combined into a single national church, and elections in the autumn, thanks to considerable Nazi intimidation, resulted in the choice of Hitler's candidate Müller as Reich bishop. The purge of Jews and left-wing sympathizers from the civil service and the professions was already under way, and a Ministry of Public Enlightenment and Propaganda had been established for Goebbels. The establishment of a Reich Chamber of Culture in September gave him formal control of all the means of publicity. Thus all the bodies most likely to resist the sway of the dictator had been quickly abolished or neutralized. No doubt the final crushing of the left consoled Hitler's allies for their own decline, and still more important was Hitler's vigorous foreign policy. The Reichstag supported this unanimously when it was allowed to meet. In the autumn Hitler left the League in protest at the non-fulfilment of his demands, and he held a plebiscite and new Reichstag elections on this issue and was overwhelmingly endorsed. Hindenburg broadcast to the nation and called on it to 'support with me and the Reich Chancellor the principle of equal rights and of peace with honour, and show the world that we have recovered, and with the help of God will maintain, German unity!'.

Two great organized bodies were untouched by Hitler, however— the army and big business. He regarded them as essential to German greatness, and had no wish to destroy either. From them, as indeed from the churches also, he wanted obedient but amicable co-operation. So though the government pressed ahead its predecessors' policies of reflation and help to agriculture, it did not implement the anti-capitalist policies of the Nazi left. Hugenberg was succeeded as minister of the economy by Dr Schmitt, head of the largest German insurance company. Schacht, the new president of the Reichsbank, was also a champion of economic orthodoxy. Nazi advocates of a corporate organization on fascist lines, subordinating the businessmen to the party, were pushed aside. A 'combat league of middle-class tradespeople' intended by them to protect the small man against monopolists was dissolved. There was mounting dissatisfaction among the Nazi rank and file at the failure to embark on the 'second revolution' against the capitalists and the old ruling class generally. Its most important leader was Ernst Röhm, the leader of the SA. He wished to get rid of the regular army and replace it with his political force, now over two million strong. He believed that German rearmament must have a 'revolutionary' basis and that the existing generals 'are the same old clods and they'll certainly lose the next war'. This was a striking opinion from a man who had himself been a regular officer, and for long the main liaison between party and army.

Röhm controlled the most powerful force within the party and Hitler was loath to quarrel with him. At the end of 1933 he and Hess, representing the party organization, were brought into the cabinet. The SA was appeased by the grant of pension rights to those killed and injured in their gutter campaigning. But indignation grew in the army, as Röhm developed his military plans and began the more serious arming of his troops. It further became known that Hindenburg's life was at last approaching its end: Hitler was determined to succeed him, and for this he needed the army's help. He had already tried to reassure military opinion with fair words and the exemption of the army from the jurisdiction of civil courts. In April 1934 he is said to have made a bargain with General von Blomberg, the minister of defence, and Fritsch and Raeder the commanders of the army and navy. It is supposed that he agreed to oppose Röhm's plans, and they agreed to back him for the succession. A conference of army leaders subsequently approved the deal. But Hitler could not bring himself to break with Röhm, and tension mounted. Conservatives disgusted at Nazi violence and tyranny and their own loss of influence plucked up courage. On 17 June Papen ventured to deliver at Marburg university a speech of protest composed for him by some young catholic intellectuals. He warned the nation against 'a permanent revolt from below' and called on it to 'join together in fraternal friendship and respect for all our fellow countrymen . . . and to silence fanatics'. When Goebbels suppressed the publication of this speech Papen threatened resignation by all the conservative ministers. Blomberg, with Hindenburg's authority, warned Hitler that unless political tension was relaxed, the president would entrust power to the army.

Hitler therefore had to crush his own left. He was helped by the fact that almost all the Nazi leaders were jealous of Röhm. Goebbels, his main ally, changed sides at the end. At the end of June a bloody purge took place, in which Röhm and other leaders of the SA were liquidated without trial. The work was mainly directed by Göring and the then relatively obscure Himmler. The force employed was the black-shirted SS,[1] a select body under Himmler's command created within the SA and with rather more pretensions to efficiency. Blomberg had prepared the way by a public declaration that the army stood behind Hitler 'who came from its ranks and remains one of ours'. The excuse for the action (which Hitler may have believed) was that Röhm was meditating a coup, and this supposed plot made it possible to cast the net more widely. Not only Gregor Strasser but Schleicher was murdered—the man who had hoped to govern through the Nazi left wing. At the same time, Papen was placed under house arrest and the authors of his famous speech were killed. He was glad to retire from office and escape to the more suitable task of ambassador in Vienna. The SA sank into decorative obscurity. Hitler did not fail to point out (now that they had served their turn) that the SA leaders were a corrupt and profligate body of thugs and plunderers (many of them were homosexual). On 2 August Hindenburg died, and the government at once promulgated a law merging the offices of chancellor and head of state. The armed forces took an oath of loyalty to Hitler —personally. His new position of 'Führer and Chancellor' was confirmed by a plebiscite in which the 38 million affirmative votes were given weight by the fact that over 5 million ventured to vote 'no' or spoil their papers.

Hitler had appeared to give ground in 1934, but he sacrificed nothing that he really valued, and he got rid of the last shred of organized opposition. The extent of his power henceforth is indeed a little hard to gauge because there seems to have been so little desire to oppose him. It is noteworthy that with relatively few exceptions German citizens—unlike those of the Soviet Union—were allowed to travel freely abroad. There was little risk of their 'defecting' or contracting democratic sympathies. However, some bodies were not entirely submissive and there was a revival of opposition from 1937, not out of hostility to Nazism but because Hitler's military and economic policies seemed to have become too ambitious for the safety of the nation. As a result, Hitler notably tightened his hold on the coercive apparatus of the state. Once more, the really dangerous protest came from the army. The generals thought that Hitler was expanding

[1] SS=Schutz Staffeln (defence squads). SA=Sturm Abteilung (storm detachment).

it faster than was compatible with efficiency, and they were terrified that he would come to a collision with the western powers before they were in a state to fight. When, at the end of 1937, he announced his intention of beginning on territorial expansion very soon there were serious protests from Fritsch, the commander-in-chief, echoed by the conservative foreign minister, Neurath. Hitler was very angry and, as in 1934, Göring and Himmler seized the opportunity to enlarge their own importance, this time at the expense of the army. First Blomberg was forced out of office, after the woman whom he had just married (with Göring's encouragement) was discovered to have been a professional prostitute. Then Fritsch was driven out, after the preferment of charges of homosexuality subsequently shown to have been fabricated. Hitler himself took over Blomberg's duties as minister of defence, appointing as his chief of staff in that capacity the entirely subservient Keitel. Fritsch's successor, Brauchitch, was likewise a man less capable of making trouble. Sixteen other generals were retired, and there were comparable changes among the civilians. Neurath and Schacht lost their jobs, and after February 1938 there were no more cabinet meetings at which surviving conservative ministers could make their voice heard.

The effect of this is visible in the ensuing Czech crisis, when Hitler was seriously determined to go to war with the west if necessary and the army was frightened as never before. Brauchitch would do nothing. His chief of staff, Beck, tried to induce the generals to resign in a body. He declared that he was 'for the Führer, against war, against boss rule', and besides greater freedom wanted a halving of the Party's income and 'more Prussian probity and simplicity'. He eventually resigned, but nobody else did. His successor, Halder, was involved in a more serious plan to stage a coup if mobilization was ordered. Several military commanders were involved in this, but they would only act if there was firm evidence that Britain and France would fight if Hitler attacked the Czechs. Envoys were sent to London to procure such evidence, and we cannot know what would have happened if they had succeeded. But the plotters showed little eagerness to seize Hitler and Berlin at the end of September, though the forces were there and popular feeling was clearly averse to war. Like all earlier oppositions to Hitler, this one had been demoralized and could only be nerved to action by an overwhelming new danger. By the time the danger really was overwhelming, even this was not enough to ensure success.

Hitler's growing ascendancy over his army was largely due to the fact that his political judgment was far better than that of the generals, and they increasingly recognized this. His power was also greatly fortified, like Stalin's, by the rise of a younger generation who owed everything to him, and whose personal advancement was their great concern. The younger officers would not follow their seniors in revolt. It was Hitler who had expanded the army and made them what they were, and they were unwilling to desert him. It was also important that Nazi beliefs had a growing hold on the younger generation, and that Hitler, despite his pledges to the army, gradually built up forces more directly under party control. He had never doubted the importance of this, but merely wished to work more cautiously than Röhm and with more concern for military efficiency. Hermann Göring, his second-in-command, had been a fighter pilot in the 1914 war. It was natural that he should be entrusted with the rebuilding of the German air force, the arm *par excellence* of the younger generation. Handsome in youth and obese in his years of power, famous for the brilliance of his uniforms and increasingly occupied in the amassing of wealth, the Reichsmarschall became something of a figure of fun. From 1938 he ranked highest among the military commanders but this was something of a consolation prize: Hitler would not crown his career by making him minister of defence. Until that time, however, nobody had contributed more to the enormous growth of the party's power in the police, in the forces and, we shall see also, in the economy. In retrospect he seems the strongest man among the subordinate Nazi leaders.

In the later years of Nazi power the pace was increasingly made by Heinrich Himmler. A former chicken farmer, whose application greatly exceeded his intelligence, he took half-baked ideas with great seriousness—astrology no less than Nazi ideology. He probably owed his increasing power to Hitler's confidence that he would remain in tame subordination. To the SS and its intelligence arm the SD, under the devilish Heydrich, he added in 1934 the Gestapo created originally by Göring. In 1936 he became minister in control of all the police of the Reich—a further great measure of centralization. The SS was essentially a pretorian guard for the protection first of the Nazi leadership and later of the Nazi state. It eventually became a strong military force independent of the army, and part of it fought at the front. It therefore renewed the party challenge which the army thought it had ended with the downgrading of the SA, and the army hated and feared it accordingly. But its significance was far wider than this: more than any other organization it was the institutional embodiment of the Nazi ideal. Like Lenin, Hitler believed that a revolutionary élite could wield decisive political influence, and that mass action was effective only under the direction of such an élite. The original Nazi movement and the SA had been built up to seize power in a democracy, and they were mass organizations whose main characteristics were simply the bad features of democracy—graft, rowdyism, mob violence and the hatred of ignorance for knowledge. The SS on the other hand, like the Bolsheviks, was a disciplined body of dedicated men, bent on the remoulding of society by systematic violence. The doctrine of race was their fundamental belief, as it was with all Nazis. But with them it did not take the merely demagogic form of a belief in German superiority. The really dedicated Nazis believed in an international élite of true Aryans, comprising some who were not Germans and leaving out a great many who were.

It was in the war that the reshaping of Europe by this supposed élite began, and Nazism finally ceased to be the conservative force that the old ruling class had hoped to make of it. But by 1939 preparations were far advanced. Concentration camps were originally set up by the SA to allow physical maltreatment at leisure, and the profitable ransoming of persons kidnapped and placed in them. There were even attempts to get rid of them as the new government broke with its more disreputable elements. But in 1934 Himmler took them over and made them efficient instruments of systematic terror and, in due course, extermination. His freedom of action was finally consolidated when in 1936 the Gestapo[1] was freed from all legal control. The Nazis did not interfere overmuch with the courts—the judges were a reactionary body, anyway, and prisoners who even so could not be convicted, need not be tried. But terror was given a judicial arm in the Special Court which sat usually in private, and the People's Court which consisted largely of party and SS nominees. The spectacular as well as the silent dispatch of the state's enemies could now be arranged.

Of course, Nazi pressure on the spiritual life of the nation steadily

[1] Geheime Staatspolizei (secret state police).

increased. Goebbels organized both the creative artists and the publicists by press and radio in the different sections of his Chamber of Culture, and he told them what to produce. This venomous lame and ugly dwarf achieved little in the fields of literature and amorous adventure in which he longed to shine, but in oratory and the organizing of propaganda his genius was surpassed only by his master's. In the arts his influence was merely deadening: innovation was condemned as 'decadent'. Music suffered least from being treated thus, and musicians as a body were on good terms with the régime. University teachers out of sympathy with it (a quarter at the very most) were got rid of. School books were rewritten, and teachers had to learn the new ideology. There was already an enormous youth movement in Weimar Germany, run by religious and other private organizations. The Nazis took this over and, until they made membership of the Hitler Youth compulsory in 1938, it was actually smaller than before. The destruction of the catholic youth movement was one of many breaches of the concordat with Rome, and the church was displeased with many Nazi measures—for instance, the law of 1933 for the sterilization of the unfit. In the encyclical 'Mit brennende Sorge' (1937), Pope Pius XI accused the German government of a breach of faith, and foresaw 'destructive religious wars' with no aim but 'extermination'. Among the protestants, too, there was a movement of secession from the authority of the Reich bishop, whose career soon ended. But in 1936–7 many rebellious clergy, notably Pastor Niemöller, were put behind bars, and the rest mostly submitted.

But it was the treatment of the Jews that most clearly pointed the way to come. The Nuremberg Laws (1935) were among the few to which the Nazis gave the added solemnity of passage by the Reichstag. The Jews were deprived of citizenship, and forbidden to marry or have sexual intercourse with Aryans. The occupations from which they were excluded already comprised public employment, farming, the stock exchange and the whole cultural field, and terrorism often deprived them of rights which legally they still might claim. 1938, the year when Nazi rule took a deeper hold all round, ended with a pogrom which served notice that the Nazis were returning to their revolutionary past. On 7 November a Jewish refugee killed a German embassy official in Paris. The Nazis responded with organized anti-Jewish rioting, in which synagogues, shops and houses were burnt down on a large scale and there were a number of murders. Twenty thousand Jews were imprisoned, a fine of a milliard marks was imposed on the whole community and they were forbidden to engage in business or practise law or medicine. Extermination was to be the next step.

The Nazi ascendancy in the world of big business was less pronounced. The discomfiture of the generals in 1938 was accompanied, it is true, by the fall of Schacht. Appointed minister of the economy in 1934, he achieved supreme power in this domain just as the generals began to decline. But in 1936 Göring became Director of the (second) Four Year Plan and emerged as a rival economic authority. The project of a gigantic new state concern (named after himself) to exploit the native low grade iron ore suggested that the party was about to invade the businessmen's domain in a big way. Schacht was increasingly concerned at the economic effects of accelerating rearmament. He gave up his ministry at the end of 1937, and his successor, Funk, was the former chief Nazi fund-raiser among businessmen and acted as Göring's tool. Schacht complained how the businessmen 'crowded into Göring's anteroom in the hope of getting orders when I was still trying to make the voice of reason heard'. Even less than the generals did business leaders try to resist the Nazis: sycophancy and large bribes were their ways of self-preservation.

But the Nazis for their part did not really interfere with the businessmen much. There were many economic controls, and in 1934 the many businessmen's associations were turned into an official corporative structure under a Reich Economic Chamber. On the other hand, the state lent enormous sums to industry, and it looked with a less jealous eye than in Weimar days on the protection of profits through monopolies and cartels. In 1937 a number of small businesses were even dissolved by law. Wages were held down, and the Labour Front, like its Italian and Soviet equivalent, did not protect the workers against the employers but concentrated on welfare work—notably through the great leisure and holiday organization Strength through Joy. The Göring steel enterprise never came to much and the most important Nazi interference with property rights was in agriculture, and that in a conservative sense. Their minister of agriculture, Walter Darré, was unusual among them in being a real expert in his subject. To preserve the peasant proprietors he made all small properties capable of sustaining a family inalienable and indivisible. They could not be foreclosed for the owner's debts, and they passed intact to one son in each family, who had then the obligation of supporting the other members. A powerful state organization promoted stable prices and increased production.

It would be wrong to conclude from this that Hitler was a tool of the capitalists. It was rather that he had only a limited interest in economics, and the views of himself and his principal associates were in this field fairly orthodox. They fully shared the deep fear of inflation which has characterized the German people and all their rulers from 1924 to the present day, and this made them reluctant to break with Schacht or to press ahead as fast as they might have done with rearmament.[1] For Hitler all human existence was based on struggle and the survival of the fittest, and in economic matters that made him a supporter of free enterprise.

The Third Reich presented to the world in 1939 a formidable appearance of monolithic uniformity (*Gleichschaltung*) and efficiency. The reality was a little different. Authority had been centralized, but it was divided between the competing personal empires of the great Nazi leaders. Many old landmarks had been destroyed, but a good part of the old social hierarchy still remained. For all these reasons, planning was often haphazard and policy, domestic and foreign, was made in fits and starts. Hitler's own ascendancy rested in part on the jealousies of his subordinates, and he was personally uninterested in political system building. He never even bothered to replace the Weimar constitution, and it remained theoretically in force. But even in retrospect his government appears uncommonly strong, remarkably intrepid and, above all, of great revolutionary potential.

The Last Years of the Third Republic

The economic collapse of the early thirties was really as fatal to the French as to the German republic, but the first took several years longer to die. The reason was partly that the crisis took longer to develop. France had concentrated in the later twenties on strengthening her currency, and had built up a large gold reserve. She surmounted the financial crisis of 1931, so fatal to Britian and Germany.

---

[1] See B. H. Klein, *Germany's Economic Preparations for War* (Harvard, 1959), Part I. Schacht remained at the Reichsbank till 1939.

Only gradually did her position deteriorate because her currency was now overvalued in terms of those no longer linked to gold. Exports fell, imports increased, home prices fell very heavily, especially for the farmers, and production and consumption went down. Eventually it was clear that the high value of the currency was not securely based on a strong economy, and there was a flight of gold abroad. Even so, as explained already, the worst evils of unemployment were avoided because there was a large immigrant population that could be repatriated.

The other factor that preserved French democracy for a time was a change in the attitude of the Communists. In the twenties they had everywhere voted indiscriminately against bourgeois governments, whether of left or right, and so had weakened the left-inclined forces that in most continental countries were the only firm defenders of democracy. This was partly done on the orders of Moscow, but it was a natural attitude on the far left anyway: its prevalence among the Italian socialists had furthered the rise of Mussolini. In Germany, Stalin was particularly anxious for the Communists to attack the Socialists because they were partisans of German reconciliation with the west. The Communists watched the Nazi rise with complacency, believing that only they could solve the economic problem, and so their turn would come next. But not only did this prove entirely false but the Nazi government ended the Weimar policy of friendship with Russia. It was Stalin's turn to look for friends in the west, and the Communists were told to ally with the moderate left against 'fascism'. This made it easier for French, than it had latterly been for German, parliamentarians to find a majority. But what was more, the majority might be all from the left instead of a combination of moderates of left and right. There would be more chance of finding policies of the necessary boldness on which all could agree. Momentum might yet be regained without the abandonment of democracy.

But the chance was never a very strong one for, even supposing that the Communists did not make trouble, the socialists and radicals of the moderate left had very different economic ideas. Both were suspicious of big business, but the radicals stood largely for the small independent producer and did not like state intervention much either. They continued to be at one with the right in wishing to defend the currency at all costs. Socialists and radicals were the victors in the

16—E.E.P.

elections of 1932, when the right lost their majority and the Communists did badly. But they proved too disunited to be able to govern, and France seemed already to be following the German path. There were repeated ministerial crises because the determination on all sides to balance the budget and defend the franc was in contradiction with the refusal of the moderate left to vote cuts in expenditure. This reflected the important place held among their supporters by employees of the state, whose jobs were threatened by the economies. The economic malaise led in 1933 to a growth of movements pressing for more strength and authority in the state. The Action Française, which had upheld this cause since the days of Dreyfus, had been weakened in 1926 by a condemnation of its views by the Vatican, and it had become too used to scurrilous opposition to be capable of constructive leadership. More important were the Croix-de-Feu, founded by La Roque—at first an ex-servicemen's organization. Notable also were splinter groups on the left, which kept their collectivism but gave it a nationalist setting. Déat of the Socialists created one of these, and so later did Doriot from the Communists. Both were to be props of the Vichy government.

An opportune scandal gave the reviving extreme right a pretext for action. Stavisky was a shady financier who had raised money by selling bonds purporting to be issued by the municipality of Bayonne. In January 1934 he committed suicide. He proved to have many accomplices in high places, and many suspected that they had had him killed to avoid disclosures. The government fell, and the incoming premier, Daladier, began a clean-up by dismissing Chiappe, the influential prefect of police in Paris. His friends swelled the ranks of the discontented, and the result was a huge riot in front of the Palais Bourbon, the meeting-place of the Chamber (6 February). This, too, caused a change of government and more, a swing to the right. As in 1926, the radicals deserted the socialists and combined with more conservative parties. The new government of Gaston Doumergue was given power to cut expenditure by decree, and thus briefly restored confidence in the franc. The premier took to appealing beyond parliament to the people by broadcast speeches. He desired to reform the constitution in a way that would have given him more the position of his English equivalent. An appeal to the country by the government was to be made easier, and it was to have the sole right to propose expenditure. This was too much for the radicals and he was over-thrown, whereat the extreme right staged a huge demonstration in his honour. In 1935 the leakage of gold began again and Laval took office, again with emergency powers and the sympathy of the extreme right. He cut not only expenditure but prices and wages as well in an attempt to save the currency. The French Brüning (to say the least) had arrived.

That the authoritarian trend was halted was due partly to the fact that the deflationary measures which it made possible merely made the depression deeper, and did not long serve even the primary con-servative purpose of protecting the currency. Developments in foreign affairs greatly helped to turn discontent into action. Laval, as we shall see, made a rather unwilling attempt to conclude an alliance with Soviet Russia against Germany, and a much more serious one to retain the friendship of Mussolini by being conciliatory over Abyssinia. This offended the British. One half of his policy led the Communists to rally to the republic; the other half led the radicals, who valued British friendship, to turn to the left again. Co-operation between socialists and Communists began at the municipal elections in the spring of 1935. A national committee then arose which organized massive demonstrations of the united left on 14 July, the great republican festival. Communists, socialists and a few radicals led by Edouard Daladier took part. They pledged themselves to unite to give 'bread to the workers, work to the young and peace to the world' and 'defend and develop democratic freedoms'. In the autumn the radical party decided to adhere to the new movement, and the communist and socialist trade unions amalgamated. Early in 1936 the radical ministers left the government and Laval resigned. In the elections of April 1936 what was now called the Popular Front won 386 seats against the 222 of the parties of the right. There were 149 socialists, 109 radicals and 72 communists (instead of 10). The socialist leader, Léon Blum, formed the next ministry—the first leader of the main socialist party ever to do so.

The new government managed in little more than a year of office to give France a decided impulse towards recovery. But, as in 1932 and 1924, the left had won the elections largely because it had united for political reasons and ignored the fact that it was not really at one on economic policy. The Front's economic slogan was 'neither deflation nor devaluation'. They hoped to restore prosperity without offending their middle-class adherents by going off gold. Their main remedy was to raise purchasing power. They expected increased demand to lead to increased production, and so to a general economic recovery which would restore strength to the franc. The workers took the initiative after the election by staging widespread strikes and occupying factories. This was as much a political as an economic demonstration, associated with the Front's pledge to nationalize certain industries. The new government had to put an end to the confusion by mediation, and Blum virtually dictated a substantial wage increase to the employers. This was followed by legislation establishing a forty-hour week without loss of earnings and holidays with pay. These measures were partly meant to spread the available amount of employment among more workers. Workers and employers agreed to establish factory committees, and a system of consultation in each industry for regulating conditions of work. Legislation provided that agreements negotiated between workers' and employers' organizations might be made binding even on those who were not parties to them. To raise farmers' incomes a state grain monopoly was instituted which doubled the price of wheat.

But the raising of prices and shortening of hours was not the way to improve the competitive position of a country whose currency was already overvalued. The nationalization of the Bank of France, suspected of having exercised a stranglehold on the economy, made no difference. The nationalization of the armaments industry did not prevent a drop in production that was to be especially serious for the French air force in the coming emergencies. In September the government was at last obliged to devalue the franc: the Bank of France was given a fund with which to maintain its value within certain limits laid down by law. A real recovery now began, but it was limited in extent by the dampening effect of the measures already taken on efficiency, and still more on the confidence of businessmen, who feared further steps towards socialism. In March 1937 the government announced a 'pause', tried to balance the budget and called in three bankers to advise it in order to reassure business opinion. But in June, unable to moderate its followers' desires, it quarrelled with them and asked parliament for powers to establish exchange controls and forced loans by decree. These measures of coercion against the capitalists were too much for the radicals of the senate, where the moderate wing of the party predominated. The government was defeated there, and succeeding ministries likewise failed to get the radicals to vote for a left-wing solution of the economic problem. By April 1938 the Popular Front was at an end.

Economically, its work was fruitfully continued by its successor, a renewed combination of radicals and conservatives presided over by Daladier. The attempt to maintain a minimum value for the franc had had to be given up, and its depreciation continued. The new government secured powers once more to remedy the ills of the economy by decree. By the autumn they had plucked up courage to use their powers to abrogate the forty-hour week. Employers might require their men to work overtime for higher rates of pay. A strike in protest against this was a failure—party because it was also a protest against Munich, which many workers in their hearts approved of. This in itself did much to restore business confidence. The ministry of finance was given to Paul Reynaud—a conservative, but the only important politician of either left or right who had not made a fetish of the currency. As early as 1933 he had urged a moderate devaluation, with reliance on sound management of the state finances to prevent inflation. He now managed to stabilize the franc at a low level. Capital that had fled abroad returned, and longer hours of work made it easier to revive production—especially by ending 'bottlenecks' due to the shortage of labour in certain industries. But when war came, France had still not quite recovered the degree of prosperity she had known in 1929, and there were still more unemployed than in 1933.

The economic situation, though mediocre, was improving. But the political situation got steadily worse. The Communists had refused to join the Blum government, and so were able to escape responsibility for its failures and denounce the moderate left as traitors. Blum's failure to help the Spanish republicans particularly incensed them. In 1939 Stalin and Hitler made friends, and Soviet policy no longer required the Communists to support the French republic. They came out in opposition to the war of 1939 and were proscribed. At the opposite extreme, the attempt to build up movements recalling the stormtroopers was suppressed by the Blum government. A conspiratorial organization, the Cagoule, was also broken up. The ultra-right appeared to consist only of some small parliamentary groups.

But conservative sympathies were moving in their direction, just as disillusioned men on the left were turning from the democratic parties to the communists. The figure of Léon Blum served especially as a focus of hatred on the right. A refined bourgeois man of letters, he was regarded as the traitor who opened the gate to social revolution: especially incriminating was the fact that he was a Jew. He was badly beaten up just before he became prime minister, and the verbal violence against him at all times was astonishing. We shall never know how well the two extremes would have done in the elections that were due in 1940. With a little luck the French republic might have survived until better times—as might the Weimar republic. But physically and morally it was in no state to fight a war and defeat was fatal to it. In June 1940 parliament turned to the aged Marshal Pétain, the hero of Verdun. After he had made peace with Germany and Italy, the two chambers in joint session conferred plenary powers on him and were indefinitely adjourned. France now had her Hindenburg, with the powers of a Hitler. Five hundred and sixty-nine parliamentarians had voted for this solution and only eighty against. As in Germany in 1933, the Communists had been removed from the scene already.

The interest of this tragic history lies mainly in the contrast between the behaviour of the French Communists at this time, and the earlier behaviour of the extreme left in Germany and Italy. Would anything have been gained if the revolutionaries in those countries had helped to defend constitutional democracy against Mussolini and Hitler? The French experiment makes it clear that there were good reasons for answering in the negative. The united left was unable to save the republic by restoring prosperity. In so far as they made any progress in this direction, it was mainly by paving the way for a recovery on orthodox capitalist lines, and so the strengthening of the enemies of the left. Also, the more the republic seemed to be kept in being by the votes of revolutionaries, the more disloyal to it did the propertied classes become. The fact remains that the republic was a little farther from crisis in 1939 than in 1935, and that solid gains had been made by the peasantry and working class. If the left had failed to restore prosperity, it was perhaps because it was not ingenious enough rather than because the balance of political forces made the thing impossible. The ideas and policy of Reynaud show that it was not entirely impossible to win sensible conservatives for a radical and forward-looking policy of the right kind. But all that is certain is that in all these western countries the revolutionary left failed to gain power for itself. In France it is particularly hard to see how it could have done so. The revolutionary forces in the towns had been repeatedly defeated there by the huge conservative forces of the middle class and peasantry. Democracy was the only feasible alternative to fascism.

4: Southern Europe and German Rearmament

When Hitler took office in 1933 Germany was virtually free both of foreign occupation and of reparations. But she was still forbidden to have more than the smallest armaments, and the substantial territorial expansion which Hitler wanted could not begin until this prohibition was overcome. In the end he was able to defy with impunity all the restrictions laid upon the German forces at Versailles. For this there were several reasons. Since Locarno the western powers had increasingly come to believe that the wisest course was to treat Germany as an equal. It was difficult to avoid carrying this policy to its logical conclusion—equality in armaments. It was hard also to reverse it merely because there had been a change of government in Germany—especially as Hitler was prolific in assurances of good intentions. Economic difficulties were at their worst in Britain and France in the years down to 1936, and neither country was eager to embark on a more vigorous foreign policy. As the duplicity of Hitler grew more obvious, attempts were nevertheless made to build up a front against him. But these were too feeble to survive the outbreak of a new crisis centred on southern Europe. Italy attacked Abyssinia, and then became involved in a Spanish civil war that increasingly became a trial of strength between the European left and right. The attempt to isolate Germany had failed.

German Rearmament Begins

In 1932 the world disarmament conference for which preparations had been in progress all through the twenties at last met. The Germans had begun to take up the armaments question as the next one on which concessions could be wrung from the allies, and plans were being laid for the re-expansion of the forces. France was on the defensive. She put forward a plan by which more powerful weapons like bombers and battleships might only be used in certain prescribed cases, and a strong international force would be created to maintain security. This was traditional French doctrine and met no more support than in 1919. There was far more sympathy for Brüning when, just before his fall, he asked that the German army might be doubled and the prohibitions on German possession of certain weapons removed in principle. Next, President Hoover proposed large specific cuts in the heavier weapons, and even fascist Italy agreed to this but not the French. Papen's government therefore withdrew from the conference until the principle of German equality with the other powers in the field of armaments was conceded. She was no longer ready to remain disarmed if no other power would disarm, and most of the other governments considered this right. The French therefore gave ground: their new plan allowed all the continental powers, including Germany, to have a short-service conscript army. In December 1932 it was agreed that the disarmament convention should give Germany 'equality of rights in a system which would provide security for all nations', and Germany returned to the conference in triumph.

Hitler therefore inherited from his predecessors a splendid diplomatic position, and it went on improving with little effort on his part. Early in 1933 the British produced a disarmament plan which specified levels of force in considerable detail and gave Germany the prospect of equality in five years. A Permanent Commission was to verify that the restrictions were being observed, and by way of compensating France for the diminution of her powers of self-defence, the prospect of United States help under the Kellogg Pact was invoked. Stimson, while secretary of state, had advanced the view that the pact bound the Americans to consult in the case of supposed aggression, and the new president, Roosevelt, accepted this view and promised not to obstruct sanctions against an aggressor. Fear of this happening had long deterred the other English-speaking countries from binding themselves to impose sanctions. After some hesitation, Hitler accepted the British draft in principle, and made a brilliant speech in May which went far to convince the world of his desire for disarmament. But the French were not satisfied. They insisted on amendments to the plan which would keep Germany disarmed for another four years and give her equality only after eight. The British and Americans tried to induce Germany to accept these proposals, but in October Hitler seized the opportunity to leave not only the disarmament conference but the League as well, with the claim that Germany had been denied justice. The German military budget for 1934–5 showed a virtual doubling of expenditure, and £10 million was allocated to the development of a prohibited arm—the air force. The other powers, too, began to rearm in 1934, and the disarmament conference petered out.

Mussolini, meanwhile, had begun to show signs of restlessness beneficial to Hitler. In March 1933 he proposed to Germany, Britain and France a pact by which they were to co-operate in the revision of the peace treaties within the framework of the League. This reflected Italy's own dissatisfaction at the peace settlement, her embarrassment at the prospect of having to take sides in a serious conflict between Germany and France and, above all, her usual desire to show herself a great power. The French had no wish to see European frontiers disturbed, but they did not want to push Mussolini into friendship with Germany. Eventually they succeeded in making the text of the treaty sufficiently meaningless to be signed without danger. But their allies in eastern Europe were terrified by this—as it now seems—anticipation of Munich. Poland was further incensed at not being invited to join herself: she, too, yearned to be treated as a great power. In November she approached Germany for an assurance that she would not use force to decide the issues between them. Hitler had been disturbed by the conclusion of a Polish-Soviet non-aggression pact in 1932.[1] He agreed to the Polish request, and a declaration was signed in January 1934. The effectiveness of France's anti-German alliances was called in question.

But France was by no means helpless, and in 1934–5 staged a diplomatic counter-offensive. Hitler's advent gave her a big new asset almost at once. Though he did not quarrel violently with Russia, relations with her cooled, and military collaboration ceased by the end of 1933. More afraid than ever of a capitalist alliance against him, Stalin seized the opportunity of Hitler's withdrawal from the League to make a declaration friendly to it. Barthou, the French foreign minister, energetically set about making something of this. He pressed for the admission of Russia to the League, with a seat on the Council, and in September 1934 secured it, unwelcome though it was

[1] E. M. Robertson, *Hitler's Pre-War Policy and Military Plans* (1963), p. 5.

to many members. He visited the capitals of France's east European friends, and put forward a plan for an 'eastern Locarno', by which Germany, Russia, Poland, Czechoslovakia and the Baltic states guaranteed each other's security. Germany politely rejected this plan, and it was also turned down by Poland, where there was now less fear of Germany and no wish to get too close to Russia. France had offered Russia a guarantee of her frontiers as an inducement to join in security measures, and what eventually came of Barthou's initiatives was the conclusion of Franco-Russian and Russo-Czech defensive alliances in May and June 1935.

Nazi turbulence by then had begun to drive Italy into the arms of France. Austria had been undergoing an economic and political collapse parallel to Germany's, and the growing Nazi movement there was eager to take advantage of this to overthrow the republic and bring about union with the new Reich. Italy was the power most strongly opposed to this. The little Austrian state protected her from German pressure very much as the demilitarized Rhineland protected France. Dr Dollfuss,[1] the Austrian chancellor and leader of the catholic party, therefore leaned increasingly on Mussolini, and on the Heimwehr, a nationalist paramilitary organization supported by Italy. Early in 1933 he ended parliamentary government, and a year later bloodily suppressed the socialist movement. Austria became an 'authoritarian corporative state', rather like Salazar's Portugal. But the process of its creation made Dollfuss many enemies. Socialists did not scruple to pass over to the Nazis in search of revenge. Nazi Germany tried to undermine his government by economic pressure and wireless propaganda. Hitler had no immediate plans for the absorbtion of Austria. This German people might be expected to work with him of their own accord, without needing to be conquered. Now and for a long time, his policy was to gain for the pro-German element a chance to assert themselves and so 'obviate the need for actual *Anschluss*'.[2] He had always wanted good relations with Italy, making himself unpopular with many other nationalists by contending that for the sake of this no attempt should be made to liberate the Germans of the south Tyrol from Italian rule. He did his best now to reassure Mussolini, who already had fairly warm feelings for his

[1] Under five feet tall: 'the Millemeternich.'
[2] Robertson, p. 14.

brother dictator. But the SA in Austria were as rowdy and insubordinate as their German brethren, and Hitler does not seem to have had the heart to check the longing for union with Germany among his compatriots.[1] At the end of July 1934 they staged a putsch in Vienna, and murdered Dollfuss.

Already in February 1934 Britain, France and Italy had declared their 'common view' that Austrian independence should be maintained. Mussolini was now furious and began to send troops to the frontier. The Nazi revolt was put down (simultaneously with the purge of the too turbulent SA in Germany) and Hitler abandoned all provocative action. Papen was sent as ambassador to restore good relations with Austria's rulers (of whom he was the German equivalent). But Italy nevertheless moved towards France. Barthou was faced with the problem of reconciling France's friends the Yugoslavs to this rapprochement with their enemies. It was when King Alexander was visiting him to discuss the question that the two men were assassinated at Marseilles. Thus perished the toughest and most resourceful French opponent of Hitler. Laval was the new foreign minister, and in January 1935 he concluded agreements with Italy settling colonial disputes and providing for general co-operation in Europe. The two powers were to consult in the event of a threat to Austrian independence, and encourage a pact between the Danubian states pledging them to abstain from intervention in each other's affairs. They also agreed to act together if any power (meaning Germany) unilaterally abandoned her obligations in respect of armaments. Britain associated herself with these objectives.

Hitler, however, soon responded by stepping up his rearmament. After leaving the League he had produced a disarmament plan of his own. In the usual fashion, the French were hostile to it, and the British and Italians tried to mediate. But the reappearance of a German air force caused the British to be apprehensive about their own security—for the first time, really, since the German fleet had been scuttled in 1919. Early in 1935 they announced a notable increase in armaments expenditure, while the French at the same time began to restore the efficiency of their army by lengthening the period of service for conscripts from one to two years. This made it desirable

---

[1] He only ceased to be an Austrian citizen in 1932, in order to stand for the German presidency.

for Hitler to move faster in order to catch up, and he was emboldened to do so by success in the plebiscite held in January 1935 to decide whether the Saar should return to German sovereignty. While the international régime established in 1919 (above p. 322) continued, he dared not infringe the peace treaty too grossly for fear that the allies would retaliate by depriving the Saarlanders of their right to opt for Germany after fifteen years. In March 1935, however, Germany officially acknowledged the existence of her air force and went on to reintroduce conscription. The peacetime strength of the German army was to be thirty-six divisions (say 550,000 men). No longer was mere parity with other powers the stated aim: these proposals would give Germany superiority over France in peace and war.

Britain, France and Italy responded with apparent vigour by a meeting of heads of government at Stresa in April. They condemned the unilateral action which Germany had taken, and reaffirmed their loyalty to the Locarno Pacts and their previous declarations concerning Austria. The Council of the League, at their invitation, issued a declaration censuring Germany, and set up a committee to consider how economic and financial sanctions might be applied against an aggressor. The Franco-Russian alliance soon followed. The front against Germany appeared to have been consolidated. If appearances had been all, German rearmament would at worst have been innocuous, neutralized by the co-operation of the other leading European powers.

In fact, it was obvious from the start that the combination against Hitler was not really very strong. To begin with, Britain and France had abandoned hope of really preventing German rearmament. Instead, they had been planning to make Germany pay a price for it by joining the 'eastern Locarno' which the French had been planning. The Stresa declaration therefore only complained weakly of 'unilateral repudiation . . . at a moment when steps were being taken to promote a freely negotiated settlement'. The desire for such a settlement was something that Hitler could exploit, particularly in the case of the British. They were directly concerned only with the growth of German air and sea power, and Hitler had as yet so little of either that he could afford to be conciliatory. He had let it be known that he would be willing to restrict his naval strength to 35 per cent of the British, and he took up the idea of an 'air Locarno', by which the western powers would guarantee each other against air attack. Anglo-German talks continued despite the German repudiation of Versailles. In May Hitler made one of his clever, conciliatory speeches, in which he offered to confine himself to parity in the air and 35 per cent of British naval strength. In June the British broke the Stresa front by concluding a naval agreement on the lines indicated, but conceding parity to Germany in submarines. Hitler's May speech had affected the other powers as well. He reassured them all by promising to respect the Locarno Pact—a treaty unlike Versailles in being voluntarily entered into. But he also complained that its meaning had been made doubtful by the conclusion of the Franco-Russian alliance. This was a shrewd appeal to conservative sentiment in France, hostile to the new bond with the Soviet government, and more was to come of it. He further promised to respect the integrity of Austria, which of course was pleasant news for Italy. It was on that side, in fact, that the Stresa front at last broke down completely—but for reasons only loosely connected with German affairs.

The Abyssinian and Rhineland Crises

By 1933 Mussolini appeared to have lived down much of his earlier intemperance. He was merely the most flamboyant of the cautious, conservative statesmen who had largely dominated Europe for a decade. His early attitude to Hitler, though sympathetic, was also patronizing. But gradually he tried to imitate and emulate him, stressing the revolutionary instead of the conservative side of fascism. He responded to economic confusion by attempts at planning and control. Entering the Spanish civil war, he did much to give it the character of an international ideological conflict. The formation of the Rome–Berlin Axis gradually led to the forming of a nazi-fascist international crusade (or disruptive movement) in which a purely political alliance was reinforced by ideological solidarity. The most notable sign of this was the introduction from 1938 of antisemitic legislation in Italy. The fascists had never previously had anything against the Jews, though they had persecuted the Slav and German minorities in the frontier provinces. Mussolini was thus trying to convert his followers into nazis. His desire to keep up with Hitler having led him into the Second World War and to defeat and overthrow, he ended as a nazi puppet, presiding over a revolutionary fascist republic.

The Abyssinian affair played an important part in all this. It led to a breach between Mussolini and the European democracies, and their attempt to restrain him by economic sanctions hastened his efforts to build up a planned economy geared to war needs. But it does not seem at first to have had much to do with Mussolini's evolution into a disrupter of Europe. It was rather more a piece of old-style colonial expansion, such as had been until lately considered quite respectable in Europe. Like Japanese aggression in China, it was largely a response to the growth of nationalism in the country to be conquered, which made peaceful penetration more difficult. The Italians had long been confident that by this latter means they could gradually make good their failure to subdue Abyssinia by force. In 1923 they had promoted Abyssinian membership of the League, in face of British opposition[1] and largely with the object of preventing any British attempt to expand in the area. In 1928 there was a friend-ship pact between the two countries, and the Italians were given a contract to build a main road from their port of Assab to Dessyé, half-way to the Abyssinian capital, Addis Ababa. But the regent, Ras Tafari, who in 1930 became the Emperor Haile Selassie, had no in-tention of becoming another King Zog of Albania. As early as 1925 he had nullified an Anglo-Italian agreement envisaging the establish-ment of spheres of influence in his country by complaining about it to the League. The work of developing the country was entrusted to no single power. The Italian highway from Assab was not built. In 1933 Mussolini lost patience and ordered General de Bono, his minister of colonies, to prepare a full-scale invasion. He maintained that he took action when he did in order to have his hands free again to oppose Hitler by the time that he was militarily strong enough to consider the conquest of Austria. This at first was the only link be-tween European and African events, and we have only Mussolini's word for it.

In December 1934 Italian troops from Somaliland clashed with a body of Abyssinians at Wal-Wal, in territory to which both states laid claim. The matter was brought before the League, and the Italians were induced, with many delays and difficulties, to allow arbitration

[1] On the legitimate ground that slavery was rife there.

in accordance with the friendship treaty of 1928 to decide who was responsible for the affray. But the League turned a deaf ear to the requests of Abyssinia, from March 1935 onward, that it investigate the big preparations for an attack upon her that were being made in the Italian colonies. This was due to the desire of the Stresa powers to keep together against Hitler. Laval, who directed French policy throughout 1935 and headed the government for most of it, was particularly eager to appease Mussolini. He was accused of having promised to support Italy's plans in the negotiations of January. This he always denied, but France did agree to sell Italy a share in Abyssinia's only railway. The British government's attitude was essentially the same. An official enquiry suggested that Italian expansion would not endanger imperial defence. The two great colonial powers felt, as with Japan, a great reluctance to oppose the imperial ambitions of other states with whom they had been able to work amicably. In June Anthony Eden, who had been appointed a special Minister for League Affairs, visited Mussolini and offered him a province of Abyssinia, to be paid for by a British cession of part of Somaliland which would give the African state its own port. In August and September Britain and France put forward plans for a sort of League protectorate over Abyssinia, behind which the Italians would be able to undertake extensive economic penetration.

The Council of the League was obliged to defer to Anglo-French policy, having no means of influencing events without their support. But Britain and France did not succeed in appeasing Mussolini, and they aroused considerable popular opposition. Italy rejected the offers made to her and on 4 September presented to the League an enormous memorandum charging the Abyssinian government with being backward and oppressive, and having committed or condoned a host of offences against Italians over a space of twenty years. On 3 October the Italian attack began. In June there had been published in Britain the results of the so-called Peace Ballot, in which over ten million voters pronounced themselves in favour of membership of the League, disarmament and economic measures against aggressors. In the general election that autumn the government found it wise to come out strongly in favour of collective security. A similar spirit was apparent in the rise of the Popular Front in France and these were only two manifestations of a movement of feeling that was strong in most countries. In September, therefore, Sir Samuel Hoare in the League Assembly pledged Britain to join in 'collective resistance' to aggression, and his lead was generally followed. When the fighting began the Council pronounced Italy to be acting in breach of the Covenant, and the overwhelming majority of the members in the Assembly pronounced themselves in favour of sanctions.

Britain and France had not really altered their policy, however. They refrained from censuring Italy in strong terms, and oddly tried to continue negotiations while applying sanctions. This was done slowly and incompletely. Three League members with special ties with Italy (Austria, Hungary and Albania) had refused to vote for measures against her, so the sanctions were not legally League measures at all, but were imposed by an informal conference of the fifty members who wanted them. This conference, of course, could only make recommendations; it had to avoid measures especially damaging to the economies of the states that would be asked to apply them, and it had to reckon with the supplies that Italy could draw from states not belonging to the League or joining in sanctions. Germany and the United States were especially important in this respect. Eventually, the supply of arms to Italy was cut off, lending to her and importing from her was forbidden, and so was the supply of certain articles which came almost exclusively from the boycotting states. The United States helped by imposing a ban on the export of arms to either side, as required by the recently passed Neutrality Act. The American government unofficially discouraged their businessmen from supplying Italy with goods involved in the boycott, and this was not done on an important scale from any quarter. But such vital commodities as oil, steel and coal were not covered by the sanctions, nor was there any move to sever diplomatic relations or close the Suez Canal. Italy, indeed, was able to mount a diplomatic offensive against Abyssinia which made it almost impossible for her to buy arms anywhere. When it became likely that an embargo on Italian oil supplies might be imposed, Laval tried to forestall it by peace proposals. He managed to win Hoare, the British foreign secretary, to a plan whereby Italy was to be given large tracts of Abyssinia, and a virtual protectorate over much of what was left. Universal execration greeted his plan of December 1935, and Hoare was driven from office and replaced by Eden. But Laval had managed to get a good deal of time wasted.

The curious double policy of Britain and France might have worked if Abyssinia had been able to hold out longer. Her troops had little beyond small arms, but they were enormously helped by the lack of roads and the abundance of mountain and desert. The initial Italian advance soon came to a halt. The stoppage of Italian exports brought a great drain on their reserves of foreign currency, sufficient to exhaust them within a year. If the Abyssinians could hold out until the summer rains stopped the fighting, Italy would have to accept a compromise, as Britain and France desired. But in the end Italy proved able to win in time. De Bono was replaced by the much more forceful Badoglio. In the new year the Italians began using gas in their air attacks: mustard gas especially did great damage to the barefoot troops and scantily clad populace of Abyssinia. From the end of January 1936 a series of great attacks from the north broke through the mountain defences. The Emperor himself suffered a decisive defeat at the end of March. Graziani was able simultaneously to advance from Somaliland, which poor communications made a secondary theatre. At the beginning of May Addis Ababa fell, the Emperor left the country in the belief that further bloodshed was useless, and his title was assumed by the King of Italy. Victory had been won by a relentless use of air and motor power, made possible by a huge effort in the construction of roads and airfields. The massive bribery of dissident local chieftains had also been important.

As the pressure on the Abyssinians mounted, so too did the pressure within the League for really effective sanctions. Oil became increasingly the test case: if Italy's tanks and aircraft could be halted, the day might be saved. After the confusion caused by the Hoare-Laval plan, an expert committee was appointed in February 1936 which quickly reported that Italy only had stocks of oil for three and a half months, that League members and the United States controlled almost all the available supplies and that if the Americans refused to join in a boycott it would nevertheless be effective if League members denied Italy the use of their tankers. The appeasers were thus deprived of their main argument against extending sanctions: that they would only work for commodities which could only be obtained from League members. At the beginning of March Eden announced that Britain would be willing to join in an oil embargo, but France insisted on a further attempt at a negotiated settlement. By the time that the belligerents had expressed their willingness to negotiate, a more urgent matter had distracted Anglo-French attention.

Germany followed a very discreet line during the Abyssinian crisis, not applying sanctions but not allowing Italy to increase purchases from her. She was rewarded by the favour of both sides. In January Mussolini told the German ambassador, Hassell, that Stresa was dead and Italy would not mind if Austria became a 'German satellite'.[1] Early in February Hitler decided that the moment had come to repudiate Locarno and regain his right to station his forces in the Rhineland. For this purpose a convenient pretext was provided by the ratification of the Franco-Russian alliance, which was so disliked by conservative opinion in France that it was only at this point laid before parliament. Also in February the British began very secret approaches to Germany on the subject of revising the Locarno Pacts. Another of their strategic enquiries had led to the conclusion that the absence of German troops from the Rhine was of no value to Britain, and they were keen to get a treaty limiting air forces instead. Hitler's first idea had been that Mussolini might take the lead in denouncing Locarno, but in the end he made the first move himself and relied on British rather than Italian sympathy. On 27 February the French chamber accepted the Russian alliance. On 7 March German troops marched into the demilitarized zone, and Hitler, in a speech before the Reichstag, justified his action but went on to offer new pacts to safeguard both his eastern and western neighbours, including an air pact. He also offered to rejoin the League, which was satisfactory to Britain but highly displeasing to Mussolini.

France and Belgium would have been within their rights in treating Germany's action as a flagrant breach of the Locarno settlement and marching against her. The French army was still very much stronger than the German and would have beaten it easily. But the French generals did not think that their peacetime strength was sufficient for this any longer and called for measures of mobilization. The French government dared not face the unpopularity which this would bring upon them. France had reached an economic and political nadir. Laval's deflationary policy had failed, and he had fallen. But the elections which were to bring the Popular Front to power had yet to be held. A caretaker ministry was in office which could not

[1] For what follows see especially Robertson, pp. 66–81.

readily give a lead. France therefore appealed to the Council of the League—the procedure laid down for cases of a suspected but not flagrant breach of the Locarno treaty. Attempts were made without success to get both Britain and Italy to take a strong line. The Council formally pronounced Germany to be in the wrong, but nothing else was done. Attempts to negotiate new agreements with Germany soon petered out: they revealed as much discord between Britain and France as between those powers and Hitler. In October the ruin of Locarno was completed by Belgium's withdrawal from it. Since the war she had been in virtual alliance with France, but she now tried to retreat into the position of neutrality which she had occupied before 1914. This, of course, was because she had lost faith in France, and it meant that France was once more open to attack from the north. Under pressure from Germany, France could contemplate no further steps to help Abyssinia. Mussolini had agreed in principle to end the war by negotiation, but he was soon able to claim that there was nobody to negotiate with. He was not effectively contradicted.

In 1936 Hitler completed the demolition of the military disabilities under which Germany had been placed in 1919. His aggressive attacks upon them, at a time when Germany was almost defenceless and her soldiers counselled caution, are a matchless example of political courage. But it will be seen that he always had good reason to believe that Britain and France would give him most of what he wanted by negotiation. What he achieved by unilateral action was mainly the avoidance of vexing conditions. The general reasons for Anglo-French complaisance have already been given. A more immediate reason for the British attitude was the selfish and stupid belief that the German army was no danger to them if limitations were placed on the German navy and air force. Of course, this had been true after 1870, but it was not merely German weakness at sea that had preserved Britain then. More important was Bismarck's preference for stability and his re-jection of frantic policies of expansion. Hitler's priorities were differ-ent. A crucial feature of French policy was their unwillingness to re-sist Hitler by force. They refused him—to start with—the legal right to rearm. But this expressed not so much the determination to hold him down as the desire not to have to fight him. France had tried to make treaties do the work of armies; when they collapsed, she was content to withdraw to her inner and real defences, the Maginot line and the still powerful but sluggish army behind it.

The desire of conservative Frenchmen (and many conservative Englishmen) to buy the help of Mussolini against Hitler was bitterly reviled by the friends of the League and Abyssinia, and has been so ever since. This is not entirely fair. With rearmament everywhere under way, the keeping of a balance of power in Europe so as to preserve the independence of its states was coming to be of great importance. It could be claimed that the destruction of what was still, despite its Emperor's efforts, a barbarous and chaotic kingdom was a small price to pay. It was unjust to sacrifice the independence of black men to preserve that of white men—but it was practicable. Africa had been carved up hitherto without setting injurious precedents for aggression in Europe: the two things, however mistakenly, were felt to be different. On the other hand, the fact remains that if France had been willing to attack Hitler when he was legally in the wrong but still without arms, she would not have had to turn to Mussolini. Even leaving that aside, the motives of the French conservatives, their whole willingness to resist Hitler, remain highly suspect. The proper way to maintain a balance of power against Hitler would have been to bring not only Italy but also the Soviet Union into a solid front against Germany. This seems to have been what Barthou was trying to do. Laval on the other hand, though he concluded the alliance with Russia, did so without enthusiasm and never strove to make it a practical reality. The unpopularity of the treaty in France was cleverly exploited by Hitler as we have seen. The growing cleavages in French society were clearly expressed in divisions on foreign policy. The left wanted friendship with Britain and Russia. The right preferred Italy, and many in the end, Laval at their head, were to be tools of the Nazis. By contrast, the more resolute Hitler and Stalin used ideology only as a tool in foreign affairs—they were not slaves to it. Mussolini was to become so, to his cost.

The crises of 1935–6 were fatal to the League, which was not taken seriously again though there were discussions about reforming it. The failure to preserve Abyssinia was aggravated when France tried to make the League the scapegoat for her own ineffectiveness on the Rhine. But the Abyssinian affair showed, on the other hand, a great strengthening of the belief in the ideals for which the League stood.

Hitherto most countries had been very reluctant to consider sanctions against aggressors, and they had wanted to avoid having to help nations remote from themselves and their interests. Though there had been occasional surges of feeling against war, the organizing of peace had mainly attracted the interest of enlightened statesmen and a smallish body of idealists. Now sanctions were tried for the first time, and fifty nations were willing to apply them. It was public opinion rather than the statesmen immediately responsible that demanded this great new departure. The country being defended was of little practical concern even to Britain and France, who had been traditionally interested in it. Especially noteworthy was the support for the League from the hitherto strongly isolationist British Dominions.

Of course, it was still only a section of the public that responded in this way. Nationalism, both aggressive and isolationist, was powerful everywhere. Italian opinion seems to have been solidly behind its government. Isolationism had strengthened in the United States, which was less active than in the Manchurian crisis.[1] The British Peace Ballot showed many more people in general favour of the League than were prepared to contemplate military action against an aggressor. These limitations were what counted at the time. But in retrospect it is the growth of support for collective security that is striking. No doubt it was mainly the popular reaction (especially on the left) to the emergence of obvious and dramatic villains, enemies of democracy and now turning to the offensive. Ideological garnishing gave collective security a savour that it had hitherto lacked. But it was too late to save the League. Instead, it began the emotional preparation among the democracies for the Second World War. Having called for sanctions in defence of Abyssinia the British public were at length to accept the need to fight for Poland—no less unthinkable in the twenties.

In 1936 the ideological conflict still existed mainly in the popular imagination. There was no secret understanding, as was commonly thought at the time, between Hitler and Mussolini. There was sympathy between them, but they helped each other mainly by accident. Italy, once Abyssinia was swallowed, wished to return to the League and be reconciled to her Stresa partners. Anglo-French policy sought

[1] Naturally enough: the Americans hated Japan, whereas there are many Italian Americans.

to promote this: sanctions were lifted and the League did not bind its members, as in the case of Manchuria, not to recognize the new settlement. Britain and France failed to induce the other members to turn the Abyssinian representative out of the Assembly—indeed, the fugitive Emperor was allowed to address it. The Italians therefore left the League. But an entirely fresh development was needed to draw Germany and Italy together—the Spanish civil war.

The Rise and Fall of the Spanish Republic

Spain was unique in Europe in experiencing a revolution by the left at the time of the great economic collapse. One, though not the only reason for Primo's fall in 1930, was the mismanagement of the finances and consequent depreciation of the peseta. The king replaced the discredited dictator by another general, and at first all went on as before. But no progress was made in the creation of a new constitutional system that looked capable of lasting. In 1931 the experiment of free municipal elections was tried, which resulted in a republican landslide in the towns. The army had little affection left for the unstable monarch who had loved it so much: his insistence on the execution of two republican officers who had rebelled was particularly resented. It withdrew its support from him and he left the country. A constituent assembly was elected which contained almost no monarchists. It established a republic governed by a single-chamber parliament, ministers responsible to it, and a president. A supreme court had power to nullify acts contrary to the constitution. Extensive autonomy was granted to Catalonia. The church was disestablished and disendowed.

The republic was an attempt to introduce freedom and democracy in a backward region of Europe at a time when industrial depression and the collapse of agricultural prices were making the rich uneasy and deepening the misery of the poor. The result was a social explosion. At first the tensions within the nation were mainly expressed in the harmless form of conflict between respectable political parties. But all the time there was a steady increase in popular revolutionary disorder. The army was loyal to the republic only as long as it was a barrier against this—some officers were not even that. In 1936 the army and the masses clashed head on, and the civil war began. Power now passed to the best organizers of force—the soldiers and the totalitarian parties of left and right. Foreign intervention tipped the scale in favour of the army and the fascists.

Power in the constituent cortes had lain with the republicans of the left—middle-class radicals and the respectable and parliamentary socialist party. They governed energetically, putting down both military conspiracy and revolutionary mobs, and at the same time developing the machinery for the settlement of industrial disputes, raising wages and limiting hours of work in the countryside, and making a start with the nationalization of the great estates. But both their social policy and their measures against the church made for energetic resistance on the right, while on the left there was growing division. The socialists were bitterly hated by the anarchists and syndicalists, hitherto the principal labour movement, who were intransigent revolutionaries and would have nothing to do with the bourgeois republic. They would neither put up candidates in elections nor vote for the candidates of other parties. They confined themselves to strikes, riots and terrorism. The socialists, for their part, used their control of the ministry of labour to favour their own trade unions at the expense of those of the syndicalists. They also failed to compensate for the electoral abstention of the syndicalists by an electoral pact with their middle-class allies in the government. The republic's electoral law was designed on the British model to favour large parties (or alliances of parties) against small. It was mainly because the right was more united that it won the elections of 1933.

With the church and the wealth of the country behind it, the new majority should have been able, on previous Spanish form, to dominate the country. That it was not able to do so was partly owing to its divisions and incompetence. There were two large parties within the majority. The so-called Radicals had helped to establish the republic and were led by a disreputable demagogue from Barcelona named Lerroux. They represented the traditional self-seeking and immobilism of the former parliamentary monarchy and could not survive in the new, more strenuous, conditions. Discredited by a particularly nasty scandal at the end of 1935, they almost disappeared from the scene. More formidable was the Ceda, a party hastily created to defend the church and the landlords. Its leader was Gil Robles, who had been prepared for the task by the Jesuits, on one of whose newspapers he had served. His model was the catholic and corporatist state being established in Austria by Dollfuss. In theory his party favoured social reform, but it was too dependent financially on the landlords to be able to do so in practice. He relished the idea of becoming a Spanish Führer, and the cult of his own personality played a large part in his movement's propaganda. His plan was to await an opportune moment and then sweep away the existing constitution, or much of it. But he entirely lacked the tactical skill shown by the successful dictators in circumventing or winning over opponents. In particular he alienated the President, Zamora, who was very conservative, but refused to play the part of Hindenburg and put him in charge of the government.

It was only to be expected that the new majority would repeal the social and anticlerical legislation of the previous parliament and so arouse great animosity on the left.[1] But they failed to hold together well and govern firmly and prudently. There was great ministerial instability. The financial situation deteriorated. The Catalans were alienated and broke into revolt when the supreme court (which had been augmented by the new rulers with their supporters) declared one of the measures of their autonomous government invalid. There was some reason in this, for a left-wing measure of land reform was in question. But the denial of autonomy to the Basques was absurd. The Basques were relatively prosperous, and so had more of a bent than most Spaniards for freedom and democracy. But they were strongly catholic and conservative as well, and had worked with the right in the elections of 1933. They were henceforth to side with the left. The majority of 1933 was gratuitously making itself enemies.

But what doomed the experiment of a conservative republic to failure was the fact that the populace was no longer apathetic. The days when it could readily be cudgelled into submission at election time were over. The electoral victory of the right in 1933 was won by an unprecedented outpouring of money and propaganda, which in the old days would not have been necessary at all. Revolutionary violence grew as the government moved to the right. There was a general strike in the summer of 1934. The entry of Ceda ministers into the government that October (the Ceda had at first been content to

---

[1] One anticlerical measure the country was well rid of. The attempt to insist on lay teachers had disrupted the schools.

support radical ministries) was the signal for revolts not only in Catalonia as mentioned but in Madrid and by the miners of the Asturias.
What was more, the left was sinking its differences. The socialists
became more revolutionary in opposition. They had originally been
the party of the comparatively prosperous town workers in the new
industries. Under the republic they had the chance to win support
among the much poorer rural masses: in competing with the anarchists they had to become more like them and shed their moderation.
This made easier the common front that was so clearly necessary.
The little communist party joined in on instructions from Moscow,
and the Popular Front began to take shape. Absent in Catalonia in
1934, it was apparent already in the Asturias, where the miners held
out far better than the other rebels. To crush them it was necessary,
as in the civil war later, to resort to colonial mercenaries: Moorish
troops and the Foreign Legion which the Spaniards, like the French,
maintained in Africa.

Early in 1936 the collapse of the radicals and the president's unwillingness to entrust power to Gil Robles made elections necessary.
The Popular Front now stretched from the middle-class republicans
to the anarchists, who for the first time decided officially to go to
the polls. They seem to have added something like a million to the
votes of the left, which beat the right by about that margin ($4\frac{3}{4}$
millions to not quite 4 millions) and gained an overwhelming majority
in seats. Unfortunately, the new majority showed itself no fitter to
govern than the outgoing one—less fit in fact than the same men had
been in 1932–3. The socialists, having moved to the left, were no
longer willing to join in a moderate, bourgeois government. Largo
Caballero, their main leader, was a veteran trade unionist converted
into a semi-revolutionary in his old age. He went back to the classic,
erroneous old-time socialist strategy of sitting back and letting 'historical inevitability' bring his party to supreme power. Azana on the
other hand, the leading bourgeois republican, was convinced that the
republic could only survive if it remained moderate. Premier in 1932–3,
he was now made president, and he was determined not to allow a
purely socialist government. The result was weak middle-class ministries, under whose nerveless rule the socialists happily awaited the
right moment for bringing down the old order, and the terrified upper
class got ready to forestall them by a military coup. This took place

in July, and was answered by popular risings everywhere. The navy and the air force remained loyal to the republic, and the people prevailed over the army in the capital and, broadly speaking, in the eastern half of the country. This included the Basque and Catalan areas and the main centres of industry and commerce, whence opposition to the old order had traditionally come. The army, however, secured large areas mainly to the westward. In the north-west this was because there was a large class of peasant proprietors, a catholic and conservative force. In the south-west it was rather for the opposite reasons. Large estates were here at their biggest, and the labourers were still too poor and degraded to offer much resistance. The army was also in control of Morocco, with its valuable stock of mercenaries.

Although the republic had come off best in the initial shock, it was ill-organized to recover what it had lost. The popular insurrection was followed by the setting up of revolutionary committees everywhere, the taking over of large industrial and agricultural properties and the summary liquidation of elements thought to be hostile. Horrible outrages against the church also characterized this revolutionary year. The other side was no less forward in the perpetration of atrocities, but they possessed organized forces as well and so were better placed to re-establish a solid government. The republicans, however, responded well to the challenge which this presented. Largo Caballero decided that his hour had come, and in September formed an effective and broad-based government. Even the anarchists revised their ideas prodigiously and soon had their representatives in it. Order was restored, the masses and the middle class in republican territory were brought to work together, and an effective army was slowly built up. Two organized states confronted each other and only a serious war could decide which should rule the country.

In this situation the older political parties lost ground to the Communists and the Falange, both insignificant until 1936, but now the men of the hour because of their essentially military outlook, their belief in discipline and organization. Both, indeed, had been most active in the south-west, where the abjectness of the population gave disciplined minorities a strong position. The Communists, obedient to their leaders and to Mocow, had seemed a very tame and bourgeois lot beside the wild anarchists and nobody had been much afraid of them. During the civil war they insisted on the need to conciliate the middle class and put efficiency first: they applied, in short, the lessons learned by the Bolsheviks after 1917. They accordingly won many middle-class supporters—careerists and men in search of strong protectors. At the same time they were no strangers to the harsher side of Communist practice, and it was largely (though by no means wholly) owing to them that the republic was equipped with the machinery of a police state for hunting down its many enemies behind the lines.[1] They also tried constantly to increase their hold on the army and the organs of government, and to undermine the other parties. Their bitterest enemies were the anarchists and left-wing socialists, who were less convinced of the need for moderation. In May 1937 there was three days' street fighting in Barcelona between the Communists and their enemies, after which the Communists tried to get the anarchists suppressed and managed to destroy a small (allegedly) Trotskyist party. The government fell and was replaced by that of the moderate socialist Negrin, with the Communists more strongly represented. Communist influence continued to mount until the spring of 1938.

The Falange on the other side were never so powerful. Founded by the son of Primo de Rivera, they were modelled on the Italian fascists, and in theory they were a revolutionary party of the left, differing from the working-class parties only in that they believed in the collaboration of classes for the national good. Their contribution to the rebel cause was twofold. They massacred supporters of the republic, and they could attempt to rival them in popular estimation by calling for social reform. They became the army's chosen political instrument and, like the Communists, they attracted a large body of support from careerists. The parties were also alike in their appeal to youth, being more dynamic and up to date than the other Spanish movements. The youth movement of the Socialists deserted *en bloc* to the Communists, and that of the Ceda deserted to the Falange. But political influence eluded the latter. Their original leader was killed in 1936. Early in 1937 Hedilla, the secretary of the party, demanded that its radical programme should be put in force. He was imprisoned. The leadership of the rebel cause lay not with a politician

---

[1] It was the rebel General Mola who gave a new term to political science by saying that he had four columns advancing on Madrid and a fifth inside the city.

but with General Franco, who had brought in Morocco and its mercenaries.

The rise of the totalitarian parties reflected the intervention in the war of the totalitarian powers. Indeed, the influence of the Communists was largely due to their being made the channel for Russian help to the republic. Germany and Italy did not so use the Falange. Both sides received both men and munitions from outside. But the international brigade that fought for the republic consisted of volunteers and the supplies sent or bought by the Russians had to be paid for. The German and Italian forces in Spain were volunteers only in name, and the assistance provided in men and materials was massive and decisive. At the start of the war the republic had command of both sea and air. German and Italian intervention deprived it of both, and its forces were steadily ground down by the opposing tanks and aircraft. Portugal also gave the rebels important aid, especially at first, when their northern and southern forces were only in communication through Portuguese territory. Of the four intervening states, Italy and Portugal had the strongest and most obvious motives. The triumph of a revolutionary republic in Spain would threaten both, while a more friendly Spain would give Mussolini a commanding position in the Mediterranean, especially against France. He had been in touch with right-wing conspirators at least since 1934. German and Russian intervention bears testimony to the ideological and strategic significance of the Spanish struggle, its ability to tip the balance of power in Europe and also the opportunity it gave for fishing in troubled waters.

It was now, in fact, that Hitler decided to base his next steps forward on co-operation with Italy and on her power to distract the western powers from Germany and her doings. The path for this was prepared by an amicable settlement with Austria. The pressure upon Italy during the Abyssinian crisis had weakened her influence here, and in May 1936 Strahremberg, her leading partisan, left the government. In July there was a 'gentlemen's agreement' between Hitler and the Austrians. Hitler promised not to interfere in Austrian internal affairs, but pro-Germans were to be admitted to the Austrian government, and Austria promised to base her policy on the fact that she 'has acknowledged herself to be a German state'. Italy was now fully ready to turn to Germany, but Hitler was still very keen to make use of Britain in his schemes. A special mission was sent there in the person of Ribbentrop, who hoped to bring off a great coup and become foreign minister. The Italians were alarmed, and a strong bid for German friendship was made by their new foreign minister the Duce's intelligent but rather frivolous son-in-law, Count Ciano. The Italians had managed to get hold of some hostile reports by the British ambassador in Berlin, printed for private circulation within the British government with an introduction by Eden pressing the need for rearmament. These seem to have made a great impression on Hitler when he was shown them. A protocol was signed by which the two powers undertook to follow a common policy in Spain and south-east Europe. On 1 November 1936 Mussolini spoke for the first time of 'an axis' around which the peace-loving states of Europe could unite. On 18 November the two powers recognized Franco's administration as the lawful government of Spain.

The Spanish affair had given Mussolini cause to sue really hard for German friendship, and it was therefore acutely embarrassing for Britain and France. The deepening ideological cleavage in the latter country gave especial poignancy there to the question of whether the Spanish republic should be helped against its foreign enemies. A compromise policy was adopted. The Blum government proposed 'non-intervention' to the powers: they were to undertake to help neither side, and were to establish a sort of blockade to prevent either side receiving aid. This plan was accepted by all the European states. Like Laval's Abyssinian policy, it has always been bitterly assailed on the left. It was particularly objectionable in depriving what all except the Axis powers regarded as the legitimate Spanish government of its undoubted right to buy arms abroad. If, however, it had been possible to apply it without upsetting Italy, it would have been a brilliantly successful policy. Had neither side received outside help, the republic would have won, and so the democracies would have kept Spain friendly without entirely losing touch with Mussolini. But the Duce was not to be deceived by such a sleight of hand. He was determined to win in Spain. 'Non-intervention' was never enforced in practice, but even this retreat by the democratic powers was insufficient to win back the Duce. His behaviour became so outrageous, anyway, that the retreat could not be carried far enough. By the summer of 1937 ships were being sunk all over the Mediterranean by submarines operating on Franco's behalf. The British navy had to fight back and the activities of the 'pirates' (known by everyone to be Italian) eventually ceased when an international conference instituted naval patrols. In this situation the efforts which the British were constantly making to improve relations with Italy came to nothing. Italian influence continued to work against good relations between Britain and Germany, and in November 1937 Italy adhered to the anti-Comintern pact of 1936 between Germany and Japan.

In Spain the republic was gradually worn down. The Basque territories, too conservative to be wholeheartedly republican, were overrun in the summer of 1937. In December the republicans staged a remarkable offensive against Teruel, north of Valencia, where there had long been a salient thrust deep into their territory. This exhausted their strength, however, and in the early months of 1938 Franco conquered Catalonia. The republicans held out until March 1939 in their remaining territory round Valencia and Madrid. Russia ceased to support them, deciding that their cause was hopeless. Eventually a section of the army overthrew the government and organized a surrender to Franco. The creation of a parliamentary republic in the unpropitious conditions of Spain was an extraordinary event, and its survival under fierce attack for so long was even more extraordinary. It never had much of the character of a liberal democracy, and the slender chances of establishing such a system were lessened by the mistakes of the moderate republicans: their immediate all-out attack on the church and their failure to keep together at crucial moments in 1933 and 1936. Conservatives in Britain and France were not unfair in denying that the civil war was a struggle to preserve free institutions. But the republic inspired enormous devotion, and its leaders showed a considerable capacity to organize and to learn from their mistakes. That is why the republic survived as long as it did and why it is fair, too, to argue that it deserved a better fate.

In 1937 the Axis was in being and it had won its first victories. France was tamely accepting the establishment of a hostile power in her rear, which she had fought to prevent in 1870. The balance of power was tipping in Germany's favour, restrained only by the quite ineffective efforts of Britain to woo Italy. The moment had come for Hitler to advance from the re-ordering of Germany to the re-ordering of Europe.

5: The Triumph of Hitler

When British and French statesmen accepted German rearmament without effective protest, the general expectation on both sides was that the clock would simply be put back to before 1914. There would be several heavily armed powers of comparable strength, and peace and equilibrium would be maintained by diplomatic jockeying between them. The situation would have many perils, but might remain fundamentally stable. But Hitler did not share the comfortable outlook of western statesmen and his own military and diplomatic experts. He wanted a great German break-through at the expense of the other powers, and in his own lifetime. He was ready in theory to wait until 1943–5, when German military strength would be fully developed. But by that time other powers, too, would be well prepared, and he was eager, if he could, to strike before then, taking advantage of any momentary weaknesses among his opponents. Although Hitler spoke in 1936 of the need to be ready for war in four years time, he acted in fact before then and while his forces were by no means fully prepared. In 1938 the defences on his western frontier had not been sufficiently rebuilt to secure his rear while he struck east. If Britain had no armoured division until 1940, Germany had only two at the time of Munich. Production of the heavy tanks which were to give her superiority in that arm began only in 1938. Aircraft production in the autumn of 1939 was about 675 a month, about the same as Britain's. Hitler relied for victory in part on temporary superiority in certain weapons such as aircraft, but still more on moral superiority—on bluff, surprises and determination. When he found that his senior subordinates did not like his methods, he disposed of them (1938) as we have seen. His brilliant opportunism fully justified itself down to 1941, and even then failed by only a narrow margin to bring him complete mastery of the European continent.

The Czech and Polish Crises

On 5 November 1937 Hitler explained his policy to his foreign minister

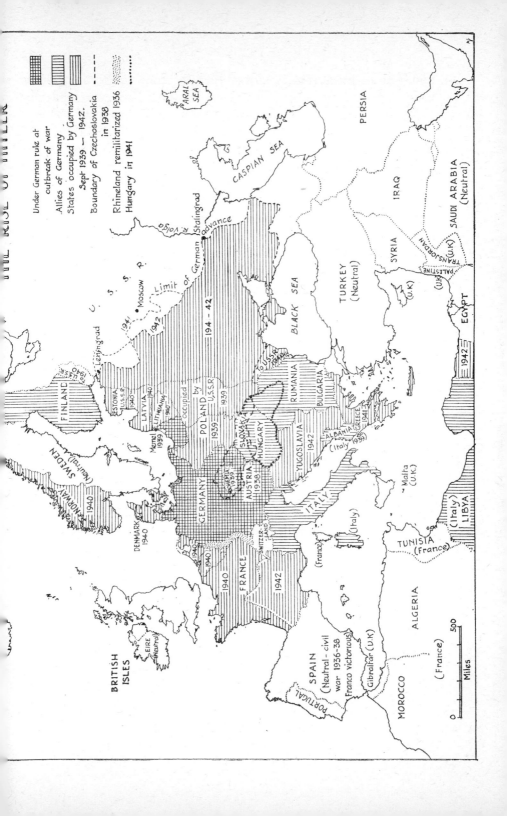

and service chiefs, and declared that the time might soon come for laying hands on Austria and Czechoslovakia. This was to be done if France and Italy went to war over Spain, or in the less likely event of civil war breaking out in France. In either event Hitler expected to be able to act without having to fight any of the great powers. The 'Hossbach memorandum',[1] in which his views were recorded, was to become after the war one of the main proofs that Hitler had always meditated aggression and that his peaceful professions were insincere. Both in court and by historians it was cited to show that Germany had a systematic plan, a timetable even, for expansion. This it does not quite do: Hitler's methods in 1938 and, still more, the events which led him to act were not what he had predicted in 1937. But that Hitler had decided, more generally, that the time would soon be ripe to do something, there seems to be no doubt.

The Spanish affair was one reason for this, and another was the situation in Russia. Hitler seems to have been much impressed by the Five-Year Plans, and even to have intensified his own economic and military preparations in 1936 in order not to be left behind by Russia. He had also concluded against her the anti-Comintern pact with the Japanese. This was a fairly platonic measure against communist subversion, to which all states were invited to accede. But the parties promised each other benevolent neutrality in the event of a Soviet attack. In 1937, however, the military purges convinced Hitler (and the British, too, to some extent) that Russia's apparently waxing power was largely a sham. He began to see Britain as the main remaining obstacle to his expansion, and was encouraged in this by Ribbentrop, who had failed to make friends with her but succeeded Neurath as foreign minister in the general turn out of timid conservatives. Japan's attack on China was important in this connection. It threatened British and American interests, and made the British more anxious to avoid entanglements in Europe. With some hesitation, Hitler accepted the new anti-British implications of German–Japanese friendship.

Thus it was that German action came to seem possible. But it was events inside Austria and Czechoslovakia that made it seem necessary. Henlein's party among the Sudeten Germans had, with German help, reached maximum strength and was eager for action. Henlein had

---

[1] Colonel Hossbach, Hitler's adjutant, took notes at the meeting.

visited Britain three times and made a good impression in official quarters. He even seems to have told Hitler that Britain and France would not intervene in defence of the Czechs.[1] It was, however, the Austrian situation that required action first. After the event, the view was commonly held that Hitler had made Austria his first victim so as to outflank the Czechs on the south. There was, in fact, no such plan, and it does not seem that Hitler was especially dissatisfied with his compromise of 1936 with the Austrians. But the Austrian nazis would not keep still, and in January 1938 evidence of serious plotting by them was discovered by the Austrian police. Shortly afterwards Papen was dismissed from his ambassadorial post as part of the general clearance of conservatives. Trying to regain the Führer's favour, he suggested a personal meeting with the Austrian chancellor, Schuschnigg, to remove causes of friction. Hitler agreed, but when he met Schuschnigg (12 February) he hectored him outrageously and forced him by threats of war to legalize the Nazi party, appoint Nazi sympathizers to the ministries of the interior, war and economics and accept close military and economic co-operation. But he also dismissed and rebuked the Austrian nazi leaders and told them that he was determined to try 'the evolutionary course'. He apparently hoped to keep Austria going as a client state, and expected his followers to acquiesce. But once more they did not, and their behaviour, now that they were free to agitate, became so outrageous that Schuschnigg had to act against them. He ordered a plebiscite on the issue of Austrian independence and sought reconciliation with the proscribed socialists. Hitler dared not allow a popular vote that was expected to go against Germany. He hastily improvised an invasion. Schuschnigg called off the plebiscite at the last moment, but it was too late. On 14 March Hitler entered Vienna in triumph.

The Austrian affair confirmed the strength of Germany's general position. Hitler had already received, as we shall see, indications of sympathy in Britain and France in the event of his putting forward east European claims in a conciliatory way. Both powers had decided to do nothing to help Austria. After the Hitler–Schuschnigg interview the Italians showed more interest in an understanding with Britain, and this was eagerly taken up by Chamberlain. His attitude caused the resignation of Eden, who was tired of Italian bad faith and

[1] Robertson, p. 105.

annoyed at finding the prime minister negotiating with them on his own account. But Chamberlain was unwilling to offer the bait of help over Austria, and the agreement which he eventually made with the Italians contained nothing of substance. Mussolini probably would not have swallowed the bait in any case. Hitler sent him a personal letter of justification by the hand of Prince Philip of Hesse, who was related to the Italian royal family. The Duce accepted what had been done, and Hitler declared with joy 'I shall never forget him for this, no matter what happens.' He was to keep his word. Early in May he paid a very successful visit to Rome. The time was clearly ripe for beginning to put pressure on the Czechs, and the Austro-German *Anschluss* had naturally made the Sudeten Germans furiously eager for action and as likely to get out of control as the Austrian nazis. At the end of March 1938 Henlein was summoned to Berlin and told (*a*) to regard himself as under German orders, (*b*) to put forward demands so extreme that the Czechs could not possibly accept them. At the end of April he duly did this in a speech at Carlsbad. He called for complete German autonomy in a Czechoslovakia remodelled as an avowedly multinational state in alliance with Germany. This, of course, would have given her the sort of satellite position which Germany had tried to force on Austria between 1936 and 1938.

Britain and France, in their unfavourable position, had fairly readily shrugged off Austria because her existence was primarily an Italian interest. But Czechoslovakia was different. She had always been a pillar of the French system of security, and she was the ally not only of that country but of Russia. But although the Russians strongly protested their readiness to honour their alliance, the French were now decidedly unwilling to do so. They had failed in 1934 to create a security system in the east embracing Poland and Rumania, as well as Russia and Czechoslovakia. Russia was therefore physically unable to help the Czechs, and as Germany rearmed it became increasingly hard for France to help, or be helped by, the Czechs and Poles. The French therefore relied for their own security increasingly on their own strength and on the help of a rearming Britain, from whom they had received a rather vague promise of support when the Rhineland was remilitarized. The implication was that the Czechs should seek safety in friendship with Hitler, as the Poles had apparently succeeded in doing. The consequential changes in French foreign policy were, however, awkward to make. Within the cabinet in 1938 there was conflict between two approaches. Georges Bonnet, the foreign minister, was simply out for an excuse for France to withdraw from the east. Premier Daladier realized that this could easily result in severe damage to French prestige and European stability, and he wanted at least enough resistance to Hitler to prevent these bad consequences.

The British had never committed themselves to the defence of the Czechs and Poles, and had always believed that the Germans had a strong case against them. They were therefore far more uninhibited in trying to improve relations with Hitler by concessions to him in the east. When he became prime minister in May 1937 Neville Chamberlain was eager to improve relations with both Rome and Berlin. He began with a personal letter to Mussolini in July, which was followed by the renewed efforts at accord with Italy already referred to. In November he sent Halifax—who later replaced Eden at the foreign office—on a personal mission to Hitler. Halifax spoke of 'possible alterations' to the east of Germany, which Britain would wish to see come through 'peaceful evolution, and that methods should be avoided which might cause far-reaching disturbances'. (Papen, mean- while, was being told in France that the peaceful penetration of Austria and Czechoslovakia would not be objected to.) Defenders of Chamberlain have usually claimed that his policy was made necessary by British weakness, and that he was buying time for rearmament. He was certainly very eager to press forward with this, though rather too easily satisfied with the progress achieved. He fully realized how the Anglo-French position had weakened, and in particular that it would be very hard to give the Czechs military help. But in 1938 he was ready to face war when his policy finally looked like breaking down, while in 1939 he went on trying to appease Hitler to the bitter end, even though he now believed that Britain was stronger. The main element in his policy was the belief that Germany had been badly treated and would behave reasonably if concessions were made to her. He would have preferred these concessions to be in the colonial and economic field, but since Hitler was interested only in Europe, he tried to satisfy him there.

In the spring of 1938 the British encouraged the Germans to make demands on the Czechs, and the British and French urged the Czechs to give way. In the last resort the British could force their policy on the French, and the French could force it on the Czechs by threatening to consider themselves absolved from pledges of military help if their advice was not followed. The Czech attitude was basically the same as that of their western 'friends'. They, too, believed themselves to be strategically isolated and doomed. The possibility of help from the Soviet Union was just as alarming, anyway, as the probability of no help at all. Though they had a powerful army, strong fortifications, and an important munitions industry, they had no intention of fighting. But they believed that Hitler would not dare to do anything to them without the acquiescence of the powers. President Beneš had been one of the most important figures in the life of the League. He retained a belief in collective diplomatic pressure and appeals to world opinion. He therefore tried to put Henlein in the wrong in order to arouse these shadowy forces against Hitler. Henlein made this task easier by his policy of refusing to be satisfied and waging a war of nerves against the Czechs.

The evolution of this Czech situation into a crisis dangerous to peace was due to the Czech efforts at self-preservation, inoffensive though these were. On 20 May the Czechs, alarmed by rumours of German troop movements, ordered partial mobilization. This immediately produced British and French warnings to Germany, and assurances of support from France and Russia—which was no doubt its purpose. But the Czechs suffered in the long run. Hitler lost his temper. He had ordered his forces to be ready to attack Czechoslovakia in the event either of a grave internal crisis there or of a quite unusually favourable diplomatic situation. Now he decided to attack, in any case, on or before 1 October. It is not entirely certain that he meant to, but he certainly seemed to be in earnest, and his generals were highly alarmed, as we have seen. So were Britain and France, as they came to realize that war was really in the wind. They became increasingly eager for the Czechs to surrender, and in July the Runciman mission was sent by Chamberlain to study the situation on the spot and press for concessions. On 4 September, therefore, Beneš played his trump card. He promised to grant the Sudeten leaders whatever they asked. They were nonplussed. What they were supposed to want was autonomy within a reconstructed Czechoslovakia. What they in fact wanted was the destruction, if not of Czechoslovakia, then at least of its existing rulers and freedom. But they could not say so without putting themselves so hopelessly in the wrong that France would hardly be able to evade coming to the help of the Czechs. They found a pretext for breaking off negotiations. On the 12th Hitler delivered a violent attack on the Czechs at the Nuremberg rally, and this was followed by a rising of the Sudetens which the Czechs quickly put down.

The Germans had succeeded both in confusing the issue and further frightening the British and French. On the 15th Chamberlain went to see Hitler, travelling by air—which in those days was a highly remarkable thing for an elderly statesman to do. Already, on the 7th, *The Times* had suggested that a way out of the crisis might be found by ceding the Sudeten areas to Germany, and this was what the prime minister now suggested to the fulminating Führer. Hitler consented to let him find out if the French and the Czechs would agree. The French did so, but they forced the British to accept a highly significant condition: they were to join in a guarantee of the Czech territory that remained. The Czechs at first refused, but they gave in when the French threatened to give them no military help if they defied Hitler. It is likely, though the point has been much contested, that the 'threat' was made at the request of the Czechs themselves,[1] to give them an excuse not to fight.

On 22 September Chamberlain returned to Germany to tell Hitler of his success. But Hitler was not pleased. His object had been to gain a plausible excuse for crushing Czechoslovakia altogether, and he was stirring up the Poles and Hungarians to attack her. Now the Czechs were to preserve their political existence by a strategic withdrawal. Hitler declared that the Sudeten Germans were being massacred and demanded immediate German occupation of the areas in dispute. For a day or two he seems to have been beside himself with rage at being cheated of his prey. His real aims were now so obvious to the democratic powers that they began to resign themselves to war. But a last attempt to satisfy him was made. The French offered to see that the Czechs left the Sudeten areas by 10 October. Chamberlain sent over a personal envoy once more, and he also turned his improved relations with Italy to account by appealing to Mussolini. The Duce was not prepared for a European war and urged Hitler to make

[1] See P. Renouvin, *Histoire des Relations Internationales*, vol. viii, part 2, pp. 135–6.

a last attempt at a settlement, promising to support him if it failed. The two dictators accordingly met Chamberlain and Daladier at Munich on the 29th—two days before Hitler's war was due to break out. Hitler's entourage was solidly for peace, and there seemed to be no enthusiasm for war among the German people either. Hitler agreed to take what was offered him. The Czechs were not even present at the negotiations. Subsequently they had to give slices of territory to Hungary and Poland also. The remains of their republic passed into the hands of men subservient to Germany, and was further weakened by the grant of autonomy to Slovakia and Ruthenia.

It goes without saying that Hitler's appetite was not sated by his gains at Munich. But for the time being his attention was concentrated on long-term plans for a fight to the finish with the western powers. Though he came increasingly to despise them, he regarded them as the prime obstacle to unlimited mastery in the east. Preparations against them were a relatively slow business. Hitler wished to be sure of the help of Mussolini, and at the time of Munich offers of a formal military alliance were made to him. But Mussolini was displeased at the continuous growth of German influence in eastern Europe, culminating in the speedy overthrow of the Munich settlement itself. He found the prospect of gains at the expense of France irresistible, however, and in May 1939 a military alliance known as the 'pact of steel' was concluded. But Mussolini explained that he would not be ready for war for four years, and Japan proved unwilling to conclude an alliance against anyone but Russia. Another difficulty was that Hitler increasingly and rightly felt that Britain rather than France was the really dangerous power in the west, and to beat her he needed more of a navy and air force. Even in May 1939 he talked at length to his military leaders about this, and 1943–4 was mentioned as the date for completing German armaments.

While these preparations were going on, Hitler's idea was to make substantial but essentially limited gains in the east. The Czechs he was determined to subjugate as soon as he could—he was furious at the thought of the reprieve which they had won at Munich. He evaded the pledge which he had given to conclude a treaty guaranteeing Czechoslovakia with the other Munich powers. He intrigued with the Slovak and Ruthenian leaders. The new servile Czech President,

Hacha, eventually made the mistake of trying to restore his authority, which had been fatal to Schuschnigg. He dismissed the Slovak and Ruthenian premiers. Hitler at once instructed these protégés of his to revolt, and when they had done so he summoned Hacha to his presence and required his abdication. On 15 March 1939 he entered Prague. The Czech lands became a German 'protectorate'. Slovakia was technically independent, but had a German garrison. Ruthenia was handed over to Hungary.

But for the time being Hitler did not propose to destroy any more states. He did desire three smallish gratifications of German vanity: the return of the towns of Memel and Danzig and the establishment of a German corridor across the Polish corridor to link East Prussia with the Reich. Negotiations with Poland over the latter points began at the end of 1938. But in return for concessions, Germany offered a defensive alliance. The cession of Ruthenia to Hungary was also a concession to Poland. It destroyed a rallying point for the Polish Ruthenes and gave Poland a common frontier with a traditional ally. The Poles were annoyed that Slovakia had not been dealt with similarly and they were unwilling to give ground, especially after Hitler had seized Memel from Lithuania by force in March. They also offended Hitler by friendly gestures to Russia and refusing to join the anti-Comintern pact. But on 25 March Hitler told Brauchitsch that he did not 'wish to solve the Danzig question by the use of force' and 'for the time being' did not 'intend to solve the Polish question', unless 'exceptionally favourable political conditions' appeared. Poland was to be kept as a dependent ally until the time was ripe for degrading her further. A very favourable economic agreement with Rumania signed in March 1939 applied this policy to her, and everywhere in the Balkans economic and ideological penetration went steadily on. To keep his end up, Mussolini annexed Albania in April 1939, deposing his own puppet Zog.

But expansion by peaceful penetration, pending the decisive blow at Britain and France later on, gradually ceased to be Hitler's policy after March 1939. The reason was the reaction in the west to his final disruption of Czechoslovakia. This convinced many not merely of his faithlessness but of his fundamentally aggressive purpose. Everything that he had done down to September 1938 could be justified in terms of righting wrongs done to Germany or people of German stock and applying principles in which the democracies themselves believed, especially the principle of self-determination. The occupation of Bohemia and Moravia could not be so justified: it was a simple expression of greed. There was a general feeling that German ambition was limitless and that to conciliate her would serve no useful purpose. The British government took the initiative in trying to halt the German advance. As early as 17 March Halifax was asking France, Russia and Poland to be ready to help Rumania. On the 31st an unconditional British guarantee of Poland was announced. Later, similar guarantees were given to Rumania and Greece, the latter being directed against Italy. From President Roosevelt there came an invitation to Hitler and Mussolini to undertake not to attack a list of no less than thirty countries. Hitler was beside himself. 'I'll cook them a stew that they'll choke on,' he is reported to have said. On 3 April he ordered his forces to have plans ready for an all-out attack on Poland by 1 September. On 28 April he answered Roosevelt in a sarcastic speech, in which he further denounced the Anglo-German naval agreement and the German–Polish non-aggression treaty.

War of some kind now seemed to be imminent, and it was no longer possible for either side to ignore the Russians—which is what in substance they had done at Munich, when they were still able to agree. Less is known about the development of Russian policy at this time than about that of any other power: speculation has been the more intense. There is clear evidence of disenchantment with the policy of trying to work with the west against Germany. In a speech on 10 March 1939 Stalin spoke angrily of the western powers, and declared that he would not let them push him into war with Germany. In April the German foreign office was visited by the Russian ambassador for the first time since his appointment nearly a year before. He told Weizsäcker, the leading permanent official, that ideological differences need not prevent good relations. In May the pro-western Litvinov was replaced as foreign minister by Molotov. This was taken as a shift in the direction of Russian foreign policy, and it also suggests that the Russians had begun to take the subject much more seriously. Molotov was one of the most important political figures in the country, which neither Litvinov nor his predecessor Chicherin had been. Subsequent events suggest that the Russians were eager to shelter themselves from the approaching war by diplomatic arrangements that would enable them to lay hands on a broad strip of extra territory in eastern Europe.

But they did not lose sight of the possibility of doing this by co-operation with the western powers. In March they proposed a conference of peace-loving states, and they showed active interest in later western proposals. This is hardly surprising, because though Ribbentrop was interested in the soundings which the Russians made in Berlin, Hitler was sceptical. There were tentative talks but little warmth on the German side till the end of July. In the west the French were fairly eager for a Russian alliance, but the British were very sceptical and dilatory. Like Hitler, they regarded Russia as of little military importance, and they were highly suspicious of her aims. In April they asked the Russians if their assistance would be 'available if desired' in resisting aggression against their neighbours. Litvinov replied with a straightforward offer of an alliance in defence of eastern Europe. Subsequent exchanges revealed that the Russians desired to assist their neighbours whether they desired it or not: as in 1934, it was proving impossible to combine against Germany powers that bitterly disliked each other. The British and French were willing to accept the Russian position in case of an actual German attack. But they would not agree to a Russian definition of 'indirect aggression' that would have allowed them to lay hands on the Baltic states even without this. Political discussions were adjourned at the end of July, and their failure was masked by the sending of a military mission to Moscow to discuss how an alliance would function if it was ever signed.

By that time German preparations against Poland were far advanced, and the Germans set about raising the temperature by propaganda and demonstrations, not least in the free city of Danzig which had a Nazi government. Hitler was at last convinced that an understanding with Russia would greatly ease his task in Poland, and the Germans pressed their friendship on the Russians. At length, on 17 August, Molotov suggested that they might, after concluding a trade treaty that was under discussion, go on to consider a non-aggression pact accompanied by an agreement on certain political questions. This was too slow for Hitler's military timetable, and he telegraphed personally to Stalin accepting Russia's terms and asking that Ribbentrop be received in Moscow at once to sign. The Russians agreed, and the ceremony took place on the 24th. To the non-aggression pact there was added a secret agreement which declared Finland, Bessarabia, Estonia and Latvia to be a Soviet sphere of influence, and Lithuania and Vilna a German. A partition of Poland was envisaged and the border defined.

Hitler was now in an outstandingly good position to crush Poland, and on 22 August he told his generals that he was determined to do it. He thought it 'highly probable' that the western powers would not fight. 'Our enemies are tiny little worms. I saw them at Munich.' The slight risk of their interfering was worth running. The 26th was fixed as the date of the attack. But Hitler's resolve was shaken by the firmness of the British and the weakness of the Italians. The British were undismayed by the Russo-German treaty, disbelieving as they did in Russian strength. They hastened to conclude a formal alliance with Poland, which had been hanging fire during the negotiations with Russia. Chamberlain wrote personally to Hitler, warning him that Britain was determined to abide by her obligations. On the 25th Mussolini let him know that his preparations were not sufficiently far advanced to enable him to go to war. Hitler thereupon postponed his attack. Earlier he had sent the British ambassador, Henderson, off to London with a strange proposal to guarantee the British Empire and disarm after the Polish question had been settled. On the 26th a better offer (not committed to paper) was sent through Dahlerus, a Swedish businessman friendly with Göring. Germany would content herself with Danzig and a 'corridor across the corridor' and would guarantee the rest of Poland.

It is just possible that Hitler for a moment really meant this or that he could have been induced to mean it, rather as he had been induced to take only part of what he wanted at Munich. Then, too, he had been restrained by Mussolini and also by Göring, now in touch with the British government through his Swedish friend. But on the 26th Hitler fixed a new date for the attack on Poland, 1 September. Most of the evidence suggests that his object in negotiating with Britain was to put Poland in the wrong and isolate her. Had he given himself a little more time, he might even have succeeded. Chamberlain remained an appeaser at heart, restrained now, however, by the change in British public feeling. In July Sir Horace Wilson, a treasury official who was his chief adviser on foreign affairs, communicated informally to the Germans a grandiose plan of British economic assistance to Germany in return for a non-aggression pact and disarmament. In August, Chamberlain was trying to get the Americans to press the Poles to make concessions, since he dared not do so himself.[1] Even Halifax and the foreign office were impressed when the Germans began to make moderate proposals. On the 28th the British replied recommending direct negotiations between Germany and Poland on frontiers and minorities, the resulting agreement to be guaranteed by the powers. They had induced the Poles to agree to this. Hitler replied by demanding that an emissary with 'full powers' be sent to Berlin on the 30th. Rather uneasily the British passed this request on, but Colonel Beck, the Polish foreign minister, declared that he would not be treated like President Hacha. Hitler's request for an envoy who could sign on the spot was indeed highly sinister. On the 31st Mussolini announced that he would call a European conference, but on 1 September Poland was invaded and Britain declared that she could not take part unless the Germans withdrew. Britain declared war on the morning of 3 September; France, having made sure that Mussolini's proposal had failed, followed suit in the afternoon.

Hitler had achieved astounding success in re-ordering the map of Europe and the balance of power without war. He now had to fight not only Poland, which he did not much mind, but also the democratic powers, whom he had intended to tackle later. The ending of the pacific stage in his advance was due to the attitude of Poland, Russia and Britain. The Poles, like the Czechs, were faced in the first place with demands that squared with the principle of self-determination and so could be made to seem acceptable to world opinion. Unlike the Czechs they refused to make concessions in order to avoid being put in the wrong—perhaps because, unlike the Czechs, they had treated their minorities badly and so were in the wrong anyway. Would-be appeasers were thus given nothing to work on.

The Russians, by offering Hitler friendship, gave him a chance to finish Poland too good to miss, whatever the consequences. Stalin has been much blamed for his change of policy in 1939, but not very justly. It must always be a prime Russian objective to secure her western frontier by keeping Germany friendly if at all possible. From the Czech crisis onward the western powers showed every sign both of

[1] A. J. P. Taylor, *Origins of the Second World War* (1961), p. 272–3.

weakness and of coldness towards the Soviet Union. It was common prudence to see if the friendly relations with Germany that had existed until 1933 could be restored. It must be remembered, too, that Russia was a 'revisionist' power like Germany: she had been forced by military weakness to accept the post-war frontiers of eastern Europe and, like the Germans, she had legitimate grievances against the Poles. There remains, however, the question whether Stalin was prudent in allowing Hitler to increase his own power: this is best considered farther on.

The Russians have their own charges against the west: that the capitalist powers wanted Hitler to attack the Soviet Union, that they betrayed Russia's friend Czechoslovakia and only went to war when Hitler attacked Poland, Russia's foe. Anti-Bolshevik feeling certainly made opinion in the west more sympathetic to Nazi Germany, which Halifax told Hitler in November 1937 was 'the bulwark of Europe against Bolshevism'. But the French at the end really wanted a Russian alliance, and if the British were sceptical it was because they doubted Russia's power. Fear of Russia had been important after 1918, when the British attempt to appease Germany really began. But by the late thirties Bolshevism seemed to be contained and Russia showed signs of early collapse. British policy towards Russia was not malevolent. But it was eminently foolish. Not only was her power underrated but the Germans were given a chance to make friends with her, of which they made good use.

For twenty years (1919–39) Britain had tried to pacify Europe by appeasing Germany, had believed that her eastern frontiers constituted a real grievance and refused to pledge herself to the defence of the Czechs and Poles. The decision to guarantee Poland in March 1939 was a revolution in British foreign policy which to some extent has determined its course ever since. It was not merely that Germany was now to be resisted. There was a repudiation of isolationism, an acceptance rightly or wrongly of the idea that unless all states are secure no state is so. Wilson had believed this in 1919; the British were now converted to it, and from it sprang their dedication after the war not merely to the United Nations but to the Atlantic Alliance and similar organizations round the world.

Appeasement in France was a policy adopted because of military and general weakness and never abandoned at heart. France honoured her obligation to Poland with reluctance, just as on the other side Mussolini knew his limitations too well to let his German friendship involve him in serious fighting. Appeasement in Britain was not adopted primarily for this sort of reason and its popularity there diminished with time, whereas in France it grew. There was much to be said for it in the Weimar period, and even afterwards it was not necessarily foolish. Europe in 1938 was mainly ruled by aggressive dictators and one could not be opposed without helping others. It was perfectly possible to arouse in Hitler a genuine interest in cooperating with Britain. Appeasing Mussolini and Stalin were not necessarily preferable alternatives. Firmness did not stop Hitler in his tracks, as is often supposed: it merely made him more bellicose. But the appeasers did not understand how to deal with dictators. Even when they were not taken in by their fair words, they failed to penetrate beneath the barrage of rhetoric which characterizes totalitarian régimes and understand the governments' motives and how they might be influenced. Chamberlain seems to have thought that Hitler was an evil man, but he could devise no way of influencing him beyond friendly persuasion. In this, however, democratic statesmen are all much alike. The anti-appeasers were not to do much better with Stalin than the appeasers had with Hitler.

The Conquest of Europe, 1939–41

Hitler was not entirely ready for war with Britain and France in 1939, and it was his policy in any case to avoid fighting a war in both east and west at the same time—the Germans commonly believed that this had been the cause of their defeat in the previous conflict. He was consoled by the belief that the democracies did not mean to fight, and their passivity during the attack on Poland seemed to confirm this. As late as 6 October he offered them peace if they would accept the new situation in eastern Europe. But success encouraged him to be more daring. Poland had quickly succumbed to air and armoured attack. Like Czechoslovakia, she had considerable industrial strength, but unfortunately the Polish army had retained its belief in the horse. At the end of a fortnight it was no more. On 28 September a new agreement with Russia regulated the partition of the country and added Lithuania to the Russian sphere of influence. Hitler had intended to preserve a satellite Polish state covering much of his sphere, but Stalin insisted on outright annexation—perhaps to widen the gulf between Hitler and the western powers. Assured of Russian friendship, Hitler had every incentive to press on at once to the destruction of the western powers. He resolved, as usual, to exploit his opportunity to the full, improvising and trusting to luck and determination where he was not sufficiently prepared. On 27 September he told his commanders of his intention to attack in the west.

True to form, Hitler terrified his generals by deciding in October for an offensive as early as the following month. By a succession of excuses they managed to get it put off until the spring. Attention shifted northwards. At the end of the year Stalin attacked Finland. Britain and France were eager to come to her help and tried to get permission for their troops to cross Scandinavia. This alarmed Hitler because it endangered Germany's main supply of iron ore, from Sweden. He was especially annoyed in February 1940 when the German supply ship *Altmark*, with British prisoners on board, was hunted down by the British in Norwegian territorial waters. In April, indeed, Britain at last decided to cut the main route for moving ore to Germany by mining the Norwegian coast. But tension in the area had subsided in March, when Finland bought peace by ceding Russia some territory. It was longer-range offensive plans which led the Germans to forestall Britain by attacking in the north in April. The German navy had become convinced that the possession of Norway, enabling them to outflank the British blockade, was essential to a successful offensive against Britain. Admiral Raeder, the naval commander-in-chief, succeeded in interesting Hitler in this idea. At first there was a project for a coup by Quisling's Nazi movement in Norway, but the eventual plan was for a surprise attack by the navy and a small force of five divisions. On 9 April the principal Norwegian towns, all ports, were secured at one blow. Denmark was occupied without resistance, thus assuring the line of communications. Britain and France sent help to the Norwegians and fighting continued there into the summer, the German fleet suffering considerable loss. But the operation, conducted by stealth in face of heavy allied naval superiority, was one of the most remarkable German successes.

The main German offensive at length began on 10 May. The original plan had been essentially a repetition of Schlieffen's. The

German right flank was to make the main attack, sweeping through Belgium, though its first objective was to be the Channel ports rather than the encirclement of the French armies. Holland, moreover, was to be attacked, mainly because the Luftwaffe[1] wanted to use it for assaults on Britain. This plan would probably have failed: warned by past experience, the British and French made plans to rush into Belgium in force the moment it was invaded. But anticipating this, Manstein, the chief of staff of the army group in the centre of the front, put forward another plan. The main attack was to be a thrust by armoured forces in his own sector. This would achieve surprise because it would cross the Ardennes, a hilly region in south-east Belgium which most people believed impassable by tanks. Its objective would be the Channel coast, and it would cut off the allied forces in Belgium from those farther south. Manstein was a relatively junior figure and most of the generals considered his views absurd. But he managed to gain access to Hitler and win his interest—in fact, Hitler ended by believing that the plan was his own idea.

The forces of Britain, France and the Low Countries were about equal to those of the Germans—135 divisions against 136. The Germans, however, had concentrated their armour—including 1,000 heavy tanks—in 10 divisions of which 7 were massed in the centre. Holland was quickly overwhelmed. Airborne troops crossed the waterways on which its defence was based. Resistance ended after the heavy air bombardment of Rotterdam. In central Belgium the allies were soon present in greater force than the Germans. But when the German armour broke through in the Ardennes the French had no reserves to oppose them, and on 20 May they reached the mouth of the Somme. Boulogne and Calais were quickly captured, and on the 28th the King of the Belgians, who commanded his forces in person, surrendered. The remaining allied forces in the north appeared to be doomed. But on the 24th the German tanks were halted. The reasons for this extraordinary step have been much debated. It seems that both Hitler and Rundstedt, the army group commander, got cold feet. Hitler had been very afraid all along of French counter-measures from the south. He now let himself be influenced by Göring, who wanted the glory of final victory to go to the Luftwaffe. In fact, the British air and naval forces succeeded

[1] Air force.

respectively in beating back the German bombers and taking off 338,000 British and French troops from Dunkirk and its beaches. But their heavy equipment had to be left behind, and for the moment they were out of the war. The British air force, too, had suffered heavily and, despite the strongest French pleas, it was not committed to the defence of France but reserved for the protection of the home country. The French forces that remained were outnumbered in any case two to one, and they soon succumbed. An armistice was signed on 21 June.

Hitler had now to deal with Britain. He had become increasingly of the opinion that she was the soul of resistance to him and would have to be reduced by force. The occupation of Norway shows the persistence of this belief. But preparations for an attack on Britain had scarcely begun. There were not even submarines enough to attempt a serious blockade. Hitler, moreover, had no real desire to take territory from the British. He even told Ciano in July that the British Empire was a necessary 'factor in world equilibrium'. He hoped that the British would accept his conquests, and confidently awaited a peace offer from them. He eventually made one himself, in a rather subdued speech in the Reichstag. But by that time he had decided that there was nothing for it but to improvise an invasion. On the insistence of the navy it was eventually decided to restrict the operation to a hop across the Straits of Dover by a force of thirteen divisions. The invasion fleet began to assemble on 1 September, with a view to a landing later in the month. By that time the British could put a land force of equal size in the field, and the Germans believed them to be stronger still. All therefore depended on winning and exploiting command of the air. The Luftwaffe began its main offensive on 13 August. It had a marked though not overwhelming superiority in numbers (the fighter strength engaged was about 950 against 700 or 800), and although it suffered severely, it at first inflicted heavier loss on the British and threatened to destroy them by attrition. But there was a failure to concentrate on this objective. Attacks on radar stations were soon given up and so, on the point of success, was the attack on the British fighters' bases and the control centres from which they were directed. Attacks were launched on London instead, and though these were very damaging they allowed the air defences to recover. Attacks on cities were planned in any case as a preliminary to the landing of troops, but the switch to them was mainly due to British attacks on Berlin. Though small, these caused much anger and alarm. Of more direct military value were the heavy British air attacks on the assembling invasion fleet and the striking defeat of the Luftwaffe on 15 September, when it tried to attack London by day instead of by night. It was apparent that British air strength could not be broken before winter weather made a landing impossible. The invasion was called off, though the offensive against the cities went on until the spring.

All this time Hitler had been itching to turn to what for him was always the ultimate objective—the creation of a great German empire in eastern Europe. There are signs that he was already thinking of an attack on Russia before the conquest of France was complete, and that he hoped at first to be able to undertake it before the end of the year. In July he told his generals that an attack on Russia would destroy one of Britain's potential allies, and by strengthening Japan it would neutralize the other, America. Planning began for an invasion in the spring. At that time there was still a firm intention of conquering Britain first. But when definite orders were issued on 18 December they were 'to crush Soviet Russia in a quick campaign before the end of the war against England'. Preparations were to be complete by 15 May. It was the most fateful of Hitler's military decisions: as in the attack on Poland, he had accepted the risk of a war on two fronts.

Before Hitler's decision could take effect, however, he suffered a frustrating series of new involvements in the affairs of southern Europe, of which the first represented an attempt to defeat Britain by flank attack while the last were an essential cause of his failure in Russia. In September 1940 Admiral Raeder tried to interest him in plans for driving the British out of the Mediterranean. He explained to the Führer that they had always considered it the pivot of their empire. Hitler had already laid the foundation of such a plan by the moderation which he had shown in dealing with France. He had allowed her to keep her fleet (disarmed) and her colonies, and the centre and south of the country were not subject to occupation. In this way he had managed to keep France's resources out of British hands. The governments of the Low Countries had fled to Britain and (as it were) brought their colonies with them. French resistance was continued only by the unofficial movement of General de Gaulle.

Some of the remoter colonies adhered to him, but north and west Africa remained loyal to the government at Vichy. In October Hitler visited his Latin satellites to invite them to join in moves against Britain, and Marshal Pétain gave him full satisfaction. But France's neighbours were displeased at the favour shown to her. Franco had offered to enter the war in June in return for large tracts of the French Empire. He was now offered territory only to the extent that France could be compensated from what Britain held. It was clear by now that Britain was far from beaten and Franco was not satisfied. Hitler, to his intense annoyance, could get nothing from him.

Mussolini had entered the war immediately before France collapsed, in order to share the spoils. To his chagrin he got nothing, and found himself obliged to fight the undefeated British. Italy, like France, now paid the penalty of having been the leading military power some years before. Her forces were obsolescent and Mussolini had realized that they would not be fit for some years for a really serious war. An invasion of Egypt at the end of the year was thrown back with heavy loss by a scratch force which conquered half Libya. Italy's East African empire was destroyed in the spring of 1941. Until then, however, Mussolini had laid aside caution in his eagerness for conquests to match Hitler's. He played a large part in the Balkan imbroglio that increasingly set both dictators and Stalin as well by the ears.

Stalin, indeed, began it. He took advantage of the fall of France to lay hands on more of the territories recognized by the Germans as his sphere of influence. The Balkan states disappeared, and Rumania had to give up Bukovina and Bessarabia. Thereupon Hungary and Bulgaria demanded territory from her too. Hitler intervened and imposed a compromise settlement. Rumania suffered an internal convulsion which toppled King Carol from his throne and ended in the dictatorship of General Antonescu, who tried to get on better terms with Hitler. He accepted a German guarantee of his remaining territory and the stationing on it of German troops. Hitler was furious at Stalin's initiative in disturbing the east: Rumania was of considerable importance to him as a source of oil. Stalin was angry, likewise, at the German occupation of Rumania and also at the appearance of German troops in Finland. Acrimonious negotiations took place at the end of the year at which the Germans offered the Russians airy prospects of expansion in the direction of the Indian Ocean at the expense of Britain, and the Russians demanded predominance in Finland, Bulgaria, Turkey and Persia. Hitler's inclination to invade Russia was much strengthened by these events.

Mussolini's jealousy was greatly inflamed by Hitler's advance into the Balkans, once mainly his own stamping-ground. When Hitler visited him in October, it was to find that he had just attacked Greece. This put the plans for an offensive against Britain out of gear, especially as the Italians were soon defeated. It gave the British bases in Greece from which they could attack the Rumanian oilfields. Hitler lost interest in the diminishing prospects of an offensive to the south, but he had to protect his oil and he considered it necessary to prevent Italy being driven out of the war. In December he ordered the preparation of an attack on Greece through Bulgaria, and he decided to reinforce the Italians in Libya. In February Bulgaria was duly occupied, and in March a pact with the Yugoslavs assured the German flank. But as a consequence of this pact the regency of Prince Paul was overthrown and the young King Peter assumed power. The new government offered the Germans a non-aggression pact in place of the semi-alliance, but Hitler completely lost his temper and decided that Yugoslavia must be destroyed. In April there was a general offensive to the south-east. Yugoslavia was destroyed in a matter of days and Greece by the end of the month. Weakened by the despatch of forces thither, the British were driven out of Libya by Rommel. An airborne attack deprived them of Crete in May. Hitler was again pressed by his navy to continue the offensive against the British. They were now badly exposed in the Middle East, and Iraq rose in their rear. He decided instead to press on with the attack on Russia. But valuable time had been lost. The launching of the offensive had to be postponed till 22 June. The delay caused by the Balkans having got out of control made it somewhat less likely that Russia could be crushed before winter.

The German plan envisaged an attack on Russia by 138 divisions, including 12 Rumanian. The Russian forces were considerably larger, but their quality was uneven and complete surprise was secured. Within three weeks von Bock's forces in the centre were at Smolensk, having covered two-thirds of the distance to Moscow. By mid August Leeb in the north was approaching Leningrad, and Rundtstedt in the south had reached the mouth of the Dnieper. In October Hitler was so confident that he ordered preparations for demobilization. But, as in the Battle of Britain, there was a fatal failure to concentrate on destroying the enemy's forces and the nerve-centres of command. The original plan, indeed, had been to concentrate on preventing the Russian forces from escaping into the interior, surrounding and destroying them near the border. A great enveloping operation between Moscow and Leningrad was to be striven for. But although large bodies of Russian troops were duly engulfed, plenty got away. The German generals thereafter considered that the way to break the back of Russian resistance was to take Moscow. It was the main centre alike of administration, the railway system and the arms industry. Hitler, however, was more interested in the conquest of the Ukraine and the Caucasus with their rich economic resources. He was also eager to capture Leningrad, the 'holy city' of the revolution. Von Bock was halted at Smolensk, and when at last he was allowed to advance again in October, the other offensives were continued as well. This was a dangerous dispersal of effort. The southern forces entered Rostov at the mouth of the Don on 21 November, but five days later they had to withdraw. Yet Bock might have got to Moscow if he had been allowed to start a little sooner. On 2 December a small German detachment reached the suburbs and was in sight of the Kremlin. By that time the city was ringed half round and the ministries had been evacuated. But in the middle of October the rain had begun to fall and the invaders were soon deep in mud. At the beginning of November the thermometer fell below freezing-point, and it was soon −8° *Fahrenheit*. Neither the German troops nor their equipment had been prepared for a winter campaign, which had not been expected. Men were frostbitten, tanks seized up, automatic weapons would not fire. Everyone began to think of what had happened to Napoleon in Russia.

On 6 December Zhukov, the new Russian commander on the Moscow front, launched an offensive with 100 divisions. Only Hitler's great determination in the ensuing weeks, his removal of any general who ventured to withdraw, prevented a catastrophic German panic. Russia, which as late as 1940 had fought very badly against Finland, had managed to recover from the purges in the army. Despite the appalling strains to which her society had been subjected there was substantial national unity in the face of the invader. The German army met a fighting spirit absent from its opponents in previous campaigns. It now faced the prospect of a long war in the east. Nor was this all. On 7 December Japan attacked the United States. Hitler had long been trying to get Japan into the war against Britain: an alliance had been signed with her in the autumn of 1940. He had accordingly given them assurances of help against the Americans, with whom he was himself on steadily worsening terms. On 11 December he declared war on them. He did so with a fairly light heart, for, like Ludendorff, he was incapacitated by his mental outlook from judging their strength aright. With their democracy, love of peace and (above all) mixture of races, they seemed to meet exactly the Hitlerian recipe for a decadent nation. At the end of 1941, therefore, Hitler was at war with two powers far stronger than those he had overthrown. Neither could be destroyed in a *blitzkrieg*, his forces and his economic organization were not prepared for a long war and he had not the resources at hand for such preparations. He was far from beaten, but his genius for improvisation was to prove unequal to taking him farther.

Hitler's 'thousand year Reich' was to perish within another four years and leave no trace, apparently, behind. But the event of 1940–1 had nevertheless a considerable part in the reshaping of Europe after the war. In the west they created a gulf between Britain and the continent, which was still unbridged a quarter of a century after. Britain managed to defend her independence and to survive as a worldwide power. Her own efforts only partly accounted for this, but her main sources of succour were outside Europe, the chief one being the United States. There was therefore no strong feeling in Britain after the war that all depended on drawing closer to her continental neighbours. France, by contrast, was overwhelmed in 1940. In the last weeks of the republic desperate appeals for help were made to both British and Americans, and made in vain. This and much else that happened during the war paved the way for a reconciliation between France and her German and Italian neighbours when they, too, had been humbled by defeat. The first seed of west European federation was sown.

In the east the German invasion was a terrible disaster for Russia. It has been said that Stalin was sensible in seeking to be on good terms with Germany. But it is obvious that this policy had its dangers. which he did too little to guard against. The destruction of France weakened his position enormously and made it very tempting for Hitler to attack him, but he seems in no way to have realized his danger. He may perhaps have been right to let Germany and France fight it out without interfering. But it was misguided of him to allow Germany to draw economic resources on a massive scale from and through Russian territory. Much more crass was the Russian disregard of the many signs that a great invasion against them was being prepared. Though they were increasing their general military strength as much as they could, they were not poised to meet the blow when it came; indeed, their first reaction was sheer incredulity. No democratic statesman was bamboozled by Hitler as completely as Stalin was.

But in the long run Stalin's blunders were curiously rewarding. The first result of the Russo-German entente of 1939–41 was to give Hitler western Europe. The ultimate result was to give Stalin eastern Europe. Hitler destroyed such independent forces as had existed between Russia and Germany and paved the way for Russian domination. By conquering France and holding the Atlantic coast of the continent strongly, he made it very much harder for the western powers to advance into Europe than it would have been if a western front had continued in existence all through. The war with Japan, which tied up so much allied shipping and landing craft, made it even harder for the western powers to keep pace. This strategic fact is reflected not only in the advance of Russian troops to key areas of central and eastern Europe before troops from the west could get there. It also greatly affected the dealings between the Russians and the western powers during the war and helps to account for concessions made by the latter to the former. Hitler therefore stands to some extent behind two of the main trends of post-war Europe. He contributed not only to the federative moves in the west but to the domination of the east by Stalin.

6: Epilogue—the Triumph of Stalin

Russia and the United States exercised increasing sway over Europe from the moment that they began to fight Hitler, even though at first he had the best of it. By 1945 they dominated the continent, and the old west-centred Europe was dead—or, at any rate, temporarily lifeless. The foundations of the post-war world were being laid in these years, just as the European settlement of the twenties had been moulded by the wartime events of 1917–18. This new world is not the concern of the present volume,[1] and the later stages of the Second World War will therefore be treated very briefly. To complete the story so far told, however, it is necessary to say in a few words why the states which Hitler dominated failed to escape their doom and why more generally western Europe was unable to save itself from destruction and forestall the establishment of Russo-American condominium.

The Entry of the United States into the War

The coming to power of Franklin Roosevelt and the Democrats in 1933 was in some ways a victory for isolationism. The Republicans were to some extent kept active in the affairs of the world by their keenness to protect American interests. Roosevelt's administration repudiated 'dollar diplomacy' as Wilson's had done. But this meant that though it showed an idealistic concern for peace and democracy it was even less inclined than its predecessor to take steps to defend them. When Japan attacked China in 1937, the United States and the members of the League vainly urged each other forward. The American response to the Abyssinian affair was the first of the Neutrality Acts (1935–7) which were designed to prevent American war materials and American shipping from going to belligerent countries, thereby inviting the sort of attack that had brought America into war in 1917. American citizens were even to be stopped from travelling

[1] See rather R. C. Mowat, *Ruin and Resurgence: 1939–65.*

on belligerent vessels, to avoid crises like that resulting from the sinking of the *Lusitania*.

There was, however, something double-edged even about this American waiver of her rights as a neutral to trade with belligerents, for which she had hitherto fought so hard. It did, indeed, ease American relations with Germany in 1939–40. American ships were barred from the war zones, and German submarines could therefore safely sink any ships they found. But it also meant a final American abandonment of objection to blockades imposed by the League against an aggressor—or indeed by anyone else. The British were able to institute a far stricter blockade in 1939 than they had in 1914, with far less American protest, though this was largely because the Americans themselves had set a precedent for it in 1917–18. Moreover, the Americans were able to indulge in most unneutral behaviour under the guise of varying their neutrality regulations. It was the President's responsibility to declare when a state of war existed, and when Japan attacked China he simply failed to do so. China was allowed to buy supplies, and American firms were officially discouraged from selling to the Japanese. After the outbreak of war in 1939, Congress modified the law by allowing belligerents to buy war materials, but they were not to be lent money for the purpose by Americans and they were to convey their purchases in their own ships.

There was, indeed, never any doubt about which side the Americans wanted to win. Wilson in 1914 had urged his countrymen to be neutral in thought and feeling. Roosevelt, however, in proclaiming neutrality, went out of his way to say that this did not interfere 'with the free expression of opinion and sympathy'. Both presidents seem to have caught the mood of the moment. Important factors making for the difference were the growing danger from Japan and the failure of Russia to march with the allies in 1939 as she had in 1914. There was no doubt this time which was the 'democratic' side. Americans had no wish to fight themselves, but Roosevelt had broken new ground by his appeal to the dictators to stop their advance in the spring of 1939. He had also appealed to the powers concerned for a peaceful settlement at the time of Munich; Wilson in 1914 had done no more than offer to act as an intermediary if desired. The fall of France was taken by Roosevelt as it ought to have been taken by

Stalin—as a threat to the security of his own nation. American pre-cautionary measures were not in fact justified by Hitler's immediate plans, as comparable moves by Russia would have been. A variety of measures were taken to help the supply of arms to Britain. In September 1940 she was given fifty old destroyers, and in return allowed the Americans to establish bases in her transatlantic posses-sions. After Roosevelt's unprecedented election for a third term in the autumn, a request came from Churchill for help on a bigger scale. At the end of the year Roosevelt launched the slogan of America 'the arsenal of democracy' and the Lend-Lease act was passed which allowed the supply of munitions on a massive scale at American expense. There was to be no problem this time of debts owed to Americans by their allies. Though there was a strong isolationist agitation against these measures, they were supported by the bulk of both parties, as was the reintroduction of conscription in September 1940.

In the course of 1941, the United States reached a condition of 'undeclared war' against Germany. To ensure the defence of their hemisphere, the Americans garrisoned the Danish possessions of Greenland and Iceland and contemplated occupying the Spanish and Portuguese islands in the Atlantic if those countries fell under Hitler's influence. A state of emergency was proclaimed in May. German submarines began to sink American ships, especially on the route to Iceland which they declared blockaded. In November Con-gress allowed American merchant ships to be armed. In August there was a joint statement of Anglo-American policy (in effect, of war aims), resulting from the meeting of Churchill and Roosevelt off the coast of Newfoundland. The 'Atlantic Charter' reaffirmed in the main the principles of the Fourteen Points. It had the merit of being vaguer, though no less stirring.

Hitler had nothing to gain by resenting all this and so war with Germany remained 'undeclared'. Japan, on the other hand, needed to make the most of the confusion in Europe while it lasted. When France fell, she made an alliance with Siam and occupied northern Indo-China. When the attack on Russia removed all danger from that side, she occupied southern Indo-China and was clearly poised for an assault on Singapore and the British and Dutch Indies. These governments and the United States therefore imposed a virtual economic blockade on her, and protracted American–Japanese negotiations followed in which each power tried to get the other to accept its policy. The Japanese navy and politicians had a healthy respect for the United States and would have been willing to accept her terms, involving the abandonment of the Chinese adventure. But the army believed that the moment for still greater adventures had come. At their behest the negotiations were interrupted by the crippling surprise attack on the American Pacific fleet at Pearl Harbour, which was accompanied by attacks on Hong-Kong and Manilla, and rapidly followed by the Japanese conquest of south-east Asia. The United States found herself fully at war in December 1941 through the volition of her enemies.

She entered it, in the tradition of Wilson, as a revolutionary force. Her real object was to destroy the German government, regarded as a threat by its very nature to the security of every country. Germany was not immediately threatening American territory and interests whereas Japan was. Yet the United States was forbearing towards Japan until her formal alliance with Germany in the autumn of 1940. American plans regarded Germany as the more formidable adversary of the two, the one that must be defeated first. For the Americans, therefore, even more than for Russia, the conflict had a strongly ideological character. Fighting for no tangible, national objective, they virtually could not be appeased. The unconditional surrender of the enemy which was to be their aim was implicit in the circumstances of their entry into the war. Without it, Stalin might have been inclined and Churchill might have been forced to make a compromise peace. Once the Americans were in there was little likelihood of the 'united nations', as they now styled themselves, doing so.

The Military Position of Germany, 1942–5

What were Hitler's chances of forcing the United Nations to tolerate him by making himself too strong to be overthrown? The German forces had been considerably weakened by the efforts of 1941. In March 1942 only 8 of the 162 divisions in the east were ready for an offensive, and the 16 armoured divisions had only 140 tanks fit for service. To repair the damage, Italy and the Balkan allies had to be called on for contingents that finally amounted to a quarter of the

Axis forces in Russia. Germany was already losing the decisive but temporary lead in preparedness on which her victories had been based and could no longer attempt the overthrow of Russia by one great stroke. But she could still mount a formidable offensive, able at least to render her impregnable. In Russia, Hitler proposed to strike at Stalingrad and the Caucasus oilfields. As in the civil war, the erstwhile Tsaritsyn was a key traffic centre through which food and fuel passed to Moscow from the south. By depriving the Russians of wheat and oil and gaining them for himself, Hitler hoped to alter the balance of forces decisively. He was also induced once more to undertake an offensive in the Mediterranean, a project which had been put off pending the fall of Russia. In 1940–1 the British had inflicted heavy punishment on the Italian navy, and the Axis forces in Libya had been ill-supplied. Now a great air offensive against Malta and the surrounding waters drove the British fleet to Egypt. Rommel's forces were brought up to strength, and the British army, too, was driven back towards Alexandria. A gigantic pincer movement threatened to engulf the Middle East and bring Germans and Japanese into contact in the Indian Ocean.

The main reason why this did not happen was that Hitler did not think of it in such terms. He could not escape from his preoccupation with Europe, and failed to nourish Rommel's offensive and undertake the conquest of Malta. In June 1942 the island was reinforced, at the cost of heavy losses. The attack on Rommel's supply lines began again and he never reached Alexandria. In Russia, Hitler's armies reached the Volga on either side of Stalingrad, and in August they were on the fringe of the oilfields round Grozny. Hitler's mistake here was to attempt the capture of both objectives: had he concentrated on either, he would have succeeded completely. November, however, saw successful counterattacks, both in Russia and in Egypt. Hitler had placed the northern flank of his offensive in the hands of his allies' troops, and the Russians were able to crush them and threaten the German forces with encirclement. Hitler eventually allowed those in the Caucasus to withdraw, but he would not give up Stalingrad, to the capture of which he attached an almost mystic significance. An army of almost 300,000 was cut off there, attempts to relieve it failed, and after unbelievably fierce fighting it was destroyed in January 1943. Rommel's army suffered a similar fate after its defeat at El

Alamein, and again Hitler's unwillingness to allow it to withdraw was an important cause. The allies meanwhile landed in French North and West Africa, and when the Germans in Tunisia capitulated in March 1943 they were left virtually masters of the Mediterranean.

A submarine offensive was a further means by which Hitler might hold off his worldwide enemies. This, too, was tried with great success, but it came too late to turn the scale: Hitler's concentration on Europe made him slow to realize the need for it. Till February 1941, Raeder was unable to keep more than 6 submarines at sea at a time. By the end of the year this had increased to 60, and 300 submarines were built in 1942. Submarines now had range enough to operate right across the Atlantic and they could overwhelm convoys by working in groups. In 1942 they sank 6 million tons of shipping. The allied invasion of North Africa was only made possible by drastic cuts in shippings to Britain. But new defensive weapons were to hand, notably radar and long-range aircraft. In April–May 1943 shipping losses fell steeply and many submarines were destroyed. In June Dönitz, the submarine commander and now head of the navy, withdrew his ships from the North Atlantic. They returned in September but, in the remainder of the year their losses were 64 against only 67 ships sunk.

1942 was the last year when Hitler could take the offensive on a big scale, but he still had great strength on the defensive. At the beginning of that year he appointed as minister of munitions Albert Speer, who had originally come to his notice as an architect. Speer proved a remarkable organizer, and it was under his direction that German arms production reached its height, increasing by 150 per cent in 1942–3. Even in 1944 the production of fighter planes almost trebled between January and September. This was accomplished despite a mounting allied air offensive against the German cities: the first raid by a thousand bombers (on Cologne) took place in May 1942 and between November 1943 and February 1944 the high explosives dropped on Berlin amounted to 22,000 tons. Of course, the Germans drew ruthlessly on the resources of the entire continent to keep up production, as will be told, but their achievement was considerable all the same. Immediate needs could only be met, however, by sacrificing the possibilities of industrial expansion and new weaponry which might have put Germany more on a level with the two great world powers. A rigid order of priorities was necessary, too, which left some important services short of supplies, notably air defence. The air attack, moreover, became more formidable as the allied powers learned to make it more selective. In 1944 they struck particularly hard at aircraft factories, oil supplies and lines of communication. German forces on land found it increasingly hard to move and the Luftwaffe was badly cramped by lack of fuel. The development of new weapons—rockets, flying bombs, jet planes—was badly delayed by judicious air attack. The remarkable operation of landing a great army in Normandy without a proper port and in face of powerful and even superior German forces was only possible because air attack impeded the movement of the German army.

In the summer of 1943 the western powers conquered the southern portion of Italy, and the Russians launched a general offensive. By the end of the year they had recovered most of the territory east of their pre-1939 frontier. In June 1944 the western powers landed in Normandy, and the Russians launched a further offensive. By the end of the year France, Belgium, most of the Balkans and all but the northern plain of Italy had been lost and the German garrisons in the Baltic states were cut off. Hitler still had 260 divisions under arms— twice as many as in 1940—and they fought well to the end. But by May 1945 they had been overwhelmed. German resistance was shortened by Hitler's continued reluctance to allow his troops to withdraw. He held on as long as he could to the Baltic region, the Balkans and Italy when he might have made things easier for himself by shortening his line and concentrating his troops. But it is doubtful if tactical mistakes made much difference. By 1944 Germany was losing the war of attrition at an alarming rate, and loss of territory only accentuated this. It laid open what remained to even intenser air attack and reduced supplies for the war effort—oil and chrome from the Balkans, for instance. Hitler in 1942 was probably too weak already to win a total victory, but he was certainly strong enough to win a breathing space which might have enabled him to develop his resources and hold his own. After that year, time was against him. The United Nations were disappointed that he took so long to destroy, and he might have prolonged the agony further. But there was little chance of his forcing a military stalemate upon them, especially as the Japanese offensive had also spent its force.

Europe under Hitler

Given that the United Nations were set on destroying Hitler and that they possessed the means to do it, the bulk of the continent would suffer devastation and be at the disposal of the victorious powers unless it could somehow get rid of him and come to terms with his opponents. But a peace of conciliation by this means was prevented by the tightening of Hitler's control over the countries he ruled. It was now, in fact, that the Nazi revolution bore its full fruit and the recasting of Europe in the Nazi image really began. This was most apparent in the conquered Slav lands. Hitler showed moderation in allowing the survival of puppet Slovak and Croat states, but in his main eastern conquests he began at once to clear the ground for permanent German settlement and domination. Himmler was given special responsibility for this in Poland in 1939, and the evacuation of Poles from the western territories annexed to Germany began. It was decided to exterminate the educated class among both the Poles and Czechs. Some of the latter were to be turned into Germans, and the rest of the population was to be a helot class of unskilled labourers. When Russia was invaded, Alfred Rosenberg, a racialist crank who was himself born one of Russia's German minority, was made minister for the eastern territories. But his authority was overshadowed by that of Himmler and, in economic matters, of Göring. The total destruction of Russian industry was contemplated. Hitler ordered that Leningrad was to be razed to the ground by the advancing army, and it was intended that all available food should be sent to Germany, the Russian townspeople being left to starve. At the end of 1941 Göring told Ciano that 'this year between twenty and thirty million persons will die of hunger in Russia. Perhaps it is well that it should be so, for certain nations must be decimated'.

This simple idea was all the policy which the Nazis felt the need of in the case of the Jews. They embarked on the 'final solution of the Jewish problem', as they called it, by extermination. Working the Jews to death was their first idea, but it was not quick enough. In their quest for speed, they used first mass shootings and then the gas chambers. In the time allowed them, they managed to account for about half the Jews of Europe: it is estimated that some $4\frac{1}{2}$ millions were killed. But though the Germans let anything up to 3 million

Russian prisoners of war die from exposure, they came to think that subject Aryans might be more use alive. Himmler remarked in 1943 that at first 'we did not value the mass of humanity as we value it to-day, as raw material, as labour'. By September 1944 there were 2 million prisoners of war employed in Germany, together with $7\frac{1}{2}$ million other foreigners, the overwhelming bulk of whom had simply been rounded up and deported thither. Their living conditions were appalling, and they might be made to work whatever hours their overseers wished. The mortality among them was high. Large firms like Krupp made full use of this labour, but they were not the only ones. Two and a half millions worked on farms. Boys were deported to be made apprentices. In 1942 Hitler ordered the supply of half a million Slav women 'to relieve the German housewife'. The occupied countries of the west were treated less ruthlessly in the matter of de-portations, but they suffered if anything more from extortion. They paid the costs of occupation to the tune of 60 milliard marks, half from France. Other tribute accounted for another 40 milliards, and payments in kind were very much greater. The reparations which Germany had had to pay after 1918 were dwarfed. The looting of art treasures was a conspicuous feature of the exactions. Göring be-lieved his private collection to be worth 50 million marks.

The Germans believed, however, that there were good elements among the subject peoples. Hitler envisaged Dutch and Scandinav-ians, even some Americans, joining the German colonists in Russia. It was to form the backbone of this colony and the enlarged Reich of which it would be so large a part that the Waffen SS was built up. At the start of the war there were three divisions of these SS men organ-ized as fighting troops; at the end there were thirty-five. Almost half of them were Germans from outside Germany, and a good many were foreigners. They were a racial and ideological élite distinct from and superior to the mass of Germans, and Hitler intended them to be the ruling class of his empire. Meanwhile they were its arch-exter-minators. But Himmler, in 1943, declared it 'a page of glory in our history' that many of them had witnessed thousands of executions and yet 'have remained decent fellows'. For he laid it down as their basic principle that 'we must be honest, decent, loyal and comradely to members of our own blood—and nobody else.'

Politically the horrible treatment of the Jews and Slavs made the

18—E.E.P.

task of Hitler's enemies much easier. Well though the Russian armies fought, there was a mass of deserters from them, and many of the peasants were ready to regard the Germans as liberators. This advantage the Germans gratuitously threw away and the partisans of a negotiated peace with Germany were few in the countries fighting her: the Germans could get nowhere with talk of the 'Bolshevik menace', which at any other time would surely have been most effective once the Russians began to advance. On the Axis side, the growing force of the Nazi revolution weakened the conservatives, who had supported the totalitarian cause from fear or self interest and were now inclined to desert it for the same reason. The SS and the party held the German army ever more closely in leading strings, and Nazis and and army together tightened their grip on the dependent allies. Finland, which had been fighting on the German side, managed to retire from the war. Rumania and Bulgaria also sued for armistices, but only when on the point of being occupied in any case. Hungary ended prostrate, a battlefield. In France the government seated at Vichy which had been left in control of the unoccupied zone was at first a fairly substantial one, commanding the loyalty of the conservatives, the acquiescence of most of the rest and the respect of the Americans who till the end hoped to preserve it. An attempt, disfigured by much anti-semitism, was made to establish a catholic and corporative state. When the Anglo-Americans landed in North Africa in 1942, Darlan, the leading Vichy representative there, came to terms with them. But in France itself the Germans responded by seizing the unoccupied zone, and the Vichy authorities could do nothing beyond sinking their fleet. They could no longer pretend to be independent, and vanished from the scene when France was invaded. This made possible the gradual creation of a new French government under de Gaulle, but he was no more in a position than Vichy had been to end the war by some other means than invasion and reconquest.

In Italy the Anglo-American advances in the Mediterranean at the end of 1942 set both the king and many leading Fascists thinking that a separate peace might be the only way to avoid complete calamity. But it was only after the invasion of Sicily in July 1943 that anything was done. Mussolini was induced to allow a meeting of the Fascist Grand Council, a body of leading dignitaries which till then had been mainly honorific. The lead was taken by Grandi, formerly foreign minister, who denounced the deformation of fascism that had taken place in the course of the thirties. On his motion the meeting resolved that the Duce's dictatorial powers ought to be surrendered to the king and Mussolini, low in health and spirits, complied. The king was already preparing to supplant him with a ministry headed by Badoglio, the conqueror of Abyssinia. But it was too late. The bulk of the Italian army was still outside the country. Disbelieving the new government's assurances of loyalty, the Germans reinforced their already considerable strength in the peninsula. Badoglio concluded an armistice with the western powers in September, but their forces were not able to land farther north than Salerno, and his were unable to hold the rest of the peninsula. They were, in any case, left leaderless by the flight of king and government to Brindisi. Most of the Italian forces were disarmed, and Italy became a battlefield, like Hungary and France. Mussolini was rescued by the Germans from the arrest in which he had been placed. A puppet government was established under him. The defeat of his protectors brought his death, but the monarchy did no better by being on the other side. It had failed to save the country and a republic replaced it after the war.

Inside Germany Hitler responded to defeat by humbling his army. After the failure to take Moscow in 1941, Brauchitsch was removed from the post of commander-in-chief of the army and Hitler himself assumed the post. Halder, the army's independent-minded though not very forceful chief of staff, was removed shortly before the fall of Stalingrad. Hitler's authority was increased hereafter, as it so often was, by the haphazard delegation of power to rival authorities. The supreme command of the army, headed by himself (OKH) controlled the eastern front. The supreme command of the armed forces, also headed by himself but left largely in charge of the dependable Jodl (OKW) controlled the remaining fronts. For good or ill, only Hitler had any control over all aspects of the fighting. He brought to the very top new men who did not share the aristocratic background and conservative views of the older officers. The most notable of these were Rommel (who in the end deserted him) and Model. Almost all the highest officers (field marshals and full generals) were removed from command in the course of the war.

The army was the only hope of those who desired to remove Hitler and make peace. There were a certain number who wanted this even while the war was going well, but the apathy of the soldiers rendered their planning dilatory and ineffectual. Indeed, the most important group among the younger men, the Kreisau Circle which gathered round the deeply religious Count von Moltke, would not plot at all. They regarded the leading conspirators as disillusioned old reactionaries incapable of building a new Germany. They looked for salvation to foreign conquest and devoted themselves to planning for the subsequent reconstruction. The most eminent figures in the active opposition were in fact elderly men who had served Hitler at first and been turned out: Beck, the former chief of staff, and Goerdeler, who had been price controller under both Brüning and Hitler, were the most notable. There was a more hopeful element among the less senior staff officers, and especially in the military intelligence service. But they found it almost impossible to win the support of generals actually in command of troops. The only force which they could control was the 'home army' (recruits, convalescents, etc.), and even that was done behind the back of its commander, General Fromm, who sat on the fence. This led the conspirators to decide that a rising must begin with the killing of Hitler: only if the generals were thereby freed from their oath to him was there any chance of their acting against the other Nazis. Several of the plotters had access to the Führer, and a remarkable number of attempts were made to kill him. One in March 1943 failed only because the bomb (British made) failed to go off. But Hitler expected attempts of this kind, and he constantly dislocated his enemies' plans by changing his arrangements at the last moment.

At last, on 20 July 1944, a bomb planted in his military headquarters in East Prussia by Count von Stauffenberg, Fromm's young chief of staff, did explode in his presence. By that time it was in any case too late to do much good. The landing in Normandy had been made, Rome had fallen, the Russians were advancing: even the fall of Hitler was unlikely to induce the United Nations to halt and negotiate with the Germans. For this reason the conspirators almost gave up the attempt, and their main reason for continuing was the forlorn one of saving the national honour. They wished to show the world that there were Germans who repudiated Hitler and were capable of opposing him. At this last hour their position began to improve. Rommel, commanding the forces in Normandy, had seen the writing on the wall and was willing to act. Moreover, he did not require the assassination of Hitler to release him for action—he was in favour of his arrest and trial. When the day came, it was in France that the conspiracy showed most life. Stülpnagel the governor of Paris, arrested the local Gestapo and SS. But misfortune and indecision dogged the plotters, as it usually does in such cases. Hitler was not killed: he was saved by the ponderousness of his conference table, under which the bomb had been placed. The conspirators in the capital failed to seize the ministries and wireless stations: partly through mere slowness, partly because they waited for confirmation of the first rumour that Hitler had been killed. Rommel was out of action, injured by an air attack shortly before. Almost everyone obeyed Hitler without question when a broadcast to the nation showed that he was still alive. Even before the plotters made their attempt, the Gestapo had been on their track and had arrested a good many. Now there was a reign of terror in which nearly 5,000 people died. The Nazis began the full onslaught on the conservatives of which they had dreamed. Men like Schacht were put in concentration camps. The army had to hand over many officers for liquidation. It was made to adopt the Nazi salute, and Guderian, now its chief of staff, required all staff officers to adhere expressly to National Socialist principles or resign. Himmler was given command of the 'home army' and, later, of an army group. The subordination of army to party was completed by the institution of political commissars on the Russian model—an institution which Hitler admired.

At length even the Nazi leaders began to interest themselves in a negotiated peace. But Hitler never showed much interest in it in his last years. He was carried foward by the impetus of the revolution which he had unleashed, his past conduct made it almost unthinkable that his opponents would treat with him and he had no intention of standing down in order to make it easier for his country to achieve peace. His last years were spent in delusive dreams of victory and the excoriation of his own people, on whom he blamed his failure. Physical decay marked the effect on him of his demonic career. In the end he was to die by his own hand in his conquered capital. His overthrow alone could have brought Europe peace without general destruction, and by the time that his military power had begun to wane, neither his subjects nor his allies were able to stand against him.

United Nations Strategy and Diplomacy

In January 1943 President Roosevelt, at the conference between himself and Churchill at Casablanca, announced that 'unconditional surrender' by the enemy was to be the aim of the war. Implicit in the whole American attitude, this policy had been recommended by a State Department subcommittee in May 1942. They argued that there would not have been another war if this had been done in 1918: the Germans had been able to contest the validity of the peace settlement by representing it as a repudiation of the armistice terms. Churchill accepted the American view with only slight misgivings.

It has been argued that the policy of 'unconditional surrender' made the task of Hitler's opponents at home impossible. It meant that the Germans were offered no reward for overthrowing Hitler comparable to the chance of peace on the basis of the Fourteen Points which had led them to dismiss the Kaiser. A moderate statement of United Nations war aims would, it is said, have produced the same result. There is, however, little reason to believe that a negotiated peace could have been achieved in this way. The essence of the situation was that none of Germany's enemies was willing to offer anything but severe terms. Stalin did argue for a time that even so a statement of their aims might be preferable, as frightening the Germans less, than the limitless demand for unconditional surrender. But, in fact, it would have taken very generous terms indeed to give any real encouragement to the German opposition. At the beginning of the war, their idea had been to get rid of Hitler in return for being allowed to keep his conquests. Because it called for the disarming of aggressors, the liberal and idealistic Atlantic Charter was unacceptable to the conspirators. One of their leaders, the ex-ambassador Hassell, wrote that it 'destroys every reasonable chance for peace'. In 1944 the hopes of many of the plotters were those of the Nazi government itself: that Russia was on the verge of quarrelling with the west. There were plans for a separate armistice on the western front, perhaps even with western forces entering Germany, while the battle in the east was allowed to continue.

United Nations spokesmen did what they could to prevent bad effects from the demand for unconditional surrender by frequently declaring that it was their intention to allow the enemy nations to survive and to enjoy the common rights that they believed all peoples should have. They made only one obvious blunder here: in the autumn of 1944 Churchill and Roosevelt approved (not for long) a scheme for the almost total destruction of German heavy industry. But in general the enemy was given all the reassurance that could honestly be offered. More was impossible, if only because the German hopes of a split between Russia and the west were by no means entirely without foundation. It was never easy for them to co-operate—but until Germany was defeated, it was not safe for them to quarrel. The events of 1939–41 were a terrible warning to both sides against failing to hold together. The alliance would have been strained if it had been necessary to announce firm peace terms: the allies could not entirely agree on them. 'Unconditional surrender' had the merit also of pledging the western powers to fight with Russia to the end. This was well, for there are signs that Stalin was the ruler most tempted by the idea of a separate peace. (The scale of Russian losses was certainly enough to make it tempting to anyone there.) Thus the United Nations neither desired, nor could they prudently offer, generous terms to Germany. Nor was there very much chance of a negotiated peace on anything much less than Hitler's terms.

The work of destruction therefore went forward until only two of the larger continental states, with a few small ones, survived. General Franco had stayed neutral, through a mixture of luck and judgment. His luck was to hold for many years. Stalin had defended his empire and now he pushed west in greater strength than any Russian ruler had hitherto done, giving Russia a European influence that she had not had since the reign of Nicholas I. It has been argued[1] that this Russian triumph was largely owing to involuntary help from the western powers. They refrained from striking north and east from Italy in force. They failed to end the war in 1944 by a quick offensive against the Ruhr. The Russians, therefore, had time and opportunity to master most of eastern Europe. This question will not be considered here for it concerns the building of the new Europe rather than the collapse of the old. But it is right in conclusion to emphasize once more the good strategic position that was Russia's inheritance from the latter. She was present on the continent; the western powers until

[1] For instance, by Chester Wilmot, *The Struggle for Europe* (1952).

1943 were not.[1] She was not at war with Japan and they were. This hampered their return to the continent by amphibious operations, and their slowness in taking the offensive against Germany in turn displeased the Russians. It was necessary to keep them contented, and the Americans were further anxious to secure their help against Japan at a later stage. Political concessions to them, for instance in the Polish question, were the result. Militarily, she was well placed to win any 'race'. In September 1944 she secured Rumania, Bulgaria and half Poland, while the western powers had only just reached the springboards in France and Italy from which offensives against the Ruhr and against Austria and Hungary might have been launched. The prospect of one in the latter place was so far from being displeasing to Stalin that he encouraged it.

In 1945 Europe was physically devastated almost from end to end. Half of it had passed from the grip of one dictator to that of another. Much of the rest was under foreign occupation, and there was a wide-spread spiritual as well as a physical collapse. But this was not the whole story. The present chapter has centred on the failure of bad or weak men to improve. It concludes the history of the thirties. Other men had been fighting among the ruins for better things and had begun to plan and even to build them. For many, if not most Europeans, 1945 brought hope not despair. The more constructive history of the forties and fifties had begun.

[1] Save at Gibraltar.

Concluding Thoughts

The period covered by this book witnessed a profound change of attitude by historians towards their subject. This has been part of a more general change in attitudes towards human knowledge and understanding. In the last century the physical scientist in particular was inclined to conceive of himself as a collector of hard, indubitable facts. These built up into regular laws, in a way that was relatively simple and clear to all and could leave no room for dispute. In this way, piece by piece, the entire Truth about the universe was being discovered. With the expansion of knowledge a more modest view has come to prevail. Facts are not simple either to perceive or to interpret. Generalizations about them are not likely to be invariably and irrefutably true. Approximations to the truth are the best that man can achieve. The progress of knowledge consists in making the approximations less obviously imperfect.

Historians have moved with the times. Writing in 1896 of the *Cambridge Modern History* which he was to edit, Lord Acton conceded that 'ultimate history we cannot have in this generation'. But he declared that 'all information is within reach, and every problem has become capable of solution'. Under the influence of such men as Wilhelm Dilthey (1833–1911) and Benedetto Croce (1866–1952) these beliefs have faded. History has come to be seen as the essentially subjective interpretation of data which by themselves impose no conclusion on the observer. Not only do the personal characteristics of historians influence the way in which they try to make sense of history, but historians writing at a particular moment are in the position of a man viewing a landscape from a particular hilltop. What he sees is not what he would see if he stood at any other point. Each generation similarly interprets past events in the light of its own insights and preoccupations. Indeed, it cannot understand the past unless it does so, and thus for each generation history has to be written anew. Some would say that there was no objective historical truth at all.

Beliefs like these make the study of the fairly recent past a more

19—E.E.P.

respectable occupation for the historian. If 'ultimate history' were possible, it might be wisest to wait a century or so before adding a period to the historian's repertoire, allowing passions to cool and giving time for every fact to be coaxed from its secret hiding-place. But if every interpretation is bound to be subjective, of its own time, and destined to be superseded, why not begin at once? There is indeed a positive advantage in doing so. Historians are much inclined to hindsight, to judging events and their importance in the light of re-mote consequences, to regarding this trend or that as 'inevitable'. Studies of events in the recent past are written without so much bene-fit of hindsight and are forced to judge events more in terms of their immediate impact. They can be a valuable corrective to studies writ-ten later. If there is any possibility of objective historical truth, it is likely to be in comparing the views which different generations have taken of the same event.

This book then is not 'ultimate history', but only what could be seen of it by one author writing at one particular time. The reader can and should discover the personal shortcomings of the author by comparing his work with that of other authors. But to what extent are the views expressed in this book especially characteristic of the time when it was written, the middle 1960s? In what ways would an author—even the same author—have treated the period differently if he had been writing about it earlier or later? Of course, in matters of detail the answer depends on the progress which historians make in writing (and reading!) monographs on the various matters under review. This cannot be predicted for the future; some glimpses of the progress made in the past are afforded in the bibliography. There remain the changes resulting simply from the changing viewpoint of the observer: it is about these that the following remarks are con-cerned.

If this book had been written during the thirties or forties, it would have been tempting for the author (whatever his own prefer-ences or opinions) to suppose that he was witnessing the demise of a 'liberal' and 'capitalist' society which had proved itself inherently un-fit to survive. His interpretation of events since 1870 might therefore have tended to stress inherent contradictions in the system, large impersonal forces tending to its ruin, and the helplessness of in-dividuals in face of them. But since 1945 the capitalist system has enormously revived in strength and vigour, and liberal beliefs are being strongly fought for. The cause of the individual against authority no longer seems quite hopeless, even in Russia. Even the Vatican is on the move. It therefore seems right to treat the crises of liberal-capitalist Europe in the period covered by this book not as inevitable but as due to human error; to stress the personal element, the mistakes of individuals, the timidity of classes, the narrowmindedness of particular parties or organizations—things which may indeed have been inevitable but which could in principle have been avoided by taking thought. Similarly, anyone writing on international relations between 1935 and 1945 or later might have been forgiven for believing that the liberal dream of universal peace enforced by the League was dead. But as noted earlier, the military situation has changed—war once more has begun to look unprofitable as well as wicked. The United Nations organization has survived intense scepticism as to its viability and intense hatred among its members; it has even done some useful work. Therefore the League has not, in this book, been cursorily dismissed as an ephemeral demonstration. It has been treated as the beginning of an important trend and given more attention therefore than what it actually did might justify. The protracted attention given in this book to the twenties reflects both this emphasis on the League and what it stood for, and the desire to study the American-inspired liberal revival closely. It was the precursor of the American-inspired revival of capitalism and democracy in our own day, and this gives a special interest to its achievements and failures.

But who knows if the present revival of capitalism and democracy will last? It would seem, like the parallel revival in the twenties, to depend on the continuance of prosperity. Governments have learned a great deal about economic management since then. But they continue to make so many mistakes that it is hard to be sure that the prosperity of the fifties and sixties has been due to good management rather than simple good luck. The luck may turn, there may be another collapse. In that case, no doubt, historians of the years since 1870 will be very likely to insist on the inherent weaknesses of capitalism and explain the calamities of the period in terms of impersonal factors rather than personal failings. It is hardly necessary to say that the future of the United Nations and of all other attempts at peacemaking remain gravely in doubt. If they turn out to have no future, any historians left alive may feel less concerned with their past.

The present liberal and capitalist revival is an affair of the 'advanced' countries. In the Afro-Asian world it has not done very well and there has been a stready trend towards dictatorships and a steady growth of communism. This is reflected in the comparatively sympathetic treatment given in the present book to governments in backward countries that were less than democratic, and in the close attention which I have tried to pay to the development of communism—another reason for saying much about the era of Wilson and Lenin. Historians are sometimes reproached for always defending the winning side—in fact, some historians deliberately do so. This seems rather excessive, but there are two sound points behind it. A certain leniency should be shown to a successful ruler if everyone who has tried to rule in a different way has failed. The influence of any successful movement on subsequent events is likely to be so great that a thorough understanding of it is essential to the historian, and this can hardly be attained unless he is in a reasonably dispassionate frame of mind. But though future events may lead historians to dispraisal of liberals and capitalists, they may also—if things go the other way—lead them to be more severe on the communists. There are some relatively backward countries where liberalism and capitalism have done well since the war: Italy and Japan are the most important. These countries were borderline cases when their post-war advance began, but it may be that in the future much poorer peoples may be lifted out of the mire without losing their freedom. Were the democratic republic of India to solve the problem of poverty there, the time might have come to be very much more severe about Stalin.

Though the historian must always be fair, there seems to be rather less need to be fair about nazis and fascists than about communists. In the thirties all three might well have seemed to the historian to be of equal significance as supplanters of liberal democracy. The Second World War showed the first two to be not merely horrible but infantile, corrupt and incapable of self-preservation. Hitler and Mussolini led their countries straight to ruin. Both men were extremely adept in the winning of power, but in their use of it they showed themselves to be no more than vicious cranks, increasingly enslaved and destroyed by their own daydreams. Some constructive economic and social work managed to get done under their rule, but for the most part this owed nothing to them or their movements. The democracies fought the war more efficiently than they did, and they have since shown themselves more creative in the arts of peace. Democratic Italy, in particular, compares favourably not only with Mussolini's Italy but with Franco's Spain. A decline in prosperity would no doubt bring a resurgence of fascism among the riff-raff and frightened conservatives. But it seems unlikely that intelligent people will ever take it seriously again, as many once did. There is only one achievement of the Axis governments which is calculated to make a democrat of the sixties envious: they could stop inflation by holding down wages. Since 1945, therefore, the nazis and fascists have been curtly dismissed by the historian as morbid symptoms of a Europe in decay, and this seems likely to continue to be the case.

Before the rise of the totalitarian movements, the main alternative to liberal democracy was provided by the upholders of tradition and of claims to obedience that were historical in character. Before 1914 the historian might have been inclined to lay great weight on the survival of the historic European monarchies as a force making for stability and continuity in a society otherwise in danger of disintegration from the rapidity of change. After 1918 he might well have thought that the fall of so many thrones and the radical break with tradition were a prime cause of the continent's ills. This view seems less attractive now and is probably destined to die out. It has been shown since 1945 that democracy, if it can be made to work at all, is the most conservative of régimes, the one most capable of protecting society from excessive and violent change. Wise conservatives have always realized this, at least since 1848, and it is likely that European conservatives as a whole will henceforth take their stand on democracy and forget the older conservative ideology. The European kings that have survived are indeed those whose dynasties were called to the throne by parliament or in some similar way. The old monarchs by divine right did not in fact manage to do the conservative job that was their historic mission. They were so preoccupied with the maintenance of their own power by applying the principle of 'divide and rule' that they failed to see that this behaviour was essentially unconservative. It exaggerated instead of diminishing the cleavages in society, and it encouraged a revolutionary spirit in certain groups by keeping them remote from power. Their successors have not necessarily been more enlightened, but they have at least had a better idea of how to maintain their authority. Historians are likely henceforth to regard the old monarchies in their last years as an encumbrance rather than as a lynchpin of society whose destruction was fatal.

The Habsburg monarchy may be an exception to this. During the last and much of the present century there was a steady growth of the belief that national independence and self-determination must form the basis of the international political order. The great multinational empire therefore came to seem increasingly an anachronism, and its destruction was predicted and accepted as inevitable. But even before its demise a contrary school of thought began to grow up, more conscious of the dangers of nationalism, and events since 1918 have done much to encourage it. The peoples of east-central Europe did not prove better able to live together when all were independent. They did not prove able either to maintain that independence: their failure to co-operate was punished by enslavement, first to the Germans and then to the Russians. Historians, therefore, are by no means tempted to condemn the Habsburgs out of hand and recent research has stressed the reluctance of their subjects to proceed to the total breakup of the Monarchy. Nationalism itself is beginning to seem an anachronism: the attempts at federation in the west suggest that Europe is turning back to the ecumenical ideal of the Holy Roman Empire, of which the Habsburgs were the last representatives. But it should be added that it is only in western Europe that nationalism is declining. Everywhere else it is on the increase and it seems to be breaking into fragments the great ecumenical movement of communism. In eastern Europe itself even the governments installed by the Russians have begun to struggle hard against the Russian yoke. Historians may well return to the opinion that nothing could withstand nationalism in that area.

One great European monarchy by divine right still survives—the oldest of all, the Papacy. It is in the Christian Democratic movements that the forces of tradition have survived and been given a modern, forward-looking application. The federalizing projects now on foot will bring political unity to most of the European area owing allegiance to Latin Christendom. The clerical parties have been strong supporters of this trend and they are likely to wield great influence if it succeeds. Perhaps it will not; or perhaps they will be swept back by a resurgence of those anticlerical forces which are another permanent feature of Latin Christendom. But at all events it seems right at present to pay great attention to the development of Christian Democracy, only fitfully powerful in the period covered by this book, but apparently one of the forces of the future.

This book has attempted, without benefit of more than a few years hindsight, to concentrate on factors that have been of high importance in the moulding of European society. When the moulding process has gone farther, some of these factors will be seen to have been more and some less important than the author at present believes. It will, no doubt, be found that he has missed some out altogether. Perhaps the only enduring value of this book lies in the mistakes which it contains: they, more than anything, could bring home to posterity how the period under discussion appeared to an observer reviewing it soon after it was over.

Select Bibliography

1. Works on the period in general

(a) *Useful short bibliographies*, intended, as is the list that follows, for English-speaking readers with a limited command of other languages, are A. Bullock and A. J. P. Taylor, *A Select List of Books on European History, 1815–1914* (Oxford, 1960); W. N. Medlicott, *Modern European History, 1789–1945* (Historical Association, 'Helps for Students of History', No. 60, 1961). There are excellent bibliographies in the general works listed under (b) and (c).

(b) *General Histories of Europe*: the best of these is L. Halphen and P. Sagnac (eds.), *Peuples et civilisations—histoire générale*. The later volumes arc:

> Vol. XVII. H. Hauser, J. Maurain and P. Benaerts, *Du Libéralisme à l'impérialisme, 1860–1878* (2nd ed., Paris, 1952).
> Vol. XVIII. M. Baumont, *L'essor industriel et l'impérialisme colonial, 1878–1904* (2nd ed., Paris, 1948).
> Vol. XIX. P. Renouvin, *La crise européenne et la premiére guerre mondiale, 1904–1918* (3rd ed., Paris, 1948).
> Vol. XX. M. Baumont, *La faillite de la paix, 1918–1939* (2 vols., Paris, 1951).

The best series in English at present is W. L. Langer (ed.), *The Rise of Modern Europe*. Unfortunately, the latest volume to appear so far is C. J. H. Hayes, *A Generation of Materialism, 1871–1900* (New York, 1941). Both these series excel in giving a balanced coverage of political, economic and cultural developments.

The series *Clio, Introduction aux études historiques* is valuable for its extensive bibliographies and accounts of the progress (or lack of it) in historical research. The last volume is P. Renouvin, E. Preclin and G. Hardy, *L'époque contemporaine* (Part II) *La paix armée et la grande guerre, 1871–1919* (Paris, 1939).

On cultural affairs a useful compendium is G. L. Mosse, *The Culture of Western Europe* (1963).

Economic history has been less fully investigated than political. It can be studied in outline in such works as S. B. Clough and C. W. Cole, *Economic History of Europe* (3rd ed., New York, 1953). J. H. Clapham, *The Economic Development of France and Germany, 1815–1914* (4th ed., 1936), gives a useful general impression of economic and social conditions in the west. Consult also P. I. Lyaschenko, *History of the National Economy of Russia to 1917* (1947). A stimulating essay on later developments is W. A. Lewis, *Economic Survey, 1919–1939* (1949). It covers Europe, Japan and the United States.

(c) *Diplomatic Histories*: the best is Vols. VI–VIII of P. Renouvin, *Histoire des relations internationales* (Paris, 1955–8). The earlier part of the period is covered in the classic works, rather too German-centred, of W. L. Langer, *European Alliances and Alignments, 1871–1890* (New York, 1931), and *The Diplomacy of Imperialism, 1890–1902* (2 vols., New York, 1935). An interesting corrective, rather densely packed with argument, is A. J. P. Taylor, *The Struggle for Mastery in Europe* (Oxford, 1954), the only volume so far completed of an *Oxford History of Modern Europe*.

(d) *National Histories:*

France. The Third Republic is graphically described in D. W. Brogan, *The Development of Modern France* (1940) and thoughtfully analysed in F. Goguel, *La politique des partis sous la iiie République* (Paris, 1946). Interesting despite its age is C. Seignobos, *L'évolution de la iiie République* (Paris, 1921), Vol. VIII of the *Histoire de France contemporaine* edited by E. Lavisse. Important aspects of the subject are covered in A. Dansette, *The Religious History of Modern France*, Vol. II (1961), and H. Sée, *Histoire économique de la France*, Vol. II (Paris, 1951).

Germany. The writings of E. Eyck provide a thoughtful treatment down to 1933. *The History of the Weimar Republic* is available in English (2 vols., Harvard, 1962–4), and *Das persönliche Regiment Wilhelms II* (Zürich, 1948) is not; of *Bismarck, Leben und Werk* (3 vols., Erlenbach-Zürich, 1941–4) there is an English abridgement, *Bismarck and the German Empire* (1950). E. Vermeil's interesting but rather intricate study *L'Allemagne contemporaine* (2 vols., Paris, 1953–2) covers 1890–1950. Important aspects are covered in G. A. Craig, *The Politics of the Prussian Army, 1640–1945* (Oxford, 1955)—very good—and W. F. Bruck, *Social and Economic History of Germany from William II to Hitler, 1888–1938* (Cardiff, 1938).

Spain. G. Brennan, *The Spanish Labyrinth* (1943) is a wonderfully illuminating account of the country's development from 1874 to 1936. A. Ramos Oliveira, *Politics, Economics and Men of Modern Spain, 1808–1946* (1946) is also vivid and penetrating, though rather opinionated.

Italy. Interesting accounts, hostile to those in power, are D. Mack Smith, *Italy, a Modern History* (Ann Arbor, 1959) covering 1860–c. 1950, and M. Hentze, *Pre-Fascist Italy* (1939). They can be balanced by reading B. Croce, *History of Italy, 1871–1915* (1929). An important aspect is covered in A. C. Jemolo, *Church and State in Italy, 1850–1950* (Oxford, 1960).

Austria–Hungary. Sparklingly reviewed in A. J. P. Taylor, *The Habsburg Monarchy, 1815–1918* (2nd ed., 1949), and with more sober detail in A. J. May, *The Habsburg Monarchy, 1867–1914* (Harvard, 1951), and R. A. Kann, *The Multinational Empire: Nationalism and National Reform in the Habsburg Monarchy, 1848–1918* (2 vols., New York, 1950). The story of these and the surrounding lands is continued after 1918 in H. Seton-Watson, *Eastern Europe between the Wars* (Cambridge, 1945).

Russia. H. Seton-Watson, *The Decline of Imperial Russia, 1855–1914* (1952), is a solid and penetrating analysis. Vol. III of P. N. Milyukov, C. Seignobos and L. Eisenmann, *Histoire de la Russie* (Paris, 1933), covers 1855–1932. There are several surveys of the Soviet period, such as D. W.

Treadgold, *Twentieth Century Russia* (Chicago, 1959). An important topic is covered in G. T. Robinson, *Rural Russia under the Old Régime* (1932). *Other Countries* important in their connections with Europe are usefully dealt with in B. Lewis, *The Emergence of Modern Turkey* (1961) and R. Storry, *A History of Modern Japan* (Penguin Books, 1960).

2. Some Works on Topics within the Period

No attempt is made to cover here all the matters discussed in this book. Subjects that can be easily investigated in interesting books are given preference. For a completer coverage see the bibliographies in (1).

Part I

Chapter 1. For the military situation after 1870 see B. H. Liddell Hart, *The Ghost of Napoleon* (1938); R. Girardet, *La société militaire dans la France contemporaine, 1815–1939* (Paris, 1939); and G. Howe, 'Gedanken zur deutschen Wehrpolitik zwischen 1871 und 1914' in W. Schüssler (ed.), *Weltmachtstreben und Flottenbau* (Witten-Ruhr, 1954)—all brief and interesting. Available in translation is G. Ritter, *The Schlieffen Plan* (1958).

Chapter 2. Some important developments of the seventies in the centre and west are considered in E. Schmidt-Volkmar, *Der Kulturkampf in Deutschland, 1871–90* (Göttingen, 1962); F. H. Brabant, *The Beginnings of the Third Republic in France* (1940); and J. Goualt, *Comment la France est devenue républicaine* (Paris, 1954)—the last an analysis of elections; also L. Eisenmann, *Le compromis austro-hongrois* (Paris, 1904)—very illuminating; and C. A. M. Hennessy, *The Federal Republic in Spain* (Oxford, 1962).

Chapter 3. F. Venturi, *Roots of Revolution* (1960) is an absorbing and moving, though very bulky, account of the Russian populists. B. H. Sumner, *Russia and the Balkans, 1870–1880* (Oxford, 1937) is an excellent book, and brings out the domestic drives behind Russian expansion. See, too, W. E. Mosse, *Alexander II and the Modernization of Russia* (1959) and H. Kohn, *Panslavism* (Notre Dame, 1953). Bismarck's reaction to the eastern crisis is best studied in W. N. Medlicott, *The Congress of Berlin and After* (1938), and *Bismarck, Gladstone and the Concert of Europe* (1957). His other difficulties are well indicated in W. Taffs, 'The War Scare of 1875', *Slavonic Review*, Vol. IX (1930–1), pp. 335–49, 632–49.

Part II

Chapter 1. M. P. Fogarty, *Christian Democracy in Western Europe, 1820–1953* (1957) is a useful guide to that subject, though mainly centred on the present day. A. J. Marder, *British Naval Policy, 1880–1905* (1940) and *From the Dreadnought to Scapa Flow* (only vol. 1 available, Oxford, 1961) are interesting; compare E. Kehr, *Schlachtflottenbau und Parteipolitik* (Berlin, 1930). *Imperialism* is the subject of a huge literature. It is instructive to compare J. A. Hobson's pioneering *Imperialism* (1902) with the contrasting view of E. Staley, *War and the Private Investor* (Chicago, 1935), and L. C. Robbins, *The Economic Causes of War* (1939). Informative are H. Feis, *Europe the World's Banker, 1870–1914* (New Haven, 1930), and C. A. Julien (ed.), *Les politiques d'expansion impérialiste* (Paris, 1949).

Chapter 2. On the matters discussed here see J. Alden Nichols, *Germany after Bismarck: the Caprivi Era, 1890–1894* (Harvard, 1958); A. Dansette *Le Boulangisme* (Paris, 1938); G. Chapman, *The Dreyfus Case* (1955)—see also R. F. Byrnes, *Anti-semitism in Modern France* (New Brunswick, 1953); T. H. von Laue, *Sergei Witte and the Industrialization of Russia* (New York, 1963).

Chapter 3. J. V. Fuller, *Bismarck's Diplomacy at its Zenith* (Harvard, 1922), and P. Joseph, *Foreign Diplomacy in China. 1894–1900* (1928) remain useful. Important recent studies of British policy are J. A. S. Grenville, *Lord Salisbury and Foreign Policy: the Close of the Nineteenth Century* (1964), and G. Monger, *The End of Isolation: British Foreign Policy, 1900–1907* (1963). The French position has been less studied, but see P. B. Mitchell, *The Bismarckian Policy of Conciliation towards France, 1875–85* (Philadelphia, 1936); Baron Nolde, *L'alliance franco-russe* (Paris, 1936).

Part III

Chapter 1. Socialism can be conveniently studied in J. Joll, *The Second International, 1889–1914* (1955), in fact, a brief conspectus of the whole movement down to 1914. The bulk of the story is told in detail, to the thirties, in G. D. H. Cole, *A History of Socialist Thought* (5 vols., 1953–60). C. E. Schorske, *German Social Democracy, 1905–17* (Harvard, 1955), is very interesting; compare A. Noland, *The Founding of the French Socialist Party, 1893–1905* (Harvard, 1956). The Russian movement is most pleasantly approached through B. Wolfe, *Three who Made a Revolution* (1956)—the lives of Lenin, Trotsky and Stalin to 1914.

Chapter 2. The picture of the west before 1914 is filled out a little by G. D. Crothers, *The German Elections of 1907* (New York, 1941); E. Weber, 'Le renouveau nationaliste en France et le glissement vers la droite', *Revue d'histoire moderne et contemporaine*, Vol. V (1958), pp. 114–28; B. R. Leaman, 'The Influence of Domestic Policy on Foreign Affairs in France' *Journal of Modern History*, Vol. XIV (1942), pp. 449–79; A. W. Salomone, *Italian Democracy, 1900–1914: the Political Scene in the Giolittian Era* (Philadelphia, 1945).

Chapter 3. B. Pares, *The Fall of the Russian Monarchy* (1939), and M. T. Florinsky, *The End of the Russian Empire* (New Haven, 1931), cover the period 1905–17 lucidly. A. G. Kogan, 'The Social Democrats and the conflict of nationalities in the Habsburg monarchy', *Journal of Modern History*, Vol. XXI (1949), pp. 204–17, brings out well the intractability of the problem. Its thorniest part is the subject of R. W. Seton-Watson, *The Southern Slav Question and the Habsburg Monarchy* (1911).

Chapter 4. N. Mansergh, *The Coming of the First World War* (1949), is the best brief book, and L. Albertini, *The Origins of the War of 1914* (3 vols., Oxford, 1952–7), is the most comprehensive and authoritative book on the subject. Among a host of works on particular topics may be mentioned E. L. Woodward, *Great Britain and the German Navy* (Oxford, 1935) vital for the British aspect; E. N. Anderson *The First Moroccan Crisis, 1904–06* (Chicago, 1930); B. E. Schmitt *The Annexation of Bosnia*

(Cambridge, 1937); I. M. Barlow, *The Agadir Crisis* (Chapel Hill, 1940); E. C. Helmreich, *The Diplomacy of the Balkan Wars* (Harvard, 1938); and J. B. Wolf, *The Diplomatic History of the Bagdad Railway* (New York, 1936).

Part IV

Chapter 1. C. R. M. F. Cruttwell, *A History of the Great War, 1914–1918* (Oxford, 1936), and C. Falls, *The First World War* (1960), are two out of several single-volume histories. The 'home front' is studied in F. P. Chambers, *The War behind the War* (1939). There are many books on the involvement of the United States. A. S. Link, *Wilson the Diplomatist* (Baltimore, 1957), is an excellent brief account of his policy and the controversies surrounding it. E. R. May, *The World War and American Isolation* (Harvard, 1959), usefully sets out the German and American sides of the story in parallel.

Chapter 2. For the fall of the Russian monarchy see under Part III, Chapter 3. What happened next is told briefly in C. Hill, *Lenin and the Russian Revolution* (1947), and, at length, in W. H. Chamberlin, *The Russian Revolution, 1917–21* (2 vols., 1935). L. Schapiro, *The Origin of the Communist Autocracy* (1955), shows how they suppressed critics among their members and allies. E. H. Carr's *History of Soviet Russia*, of which seven volumes have so far appeared (1950–64), is an interesting analytical account; in moderate doses it is easy to read. Brest Litovsk is vividly treated in J. W. Wheeler-Bennett, *The Forgotten Peace* (1939).

Chapter 3. R. Coper, *Failure of a Revolution: Germany in 1918–19* (1955), and A. J. Berlau, *The German Social Democratic Party, 1914–21* (New York, 1949), are critical of the republican leadership. A key figure in it is studied in K. Epstein, *Matthias Erzberger and the Dilemma of German Democracy* (New York, 1959). Much additional material on a key institution comes in J. W. Wheeler-Bennett, *The Nemesis of Power, the German Army in Politics, 1918–1945* (1953). For a parallel story see Z. A. B. Zeman, *The Breakup of the Habsburg Empire, 1914–1918* (1961). An important figure in Chapters 3–4 is briefly treated in J. H. Jackson, *Clemenceau and the Third Republic* (1946).

Chapter 4. For Wilson at Paris and afterwards see, besides Link (above under Chapter 1), T. A. Bailey, *Wilson and the Peacemakers* (New York, 1947), combining two earlier works: *Woodrow Wilson and the Lost Peace* and *Woodrow Wilson and the Great Betrayal*. S. P. Tillman, *Anglo-American Relations at the Paris Peace Conference of 1919* (Princeton, 1961), is an interesting account of an important theme. The famous tract on reparations by J. M. Keynes, *The Economic Consequences of the Peace* (1919), is interestingly attacked in E. Mantoux, *The Carthaginian Peace, or the Economic Consequences of Mr. Keynes* (1946). The atmosphere of the conference is well conveyed by a participant in H. Nicolson, *Peacemaking, 1919* (1933).

Chapters 5 and 7. Several of the books listed under Chapters 2–4 will be seen to cover this period also. Carr takes the Russian story to *c.* 1926 so far; see further, I. Deutscher, *Trotsky, the Prophet Armed, 1879–1921*

(1954), and *The Prophet Unarmed, 1921–9* (1959). Important aspects of post-war diplomacy are covered in F. P. Walters, *A History of the League of Nations* (2 vols., 1952); W. M. Jordan, *Great Britain, France and the German Problem, 1918–1939* (1943); H. W. Gatzke, *Stresemann and the Rearmament of Germany* (Baltimore, 1954); R. H. Ullman, *Anglo-Soviet Relations, 1917–21* (One volume available so far, *Intervention and the War*, Princeton, 1961); E. H. Carr, *German-Soviet Relations between the Two World Wars, 1919–1939* (Oxford, 1952).

Chapter 6. A. Rossi, *The Rise of Italian Fascism, 1918–22* (1938), is the fullest account available of that subject. The religious element in inter-war Italian politics can be studied in R. A. Webster, *Christian Democracy in Italy, 1860–1960* (1961), and D. A. Binchy, *Church and State in Fascist Italy* (1940).

Part V

Chapter 1. The onset of the financial crisis in Europe and America and the helplessness of the politicians can be followed in J. K. Galbraith, *The Great Crash, 1929* (New York, 1954), and E. W. Bennett, *Germany and the Diplomacy of the Financial Crisis, 1931* (Harvard, 1962).

Chapter 2. Useful works on the still mysterious subject of Stalin's Russia include I. Deutscher, *Stalin, a political Biography* (Oxford, 1949); M. Fainsod, *Smolensk under Soviet Rule* (Harvard, 1958); S. N. Prokopovich, *Histoire économique de l'U.R.S.S.* (Paris, 1952); J. Erickson, *The Soviet High Command, a Military-Political History, 1918–41* (1962). On the return of trouble in the Far East, see S. R. Smith, *The Manchurian Crisis, 1931–32* (New York, 1948).

Chapters 3 to 6. Nazi Germany can best be approached in A. Bullock's masterly *Hitler, A Study in Tyranny* (revised ed., Penguin Books, 1962), supplemented by W. Shirer, *The Rise and Fall of the Third Reich* (1960), voluminous and illuminated by personal recollections. But it is instructive to compare the conventional views of Shirer with such recent works as E. M. Robertson, *Hitler's Prewar Policy and Military Plans, 1933–9* (1963), and B. H. Klein, *Germany's Economic Preparations for War* (Harvard, 1959). Z. A. B. Zeman has studied *Nazi Propaganda* (1964). There are two massive German works on the overthrow of democracy there by K. D. Bracher, *Die Auflösung der Weimarer Republik* (Stuttgart, 1957), and (with W. Sauer and G. Schultz) *Die Nationalsozialistische Machtergreifung* (Köln, Opladen, 1960). H. R. Trevor-Roper has described *The Last Days of Hitler* (1947).

Chapters 4, 5. Noteworthy works on the antecedents of the Second World War include E. Wiskemann, *The Rome–Berlin Axis* (1949); J. W. Wheeler-Bennett, *Munich, Prologue to Tragedy* (1948); W. Hofer, *War Premeditated, 1939* (1955); L. B. Namier, *Diplomatic Prelude, 1938–1939* (1948). For criticism of the orthodox approach to this subject see T. D. Williams, 'The Historiography of World War II', *Historical Studies* (Dublin, 1958), pp. 33–49.

Chapters 1, 4, 6. For the wars of the period see H. Thomas, *The Spanish Civil War* (1961), and, e.g., J. F. C. Fuller, *The Second World War, 1939–45*

(1954); H. A. Jacobsen, *1939–45, Der Zweite Weltkrieg in Chronik und Dokumenten* (Darmstadt, 1959). For American re-involvement see W. L. Langer and S. E. Gleason, *The Challenge to Isolation, 1937–1940* (1952), and *The Undeclared War, 1940–1941* (1953). For wartime diplomacy see especially H. Feis, *Churchill, Roosevelt, Stalin* (Princeton, 1957). For the eclipse of France see, e.g., R. Aron, *Histoire de Vichy* (Paris, 1954).

The *Concluding Thoughts* owe much to the stimulus of reading E. H. Carr, *What is History?* (1961).

Notes

Place of publication is London unless otherwise stated.

Where a translation into English exists, the original edition of works in foreign languages has not usually been noticed.

Index